MyReadingLab™: Improving Reading Through Personalized Learning Experiences

In an ideal world, an instructor would work with each student to help improve reading skills with consistent challenges and rewards. Without that luxury, MyReadingLab offers a way to keep students focused and accelerate their progress using comprehensive pre-assignments and a powerful, adaptive study plan.

Flexible Enough to Fit Every Course Need

MyReadingLab can be set up to fit your specific course needs, whether you seek reading support to complement what you do in class, a way to administer many sections easily, or a self-paced environment for independent study.

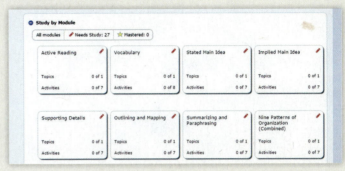

Learning in Context

In addition to distinct pre-loaded learning paths for reading/writing skills practice and reading level practice, MyReadingLab incorporates numerous activities for practice and readings from the accompanying textbook. This makes the connection between what's done in and out of the classroom more relevant to students.

NEW! Learning Tools for Student Engagement

Create an Engaging Classroom

Learning Catalytics is an interactive, student-response tool in MyReadingLab that uses students' smartphones, tablets, or laptops, allowing instructors to generate class discussion easily, guide lectures, and promote peer-to-peer learning with real-time analytics.

Build Multimedia Assignments

MediaShare allows students to easily post multimodal assignments for peer review and instructor feedback. In both face-to-face and online courses, MediaShare enriches the student learning experience by enabling contextual feedback to be provided quickly and easily.

Direct Access to MyLab

Users can link from any Learning Management System (LMS) to Pearson's MyReadingLab. Access MyLab assignments, rosters and resources, and synchronize MyLab grades with the LMS gradebook.

Visit www.myreadinglab.com for more information.

College Reading and Study Skills

College Reading and Study Skills

Thirteenth Edition

KATHLEEN T. McWHORTER
Niagara County Community College

BRETTE McWHORTER SEMBER

PEARSON

Boston Columbus Indianapolis New York San Francisco
Amsterdam Cape Town Dubai London Madrid Milan Munich Paris Montréal Toronto
Delhi Mexico City São Paulo Sydney Hong Kong Seoul Singapore Taipei Tokyo

Vice President/Editorial Director: Eric Stano
Program Manager: Anne Shure
Development Editor: Janice Wiggins
Product Marketing Manager: Jennifer Edwards
Executive Field Marketing Manager: Joyce Nilsen
Media Producer: Jessica Kajkowski
Content Specialist: Julia Pomann
Media Editor: Kelsey Loveday
Project Manager: Donna Campion

Text Design, Project Coordination, and Electronic Page Makeup: Lumina Datamatics, Inc.
Program Design Lead: Heather Scott
Cover Designer: Tamara Newnam
Cover Illustration: Mark Skalny/Shutterstock
Senior Manufacturing Buyer: Roy L. Pickering, Jr.
Printer/Binder: RR Donnelley/Kendallville
Cover Printer: Phoenix Color/Hagerstown

Acknowledgments of third-party content appear on page[s] 447–452, which constitute an extension of this copyright page.

PEARSON, ALWAYS LEARNING, and MYREADINGLAB are exclusive trademarks owned by Pearson Education, Inc. or its affiliates in the United States and/or other countries.

Unless otherwise indicated herein, any third-party trademarks that may appear in this work are the property of their respective owners and any references to third-party trademarks, logos, or other trade dress are for demonstrative or descriptive purposes only. Such references are not intended to imply any sponsorship, endorsement, authorization, or promotion of Pearson's products by the owners of such marks, or any relationship between the owner and Pearson Education, Inc., or its affiliates, authors, licensees, or distributors.

10 9 8 7 6 5 4 3 2 1—V011—19 18 17 16

PEARSON

www.pearsonhighered.com

Student Edition ISBN-10:   0-13-411170-2
Student Edition ISBN-13: 978-0-13-411170-4

A la Carte Edition ISBN 10:   0-13-411198-2
A la Carte Edition ISBN 13: 978-0-13-411198-8

BRIEF CONTENTS

CONTENTS

Part Two: Using College Textbooks 78

Part Three: Essential Reading Skills 146

PREFACE

Across twelve editions, *College Reading and Study Skills* has demonstrated that reading and study skills are inseparable. A student must develop skills in each area in order to handle college work successfully. With this goal in mind, I have tried to provide complete coverage of both reading and study skills throughout and to show their relationship and interdependency. In doing so, my emphasis has been on direct instruction. My central aim is to teach reading and study through a how-to approach.

NEW TO THE THIRTEENTH EDITION

The primary thrust of the revision is to create a stronger emphasis on college textbook reading and to provide a realistic and practical skill application model using a classroom textbook simulation. Specific changes include the following:

NEW STRONGER EMPHASIS ON COLLEGE TEXTBOOK READING SKILLS. Chapter 6, "Active Reading Strategies," has been expanded and reorganized to include skills for before reading, during reading, and after reading. A new textbook excerpt has been added to enable students to apply skills as they learn them.

NEW CLASSROOM SIMULATION OF TEXTBOOK READING AND WRITING SKILLS. In place of the sample textbook chapter, Part Seven now features a unique classroom simulation built around a textbook chapter excerpt. The simulation integrates and applies skills taught throughout *College Reading and Study Skills* to actual textbook material. It simulates the assignments, tasks, skills, processes, and outcome assessments that students are expected to face in college classrooms. The excerpt from a sociology textbook is treated as a classroom reading assignment. Students prepare for a class lecture on the assignment, preview the assignment, evaluate its learning aids, activate their background knowledge, read the assignment, review the assignment, participate in simulated class activities, write about the assignment, take quizzes based on the assignment, and prepare for an exam on the assignment.

NEW THEMATIC READINGS. Part Six of the book contains nine readings, grouped according to three themes. All existing readings have been replaced with current and engaging readings. Each theme contains one textbook excerpt. Theme A, Controversies in Science, considers the following topics: designer babies, the massive concentration of plastic in oceans, and consequences of global warming. Theme B, Health Issues, addresses concerns about the marketing of human kidneys, use of the Internet by doctors to provide medical care, and patient use of the Internet to obtain self-help. Finally, Theme C, on the Internet and Communication, offers readings on what happens when kids don't have the Internet at home, use of smartphones in developing countries, and social networking.

REVISED USING COLLEGE TEXTBOOKS FEATURE. Titled "Using College Textbooks," this feature appears in every chapter and is intended to demonstrate relevance and application of chapter content to college textbooks. Using textbook excerpts from a wide range of disciplines, this feature guides students in integrating and applying the skills taught in each chapter to textbooks used in their other courses. Each feature has been revised to be more engaging and interactive.

NEW SUCCESS WORKSHOPS. The college classroom is changing, and students need new skills to meet the challenges they face. To meet this need, three new Success Workshops titled "Think Critically about Course Content," "Improving Your Reading Rate and

Flexibility," and "Working with New Course Formats: Online, Hybrid, and Flipped Courses" have been added. The workshop that covers managing stress has also been thoroughly revised.

NEW CHAPTER REORGANIZATION. Numerous chapters have been combined and moved forward in the book to provide a more logical progression of skills. Former Chapters 1 and 2 have been combined into a new Chapter 1 titled "First Steps to Academic Success." Chapters 11 and 12 on vocabulary have also been combined into a new Chapter 7 titled "Expanding Your Vocabulary," providing more efficient and unified coverage. Chapters on textbook reading and learning have been moved forward in the book as students need these skills immediately in order to be successful in the college semester. The chapter on reading rate has been dropped, and a new Success Workshop has been added to cover this content.

ESSENTIAL SKILLS ARE PROVIDED EARLIER. Because note taking and textbook reading skills, including highlighting, outlining, summarizing, and mapping, are essential college survival skills, the chapters have been reordered to present these skills earlier in the book.

UPDATED TEXTBOOK SELECTIONS FOR EXERCISES. All selections have been checked for reading level; many have been replaced with excerpts from the most up-to-date editions of textbooks.

REVISED ANNOTATED INSTRUCTOR'S EDITION. For instructors, the Annotated Instructor's Edition is an exact replica of the student text with answers provided on the page.

NEW LEXILE MEASURES. A Lexile® measure is the most widely used reading metric in U.S. schools. The reading levels of the longer selections are indicated using Lexile measures in the Annotated Instructor's Editions of all Pearson's reading books, as is the reading level of content in MyReadingLab. See the Annotated Instructor's Edition of *College Reading and Study Skills* and the Instructor's Manual for more details.

CONTENT OVERVIEW

College Reading and Study Skills, Thirteenth Edition, presents the basic strategies for college success, including time management, analysis of learning style, active reading, and note taking. The text offers strategies for strengthening literal and critical comprehension, as well as improving vocabulary skills. Students also discover methods for reading and learning from textbook assignments, including outlining and summarizing, and for taking exams. The reading and study skills I have chosen to present are those most vital to students' success in college. Each unit teaches skills that are immediately usable—all have clear and direct application to students' course work.

Because I believe that critical thinking and reading skills are essential to college success, these skills are emphasized in the text. I introduce students to critical thinking skills by explaining Bloom's hierarchy of cognitive skills early and then showing their academic application throughout the text. *College Reading and Study Skills* offers direct skill instruction in critical reading and includes key topics such as making inferences, asking critical questions, analyzing arguments, and evaluating Internet sources.

The units of the text are interchangeable, which enables the instructor to adapt the material to a variety of instructional sequences.

SUCCESS WORKSHOPS. Appearing at the beginning of Parts One through Five, the Success Workshops use a fun, lively, and accessible format to provide students with skills that will directly and immediately contribute to their college success. Topics include acclimating to the college environment, managing one's electronic life, strengthening concentration, improving reading rate and flexibility, thinking critically about course content, polishing one's academic image, stress management, and working with new course formats: online, hybrid, and flipped courses.

PART ONE: BUILDING A FOUNDATION FOR ACADEMIC SUCCESS. This section provides an introduction to the college experience and presents skills, habits, and attitudes that are essential to academic success. In Chapter 1 students learn to assess their learning style and develop active learning strategies. Chapters 2 and 3 focus on classroom skills: note taking and classroom communication. The Success Workshops in Part One are Learn About Your Courses and Your Campus Resources and Manage Your Electronic Life.

PART TWO: USING COLLEGE TEXTBOOKS. The chapters in this section teach students to read and learn from college textbook assignments. Chapter 4 teaches students how to identify and organize what they learn using paraphrasing, highlighting, marking, outlining, summarizing, and mapping. Chapter 5 discusses the learning and memory processes and the principles on which many of the skills presented throughout the text are based. The Success Workshops in Part Two are Working with New Course Formats: Online, Hybrid, and Flipped Courses and Strengthen Your Concentration.

PART THREE: ESSENTIAL READING SKILLS. This section focuses on the development of reading skills for both textbooks and other common academic reading assignments. In Chapter 6 students learn active reading strategies for before, during, and after reading. Students are shown methods of learning specialized vocabulary and discover systems for vocabulary learning in Chapter 7. Chapter 8 focuses on paragraph reading skills. Chapter 9 focuses on recognizing thought patterns. The Success Workshop in Part Three is Improving Your Reading Rate and Flexibility.

PART FOUR: THINKING CRITICALLY AS YOU READ. Critical thinking is the focus of the two chapters in this section. Chapter 10 emphasizes evaluation of an author's message. It includes making inferences, distinguishing between fact and opinion, recognizing tone, evaluating data and evidence, and analyzing arguments. Chapter 11 focuses on evaluating an author's techniques: connotative and figurative language, missing information, generalizations, assumptions, and manipulative language. The Success Workshop in Part Four is Think Critically About Course Content.

PART FIVE: STRATEGIES FOR ACADEMIC ACHIEVEMENT. The purpose of this section is to help students handle academic assignments and exams. Chapter 12 focuses on reading and evaluating academic sources such as periodicals, nonfiction, and scholarly works. In Chapters 13 and 14, students learn specific strategies for preparing for and taking objective tests, standardized tests, and essay exams, as well as for controlling test anxiety. The Success Workshops in Part Five are Polish Your Academic Image and Manage Stress.

PART SIX: THEMATIC READINGS. This section contains nine readings, grouped according to three themes: controversies in science, health issues, and the Internet and communication. These readings, which represent the kind of texts that may be assigned in academic courses, provide students with an opportunity to apply skills taught throughout the text.

PART SEVEN: CLASSROOM SIMULATION: TEXTBOOK READING AND WRITING. Finally, a textbook chapter taken from an introduction to sociology college text, titled "Race and Ethnicity," allows students to work with actual textbook material to apply skills taught throughout the text. The chapter is representative of college textbooks, of the learning aids they contain, and of classroom activities built around chapter reading assignments.

SPECIAL FEATURES

The following features enhance the text's effectiveness and directly contribute to students' success:

- **Learning Style.**   The text emphasizes individual student learning styles and encourages students to adapt their reading and study techniques to suit their learning characteristics, as well as the characteristics of the learning task.
- **Reading as a Process.**   This text emphasizes reading as a cognitive process. Applying the findings from the research areas of metacognition and prose structure analysis, students are encouraged to approach reading as an active mental process of selecting, processing, and organizing information to be learned.
- **Metacognition.**   Students are encouraged to establish their concentration, activate prior knowledge, define their purposes, and select appropriate reading strategies prior to reading. They are also shown how to strengthen their comprehension, monitor that comprehension, select what to learn, and organize information. They learn to assess the effectiveness of their learning, revise and modify their learning strategies as needed, and apply and integrate course content.
- **Skill Application.**   Students learn to problem-solve and explore applications through case studies of academic situations included at the end of each chapter. The exercises are labeled "Applying Your Skills." "Discussing the Chapter" questions ask students to reflect on how the advice in the chapter will work in their assignments. "Analyzing a Study Situation" questions present students with mini-cases and ask them how to best approach an academic challenge. Finally, "Working on Collaborative Projects" exercises provide opportunities for group work.
- **Learning Experiments/Learning Principles.**   Each chapter begins with an interactive learning experiment designed to engage students immediately in an activity that demonstrates a principle of learning that will help students learn the chapter content. The student begins the chapter by doing, not simply by beginning to read.
- **Chapter Learning Goals.**   Each chapter opens with chapter learning objectives that correspond to the major headings in the chapter.
- **Interactive Assignments.**   The Success Workshops, the Learning Experiments at the beginning of each chapter, and the Using College Textbooks feature engage students and function as interactive learning opportunities.
- **Writing to Learn.**   The text emphasizes writing as a means of learning. Writing-to-learn strategies include paraphrasing, self-testing, outlining, summarizing, and mapping.
- **Realistic Reading Assignments.**   Exercises often include excerpts from college texts across a wide range of disciplines, providing realistic examples of college textbook reading. Furthermore, "Using College Textbooks" sections guide students in making the most of their textbooks.
- **Thematic Readings.**   Nine readings, grouped according to three themes, are contained in Part Six. These readings provide realistic materials on which to apply skills taught in the text. They also provide students with an essential link between in-chapter practice exercises and independent application of new techniques in their own textbooks, as well as valuable practice in synthesizing and evaluating ideas.
- **Self-Test Chapter Summaries.**   Linked to the chapter's learning goals, the chapter summaries use an interactive question–answer format that encourages students to become more active learners.
- **Quick Quizzes.**   A multiple-choice quick quiz is included at the end of each chapter. Each quiz assesses mastery of chapter content, provides students with feedback on their learning, and prepares students for further evaluation conducted by their instructor.
- **Visual Appeal.**   The text recognizes that many students are visual learners and presents material visually, using maps, charts, tables, and diagrams.

THE TEACHING AND LEARNING PACKAGE
Book-Specific Ancillary Materials

- **Annotated Instructor's Edition.** This supplement is an exact replica of the student text with answers provided. ISBN: 0-13-410522-2.
- **Instructor's Manual.** This supplement, created by Mary Dubbé, contains teaching suggestions for each chapter along with numerous tests formatted for easy distribution and scoring. It includes a complete answer key, strategies for approaching individual chapters, a set of overhead projection materials, and suggestions for integrating the many Pearson ancillaries. Online only. ISBN: 0-13-411196-6.
- **Test Bank.** This supplement, created by Jeanne Jones, includes content-based chapter quizzes and mastery tests to enable students to apply skills taught in every chapter. Online only. ISBN: 0-13-411194-X.
- **Pearson MyTest.** This supplement is created from the Test Bank and is a powerful assessment generation program that helps instructors easily create and print quizzes, study guides, and exams. Select Pearson's questions and supplement them with your own questions. Available at www.pearsonmytest.com. ISBN: 0-13-411193-1.
- **PowerPoint Presentations.** This supplement, created by Jeanne Jones, contains a presentation for each chapter structured around the chapter learning objectives. You can use these presentations as is or edit them to suit your lecturing style. Available for download from the Instructor Resource Center. ISBN: 0-13-411187-7.
- **Answer Key.** The Answer Key contains the solutions to the exercises in the student edition of the text. Available for download from the Instructor Resource Center. ISBN: 0-13-410506-0.

ACKNOWLEDGMENTS

In preparing this edition, I appreciate the excellent ideas, suggestions, and advice provided by reviewers: Elizabeth Walker, Labette Community College; Cynthia Galvan, Milwaukee Area Technical College; Dina Levitre, Community College of Rhode Island; Alexis Shuler, The University of Akron; Stacey Kartub, Washtenaw Community College; Constance Yates, Missouri State University; Susan Silva, El Paso Community College; Elizabeth O'Scanlon, Santa Barbara City College; and Kathy Petroff, St. Louis Community College – Forest Park.

The editorial staff at Pearson deserve special recognition and thanks for the guidance, support, and direction they have provided. In particular I wish to thank Janice Wiggins, my development editor, for her valuable advice and assistance, Gillian Cook, senior development editor, for overseeing the project, and Eric Stano, VP and editorial director, English, for his enthusiastic support of the revision.

KATHLEEN T. MCWHORTER

LEARN ABOUT YOUR COURSES AND YOUR CAMPUS RESOURCES

Did You Know?

⊃ The average graduate of a four-year college earns $29,250 more per year than the average high school graduate.[1]

⊃ Employers value a college education and are willing to contribute to their employees' tuition. Nine percent of financial aid given to undergraduates comes from employers. Twenty-two percent of graduate students and professional degree students receive assistance from their employers.[2]

These statistics indicate that the confusion and stress you may experience as you begin college are well worth it!

What should you do in your first week on campus? In addition to attending your classes, meeting your instructors, and getting your textbooks and supplies, you also need to familiarize yourself with the requirements of your courses as well as the resources and services that your college offers to students.

WHAT DO YOUR COURSES REQUIRE?

During the first week of class, you will learn what your instructor expects and what you must do to earn a grade and receive credit for the course. Often, most of this information is contained in the course syllabus—a handout distributed on the first day or in the first week of class (and often available online as well). After reading and studying the syllabus, file it in a safe place so that you can refer to it later.

WHAT INFORMATION IS INCLUDED IN A COURSE SYLLABUS?

Examine the course syllabus on the next page and make a mental note of the information it contains.

---

[1]http://www.bls.gov/emp/ep_table_education_summary.htm
[2]http://nces.ed.gov/pubs2013/2013165.pdf

Course Syllabus

Course Number: BIO 201

Course Name: Human Anatomy and Physiology I

Instructor: Dr. Jack Eberhardt

Prerequisite: BIO 102 with a grade of C or higher

Office Location: 322 Olympic Towers

Office Hours: MWF 1–3

E-mail: jeberhardt@mcc.edu

Note: It may take up to 48 hours to receive a response to any e-mails sent to me. Please do not send text messages; you will not receive a response.

Course page: BIO201-2 on BlackBoard. Note: I do not monitor the discussion board. Please do not ask me questions on the discussion board; you will not receive a response.

Course Objectives:

1. To identify the major parts of a cell and know their functions.

2. To understand the structure and function of the human organ systems.

3. To learn the types of human body tissues and understand their functions.

4. To perform laboratory activities for collection and analysis of experimental data.

....

Course Grade: Grades will be based on three multiple-choice exams and twelve weekly laboratory reports. Exam questions are based on lecture notes, textbook assignments, and the lab manual. The exams will test factual knowledge as well as critical thinking skills.

....

Exams will be held on October 17, November 15, and December 8.

....

Lab manuals will be due on Sept. 23 and 30; October 7, 14, 21, and 28; November 5, 12, 19, and 26; and December 4 and 11.

....

Attendance: Regular attendance is required for both lecture and laboratory. If you miss a class, you should get the missed material from a classmate. I will post any PowerPoint presentations that I use on the course page; however, not all lectures are accompanied by a PowerPoint presentation. You are responsible for learning the content of any material covered in the lectures, whether this material appears on the course page or not. Make-up labs will not be allowed. If you miss an exam or a lab, you must provide written documentation to explain your absence. If you fail to do so, a grade of zero will be entered.

....

Tentative Lecture Schedule:

DATE	TOPIC	CHAPTER
Sept. 16	Course Introduction, The Scientific Method	1
Sept. 21	Atoms, molecules, water, Chemical bonding	1, 2

....

>>

WHAT CAN YOU LEARN FROM ONE OF YOUR SYLLABI?

Now it's your turn to analyze a syllabus from one of your classes. What did you learn about how your course will be conducted? What additional important information does your syllabus contain? Does the syllabus include any surprising or unexpected information?

Perhaps the most important information on your syllabus is the listing of assignments, exams, and due dates. Instructors expect you to manage your time wisely and meet all due dates. Take time at the beginning of each semester to enter due dates into an electronic or printed calendar/planner, refer to that calendar/planner every day, and plan your life (including work, school, and family responsibilities) to meet your due dates.

WHAT RESOURCES AND SERVICES DOES YOUR COLLEGE OFFER?

Don't wait until you are desperate for help to learn about campus resources; be proactive and learn about them early in the semester. You will be pleasantly surprised at the number and variety of resources and services that are available to you, usually free of charge.

Now answer the following questions about your campus resources. Perhaps you can pair up with a partner and explore your campus together. You will likely find many of these answers on your school's Web site, often under a heading such as "Student Resources." Simply knowing that the resources exist is not enough; you need to know where they are and how to access them.

1. What are the hours of your college library?
2. How would you find out the last date by which you can withdraw from a course without academic penalty?
3. Where do you go or whom do you see to change from one major (or curriculum) to another?
4. What services does the student health office provide?
5. Who is your advisor and where is his or her office located on campus?
6. What assistance is available in locating part-time jobs on or off campus?
7. How would you find a tutor for a course in which you are having difficulty?
8. Where is the financial aid office and how can I see if I am qualified for scholarships or other assistance?

WHERE CAN YOU FIND INFORMATION ON COLLEGE REGULATIONS AND POLICIES?

The college catalog is your primary source of information for staying in and graduating from college. Be sure to obtain a current edition or access it online. It is your responsibility to know and work within the college's regulations, policies, and requirements to obtain your degree. Although faculty advisors are available to provide guidance, you must be certain that you are registering for the right courses in the right sequence to fulfill the requirements for your degree. Keep the catalog that is in effect during your freshman year. It is considered the catalog of record and will be used to audit your graduation requirements. A complete catalog usually provides the following information:

Academic rules and regulations	Course registration policies, grading system, class attendance policies, academic dismissal policies, policies regarding cheating and plagiarism
Degree programs and requirements	Degrees offered and outlines of the degree requirements for each major or minor
Course descriptions	A brief description of each course, the number of credits, and course prerequisites (Note: Not all courses listed are offered each semester.)
Student activities and special services	Student organizations, clubs and sports, student governance system, and special services

WHAT INFORMATION CAN YOU FIND ON YOUR COLLEGE'S WEB SITE?

Use your college's catalog and/or Web site to answer the following questions.

1. Does the college allow you to take courses on a Pass/Fail or Satisfactory/Unsatisfactory basis? If so, what restrictions or limitations apply?
2. On what basis are students academically dismissed from the college? What criteria apply to readmission?
3. What is the institution's policy on transfer credit?
4. What rules and regulations apply to motor vehicles on campus?
5. List five extracurricular programs or activities the college sponsors.
6. What foreign languages are offered?
7. What systems/media does the college use to notify you of on-campus emergencies or other essential information?
8. What courses are required in your major or curriculum? Are any general education courses required? If so, what are they?

LEARN!

Learn about your campus resources.

   Engage with your instructors to learn their expectations.

     Access the school's Web site to locate important information.

       Refer to syllabi frequently throughout the term.

         Negotiate the course schedule to plan your education and life.

SUCCESS
WORKSHOP
2

MANAGE YOUR ELECTRONIC LIFE

Did You Know?

↪ Students spend an average of 101 minutes per day on Facebook.[1]

↪ Online courses are growing: 6.7 million students reported taking at least one online class in 2012.[2] The top three programs of study in online learning are business, health care, and computer science.[3]

The revolution has occurred. Technology is all around us, and it has become a powerful tool for learning. Computers, laptops, tablets, and smartphones offer convenient ways of learning, reviewing, collaborating, and studying. Learning to make these fun tools work *for you* instead of *against you* will be a key to your success in college and beyond.

IS TECHNOLOGY AFFECTING YOUR ABILITY TO CONCENTRATE?

Is technology helping you manage your life, or is it a source of distraction? Analyze the impact of technology on your daily life by answering the following questions. You will get a sense of the type and number of electronic distractions in your life and how they affect your ability to focus.

1. How many text messages do you send and receive per day? _____ How many of these are "important"? _____ Do you stop what you are doing to check your cell phone the second a text message arrives? _____ Have you ever texted while driving? _____

2. How many e-mails do you send and receive per day? _____ How many of these are valuable in terms of communicating important information? _____ How many are purely for entertainment or socializing? _____ How much time do you spend each day on e-mail unrelated to your college work or your job? _____

3. How many calls do you receive on your cell phone each day? _____ Do you leave your cell phone on all the time? _____ Do you answer it every time it rings, even

[1] http://www.huffingtonpost.com/2013/06/25/college-students-facebook-study_n_3497733.html
[2] Elaine Allen & Jeff Seaman. Changing Course: Ten Years of Tracking Online Education in the United States. Babson Survey Research Group, 2013. http://files.eric.ed.gov/fulltext/ED541571.pdf
[3] http://www.learninghouse.com/cic2013-report/

when you're in class or studying? _____ Do you ever use your cell phone as a way to procrastinate? _____ How often do you play games on your cell phone or use your phone to entertain yourself, procrastinate, or pass the time? _____

4. How many hours a day do you spend surfing the Internet or posting on social networking sites like Facebook, tweeting on Twitter, or uploading pictures to photo-sharing sites like Snapchat or Instagram? _____ Do these activities affect your studying, concentration, and grades? _____ If so, how? _____

HOW DO DISTRACTIONS INTERFERE WITH YOUR LEARNING?

Learning is a process of connecting new information with what you have already learned, which is stored in your memory. When you encounter a new piece of information while reading, your mind files it by attaching it to what you have already learned. This is an amazing process that resembles the way we physically file (store) information in folders on our computer or in a file cabinet.

If you interrupt the storage process by stopping to check a text message, then new information will be lost rather than stored (remembered). In order to store the new information, you will have to go back to your original task, refocus, figure out where you left off, and read the material again so that your brain can reset. So you can see that checking text messages while studying is not only a time-waster; it also makes your study time less productive. You learn less when you allow yourself to be interrupted.

HOW CAN YOU MAKE TECHNOLOGY WORK FOR YOU?

How do you eliminate the distractions of technology so that you can use technology to your advantage?

Mobile Devices. Turn off the ringer, vibrator, and text notifications while studying and attending class. If you cannot resist the temptation to check your messages, put the device in another room while you are working at home, or leave it in your car or dorm room while you are in class.

E-mail. E-mail is an efficient way of communicating with your instructor or classmates when you cannot talk with them face-to-face or by phone. Be sure to check your e-mail occasionally during the day—perhaps during lunch or between classes—to make sure you are receiving important information.

Text Messages. Text messages have become the primary means of communication for many college students. Although text messages are quick to compose and quick to read, you should refrain from writing or reading them when you are working on your assignments at home or during class time. Make your study time a "text-free" time.

Apps. Many devices and phones offer applications, or "apps," that are helpful in your studies. You can download free (or inexpensive) dictionaries, encyclopedias, grammar guides, calendars and schedulers, and a host of other apps that can help with your studies. Put these apps on your main screen, and put your social or entertainment apps (such as Facebook) on a later screen.

Social Media and Webcams. In some classes, you will be expected to work as a group to discuss topics or collaborate on projects. Programs like Skype make it easy for a group to "meet" when everyone is online at the same time. Leave your webcam off during all other study times. Set up a course or group study page on Facebook and use it to share information with classmates, study for exams, or exchange study tips and suggestions.

DOES LIMITING SOCIAL TECHNOLOGY IMPROVE YOUR WORK?

Commit to following the advice in this workshop for one week. At the end of the week, assess your progress. Did you accomplish more and better-quality work? Were you more focused in class and during your study sessions? Did you get better grades on your assignments? Did you get your assignments done more quickly? Did you feel more in control of the technology in your life?

HOW CAN I TAKE CHARGE OF TECHNOLOGY IN MY LIFE?

- Remember that technology is a tool you use, not something that controls or directs your behavior.
- Create separate zones, school and social, to allow you to use technology more effectively.
- Reserve some time each day to "unplug" and be technology free—especially before bedtime.

CONCENTRATE!

Control distractions.

  Overcome the desire to post on social media while studying.

    Notice and manage your surroundings.

      Create and keep to a schedule.

        E-mail only when necessary.

          Narrow your concentration to focus on one thing at a time.

            Turn off the phone.

              Resist the temptation to procrastinate.

                Avoid loud, crowded places.

                  Text wisely.

                    Engage with the assignment and course content.

First Steps to Academic Success

LEARNING GOALS

In this chapter you will learn to

1 Establish goals and manage your valuable time.

2 Analyze your learning style.

3 Understand instructors' teaching styles.

4 Meet instructors' expectations.

5 Use active learning strategies.

6 Explain and illustrate critical thinking.

LEARNING EXPERIMENT

1 Study the photograph on the right for one minute.

2 Draw a sketch of one of the people in the photograph.

3 Write two or three sentences describing this person.

4 Compare your drawing and description with those of your classmates by quickly passing them around the room.

The Results

No doubt, some sketches were much better than others. Some were detailed, accurate likenesses; others may have resembled stick figures. Some descriptions were detailed; others were not. You can conclude that some students have stronger artistic ability than others. Some students have stronger verbal abilities than others. Which students do you expect will do well in an art class? Who will do better on essay exams? Who might consider a career in graphic design?

Learning Principle: What This Means to You

You have strengths and weaknesses as a learner; you should capitalize on your strengths and strive to overcome your weaknesses. In this chapter you will learn to identify strengths and weaknesses, manage your time, and choose study methods accordingly. You will also discover that instructors have unique teaching styles and discover how to adapt to them. Finally, you will learn what kinds of learning and thinking your instructors expect of you.

ESTABLISHING GOALS AND MANAGING YOUR VALUABLE TIME

Like most students, you are likely dividing your time among school, family, household responsibilities, friends, and possibly a job. Finding a way to manage your time effectively will help you feel less stressed and more comfortable in all aspects of your life.

It is important to set goals and manage time because

- setting goals can keep you on track, motivate you, and help you measure your progress.
- managing your time allows you to balance your course work with family, work, and social activities.
- managing your time allows you to make steady progress on long-term projects instead of being surprised by rapidly approaching due dates.

Goal 1

Establish goals and manage your valuable time.

Establishing Your Goals and Priorities

One of the first steps in getting organized and succeeding in college is to set your priorities—to decide what is and what is not important to you. For most college students, finding enough time to do everything they *should* do and everything they *want* to do is nearly impossible. They face a series of conflicts over the use of their time and are forced to choose among a variety of activities. Here are a few examples:

Want to do:		Should do:
• **Take family to park**	vs.	**Finish psychology reading assignment**
• **Go to hockey game**	vs.	**Work on term paper**
• **Go out with friends**	vs.	**Get a good night's sleep**

One of the best ways to handle such conflicts is to identify your goals. Ask yourself: What is most important to me? What activities can I afford to give up? What is least important to me when I am pressured for time? For some students, studying is their first priority. For students with family or work responsibilities, caring for a child or being available for their shift might be their first priority, and attending college is next in importance.

HOW TO DISCOVER YOUR PRIORITIES

1. **Make a list of the ten most joyous moments in your life.** A phrase or single sentence of description is all that is needed.
2. **Ask yourself: What do most or all of these moments have in common?**
3. **Try to write answers to the question above by describing why the moments were important to you—what you got out of them.** (Sample answers:

helping others, competing or winning, creating something worthwhile, proving your self-worth, connecting with nature, and so forth.)

4. **Your answers will provide a starting point for defining your life goals.**

DEFINING GOALS BASED ON YOUR PRIORITIES In defining your goals, be specific and detailed. Use the following guidelines.

- **Your goals should be positive (what you want) rather than negative (what you don't want).** Don't say "I won't ever have to worry about credit card balances and bill collectors." Instead, say "I will have enough money to live comfortably."
- **Your goals should be realistic.** Unless you have strong evidence to believe you can do so, don't say you want to win an Olympic gold medal in swimming. Instead, say you want to become a strong, competitive swimmer.
- **Your goals should be achievable.** Don't say you want to earn a million dollars a year; most people don't earn that much. Set more achievable, specific goals, such as "I want to buy a house by the time I am 30."
- **Your goals should be worth what it takes to achieve them.** Becoming an astronaut or a brain surgeon takes years of training. Are you willing to invest that amount of time?
- **Your goals should include a** time frame. The goal of earning a bachelor's degree in accounting should include a date by which you want to have the degree.
- **Expect your goals to change as your life changes.** The birth of a child or the loss of a loved one may cause you to refocus your life.

Tip *Time frame* means the length of time from the beginning to the end of an activity.

College can provide you with the self-awareness, self-confidence, knowledge, skills, practice facilities, degrees, friendships, and business contacts that can help you achieve your life goals.

You will find that clearly establishing and pursuing your goals eliminates much worry and guilt. You'll know what is important and feel that you are on target, working steadily toward the goals you have established.

Exercise 1

DIRECTIONS   Write a list of five to ten goals.

_____

_____

_____

_____

_____

Exercise 2

DIRECTIONS   For each of your life goals listed in Exercise 1, explain how attending college will help you achieve that goal.

_____

_____

_____

_____

_____

Analyzing Your Time Commitments

To make your time commitments reflect your priorities, you must determine how much time is available and then decide how you will use it.

Let's begin by making some rough estimates to help you see where your time goes each week. Fill in the chart in Figure 1-1, making reasonable estimates. After you've completed the chart, total your hours per week and write the answer in the space marked "Total committed time per week." Next, fill in that total below and complete the subtraction.

> 168   hours in one week
>
> _____ total committed time
>
> _____ hours available

Are you surprised to see how many hours per week you have left? Now answer this question: Do you have enough time available for reading and studying? As a rule of thumb, most instructors expect you to spend two hours studying for every hour spent in class. Complete the following multiplication for your class schedule this term:

> _____ hours spent in class × 2 = _____ study hours needed

Do you have this much time available each week? If your answer is no, then you are overcommitted. If you are overcommitted, ask yourself: Can I drop any activity or do it in less time? Can I reduce the number of hours I work, or can another family member split some time-consuming responsibilities with me? If you are unable to reduce your committed time, talk with your advisor about taking fewer courses.

If you are overcommitted, now is the time to develop a weekly schedule that will help you use your available time more effectively. You are probably concerned at this point, however, that your time analysis did not take into account social and leisure activities. That omission was deliberate.

Although leisure time is essential to everyone's well-being, it should not take precedence over college work. Fortunately, most students who develop and follow a time schedule for accomplishing their course work are able to handle family and community obligations and still have time left for leisure and social activities. They also find time to become involved with campus groups and activities—an important aspect of college life.

	HOURS PER DAY	HOURS PER WEEK
Sleep	_____	_____
Breakfast	_____	_____
Lunch	_____	_____
Dinner	_____	_____
Part- or full-time job	_____	_____
Time spent in class	_____	_____
Transportation time	_____	_____
Personal care (dressing, shaving, etc.)	_____	_____
Household/family responsibilities (cooking dinner, driving sister to work, etc.)	_____	_____
Sports	_____	_____
Other priorities	_____	_____
Total committed time per week		_____

FIGURE 1-1
Weekly Time Commitments

Building a Term Plan

A term plan lists all your unchanging commitments. These may include class hours, transportation to and from school and work, family commitments, religious obligations, job hours (if they are the same each week), sleep, meals, and sports. A form for a term plan is shown in Figure 1-2. You'll use your term plan to build weekly time schedules. Adjust your schedule each week as necessary.

	Monday	Tuesday	Wednesday	Thursday	Friday	Saturday	Sunday
7:00							
8:00							
9:00							
10:00							
11:00							
12:00							
1:00							
2:00							
3:00							
4:00							
5:00							
6:00							
7:00							
8:00							
9:00							
10:00							
11:00							

FIGURE 1-2
Term Plan

If you prefer to keep your schedule electronically, use an electronic calendar or scheduler on your laptop or cell phone. These applications can send you reminders about important deadlines and dates. They can also help you keep track of key dates throughout the course of the term (for example, scheduled exams and due dates for papers).

DIRECTIONS Use the form shown in Figure 1-2 or a computer software program to build your own term plan. ●

Exercise 3

Building Your Weekly Schedule

A weekly schedule is a plan that shows when and what you will study. It includes specific times for studying particular subjects as well as specific times for writing papers, conducting library research, and completing homework assignments for each course.

At the beginning of each week, decide what you need to accomplish that week, given your unchanging commitments. Consider upcoming quizzes, exams, and papers. A weekly schedule will eliminate the need to make frustrating last-minute choices between "should" and "want to" activities. The sample weekly time schedule in Figure 1-3 was developed by a first-year student. Her unchanging commitments are shown in yellow. Her weekly study adjustments are shown in lavender. Read the schedule carefully, noticing how the student reserved time for studying for each of her courses.

TIPS FOR CREATING A WEEKLY SCHEDULE Now that you have seen a sample weekly schedule, you can build your own, using the following guidelines.

1. **Before the week begins, assess the upcoming week's workload.** Reserve a specific time for this activity. Sunday evening works well for many students. Check your course management system or your class Web site for updates and new assignments. Review your long-term or electronic planner for upcoming quizzes, exams, papers, and assignments.
2. **Write in any appointments, such as with the doctor or for a haircut.** Add in new commitments such as babysitting or helping a friend.
3. **Estimate the amount of time you will need for each of your courses.** Add extra time if you have an important exam or if the amount of reading is particularly heavy. Block in study times for each course.
4. **Plan ahead.** If there's a paper due next week that requires library research, schedule time to begin your research. If you work on a shared computer (for example, in a computer lab), make sure you reserve access in advance.
5. **Block out reasonable amounts of time, especially on weekends, for having fun and relaxing.** For example, mark off the time to watch a movie or allocate time for exercise.
6. **Build into your schedule a short break before you begin studying each new subject.** Your mind needs time to refocus—to switch from one set of facts, problems, and issues to another.
7. **Include short breaks when you are working on just one assignment for a long period of time.** A 10-minute break after 50 to 60 minutes of study is reasonable.
8. **Set aside a specific time each week for developing next week's plan.** Also be sure to review your prior week's performance.

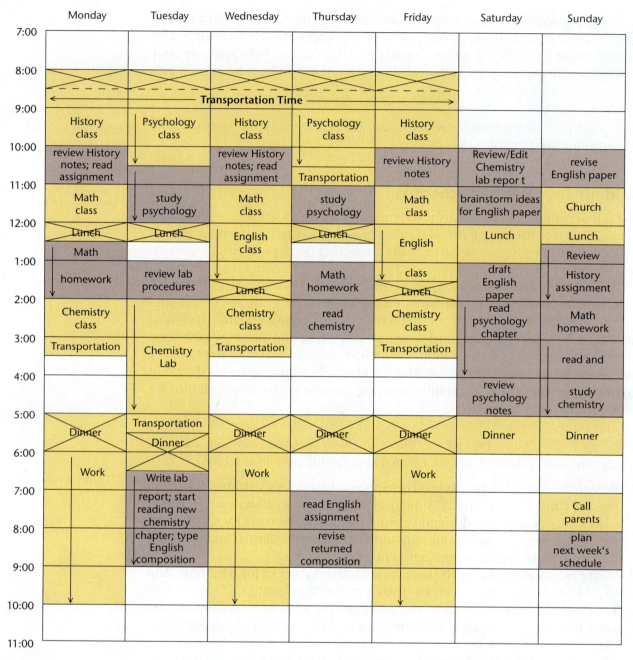

FIGURE 1-3
Sample Weekly Time Schedule

WHEN TO STUDY WHICH SUBJECTS The order in which you study various subjects and complete various tasks does matter. Use the suggestions on the next page to use your study time effectively.

Keeping to your weekly schedule will mean saying no. When friends call and want to chat at a time you planned to study, you will have to refuse. When a friend or family member asks you to do a favor—such as running an errand—you will have to refuse, but you can suggest some alternative times when you will be free. You will find that your friends and family accept your constraints and respect you for being conscientious.

GETTING THE MOST OUT OF YOUR STUDY TIME

1. **Study difficult subjects first.** It's tempting to get easy tasks and short assignments out of the way first, but resist this temptation. When you start studying, your mind is fresh and alert and you are at your peak of concentration. This is when you are best equipped to handle difficult subjects. Thinking through complicated problems or studying complex ideas requires maximum brain power, and you have the most brain power at the beginning of a study session.

2. **Leave the routine and more mechanical tasks for later in the evening.** Activities such as printing out papers or alphabetizing a bibliography for a research paper do not require a high degree of concentration and can be left until you are tired.

3. **Schedule study for a particular course close to the time when you attend class.** Plan to study the evening before the class meets or soon after the class meeting. If a class meets on Tuesday morning, plan to study Monday evening or Tuesday afternoon or evening.

4. **When reading or studying a particular subject, try to schedule two or three short, separate blocks of time for that course.** One long, continuous block can be fatiguing.

5. **Schedule study sessions at times when you know you are usually alert and feel like studying.** Do not schedule a study time early on Saturday morning if you are not a morning person, and try not to schedule study time late in the evening if you are usually tired after 8 P.M.

6. **Plan to study at times when your physical surroundings are quiet.** If the dinner hour is a rushed and confusing time, don't attempt to study then if alternative times are available. Eliminate distractions. Turn off your cell phone, disable instant messaging, and log out of social media sites.

Visual Thinking
APPLYING SKILLS

How could this student study more efficiently?

DIRECTIONS Using the term plan you wrote in Exercise 3, create a plan for next week. ●

Exercise 4

Using Time-Saving Tips to Manage a Busy Schedule

Here are a few suggestions that will help you to make the best use of your time.

1. **Use your smart phone's calendar.** Track tests, due dates for papers, and study group meetings. Set reminders to be notified of important deadlines.

2. **Set priorities.** Some students work on one project until they are exhausted and leave remaining assignments unfinished. A better approach is to decide what is most important to complete immediately and which assignments could, if necessary, be completed later.

3. **Use spare moments.** Think of all the time you spend waiting. You wait for a class to begin, for a ride, for a pizza to arrive. Instead of wasting this time, you could use it to review a set of lecture notes, work on review questions at the

end of a chapter, or review a chemistry lab setup. Always carry with you something you can work on in spare moments.

4. **Combine activities.** Busy students soon learn that it's possible to combine some daily chores with routine class assignments. Some students, for example, are able to do laundry and between loads outline a history chapter or work on routine assignments. Others review formulas for math or science courses or review vocabulary cards for language courses while riding a bus.

5. **Use lists to keep yourself organized and to save time.** A daily to-do list is helpful in keeping track of what needs to be done. As you think of tasks you need to do (whether related to coursework or not), jot them down or track them in the notes app in your phone. Then look over the list each morning and try to find the best way to get everything done. For instance, you may find that you can stop at the post office on the way to class, thus saving yourself an extra trip.

6. **Recognize when you're trying to do too much.** If you find your schedule is becoming too hectic or unmanageable, or if you are facing pressures you can't handle, consider dropping a course. Don't be too concerned that this will put you behind schedule for graduation. More than half of all college students take longer than the traditional time expected to earn their degrees. You may be able to pick up the course later during a summer or winter session or carry a heavier load during another semester.

Controlling the Tendency to Procrastinate

Have you ever felt that you should work on an assignment, and even wanted to get it out of the way, but you could not get started? If so, you have procrastinated—put off tasks that need to be done. We often put off tedious, difficult, or uninteresting tasks. However, it is often these very tasks that are essential to success in college courses. The following suggestions can help you overcome or control a tendency to procrastinate.

HOW TO FIGHT PROCRASTINATION	
Do you . . .	**Try this:**
Get distracted?	• Turn off the television. • Set your cell phone to silent (or put it in your backpack or another room). • Close social media. • Clear your desk; get rid of clutter; move other unfinished projects out of sight. • Avoid stimulus overload—don't listen to music while attempting to study in a busy and loud student lounge, for example.
Feel overwhelmed by the task?	• Break the task into manageable parts; this will make the task seem doable. Work on one piece at a time.
Try to avoid the task?	• Don't spend time on easy tasks like cleaning because they're easier than studying. • Sit and stay at your desk. Study in a library, where distractions and temptations are minimized.

REGARDLESS OF WHAT YOU DO, START! If you are having difficulty getting started, do something other than sit and stare, regardless of how trivial it may seem. The following tips will help you get started.

JUMP START!

- Start with a small task that takes very little time, such as rereading a specific assignment.
- Start with easy-to-do tasks, such as making a list of what needs to be done.
- Give yourself five minutes to get started. Once you are involved with the task, it will be easier to continue.

RECOGNIZE WHEN YOU NEED MORE INFORMATION Sometimes procrastination is a signal that you lack skills or information. You may be avoiding a task because you're not sure how to do it. You may not really understand why a certain procedure is used to solve a particular type of math problem, for example, so you feel reluctant to do math homework. Similarly, selecting a topic for a term paper may be difficult if you aren't certain of the paper's purpose or expected length. Overcome such stumbling blocks by discussing them with classmates or with your professor.

Thinking Positively

As you begin a task, it is easy to get discouraged by negative thoughts. A positive attitude will make the task more enjoyable (or at least less painful). Use the following tips to help you avoid negative thoughts.

HOW TO STAY POSITIVE

If you think . . .	Try telling yourself . . .
This is boring.	I'll be able to stick with this (and give myself a reward when I finish).
I can't wait to finish.	It will feel great to have this job done.
I'll never be able to remember all of this.	I'll highlight what is important for later review.
This is not useful to learn anyway.	My instructor would not assign this if it weren't important.
If I didn't have to do this, I could be _____.	When this task is finished, I'll find time to _____.

DIRECTIONS Read each situation described, and then answer the questions that follow. Discuss your responses with another student, or write your answers in the spaces provided.

Exercise 5

Collaboration

1. In analyzing his amount of committed time, Zabir filled in a weekly chart, in hours, as follows:

Sleep	56
Breakfast, lunch, dinner (total)	14
Job	35
Time in classes	23
Transportation	10
Personal care	15
Household/family	20
Study time	30
Total	203

Zabir is overcommitted; his total commitments add up to more hours than there are in a week (168). He has to have at least a part-time job in order to pay for school. He is working toward a degree in science lab technology, so he must spend a lot of class hours in lab. He estimates that he needs 30 hours of study time per week to maintain a high B average this semester. It is also important for him to have some time for leisure and recreation. Look at his chart again. What are his choices? Try to find as many alternatives as you can.

_____

_____

_____

_____

2. Tiffany is a serious student but is having difficulty with her accounting course. She has decided to spend all day Sunday studying accounting. She plans to lock herself in her room and not come out until she has reviewed four chapters. What is wrong with her approach? What study plan would be more effective?

_____

_____

_____

_____

3. Mark realizes that he has three assignments that must be completed in one evening. The assignments are to revise an English composition, to read and highlight ten pages in his anatomy and physiology text, and to learn a set of vocabulary words for his sociology course. He decides to get the sociology assignment out of the way first, to do the English composition next (because English is one of his favorite subjects), and then to read the anatomy and physiology text. Evaluate Mark's plan of study.

_____

_____

_____

_____

4. You are taking a course in music appreciation, and your instructor sometimes unexpectedly asks you to listen to a certain part of a concert or watch a particular program online. You cannot predict when these assignments will be given or when you will need to complete them. What could you do to include them in your weekly study schedule?

_____

_____

5. Carlos is registered for the following courses, which meet at the times indicated:

Business Management 109	T-Th 12–1:30 P.M.
English 101	M-W-F 11 A.M.–12 Noon
Math 201	T-Th 9–10:30 A.M.
Biology 131	Class M-W-F 2–3 P.M.; Lab W 3–5 P.M.
Psychology 101	M-W-F 9–10 A.M.

6. The workload for each course is as follows:

Business Management	Two chapters assigned each week; midterm and final exams; one term paper due at the end of the semester
English	One 250-word essay per week
Math	A homework assignment for each class, which takes approximately one hour to complete; a quiz each Thursday
Biology	Preparation for weekly lab; one chapter to read per week; a one-hour exam every three weeks
Psychology	One chapter to read per week; one library reading assignment per week; four exams throughout the semester

Because Carlos has a part-time job, he has the following times available for study:

Between his classes
Evenings: Tuesday, Wednesday
Afternoons: Monday, Thursday, and Friday
Weekends: Saturday morning, all day and evening Sunday

What study schedule would you recommend for Carlos? Indicate the times he should study each subject and what tasks he should work on. Use a blank term plan (Figure 1-2) to plan a schedule for Carlos.

_____

_____

_____

ANALYZING YOUR LEARNING STYLE

It is important to analyze you learning style because:

- You will understand your strengths and weaknesses as a learner and understand how to choose study methods accordingly.
- You will realize why you learn more easily from some instructors than from others.
- You will discover what kinds of learning and thinking are expected in college.

Goal 2

Analyze your learning style.

How to Analyze Your Learning Style

Have you noticed that some types of tasks are easier to complete than others? Have you found that a study method that works well for a classmate does not work as well for you? These differences can be explained by *learning style*. Just as you have a unique personality, you also have a unique learning style. People differ in how they learn and in the methods and strategies they use to learn. Learning style can also explain why certain assignments are difficult and other learning tasks are easy.

The following questionnaire will help you understand your personal learning styles. Complete the Learning Style Questionnaire before continuing.

Learning Style Questionnaire

DIRECTIONS Each item presents two choices. Select the alternative that best describes you. In cases where neither choice suits you, select the one that is closer to your preference. Write the letter of your choice on the line to the left of each item.

PART ONE

_____ 1. I would prefer to follow a set of
    a. oral directions.
    b. print directions.

_____ 2. I would prefer to
    a. attend a lecture given by a famous psychologist.
    b. read an online article written by the psychologist.

_____ 3. When I am introduced to someone, it is easier for me to remember the person's
    a. name.
    b. face.

_____ 4. I find it easier to learn new information using
    a. language (words).
    b. images (pictures).

_____ 5. I prefer classes in which the instructor
    a. lectures and answers questions.
    b. uses PowerPoint illustrations and videos.

_____ 6. To follow current events, I prefer to
    a. listen to the news on the radio or watch a TV or Web broadcast.
    b. read the news in print or online.

_____ 7. To learn how to repair a flat tire, I would prefer to
    a. listen to a friend's explanation.
    b. watch a demonstration.

PART TWO

_____ 8. I prefer to
    a. work with facts and details.
    b. construct theories and ideas.

_____ 9. I would prefer a job that involved
    a. following specific instructions.
    b. reading, writing, and analyzing.

_____ 10. I prefer to
    a. solve math problems using a formula.
    b. discover why the formula works.

_____ 11. I would prefer to write a term paper explaining
    a. how a process works.
    b. a theory.

_____ 12. I prefer tasks that require me to
    a. follow careful, detailed instructions.
    b. use reasoning and critical analysis.

_____ 13. For a criminal justice course, I would prefer to
    a. discover how and when a law can be applied.
    b. learn how and why it became law.

_____ 14. To learn more about the operation of a digital camera, I would prefer to
    a. work with several types of digital cameras.
    b. understand the principles on which it operates.

PART THREE

_____ 15. To solve a math problem, I would prefer to
   a. draw or visualize the problem.
   b. study a sample problem and use it as a model.

_____ 16. To remember something best, I
   a. create a mental picture.
   b. write it down.

_____ 17. Assembling a bicycle from a diagram would be
   a. easy.
   b. challenging.

_____ 18. I prefer classes in which I
   a. handle equipment or work with models.
   b. participate in a class discussion.

_____ 19. To understand and remember how a machine works, I would
   a. draw a diagram.
   b. write notes.

_____ 20. I enjoy
   a. drawing or working with my hands.
   b. speaking, writing, and listening.

_____ 21. If I were trying to locate an office on an unfamiliar university campus, I would prefer
   a. a map.
   b. a set of printed directions.

PART FOUR

_____ 22. For a grade in biology lab, I would prefer to
   a. work with a lab partner.
   b. work alone.

_____ 23. When faced with a difficult personal problem, I prefer to
   a. discuss it with others.
   b. resolve it myself.

_____ 24. Many instructors could improve their classes by
   a. including more discussion and group activities.
   b. allowing students to work on their own more frequently.

_____ 25. When listening to a lecturer or speaker, I respond more to
   a. the person presenting the ideas.
   b. the ideas themselves.

_____ 26. When on a team project, I prefer to
   a. work with several team members.
   b. divide up tasks and complete those assigned to me.

_____ 27. I prefer to shop and do errands
   a. with friends.
   b. by myself.

_____ 28. A job in a busy office is
   a. more appealing than working alone.
   b. less appealing than working alone.

PART FIVE

_____ 29. To make decisions, I rely on
   a. my experiences and gut feelings.
   b. facts and objective data.

_____ 30. To complete a task, I
   a. can use whatever is available to get the job done.
   b. must have everything I need at hand.

_____ 31. I prefer to express my ideas and feelings through
   a. music, song, or poetry.
   b. direct, concise language.

_____ 32. I prefer instructors who
   a. allow students to be guided by their own interests.
   b. make their expectations clear and explicit.

_____ 33. I tend to
   a. challenge and question what I hear and read.
   b. accept what I hear and read.

_____ 34. I prefer
   a. essay exams.
   b. objective exams.

_____ 35. In completing an assignment, I prefer to
   a. figure out my own approach.
   b. be told exactly what to do.

To score your questionnaire, record the total number of times you selected choice *a* and the total number of times you selected choice *b* for each part of the questionnaire. Record your totals in the scoring grid provided.

SCORING GRID

Part	Total Number of Choice *a*	Total Number of Choice *b*
Part One	_____ Auditory	_____ Visual
Part Two	_____ Applied	_____ Conceptual
Part Three	_____ Spatial	_____ Verbal
Part Four	_____ Social	_____ Independent
Part Five	_____ Creative	_____ Pragmatic

Now circle your higher score for each part of the questionnaire. The word below the score you circled indicates an aspect of your learning style. Scores in a particular row that are close to one another, such as a 3 and a 4, suggest that you do not exhibit a strong, clear preference for either aspect. Scores that are farther apart, such as a 1 and a 6, suggest a strong preference for the higher-scoring aspect. The next section describes these aspects and explains how to interpret your scores.

Interpreting Your Scores

The questionnaire was divided into five parts; each part identifies one aspect of your learning style. These five aspects are explained below.

PART ONE: AUDITORY OR VISUAL LEARNERS This score indicates the sensory mode you prefer when processing information. Auditory learners tend to learn more effectively through listening. Visual learners process information by seeing it in print or other visual modes, including films, pictures, or diagrams. If you have a higher score in auditory than visual, you tend to be an auditory learner. That is, you tend to learn more easily by hearing than by reading. A higher score in visual suggests strengths with visual modes of learning.

PART TWO: APPLIED OR CONCEPTUAL LEARNERS This score describes the types of learning tasks and learning situations you prefer and find easiest to handle. If you are an applied learner, you prefer tasks that involve real objects and situations. Practical, real-life learning situations are ideal for you. If you are a conceptual learner, you prefer to work with language and ideas; practical applications are not necessary for understanding.

PART THREE: SPATIAL OR VERBAL LEARNERS This score reveals your ability to work with spatial relationships. Spatial learners are able to visualize, or mentally see, how things work or how they are positioned in space. Their strengths may include drawing, assembling things, or repairing. Verbal learners tend to rely on verbal or language skills, rather than skills in positioning things in space.

PART FOUR: SOCIAL OR INDEPENDENT LEARNERS This score reveals your preferred level of interaction with other people in the learning process. If you are a social learner, you prefer to work with others—both peers and instructors—closely and directly. You tend to be people oriented and to enjoy personal interaction. If you are an independent learner, you prefer to work and study alone. You tend to be self-directed or self-motivated and often are goal oriented.

PART FIVE: CREATIVE OR PRAGMATIC LEARNERS This score describes the approach you prefer to take toward learning tasks. Creative learners are imaginative and innovative. They prefer to learn through discovery or experimentation. They are comfortable taking risks and following hunches. Pragmatic learners are practical, logical, and systematic. They seek order and are comfortable following rules.

DIRECTIONS   Write a paragraph describing yourself as a learner. Include aspects of your learning style and give examples from everyday experience that confirm your profile. Explain any results of the Learning Style Questionnaire with which you disagree. ●

Exercise 6

Developing an Action Plan for Learning

Now that you know more about *how* you learn, you are ready to develop an action plan for learning what you read. Figure 1-4 lists each aspect of learning style and offers suggestions for how to learn from a reading assignment. To use the figure:

1. Circle the five aspects of your learning style for which you received higher scores. Disregard the others.
2. Read through the suggestions that apply to you.
3. Place a check mark in front of the suggestions you think will work for you. Choose at least one from each category.
4. List the suggestions you chose in the following Action Plan for Learning box.

FIGURE 1-4
Learning Strategies
for Various Learning
Styles

AUDITORY	VISUAL
1. Record review notes.	1. Use mapping (see Chapter 4).
2. Discuss/study with friends.	2. Use visualization.
3. Talk aloud when studying.	3. Use online resources if available.
4. Record lectures.	4. View videos when available.
5. Listen to audio recordings about the subject matter (podcasts, MP3s).	5. Draw diagrams, charts, and maps.

APPLIED	CONCEPTUAL
1. Associate ideas with their application.	1. Use outlining.
2. Take courses with a lab or practicum.	2. Focus on thought patterns (see Chapter 9).
3. Think of practical situations to which learning applies.	3. Organize materials into rules and examples.
4. Use case studies, examples, and applications to cue your learning.	

SPATIAL	VERBAL
1. Draw diagrams; make charts and sketches.	1. Record steps, processes, and procedures in words.
2. Use outlining.	2. Write summaries.
3. Use visualization.	3. Translate diagrams and drawings into language.
4. Use mapping (see Chapter 4).	4. Write your interpretations next to textbook drawings, maps, and graphics.

SOCIAL	INDEPENDENT
1. Interact with the instructor.	1. Use online tutorials if available.
2. Find a study partner.	2. Enroll in courses using a traditional lecture–exam format.
3. Form an in-person or online study group.	3. Consider independent study courses.
4. Take courses involving class discussion.	4. Purchase review books, study guides, and online self-tutorial packages, if available.
5. Work with a tutor.	
6. Use social media to trade study tips with classmates.	

CREATIVE	PRAGMATIC
1. Take courses that involve exploration, experimentation, or discussion.	1. Write lists of steps, processes, and procedures.
2. Use annotation to record impressions and reactions.	2. Write summaries and outlines.
3. Ask questions about chapter content and answer them.	3. Use a structured study environment.
	4. Focus on problem-solving and logical sequence.

ACTION PLAN FOR LEARNING

Learning Strategy 1 _____

_____

Learning Strategy 2 _____

_____

Learning Strategy 3 _____

_____

Learning Strategy 4 _____

_____

Learning Strategy 5 _____

_____

Now that you have listed suggestions to help you learn what you read, the next step is to experiment with these techniques, one at a time. (You may need to refer to the chapters listed in parentheses in Figure 1-4 to learn or review how a certain technique works.) Use one technique for a while, then move on to the next. Continue using the techniques that seem to work; work on revising or modifying those that do not. Do not hesitate to experiment with other techniques listed in the figure; you may find other techniques that work well for you.

Developing Strategies to Overcome Limitations

You should also work on developing the weaker aspects of your learning style. Make a conscious effort to work on improving areas of weakness as well as taking advantage of your strengths. Your learning style is not fixed or unchanging; you can improve areas in which you had low scores. Although you may be weak in auditory learning, for example, many of your professors will lecture and expect you to take notes. If you work on improving your listening and note-taking skills, you will learn better from lectures.

Several Words of Caution

Ideally, through activities in this section and the use of the questionnaire, you have discovered more about yourself as a learner. However, several words of caution are in order.

1. The questionnaire is a quick and easy way to discover your learning style. Other more formal and more accurate measures of learning style are available. These include *Kolb's Learning Style Inventory* and the *Myers–Briggs Type Indicator*. These tests may be available through your college's counseling, testing, or academic skills centers.
2. There are many more aspects of learning style than those identified through the questionnaire in this chapter. To learn more about other factors affecting learning, see one or both of the tests listed in point 1.

3. Learning style is *not* a fixed, unchanging quality. Just as personalities can change and develop, so can learning style change and develop through exposure, instruction, or practice. For example, as you attend more college lectures, your skill as an auditory learner may be strengthened.

4. You probably will not be clearly strong or weak in each aspect. Some students, for example, can learn equally well spatially and verbally. If your scores on one or more parts of the questionnaire were quite close, then you may have strengths in both areas.

5. When students discover the features of their learning style, they usually recognize themselves. A frequent comment is "Yep, that's me." However, if for some reason you feel the description of yourself as a learner is incorrect, then do not make changes in your learning strategies on the basis of the questionnaire results. Instead, discuss your style with your instructor or consider taking one of the tests listed in point 1.

Goal 3

Understand instructors' teaching styles.

UNDERSTANDING YOUR INSTRUCTORS' TEACHING STYLES

Just as each student has an individual learning style, each instructor also has a teaching style. Some instructors, for example, have a teaching style that promotes social interaction among students. An instructor may organize small-group activities, encourage class participation, or require students to work in pairs or teams to complete a specific task. Other instructors offer little or no opportunity for social interaction, as in a lecture class. Some instructors are very applied; they teach by example. Others are more conceptual; they focus on presenting ideas, rules, and theories. In fact, the same five categories of learning styles identified on pages 24–25 can be applied to teaching styles as well.

To an extent, of course, the subject matter also dictates how the instructor teaches. A biology instructor, for instance, has a large body of factual information to present and may feel he or she has little time to schedule group interaction.

Comparing Learning and Teaching Style

Once you are aware of your learning style and consider the instructor's teaching style, you can begin to understand why you learn better from one instructor than from another and why you feel more comfortable in certain instructors' classes than in others. When aspects of your learning style match aspects of your instructor's teaching style, you are on the same wavelength, so to speak; the instructor is teaching the way you learn. However, when your learning style does not correspond to an instructor's teaching style, you may not be as comfortable, and learning will be more of a challenge. You may have to work harder in that class by taking extra steps to reorganize or reformat the material into a form better suited to your learning style. The following sections present each of the five categories of learning–teaching styles and suggest how you might adapt to accommodate each type of teaching style.

AUDITORY–VISUAL If your instructor announces essential course information (such as paper assignments, class projects, or descriptions of upcoming exams) orally and you are a visual learner, you should be sure to record as much information as possible in your notes. If your instructor relies on lectures to present new material not included in your textbook, taking complete lecture notes is especially important. If your instructor uses numerous visual aids and you tend to be an auditory learner, consider recording summaries of these visual aids.

APPLIED–CONCEPTUAL If your instructor seldom uses examples, models, or case studies and you are an applied learner, you need to think of your own examples to make the course material real and memorable to you. Leave space in your class notes to add examples. Add them during class if they come to mind; if not, take time as you review your notes to add examples. If your instructor uses numerous demonstrations and examples and you are a conceptual learner, you may need to leave space in your class notes to write in rules or generalizations that state what the examples are intended to prove.

SPATIAL–VERBAL If you are a spatial learner and your instructor has a verbal teaching style (he or she lectures), then you will need to draw diagrams, charts, and pictures to learn the material. If you are a verbal learner and your instructor is spatial (he or she frequently uses diagrams, flowcharts, and so forth), then you may need to translate the diagrams and flowcharts into words in order to learn them.

SOCIAL–INDEPENDENT If your instructor organizes numerous in-class group activities and you tend to be an independent learner, then you will need to spend time alone after class reviewing the class activity, making notes, and perhaps even repeating the activity by yourself to make it more meaningful. If your instructor seldom structures in-class group activities and you tend to be a social learner, try to arrange to study regularly with a classmate or create or join an in-person or online study group.

CREATIVE–PRAGMATIC Suppose your instructor is very systematic and structured in his or her lectures, and, as a creative learner, you prefer to discover ideas through experimentation and free-flowing discussion. In this case, you should consider creating a column in your class notes to record your responses and creative thoughts or reserving the bottom quarter of each page for such annotations. If your instructor is creative and tends to use a loose or free-flowing class format, and you tend to be a pragmatic learner, you may need to rewrite and restructure class notes. If your instructor fails to give you specific guidelines for completing activities or assignments, you should ask for more information.

DIRECTIONS Analyze your instructors' teaching styles by completing the following chart for the courses you are taking this semester. List as many teaching characteristics as you can, but do not try to cover every aspect of learning–teaching style.

Exercise 7

	Course	Instructor's Name	Teaching-Style Characteristics
1.			
2.			
3.			
4.			
5.			
6.			

Exercise 8

DIRECTIONS   After you have completed the chart in Exercise 7, select one of your instructors whose teaching style does not match your learning style. Write a paragraph describing the differences in your styles. Explain how you will change your study methods to make up for these differences. ●

Goal 4

Meet instructors' expectations.

MEETING YOUR INSTRUCTORS' EXPECTATIONS

Whether you have just completed high school or are returning to college with work experiences or family responsibilities, you will face new demands and expectations in college. The following sections describe your instructors' expectations.

Visual Thinking
APPLYING SKILLS

What does this student's comment reveal?

Take Responsibility for Your Own Learning

In college, learning is mainly up to you. Instructors function as guides. They define and explain what is to be learned, but they expect you to do the learning. Weekly class time is far shorter than in high school. For this reason, college class time is used primarily to introduce content and to discuss ideas. Instructors expect you to learn the material and to be prepared to discuss it in class. *When*, *where*, and *how* you learn are your choices. Be sure to take into account the five aspects of your learning style as you make these choices.

Focus on Concepts, Not Facts

Each course you take will require you to learn a great many facts, statistics, dates, definitions, formulas, rules, or principles. It is easy to become a robot learner—memorizing facts from texts and lectures and then recalling them on exams and quizzes. However, factual information is only a starting point, a base from which to approach the real content of a course. Most college instructors expect you to go beyond facts to analysis—to consider what the collection of facts and details *means*. To avoid focusing too intensely on facts, be sure to keep the following questions in mind as you read and study.

- Why do I need to know this?
- Why is this important?
- What principle or trend does this illustrate?
- How can I use this information?
- How does this fit in with other course content?

Focus on Ideas, Not "Right Answers"

Through previous schooling, many students have come to expect their answers to be either right or wrong. They assume that their mastery of the course is measured by the number of "right answers" they have learned. For this reason, they may be lost when faced with an essay question such as the following:

> Defend or criticize the arguments that are offered in favor of capital punishment. Refer to any readings that you have completed.

There is no one right answer to this question. You can either defend the arguments or criticize them. The instructor who asks this question expects you to think and to provide a reasoned, logical, consistent response that draws on information you have acquired through your reading. Here are a few more examples of questions for which there are no single correct answers.

> Would you be willing to reduce your standard of living by 15 percent if the United States could thereby eliminate poverty? Defend your response.

> Imagine a society in which everyone has exactly the same income. You are the manager of an industrial plant. What plans, policies, or programs would you implement to motivate your employees to work?

Evaluate New Ideas

Throughout college you will continually encounter new ideas; you will agree with some and disagree with others. Don't accept or reject a new idea, however, until you have really explored it and have considered its assumptions and implications. Ask questions such as these:

- What evidence is available to support this idea?
- What opposing evidence is available?
- How is my personal experience related to this idea?
- What additional information do I need in order to make a decision?

Tip An *assumption* is a firm belief that something is true even without all the evidence to prove it. An *implication* is an idea that's suggested but not stated directly. If your roommate says, "Take your umbrella today," he or she is implying that it's going to rain soon.

DEVELOPING ACTIVE LEARNING STRATEGIES

Your instructors expect you to become an active learner, illustrated by the following situation.

Goal

Use active learning strategies.

> A first-year student who had always thought of himself as a B student was getting low C's and D's in his business course. The instructor gave weekly quizzes; each was a practical problem to solve. Every week the student memorized his lecture notes and carefully reread the assigned chapter in his textbook. When he spoke with his instructor about his low grades, the instructor told him that his study methods were not effective and that he needed to become more active and involved with the subject matter. Memorizing and rereading are passive approaches, the instructor said, suggesting that the student try instead to think about content, ask questions, anticipate practical uses of the theory, solve potential problems, and draw connections among ideas.

Active Versus Passive Learning

How did you learn to ride a bike, play racquetball, or change a tire? In each case you learned by doing, by active participation. College learning requires similar active involvement and participation. Active learning is expected in most college courses and can often make the difference between barely average grades and top grades.

Figure 1-5 lists common college learning situations and contrasts the responses of passive and active learners. The examples in Figure 1-5 show that passive learners do not carry the learning process far enough. They do not go beyond what instructors tell them to do. They fail to think about, organize, and react to course content.

Active Learning Strategies

When you study, you should be thinking about and reacting to the material in front of you. This is how to do so:

1. **Ask questions about what you are reading.** You will find that asking questions helps to focus your attention and improve your concentration.
2. **Consider the purpose behind assignments.** Why might a sociology assignment require you to spend an hour at the primate exhibit of the local zoo, for example?
3. **Try to see how each assignment fits with the rest of the course.** For instance, why does a section called "Amortization" belong in a business mathematics textbook chapter titled "Business and Consumer Loans"?
4. **Relate what you are learning to what you already know from the course and from your background knowledge and personal experience.** Connect a law in physics with how your car's brakes work, for example.
5. **Think of examples or situations in which you can apply the information.**

Throughout the remainder of this text, you will learn many strategies for becoming an active learner. Active learning also involves active reading. In Chapter 6 you will learn specific strategies for becoming an active reader.

FIGURE 1-5
Characteristics of Passive and Active Learners

ACTIVITIES	PASSIVE LEARNERS	ACTIVE LEARNERS
Class lectures	Write down what the instructor says	Decide what is important to write down
Textbook assignments	Read	Read, think, ask questions, try to connect ideas
Studying	Reread	Consider learning style, make study sheets, create outlines, predict exam questions, look for trends and patterns, use online resources
Writing class assignments	Only follow the professor's instructions	Try to discover the significance of the assignment, look for the principles and concepts it illustrates
Writing term papers	Do only what is expected to get a good grade	Try to expand their knowledge and experience with a topic and connect it to the course objective or content

DIRECTIONS Consider each of the following learning situations. Answer each question by suggesting active learning approaches.

1. Your history professor returns a graded exam to you. How could you use it as a learning device? _____

_____

_____

2. You have been assigned to read "Letter from Birmingham Jail" by Martin Luther King, Jr., for your English composition class. What questions would you try to answer as you read? _____

_____

3. Your biology course requires a weekly lab. How would you prepare for attending this lab? _____

_____

4. Your sociology instructor has assigned an article from *The New York Times* on crime in major U.S. cities. How would you record important ideas? _____

_____

THINKING CRITICALLY

Goal 6

Explain and illustrate critical thinking.

In college, your instructors expect you not only to learn actively, but also to think critically. A first step in becoming a critical thinker is to become familiar with the types of thinking that college instructors demand. Figure 1-6 lists six levels of thinking in order of increasing complexity. Based on a progression of thinking skills developed by Benjamin Bloom and revised by Lorin Anderson, they are widely used by educators in many academic disciplines.

FIGURE 1-6
Levels of Thinking

LEVEL	EXAMPLES
REMEMBERING: recalling information, repeating information with no changes	Recalling dates, memorizing definitions for a history exam
UNDERSTANDING: understanding ideas, using rules, and following directions	Explaining a mathematical law, knowing how the human ear functions, explaining a definition in psychology
APPLYING: applying knowledge to a new situation	Using knowledge of formulas to solve a new physics problem
ANALYZING: seeing relationships, breaking information into parts, analyzing how things work	Comparing two poems by the same author
EVALUATING: making judgments, assessing the value or worth of information	Evaluating the effectiveness of an argument opposing the death penalty
CREATING: putting ideas and information together in a unique way, creating something new	Designing a Web page

The *remembering* level of thinking is basically memorization; this is something you've been doing for years. The *understanding* level is also familiar. If you are able to explain how to convert fractions to decimals, then you are thinking at the comprehension (*understanding*) level. At the *applying* level, you apply to a new situation information that you have memorized and understood. When you use your knowledge of punctuation to place commas correctly in a sentence, you are functioning at the application level. The *analyzing* level involves examining what you have learned and studying relationships. When you explain how a microscope works, you are analyzing its operation. *Evaluating* involves making judgments. When you decide what is effective and what is ineffective in a classmate's presentation in a public speaking class, you are evaluating the presentation. The *creating* level requires you to put ideas together to form something new. When you write a paper by drawing on a variety of sources, you are synthesizing sources to create something completely new.

The last three levels—analyzing, evaluating, and creating—involve *critical thinking*. Critical thinking requires you to interpret and evaluate what you hear and read, rather than accept everything as "the truth." The term *critical* does not mean "negative." Rather, it means "analytical" and "probing"—that is, thinking more deeply about the subjects you study.

The benefits of critical thinking extend beyond your college courses. In your everyday life, critical thinking skills will help you

- become a savvy consumer and make good financial choices.
- understand when companies are trying to manipulate you with their advertising or public-relations efforts.
- resolve conflicts or come to acceptable compromises.
- solve problems and make decisions using a logical, step-by-step process.

Tip *Synthesizing* means "combining." The word part *syn-* means "together" or "with."

APPLYING LEVELS OF THINKING

Reading and Levels of Thinking

As you read, be sure to think at each level. Here is a list of questions to help you read and think at each level.

Level of Thinking	Questions
REMEMBERING	What information do I need to learn?
UNDERSTANDING	What are the main points and how are they supported?
APPLYING	How can I use this information?
ANALYZING	How is this material organized? How are the ideas related?
	How are the data presented in graphs, tables, and charts related? What trends do they reveal?
EVALUATING	Is this information accurate, reliable, and valuable? Does the author prove his or her points?
CREATING	How does this information fit with other sources (class lectures, other readings, your prior knowledge)?

DIRECTIONS   Identify the level or levels of thinking that each of the following tasks demands.

1. Retelling a favorite family story to your nieces and nephews

   _____

2. Using the principles of time management discussed earlier in this chapter to develop a weekly study plan

   _____

3. Learning the names of the U.S. presidents since World War II

   _____

4. Reorganizing your lecture notes by topic

   _____

5. Writing a letter to the editor of your hometown newspaper praising a recently passed city ordinance that restricts new toxic-waste disposal sites

   _____

6. Writing a term paper that requires library and online research

   _____

7. Using prereading techniques when reading your speech communication textbook

   _____

8. Listening to speeches by two candidates who are running for mayor and then deciding which one gets your vote

   _____

9. Watching several hours of TV programming to determine the amount of time given to commercials, to public service announcements, to entertainment programs, and to news

   _____

10. Writing an article for the campus newspaper explaining why on-campus parking is inadequate

   _____ •

DIRECTIONS   Read "Dimensions of Nonverbal Communication" and answer the questions that follow.

Dimensions of Nonverbal Communication

In recent years, research has reemphasized the important role of physical, or nonverbal, behaviors in effective oral communication. Basically, three generalizations about nonverbal communication should occupy your attention when you are a speaker:

1. *Speakers reveal and reflect their emotional states through their nonverbal behaviors.* Your listeners read your feelings toward yourself, your topic, and your audience from your facial expressions. Consider the contrast between a speaker who walks to the front of the room briskly, head held high, and one who shuffles, head bowed and arms hanging limply.

Communications scholar Dale G. Leathers summarized a good deal of research into nonverbal communication processes: "Feelings and emotions are more accurately exchanged by nonverbal than verbal means. . . . The nonverbal portion of communication conveys meanings and intentions that are relatively free from deception, distortion, and confusion."

2. *The speaker's nonverbal cues enrich or elaborate the message that comes through words.* A solemn face can reinforce the dignity of a funeral eulogy. The words "Either do this or do that" can be illustrated with appropriate arm-and-hand gestures. Taking a few steps to one side tells an audience that you are moving from one argument to another. A smile enhances a lighter moment in your speech.

3. *Nonverbal messages form a reciprocal interaction between speaker and listener.* Listeners frown, smile, shift nervously in their seats, and engage in many types of nonverbal behavior. . . . There are four areas of nonverbal communication that concern every speaker: (a) *proxemics,* (b) *movement and stance,* (c) *facial expressions,* and (d) *gestures.*

—Gronbeck et al., *Principles of Speech Communication,* pp. 217–218

1. **Remembering:** What are the three generalizations?

_____

_____

_____

2. **Understanding:** Explain how a speaker can reveal his or her emotional state.

_____

3. **Applying:** Give an example (not used in the excerpt) of how a speaker can reveal his or her emotional state.

_____

_____

4. **Analyzing:** If nonverbal communication is relatively free of deception, is it possible to tell a lie using body language?

_____

_____

5. **Evaluating:** How is this information useful and important to me in a public speaking class?

_____

_____

_____

6. **Creating:** To what extent is this information consistent with what I already know about nonverbal messages?

_____

_____

DIRECTIONS   Read the textbook selection "Race and Ethnicity," in Part Seven, pages 425–438. Then write two questions that require thinking at each of the levels we have discussed (a total of 12 questions). ●

Exercise 12

USING COLLEGE TEXTBOOKS
Keeping Up with Reading Assignments

An important part of time management is keeping up with textbook reading assignments. It is easy to let assignments slide, especially when your instructor is not checking to be sure you have completed them.

Use the following suggestions to keep up with assigned reading.

USE AND MARK YOUR SYLLABUS

A syllabus (see the Success Workshop on page 2) often contains a list of assigned chapters along with the week they are due. Use the margins of the syllabus to mark when you plan to complete each assignment, and check it off when complete. Subdivide long chapters into sections to be completed on different days. Here is an excerpt from a syllabus for an art course.

Week 1	Chapter 1 The Nature of Art		✓ 9/15
Week 2	Chapter 3 Visual Elements of Art	pp. 112-130	✓ 9/19
		pp. 131-148	✓ 9/21
Week 3	Chapter 4 Principles of Art	pp. 149-160	9/26
		pp. 161-175	9/28

Textbook Exercise 1: Working with Your College Textbook

Choose a chapter that you have been assigned in another course. Subdivide it into sections and create a schedule for reading and completing the chapter.

ANNOTATE THE TEXT'S TABLE OF CONTENTS

Keep track of when assignments are due and when you have completed them using the book's table of contents, as shown on the next page. Feel free to add notes to yourself indicating sections that need further review or those that you had difficulty with.

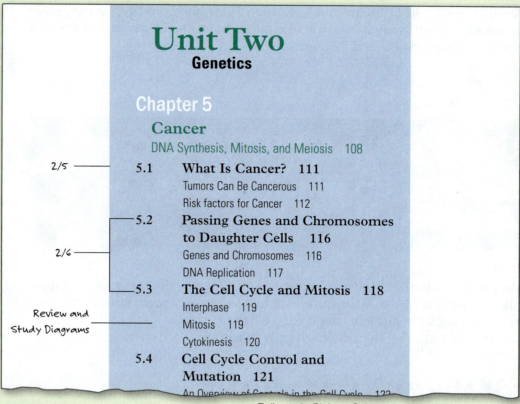

— Belk, et al., *Biology: Science for Life with Physiology*, 3e

Experiment with the two methods covered here and on the previous page of keeping track of reading assignments. Decide which one works better and use it for several weeks.

Textbook Exercise 2: Annotate A Chapter From Your College Textbook

Use the method described on this and the previous page to annotate the table of contents for this textbook.

FURTHER PRACTICE WITH TEXTBOOK READING

Textbook Exercise 3 : Textbook Chapter

Below is a section of a syllabus that assigns the textbook chapter contained in Part Seven: Classroom Simulation: Textbook Reading and Writing (p. 422). The syllabus shows topics to be studied over a one-week period.

Feb 13: Lecture on Race and Ethnicity. Read the Chapter Overview and The Social Meaning of Race and Ethnicity.
Feb 15: Lecture on Prejudice, Stereotypes, and Discrimination. Read the remainder of the "Race and Ethnicity" chapter.
Feb 17: Quiz on Chapter 11: Race and Ethnicity

Using the guidelines on pages 37–38, annotate the table of contents below according to the syllabus.

Textbook Exercise 4 : Your College Textbook

Choose a textbook that you are using in one of your other courses. Using the syllabus for that course, annotate your textbook's table of contents according to the guidelines on pages 37–38.

SELF-TEST SUMMARY

Goal 1

Why should you set goals and manage your time?

Establishing your goals will eliminate conflicts and keep you focused. Begin by establishing your priorities and following them to achieve your academic goals. Next, compare the time you have allotted to various commitments with the priorities you have assigned to those activities. Finally, build a term plan that you will adjust weekly. Analyze how you spend your time each week on nonacademic tasks to determine if you have enough time for classes, studying, and homework. Use your time wisely and control the tendency to procrastinate.

Goal 2

Why should you analyze your learning style?

Analyzing your learning style can help you understand why you learn better from one instructor than another and why some courses are easier than others. Building an awareness of how you learn best and what your limitations are can help you study more effectively and become a more efficient learner.

Goal 3

Why is it important to analyze your instructors' teaching styles?

You may need to make changes in how you learn to suit each instructor's teaching style.

Goal 4

What do instructors expect of college students?

In college, instructors expect students to set their own operating rules, take responsibility for their own learning, and focus on and evaluate ideas and concepts.

Goal 5

What does "becoming an active learner" mean?

Active learning is essential to success in college. To become a more effective learner, you should get actively involved with reading assignments, lectures, and class activities by (a) asking questions about class presentations and reading assignments, and (b) looking for the purpose of learning the information presented.

Goal 6

What is critical thinking and why is it important?

College instructors expect their students to read and think critically. There are six levels of thinking: remembering, understanding, applying, analyzing, evaluating, and creating. The last three of these are critical thinking skills. Many classroom activities, such as exams, papers, and discussions, require reading and thinking at these levels.

APPLYING | YOUR SKILLS

DISCUSSING THE CHAPTER

1. What are the advantages of working on assignments in several short sessions over a period of time rather than in one longer session all at once?
2. What are some of the ways that you can use spare moments and combine activities to help you save time?
3. How do learning styles relate to choice of major or choice of profession? Discuss majors and jobs that may be most appropriate or inappropriate for the various learning styles.
4. Take a look at the tests you've taken so far in college. Determine which of Benjamin Bloom's types of thinking are present in each exam question. Brainstorm some study strategies to help you prepare for questions in each category.

ANALYZING A STUDY SITUATION

DIRECTIONS Working in groups of three or four students, analyze the following situation. Discuss answers to the questions that follow.

A history professor has just returned graded midterm exams to her class. One student looks at the grade on the first page, flips through the remaining pages while commenting to a friend that the exam was "too picky," and files it in her notebook. A second student reviews his exam for grading errors and notices one error. Immediately, he raises his hand and asks for an adjustment to his grade. The instructor seems annoyed and tells the student she will not use class time to dispute individual grades. A third student reviews her exam bluebook to identify a pattern of error; on the cover of the bluebook, she notes topics and areas in which she is weak.

1. Compare the three students' responses to the situation.
2. What does each student's response reveal about his or her approach to learning?
3. Analyze the student's response to the instructor's error in grading. What alternatives might have been more appropriate?
4. At what level(s) of thinking was each of the three students functioning?

WORKING ON COLLABORATIVE PROJECTS

DIRECTIONS Working in groups of two or three, prepare a "Need to Know" list for new students on your campus. Include information you have discovered so far about learning and studying in college. Groups should compare and compile lists and may wish to prepare a handout for next semester's class, post information on the campus Web site, or submit the final list to the college newspaper for publication or to the director of student orientation for use with incoming students.

Quick | Quiz

DIRECTIONS   Write the letter of the choice that best completes each statement in the space provided.

CHECKING YOUR RECALL

_____ 1. If you are taking 12 hours of classes, you should expect to study each week for at least

   a. 6 hours.
   b. 12 hours.
   c. 24 hours.
   d. 30 hours.

_____ 2. An example of an effective time-saving technique is

   a. waiting as long as possible to complete an assignment.
   b. reviewing class notes while riding on the bus.
   c. eliminating optional assignments from your weekly plan.
   d. studying with a friend.

_____ 3. It is usually best to study for a difficult course

   a. in two or three short blocks of time rather than in one long block.
   b. only when you really feel like it.
   c. after a warm-up session.
   d. after you have studied for your easier courses.

_____ 4. The primary value of identifying your learning style is that it can help you

   a. become interested in what you are studying.
   b. develop and maintain your concentration.
   c. become more efficient in how you study.
   d. increase your reading rate.

_____ 5. An active learner would do all of the following _except_

   a. read, think, ask questions, and try to connect ideas.
   b. predict exam questions and look for trends and patterns.
   c. do only what is expected to get a good grade.
   d. try to discover the significance of the assignment and look for the principles and concepts it illustrates.

APPLYING YOUR SKILLS

_____ 6. Sarah has an economics examination tomorrow. She has been cramming for four hours straight and is starting to panic. Which of the following suggestions would _not_ have helped Sarah to study more effectively?

   a. studying her easier topics first
   b. studying in short blocks of time, rather than in one long block
   c. taking a ten-minute break for each hour that she studies
   d. scheduling her study session at a time when she is alert and feels like studying

_____ 7. Tonight, Justine needs to prepare for a math midterm examination that she'll take tomorrow, make vocabulary flash cards for tomorrow's Russian class, and read three chapters in a novel for her English class in two days. In what order should she attack these assignments?

   a. math, Russian, English
   b. math, English, Russian
   c. Russian, math, English
   d. English, Russian, math

_____ 8. Craig learns best using diagrams, charts, and sketches. He frequently uses outlining, visualization, and mapping to help him organize the ideas presented in his classes. Craig can best be described as a

   a. verbal learner.
   b. auditory learner.
   c. spatial learner.
   d. applied learner.

_____ 9. On her physics test, Janiece will be expected to use her knowledge of formulas to solve a new physics problem. Janiece's test will require her to use which level of thinking?

   a. remembering
   b. applying
   c. analyzing
   d. evaluating

_____ 10. Amelia is taking a biology class in which the instructor relies on lectures to present information. Because the course covers so much material, the instructor does not have time to schedule group interaction. If Amelia were a social learner, it would be most helpful for her to

   a. drop the class immediately because it doesn't suit her learning style.
   b. spend time alone after class, reviewing the lecture.
   c. form an online study group with students from her class.
   d. record lectures to listen to by herself later.

Taking Notes in Class

LEARNING GOALS

In this chapter you will learn to

1 Sharpen your listening skills.

2 Prepare for a class lecture.

3 Take lecture notes.

4 Edit your notes.

5 Study your notes.

LEARNING EXPERIMENT

1 Ask a friend to read each of the following paragraphs aloud (or your instructor may choose to read them). While paragraph 1 is read to you, just listen. While and after paragraph 2 is read to you, write a set of notes that contain its most important ideas.

Paragraph 1

Did you know that use of empty space is a form of communication? How humans use space can communicate as loudly as words and phrases. How close or how far away you stand from another person communicates a message. Research by Edward Hall identifies four types of distance, each of which defines the relationship you establish with others. The first, intimate distance, is not considered appropriate in public (except in crowded places, such as elevators). Family members and spouses may use the intimate distance. Personal distance is the space around you that no one invades unless invited, such as to shake hands. Social distance is the distance at which you operate in daily living—sitting in classrooms, attending a play, shopping, and so forth. The fourth type, public distance, is used when you are not involved with another person.

Paragraph 2

Communication occurs with words and gestures, but did you know it also occurs through sense of smell? Odor can communicate at least four types of messages. First, odor can signal attraction. Animal species give off scents to attract members of the opposite sex. Humans use fragrances to make themselves more appealing or attractive. Second, smell communicates information about tastes. The smell of popcorn popping stimulates the appetite. If you smell a chicken roasting you can anticipate its taste. A third type of smell communication is through memory. A smell can help you recall an event months or even years ago, especially if the event is an emotional one. Finally, smell can communicate by creating an identity or image for a person or product. For example, a woman may wear only one brand of perfume. Or a brand of shaving cream may have a distinct fragrance, which allows users to recognize it.

2 Wait 24 hours, or until the next class session; then, without reading either paragraph or looking at your notes, answer the following questions.

Paragraph 1

Name the four types of distances discussed in the paragraph.

Paragraph 2

Name the four messages that smell can communicate.

Check your answers using the Answer Key at the bottom of page 62.

The Results

You probably got more information correct for paragraph 2 than you did for paragraph 1. Why?

Because you listened to paragraph 2 and took notes. In doing so, you used three sensory modes: hearing (listening), touching (writing), and seeing (reading your notes). For paragraph 1, you used only one sensory mode: hearing.

Learning Principle: What This Means to You

You have five senses—five ways of taking in information from the world around you: sight, touch, smell, sound, and taste. **The more senses you use to learn something, the easier it will be to learn.** When you listen to a college lecture, you are using only one sensory mode. If you take notes on the lecture as you listen, you are using your sense of touch as well as your sense of hearing. When you reread the notes after you have written them, you are employing a third sensory mode—sight. In this chapter you will learn how to take notes effectively, how to edit them, and how to develop a system to study them.

Goal 1

Sharpen your listening skills.

SHARPENING YOUR LISTENING SKILLS

The first step in taking good lecture notes is to sharpen your listening skills. The average adult spends 31 percent of each waking hour listening. By comparison, 7 percent is spent on writing, 11 percent on reading, and 21 percent on speaking. Listening, then, is an essential communication skill. During college lectures, listening is especially important; it is your primary means of acquiring information.

Have you ever found yourself not listening to a professor who was lecturing? Her voice was loud and clear, so you certainly could hear her, but you weren't paying attention—you tuned her out. This situation illustrates the distinction between hearing and listening. Hearing is a passive, biological process in which the ear receives sound waves. In contrast, listening is an intellectual activity that involves the processing and interpretation of incoming information. Listening must be intentional, purposeful, and deliberate. You must plan to listen, have a reason for listening, and carefully focus your attention. Use the suggestions in the following box to sharpen your listening skills.

Goal 2

Prepare for a class lecture.

PREPARING FOR A CLASS LECTURE

Before you attend a lecture class, you should become familiar with the main topic of the lecture and be aware of important subtopics and related subjects.

HOW TO IMPROVE YOUR LISTENING SKILLS

1. **Approach listening as a process similar to reading.** Listening, like reading, is a comprehension process in which you grasp ideas, assess their importance, and connect them to other ideas. All the reading comprehension skills you will develop in Part Three of this text are useful for listening as well.

2. **Focus on content, not delivery.** It is easy to become so annoyed, upset, charmed, or engaged with the lecturer as an individual that you fail to comprehend his or her message. Force yourself to focus on the content of the lecture.

3. **Focus on ideas as well as facts.** If you concentrate on recording and remembering separate, unconnected facts, you will not be able to integrate all these facts into a coherent whole. In addition to facts, listen for ideas, significant trends, and patterns.

4. **Listen carefully to the speaker's opening comments.** Here the speaker may establish connections with prior lectures, identify his or her purpose, or describe the lecture's content or organization.

5. **Attempt to understand the lecturer's purpose.** Is it to present facts, raise and discuss questions, demonstrate a trend or pattern, or present a technique or procedure?

6. **Fill the gap between rate of speech and rate of thinking.** Has your mind ever wandered during a lecture? The rate of speech is much slower than the speed of thought. The average rate of speech is around 125 words per minute, whereas the rate at which you can process ideas is more than 500 words per minute. To listen most effectively, use this gap to think about lecture content. Anticipate what is to follow, think of situations in which the information might be applied, or pose questions.

Tip *Anticipate* means "to predict, to state what you think will happen in the future."

Understanding the lecture and taking notes will be easier if you have some idea of what the lecture is about. If your instructor assigns a textbook chapter that is related to the lecture, try to read the assignment before attending. If you are unable to read the entire chapter before class, at least preview the chapter to become familiar with the topics it covers. (You will learn about previewing in Chapter 6.) If no reading assignment is given in advance, check your syllabus or course outline to determine the topic of the lecture. Then preview the sections of your text that are about the topic.

Once you arrive at a lecture class, get organized before it begins. Take your coat off and have your computer, tablet, textbook, or notebook and pen ready to use. While waiting for class to begin, try to recall the content of the previous lecture: Think of three or four key points that were presented. Check your notes, if necessary. This process will activate your thought processes, focus your attention on course content, and make it easier for you to begin taking notes right away.

HOW TO TAKE LECTURE NOTES

Goal 3

Take lecture notes.

A good set of lecture notes must accomplish three things. First, and most important, your notes must serve as a record or summary of the lecture's main points. Second, they must include enough details and examples to help you recall the information several weeks later. Third, your notes must in some way show the relative importance of ideas presented and the organization of the lecture.

Record Main Ideas

The main ideas of a lecture are the points the instructor emphasizes and elaborates on. They are the major ideas that the details, explanations, examples, and general discussion support. Instructors can give clues to what is important in a lecture. The box on the next page suggests a few ways in which speakers show what is important.

Exercise 1

DIRECTIONS   Select one of your instructors and analyze his or her lecture style. Attend one lecture, and, as you take notes, try to be particularly aware of how he or she lets you know what is important. After the lecture, write a paragraph analyzing your instructor's lecture technique. ●

Record Details and Examples

A difficult part of taking notes is deciding how much detail to include with the main ideas. Obviously, you cannot write down everything; lecturers speak at

HOW SPEAKERS GIVE CLUES

When the lecturer . . .	The lecturer means . . .
Slows down or speaks more loudly	This is important! Try to record the speaker's exact words.
Lists or numbers points ("There are five causes . . . ," "Six solutions are . . . ," etc.)	Each of the points is equally important.
Makes a direct announcement ("One important fact . . . ," "Be sure to remember . . .")	This is information you should learn. It may appear on an exam.
Uses nonverbal clues (pointing, pounding the desk, walking toward the audience, etc.)	He or she feels strongly about the idea or wants to emphasize its importance.
Writes on the blackboard or whiteboard	He or she wants you to pay attention and copy the writing in your notes.
Uses PowerPoint slides	The information presented on the slides has been selected as particularly important.
Asks questions (either verbally or projected on a screen)	He or she is emphasizing the question's importance and may use this technique to provoke critical thinking (possible essay exam questions).
Distributes or posts online an outline of or note-taking guide for the lecture	The material is complex or he or she is aware that students may need help grasping the lecture's organization.

the rate of about 125 words per minute. Even if you could take shorthand, it would be nearly impossible to record everything the lecturer says. As a result, you have to be selective and record only particularly important details. As a rule of thumb, try to write down a brief phrase for each detail that directly explains or clarifies a major point.

If an instructor gives you several examples of a particular law, situation, or problem, be sure to write down, in summary form, at least one example. Record more than one if you have time. Although it may seem that you completely understand what is being discussed during the lecture, you will find that a few weeks later you really do need the example to boost your recall.

Tip A *rule of thumb* is a rough estimate based upon experience.

Record the Organization of the Lecture

As you write down a lecture's main ideas and important details, try to organize or arrange your notes so that you can easily see how the lecture is organized. By recording the lecture's organization, you will be able to determine the relative importance of ideas, and you will know what to pay the most attention to as you study and review for an exam.

A simple way to show a lecture's organization is to use indentation. Retain a regular margin on your paper or document. Start your notes on the most important of the topics at the left margin. For less important main ideas, indent your notes slightly. For major details, indent slightly more. Indent even more for examples and other details. The rule of thumb to follow is this: the less important the idea, the more it should be indented. Your notes might be organized like the sample that follows.

> **MAJOR TOPIC**
> Main idea
>   detail
>   detail
>   example
> Main idea
>   detail
>   detail
>   detail
> **MAJOR TOPIC**
> Main idea
>   detail
>   example

This indentation system, like a more formal outline, shows at a glance how important a particular fact or idea is. If the organization of a lecture is obvious, you may wish to use a number or letter system in addition to indenting.

Lectures are often organized using patterns: comparison–contrast, cause–effect, time sequence, classification, definition, or enumeration. Figure 2-1 lists tips for "customizing" your note taking to each of these patterns. An entire lecture may be organized using one pattern; a history lecture, for example, may use the time sequence pattern throughout. More often, however, several patterns will be evident at various points in a lecture. A psychology professor, for instance, may discuss definitions of motivation and compare and contrast different motivational theories. (Refer to Chapter 9 for a review of organizational patterns and the directional words that signal them.)

The notes in Figure 2-2 and Figure 2-3 were taken on the same lecture. One set of notes is thorough and effective; the other is lengthy and does not focus on key ideas. Read and evaluate each set of notes.

Tip *Classification* is a way of organizing ideas by dividing the general subject into its parts (for example, dividing sensory experience into its five sources).

FIGURE 2-1
Using Patterns in Lecture Note Taking

PATTERN	NOTE-TAKING TIPS
Comparison–contrast	Record similarities, differences, and basis of comparison; use two columns or make a chart.
Cause–effect	Distinguish causes from effects; use diagrams.
Sequence or order	Record dates; focus on order and sequence; use a time line for historical events; draw diagrams; record in order of importance; outline events or steps in a process.
Classification	Use outline form; list characteristics and distinguishing features.
Definition	Record the general category or class, then list distinguishing characteristics; include several examples.
Listing or Enumeration	Record in list or outline form; record the order of presentation.

Copyright © 2017 by Pearson Education, Inc.

FIGURE 2-2
Notes Showing
Lecture Organization

A. Social Stratification   Soc. 106
   Defs   9/16
   Soc. Strat. —hierarchy of ranks that exist in society
   Status —criteria to find positions in soc.
        2 types
              1. ascribed status—handed down; inherited
                 ex.: titles, race, wealth, ethnic background
              2. achieved status—things you control
                 ex.: education, jobs
B. Social Mobility
   Def. —how indiv. moves in hierarchy
        —amt. of movement depends on society
   2 Types
        1. caste—ex.: India—no mobility—you inherit class + status
        2. open—large amt. of achieved status—great mobility—ex.: USA.

FIGURE 2-3
Less Effective,
Unfocused Lecture
Notes

Social Stratification
   Social stratification—defined as the ranks that exist in society—the position that any person
   has—ascribed status—it is handed down—

   example: titles. A second kind is achieved—it is the kind you decide for yourself.
   Social stratification is important in understanding societies. How a person moves up and
   down + changes his social status is called mobility. Some societies have a lot of mobility.
   Others don't have any—example is India.

   There are 2 kinds of movement.
        1. Caste system is when everybody is assigned a class and they must stay there
           without any chance to change.
        2. Open—people can move from one to another. This is true in the United
           States.

Make Note Taking Easier

If you record main ideas, details, and examples using the indentation system to
show the lecture's organization, your notes will be adequate. However, there are
some tips you can follow to make note taking more effective, to make your notes
more complete, and to make study and review easier.

**USE A STANDARD-SIZED NOTEBOOK OR A SIMPLE, CLEAR COMPUTER
FONT** Paper smaller than 8½ by 11 inches doesn't allow you to write much on a
page, and it is more difficult to see the overall organization of a lecture if you have
to flip through a lot of pages.

**KEEP A SEPARATE NOTEBOOK OR COMPUTER FOLDER FOR EACH
COURSE** You need to keep your notes for each course together so that you can
review them easily.

DATE YOUR NOTES For easy reference later, be sure to date your notes. Your instructor might announce that an exam will cover everything presented after, for example, October 5. If your notes are not dated, you will not know where to begin to study.

LEAVE BLANK SPACES To make your notes more readable and to make it easier to see the organization of ideas, leave plenty of blank space. If you know you missed a detail or definition, leave additional blank space. You can fill it in later by checking with a friend or referring to your text. Word processing programs make it easy to add more blank space whenever you want to.

MARK ASSIGNMENTS Occasionally an instructor will announce an assignment or test date in the middle of a lecture. Of course you will jot it down, but be sure to mark "Assignment" or "Test Date" in the margin so that you can find it easily and transfer it to your assignment notebook. If you are taking notes on a computer, you can use a color to highlight the assignments.

MARK IDEAS THAT ARE UNCLEAR If an instructor presents a fact or idea that is unclear, put a question mark in the margin. Later, ask your instructor or another student about this idea.

SIT IN THE FRONT OF THE CLASSROOM Especially in large lecture halls, it is to your advantage to sit near the front. In the front you will be able to see and hear the instructor easily—you can maintain eye contact and observe his or her facial expressions and nonverbal clues. If you sit in the back, you may become bored, and it is easy to be distracted by all the people in front of you.

DON'T PLAN TO RECOPY YOUR NOTES Some students take each day's notes in a hasty, careless way and then recopy them in the evening. These students feel that recopying helps them review the information. Actually, recopying often becomes a mechanical process that takes a lot of time but very little thought. Time spent recopying can be better spent reviewing the notes in a manner that will be suggested later in this chapter. If, however, you are reorganizing and expanding upon your notes and not just copying them, then rewriting can be useful.

RECOGNIZE THAT RECORDING AND RE-WATCHING LECTURES IS TIME-CONSUMING In an effort to get complete and accurate notes, some students record lectures. After the lecture, they play it back and edit their notes, starting and stopping the machine as needed. Or they may re-watch a lecture video that an instructor has posted on the course Web site (new "lecture capture" technologies allow instructors to record their lectures easily). Re-watching lectures is time-consuming, but some students find it a helpful way to build their confidence, improve their note-taking, and assure themselves that their notes are complete. If you decide to record, do so sparingly. Unless your notes are incomplete, listening to a recording requires a great deal of time and often yields little gain. *If you plan to record, be sure to ask your instructor for permission to do so.*

USE ABBREVIATIONS To save time, use abbreviations instead of writing out long or frequently used words. If you are taking a course in psychology, you do not want to write out *p-s-y-c-h-o-l-o-g-y* each time the word is used. It would be much faster to use the abbreviation *psy*. Try to develop abbreviations that are appropriate for the subject areas you are studying. The abbreviations shown in Figure 2-4, devised by

COMMON WORDS	ABBREVIATION	SPECIALIZED WORDS	ABBREVIATION
and	+	organization	org.
with	w/	management	man.
compare comparison	comp.	data bank	D.B.
		structure	str.
importance	imp't	evaluation	eval.
advantage	adv	management by objective	MBO
introduction	intro	management information system	MIS
continued	cont.	organizational development	OD
		communication simulations	comm/sim

FIGURE 2-4
Abbreviations for Use in Note Taking

a student in business management, will give you an idea of the possibilities. Note that both common and specialized words are abbreviated.

As you develop your own set of abbreviations, be sure to begin gradually. It is easy to overuse abbreviations and end up with notes that are so cryptic as to be almost meaningless.

Exercise 2

DIRECTIONS   Select one set of lecture notes from a class you recently attended. Reread your notes and look for words or phrases you could have abbreviated. Write some of these words and their abbreviations in the spaces provided.

Word

Abbreviation

_____   _____

_____   _____

_____   _____

_____   _____

_____   _____

_____   _____

TAKE NOTES IN ONLINE COURSES   If you take online or hybrid (a combination of in-person and online) courses, you may have to watch lectures "in real time." When watching lectures online, act as if you are in a physical classroom. Take notes just as you would if you were attending the lecture in person.

SHARE NOTES WITH STUDY GROUPS   Before exams, trade notes with other students in an in-person or online study group. You will almost certainly pick up on key points that you missed.

FIGURE 2-5
Adapting Note Taking
to Your Learning Style

LEARNING CHARACTERISTIC	NOTE-TAKING STRATEGY
Auditory	Take advantage of your advantage! Take thorough and complete notes.
Visual	Work on note-taking skills; practice by recording a lecture or watching a pre-recorded lecture; analyze and revise your notes.
Applied	Think of applications (record as annotations). Write questions in the margin about applications.
Conceptual	Discover relationships among ideas. Watch for patterns.
Spatial	Add diagrams and maps, as appropriate, during editing.
Nonspatial	Record a lecture's diagrams and drawings—but translate into language during editing.
Social	Review and edit notes with a classmate. Compare notes with others.
Independent	Choose seating close to the instructor; avoid distracting groups of students.
Creative	Annotate your notes, recording impressions, reactions, spinoff ideas, and related ideas.
Pragmatic	Reorganize your notes during editing. Pay attention to the lecturer's organization.

CREATE A CODE SYSTEM Devise a system by which you record or mark specific types of information in specific ways. For example, number the items in a list, write "ex" next to each example, or put question marks next to ideas you don't understand.

MAKE THE MOST OF YOUR LEARNING STYLE By adapting your note-taking strategies to take advantage of your learning style, you will make study and review easier. Figure 2-5 above offers some suggestions for tailoring your note taking to your learning style.

Overcoming Common Note-Taking Problems

Instructors present lectures differently, use various lecture styles, and organize their subjects in different ways. Figure 2-6 identifies common problems associated with lecture note taking and offers possible solutions.

Goal 4

Edit your notes.

HOW TO EDIT YOUR NOTES

After you have taken a set of lecture notes, do not assume that they are accurate and complete. Most students find that they missed some information and were unable to record as many details or examples as they would have liked. Even very experienced note takers face these problems. Fortunately, the solution is simple. Don't plan on taking a final and complete set of notes during the lecture. Instead, record just enough during the lecture to help you remember a main idea, detail,

FIGURE 2-6
Common Note-Taking
Problems

PROBLEM	SOLUTIONS
"My mind wanders and I get bored."	Sit in the front of the room. Be certain to preview assignments. Think about questions you expect to be answered in the lecture.
"The instructor talks too fast."	Develop a shorthand system; use abbreviations. Leave blanks and fill them in later.
"The lecturer rambles."	Preview correlating text assignments to determine organizing principles. Reorganize your notes after the lecture.
"Some ideas don't seem to fit anywhere."	Record them in the margin or in parentheses within your notes, and think about them later during editing.
"Everything seems important."; "Nothing seems important."	You have not identified key concepts and may lack necessary background knowledge (see Chapter 6)—you do not understand the topic. Preview related text assignments.
"I can't spell all the new technical terms."	Write them phonetically, the way they sound. Fill in correct spellings during editing.
"The instructor uses terms without defining them."	Write the terms as they are used; leave space to record definitions later, when you can consult the text glossary or a dictionary.
"The instructor reads directly from the text."	Mark passages in the text; write the instructor's comments in the margin. Record page references in your notes.

or example. Leave plenty of blank space; then, if possible, sit down immediately after the lecture and review your notes. Fill in the missing information. Expand, or flesh out, any details or examples that are not fully explained. This process is called **editing**. It is essentially a process of correcting, revising, and adding to your notes to make them complete and more accurate. Editing notes for a one-hour lecture should take no more than five or ten minutes.

If you are unable to edit your notes immediately after a lecture, it is critical that you edit them that evening. The more time that lapses between note taking and editing, the less effective editing becomes. Also, the greater the time lapse, the more facts and examples you will be unable to recall and fill in.

The sample set of lecture notes in Figure 2-7 (see next page) has been edited. The notes taken during the lecture are in black; the additions and changes made during editing are in color. Read the notes, noticing the types of information added during editing.

Editing is also a time for you to think about the notes you've taken—to move beyond the literal knowledge and comprehension levels of thought to the levels that involve critical thinking.

Integrating Text and Lecture Notes

A continual problem students wrestle with is how to integrate lecture and text-book notes. The computer offers an ideal solution to the integration of text and lecture notes. The cut-and-paste option enables you to move pieces (sections) of your notes to any desired place in the document. You can also cut and paste a section from an e-book into your course notes. Thus, you can easily integrate text and lecture notes on each major topic.

FIGURE 2-7
Edited Lecture Notes

Anxiety + Defense Mechanisms   10/12

I. Anxiety generalized
        def gen fear or worry
    Levels
        1. Moderate - productive
                athletes - higher level of phys. functioning
                test-taking - certain am't helps - keeps you alert
        2. Extreme - uncomfortable ex.: nauseated
                - extremely nervous, hands shaking
                - can be reduced by defense mechanism

II. Defense Mech   scious
        def - uncon devices to protect self and/or keep self
                under control
                ex.: student who is hostile toward teacher
                explains it to himself by saying that "the
    Types of Def. Mechanism   teacher hates me"
        1. Repression - to drive out of consciousness
            ex.: student - math instructor   student forgets
                to keep app't with math instructor because
                he's afraid he will be told he is failing the
                course.   to anxiety
        2. Regression - reaction by going back to less
            mature behavior
            ex.: college student applying for job but
                doesn't get it - pouts + says the
                interviewer cheated + hired son of
                his best friend.

Taking Notes on Your Laptop

If you take notes electronically, use the following tips to make the process work for you.

- Make sure you can plug in your laptop or that you have sufficient battery power.
- Set up a folder for each course. Create a separate file for each day's notes; include the date of the lecture in naming the file.
- Save your document frequently, so you don't lose anything.
- Keep a pen and paper handy to record diagrams, drawings, and figures.
- Don't allow distracting programs such as e-mail and instant messaging to compete for your attention.
- Don't risk interrupting class with annoying beeps and buzzes. Turn the sound off.

APPLYING LEVELS OF THINKING

Editing Notes and Levels of Thinking

As you edit your notes, keep the following questions in mind.

Level of Thinking	Questions
Applying	How can I use this information?
Analyzing	How do these notes fit with other lectures? With the textbook assignment?
Evaluating	How useful is this information? Was it clear and well presented? What additional information do I need? What don't I fully understand?
Creating	What does this all mean? How can I summarize it?

Do not hesitate to add marginal notes, jot down questions, add reactions, draw arrows to show relationships, and bracket sections that seem confusing. Then ask your instructor about them during the next classroom or online session. For more information about these levels of thinking, see Chapter 1.

HOW TO STUDY YOUR NOTES

Goal 5

Study your notes.

Taking and editing lecture notes is only part of what you must do to learn from lectures. You also have to learn and review the material in the notes in order to do well on exams. Rereading is not an efficient review technique because it takes too much time relative to the amount you learn. To identify what is important, sort out what you will learn and study from all the rest of the information you have written in your notes. You also need a way of checking yourself—of deciding whether you have learned the necessary information.

To study lecture notes, you can use a system called the recall clue system.

The Cornell Note-Taking Recall Clue System

Developed at Cornell University, the recall clue system helps make the review and study of lecture notes easier and more effective. To use the recall clue system, follow these steps.

1. **Leave a two-inch margin at the left side of each page of notes.** If you take notes on your laptop, create a template that includes a two-column format.
2. **Write nothing in the margin while you are taking notes.**
3. **After you have edited your notes, fill in the left margin with words and phrases (recall clues) that briefly summarize the notes.**

The recall clues should be words that will trigger your memory and help you recall the complete information in your notes. These clues function as memory tags. They help you retrieve from your memory any information that is labeled

FIGURE 2-8
Lecture Notes with
Recall Clues Added

Numerical Properties of Atoms   Chem 109
                                                          2/9
   I. Prop. related to Temperature + Heat

melting point   A. Melting Point
                        - when particles in a solid move fast
                          enough to overcome forces holding them
                          together - temp at which this happens =
                          melting point

freezing point   - Freezing Pt. -temp at which forces
                          attracting particles to one another hold
                           particles together

heat of fusion   - Heat of Fusion -amt. of heat req'd. to
                          melt one gram of any substance
                          at its melting pt.

boiling point   B. Boiling Point
                        - Point at which molecules of a liquid
                          begin to escape as gas

heat of vap.   - Heat of vaporization -amt. of heat req'd.
                          to change one gram of liquid to a gas
                          at its boiling pt.

condensation pt.   - Condensation Pt. - point at which gas,
                          cooling, changes back to liquid

specific heat   C. Specific Heat
                           ex. beach -sand hot, water cold- why?
                           Sand + H_2O have different spec. heat
                        def. -am't. of heat needed to raise temp.
                         of a spec. mass of substance by a
                        certain am't.

formula for S.h.   formula - S.h. = heat in cals.
                                  mass in grams x temp. diff. in °C

                        S.h.   = $\dfrac{cal}{g \times °C}$

with these tags. Figure 2-8 shows a sample of notes in which the recall clue system has been used. When you are taking an exam, the recall clues from your notes will work automatically to help you remember necessary information.

A variation on the recall clue system is to write questions rather than summary words and phrases in the margin (see Figure 2-9). The questions

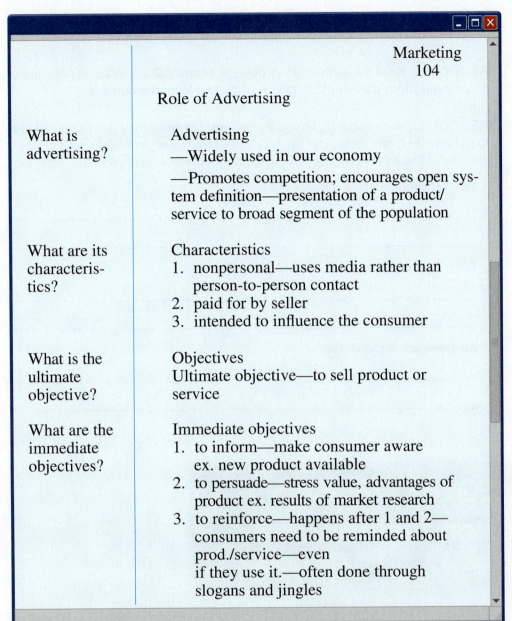

FIGURE 2-9
Lecture Notes with Recall Questions Added

(Contents of figure:)

Marketing 104

Role of Advertising

What is advertising?

Advertising
—Widely used in our economy
—Promotes competition; encourages open system definition—presentation of a product/service to broad segment of the population

What are its characteristics?

Characteristics
1. nonpersonal—uses media rather than person-to-person contact
2. paid for by seller
3. intended to influence the consumer

What is the ultimate objective?

Objectives
Ultimate objective—to sell product or service

What are the immediate objectives?

Immediate objectives
1. to inform—make consumer aware ex. new product available
2. to persuade—stress value, advantages of product ex. results of market research
3. to reinforce—happens after 1 and 2— consumers need to be reminded about prod./service—even if they use it.—often done through slogans and jingles

trigger your memory and enable you to recall the information that answers your question. The use of questions enables you to test yourself, simulating an exam situation.

Studying Your Notes Using the Cornell Note-Taking Recall Clue System

To study your notes using the recall clue system, cover up the notes with a sheet of paper, exposing only the recall clues in the left margin. Next, read the first recall clue and try to remember the information in the notes beside it. Then slide the paper down and check that portion to see whether you remembered all the important facts. If you remembered only part of the information, cover up that portion of your notes and again check your recall. Continue checking until you are satisfied that you can remember all the important facts. Then move on to the next recall clue on the page, following the same testing–checking procedure.

Exercise 3

DIRECTIONS   Read the sample set of notes in Figure 2-2. Fill in the recall clues or formulate questions that would help you study and learn the notes. ●

Exercise 4

DIRECTIONS   For each course you are taking this semester, use the recall clue system for at least one week. Use the recall clues to review your notes several times. At the end of the week, evaluate how well the system works for you.

1. What advantages does it have?

_____

_____

2. Did it help you remember facts and ideas?

_____

_____

3. Are there any disadvantages?

_____

_____ ●

USING COLLEGE TEXTBOOKS
Taking Notes on Textbook Readings

In addition to taking notes on lectures and class discussions, you need to take notes on your textbook reading assignments. Notes are valuable study tools, and the actual writing of the notes strengthens your retention and recall of the information. Be sure to include the following in your notes:

1. **Definitions.** Include definitions of important terms or concepts.
2. **Main ideas.** Write down the main idea of each paragraph.
3. **Examples.** Include examples for difficult concepts.
4. **Processes.** Outline processes that are described in the text.

You can take notes in the margins of your book, in a notebook, or on your computer. Be sure to identify the pages to which the notes refer. Refer to your notes during class or immediately after class, adding marginal notes or highlighting to indicate points your instructor emphasized.

The following annotated textbook page shows the marginal notes a student made while reading. Also shown is a set of notes she took on this page, and then later edited.

TEXTBOOK EXCERPT

Why Do People Become Vegetarians?

When discussing vegetarianism, one of the most often-asked questions is why people would make this food choice. The most common responses are included here.

Religious, Ethical, and Food-Safety Reasons

Some make the choice for religious or spiritual reasons. Several religions prohibit or restrict the consumption of animal flesh; however, generalizations can be misleading. For example, while certain sects within Hinduism forbid the consumption of meat, perusing the menu at an Indian restaurant will reveal that some other Hindus regularly consume small quantities of meat, poultry, and fish. Many Buddhists are vegetarians, as are some Christians, including Seventh-Day Adventists.

Some religious sects may prohibit meat

Many vegetarians are guided by their personal philosophy to choose vegetarianism. These people feel that it is morally and ethically wrong to consume animals and any products from animals (such as dairy or egg products) because they view the practices in the modern animal industries as inhumane. They may consume milk and eggs but choose to purchase them only from family farms where they believe animals are treated humanely.

Personal choice based on moral outrage at inhumane treatment of animals.

There is also a great deal of concern about meat-handling practices, because contaminated meat is allowed into our food supply. For example, in 1982, there was an outbreak of severe bloody diarrhea that was eventually traced to bacteria in burgers served at a fast-food restaurant. Several people became seriously ill and one child died after eating the hamburgers. Another concern surrounding beef is the possibility that it is tainted by the microbes that cause *mad cow disease*.

What is mad cow disease?

Ecological Reasons

Many people choose vegetarianism because of their concerns about the effect of meat industries on the global environment They argue that cattle consume large quantities of grain and water, require grazing areas that could be used for plant food production, destroy vulnerable ecosystems including rain forests, and produce wastes that run off into surrounding bodies of water. Meat industry organizations argue that such effects are minor and greatly exaggerated. One area of agreement that has recently emerged focuses the argument not on *whether* we eat meat but on *how much* meat we consume. The environmental damage caused by the raising of livestock is due in part to the large number of animals produced. When a population reduces its consumption of meat, reduced environmental damage follows. In addition to the environmental benefits, eating less meat may also reduce our risk for chronic diseases such as heart disease and some cancers.

How much meat is too much?

—Thompson, *Nutrition for Life*, pp. 148–150

EXCERPT FROM NOTES

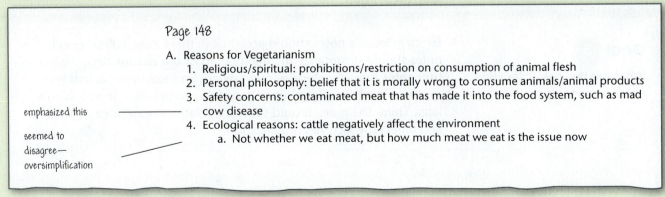

Page 148

A. Reasons for Vegetarianism
   1. Religious/spiritual: prohibitions/restriction on consumption of animal flesh
   2. Personal philosophy: belief that it is morally wrong to consume animals/animal products
   3. Safety concerns: contaminated meat that has made it into the food system, such as mad cow disease
   4. Ecological reasons: cattle negatively affect the environment
      a. Not whether we eat meat, but how much meat we eat is the issue now

emphasized this

seemed to disagree— oversimplification

Textbook Exercise 1: Evaluate the Notes

Evaluate the annotations and notes shown on the previous page. Would you find them useful for studying? What changes would you make, if any?

FURTHER PRACTICE WITH TEXTBOOK READING

Textbook Exercise 2: Sample Textbook Chapter

Read the section titled "Theories of Prejudice" (p. 435) in the sample textbook chapter and take notes on it.

Textbook Exercise 3: Your College Textbook

Choose a reading assignment you have been given in a textbook for another course. Take notes when you read the assignment.

SELF-TEST SUMMARY

Goal **1** How can you improve your listening skills?	Taking good lecture notes depends on good listening skills. To make your listening more intentional, purposeful, and deliberate, you should focus on content and ideas, not on the speaker's style or on facts alone; pay attention to opening statements; look for the speaker's purpose; and prevent your mind from wandering by focusing your concentration and attention.
Goal **2** How should you prepare for a lecture?	Because many college instructors expect you to remember and apply the facts and ideas in their class lectures, it is a good idea to become familiar with the topic before the lecture. Be sure to read (or at least preview) the assignment. Get to class early enough to settle in and prepare to listen.
Goal **3** What are the characteristics of effective lecture notes?	Effective lecture notes should accomplish three things. First, good notes should summarize the main points of the lecture. Second, lecture notes should include enough details and examples so that you can recall and completely understand the information several weeks later. Third, the notes should show the relative importance of ideas and reflect the lecture's organization.

Goal **4**	After taking a set of lecture notes, it is necessary to correct, revise, fill in missing or additional information, and expand your notes. This editing process results in clearer, more accurate notes.
Why should you edit your lecture notes?	

Goal **5**	The recall clue system is a way of making study and review easier and more effective. During note taking, leave blank a two-inch margin at the left of each page of notes. Later, as you reread your notes, write in the margin words and phrases that briefly summarize the notes. These phrases, or recall clues, trigger your memory and help you recall information in the notes.
How should you study your lecture notes?	

APPLYING | YOUR SKILLS

DISCUSSING THE CHAPTER

1. What is the difference between hearing and listening? Is it similar to the distinction between reading and understanding?
2. What goals must a good set of lecture notes accomplish?
3. Why is the recall clue system effective in helping you study?
4. Use Figure 2-5 to determine note-taking strategies that are appropriate for your learning style. How can you use these strategies in this class?

ANALYZING A STUDY SITUATION

DIRECTIONS Working in groups of three or four students, analyze the following situation. Discuss answers to the questions that follow.

Jan is taking an American government course in which class lectures are very important. She has trouble following the lectures and knowing what is important because her instructor does not follow the textbook and often digresses from the topic. The instructor lectures at a fast pace, so Jan feels she is missing important information.

1. What advice would you give Jan for taking lecture notes?
2. How should she study and review her notes?
3. What thought patterns could she expect to find in an American government course?
4. Should Jan record the lectures or re-watch her instructor's captured lectures?
5. Would rewriting or editing her notes be helpful? If so, what changes should she make?

Tip *Digress* means "to write or talk about a subject that's not related to the idea(s) being discussed."

WORKING ON COLLABORATIVE PROJECTS

DIRECTIONS   Bring two sets of lecture notes to class. The first set should be notes taken *before* this chapter on note taking was assigned. The second should be a set of notes taken *after* this chapter was assigned and should contain editing and recall clues. Work with a partner to assess each other's progress and suggest areas for further improvement.

Answer Key for Learning Experiment
Paragraph 1: intimate, personal, social, public
Paragraph 2: attraction, taste, memory, identity

Quick | Quiz

DIRECTIONS Write the letter of the choice that best completes each statement in the space provided.

CHECKING YOUR RECALL

_____ 1. A speaker's opening comments typically
  a. identify the organization and purpose of the lecture.
  b. do not contain any important information.
  c. consist only of personal or humorous stories told to get the audience's attention.
  d. will be repeated at the conclusion of the lecture.

_____ 2. The gap between rate of speech and rate of thinking is such that the
  a. speaker has a distinct advantage.
  b. listener has to strain to follow along.
  c. speaker has to allow time for listeners to catch up.
  d. listener has time to think of other things.

_____ 3. One difference between listening and hearing is that listening is
  a. purely biological.
  b. passive.
  c. unintentional.
  d. purposeful.

_____ 4. Instructors often signal what is important during a lecture by doing all of the following _except_
  a. increasing their rate of speech.
  b. changing the tone or pitch of their voices.
  c. writing on the board.
  d. listing or numbering points.

_____ 5. Recall clues are intended primarily to
  a. aid your ability to retrieve information.
  b. identify the patterns used in a particular lecture.
  c. reduce the amount of information you must learn.
  d. organize your lecture notes.

APPLYING YOUR SKILLS

_____ 6. Pedro is reviewing the psychology notes he took in class today. The best way for Pedro to review his notes is to
  a. copy his notes over to make them more legible.
  b. expand on details that he didn't have time to write down.
  c. revise his notes while listening to a recording of the lecture.
  d. read his notes aloud over and over.

_____ 7. Craig is having trouble taking good notes because his instructor speaks too quickly for him. All of the following strategies might help him _except_
  a. recording the lectures.
  b. using abbreviations.
  c. sitting at the back of the class.
  d. leaving blanks in his notes for filling in missing information later.

_____ 8. Anwali is editing the notes she took during her biology class this morning. This means that Anwali is
  a. grouping the ideas in her notes into paragraphs.
  b. copying the notes over so that they are neater.
  c. memorizing the facts in the notes.
  d. correcting, revising, and adding to her notes to make them more complete and accurate.

_____ 9. Derek is trying to improve his listening skills during lectures. Derek should try to
  a. focus on delivery, not content.
  b. memorize unconnected facts.
  c. identify main ideas, relationships, and trends.
  d. come up with mnemonic devices.

_____ 10. Kimberly has arrived early for an English lecture. The most effective use of her time would be to
  a. review the homework assignment due that day.
  b. begin reading the next textbook chapter assignment.
  c. review her notes from the previous lecture.
  d. chat with friends until the class begins.

3

Communicating in the Classroom

LEARNING GOALS

In this chapter you will learn to

1 Listen critically.

2 Ask and answer questions during class.

3 Participate in class discussions.

4 Work on collaborative activities.

5 Make oral presentations.

6 Communicate with your professors.

LEARNING EXPERIMENT

1 Select two upcoming lectures for another course.

2 Use the strategies you learned in Chapter 2 to take notes on each lecture.

3 For one lecture, exchange your notes with a partner in that class. Take a few minutes to read each other's notes.

4 Develop three meaningful questions about your partner's notes. Take turns asking and answering each other's questions.

5 For the second lecture, reread your notes, but do not exchange notes with a classmate. Write three questions that could be asked about your notes.

6 After two days, review both sets of notes. Which set seems more familiar? For which do you recall more information? On which set would you feel more prepared to take a quiz?

The Results

You probably felt better prepared with the first set of notes than with the second because you interacted with a classmate about the notes' contents. You not only read the notes, you also talked about them and exchanged ideas.

Learning Principle: What This Means to You

Talking about course content and exchanging ideas with others facilitates learning. Communicating with classmates in a classroom setting—whether in person or online—also prepares you for on-the-job teamwork. In this chapter you will learn to communicate with classmates in a variety of situations. You will also learn about asking and answering questions in class, participating in class discussions, working on group activities, and communicating with your professor.

LISTENING CRITICALLY

Goal 1

Listen critically.

Listening is an important part of classroom communication. In order to respond to what is going on in class, you have to understand and evaluate it. Your first task, then, is to absorb and learn the information presented. (See Chapter 2 for information on taking lecture notes and developing recall clues to learn them.) Another equally important task is thinking critically about what your instructor presents and what other students say. Avoid the following obstacles to critical listening:

1. **Closed-mindedness.** In your classrooms you will hear many ideas that you disagree with, and you will meet people who have different values than you do. What others believe about what is right or wrong about the course subject matter—or about life in general—may not reflect your own beliefs. Avoid prejudging a speaker, and keep an open mind. Delay your judgment until the speaker has finished and you fully understand the speaker's message and intentions. If you are taking an online course, you have the advantage of taking a few minutes to reread someone's posting before jumping in hastily with your own reaction.

2. **Selective listening.** Some students hear only what they want to hear. That is, they pay attention to ideas they agree with and may misinterpret or even ignore ideas with which they disagree. Selective listening often occurs when the topic has political, religious, or moral elements. To avoid selective listening, first recognize your own biases. A **bias** (as we'll discuss in Chapter 10) is a very strong feeling or inclination toward a particular point of view. Make a deliberate effort to recognize when a speaker's viewpoint conflicts with your own bias about an issue—and do not let your own bias block your understanding of that opposing viewpoint. If your feelings are very strong, try taking notes or writing an outline of the speaker's viewpoints to keep yourself constructively engaged and open-minded.

3. **Judging the speaker instead of the message.** Focus on the message, not the person delivering the message. Try not to be distracted by mannerisms, dress, or the method of delivery (pauses, tone of voice, grammatical errors in online postings, and so forth).

4. **Lack of audience awareness.** Don't get so caught up in what you're saying that you lose sight of your audience and their reactions. Be sensitive to the feelings and viewpoints of other class members—try not to be bullying, argumentative, or overly emotional in your verbal responses or other reactions. When making a point or offering a comment, watch both your instructor and classmates. Their responses will show whether they understand you or need further information, whether they agree or disagree, whether you have caused offense, and whether they are interested or uninterested. You can then decide, based on these responses, whether you made your point effectively or whether you need to explain or defend your argument more carefully.

Exercise 1
Collaboration

DIRECTIONS   Working with a classmate, identify at least three or four class discussion topics for which it would be important to keep an open mind and avoid selective listening. ●

Goal 2

Ask and answer questions during class.

ASKING AND ANSWERING QUESTIONS

Framing clear, direct answers to questions asked by your instructors or classmates is a skill worth developing. Effective questioning is important in college classes, but it is also an important workplace skill. Use the following suggestions to strengthen your questioning and answering skills.

1. **Conquer the fear of asking questions.** Many students are hesitant to ask or answer questions. They fear that their questions may seem dumb or that their answers may be incorrect. However, you will find that once you've asked a question, other students will be glad you asked because they had the same question in mind. Answering questions posed by your instructor gives you an opportunity to evaluate how well you have learned or understood course content as well as to demonstrate your knowledge.

2. **As you read an assignment, jot down several questions that might clarify or explain it better.** Bring your list to class and ask the questions at an appropriate time.

3. **When you ask a question, state it clearly and concisely.** Don't ramble or make excuses for asking.

4. **Remember, most instructors invite and respond favorably to questions. If your question is a serious one, it will be received positively.** Don't pose questions for the sake of asking a question. Class time is limited and valuable.

5. **In answering questions, think your responses through before you volunteer them.**

Tip *Critiquing format* means "talking or writing about how good or bad the organization and/or design of something is" or "evaluating its method of presentation."

Exercise 2
Collaboration

DIRECTIONS   Select a reading assignment from one of your other courses. Practice asking and answering questions with a student from that class. Take turns critiquing format, content, and delivery of both questions and answers. ●

Exercise 3

DIRECTIONS   In one of your classes this week, pay attention to the types of questions and comments the students make. Which seem most helpful to the class as a whole? Which seem less important? Which seem to interrupt the class more than contribute to it? Why? ●

Goal 3

Participate in class discussions.

PARTICIPATING IN CLASS DISCUSSIONS

Participation in class means more than being interested, prepared, and alert. To participate you must be actively involved in class discussions. Participating in class has a number of advantages.

1. **Participation will help you concentrate and focus.**

2. **Participation will help you sort out what you know and what you don't yet know.** By talking about ideas, you will discover which ideas you are knowledgeable about and which you need to study further.

3. You will be better prepared for exams and quizzes because you have already put the course content into your own words.
4. Participation gives you practice in speaking before a group—a skill you will definitely need in the workplace.
5. Learning the etiquette of participation in a discussion will help you contribute more effectively to online discussions in both academic and nonacademic settings.

Finding Out What Your Instructor Expects

Before participating in a discussion, be sure to understand your instructor's expectations. Check your syllabus or course management Web site to find out what percentage of your grade is determined by the level and quality of your participation. Also find out answers to the following questions:

- Are you expected to react to assigned readings?
- Are you expected to respond to lecture content?
- Are you expected to react to other students' comments?
- Are personal opinions welcome, or should you limit your response to factual information?
- Are online discussions part of the course?

Preparing for Class Discussions

Preparing for a class discussion demands more time and effort than getting ready for a lecture class does. In a lecture class, most of your work comes *after* the class, editing your notes and using the recall clue system to review them. The opposite is true for discussion courses, for which most of your work is done *before* you go to class. Be sure to spend considerable time reading, thinking, and making notes. You will perform better in a class discussion if you prepare in advance. Use the following strategies to be prepared.

1. **Read the assignment.** Usually a class discussion is about a particular topic. Frequently, instructors give textbook, library, or online reading assignments that provide background information or acquaint you with the issues. Read these materials carefully; don't just skim them.
2. **Mark and highlight important ideas as you read.** Doing so will allow you review the material just before class begins and to locate ideas quickly during the discussion.
3. **Take notes during the discussion.** Notes are essential to effective participation.
4. **Ask critical thinking questions.** Class discussions seldom center around factual information. Instead, they usually focus on the application, analysis, synthesis, and evaluation of ideas and information. To prepare for discussions, then, start with the following critical thinking questions:

   - How can I use this information? To what situations is it applicable?
   - How does this information compare with other information I have read or learned on the same topic?
   - What is the source of the material?

- Is the material fact or opinion?
- What is the author's purpose?
- Is the author biased?
- Is relevant and sufficient evidence provided?

Exercise 4

DIRECTIONS   Working alone or with a classmate, develop a set of notes that contains a list of ideas and concepts presented in the sample textbook chapter in Part Seven that you could share in a group discussion. ●

Exercise 5

DIRECTIONS   Prepare for one of your other classes as though it will take the form of a class discussion. Apply the critical thinking questions above to the reading you do before the class meets, and make notes for the discussion. Whether the class actually takes the format of a lecture or a discussion, afterward think about how preparing in this way aided you in comprehending the class. ●

Participating in Online Discussions

Use the following tips to make the most of online discussions.

- Become familiar with the software or course management system before you attempt to post messages. You can also get help from your campus computer center or ask classmates for help.
- Read all previous posts before posting your comments. You want to be sure someone else has not already said what you plan to say.
- Make your comments easy to read. Use correct spelling and grammar and format your comment using spacing, boldfaced print, numbered lists, and so on.
- Place your comments within a context. Make it clear whether you are responding to another posting (if so, give date and name), a reading assignment (give chapter or page), or a lecture (give date).

Getting Involved in Class Discussions

Some students wonder when it is appropriate to speak in class. Say something when

- you can ask a serious, thoughtful question.
- someone asks a question that you can answer.
- you have a comment or suggestion to make about what has already been said.
- you can supply additional information that will clarify the topic under discussion.
- you can correct an error or clarify a misunderstanding.

To get more involved in classroom communication (both in person and online), try the strategies in the following box.

PARTICIPATING CONSTRUCTIVELY IN CLASS DISCUSSIONS

- **Even if you are reluctant to speak before a group, try to say something early in the discussion.**
- **Make your comments brief and to the point.** Do not tell lengthy personal anecdotes.
- **Try to avoid getting involved in direct exchanges or disagreements with individual class members.**
- **Do not interrupt other speakers.** Signal to your instructor or moderator that you would like to be recognized to speak, if necessary.
- **Avoid talking privately with, making comments to, or chatting on social media with another student while the discussion is taking place.**
- **Do not monopolize the discussion.** Give others a chance to express their ideas.

DIRECTIONS Review the "Action Plan for Learning" you developed in Chapter 1 (p. 27). Which of your strategies could help you communicate more actively and constructively in the classroom? ●

Exercise 6

Recording and Reviewing Classroom Communication

Class discussions contain important ideas and information. Some of the information may be included on tests or exams; other information may be useful in other discussions, when writing papers, or for completing class assignments. Be sure to develop a note-taking system for keeping track of this information. Consider the following points:

- Taking notes while participating in the discussion leaves you less time to listen. Plan on recording only the main points during class and filling in the details later.
- It is a good idea to review your notes and fill in details as soon as possible after the discussion before forgetting occurs.
- Noting the speaker's name in the margin may help you recall his or her comments more vividly.
- While online discussions are always available for you to review by tracking back through the discussion, it is time-consuming to do so. Instead, write a brief summary of each topic, daily or weekly, depending on the number of posts.

WORKING ON COLLABORATIVE ACTIVITIES

Goal

Work on collaborative activities.

Many assignments and class activities involve working with a small group of classmates. Group activities help students to learn from one another, giving them a window into the group members' thinking processes and asking them to evaluate the group members' ideas. For example, a sociology instructor might divide the class into groups and ask each group to brainstorm solutions to the economic or social problems of the elderly. Your political science professor might create a panel to discuss ways to increase voter participation.

Group activities develop valuable skills in interpersonal communication that are essential in your career. However, some students are reluctant to work in groups; they dislike having their grade depend on the performance of others. Use the following suggestions to help your group function effectively.

1. **Select alert, energetic classmates** if you are permitted to choose your group members.
2. **Be an active, responsible participant.** Accept your share of the work and expect others to do the same. Establish a serious tone to cut down on wasted time.
3. **Take a leadership role.** Organization and direction are essential for group productivity, and leadership roles are valuable experiences for your career.
4. **Take advantage of individual strengths and weaknesses.** For instance, a person who seems indifferent or easily distracted should not be assigned the task of recording the group's findings. The most organized, outgoing member might be assigned the task of making an oral report to the class.

Exercise 7

DIRECTIONS   Suppose you are part of a five-member group that is preparing for a panel discussion on animal rights. One group member is very vocal and opinionated. You fear she is likely to dominate the discussion. Another group member is painfully shy and has volunteered to do double research if he doesn't have to speak much during the discussion. A third member appears uninterested and tends to sit back and watch as the group works and plans. How should the group respond to each of these individuals? List several possible solutions to each problem. ●

Goal

Make oral presentations.

MAKING ORAL PRESENTATIONS

Oral presentations may be done in groups or individually. Groups may be asked to report their findings, summarize their research, or describe a process or procedure. Individual presentations are often summaries of research papers, reviews or critiques, or interpretations of literary or artistic works. Use the following suggestions to make effective oral presentations.

1. **Understand the purpose of the assignment.** Analyze it carefully before beginning to work.
2. **Research your topic thoroughly.** Collect and organize your information.
3. **Prepare outline notes.** Record only key words and phrases.
4. **Consider using visual aids in your presentation.** Depending on the type of assignment as well as on your topic, diagrams, photographs, or demonstrations may be appropriate and effective in maintaining audience interest.
5. **Anticipate questions your audience may ask.** Review and revise your notes to include answers.
6. **Practice delivering your presentation to build your confidence and help you overcome nervousness.** First, practice aloud several times by yourself. Time yourself to be sure you are within any limits. Then practice in front of friends and ask for criticism. Finally, record your presentation. Play it back, looking for ways to improve it.
7. **Deliver your presentation effectively.** Engage your audience's interest by maintaining eye contact; look directly at other students as you speak. Make a deliberate effort to speak slowly; when you are nervous, your speech tends to speed up. Be enthusiastic and energetic.

Figure 3-1 answers some commonly asked questions about making oral presentations.

QUESTIONS	ANSWERS
1. How can I overcome the fear of public speaking?	• Practice delivering your speech before you make your presentation. Practice speaking slowly and distinctly, taking deep breaths, and pausing.
2. How can I make sure my presentation is interesting?	• Vary the content. For example, you could start off by telling an interesting story or engaging the class's attention by posing a thoughtful question. • Use visual aids such as a whiteboard, a projector, or a chart that you've designed to help you maintain the interest of your audience.
3. What if, during my presentation, the instructor and/or the class starts to show signs of boredom?	• Change the tone or pitch of your voice. • Recapture your audience's interest by engaging them in the presentation. Pose a question, for example. • Make eye contact with restless individuals.
4. What do I do if I "go blank"?	• Write brief notes. If you suddenly "go blank," all you need to do is look at your notes. • Ask whether there are any questions. Even if there aren't, this pause will give you time to think about what to say next.

FIGURE 3-1
Questions and Answers About Oral Presentations

Visual Thinking
APPLYING SKILLS

Analyze the students in this lecture class. Which students seem to be serious active listeners? Which are not? Identify the behaviors that are not productive.

DIRECTIONS Develop a checklist of five to ten different criteria that you could use to evaluate how effective an oral presentation is. The next time you are asked to make an oral presentation, use your checklist to evaluate a practice session. ●

Exercise 8

DIRECTIONS You are asked to make a three-minute oral presentation on how to study for a particular course you are taking this semester. Prepare a set of outline notes for your presentation, and practice delivery of your presentation. Then answer the following questions:

1. How did you organize your presentation?

2. Did preparation of your presentation force you to analyze how you learn in the course you chose?

3. How did you improve your presentation through practice? ●

Exercise 9

Goal 6

Communicate with your professors.

COMMUNICATING WITH YOUR PROFESSORS

Your instructors are valuable resources, and you can learn a great deal by communicating with them beyond formal in-class attendance. Here are some options.

1. **Office hours.** Most professors hold office hours—times when they will be in their office and available to students. You can use office hours to discuss your progress in the course, ask for help, or seek advice. Office hours are an opportunity to build a relationship with your professors.
2. **E-mail.** Many professors give students an e-mail address at which to contact them. Some professors check their e-mail daily; others do so as little as once or twice a week. Until you are certain a professor checks his or her e-mail frequently, do not send time-sensitive information. Check the syllabus for more information about the instructor's philosophy of reading and responding to e-mail.
3. **Phone.** Be cautious with professors' phone numbers, and always call at appropriate times. It's all right to call an office number at 2 A.M., but not a home number.
4. **Text messages.** Most professors prefer not to communicate with students via text messages. If you have one who accepts text messages, be respectful of the professor's wishes regarding the frequency and timing of text messages.

When communicating with professors electronically, use a more formal level of communication than you would use for friends and family. Do not be overly friendly or familiar. Use correct grammar, spelling, capitalization, and punctuation; avoid slang.

USING COLLEGE TEXTBOOKS
Preparing for Class Discussions

Frequently, instructors assign textbook readings to introduce a topic, expose you to different viewpoints about an issue, or indicate some aspects of a problem. To prepare for a class discussion, make notes about the following, writing either in the margin of the text or on a separate sheet of paper or in a computer file:

- **Ideas, concepts, or viewpoints you do not understand.** Keep a list of these and use it as a guide to ask questions during class.
- **Points with which you strongly agree or disagree.** Making notes about these points will give you some ideas to start with if your instructor asks you for a reaction to the reading.
- **Good and poor examples.** These will give you something concrete to point to when discussing your reactions to the reading.
- **Strong and weak arguments.** As you read, try to follow the line of reasoning and evaluate any arguments presented. Make notes about your evaluations. These will remind you of points you may want to make during a class discussion.

The following is an excerpt from a sociology textbook, along with sample marginal notes one student made in preparation for a class discussion.

Slaves in Tulsa

Could slavery still exist in the United States? According to Kevin Bales, the United States imports about *50,000 slaves* every year. In February 2002, the Midwestern city of Tulsa, Oklahoma, was shocked to learn that they had slaves working in their midst. Workers recruited by a Mumbai (formerly Bombay), India, company *signed contracts for labor overseas*. Many paid the company a fee of more than $2,000 to gain employment in the United States. Workers flew to Tulsa where they worked as welders for an industrial equipment manufacturer.

Where are the rest of these slaves?

These workers left their country with a promise of long-term residency, good jobs, and high pay. What they found was significantly different. The group lived in barracks on the factory grounds, sometimes working 12-hour days and earning as little as $2.31 an hour. The company's food was substandard, and many workers had to share beds because of a shortage of space. In the dormitory, a sign stated that workers who left the grounds could be sent back to India and that armed guards patrolled the grounds. Many also reported verbal threats and deliberate intimidation to keep the workers on the property.

What is the definition of a slave?
These people are not owned. How is this slavery? May be it is unlawful imprisonment instead.

After the situation became public, many local community members helped the Indian workers find legitimate jobs, and immigration hearings allowed them to legally stay in the country. With new jobs, the workers now seek to make their American dream come true. This case has a *happy ending*, largely because it occurred in a country with a free press and a strong government. Unfortunately, most contract labor occurs in countries without either of these two important components.

Happy ending? What about their families? Were they allowed to come to the United States? What happened to workers who wanted to go back to their own country?

—adapted from Carl, *THINK Sociology*, p. 143

Textbook Exercise 1: Respond to the Reading

Reread "Slaves in Tulsa." Identify (1) any concepts or ideas you do not understand, (2) points with which you strongly agree or disagree, (3) good and poor examples, and (4) strong and weak arguments.

FURTHER PRACTICE WITH TEXTBOOK READING

Textbook Exercise 2: Sample Textbook Chapter

Read the box titled "Hard Work: The Immigrant Life in the United States" in the textbook chapter on page 432, and make notes to prepare for a class discussion. Then answer the following questions.

- What is the purpose of the box?
- Why is the story of Manuel Barrera included?
- Write an answer to each of the "What Do You Think? questions.

Textbook Exercise 3: Your College Textbook

Choose an assignment given by one of your instructors and make notes on it as if you were preparing for a class discussion on the topic.

SELF-TEST SUMMARY

Goal **1**

Why is it important to listen critically in class?

Critical listening enables you to respond thoughtfully and participate meaningfully.

Goal **2**

What strategies can you use to strengthen your questioning and answering skills?

While reading an assignment, write down questions, and bring the list to class. Be clear and concise. Ask serious questions, and think through your responses before volunteering them.

Goal **3**

Why is participation in class discussions important, and what strategies can improve your involvement in class discussions?

Participation improves concentration and focus. It gives you practice in speaking before groups. Try to say something early in the discussion. Be brief and concise, avoid direct exchanges with individuals, and do not monopolize the discussion or interrupt other speakers. Jot down ideas as the discussion is going on and organize your remarks before speaking. Watch the group's responses as you speak.

Goal **4**

For group activities, how can you help the group function most effectively?

Choose group members who are alert and energetic. Participate actively and responsibly and take a leadership role. Make the most of individual strengths and weaknesses.

Goal **5**

How do you make an effective oral presentation?

Understand the purpose of the assignment. Research the topic thoroughly and prepare outline notes. Use visual aids if appropriate. Anticipate questions from the audience. Practice making the presentation, and deliver it as effectively as possible.

Goal **6**

How can you communicate effectively with your professors?

Most professors hold office hours during which you can meet with them. Your professors are likely also available by e-mail or phone. Be sure to use a professional tone and call, e-mail, or text only at appropriate hours.

APPLYING YOUR SKILLS

DISCUSSING THE CHAPTER

1. Discuss what members of a class should and should *not* do when one class member continually dominates the class discussion or fills class time with unimportant questions.
2. Discuss what classmates could do to help a student who is afraid to make a required oral presentation.
3. Suppose you are a member of a group that must prepare a group project. The group has chosen a topic that you are certain does not meet the instructor's requirements. What courses of action might you take?

ANALYZING A STUDY SITUATION

Martha is taking an interpersonal communication course in which the instructor allows students to select from a menu of activities that earn points that determine their final grade. Each student must choose at least three different activities. The activities include quizzes, a final exam, oral reports, group projects, research papers, panel discussions, interviews with community leaders, and leading class discussions.

Because Martha is not confident about her writing skills and gets nervous when taking exams, she selected oral reports, group projects, and panel discussions. Martha is a shy, quiet, self-directed person. She is well organized and feels most comfortable when she knows exactly what to expect and is in control of details.

1. Evaluate Martha's choice of activities.
2. What advice would you give Martha for how to be successful with each of her choices?

WORKING ON COLLABORATIVE PROJECTS

DIRECTIONS   Five or six class members should volunteer to participate in a panel discussion on a current controversial issue. The panel members should meet to plan their panel discussion while the rest of the class observes. The observers should critique the panel group's planning, efficiency, and interaction. Your instructor may "plant" problem panel members.

Quick Quiz

DIRECTIONS Write the letter of the choice that best completes each statement in the space provided.

CHECKING YOUR RECALL

_____ 1. All of the following strategies can help you avoid obstacles to critical listening *except*

    a. keeping an open mind about a speaker or a topic.
    b. recognizing your own biases.
    c. practicing selective listening.
    d. observing the responses of the audience.

_____ 2. Preparing for and participating in class discussions allows you to do all of the following *except*

    a. avoid reading assigned material.
    b. practice speaking in front of groups.
    c. be better prepared for exams and quizzes.
    d. sort out what you know and what you need to study further.

_____ 3. The best way to prepare for a class discussion is to

    a. quickly skim through the reading assignment.
    b. talk to classmates about their views on the topic.
    c. focus on factual information about the topic.
    d. mark and highlight key ideas in the reading assignment.

_____ 4. In class discussions, you should use all of the following strategies *except*

    a. try to say something early in the discussion.
    b. try to involve other class members in direct exchanges.
    c. make your comments brief and to the point.
    d. watch the group's responses as you speak.

_____ 5. When you are preparing an oral presentation, your first step should be to

    a. understand the purpose of the assignment.
    b. decide on what kind of visual aids you will use.
    c. collect and organize your information.
    d. anticipate questions your audience may ask.

APPLYING YOUR SKILLS

_____ 6. Isaac is trying to improve his questioning and answering skills in class discussions. One strategy he should adopt is to

    a. wait until someone else in the class asks the question he is thinking of.
    b. answer a question only if he is positive his answer is correct.
    c. jot down questions as he is reading an assignment and bring the list to class.
    d. repeat a question that has already been asked.

_____ 7. Sydney will be participating regularly in online discussions for a health and nutrition class. She should plan to do all of the following *except*

    a. become familiar with the software before she posts messages.
    b. think through what she wants to say before she says it.
    c. avoid reading previous posts so she is not influenced by what others have said.
    d. indicate whether her comments are in response to an assignment or a lecture.

_____ 8. If your instructor asks the class to form small groups for a project, you can help your group function effectively by doing all of the following *except*

    a. taking a leadership role.
    b. selecting alert, energetic classmates for the group.
    c. joking with group members about the assignment to make it more fun.
    d. accepting your share of the work and expecting others to do the same.

_____ 9. Joanna is nervous about making an oral presentation for her sociology class. Her first step should be to

    a. practice her presentation aloud several times by herself.
    b. practice her presentation in front of her friends.
    c. practice by writing out the speech several times.
    d. practice answering possible questions about her presentation.

_____ 10. When you want to communicate with a professor outside of class, you should remember that

    a. most professors typically use text messages to communicate with students.
    b. you can use your professor's office hours to ask for help in the course.
    c. e-mail is always best for sending your professors time-sensitive information.
    d. it is fine to use informal language in electronic communications with professors.

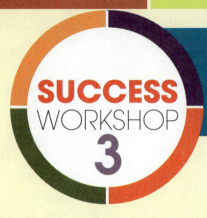

SUCCESS
WORKSHOP
3

WORKING WITH NEW COURSE FORMATS: ONLINE, HYBRID, AND FLIPPED COURSES

Did You Know?

⟳ One study found that the greatest challenges for online students are getting behind and not being able to catch up, not understanding the requirements of the course (for example, having to start and finish on a certain day), and having too many other responsibilities.[1]

⟳ A chemical engineering major at Villanova University said his exam scores went up 10 percentage points over the term in his courses that used the flipped classroom model. He said, "Everything kind of tied together as you were moving forward."[2]

As the information above indicates, new course formats have become a common part of the college experience. How can you use the new course formats to stimulate your learning?

WHAT ARE ONLINE AND HYBRID COURSES?

Many colleges offer online courses (which are conducted exclusively online) or hybrid courses (which combine online coursework with occasional required

on-campus sessions or meetings). Doing well in online and hybrid courses requires a great deal of independence and self-direction, as well as the ability to work in electronic teams.

Avoid taking online or hybrid courses during your first semester or first year of college. Attending traditional, in-person courses helps you learn what is expected in college classes. Once you are familiar with college expectations, you will be better prepared to take online courses.

---

[1]M. Fetzner, "What Do Unsuccessful Online Students Want Us to Know?" *Journal Of Asynchronous Learning Networks* 17, no. 1 (2013): 13–27.
[2]http://www.usnews.com/news/stem-solutions/articles/2014/08/05/taking-a-page-from-humanities-college-engineering-gets-flipped

HOW CAN YOU SUCCEED IN ONLINE COURSES?

To maximize your success in online and hybrid courses, use the following suggestions.

Read, read, read. Reading is your primary source of information in online courses; you read textbooks and communications from professors and other students. If you do not like reading on screen, print the course materials and read them that way.

Develop a support network. If you like or need personal contact or in-person support from other students, find a friend who will register for the same online course. Use the course Web page or social media to stay in touch with and collaborate with classmates. Use social media to focus on course content; do not use it to avoid coursework.

Keep up with the work. Most students who fail online courses do so because they fall hopelessly behind with the required reading and written assignments and cannot catch up. Devote specific hours each week to the online course. Make a work/study schedule and follow it as you would for any other class.

Keep your focus. Turn off music and other distractions while working on your computer for your online course. Turn off your smart phone. Close windows on your Internet browser that are not relevant to your coursework. If you use Skype, use it during study time to discuss course content. Go "invisible" to friends who are not in your class.

Get to know your professors. Even though you may never meet your instructor in person, you can still build a relationship with your professor by asking questions during live broadcasts and by posting questions. (Be sure to follow any rules that the instructor has established regarding communication etiquette or protocols.) Talking with your instructors also helps you establish an academic reputation as a conscientious and interested student (see Success Workshop 7: Polish Your Academic Image).

WHAT IS A COURSE MANAGEMENT SYSTEM?

Most online courses take place within a computer-based course management system (such as Moodle, Sakai, Canvas, or BlackBoard). The system usually contains the course syllabus (see Success Workshop 1: Learn About Your Courses and Your Campus Resources), lists of assignments, announcements of quizzes and exams, and so forth. It also allows you to communicate directly with classmates and with your professor. Instructors typically ask students to complete and submit assignments and exams electronically via the course management system, which the instructor also uses to grade and return assignments to you.

Most course management systems are multimedia experiences. Through them you can read an e-book, watch videos, take quizzes to assess your understanding of course materials, download image or text files, and link to Web sites that house additional course materials.

If your online course requires you to use a specific course management system, do the following:

- Sign up early, following the instructions on the home page carefully.

- Keep track of your username and password. Most calls to technical support come from students who have forgotten this information.

- Be sure that you are using the most up-to-date release of the system and that you are running it on the recommended Internet browser. (For example, some systems may indicate that they are most stable on Firefox or Chrome and not recommended for Internet Explorer or Safari.) If you do not have the recommended browser, download it and make it your default browser.

Now answer the following questions about online courses at your school.

1. List a few required courses that are offered online. Choose one in which you might be interested.
2. Compare the syllabus with that of a traditional (in-person) course. How are the syllabi similar? How are they different?
3. Does the course require you to use a course management system? If so, which one? Is your computer currently set up to meet the requirements of the course management system?
4. How will your final grade be determined?
5. Is the course completely online, or will you be required to meet with your instructor and/or classmates at some point during the term?

WHAT ARE THE BENEFITS OF FORMING AN ONLINE STUDY GROUP?

An online study group can help you feel less isolated, especially if you are a social person. You and a group of virtual classmates can use online study sessions to review, quiz one another, and study for exams. If the class course management system does not support online study groups, try setting up a class-specific Facebook page (or use another type of social media). When posting to the page or interacting with the group, stay focused on the course content. Don't post anything that will not help the members of your study group get a better grade in the course.

WHAT IS A "FLIPPED CLASSROOM"?

Instructors in many disciplines have begun to experiment with a new teaching technique called the **flipped classroom**. In this model, students learn most of the course's basic concepts before coming to class. The flipped classroom often has a substantial online component. Students may read online materials, watch videos, complete interactive exercises, take online quizzes to assess their understanding of key ideas, and examine PowerPoint slides that summarize important terms and research. Class sessions are then devoted to examining topics in more detail, clarifying difficult topics, engaging in discussion or debate, or other activities that require active student involvement.

Here are some suggestions for learning in a flipped environment.

Complete all required activities before coming to class. Do not skip any part of the pre-meeting assignment; by doing so you may miss learning important topics that you will be required to discuss during class.

Form a study group that meets to review the course materials before each session or at key points in the term. Most flipped classrooms require collaboration; participating in a study group is good practice.

When watching instructional videos, eliminate all distractions and concentrate on the topic being discussed. Pay close attention to the way sample problems are solved. Watch the video as many times as you need to; don't expect that you will always understand everything after watching a video only once.

Speak up in class. Class sessions are your only opportunity to get clarification on materials you do not understand. You will be tested on these materials; it is your responsibility to make sure you understand them.

Now answer the following questions about "flipped classrooms."

1. How does a flipped learning environment require you to take charge of your learning?
2. In what types of courses do you think a flipped environment would work best? Why?
3. Does the idea of attending a flipped class appeal to you? Why or why not?
4. What do you think the instructor's role in a flipped classroom is or should be?
5. Do you think a flipped environment would work better in an introductory class or in a class for majors only? Explain.

ONLINE!

Opportunities to take classes that might not otherwise fit into your schedule.

New experiences with evolving educational technologies.

Learning that requires self-direction and strong organizational skills.

Interactive media elements in the online environment.

Nighttime and weekend classes become possible and convenient.

Enhanced digital skills that carry over to the workplace.

SUCCESS WORKSHOP 4

STRENGTHEN YOUR CONCENTRATION

Did You Know?

➲ A recent survey asked students how they use their digital devices in class. The responses were as follows: 86 percent texted, 68 percent checked e-mail, 66 percent used social networks, and 8 percent played games.[1]

➲ Getting 30 minutes of exercise a day can lead to higher levels of concentration and stamina.[2]

As these statistics show, students face many distractions that may interfere with their studies. Fortunately, some basic techniques can help you improve your focus and concentration.

WHY IS IT IMPORTANT TO STRENGTHEN YOUR CONCENTRATION?

Every assignment that you do in college requires concentration. Whether you are writing a paper, reading a chapter, working on a project, or listening to a lecture, you will have to keep your mind on your work if you expect to learn. No matter how intelligent you are, or what skills and talents you possess, you cannot succeed if you can't focus on the task at hand.

WHAT IS WRONG WITH THIS PICTURE?

Why could this student be having trouble concentrating? List as many reasons as you can think of below.

_____

_____

_____

[1]http://newsroom.unl.edu/releases/2013/10/23/UNL+study+shows+college+students+are+digitally+distracted+in+class

[2]http://www.cimaglobal.com/Thought-leadership/Newsletters/Velocity-e-magazine/Velocity-2011/Velocity-April-2011/Read-the-best-studying-tips/

HAVE YOU EVER SAID OR THOUGHT . . .

"I just can't seem to concentrate!"

"I've got so much reading to do; I'll never be able to catch up!"

"I try to study, but I can't sit still."

"I waste a lot of time just trying to get started."

"When I'm trying to study, I find myself surfing the Web or catching up with friends on Facebook."

"My brain shuts off the minute I encounter something challenging, long, or complicated."

If you have, consider the following suggestions for improving your study surroundings and focusing your attention.

HOW CAN YOU CREATE A WORKABLE STUDY ENVIRONMENT?

- Choose a place with minimal distractions, such as a basement, library, or attic. Avoid studying in student centers or cafeterias, which tend to be noisy and frenetic.
- Establish a study area with a table or desk that is yours alone for study.
- Control noise levels. Determine how much background noise, if any, you can tolerate, and choose a place best suited to you.
- Put away all electronic devices that are not necessary for study, such as your iPad or cell phone.
- Eliminate distracting clutter. Get rid of photos, stacks of bills, mementos, and so forth.
- Have necessary supplies at your fingertips: dictionaries, pens and pencils, calculator, calendar, watch or clock.

WHAT DO YOU NEED TO CHANGE IN YOUR STUDY ENVIRONMENT?

Write a check mark next to each suggestion in the preceding section that you could use to improve your study area. Plan the changes you will make, assigning one task that you will do on each of the next three days.

HOW CAN YOU FOCUS YOUR ATTENTION?

- Establish goals and time limits for each assignment. Deadlines will keep you motivated and create a sense of urgency, making you less likely to daydream or become distracted.
- Reward yourself. Use rewards such as checking your messages or eating a healthy snack when you complete a substantial task.

- Use writing to keep yourself mentally and physically active. Highlighting, outlining, and note taking will force you to keep your mind on the material you are reading.

- Vary your activities. Avoid working on one type of activity for a long period of time. Instead, alternate between writing, reading, reviewing, and solving math problems, for example.

- Keep a distractions list. As distracting thoughts enter your mind, jot them on a notepad. You may, for example, think of your mother's upcoming birthday as you're reading your psychology textbook. Writing it down will help you remember it and will eliminate the distraction.

- End on a positive note before you get too tired or frustrated. For long-term projects, stop at a point at which it will be easy to pick up again.

- Check your concentration. Each time your mind wanders, place a light check mark on the page or a sheet of scrap paper. When the number of check marks increases, you'll know it's time to take a break or vary your activities.

IN WHAT WAYS CAN YOU SHARPEN YOUR FOCUS?

Make a plan here for trying out each idea on this and the previous page for a week to see which you find most helpful. If you can think of other helpful ideas, add them to your plan.

Week 1 _____

_____

_____

Week 2 _____

_____

_____

Week 3 _____

_____

_____

Week 4 _____

_____

_____

Week 5 _____

_____

_____

WHAT WORKED AND WHAT DIDN'T?

To learn from what you do, you need to keep track of what works and what does not. Of the various ideas you have tried, which were the most helpful? Which weren't as helpful? For the ideas that didn't work as well, can you think of different ways to put them into action that might work better for you? Keep experimenting until you think you have made full use of all suggestions and **remember to . . .**

FOCUS!

Figure out how to make your study area work for you.

  Organize your assignments to vary your activities.

    Concentrate on one task at a time.

      Use writing, highlighting, and note taking to stay engaged in study.

        Set goals and time limits for each assignment.

Identify and Organize What to Learn

LEARNING GOALS

In this chapter you will learn to

1 Use paraphrasing to restate ideas.

2 Highlight textbooks.

3 Mark textbooks.

4 Outline to organize information.

5 Summarize to condense information.

6 Map to visualize ideas.

7 Avoid plagiarism.

LEARNING EXPERIMENT

1 Read the following description of the steps involved in a conversation.

Conversation takes place in at least five steps: opening, feedforward, business, feedback, and closing. It is convenient to divide any act—and conversation is no exception—into chunks or stages and view each stage as requiring a choice of what to say and how to say it. In this model the conversation process is divided into five steps, each of which requires that you make a choice as to what you'll do. The first step is to open the conversation, usually with some kind of greeting: "Hi. How are you?" "Hello, this is Joe." It is a message that establishes a connection between two people and opens the channels for more meaningful interaction. At the second step, you usually provide some kind of feedforward, which gives the other person a general idea of the conversation's focus: "I've got to tell you about Jack," "Did you hear what happened in class yesterday?" or "We need to talk about our vacation plans." At the third step, you talk "business," the substance or focus of the conversation. The term "business" is used to emphasize that most conversations are goal directed; you converse to fulfill one or several of the general purposes of interpersonal communication: to learn, relate, influence, play or help. The fourth step is the reverse of the second. Here you reflect back on the conversation to signal that as far as you're concerned the business is completed: "So you want to send Jack a get-well card," "Wasn't that the craziest class you ever heard of?" or "I'll call for reservations, and you'll shop for what we need." The closing is the goodbye, which often reveals how satisfied the persons were with the conversation. "I hope to talk again soon" or "Don't call us, we'll call you."

—adapted from DeVito, *The Interpersonal Communication Book*, p. 266

2 Now, draw a diagram or write an outline that explains the process of conversation.

The Results

Did drawing the diagram or writing the outline help you learn or understand the steps in conversation? Why? In order to diagram or outline, you had to grasp the process and make it fit within a framework. Through these activities you were consolidating, or putting together, the information.

You organized it and made connections among the ideas presented.

Learning Principle: What This Means to You

Consolidation is a process in which information settles, gels, or takes shape. The key to learning large amounts of information is to organize and consolidate it. Basically, consolidation involves looking for patterns, differences, similarities, or shared characteristics and then grouping, rearranging, and reducing the information into manageable pieces. For academic learning, writing is often an effective way to consolidate what you've learned. In this chapter you will learn several methods of consolidating information found in textbooks: paraphrasing, highlighting, annotating, outlining, summarizing, and mapping. You will also learn to avoid plagiarism by carefully recording sources you use.

PARAPHRASING

A **paraphrase** is a restatement of a passage in your own words. The author's meaning is retained, but your wording, *not* the author's, is used. We use paraphrasing frequently in everyday speech. For example, when you relay a message from one person to another, you convey the meaning but do not use the person's exact wording. A paraphrase can be used to make a passage's meaning clearer and more concise. A paraphrase, then, moves you from a knowledge level in which you can recall information to a comprehension level in which you understand the ideas presented.

Paraphrasing is appropriate when . . .

- **Exact detailed comprehension is required.** Working through a passage line by line will strengthen your comprehension. You might paraphrase the steps in solving a math problem or a process in biology, for example.
- **Reading material is difficult or complicated.** If you can express the author's ideas in your own words, you can be sure you understand it. If you cannot paraphrase it, you will know your comprehension is incomplete. See Figure 4-1.
- **Material is stylistically complex or uses complicated or unfamiliar language.** Paraphrasing will help you break though the language barrier and express the content as simply as possible.

Goal

Use paraphrasing to restate ideas.

HOW TO PARAPHRASE EFFECTIVELY

Use the following suggestions to paraphrase effectively.

1. Read slowly and carefully, and read the material through entirely before writing anything.
2. As you read, pay attention to exact meanings and relationships among ideas.
3. As you begin to write your paraphrase, read each sentence and express the key idea in your own words.
4. Reread the original sentence; look away and write your own sentence; then reread the original and add anything you missed.
5. Don't try to paraphrase word by word; instead, work with ideas.
6. For words or phrases that you are unsure of or are not comfortable using, check a dictionary to locate a more familiar meaning.
7. You may combine several original sentences into a more concise paraphrase.
8. When finished, reread your paraphrase and compare it with the original for completeness and accuracy.

FIGURE 4-1
A Comparison of Paraphrases of Difficult, Complicated Material

PASSAGE: NEURONS

Individual neurons do not form a continuous chain, with each neuron directly touching another, end to end. If they did, the number of connections would be inadequate for the vast amount of information the nervous system must handle. Instead, individual neurons are separated by a minuscule space called the synaptic cleft, where the axon terminal nearly touches a dendrite or the cell body of another. The entire site—the axon terminal, the cleft, and the membrane of the receiving dendrite or cell body—is called a synapse. Because a neuron's axon may have hundreds or even thousands of terminals, a single neuron may have synaptic connections with a great many others. As a result, the number of communication links in the nervous system runs into the trillions or perhaps even the quadrillions.

Although we seem to be born with nearly all the neurons we will ever have, many synapses have not yet formed at birth. Research with animals shows that axons and dendrites continue to grow as a result of both physical maturation and experience with the world, and tiny projections on dendrites called spines increase both in size and in number. Throughout life, new learning results in the establishment of new synaptic connections in the brain, with stimulating environments producing the greatest changes (Greenough & Anderson, 1991; Greenough & Black, 1992). Conversely, some unused synaptic connections are lost as cells or their branches die and are not replaced (Camel, Withers, & Greenough, 1986). The brain's circuits are not fixed and immutable; they are continually developing and being pruned in response to information and to challenges and changes in the environment.

—Wade and Tavris, *Psychology*, pp. 124–125

Paraphrase 1: Demonstrates Lack of Understanding
Neurons don't connect with each other because it would be too much information for the nervous system. They have trillions or even quadrillions of links and hundreds or thousands of terminals. They also have clefts, membranes, and synapses—the receiving dendrite or cell body. We seem to be born with all of them that we will ever have. Spines or dendrites become more and bigger, and some of their branches aren't replaced. The brain's circuits cannot be fixed, but are pruned.

Paraphrase 2: Demonstrates Understanding
Neurons are separated from each other by tiny spaces or clefts between the axon of one and the dendrite of another. These three parts make up a synapse. Because of synapses, neurons can make more connections with one another than if they had to touch. This allows for trillions of links in the nervous system. The number of synapses we have is constantly changing. Unused connections vanish, and learning causes our axons and dendrites to grow and make new synaptic connections.

DIRECTIONS Write a paraphrase for each of the following excerpts.

Exercise 1

1. The tides are important for several reasons. Tidal mixing of nearshore waters removes pollutants and recirculates nutrients. Tidal currents also move floating animals and plants to and from their usual breeding areas in estuaries to deeper waters. People who fish frequently follow tidal cycles to improve their catch, because strong tidal currents concentrate bait and smaller fish, thus attracting larger fish. When sailing ships were more common, departures or arrivals in a harbor had to be closely linked to the tidal cycle.

   —Ross, *Introduction to Oceanography*, p. 239

2. The *stomach* is a muscular sac that churns the food as it secretes mucus, hydrochloric acid, and enzymes that begin the digestion of proteins. The food is meanwhile sealed in the stomach by two sphincters, or rings of muscles, one at either end of the stomach. After the mixing is completed, the lower sphincter opens and the stomach begins to contract repeatedly, squeezing the food into the small intestine. A fatty meal, by the way, slows this process and makes us feel "full" longer. This is also why we're hungry again so soon after a low-fat Chinese dinner.

   The *small intestine* is a long convoluted tube in which digestion is completed and through which most nutrient products enter the bloodstream. Its inner surface is covered with tiny, fingerlike projections called *villi*, which increase the surface area of the intestinal lining. Furthermore, the surface area of each villus is increased by about 3000 tiny projections called *microvilli*. Within each villus is a minute lymph vessel surrounded by a network of blood capillaries. While the digested products of certain fats move directly into the lymph vessel, the products of protein and starch digestion move into the blood capillaries.

   —Wallace, *Biology: The World of Life*, p. 443

   Tip *Minute* means "very small." The word is pronounced [my-noot] and stressed on the second syllable. Don't confuse it with *minute* [min-nut], meaning 60 seconds.

3. *Section 7.* (1). All bills for raising revenue shall originate in the House of Representatives; but the Senate may propose or concur with amendments as on other bills.

   (2). Every bill which shall have passed the House of Representatives and the Senate, shall, before it become a law, be presented to the President of the United States; if he approve he shall sign it, but if not he shall return it, with his objections to that House in which it shall have originated, who shall enter the objections at large on their journal, and proceed to reconsider it. If after such reconsideration two thirds of that House shall agree to pass the bill, it shall be sent, together with the objections, to the other House, by which it shall likewise be reconsidered, and if approved by two thirds of that House, it shall become a law. But in all such cases the votes of both Houses shall be determined by yeas and nays, and the names of the persons voting for and against the bill shall be entered on the journal of each House respectively. If any bill shall not be returned by the President within ten days (Sundays excepted) after it shall have been presented to him, the same shall be a law, in like manner as if he had signed it, unless the Congress by their adjournment prevent its return, in which case it shall not be a law.

   —U.S. Constitution. United States Congress ●

Exercise 2

DIRECTIONS Write a paraphrase of "Prejudice and Discrimination: The Vicious Circle" in Part Seven, on page 437. ●

Exercise 3

DIRECTIONS Write a paraphrase of a two- or three-paragraph excerpt from one of your textbooks. Choose a passage that is difficult or stylistically complex. ●

Goal 2

Highlight textbooks.

HIGHLIGHTING

As you have already discovered, most college courses involve lengthy and time-consuming reading assignments. Just completing the reading assignments is a big job. Have you begun to wonder how you will ever go back over all those textbook chapters when it's time to prepare for an exam?

Let's suppose that it takes you at least four hours to carefully read a 40-page chapter. Assume that your text has ten chapters of approximately 40 pages each. It would take a total of 40 hours, then, to read completely through the text once. Suppose that your instructor is giving a final exam that covers the entire text. If the only thing you did to prepare for the final was to reread the whole text, then it would take close to another 40 hours to study for the exam; and an additional reading is no guarantee that you will pass or do well on the exam.

Now consider this: If you had highlighted and marked important ideas and facts as you were first reading the chapters, you would then have to read and study only what you marked. If you had marked or highlighted 15 to 20 percent of the chapter material, you would have cut your rereading time by 80 to 85 percent, or 32 hours! Of course, to prepare effectively for the exam, you would have to review in other ways besides rereading, but you would have time left to do this.

How to Highlight Textbooks

To highlight textbooks effectively, use the following guidelines.

1. **Read first; then highlight.** As you are developing skill in highlighting, it is better to read a paragraph or section first and then go back and highlight what is important to remember and review. Later, when you've had more practice highlighting, you may be able to highlight while you read. If you are reading on an e-reader or tablet, use the highlighter function.
2. **Read the boldfaced headings.** Headings are labels that announce the overall topics contained in a section. Use the headings to form questions that you expect to be answered in the section.
3. **After you have read the section, go back and highlight the parts that answer your questions.** These will be parts of sentences that express the main ideas, or most important thoughts, in the section. In reading and highlighting the following section, you could form questions like those suggested and then highlight as shown.

Questions to Ask

What are primary groups?

What are secondary groups?

PRIMARY AND SECONDARY GROUPS

It is not at all surprising that some students used their families as a reference group. After all, families are the best examples of the groups Charles Cooley called *primary* chiefly because they "are fundamental in forming the social nature and ideals of the individual." In a primary group the individuals interact informally, relate to each other as whole persons, and enjoy their relationship for its own sake. This is one of the two main types of social groups. In the other type, a secondary group, the individuals interact formally, relate to each other as players of particular roles, and expect to profit from each other.

—Thio, *Sociology*, p. 100

4. **As you identify and highlight main ideas, look for important facts that explain or support the main idea, and highlight them too.**
5. **When highlighting main ideas and details, do not highlight complete sentences.** Highlight only enough so that you can see what is important and so that your highlighting makes sense when you reread. Note how only key words and phrases are highlighted in the following passage.

GOSSIP

There can be no doubt that everyone spends a great deal of time gossiping. In fact, gossip seems universal among all cultures, and among some it's a commonly accepted ritual. Gossip refers to third party talk about another person; the word *gossip* "now embraces both the talker and the talk, the tattler and the tattle, the newsmonger and the news mongering." Gossip is an inevitable part of daily interactions; to advise anyone not to gossip would be absurd. Not gossiping would eliminate one of the most frequent and enjoyable forms of communication.

In some instances, however, gossip is unethical. First, it's unethical to reveal information that you've promised to keep secret. Although this principle may seem too obvious to even mention, it seems violated in many cases. For example, in a study of 133 school executives, board presidents, and superintendents, the majority received communications that violated an employee's right to confidentiality. When it is impossible to keep something secret (Bok offers the example of the teenager who confides a suicide plan), the information should be revealed only to those who must know it, not to the world at large. Second, gossip is unethical when it invades the privacy that everyone has a right to, for example, when it concerns matters that are properly considered private and when the gossip can hurt the individuals involved. Third, gossip is unethical when it's known to be false and is nevertheless passed on to others.

—DeVito, *The Interpersonal Communication Book*, p. 191

Aspects of Effective Highlighting

For your highlighting to be effective and useful for study and review, it must follow four specific guidelines.

1. **The right amount of information must be highlighted.**
2. **The highlighting must be regular and consistent.**
3. **It must be accurate.**
4. **It must clearly reflect the content of the passage.**

Suggestions for implementing these guidelines and examples of each are given in the following paragraphs.

HIGHLIGHT THE RIGHT AMOUNT Students frequently make the mistake of highlighting either too much or too little. If you highlight too much, the passages you have marked will take you too long to reread when you are studying later. If you highlight too little, you won't get any meaning from your highlighting as you review it.

TOO MUCH HIGHLIGHTING

Tip *Bone of contention* is an idiom referring to something people disagree about and are arguing about.

Iran, which had served as an area of competition between the British and the Russians since the nineteenth century, became a bone of contention between the United States and the Soviet Union after World War II. As the result of an agreement between the British and the Russians in 1941, Shah Mohammad Reza Pahlavi (1919–1980) gained the Iranian throne. After the war he asked foreign troops to withdraw from his country, but following the slow return of the Soviet army to its borders, aggressive activities of the Iranian Communist party (Tudeh), and an assassination attempt on the Shah's life, Iran firmly tied itself to the West.

—Wallbank et al., *Civilization Past and Present*, pp. 1012–1013

TOO LITTLE HIGHLIGHTING

Iran, which had served as an area of competition between the British and the Russians since the nineteenth century, became a bone of contention between the United States and the Soviet Union after World War II. As the result of an agreement between the British and the Russians in 1941, Shah Mohammad Reza Pahlavi (1919–1980) gained the Iranian throne. After the war he asked foreign troops to withdraw from his country, but following the slow return of the Soviet army to its borders, aggressive activities of the Iranian Communist party (Tudeh), and an assassination attempt on the Shah's life, Iran firmly tied itself to the West.

EFFECTIVE HIGHLIGHTING

Iran, which had served as an area of competition between the British and the Russians since the nineteenth century, became a bone of contention between the United States and the Soviet Union after World War II. As the result of an agreement between the British and the Russians in 1941, Shah Mohammad Reza Pahlavi (1919–1980) gained the Iranian throne. After the war he asked foreign troops to withdraw from his country, but following the slow return of the Soviet army to its borders, aggressive activities of the Iranian Communist party (Tudeh), and an assassination attempt on the Shah's life, Iran firmly tied itself to the West.

The highlighting in the first passage does not distinguish important from unimportant information. In the second passage, only the main point of the paragraph is highlighted, but not enough detail is included. The highlighting in the third passage is effective; it identifies the main idea of the paragraph and includes enough details to make the main idea clear and understandable.

As a rule of thumb, try to highlight no more than one-quarter to one-third of each page. This number will vary, of course, depending on the type of material you are reading.

DEVELOP A REGULAR AND CONSISTENT SYSTEM OF HIGHLIGHTING To develop a system for deciding what type of information you will highlight and how you will mark it, use the following guidelines.

• First, decide what type of information you want to mark: for example, only main ideas, details, new terminology, key names or dates, or any combination of these.

- Second, determine how you will distinguish each type of information. Perhaps you will highlight main ideas in yellow, key terms in blue. Another approach is to use asterisks and brackets to call attention to the main points.
- Third, be sure to use consistently whatever system and type of highlighting you decide on so that you will know what your highlighting means when you review it. If you sometimes mark details and other times highlight only main ideas, at review time you will find that you are unsure of what passages are marked in what way.

Each of the following paragraphs has been highlighted using one of the suggested systems. You will notice that the paragraphs vary in the type of information marked in each.

VERSION 1: USE OF COLOR

MONOCHRONISM AND POLYCHRONISM

Another important cultural distinction exists between **monochronic and polychronic time orientations**. Monochronic peoples or cultures such as those of the United States, Germany, Scandinavia, and Switzerland schedule one thing at a time. These cultures compartmentalize time and set sequential times for different activities. Polychronic peoples or cultures such as those of Latin America, the Mediterranean, and the Arab world, on the other hand, schedule multiple things at the same time. Eating, conducting business with several different people, and taking care of family matters may all go on at once. No culture is entirely monochronic or polychronic; rather, these are general or preponderant tendencies. Some cultures combine both time orientations; in Japan and in parts of American culture, for example, both orientations can be found.

—DeVito, *Essentials of Human Communication*, p. 125

VERSION 2: USE OF BRACKETS AND ASTERISKS

MONOCHRONISM AND POLYCHRONISM

Another important cultural distinction exists between **monochronic** and **polychronic time orientations**. Monochronic peoples or cultures such as those of the United States, Germany, Scandinavia, and Switzerland schedule one thing at a time. These cultures compartmentalize time and set sequential times for different activities. Polychronic peoples or cultures such as those of Latin America, the Mediterranean, and the Arab world, on the other hand, schedule multiple things at the same time. Eating, conducting business with several different people, and taking care of family matters may all go on at once. No culture is entirely monochronic or polychronic; rather, these are general or preponderant tendencies. Some cultures combine both time orientations; in Japan and in parts of American culture, for example, both orientations can be found.

Exercise 4

DIRECTIONS Read the following passage. Then evaluate the effectiveness of the highlighting, making suggestions for improvement.

SCARCITY OF HUMAN FOSSILS

Unfortunately humans are a maddeningly poor source of fossils. In 1956, the paleontologist G. H. R. von Koenigswald calculated that if all the then-known fragments of human beings older than the Neanderthal people were gathered together they could be comfortably displayed on a medium-sized table. Although many more fossils of early hominids have been found since then, discoveries are still rare.

Why are human fossils so scarce? Why can one go to good fossil sites almost anywhere in the world and find millions of shell remains or thousands of bones of extinct reptiles and mammals, while peoples earlier than Neanderthal are known from only a handful of sites at which investigators, working through tons of deposits, pile up other finds by the bushel basket before recovering a single human tooth?

There are many reasons. First, the commonness of marine fossils is a direct reflection of the abundance of these creatures when they were alive. It also reflects the tremendous span of time during which they abounded. Many of them swarmed through the waters of the earth for hundreds of millions of years. When they died, they sank and were covered by sediments. Their way of life—their life in the water—preserved them, as did their extremely durable shells, the only parts of them that now remain. Humans, by contrast, have never been as numerous as oysters and clams. They existed in small numbers, reproduced slowly and in small numbers, and lived a relatively long time. They were more intelligent than, for example, dinosaurs and were perhaps less apt to get mired in bogs, marshes, or quicksands. Most important, their way of life was different. They were not sea creatures or exclusively riverside browsers but lively, wide-ranging food-gatherers and hunters. They often lived and died in the open, where their bones were gnawed by scavengers, were trampled on, and were bleached and decomposed by the sun and rain. In hot climates, particularly in tropical forests and woodlands, the soil is likely to be markedly acid. Bones dissolve in such soils, and early humans who lived and died in such an environment had a very poor chance of leaving remains that would last until today. Finally, human ancestors have been on earth only a few million years. There simply has not been as much time for them to leave their bones as there has been for some of the more ancient species of animals.

—Campbell and Loy, *Humankind Emerging*, pp. 22–23 ●

Exercise 5

DIRECTIONS   Read each passage and then highlight the main ideas and important details in each. You may want to try various systems of highlighting as you work through this exercise.

1. **Why We Worry About the Wrong Things**

Nowadays we often worry about things that have a low probability of killing us and ignore things that have a much higher probability of doing us in. We worry more, for example, about being murdered by others than about killing ourselves, even though twice as many Americans commit suicide every year than are murdered. We worry about being struck by lightning during a thunder storm, while more than 10 times as many Americans die from falling out of bed. We are more afraid of dying in an airline accident than on the highway, although more than 500 times as many people die in car wrecks as in plane crashes. We are not shaken up over the likelihood of getting the common flu, which annually contributes to 36,000 deaths in the United States. We are not scared, either, by the cholesterol in our hamburger that contributes to heart disease killing 700,000 Americans a year.

Why, then, do we worry so much about those things that threaten us less than other things? One reason is the dread of prolonged pain or suffering. Thus we are more afraid of AIDS than heart disease because AIDS may take years for the patient to die but heart disease can kill in seconds. Another reason is that unfamiliar threats such as avian flu appear more frightening than familiar ones like the common flu. A third reason is the lack of control, which may explain the decision to drive rather than fly. Behind the wheel, you are in charge, but as an airline passenger, you are at the mercy of the pilot.

—adapted from Thio, *Sociology*, p. 105

2. DNA Fingerprinting and Forensics

DNA fingerprinting has become a vital tool in forensic medicine (the application of medical knowledge to questions of law). For example, DNA fingerprinting is used to identify "John and Jane Does," unknown human remains. The U.S. military takes blood and saliva samples from every recruit so it can identify soldiers killed in the line of duty. DNA fingerprinting can also identify victims of mass disasters such as airplane crashes. The World Trade Center tragedy called for genetic analysis on an unprecedented scale.

DNA fingerprinting can prove that a suspect was actually at the scene of a crime. In the United States, some communities now require certain criminal offenders to provide DNA samples, which are classified and stored. DNA profiles can also establish innocence. At least 10 people in the United States have been released from death row after genetic evidence exonerated them.

DNA fingerprinting can also verify relationships in cases of disputed property, identify long-lost relatives, and establish paternity, even in paternity cases that are centuries old. For example, historians have fiercely debated whether Thomas Jefferson, our third president, fathered any children by his slave Sally Hemings. Modern DNA researchers entered

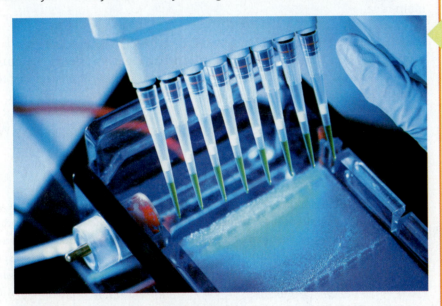

Visual Thinking
ANALYZING IMAGES

What would you highlight or what notes would you make after studying the photograph and caption?

Scientist using DNA electrophoresis.
"DNA retrieval can become a race against time."

This process involves cutting DNA into fragments and sorting them by length. Scientists then search for a repeating sequence or pattern, which constitutes a person's unique DNA profile. A person's known DNA is then compared with DNA samples collected at crime scenes.
(adapted from same source as passage—Marieb)

the fray by profiling Jefferson's Y chromosome. A comparison of 19 genetic markers on the Jefferson Y chromosomes and those of Hemings' descendants found identical matches between the Jefferson line and Hemings' youngest son. Could it be chance? Hardly!

—Marieb, *Essentials of Human Anatomy & Physiology*, p. 58 ●

HIGHLIGHT ACCURATELY A third guideline for marking textbooks is to be sure that the information you highlight accurately conveys the content of the paragraph or passage. In a rush, students sometimes overlook the second half of the main idea expressed in a paragraph, miss a crucial qualifying statement, or mistake an example or (worse yet) a contrasting idea for the main idea. Read the following paragraph and evaluate the accuracy of the highlighting.

It has long been established that the American legal court system is an open and fair system. Those suspected to be guilty of a criminal offense are given a jury trial in which a group of impartially selected citizens are asked to determine, based upon evidence presented, the guilt or innocence of the person on trial. In actuality, however, this system of jury trial is fair to everyone except the jurors involved. Citizens are expected and, in many instances, required to sit on a jury. They have little or no choice as to the time, place, or any other circumstances surrounding their participation. Additionally, they are expected to leave their job and accept jury duty pay for each day spent in court in place of their regular on-the-job salary. The jury must remain on duty until the case is decided.

The highlighting indicates that the main idea of the paragraph is that the American court system is open and fair. The paragraph starts out by saying that the legal system has long been established as fair, but then it goes on to say (in the third sentence) that the system is actually unfair to one particular group—the jury. In this case, the student who did the highlighting missed the real main statement of the paragraph by mistaking the introductory contrasting statement for the main idea.

MAKE YOUR HIGHLIGHTING UNDERSTANDABLE FOR REVIEW As you highlight, be certain that your highlighting clearly reflects the content of the passage so that you will be able to reread and review it easily. Try to highlight enough information in each passage so that the passage reads smoothly when you review it.

Read these two examples of highlighting of the same passage. Which highlighting is easier to reread?

VERSION 1

Capital may be thought of as manufactured resources. Capital includes the tools and equipment that strengthen, extend, or replace human hands in the production of goods and services. Hammers, sewing machines, turbines, bookkeeping machines, and component parts of finished goods—all are capital goods. Even the specialized skills of trained workers can be thought of as a kind of human capital. Capital resources permit "roundabout" production: producing goods indirectly with a kind of tool rather than directly by physical labor.

To construct a capital resource requires that we postpone production of consumer goods and services today so that we can produce a tool that will enable us to produce more goods and services in the future. To postpone production of wanted goods and services is sometimes a painful decision, particularly when people are poor and in desperate need of goods and services today.

—McCarty, *Dollars and Sense*, pp. 213–214

VERSION 2

Capital may be thought of as manufactured resources. Capital includes the tools and equipment that strengthen, extend, or replace human hands in the production of goods and services. Hammers, sewing machines, turbines, bookkeeping machines, and component parts of finished goods—all are capital goods. Even the specialized skills of trained workers can be thought of as a kind of human capital. Capital resources permit "roundabout" production: producing goods indirectly with a kind of tool rather than directly by physical labor.

To construct a capital resource requires that we postpone production of consumer goods and services today so that we can produce a tool that will enable us to produce more goods and services in the future. To postpone production of wanted goods and services is sometimes a painful decision, particularly when people are poor and in desperate need of goods and services today.

A good way to check to see if your highlighting is understandable for review is to reread only your highlighting. If parts are unclear right away, you can be sure it will be more confusing when you reread it a week or a month later. Be sure to fix ineffectual highlighting in one paragraph before you continue to the next paragraph. (And note: The highlighting in the second paragraph is more effective because it is easier to read. The student has highlighted verbs, and in doing so makes the highlights read like full sentences that will be easy to review.)

CHECKING YOUR HIGHLIGHTING

To test the effectiveness of your highlighting, ask yourself the following questions.

1. Have I highlighted the right amount or have I highlighted too much or too little information?
2. Have I used a regular and consistent system for highlighting?
3. Does my highlighting accurately reflect the meaning of the passage?
4. As I reread my highlighting, is it easy to follow the train of thought, or does the passage seem like a list of unconnected words?

DIRECTIONS Read the entire section titled "Theories of Prejudice" in Part Seven on pages 435–436. Highlight the main ideas and important details. When you have finished, test your highlighting by asking the four questions in the "Checking Your Highlighting" box above. Make any changes that will make your highlighting more consistent, accurate, or understandable. ●

Exercise 6

DIRECTIONS Choose a three- to four-page passage from one of your textbooks. Read the selection and highlight the main ideas, the important details, and any key terms that are introduced. When you have finished, test your highlighting by asking the four questions listed in the "Checking Your Highlighting" box above, and make any changes that will improve your highlighting. ●

Exercise 7

MARKING A TEXTBOOK

Goal 3

Mark textbooks.

As you were highlighting paragraphs and passages in the preceding section, you may have realized that highlighting alone is not sufficient, in many cases, to separate main ideas from details and both of these from new terminology. You may have seen that highlighting does not easily show the relative importance of ideas or indicate the relationship between facts and ideas. Therefore, it is often necessary to mark (or annotate), as well as highlight, selections that you are reading. Suggestions for marking are shown in Figure 4-2. If you are reading your textbook with an e-reader, use the annotation or note function to mark it.

FIGURE 4-2
Textbook Marking

Type of Marking		Example
Circling unknown words	def	. . . redressing the apparent (asymmetry) of their relationship . . .
Marking definitions	def	To say that the balance of power favors one party over another is to introduce a disequilibrium
Marking examples	ex	. . . concessions may include negative sanctions, trade agreements . . .
Numbering lists of ideas, causes, reasons, or events		. . . components of power include ① self-image, ② population, ③ natural resources, and ④ geography
Placing asterisks next to important passages	*	Power comes from three primary sources . . .
Putting question marks next to confusing passages	?→	. . . war prevention occurs through institutionalization of mediation . . .
Making notes to yourself	check def in soc text	. . . power is the ability of an actor on the international stage to . . .
Marking possible test items	T	There are several key features in the relationship . . .
Drawing arrows to show relationships	↻	. . . natural resources . . . control of industrial manufacturing capacity
Writing comments, noting disagreements and similarities	Can terrorism be prevented through similar balance?	. . . war prevention through balance of power is . . .
Marking summary statements	Sum	. . . the greater the degree of conflict, the more intricate will be . . .

Writing Critical Comments

When you highlight, you are operating at the knowledge and comprehension levels of thinking (see Chapter 1, p. 33). Marking is an opportunity to record your thinking at other levels.

APPLYING LEVELS OF THINKING

Marking and Levels of Thinking

Here are some examples of the kinds of marginal notes you might make.

Level of Thinking	Marginal Notes
Applying	Jot notes about how to use the information.
Analyzing	Draw arrows to link related material.
Evaluating	Comment on the worth, value, relevance, and timeliness of ideas.
Creating	Record ideas about how topics fit together; make notes connecting material to lectures; condense ideas into your own words.

Writing Summary Notes

Writing summary words or phrases in the margin of your textbook is one of the most valuable types of textbook marking. The process of pulling ideas together and summarizing them in your own words forces you to think and evaluate as you read and makes remembering easier. Writing summary phrases is also a good test of your understanding. If you cannot state the main idea of a section in your own words, you probably do not understand it clearly. This realization can serve as an early warning signal that you may not be able to handle a test question on that section.

The following sample passage has been included to illustrate effective marking of summary phrases. First, read through the passage. Then look at the marginal summary clues.

WEIGHT TRENDS ON CAMPUS

Most first-year students do gain some weight once they start college—usually about 7 to 8 pounds. More importantly, this weight often doesn't disappear once the first year is over. Instead, many students gain a few more pounds every year of college. One study found that 23% of students were classified as overweight their first year, and that number grew to about 28% by their fourth year. Male students experienced weight gain more often—about 35% of them qualified as overweight, compared to about 20% of female students. In another survey, about 50% of college students said they were trying to lose weight.

What's the big culprit behind campus weight gain? While excess calories clearly contribute, a decline in physical activity also appears to be a major factor. Female students, for example, often find that their level of physical activity drops substantially in college. For all students, larger amounts of time spent watching television and smaller amounts of physical activity have been closely linked with excess weight.

The problem is compounded by the fact that more students are starting college at heavier weights than ever before. About 17% of American adolescents between the ages of 12 and 19 are overweight, compared to 5% in 1970. Another 17% carry enough extra pounds to put them at serious risk of becoming overweight. For many, these problems start during early childhood, with about 14% of children between the ages of 2 and 5 qualifying as overweight. As the number of overweight children climbs, so do cases of childhood diabetes and high blood pressure, conditions once largely limited to adults. Overweight children are far more likely to carry extra pounds into adulthood.

—Lynch et al., *Choosing Health*, p. 122

Margin notes:
- 7–8 lb average weight gain first year of college
- 28% overweight by year 4
  Male students gain more than female
- Reasons: excess calories, decline in activity (particularly women), and TV
- More people start college overweight than before, due to childhood obesity

Summary notes are most effective in passages that contain long and complicated ideas. In these cases, it is often simpler to write a summary phrase in the margin than to highlight a long or complicated statement of the main idea and supporting details.

To write a summary clue, try to think of a word or phrase that briefly and accurately states a particular idea presented in the passage. Summary words should trigger your memory of the content of the passage.

Exercise 8

DIRECTIONS Read the following textbook selection. Then mark as well as highlight important information contained in the passage.

WHAT IS CANCER?

The term cancer is used to identify a group of more than 100 diseases characterized by uncontrolled growth and spread of abnormal cells. The most common type for both men and women is lung cancer, with skin, breast, prostate, and colorectal cancers also occurring in large numbers. The types differ not only in where they occur in the body, but also in their causes, treatments, and prognoses. Carcinomas—cancers of epithelial cells that line the internal and external cavities of the body, including the glands—represent almost 80 to 90 percent of all cancers in adults. Sarcomas, or cancers of the connective tissue, occur in bone and muscle. Lymphoma, including both Hodgkin's disease and non-Hodgkin's lymphoma, is the third most frequently diagnosed cancer in children. Leukemia differs from the other types of cancer in that it does not result in a tumor. It is an aggressive cancer of the white blood cells formed in the bone marrow.

Cancer is responsible for 22.8 percent of all deaths in the United States, making it the second leading cause of death, behind heart disease. Even though the death rate from cancer has declined slightly since 2004, an estimated 577,190 Americans died of cancer in 2012, or 1,500 per day. About one-third of these cancer deaths in 2012 were related to overweight or obesity, physical inactivity, and poor diet.

—Blake et al., *Nutrition*, p. 329 ●

Exercise 9

DIRECTIONS Turn to "Theories of Prejudice" on pages 435–436 in Part Seven that you highlighted to complete Exercise 6. Review the section and add marking and summary words that would make the section easier to study and review. ●

Exercise 10

DIRECTIONS Choose a three- to four-page excerpt from one of your textbooks. Highlight and mark main ideas, important details, and key terms. Include summary words, if possible. ●

Goal ④

Outline to organize information.

ORGANIZING BY OUTLINING

Outlining is an effective way of organizing the relationships among ideas. From past experiences, many students think of an outline as an exact, detailed, organized listing of all information in a passage; they see outlining as routine copying of information from page to page and, therefore, avoid doing it.

Actually, an outline should *not* be a recopying of ideas. Think of it, instead, as a means of pulling together important information and showing how ideas interconnect. An outline is a form of note taking that provides a visual picture of the structure of ideas.

Outlining allows you to think about the material you read and to sort out the important ideas from those that are less important. Because it requires you to express ideas in your own words and to group them, outlining reveals whether you have understood what you read. Finally, thinking about, sorting, and expressing ideas in your own words is a form of repetition that helps you to remember the material.

WHEN TO USE OUTLINING

Outlining is useful in a variety of situations.

- **When you are using reference books or reading books you do not own, outlining is an effective way of taking notes.**
- **When you are reading material that seems difficult or confusing, outlining forces you to sort ideas, see connections, and express them in your own words.**
- **When you are asked to write an evaluation or critical interpretation of an article or essay, it is helpful to briefly outline the factual content.** The outline will reflect the development and progression of thought and will help you analyze the writer's ideas.
- **In courses where order or process is important, an outline is particularly useful.** In a data processing course, for example, in which various sets of programming commands must be performed in a specified sequence, making an outline is a good way to organize the information.
- **In the natural sciences, in which classifications are important, outlines help you record and sort information.** In botany, for example, one important focus is the classification and description of various plant groups. Making an outline will enable you to list subgroups within each category and to keep track of similar characteristics.

How to Develop an Outline

To be effective, an outline must show (1) the <u>relative</u> importance of ideas and (2) the relationship between ideas. The easiest way to achieve these goals is to use the following format.

> I.   First major topic
>   A. First major idea
>   1. First important detail
>   2. Second important detail
>   B. Second major idea
>   1. First important detail
>   a. Minor detail or example
>   2. Second important detail
> II. Second major topic
>   A. First major idea

Tip *Relative* means "having a particular quality when compared to something else." (Here, it means deciding which ideas are more important and which are less important.)

Note that the more important ideas are closer to the left margin, while less important details are indented toward the middle of the page. A quick glance at an outline indicates what is most important and how ideas support or explain one another. If you are creating an outline on computer, the Tab key makes indenting easy and consistent.

DEVELOPING AN OUTLINE

Here are a few suggestions for developing an effective outline.

1. **Don't get caught up in the numbering and lettering system.** Instead, concentrate on showing the relative importance of ideas. How you number or letter an idea is not as important as showing the other ideas that it supports or explains. Don't be concerned if some items don't fit exactly into outline format.

(Continued)

2. **Be brief. Use words and phrases, never complete sentences.** Abbreviate where possible.
3. **Use your own words rather than lifting most of the material from the text.** You can use the author's key words and the specialized terminology of the discipline.
4. **Be sure that all information underneath a heading supports or explains it.**
5. **All headings that are aligned vertically should be of equal importance.**

Now study the sample outline in Figure 4-3, which is based on the section titled "Minorities" in Part Seven on pages 430–431.

How Much Information to Include

Before you begin to outline, decide how much information to include. An outline can be very brief and cover only major topics. At the other extreme, it can be very detailed, providing an extensive review of information. To determine the right amount of detail, determine your purpose for writing the outline. Ask yourself: What do I need to know? What type of test situation, if any, am I preparing for?

Exercise 11

DIRECTIONS Read each of the following passages and complete the outline that follows it.

1. **FIBROMYALGIA**

   Although there are many diseases today that seem to defy our best medical tests and treatments, one that is particularly frustrating is fibromyalgia, a chronic, painful,

FIGURE 4-3
A Sample Outline

I. Minorities
   A. Minority—cat. of people set apart by society based on phys. or cultural differences
      1. Can be based on race, ethnicity, or both
      2 2011: majority of births in US were racial/ethnic minorities
      3. By 2043, minorities will be the majority in the US
   B. Characteristics of minorities
      1. Distinctive identity
         a. May be based on phys. or cultural traits
      2. Subordination
         a. lower levels of income, occ prestige, school—stratification
   C. Exceptions
      1. Not all minorities are disadvantaged
      2. Race/ethnicity often serves as master status (person's key status)
   D. Numbers
      1. Usually a small portion of a population
      2. Exceptions
         a. Black people in South Africa
         b. Women in the US

rheumatoid-like disorder that affects as many as 5 to 6 percent of the general population. Persons with fibromyalgia experience an array of symptoms including headaches, dizziness, numbness and tingling, itching, fluid retention, chronic joint pain, abdominal or pelvic pain, and even occasional diarrhea. Suspected causes have ranged from sleep disturbances, stress, emotional distress, and viruses, to autoimmune disorders; however, none have been proven in clinical trials. Because of fibromyalgia's multiple symptoms, it is usually diagnosed only after myriad tests have ruled out other disorders. The American College of Rheumatology identifies the major diagnostic criteria as:

- History of widespread pain of at least 3 months' duration in the axial skeleton as well as in all four quadrants of the body.
- Pain in at least 11 of 18 paired tender points on digital palpitation of about 4 kilograms of pressure.

—adapted from Donatelle, *Health: The Basics*, p. 346

Tip *Autoimmune disorders are conditions in which substances that normally prevent illness in the body instead attack and harm parts of it.*

Tip *Myriad means "a great many."*

I. Fibromyalgia—chronic rheumatoid-like disorder

   A. Affects _____ % of population

   B. Symptoms

      1. headaches, _____, numbness, tingling, itching, _____, joint pain, abdominal or _____ pain, diarrhea

   C. Suspected _____

      1. Sleep disturbances, _____, _____, viruses, autoimmune disorders

   D. Major diagnostic criteria

      1. _____

         _____

      2. _____

         _____

2. GATHERING DATA IN FOREIGN COUNTRIES

Conducting market research around the world is big business for U.S. firms. Among the top 50 U.S. research firms, over 40 percent of revenues come from projects outside the United States. However, market conditions and consumer preferences vary widely in different parts of the world, and there are big differences in the sophistication of market research operations and the amount of data available to global marketers.

For these reasons, choosing an appropriate data collection method is difficult. In some countries many people may not have phones, or low literacy rates may interfere with mail surveys. Local customs can be a problem as well. Offering money for interviews is rude in Latin American countries. Saudi Arabia bans gatherings of four or more people except for family or religious events, and it's illegal to stop strangers on the street or knock on the door of someone's house! Cultural differences also affect responses to survey items. Both Danish and British consumers, for example, agree that it is important to eat breakfast, but the Danish sample may be thinking of fruit and yogurt whereas the British sample is thinking of toast and tea. Sometimes these problems can be overcome by involving local researchers in decisions about the research design, but even so care must be taken to ensure that they fully understand the study's objectives and can relate what they find to the culture of the sponsoring company.

Another problem with conducting marketing research in global markets is language. It is not uncommon for researchers to mistranslate questionnaires, or for entire subcultures within a country to be excluded from research. For example, there are still large areas in Mexico where native Indian tribes speak languages other than Spanish, so researchers may bypass these groups in surveys. To overcome these difficulties, researchers use a process called *back-translation*, which requires two steps. First, a questionnaire is translated into the second language by a native speaker of that language. Second, this new version is translated back into the original language to ensure that the correct meanings survive the process. Even with precautions such as these, however, researchers must interpret data obtained from other cultures with care.

—Solomon, *Marketing*, p. 135

I.   Market research in foreign countries
  A.   Big business for U.S. firms
    1.   _____ of U.S. research firms' revenue comes from foreign projects
    2.   _____ and consumer preferences vary widely
    3.   differences in sophistication and _____
  B.   Choice of data collection methods
    1.   no _____
    2.   _____
    3.   _____ customs
    4.   cultural differences affect _____
    5.   problems may be overcome by using _____
  C.   Language problems
    1.   _____
    2.   _____
    3.   overcome problems using back-translation
      a.   _____
      b.   _____ •

Exercise 12

DIRECTIONS   Turn to the section titled "Prejudice and Stereotypes" in Part Seven on pages 432–436. Write a brief outline of the section. •

Exercise 13

DIRECTIONS   Choose a section from one of your textbooks and write a brief outline that reflects the organization and content of that section. •

Goal 5

Summarize to condense information.

SUMMARIZING: CONDENSING IDEAS

A **summary** is a brief statement or list of ideas that identifies the major concepts in a reading selection. Its main purpose is to record the most important ideas in an abbreviated and condensed prose form, with complete sentences in a complete paragraph. A summary is briefer and less detailed than an outline. It goes one step beyond an outline by pulling together the writer's thoughts and considering what they mean as a whole. Summarizing encourages you to consider such questions as "What is the writer's main point?" and "How does the writer prove or explain his or her ideas?" It is also a valuable study technique that will clarify the material.

WHEN TO USE SUMMARIES

Summaries are particularly useful when factual, detailed recall is not needed.

- **Use summaries to prepare for essay exams.** Because essay-exam questions often require you to summarize information you have learned on a particular topic, writing summaries is a good way to practice taking the exam.

- **Use summaries when you read literature.** Writing a plot summary (describing who did what, when, and where) for fiction and a content summary for nonfiction will help you master the literal content.

- **A brief summary is a useful study aid for collateral reading assignments.** In many college courses, instructors give additional reading assignments to supplement information in the text, to present a different or opposing viewpoint, to illustrate a concept, or to show practical applications.

- **Summarize laboratory reports or demonstrations.** Laboratory reports often include a summary. Writing and reviewing your summaries is an efficient way of recalling the purposes, procedures, and outcomes of lab and classroom experiments.

How to Summarize

A good summary records ideas, not just facts. The box on page 106 titled "How to Summarize" lists tips for writing summaries. Before reading them, read the selection titled "Causes of Ulcers" and the sample summary shown in Figure 4-4.

CAUSES OF ULCERS

For decades, physicians believed that experiencing high levels of stress, drinking alcohol, and eating spicy foods were the primary factors responsible for ulcers. But in 1982, Australian gastroenterologists Robin Warren and Barry Marshall detected the same species of bacteria in the majority of their patients' stomachs. Treatment with an antibiotic effective against the bacterium, *Helicobacter pylori (H. pylori)*, cured the ulcers. It is now known that *H. pylori* plays a key role in development of most peptic ulcers. The hydrochloric acid in gastric juice kills most bacteria, but *H. pylori* is unusual in that it thrives in acidic environments. Approximately 40% of people have this bacterium in their stomach, but most people do not develop ulcers. The reason for this is unknown.

Prevention of infection with *H. pylori*, as with any infectious microorganism, includes regular hand-washing and safe food-handling practices. Because of the role of *H. pylori* in ulcer development, treatment usually involves antibiotics and acid-suppressing medications. Special diets and stress-reduction techniques are no longer typically recommended because they do not reduce acid secretion. However, people with ulcers should avoid specific foods that cause them discomfort.

Although most peptic ulcers are caused by *H. pylori* infection, some are caused by prolonged use of nonsteroidal anti-inflammatory drugs (NSAIDs); these drugs include pain relievers such as aspirin, ibuprofen, and naproxen sodium. They appear to cause ulcers by suppressing the secretion of mucus and bicarbonate, which normally protect the stomach from its acidic gastric juice. Ulcers caused by NSAID use generally heal once a person stops taking the medication.

—Thompson and Manore, *Nutrition for Life*, p. 59

FIGURE 4-4
A Sample Summary

Stress, alcohol, and spicy foods used to be blamed for causing ulcers, but in 1982, gastroenterologists identified the bacterium <u>Helicobacter pylori (H. pylori)</u> as key to most peptic ulcers. <u>H. pylori</u> thrives in acidic environments. About 40% of people have <u>H. pylori</u> in their stomach, but for unknown reasons most people do not get ulcers. Infection with <u>H. pylori</u> can be prevented by regular hand-washing and safe food handling. Infections are treated with antibiotics and acid-suppressing medications. People with ulcers should avoid foods that cause discomfort. Peptic ulcers may also be caused by prolonged use of nonsteroidal anti-inflammatory drugs (NSAIDs), such as aspirin, ibuprofen, and naproxen sodium, which suppress the secretion of protective mucus and bicarbonate in the stomach. These ulcers usually heal once a person stops taking the NSAID.

HOW TO SUMMARIZE

1. **Define your purpose.** Before writing a summary, take a moment to consider your purpose for writing it. Your purpose will help you determine how much and what kind of information you want to include in your summary. Gear your summary toward what you are trying to learn from the selection. In the sample summary in Figure 4-4, the student's purpose is to understand the causes of ulcers.

2. **Identify the main point.** When you begin to write a summary, first identify the author's main idea. Once you find it, write a statement that expresses it. This statement will help you to focus your summary. In the summary in Figure 4-4, the main point is that spicy foods used to be thought to cause ulcers, but now a strain of bacteria has been identified as the cause.

3. **Include key supporting information.** After you have located the main point, look for the most important information used to support the main idea. Include only key reasons, facts, or events. In Figure 4-4, why the bacteria thrive in the stomach and how infections can be prevented are included.

4. **Identify key definitions.** Include definitions of key terms, new principles, theories, or procedures. As you write the summary, underline or highlight essential words or phrases as you define them so that you will be able to locate them easily when reviewing.

5. **Evaluate the importance of details and examples.** You will probably want to include some details in your summary; however, the amount of detail needed will vary depending on the type and amount of recall you need. It can be useful to include examples when you have difficulty understanding a concept.

6. **Consider the author's attitude and approach.** It may be appropriate to include the author's attitude and approach toward the subject, depending on the type of material you are summarizing. Additionally, you may want to include the author's purpose for writing.

7. **Keep your summary objective and factual.** Think of it as a brief report that reflects the writers' ideas and does not include your own evaluation of them. You are not writing an analysis of the passage; you're simply trying to boil down the basic facts and information presented in the passage.

DIRECTIONS   After reading each selection, circle the letter of the choice that best summarizes it.

Exercise 14

1. **LEARNING INFLUENCES OUR FOOD CHOICES**

   Pigs' feet, anyone? What about blood sausage, stewed octopus, or tripe? These are delicacies in various European cultures, whereas the meat of horses, dogs, monkeys, and snakes are enjoyed in different regions of Asia. Would you eat grasshoppers? If you'd grown up in certain parts of Africa or Central America, you probably would. That's because our preference for particular foods is largely a *learned* response: The cultures in which we are raised teach us what plant and animal products are appropriate to eat. If your parents fed you cubes of plain tofu throughout your toddlerhood, then you are probably still eating tofu now.

   That said, early introduction to foods is not essential. We can learn to enjoy new foods at any point in our lives. Immigrants from developing nations settling in the United States or Canada often adopt a typical Western diet, especially when their traditional foods are not readily available. This happens temporarily when we travel. The last time you were away from home, you probably enjoyed sampling a variety of dishes that were not normally part of your diet.

   We can also "learn" to dislike foods we once enjoyed. For example, if we experience an episode of food poisoning after eating undercooked scrambled eggs, we may develop a strong distaste for all types of cooked eggs. Many adults who become vegetarians do so after learning about the treatment of animals in slaughterhouses. They may have eaten meat daily when they were young but could not imagine ever eating it again.

   —Thompson and Manore, *Nutrition for Life*, pp. 42–43

   a. We make our food choices depending on what we grew up eating and on our experiences as an adult. We learn from our culture what foods are good to eat. We can also learn to enjoy different foods, whether we are new to a country or simply traveling there.

   b. Our preference for certain foods is mostly learned from the cultures in which we are raised. However, we can learn to like or dislike new foods at any time in our lives as a result of exposure to new foods or information or experiences.

   c. People have different food preferences because their cultures teach them what is appropriate to eat. Pigs' feet, blood sausage, stewed octopus, and tripe are delicacies in some European cultures. People in different areas of Asia eat the meat of horses, dogs, monkeys, and snakes, and grasshoppers are food in certain parts of Africa and Central America. Similarly, if you grew up eating tofu, you probably still eat it.

   d. We learn to prefer certain foods because of how we were raised. We learn to dislike other foods because we have bad experiences, such as food poisoning, or because we learn new information, such as finding out about the treatment of animals at slaughterhouses.

2. **DESIGNING YOUR FITNESS PROGRAM**

   Once you commit yourself to becoming physically active, you must decide what type of fitness program is best suited to your needs. Good fitness programs are designed to improve or maintain cardiorespiratory fitness, flexibility, muscular strength and endurance, and body composition. A comprehensive program could include a warm-up period of easy walking followed by stretching activities to improve flexibility, then selected strength development exercises, followed by performance of an aerobic activity for 20 minutes or more, and concluding with a cool-down period of gentle flexibility exercises.

The greatest proportion of your exercise time should be spent developing cardiovascular fitness, but you should not exclude the other components. Choose an aerobic activity you think you will like. Many people find cross training—alternate-day participation in two or more aerobic activities (i.e., jogging and swimming)—less monotonous and more enjoyable than long-term participation in only one aerobic activity. Cross training is also beneficial because it strengthens a variety of muscles, thus helping you avoid overuse injuries to muscles and joints.

—Donatelle, *Health: The Basics*, p. 282

a. A good fitness program includes a warm-up period of easy walking, stretching, strength development exercises, a 20-minute aerobic activity, and a cool-down period of flexibility exercises.

b. Good fitness programs improve or maintain cardiorespiratory fitness, flexibility, muscular strength and endurance, and body composition. A program's focus should be on cardiovascular fitness but should include other components. Cross training, alternate-day participation in two or more aerobic activities, strengthens a variety of muscles.

c. It is important to choose a fitness program that is best suited to your needs. You should choose an aerobic activity you like. Cross training reduces boredom and is more enjoyable than just one aerobic activity. It helps avoid overuse injuries to muscles and joints as well.

Visual Thinking
ANALYZING IMAGES

How does this graphic enhance the passage "Designing Your Fitness Program"?

FIGURE A
Calories Burned by Different Activities

The harder you exercise, the more energy you expend. Estimated calories burned for various moderate and vigorous activities are listed for a 30-minute bout of activity.

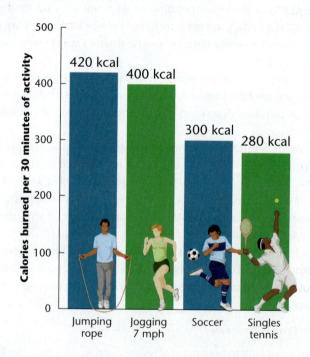

Calories burned per 30 minutes of activity

- Jumping rope: 420 kcal
- Jogging 7 mph: 400 kcal
- Soccer: 300 kcal
- Singles tennis: 280 kcal

d. Cardiovascular fitness is the most important component of a fitness program. A cool-down period is recommended. Jogging and swimming are two aerobic activities that can be done together in cross training. A comprehensive fitness program will include the different components of body composition. ●

Exercise 15

DIRECTIONS Read each of the following selections and then complete the summaries that follow them by filling in the blanks.

1. **TSUNAMI OR SEISMIC SEA WAVE**

An occasional wave that momentarily but powerfully influences coastlines is the tsunami. Tsunami is Japanese for "harbor wave," named for its devastating effect where its energy is focused in harbors. Tsunami often are reported incorrectly as "tidal waves," but they have no relation to the tides. They are formed by sudden, sharp motions in the sea floor, caused by earthquakes, submarine landslides, or eruptions of undersea volcanoes. Thus, they properly are called *seismic sea waves*.

—Christopherson, *Geosystems*, p. 470

Summary: A _____ (also called a tsunami) is a wave that

powerfully influences coastlines and is formed by _____

_____ caused by _____

_____ . It has devastating effects on _____ .

2. **TYPES OF EVIDENCE PRESENTED IN COURT**

The outcome of a trial usually hinges on the presentation of evidence. Attorneys for the prosecution and defense have two major types of evidence they can offer in support of their case: demonstrative evidence and testimonial evidence. Demonstrative evidence consists of physical objects—for example, the bloody glove presented in the O.J. Simpson trial, a weapon, fingerprints, blood samples, DNA, stolen property, tire or shoe prints, business records, computer files, and written or videotaped confessions. Testimonial evidence consists of oral evidence given under oath either in the courtroom or in depositions taken before attorneys for both sides and recorded by a court reporter.

—Barlow, *Criminal Justice in America*, p. 439

Summary: Two types of _____ can be presented in court. _____

_____ is physical objects. Testimonial evidence is _____

_____ or _____ .

3. **STORE IMAGE**

When people think of a store, they often have no trouble portraying it in the same terms they might use in describing a person. They might use words like *exciting, depressed, old-fashioned, tacky,* or *elegant.* Store image is how the target market perceives the store—its market position relative to the competition. For example, Bloomingdale's department store is seen by many as chic and fashionable, especially compared to a more traditional competitor such as Macy's. These images don't just happen. Just as brand managers do for products, store managers work hard to create a "personality."

—Solomon and Stuart, *Marketing*, p. 418

Summary: _____ is how the target market perceives _____ and is its

market position relative to _____. Store managers must work hard to

create _____.

4. **HAY FEVER**

Perhaps the best example of a chronic respiratory disease is hay fever. Usually considered to be a seasonally related disease (most prevalent when ragweed and flowers are blooming), hay fever is common throughout the world. Hay fever attacks, which are characterized by sneezing and itchy, watery eyes and nose, cause a great deal of misery for countless people. Hay fever appears to run in families, and research indicates that lifestyle is not as great a factor in developing hay fever as it is in other chronic diseases. Instead, an overzealous immune system and an exposure to environmental allergens including pet dander, dust, pollen from various plants, and other substances appear to be the critical factors that determine vulnerability. For those people who are unable to get away from the cause of their hay fever response, medical assistance in the form of injections or antihistamines may provide the only possibility of relief.

—Donatelle, *Health: The Basics*, p. 338

Summary: Hay fever is a _____ that is seasonally related

and common _____. It is characterized by _____

_____. It runs in families and is not affected by _____.

Overzealous immune systems and _____ determine

vulnerability. It can be treated with _____.

5. **AGING AND CULTURE**

Culture shapes how we understand growing old. In low-income countries, old age gives people great influence and respect because they control most land and have wisdom gained over a lifetime. A preindustrial society, then, is usually a gerontocracy, a form of social organization in which the elderly have the most wealth, power, and privileges.

But industrialization lessens the social standing of the elderly. Older people typically live apart from their grown children, and rapid social change renders much of what seniors know obsolete, at least from the point of view of the young. A problem of industrial societies, then, is ageism, prejudice and discrimination against the elderly.

—Macionis, *Society: The Basics*, p. 77

Summary: _____ affects how we regard aging. _____ societies

are usually gerontocracies, where the elderly have the most _____

_____. In _____ societies, the elderly live apart from their families and

have obsolete knowledge. _____, which means prejudice and _____

against older people, becomes a problem. ●

DIRECTIONS Read the following selection and then complete the summary by filling in the blanks.

CUTTING THROUGH THE PAIN

When some people are unable to deal with the pain, pressure, and stress they experience in everyday life, they may resort to self-injury in order to cope. Self-injury, also termed self-mutilation, self-harm, or nonsuicidal self-injury (NSSI), is the act of deliberately harming one's body in an attempt to cope with overwhelming negative emotions. Self-injury is a coping mechanism; it is not an attempt at suicide. The most common method of self-harm is cutting (with razors, glass, knives, or other sharp objects). Other methods include burning, bruising, excessive nail biting, breaking bones, pulling out hair, and embedding sharp objects under the skin. Seventy-five percent of those who harm themselves do so in more than one way.

Researchers estimate that between 2 and 8 million Americans have engaged in self-harm at some point in their lives and the prevalence of NSSI in college students is reported between 17 and 38 percent. Many people who inflict self-harm suffer from larger mental health conditions and have experienced sexual, physical, or emotional abuse as children or adults. Self-harm is also commonly associated with mental illnesses such as borderline personality disorder, depression, anxiety disorders, substance abuse disorders, post-traumatic stress disorder, and eating disorders.

—Donatelle, *Health: The Basics*, p. 41

Summary: Self-harm or _____ (NSSI) is a _____ to pain, pressure and stress as a way to manage _____. It is not a _____. _____ is the most common method. Other examples are burning, bruising, nail biting, breaking bones, and so on. 75% of those who use NSSI do so _____. Between 2 and 8 million Americans have _____ ____. _____ of college students engage in it. Many people who engage have other _____ or have experienced abuse. ●

DIRECTIONS Write a summary of the feature titled "Hard Work: The Immigrant Life in the United States," which begins on page 432 in Part Seven. ●

DIRECTIONS Refer to the section from one of your textbooks that you used to complete Exercise 13 on page 104. Write a summary of the information presented in this section. ●

MAPPING: A VISUAL MEANS OF ORGANIZING IDEAS

Goal 6

Map to visualize ideas.

Mapping is a visual method of organizing information. It involves drawing diagrams to show how ideas or concepts are related. Many students draw maps by hand, but some prefer to draw them electronically. Most word processing programs include tools that can help you visually organize your ideas. Look for "Diagram," "AutoShapes," and "Organization Charts" on the drop-down "Insert" menu of your word processing program.

HOW TO DRAW MAPS

Use the following steps to draw a map.

1. Identify the overall topic or subject. Write it in the center or at the top of the page.
2. Identify the major supporting information that is related to the topic. Write each fact or idea and connect it with a line to the central topic.
3. When you discover a detail that further explains an idea already mapped, draw a new line branching from the idea it explains.

Maps can take numerous forms. You can draw them in any way that shows the relationships among ideas. Figure 4-5 shows the types of information to include in a map, depending on the desired level of detail. Figure 4-6 shows two sample maps. Each was drawn to show the organization of Chapter 9 of this text. Refer to pages 233–257; then study each map.

WHEN TO USE MAPS

Maps are particularly well suited to the following situations.

- **Use maps if you are a visual learner.** You will be able to close your eyes and visualize the map.
- **Use maps for complicated processes and procedures that contain numerous steps.**
- **Use maps for material that is difficult to organize.** Constructing the map will help you see connections between ideas.
- **Use maps for physical objects.** Drawing a diagram of a piece of equipment or of the human skeletal system is an effective study method.

FIGURE 4-5
A Model Map

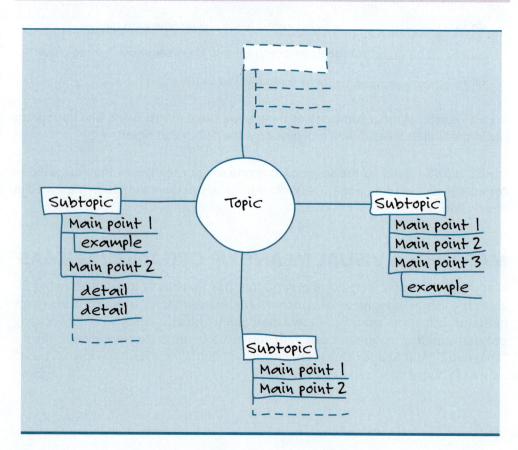

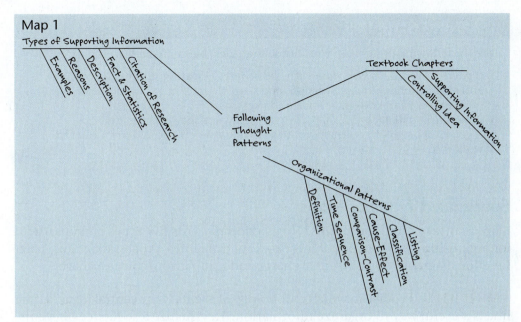

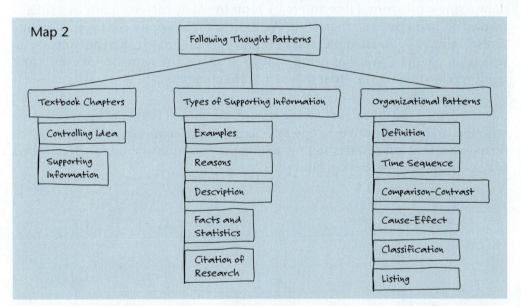

FIGURE 4-6
Two Maps for the Same Information, Organized in Different Styles

DIRECTIONS   Draw a map showing the organization of any section of Chapter 1 in this text. ●

Exercise 19

DIRECTIONS   Turn to the section titled "The Social Meaning of Race and Ethnicity" on pages 427–431 in Part Seven. Draw a map showing how the textbook section is organized. ●

Exercise 20

DIRECTIONS   Choose a section from one of your textbooks. Draw a map that reflects its organization. ●

Exercise 21

Specialized Types of Maps

Maps may take numerous forms. This section presents five types of maps useful for organizing specific types of information: time lines, process diagrams, part/function diagrams, organizational charts, and comparison–contrast charts.

TIME LINES In a course in which chronology of events is the central focus, a time line is a useful way to organize information. To visualize a sequence of events, draw a single horizontal line and mark it off in yearly intervals, just as a ruler is marked off in inches, and then write events next to the appropriate year. The time line in Figure 4-7, for example, was developed for an American history course in which the Vietnam War was being studied. It shows the sequence of events and helps you to visualize the order in which things happened.

Exercise 22

DIRECTIONS   The following passage reviews the ancient history of maps. Read the selection, and then draw a time line that helps you visualize these historical events. (Remember that B.C.E. refers to time before the common era, and such numbers increase as time moves back in history.)

FIGURE 4-7
A Time Line

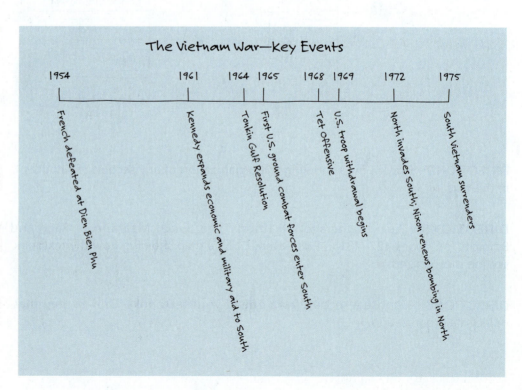

In Babylonia, in approximately 2300 B.C.E., the oldest known map was drawn on a clay tablet. The map showed a man's property located in a valley surrounded by tall mountains. Later, around 1300 B.C.E., the Egyptians drew maps that detailed the location of Ethiopian gold mines and that showed a route from the Nile Valley to the mines. The ancient Greeks were early mapmakers as well, although no maps remain for us to examine. It is estimated that in 300 B.C.E. they drew maps showing the earth to be round. The Romans drew the first road maps, a few of which have been preserved for study today. Claudius Ptolemy, an Egyptian scholar who lived around 150 C.E., drew one of the most famous ancient maps. He drew maps of the world as it was known at that time, including 26 regional maps of Europe, Africa, and Asia. ●

PROCESS DIAGRAMS In the natural sciences, as well as in other courses such as economics and data processing, processes are an important part of course content. A diagram that visually presents the steps, variables, or parts of a process will aid learning. A biology student, for example, might draw Figure 4-8, which describes the food chain and shows how energy is transferred through food consumption. Note that this student included an example, as well as the steps in the process, to make the diagram clearer.

Exercise 23

DIRECTIONS The following paragraph describes the process through which mosquitoes spread malaria. Read the paragraph, and then draw a process diagram that shows how this process occurs.

Malaria, a serious tropical disease, is caused by parasites, or one-celled animals, called protozoa. These parasites live in the red blood cells of humans as well as in female anopheles mosquitoes. These mosquitoes serve as hosts to the parasites and carry and spread malaria. When an anopheles mosquito bites a person who already has malaria, it ingests the red blood cells that contain the malaria parasites. In the host mosquito's body, these parasites multiply rapidly and move to its salivary glands and mouth. When the host mosquito bites another person, the malaria parasites are injected into the victim and enter his or her bloodstream. The parasites again multiply and burst the victim's blood cells, causing anemia. ●

PART/FUNCTION DIAGRAMS In courses that deal with the use and description of physical objects, labeled drawings are an important learning tool. In a human anatomy and physiology course, for example, the easiest way to study the parts and functions of the inner, middle, and outer ear is to use a drawing of the ear. You can study the material and make a sketch of the ear, then test your recall of ear parts and their functions. Refer to Figure 4-9 for a sample part/function diagram.

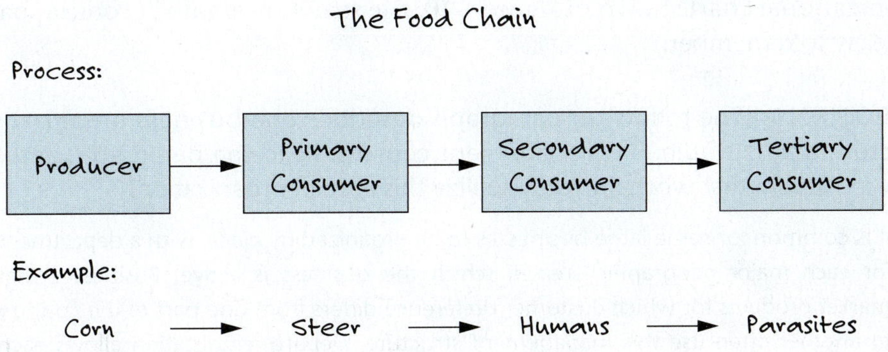

FIGURE 4-8
A Process Diagram

The Food Chain

Process:

Producer → Primary Consumer → Secondary Consumer → Tertiary Consumer

Example:

Corn → Steer → Humans → Parasites

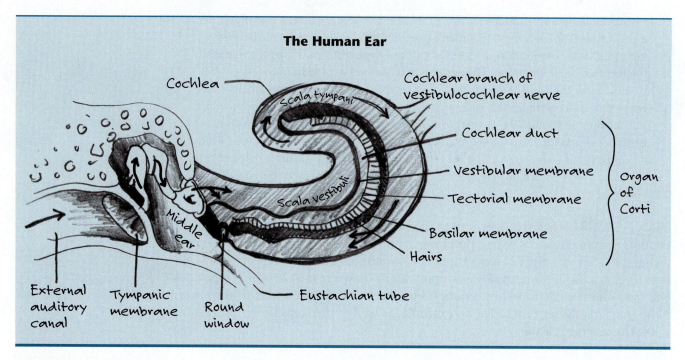

FIGURE 4-9
A Part/Function Diagram

Exercise 24

DIRECTIONS   The following paragraph describes Earth's structure. Read the paragraph and then draw a diagram that will help you visualize how Earth's interior is structured.

> At the center is a hot, highly compressed inner core, presumably solid and composed mainly of iron and nickel. Surrounding the inner core is an outer core, a molten shell primarily of liquid iron and nickel with lighter liquid material on the top. The outer envelope beyond the core is the mantle, of which the upper portion is mostly solid rock in the form of olivine, an iron–magnesium silicate, and the lower portion chiefly iron and magnesium oxides. A thin coat of metal silicates and oxides (granite), called the crust, forms the outermost skin.
>
> —Berman and Evans, *Exploring the Cosmos*, p. 145 ●

ORGANIZATIONAL CHARTS When you are reviewing material that discusses relationships and structures, organizational charts are useful study aids. Suppose that in a business management course, you are studying the organization of a small temporary clerical employment agency. If you drew and studied the organizational chart shown in Figure 4-10, the structure would become apparent and easy to remember.

Exercise 25

DIRECTIONS   The following paragraph describes one business organizational structure that is studied in management courses. Read the paragraph, and then draw a diagram that will help you visualize this type of organization.

> It is common for some large businesses to be organized by *place*, with a department for each major geographic area in which the business is active. Businesses that market products for which customer preference differs from one part of the country to another often use this management structure. Departmentalization allows each

region to focus on its own special needs and problems. Often the president of such a company appoints several regional vice presidents, one for each part of the country. Then each regional office is divided into sales districts, each supervised by a district director. ●

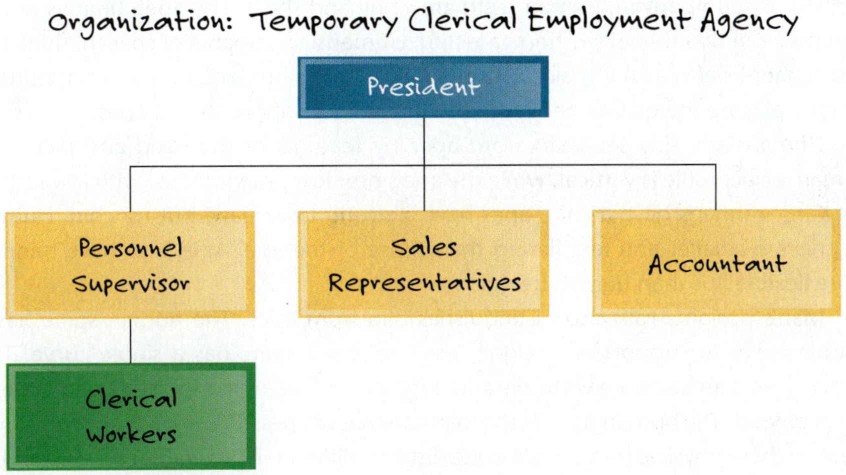

Organization: Temporary Clerical Employment Agency

FIGURE 4-10
An Organizational
Chart

COMPARISON–CONTRAST CHARTS Based on the categorization principle of learning, a comparison–contrast chart divides and groups information according to similarities, common characteristics, and/or differences. Suppose that in a marketing and advertising course, you are studying three types of market survey techniques: mail, telephone, and personal interviews. You are concerned with factors such as cost, level of response, time, and accuracy. In your text, this information is discussed in paragraph form. To learn and review this information in an efficient manner, you could draw a chart like the one shown in Figure 4-11.

FIGURE 4-11
A Comparison–
Contrast Chart

MARKET SURVEY TECHNIQUES

Type	Cost	Response	Accuracy
Mail	usually the cheapest	higher than phone or personal interview	problems with misunderstanding directions
Phone	depends on phone service	same as personal interview	problems with unlisted phones and homes w/ out phones
Personal interview	most expensive	same as phone	problems with interview honesty when asking personal or embarrassing questions

DIRECTIONS The following passage describes the major physical differences between humans and apes. Read the selection, and then arrange the information into a comparison–contrast chart that would make the information easy to learn.

Exercise 26

Numerous physical characteristics distinguish humans from apes. While apes' bodies are covered with hair, the human body has relatively little hair. While apes often use both their hands and feet to walk, humans walk erect. Apes' arms are longer than their legs, while just the reverse is true for humans. Apes have large teeth, necessary for devouring coarse, uncooked food, and long canine teeth for self-defense and fighting. By comparison, human teeth are small and short. The ape's brain is not as well developed as that of the human being. Humans are capable of speech, thinking, and higher-level reasoning skills. These skills enable humans to establish culture, thereby placing the quality and level of human life far above that of apes.

Humans are also set apart from apes by features of the head and face. The human facial profile is vertical, while the ape's profile is *prognathous*, with jaw jutting outward. Humans have a chin; apes have a strong lower jaw, but no chin. Human nostrils are smaller and less flaring than those of the ape. Apes also have thinner, more flexible lips than human beings.

Man's upright walk also distinguishes him from apes. The human spine has a double curve to support his weight, while an ape's spine has a single curve. The human foot is arched both vertically and horizontally but, unlike the ape's, is unable to grasp objects. The human torso is shorter than that of apes. It is important to note that many of these physical traits, while quite distinct, differ in degree rather than in kind. ●

Goal 7

Avoid plagiarism.

AVOIDING PLAGIARISM

As you write paraphrases, summaries, and outlines of material you read, it is important that you be careful to avoid plagiarism.

Plagiarism means borrowing someone else's ideas or exact wording without giving that person credit. If you take information on Frank Lloyd Wright's architecture from a reference source, but do not indicate where you found it, you have plagiarized. If you take the six-word phrase "Martinez, the vengeful, despicable drug czar" from an online news article without putting quotation marks around it and noting the source, you have plagiarized. Plagiarism is intellectually dishonest because you are taking someone else's ideas or words and passing them off as your own.

You need to identify your sources for two reasons: (1) to help readers find a source if they want to look into that author's ideas further and (2) to give credit to the person who originally wrote the material or thought of the idea.

The Internet, while a remarkable source of information, has unfortunately contributed to an increase in plagiarism—both accidental and deliberate. The Internet makes it easy to copy something and paste it into your own paper without giving credit to the original source. Numerous Web sites offer student papers for sale; using these papers and submitting them as your own is also considered plagiarism.

WHAT CONSTITUTES PLAGIARISM

- Plagiarism is the use of another person's words without giving credit to that person.
- Plagiarism uses another person's theory, opinion, or idea without listing where the information was taken from.
- Plagiarism results when another person's exact words are not placed inside quotation marks. Both the quotation marks and a citation (reference) to the original source are needed.
- Paraphrasing (rewording) another person's words without giving credit to him or her is plagiarism.

(Continued)

- Using facts, data, graphs, charts, and so on without stating where they were taken from is plagiarism.
- Using commonly known facts or information is not plagiarism and you need not give a source for your information. For example, the fact that Neil Armstrong set foot on the moon in 1969 is widely known and so does not require documentation.

There are academic penalties for plagiarism. You may receive a failing grade on your paper or you may fail the entire course. At some institutions you can even be academically dismissed.

AVOIDING PLAGIARISM

Use the following suggestions to avoid unintentional plagiarism.

- If you copy exact words from any source, put them in quotation marks in your notes, along with the publication information: the author, title, publisher, date of publication, and page number of the source, or, for Web sites, the author, name of the site or page, date of publication, URL, and date of access. Be sure to consult a style manual for details on how to indicate in your paper which material is borrowed and how to set up a list of the works you used in your paper.
- List sources for all the information you include in your notes regardless of whether it takes the form of direct quotations, paraphrases, or summaries of someone else's ideas.
- Never copy and paste directly from a Web site into your paper without enclosing the words in quotation marks and listing the source.
- List the source for any information, facts, ideas, opinions, theories, or data you use from a Web site.
- When paraphrasing someone else's words, change as many words as possible and try not to follow the exact same organization. Credit where the information came from.
- Write paraphrases without looking at the original text so you will rephrase it in your own words.

DIRECTIONS   Read the following passage from *Sociology for the Twenty-First Century* by Tim Curry, Robert Jiobu, and Kent Schwirian, p. 207. Then place a check mark next to each statement that is an example of plagiarism.

Exercise 27

Currently, Mexican Americans are the second-largest racial or ethnic minority in the United States, but by early in the next century they will be the largest group. Their numbers will swell as a result of continual immigration from Mexico and the relatively high Mexican birth rate. Mexican Americans are one of the oldest racial-ethnic groups in the United States. Under the terms of the treaty ending the Mexican-American War in 1848, Mexicans living in territories acquired by the United States could remain there and were to be treated as American citizens. Those that did stay became known as "Californios," "Tejanos," or "Hispanos."

_____ a. Mexican Americans are the second-largest minority in the United States. Their number grows as more people emigrate from Mexico.

_____ b. After the Mexican-American War, those Mexicans living in territories owned by the United States became American citizens and were called "Californios," "Tejanos," and "Hispanos" (Curry, Jiobu, and Schwirian, 207).

_____ c. "Mexican Americans are one of the oldest racial-ethnic groups in the United States."

_____ d. The Mexican-American War ended in 1848.

USING COLLEGE TEXTBOOKS
Knowing What Is Important and Identifying Supporting Details

Textbook authors often help you identify main ideas and their major supporting details, and thereby signal what you should highlight and mark, by using in-chapter focus questions, end-of-chapter review questions, and end-of-chapter summaries. Here are some ways to use each.

1. **In-chapter Focus, Key, or End-of-Section Questions.** Focus or key questions appear at the beginning of the chapter or before or after each major section of a chapter. At the beginning of a chapter, they may appear along with a set of learning objectives. Their purpose is to focus your attention on what is important and provide a way for you to test your recall. They may be labeled in a variety of ways: "Learning Checks," "Spotlight on Key Ideas," and so forth. Here are two ways to use them.

   - **Read focus or key questions before you read the chapter.** It is also helpful to read the questions that correspond to a section before you read the section. The questions often serve as a list of what you are supposed to know when you finish reading.

   - **Answer end-of-section questions as you come to them.** Some students answer them mentally; others annotate the chapter; others answer them in their notes. It is usually better to write the answers than to just mentally think them through. By writing the answers, you will remember more, and you will also have a written record to use for later review.

   Here are a few samples from various textbooks.

▼ Chapter **Focus**

Personal Selling, pp. 181–182 ⟵ **Objective 1.** What are the advantages and disadvantages of personal selling?

Personal Selling Process, pp. 182–184 ⟵ **Objective 2.** What is the standard selling process used by virtually every company?

—Levens, *Marketing*, p. 180

Textbook Exercise 1: Using Focus Questions

Suppose you get a job selling new cars. You want to know the step-by-step process involved in meeting customers and selling them a car. Which pages of Levens's *Marketing* textbook should you consult?

SECTION 13.4 Review Questions

1. Describe the three layers of tissue that make up the heart.
2. What is an aneurysm?
3. What are actions that people can take to prevent myocardial infarction?

—Thomson and Manore, *Nutrition*, p. 39

Textbook Exercise 2: Understanding Review Questions

For each of the questions above, identify whether it asks you (a) for the definition of a vocabulary word, (b) to apply your knowledge to a real-world situation, or (c) to label and describe components.

TEST YOURSELF

Are these statements true or false? Circle your guess.

1. Your stomach is the primary organ responsible for telling you when you are hungry. **TRUE or FALSE**
2. The entire process of digestion and absorption of one meal takes about 24 hours. **TRUE or FALSE**
3. Some types of bacteria actually help keep our digestive system healthy. **TRUE or FALSE**
4. Most ulcers result from a type of infection. **TRUE or FALSE**
5. Irritable bowel syndrome is a rare disease that mostly affects older people. **TRUE or FALSE**

—Badasch and Chesebro, *Health Science Fundamentals*, p. 356

Textbook Exercise 3: Using Test Questions

Which level of thinking do the above statements require: remembering, analyzing, or evaluating?

2. **End-of-Chapter Review Questions.** Some textbooks present end-of-chapter review questions in the form of simple questions; others use a multiple-choice or true/false format. Regardless of format, these questions are designed to help you understand what is important to learn in the chapter and to test your recall. Here are some tips for how to use them.

- **Preview the end-of-chapter review questions before you start the chapter.** The questions will point to the most important information in the chapter. Open-ended questions are often better guides than multiple-choice or true/false questions.
- **Answer all the questions when you finish the chapter.** Doing so will help you self-test your understanding of the chapter and point to your areas of strength and weakness. Also check the Web-based materials that accompany the textbook; they often include additional questions and quizzes to help you learn.

- **Use both the questions and your written answers when reviewing for exams.** Read the questions, cover your answers, and test yourself to see if you can recall the answers.

Here are a few samples of review questions from textbooks:

Questions for Review

1. How have textile imports taken such a big market share in the United States?
2. What has been the textile industry's response to imports?
3. How does modern marketing differ from textile marketing in the past, when only natural fabrics were available?

—Frings, *Fashion*, p. 158

Textbook Exercise 4: Understand Key Vocabulary

Answering the above questions correctly requires you to understand key vocabulary terms. What exactly are textiles? What are imports?

Learning the Basics

1. Define the term *metabolism*.
2. List three common cellular substances that can pass through cell membranes unaided.
3. Macronutrients _____.

A. include carbohydrates and vitamins; **B.** should comprise a small percentage of a healthful diet; **C.** are essential in minute amounts to help enzymes function; **D.** include carbohydrates, fats, and proteins; **E.** are synthesized by cells and not necessary to obtain from the diet

—Belk and Maier, *Biology*, p. 78

Textbook Exercise 5: Reading the Assignment

Suppose your instructor gives the above three questions on a "pop quiz" in class. What are your odds of getting a decent grade on the quiz if you haven't read the assignment?

MORE TOPICS FOR WRITING

1. Choose a story from this chapter. Describe your experience of reading that story, and of encountering its symbols. At what point did the main symbol's meaning become clear? What in the story indicated the larger importance of that symbol?
2. From any story in this book, select an object, or place, or action that seems clearly symbolic. How do you know? Now select an object, place, or action from the same story that clearly seems to signify no more than itself. How can you tell?

—Kennedy and Gioia, *Literature*, p. 258

Textbook Exercise 6: Understanding Writing Assignments

In which ways do the two writing assignments on the previous page require you to use all six levels of thinking?

3. **Summaries.** These brief reviews appear at the end of chapter sections or at the end of the entire chapter. They help you review and understand the main points of the chapter. Here are some tips for how to use them.

   - **Compare summaries.** Write your own summary and compare it to the provided summary to determine whether you have understood the reading and taken away the main points.
   - **Use summaries to create outlines.** You can use the main points in a summary to help you create a detailed outline of the chapter.

Here is a sample from a chapter summary. You can find other samples in the "Self-Test Summary" at the end of this chapter (pages 124–125) and in the sample textbook reading on page 438.

CHAPTER SUMMARY

What Is Abnormality?

12.1   Describe how mental illness has been explained in the past and how abnormal behavior and thinking are defined today.

- Psychopathology is the study of abnormal behavior and psychological dysfunction.
- In ancient times holes were cut in an ill person's head to let out evil spirits in a process called trephining. Hippocrates believed that mental illness came from an imbalance in the body's four humors, whereas in the early Renaissance period the mentally ill were labeled as witches.
- Abnormality can be characterized as thinking or behavior that is statistically rare, deviant from social norms, causes subjective discomfort, does not allow day-to-day functioning, or causes a person to be dangerous to self or others.
- In the United States, *insanity* is a legal term, not a psychological term.

—Ciccarelli and Nolan, *Psychology: An Exploration*, p. 484

Textbook Exercise 7: Using a Summary

Underline the three key vocabulary terms that are defined in the above summary.

FURTHER PRACTICE WITH TEXTBOOK READING

Textbook Exercise 8: Sample Textbook Chapter

Read and answer the questions numbered 11.1, 11.2, and 11.3 in the sample textbook chapter in Part Seven (pages 427, 432, and 436).

Textbook Exercise 9: Your College Textbook

Choose a textbook chapter that you have been assigned to read for one of your other courses. When you have completed the chapter, answer the review questions at the end to test your knowledge of the material. Make note of the questions you did not answer correctly and review that material.

SELF-TEST SUMMARY

Goal 1

Why should you use paraphrasing to restate ideas?

Paraphrasing, the restatement of a passage's ideas in your own words, is a particularly useful strategy for recording meaning and checking your comprehension of detailed, complex, or precise passages. When you use your own words rather than the author's, you demonstrate your understanding of the original work.

Goal 2

What guidelines should you follow for effective highlighting?

Highlight the right amount. Develop a regular and consistent system of highlighting. Highlight accurately. And make your highlighting understandable for later review. It is also wise to have a system for marking as well as highlighting.

Goal 3

Why should you supplement your textbook highlighting with marking?

Marking (annotating) involves using marginal notes, summary words, and symbols that make a passage easier to review. Marking can help you to organize the information you have highlighted by showing the relative importance of facts and ideas or the relationships between them.

Goal 4

What is an outline and what are its advantages?

Outlining is a way to organize information to indicate the relative importance of ideas and the relationships among them. A good outline helps you sort ideas, test your understanding, and recall the material.

Goal 5

What is a summary and what are its advantages?

Summarizing is the process of recording a passage's most important ideas in a condensed, abbreviated form. A summary not only helps you organize the facts and ideas presented in the text but also helps you think critically.

Goal 6 What is mapping and what are its advantages?	Mapping creates a visual representation of information and shows relationships. Five types of concept maps are time lines, process diagrams, part/function diagrams, organizational charts, and comparison–contrast charts. Mapping enables you to adjust to both the information you are recording and its unique organization. Grouping and consolidating information in different ways makes it easier to learn and remember.
Goal 7 How do you avoid plagiarism?	To avoid plagiarism, be sure to credit every idea you take from someone else's work by providing a citation. List sources for all the information you include in your notes, regardless of whether it takes the form of direct quotations, paraphrases, or summaries. Never copy and paste directly from a source without enclosing the selection in quotation marks.

APPLYING YOUR SKILLS

DISCUSSING THE CHAPTER

1. Highlighting becomes more challenging as the density of the reading selection increases. Discuss the systems you use to highlight and mark texts in various subject areas.
2. In what types of learning situations are summaries most helpful to you? How and when have you used summaries in the past? What makes a summary particularly effective?
3. List some learning situations in which time lines, process diagrams, part/function diagrams, organizational charts, and comparison–contrast charts can be helpful to you and your classmates.

ANALYZING A STUDY SITUATION

Ken's courses this semester include History of the British Empire, Business Management, Biology, and Introduction to Anthropology. The history course requirements include several reading assignments from books placed on reserve in the library and an essay final exam. The anthropology course content includes several textbook chapters and lectures explaining how humans evolved and the relationships of other species to humans; a short-answer and essay final exam will be given. The biology course involves textbook reading, lectures, labs, and multiple-choice exams. The business management course focuses, in part, on the organization and structure of corporations; two multiple-choice and true/false exams will be given.

1. In which course(s) do you think Ken will need to use outlining? Why?
2. In which course(s) do you think Ken will need to use summarizing? Why?
3. Recommend a mapping strategy Ken might use for each course. Explain why each recommended approach is appropriate.

WORKING ON COLLABORATIVE PROJECTS

DIRECTIONS   Your instructor will choose a reading from Part Six and divide the class into three groups. Members of one group should outline the material, another group should draw maps, and the third should write summaries. When the groups have completed their tasks, the class members should review one another's work. Several students should read their summaries aloud, draw their maps, and write their outlines on the chalkboard. Discuss which of the three methods seemed most effective for the material and how well prepared each group feels for (1) an essay exam, (2) a multiple-choice exam, and (3) a class discussion.

Quick Quiz

DIRECTIONS   Write the letter of the choice that best completes each statement in the space provided.

CHECKING YOUR RECALL

_____ 1. Outlining requires you to do all of the following *except*

a. think about the material you read.
b. decide the relative importance of ideas.
c. put ideas into your own words.
d. include your opinion of the information.

_____ 2. The main purpose of a summary is to

a. reflect the organization of ideas.
b. present a brief review of information.
c. raise questions about the material.
d. provide a detailed record of content.

_____ 3. The most useful type of map for organizing information according to similarities of common characteristics is

a. an organizational chart.
b. a process diagram.
c. a comparison–contrast chart.
d. a time line.

_____ 4. The primary purpose of highlighting is to

a. increase your reading rate.
b. make review and study more efficient.
c. learn to highlight the right amount.
d. increase your review time.

_____ 5. One difference between highlighting and marking is that, typically,

a. highlighting shows the relative importance of ideas.
b. highlighting indicates the relationship between facts and ideas.
c. marking requires you to operate at higher levels of thinking.
d. marking can be done without reading the text.

APPLYING YOUR SKILLS

_____ 6. Oliver is trying to decide what he should highlight in his psychology text. In making his decision, he should pay particular attention to

a. paragraph length.
b. page layout.
c. graphics.
d. boldfaced headings.

_____ 7. Four students created outlines from a chapter in their economics text. Which student probably created the most effective outline?

a. Ron included only the information that fit into the outline format he chose.
b. Emily focused on outlining the author's attitudes.
c. Michel ensured that his outline expressed at least four levels of ideas.
d. Li-Min showed the relative importance of ideas.

_____ 8. Dominique needs to complete the following tasks. The task for which writing a summary would be most helpful would be

a. preparing for an essay exam in sociology.
b. keeping track of the steps to follow in solving calculus problems.
c. learning a list of terms and definitions for a biology course.
d. learning the characteristics of different types of mental illness for a psychology class.

_____ 9. Mimi is taking a sociology course in which the focus is social problems. Her instructor has distributed a list of articles, of which she is expected to read ten. The most effective way for her to record the information from her reading would be to prepare

a. a detailed outline of each article.
b. index cards for each article.
c. a summary of each article.
d. a time line to organize the articles.

_____ 10. Rashida has finished highlighting and marking a chapter in her physics text and is now writing summary notes. If Rashida is working effectively, she is most likely

a. pulling ideas together and summarizing them in her own words.
b. taking notes based only on the summary of a chapter.
c. highlighting a long or complicated section first.
d. recording her impression of the material's value.

Learning and Memory

LEARNING GOALS

In this chapter you will learn to

1 Cope with forgetting.

2 Understand how learning and memory work.

3 Develop effective learning strategies.

4 Review effectively.

LEARNING EXPERIMENT

1 Suppose you wanted to become a better swimmer. What would you do? List some ideas here:

_____

_____

_____

2 Now read the following paragraph, which explains the physics of swimming, and examine the accompanying photograph.

For every action, there's an equal and opposite reaction. Swimmers move *forward* by pushing *back* against the water (instead of pushing *up* and *out* as many do). The greater the resistance of the water, the greater the forward thrust. And since still water provides greater resistance than water that's already moving backward, the old straight-arm pull isn't the most efficient way to swim. The most effective stroke, instead, is one that's curved so that you're always pushing against a column of "new" or still water. Resistance in the right places is a swimmer's friend. In the wrong places, though, it's an enemy, and it's known as drag. In order to move through water most efficiently, your body must pose as little resistance (drag) as possible. This is called streamlining. To streamline your body, keep it generally horizontal along the central axis (your spine) so that all your energy is used for propelling your body *directly forward*, and none is wasted by moving it vertically, to the side, or even backward.

—Katz, *Swimming for Total Fitness*, p. 99

3 Would the paragraph and/or photograph above help you become a better swimmer? Why or why not?

The Results

You probably agreed that the paragraph and photograph would be useful. Why? They explain how the process works and offer suggestions about how to position your body to move through the water more efficiently.

Learning Principle: What this Means to You

By reading about the dynamics of swimming, you received an overview of the process. **If you understand how a process works, you will be able to put it to use more easily.** In this chapter you will learn how memory works, as well as many practical suggestions for improving your memory. After you have completed this chapter you will be better prepared to learn from both lectures and textbooks.

FORGETTING

Forgetting, which is defined as the loss of information stored in memory, is a normal, everyday occurrence. Psychologists have extensively studied the rate at which forgetting takes place. For most people, forgetting occurs very rapidly right after learning and then levels off over time. In other words, unless you are one of the lucky few who remember almost everything they hear or read, you will forget a large portion of the information you learn unless you do something to prevent it.

Fortunately, certain techniques can prevent or slow down forgetting. These techniques are the focus of this text. Throughout the text, you will learn techniques that will enable you to identify what to learn (pick out what is important) and to learn it in the most effective way. Each technique is intended to help you remember more and to slow down your rate of forgetting. For instance, in Chapter 2 you learned how taking notes during class lectures can help you learn and remember the lecture. In Chapter 6 you will learn a reading system for learning and remembering more.

Why Forgetting Occurs

There are two common reasons why forgetting occurs: disuse and interference.

Disuse: Use it or lose it! If you do not use information, you tend to forget it. For example, if you don't use a friend's phone number, you tend to forget it. If you use it frequently, you will remember it. To make sure you do not forget information you have learned, be sure to use it. Periodic review, discussed later in this chapter, will help keep information fixed in your memory.

Interference. Interference occurs when new or existing knowledge hinders recall. One type of interference occurs when something new you have learned prevents you from remembering something old you have already learned. If you start studying Spanish, you may find you have difficulty remembering the French you already learned. This type of interference occurs when the new learning is very similar to the old learning. To minimize the effects of interference, try not to study similar subjects back-to-back.

Another type of interference occurs when something you have already learned prevents you from learning something new. For example, in a history course if you studied World War I and then World War II, you might have trouble

Goal 1

Cope with forgetting.

remembering events in World War II. To prevent this type of interference, you may have to review the new learning to keep it fresh in your memory. Refer to the section of this chapter titled "How to Review," page 138.

Exercise 1

DIRECTIONS   For each of the following situations, use the information on this page and the previous page on forgetting to explain why the student was experiencing difficulty.

1. Allan was taking both sociology and psychology. Why did he forget what he studied yesterday in sociology after he attended his psychology class today?

   _____

   _____

   _____

2. Maria carefully read and highlighted each chapter in her business marketing text. She worked hard each week on the assigned chapters but never looked back at what she had already learned. When an exam was announced, she found she had to relearn much of the information. Why did she forget it?

   _____

   _____

3. Kim was taking a history course. She reviewed her lecture notes each afternoon, right after class, and was confident she had learned the information. When an exam was announced, she found she had to relearn a great deal of information. Why did she forget it?

   _____

   _____

   _____

Goal 2

Understand how learning and memory work.

AN OVERVIEW OF THE LEARNING AND MEMORY PROCESS

Three stages are involved in the memory process: encoding, storage, and retrieval. Figure 5-1 is a visual model of the learning and memory processes. Refer to it frequently as you read the sections that explain each stage.

How Encoding Works

Every waking moment, your mind is bombarded with a variety of impressions of what is going on around you. Your five senses—hearing, sight, touch, taste, and smell—provide information about your surroundings. Think for a moment of all the signals your brain receives at a given moment. If you are reading, your eyes transmit the visual patterns of the words. But you may also hear a door slamming, a clock ticking, or a dog barking. Your sense of smell may detect perfume or cigarette smoke. Your sense of touch may signal that a pen you are using to underline

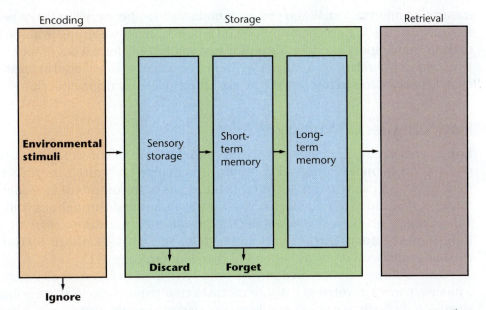

FIGURE 5-1
A Model of Memory

will soon run out of ink or that the room is chilly. When you listen to a classroom lecture, you are constantly receiving stimuli—from the professor, from students around you, and from the lecture hall. During **encoding**, all these environmental stimuli are transmitted to your brain for very brief sensory storage and interpretation. It is easy to be distracted by competing stimuli.

How Sensory Storage Works

Information received from your five senses is transmitted through the nervous system to the brain, which accepts and interprets it. The information stays briefly in the nervous system while the brain interprets it; this short period of interpretation is known as **sensory storage**.

How does your mind handle the barrage of information conveyed by your senses? Thanks to **selective attention**, your brain automatically sorts out the more important signals from the trivial ones. Trivial signals, such as insignificant noises around you, are ignored or discarded. Through the skills of concentration and attention, you can train yourself to ignore other, more distracting signals, such as a dog barking or people talking in the background.

Although your sensory storage accepts all information, data are kept there only briefly, usually less than a few seconds. Then the information fades, decays, or is replaced with new, incoming stimuli. The function of sensory storage, then, is to retain information long enough for you to selectively interpret it and send it to your short-term memory.

How Short-Term Memory Works

Short-term memory holds the information that was sent from your sensory storage system. It is used to store information you wish to retain for only a few seconds. If you look up a phone number on the Internet, for example, it is stored in your short-term memory until you dial it. A lecturer's words are retained until you can record them in your notes.

Most researchers agree that short-term memory lasts much less than a minute—perhaps 20 seconds or less. Information can be maintained longer if you practice or *rehearse* the information. When you are introduced to someone, you will not be able to remember the person's name unless you repeat it, thereby learning it, at the time of the introduction. Otherwise, incoming information will force it out of your short-term memory. Similarly, you will not be able to remember what you read in a textbook chapter or heard in a lecture unless you take action to learn and remember it.

How Long-Term Memory Works

Long-term memory is a relatively permanent store of information. Unlike short-term memory, long-term memory is nearly unlimited in both span (length) and capacity (size). It contains hundreds of thousands of facts, details, impressions, and experiences that you have accumulated throughout your life. For textbook reading, the key is deciding *what* information to store in your long-term memory. Textbooks do offer help. See "Using College Textbooks: Deciding What to Learn" at the end of this chapter, page 141.

Once information is stored in your long-term memory, you recall it through a process known as **retrieval**. Academic tasks that require you to retrieve knowledge include math or science problems, quizzes and exams, and papers. Retrieval is tied to storage. The manner in which information is stored in your memory affects its availability and how easily you can retrieve it.

Visual Thinking
APPLYING SKILLS

What types of sensory information compete for your attention in this lecture class? How can you ignore them?

Exercise 2

DIRECTIONS Use your knowledge of the memory process to answer the following questions.

1. Observe and analyze the area in which you are sitting. What sensory impressions (sights, sounds, touch sensations) have you been ignoring as a result of selective attention?

   _____

   _____

2. Can you remember what you ate for lunch three Tuesdays ago? If not, why not?

   _____

3. Explain why two people are able to carry on a deep conversation at a crowded, noisy party.

_____

4. Explain why someone who looks up an address and then walks into another room to write it on an envelope may forget the address.

_____

_____

5. Suppose you are reading a section of your history textbook. You come across an unfamiliar word and look up its meaning. Once you have looked up the word, you find that you must reread the section. Why?

_____

_____

_____

LEARNING STRATEGIES

You have to learn something before you can remember it. The manner in which you take in information determines how well you can remember it. Use the following suggestions for learning information the first time.

Get Focused

You will learn more in less time if you get focused before you begin. Instead of jumping right into a new chapter or series of class notes, use the tips in the box below to zero in on the task.

Goal

Develop effective learning strategies.

HOW TO GET FOCUSED	
Strategy	**Why It Works**
Avoid competing visual information. Competing visual information may include a television, a computer or phone screen, or a window overlooking a busy scene.	Any visual information pulls your eye and your mind away from the material you are trying to learn.
Identify your purpose. Is your purpose to prepare for an exam, write a research paper, or participate in a class discussion?	Knowing why you are learning creates a focused mind-set and will help you decide what to learn.
Decide what types of information you need to learn. Are dates, events, definitions, statistics, or research findings important? What is less important? Use your syllabus to help you.	It is impossible to learn every fact in a textbook chapter or lecture. You are making the task doable by focusing on essential information.
Use previewing (see Chapter 6).	You will remember more of what you read if you are familiar with its content and organization before you begin.

Tip A _strategy_ is a plan for an action or series of actions designed to achieve a specific goal, such as getting a good grade in biology.

Learn As Efficiently as Possible

Many students spend hours studying but do not get the grades they want. The key is not to simply spend time learning; rather, it is to use the right strategies to make the most of your study time. The strategies in the box below will help you optimize your study time.

HOW TO OPTIMIZE YOUR STUDY TIME

Strategy	Why It Works
Use numerous sensory channels. Don't just read. Also use writing, listening, and speaking. Take notes, repeat information aloud, and listen to classmates talk about the material.	Processing the information through different channels gives your brain numerous ways to take in and organize the information.
Learn in your own words. When taking notes, avoid copying or repeating information word-for-word from textbooks or recording exactly what is said in a lecture.	By explaining ideas in your own words, you will test your understanding and create your own mental circuits for learning the information.
Connect new information with old information you have already learned. For example, you might learn the steps in developing a business plan by associating them with how your family began its florist business.	The associations you build with old information work as links or springboards that lead you to and help you remember the new material.
Take advantage of your learning style (see Chapter 1).	Your learning style suggests your strengths as a learner. Its components point you toward the most efficient and best ways for you to learn.

Use Visualization

Even if you are not a visual learner, visualizing certain types of information is the best way to learn them. Visualizing means creating a mental picture of something in your mind. Your picture or image should include as much relevant information as possible. A student taking an anatomy and physiology class drew the sketch shown in Figure 5-2 to help her learn the parts of the human brain. She first drew it on paper and then she visualized, or mentally drew, the brain diagram to help her remember the parts.

Visualization makes remembering easier because related information is stored in one unified image, and, if you can recall any part of that mental picture, you will be able to retrieve the whole picture.

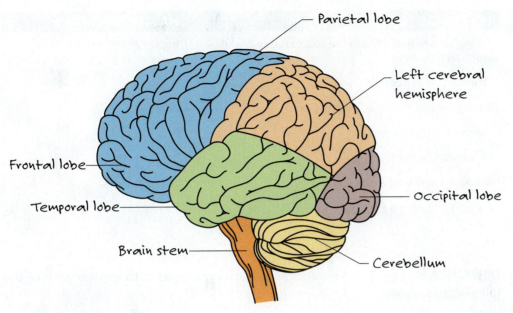

FIGURE 5-2
Sketch of Brain

Organize Information by Chunking

Learning a large number of individual facts or pieces of information is often a difficult, frustrating task. Instead of overloading your memory with numerous individual facts, learn organized, meaningful sets of information that you can store as one chunk. Have you ever wondered why Social Security numbers and phone numbers have dashes? The dashes divide the information into chunks, making them easier to remember.

To organize information, keep the following suggestions in mind.

- **Discover how the material you are studying is connected.** Search for some organizing principle. In studying basic business management skills, for example, you may discover that you can chunk them into technical skills, interpersonal relations skills, and decision-making skills.
- **Look for similarities and differences.** If you are studying types of businesses, compare and contrast the following chunks: structure, operation, and efficiency of each type.
- **Look for sequences and for obvious divisions or breaking points within the sequences.** For example, if you are studying the overfishing of oceans as part of an environmental studies class, you could chunk the information into past practices, current policies, and unsolved problems.

Use Effective Study Strategies

You can learn more effectively and in less time if you use the right study methods. Table 5-1 provides an easy reference guide to the learning strategies covered in this text.

TABLE 5-1
Reference Guide to
Learning Strategies

LEARNING STRATEGY	CHAPTER REFERENCE
Taking lecture notes, using the recall clue system to study lecture notes	Chapter 2
Highlighting textbooks	Chapter 4
Outlining, summarizing, and mapping	Chapter 4
Using the SQ3R system	Chapter 6
Previewing, active reading	Chapter 6
Recognizing thought patterns	Chapter 9
Studying for exams	Chapter 13

Exercise 3

DIRECTIONS   Use your knowledge of learning strategies to explain each of the following situations.

1. A business instructor plans to lecture on the process of analyzing job stress. Before class, she draws a diagram of this process on the chalkboard. During the lecture she refers to it frequently. Why did the instructor draw the diagram?

   _____

   _____

   _____

   _____

2. A political science instructor is discussing an essay on terrorism. He begins the discussion by asking his students to recall recent terrorist acts and what the response to them was. How is the instructor helping his students learn the content of the essay?

   _____

   _____

   _____

3. A student in a health-care degree program was studying conflict resolution. She had to learn ten different resolution strategies. How could she learn them effectively?

   _____

   _____

   _____

   _____

   _____

   _____

   _____

4. One group of students read a psychology chapter and took notes on it. Another group read the chapter and took notes as well, but they also discussed the material in a study group. Why did the second group score higher on the exam that was based on that chapter?

_____

_____

_____

_____

_____

5. A business management student was studying the decision-making process. She grouped the steps into three categories: data gathering, analysis, and resolution. What learning technique did she use?

_____

DIRECTIONS   Discuss techniques that might help you learn the following sets of information.

Exercise 4

1. the process of amending the Constitution (in an American government course)

_____

2. the factors that influence market price (in an economics course)

_____

3. different forms of mental illness (in a psychology course)

_____

4. ways to recognize and distinguish the different types of figurative language (in a literature course)

_____

5. the process of cell division (in a biology course)

_____

6. important terms for an introductory sociology course

_____

7. the different types of white collar crimes and their cost to society (in a criminology course)

_____

_____

8. a comparison of the different kinds of psychoactive drugs (in a health course)

_____

_____

Goal 4

Review effectively.

REVIEW

Some students think that as long as they spend time studying, they will get good grades. That is not necessarily the case. This section will teach you when to review and how to get the most out of your review time.

When to Review

It is very important to plan *when* to study and review so that you get the most out of the time you spend.

IMMEDIATE REVIEW   Forgetting occurs most rapidly right after learning. **Immediate review** means reviewing new information as soon as possible after you hear or read it. Think of immediate review as a way of fixing in your mind what you have just learned. Here are some ways to use immediate review:

- **Review your lecture notes as soon as possible after taking them.** This review will help the ideas stick in your mind.
- **Review a textbook chapter as soon as you finish reading it.** Do this by rereading each chapter heading and then rereading the summary.
- **Review all new course materials again at the end of each day.** This review will help you pull together information and make it more meaningful.

PERIODIC REVIEW   Most college semesters are three or four months long. You cannot realistically expect to remember what you learned early in the semester, especially since you are continuing to learn more new information, unless you take active steps to do so. To keep from forgetting what you learned early in the semester, you will need to review it several times throughout the semester. **Periodic review** means returning to and quickly reviewing previously learned material on a regular basis. You should establish a periodic review schedule in which you quickly review course materials every three weeks or so.

FINAL REVIEW   **Final review** means making a last check of material before a test or exam. A final review should not be a lengthy session; instead, it should be a quick once-over of everything you have learned. Be sure to schedule your final review as close as possible to the exam in which you will need to recall the material.

How to Review

The worst way to review what you have learned is to simply reread it. Rereading textbook chapters and entire sets of lecture notes is time-consuming and produces very poor results. Use the following suggestions to improve your review efficiency.

SCHEDULE SHORT REVIEW SESSIONS   While it is tempting to cram, you will learn more quickly if you schedule several short review sessions rather than one long one. If possible, spread your review over several days, with short sessions scheduled for each day.

TEST YOURSELF BY ANTICIPATING EXAM QUESTIONS   Make up questions and write the answers to them. Study with another student and ask each other questions. Turn the headings in your textbook into questions and answer them. For more about these techniques, see the section on guide questions in Chapter 6, page 158. The recall clue system for note taking in Chapter 2, page 55, is another way to test yourself. For more on preparing for exams, see Chapter 13.

DEVELOP RETRIEVAL CLUES A **retrieval clue** is a tag that enables you to pull a piece of information from your memory. Think of your memory as having slots or compartments in which you store information. If you can name or label what is in the slot, you will know where to look for the information that is located in that slot. For example, if you have a memory slot labeled "environmental problems" in which you store information related to pollution and its problems, causes, and solutions, you can retrieve information on air pollution by locating the appropriate memory slot. Developing retrieval clues involves selecting a word or phrase that summarizes or categorizes several pieces of information. For example, you might use the phrase "motivation theories" to organize information for a psychology course on instinct, drive, cognitive, arousal, and opponent-process theories.

SIMULATE TEST SITUATIONS Practice retrieving learned information by simulating test conditions. If you are studying for a math exam, prepare by solving problems. If an exam in your horticulture class requires you to identify certain plants, then study photos and characteristics of plants. Be sure to model your practice on the event for which you are preparing. Your practice should entail the same type of activity and have the same time limit.

> **Tip** *Simulate* means "to produce something that is not real or original but seems to be." A *simulation* is *similar* to the original.

OVERLEARN It is tempting to stop studying as soon as you feel you have learned a given body of information. However, to ensure complete, thorough learning, it is best to plan a few more review sessions. When you learned to drive a car, you did not stop practicing parallel parking after the first time you did it correctly. Similarly, for a botany course, you should not stop reviewing the process of photosynthesis at the moment you feel you have mastered it. Instead, use additional review to make the material stick in your mind.

CONSIDER PHYSICAL SURROUNDINGS It is easier to recall information when you are in the same setting in which you learned it. Consider reviewing your notes in the lecture hall in which you took them. Also, if possible, study in the room in which you will take a particular exam.

USE MEMORIZATION Memorization is one of the least effective ways of learning, but there is plenty of material that must be learned this way. In chemistry, you have to memorize parts of the periodic table. In history, you need to memorize dates and historical events. Here are some useful memorization techniques.

- *Mnemonics* **are memory tricks or aids that you devise to help you remember information.** Mnemonics include rhymes, acronyms, words, nonsense words, sentences, and mental pictures that aid in the recall of facts. Do you remember this rhyme? "Thirty days hath September, / April, June, and November. / All the rest have thirty-one / except February, alone, / which has twenty-eight days clear / and twenty-nine in each leap year." The rhyme is an example of a mnemonic device. It is a quick and easy way of remembering the number of days in each month of the year. You may have learned to recall the colors of the rainbow by remembering the name *Roy G. Biv*; each letter in this name stands for one of the colors that make up the spectrum: *Red*, *Orange*, *Yellow*, *Green*, *Blue*, *Indigo*, *Violet*.

- **Another memory device is called** *method of loci.* It involves selecting a familiar object, such as your home or car, and associating items to be remembered with areas in the object. For example, suppose you are trying to remember the four components of language: phonemes, morphemes, syntax, and semantics. Begin by picturing the first location, say the hood of your car. Place phonemes on the hood. Then move to the windshield; place morphemes on the windshield. Place syntax on the steering wheel and semantics on the dashboard. To learn the four components of language, visualize the first location and think of phonemes, associating them together, and so forth. To recall the components, take an imaginary tour of your car. When you think of the hood, you will think of phonemes.

Exercise 5

DIRECTIONS   Use your knowledge of the memory process to answer the following questions.

1. On many campuses, weekly recitations or discussions are scheduled for small groups to review material presented in large lecture classes. What learning function do these recitation sections perform?

   _____

   _____

2. After lecturing on the causes of domestic violence, a sociology instructor showed her class a video of an incident of domestic violence. What learning function(s) did the film perform? How would the video help students remember the lecture?

   _____

   _____

3. A student spends more time than anyone else in her class preparing for the midterm exam, yet she cannot remember important definitions and concepts at the time of the exam. Offer several possible explanations of her problem.

   _____

   _____

   _____

   _____

4. A sociology student is studying a chapter on age and the elderly. The exam based on that chapter will contain both multiple-choice items and an essay question. How should she test herself in preparation for the exam?

   _____

   _____

   _____

5. One student studied for his math exam for three hours the night before the exam. Another student studied for one hour on each of three days before the exam. He studied by creating and solving sample problems. Which student do you think did better on the exam? Why?

_____

_____

_____

_____

_____

Exercise 6

DIRECTIONS Apply your knowledge of memorization techniques by completing each of the following activities.

1. Make up a rhyme or nonsense word to help you learn something you need to remember for one of your other courses.

2. Use the method of loci technique to remember the last names of your classmates. Then try it out on material for one of your other courses.

Exercise 7

Collaboration

DIRECTIONS Identify your most difficult course. Consider the material you are required to learn and review for the next major test. Spend some time organizing textbook and lecture material that you are sure will be on that test. Make a study plan that uses at least four of the techniques described in this chapter. Show your work to a classmate. Both of you should then offer each other suggestions to make studying more effective.

Exercise 8

DIRECTIONS Select two or more learning strategies starting on page 133 and apply them to the section of the sample textbook chapter titled "Prejudice and Stereotypes" (pp. 432–436). Use immediate review when you finish. Review the material periodically. Evaluate the effectiveness of the techniques you have chosen.

USING COLLEGE TEXTBOOKS
Deciding What to Learn

One of the most challenging tasks facing college students is deciding what to learn in each of their textbooks. Realistically, you cannot learn every fact in every one of your textbooks. Fortunately, your textbooks offer plenty of guidance. They contain numerous features to help you pick out what is important.

One useful feature is chapter objectives. These may be labeled "Learning Objectives," "Chapter Objectives," or "Learning Goals," as they are called in this text. Chapter objectives list what you should know when you have finished reading a chapter. Often they correspond or relate to the course objectives that appear on your course syllabus. Read the objectives once before you read the chapter, as part of your preview. Then, after you have finished the chapter, use them to test yourself by writing notes that summarize what you have learned about each objective.

CHAPTER OBJECTIVES

After reading this chapter, you should be able to:

1. Discuss the unique design considerations of various accessories
2. Describe production methods for the major accessories
3. Explain accessory design and production centers
4. Discuss aspects of marketing for accessories
5. Explain fur garment production

—Frings, *Fashion*, p. 80

LEARNING OBJECTIVES

After studying this chapter, you will be able to:

1. Explain how to adapt to your audiences when writing reports and proposals, and provide an overview of the process of drafting report content
2. Provide an overview of the process of drafting proposal content, and list six strategies to strengthen proposal argument

—Thill and Bovee, *Excellence in Business Communication*, p. 355

UPON COMPLETING THIS CHAPTER, YOU WILL BE ABLE TO:

- Describe the scale of urbanization
- Assess urban and suburban sprawl
- Outline city and regional planning and land use strategies
- Evaluate transportation options
- Describe the roles of urban parks
- Analyze environmental impacts and advantages of urban centers
- Assess urban ecology, green building efforts, and the pursuit of sustainable cities

—Withgott and Brennan, *Environment*, p. 343

Textbook Exercise 1: Using Learning Objectives

For each set of learning objectives above, predict the key topics of each chapter and provide a title for the chapter. For example, for the first set of objectives from Frings' **Fashion** textbook, the chapter title might be "Accessories and Fur Garments."

FURTHER PRACTICE WITH TEXTBOOK READING

Textbook Exercise 2: Sample Textbook Chapter

Learning goals can take various forms. In the sample textbook chapter in Part Seven, the goals take the form of learning objectives and appear just under the chapter title on page 425. Use these objectives to guide you as you read the chapter; they list what you need to learn. Turn each objective into a question, and answer each question as you finish the section to which it corresponds. Then, when you have finished reading the chapter, answer all four questions again. Notice that the summary (titled "Making the Grade") on page 438 provides an outline of key concepts for each learning objective. Use this summary to verify that you have answered each question accurately and completely.

Textbook Exercise 3: Your College Textbook

Choose a textbook that you are using in one of your other courses. Read a chapter. If it contains chapter objectives or learning goals, use them to test yourself by writing a set of notes summarizing the information you learned for each goal. If the chapter does not contain objectives or goals, use the chapter headings and summary to write a set of goals. Then test yourself.

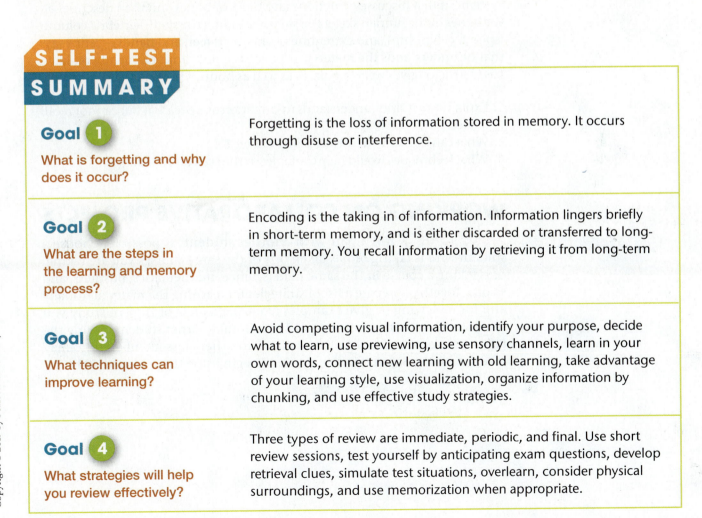

SELF-TEST SUMMARY

Goal 1

What is forgetting and why does it occur?

Forgetting is the loss of information stored in memory. It occurs through disuse or interference.

Goal 2

What are the steps in the learning and memory process?

Encoding is the taking in of information. Information lingers briefly in short-term memory, and is either discarded or transferred to long-term memory. You recall information by retrieving it from long-term memory.

Goal 3

What techniques can improve learning?

Avoid competing visual information, identify your purpose, decide what to learn, use previewing, use sensory channels, learn in your own words, connect new learning with old learning, take advantage of your learning style, use visualization, organize information by chunking, and use effective study strategies.

Goal 4

What strategies will help you review effectively?

Three types of review are immediate, periodic, and final. Use short review sessions, test yourself by anticipating exam questions, develop retrieval clues, simulate test situations, overlearn, consider physical surroundings, and use memorization when appropriate.

APPLYING | YOUR SKILLS

DISCUSSING THE CHAPTER

1. What strategies do you use to remember the following types of information: people's names, recipes, directions, steps in a process, a child's lullaby? Use the chapter's information to explain why different strategies are needed for these different types of information.
2. Imagine that you are learning about the culture of an African people, the artistic style of Monet, and the chemical differences between acids and bases. What could you do to learn the information in each of these situations?
3. Give some examples of mnemonic devices that you have used to help you store information.

ANALYZING A STUDY SITUATION

Carlos is having difficulty with his human anatomy and physiology course. He feels overwhelmed by the volume of facts and details, as well as the new terminology he must learn. His next assigned chapter is "The Skeletal System." It first discusses functions and types of bones and then describes all the bones in the human skeletal system, including the skull, vertebral column (spine), pelvis (hip), and extremities (arms, legs, feet, and hands). Carlos says that he understands the material as he reads it but cannot remember it later. His instructor gives weekly quizzes as well as hour-long exams.

1. Explain why Carlos understands information as he reads it but cannot recall it later.
2. What can Carlos do to correct his lack of recall?
3. What techniques would help Carlos learn the skeletal system?

WORKING ON COLLABORATIVE PROJECTS

DIRECTIONS Form a pair with another student. If possible, choose a student who is taking or has taken one of the same courses you are taking, or is taking a course in the same field (science, mathematics, business, and so on). Together, prepare a list of strategies for learning the material initially and for reviewing it; give examples from the course or field of study you share. Include strategies that would be helpful to other students taking the course. Make your strategy list available to other class members who may take the course. Select two strategies and begin using them immediately.

Quick Quiz

DIRECTIONS Write the letter of the choice that best completes each statement in the space provided.

CHECKING YOUR RECALL

_____ 1. All of the following are types of review *except*

    a. immediate review.
    b. purposeful review.
    c. periodic review.
    d. final review.

_____ 2. Information remains in your short-term memory for no longer than

    a. a minute.
    b. an hour.
    c. a day.
    d. a week.

_____ 3. Mnemonics involves

    a. making up rhymes or words to help you remember information.
    b. visualizing an event as it happened.
    c. connecting new information with already learned facts.
    d. grouping ideas together based on similar characteristics.

_____ 4. During selective attention, your brain

    a. classifies information into groups or sets.
    b. practices information to learn it.
    c. automatically sorts out important information from trivial signals.
    d. sends information to long-term memory.

_____ 5. If you are unable to explain information in your own words, it is a sign that

    a. you do not understand it.
    b. you did not review it properly.
    c. you did not connect new learning with previous learning.
    d. interference has occurred.

APPLYING YOUR SKILLS

_____ 6. Luis has just attended a chemistry lecture. He had difficulty learning the material in the chemistry class because he had just come from his biology class. Luis experienced

    a. interference.
    b. disuse.
    c. selective attention.
    d. sensory storage.

_____ 7. Taylor is studying in his apartment while his roommates are home. He is concentrating on his studies and ignoring his roommates' chatter and laughter. Taylor is practicing

    a. overlearning.
    b. selective attention.
    c. retrieval.
    d. periodic review.

_____ 8. In her Introduction to Music elective, Katie uses the saying "Every good boy deserves fudge" to help her remember the line notes of the treble clef. This memory trick is an example of

    a. competing stimuli.
    b. a sensory channel.
    c. a visualization.
    d. a mnemonic device.

_____ 9. Zachary has just finished reading a textbook chapter on the causes of World War I. The most effective way for Zachary to store the information he has just learned is for him to

    a. immediately reread the chapter.
    b. move on to a completely different subject.
    c. read the next chapter.
    d. reread the chapter headings and the summary.

_____ 10. If Rosa wanted to develop retrieval clues to help her learn material for her geology class, she would specifically try to

    a. overlearn the material.
    b. store the information in short-term memory.
    c. choose a word or phrase that summarizes several pieces of information.
    d. connect the information with her personal experience.

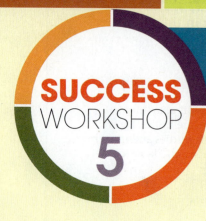

SUCCESS
WORKSHOP
5

IMPROVING YOUR READING RATE AND FLEXIBILITY

Did You Know?

○ The typical business course requires 7 hours of reading per week. Social science courses typically require 8 hours of reading per week; so do courses in the arts and humanities.[1]

○ Students cite "not enough time to read everything assigned" as their number-one challenge in completing their coursework.[2]

Reading makes up the bulk of most students' workloads. How can you get all of your assigned reading done in the allotted time?

WHAT ARE READING RATE AND FLEXIBILITY?

The best readers sometimes read quickly and sometimes read slowly. You should strive to improve your **reading rate**, the speed at which you read, in order to become a more efficient reader. But you should also aim to increase your **reading flexibility**. When you are a flexible reader, you adjust how you read to suit what you are reading and why you are reading it.

HOW CAN YOU IMPROVE YOUR READING RATE?

1. **Eliminate bad reading habits.** If you can eliminate the three most common bad reading habits—moving your head, moving your lips, and keeping your place on the line with your finger—you will be well on your way to improving your reading rate and flexibility.

2. **Preview what you are reading.** If you familiarize yourself with the organization and content of the material before you read it, you will be able to anticipate the flow of ideas and you will find yourself able to read the material more quickly. See Chapter 6 to learn how to preview.

3. **Read in meaning clusters.** Good readers often combine words that naturally go together. As you read, try not to think of a sentence as a string of single words. Instead, think of it as several word clusters or phrases. Group

---

[1]http://nsse.iub.edu/html/annual_results.cfm, Table 2.
[2]Georgeana Stratton, "Does Increasing Textbook Portability Increase Reading Rates or Academic Performance?" *Inquiry* 16, no. 1 (2011): 5–16.

words that make sense together: group words with the words they explain or modify.

4. **Pace yourself.** Pacing means pushing yourself to read faster than your normal speed while maintaining your level of comprehension. To pace yourself you can

   - **Use an index card** to "push" you down a print page, covering up lines as you read them.
   - **Use the scroll key when reading online** to force yourself to move rapidly down the page.

Remember: Be sure to monitor your comprehension as you work at increasing your speed. Your goals are to increase your speed *and* to remember and understand what you read.

HOW CAN YOU IMPROVE YOUR READING FLEXIBILITY?

Reading flexibility involves adjusting your reading strategies, reading rate, and level of comprehension to suit the task, the material, and your background knowledge. To become a flexible reader, you must make a decision about how you will read a given piece of material. For example, you would read an article in *People* magazine much more quickly than you would read a chapter in a biology textbook. You need to achieve a higher level of comprehension with the biology textbook because you'll be tested on that reading. In contrast, you won't be tested on the contents of the *People* article. To improve your reading flexibility, use the following two steps:

1. **Assess difficulty.** The first step in determining how to read a given piece of writing is to assess its difficulty. The easiest way to assess difficulty is to preview the reading. Use the following checklist to determine difficulty.

CHECKLIST TO EVALUATE DIFFICULTY		
Format	**Vocabulary Level**	**Your Background Knowledge**
• helpful	• difficult vocabulary	• strong
• difficult to follow	• understandable vocabulary	• moderate
		• weak
Graphic/Visual Aids	**Subject Matter**	**Your Physical/Mental State**
• yes	• complex	• alert
• no	• understandable	• moderately alert
	• familiar	• distractible
Typographical Aids	**Length**	**Your Interest Level**
• yes	• short	• high
• no	• moderate	• moderate
	• long	• low
Language Features	**Organization**	
• short sentences and paragraphs	• strong	
• long sentences and paragraphs	• moderate	
	• weak	

2. **Define your purpose.** Different reading situations require different levels of comprehension and recall. Your reading can range from paying careful, close attention to a very brief, quick reading for only main ideas. You will find that as your comprehension decreases, your rate increases. The following table summarizes types of reading material, purposes for reading, and levels of comprehension required.

THE RELATIONSHIPS AMONG TYPE OF READING MATERIAL, PURPOSE, AND COMPREHENSION

Type of Material	Purpose for Reading	Desired Level of Comprehension
Poetry, legal documents, argumentative writing	Analyze, criticize, evaluate	Complete (100%)
Textbooks, manuals, research documents	High comprehension and recall for exams, writing research papers, following directions	High (90–100%)
Novels, paperbacks, newspapers, magazines, blogs, social networking sites	Entertainment, enjoyment, general information	Moderate (69–90%)
Reference materials, catalogs, magazines, nonfiction, Web sites	Overview of material, locating specific facts, review of previously read material	Low (60% or below)

ASSESSING DIFFICULTY AND DEFINING YOUR PURPOSE

Choose a reading selection or assignment and review the Checklist to Evaluate Difficulty on the previous page and The Relationships Among Type of Reading Material, Purpose, and Comprehension above. Then answer the following questions.

1. Will the selection be easy to read, difficult to read, or of moderate difficulty? On which elements of the reading do you base your evaluation?

_____

_____

2. What is your purpose for reading, and what is your desired level of comprehension? Explain.

_____

_____

READ!

Read efficiently and flexibly.

   Evaluate difficulty and adjust your rate accordingly.

      Always preview an assignment before reading it.

         Define your purpose for reading.

Active Reading Strategies

LEARNING GOALS

In this chapter you will learn to

1. Preview before you read.

2. Discover what you already know about a topic.

3. Define your purpose for reading.

4. Check your comprehension.

5. Strengthen your comprehension of text.

6. Review after reading.

7. Strengthen your comprehension of visual aids.

8. Use and adapt the SQ3R system to fit your needs.

LEARNING EXPERIMENT

1. In the space below, draw the front of a one-dollar bill.

2. Find a one-dollar bill and compare your drawing with it. Notice the features you did not include.

The Results

Although hundreds of one-dollar bills have passed through your hands over the years, you probably did not recall very many features. Why? You did not recall these features because you did not plan to remember them.

Learning Principle: What This Means to You

We remember what we intend to remember. If you do not decide what you should remember before reading an assignment, your recall is likely to be poor. However, if you decide what you need to know before you start reading, your recall will be much higher. This chapter demonstrates several techniques that will help you become an active reader. Specifically, you will learn to preview before reading, to discover what you already know about the topic, and to define your purposes for reading. You will also learn to monitor and strengthen your comprehension while and after you read, read graphics, and use an effective system, SQ3R, to increase how well you read and remember textbook content.

PREVIEWING AND PREDICTING BEFORE READING

Before reading, you should make predictions, or educated guesses, about the material. You might make predictions about how difficult or interesting the material will be, what topics will be discussed, or how the author will approach the subject. You might also anticipate how the material will be organized—how it progresses from one idea to another.

Your overall purposes in previewing are to identify the most important ideas in the material and note their organization. You look only at specific parts and skip over the rest. The portions to look at in previewing a textbook chapter are described in the following box. Later you will learn how to adapt this procedure to other types of material.

HOW TO PREVIEW A TEXTBOOK CHAPTER

1. **Read the title and subtitle.** The title provides the overall topic of the chapter. The subtitle suggests the specific focus, aspect, or approach toward the overall topic. Also note objectives or outlines, if provided.

2. **Read the lead-in or introduction.** If it is extremely long, read just the first paragraph. The introduction, or first paragraph if there is no introduction, serves as a lead-in to the chapter. It gives you an idea of where the material starts and where it is going.

3. **Read each boldfaced heading and the first sentence that follows it.** Headings announce the major topic of each section. The first sentence frequently tells you what the passage is about or states the central thought. However, in some types of material, the first sentence does not function as a central thought. Instead, the opening sentence may function as a transition or lead-in statement, or it may be designed to catch your interest. If the first sentence seems unimportant, read the last sentence, which often states or restates the central thought.

4. **Read titles of maps, charts, or graphs.** Also read the captions for pictures and the legends on graphs, charts, and tables. (Legends provide detailed information about what the symbols—figures, shapes, lines, colors, etc.—on a visual mean.) Be sure to notice sidebars, marginal notes, boxed material, and annotations on figures and diagrams.

5. **Read the last paragraph or the summary.** The last paragraph usually gives a condensed view of the selection and helps you identify key ideas. Often the summary outlines the selection's key points.

6. **Note any typographical and graphical aids.** *Italic* (slanted) or **boldfaced** type often emphasizes important terms and definitions by distinguishing them from the rest of the passage. Note any material that is numbered 1, 2, 3, lettered a, b, c, or presented in list form.

7. **Read the end-of-selection materials.** These might include references, study questions, vocabulary lists, or biographical information about the author. These materials will be useful later as you read and study the selection. Study questions often indicate what is important in the chapter. If a vocabulary list is included, rapidly skim through it to identify terms you need to learn as you read.

Demonstration of Previewing

Figure 6-1 on the next page presents an excerpt from an introductory marketing textbook. Everything that you should look at or read has been shaded. Preview this excerpt now, reading only the shaded portions of each page.

FIGURE 6-1
A Demonstration of Previewing

SOCIAL NETWORKING

One of the most exciting developments in the marketing world is the evolution of how consumers interact with marketers. The tremendous acceleration of social networking fuels this fire. In a social network a user represents him- or herself via a profile on a Web site and provides and receives links to other members of the network to share input about common interests.

SOCIAL MEDIA IS EVERYWHERE

Social media has become part of all facets of our lives. The odds are you and most of your classmates checked your Facebook page before (or during?) class today. You probably used Twitter or FourSquare at some point in the day as well to let people know where you were, check news, or find out what your friends were doing.

Social media platforms like this are very hot today. More and more advertisers realize that these sites are a great way to reach an audience that tunes in regularly and enthusiastically to catch up with friends, check out photos of what they did at that outrageous party Saturday night, proclaim opinions about political or social issues, or share discoveries of new musical artists.

WEB 2.0

Social networking is an integral part of what many call Web 2.0, which is like the Internet on steroids. The key difference between Web 1.0 and the new version is the interactivity we see among producers and users, but these are some other characteristics of a Web 2.0 site:

- **It improves as the number of users increases.** For example, Amazon's ability to recommend books to you based on what other people with similar interests have bought gets better as it tracks more and more people who are entering search queries.

- **Its currency is eyeballs.** Google makes its money by charging advertisers according to the number of people who see their ads after they type in a search term.

- **It's version-free and in perpetual beta.** Unlike static Web sites or books, content is always a work in progress. Wikipedia, the online encyclopedia, gets updated constantly by users who "correct" others' errors.

- **It categorizes entries according to folksonomy rather than "taxonomy."** In other words, sites rely on users rather than preestablished systems to sort contents. Listeners at Pandora.com create their own "radio stations" that play songs by artists they choose as well as other similar artists.

This last point highlights a key change in the way some new media companies approach their businesses: Think of it as marketing strategy by committee. The wisdom of crowds perspective (from a book by that name) argues that under the right circumstances, groups are smarter than the smartest people in them. If this is true, it implies that large numbers of (non-expert) consumers can predict successful products.

—adapted from Solomon, Marshall, and Stuart,
Marketing: Real People, Real Choices, pp. 25–27

Exercise 1

DIRECTIONS   Answer each of the following questions after you have previewed the reading titled "The Cult of Celebrity" in Figure 6-2 below. Do *not* read the entire selection. Mark *T* after statements that are true and *F* after those that are false. Do not look back in the reading to locate the answers. When you finish, check your answers in the answer key at the end of the chapter, page 179, and write your score in the space indicated.

1. Being a celebrity is based on outstanding achievement or accomplishment.   _____

2. A celebrity is a person well known in science, politics, or entertainment.   _____

3. Early movie studios catered to a universal need for fairy tales with a rags-to-riches theme.   _____

4. Motion picture studios promoted their stars as "regular people" whose "job" is acting.   _____

5. People are fascinated by celebrities because people want to be entertained.   _____

Score (number right): _____ ●

FIGURE 6-2
Sample Textbook
Selection

THE CULT OF CELEBRITY

What Is a Celebrity?

According to historian Daniel Boorstin, a celebrity can be defined as a person well known in one of a wide variety of fields such as science, politics, or entertainment. In other words, Barack Obama, Pope Francis, and even Lady Gaga are legitimate celebrities. Being a celebrity today, however, doesn't necessarily mean that it's based on some sort of outstanding achievement or accomplishment.

The entertainment industry, in particular, is fueled by the constant publicizing and glorification of personalities. Individuals such as movie stars, pop music divas, television personalities, and talk show hosts generate a great deal of publicity in the media and on the Web, but today's celebrity status is often only temporary, as there are continually new celebrities who try to take the place of established icons in the public's esteem and interest.

Stephen Cave, reviewing a number of books about fame and celebrity in the *Financial Times*, makes several observations. First, he says, "Fame is a product of certain industries—most notably the mass entertainment business—not a gold star given by the good fairy to the deserving." He goes on, "Fame is not what it used to be . . . Now it is heaped on anyone who is runner-up in a television talent show, subsequently strips for a lads' magazine, then writes their life story at age 25 while on day-release from rehab." Cave continues, "But the fame trade has indeed changed. The rise of instant communications, digital media and mass literacy have all fueled the market for stars. Dedicated TV channels, websites, and magazines such as *Heat* and *People* have exponentially increased the speed and volume of celebrity gossip—and the number of celebrities."

An example of the media's fixation on celebrity was the coverage of the death of pop star Michael Jackson in mid-2009. In the 24 hours after his death, the Pew Research Center for Excellence in Journalism found that 60 percent of the total news coverage was devoted to his death, his life story, and his legacy. The coverage eclipsed all other major news stories such as health care reform, major political violence in Iran, and the greenhouse gas bill.

The three-hour memorial service for Jackson at Staples Center in Los Angeles, however, seemed to confirm the media's assessment that there was tremendous public interest in the story. *The New York Times* dubbed it "one of the most watched farewells in history" because the service attracted a television audience of 31 million and almost 8 million online viewers. Later that day, 20 million watched the prime-time specials offered by the major TV networks.

FIGURE 6-2
(Continued)

The death of a celebrity, particularly under unusual circumstances, generates massive media coverage, but so does the birth of a child to the "right" celebrity couple. Angelina Jolie and Brad Pitt, for example, received $14 million from *People* magazine for an exclusive interview and photos of their newborn twins in 2008. It was the best-selling issue of *People* in seven years.

More recently, the birth of Britain's Prince George in 2013 also generated a media frenzy. On a more somber note, the passing of Nelson Mandela in December 2013 generated more than two weeks of worldwide coverage about his life and march to freedom from 27 years in prison to becoming the first Black president of a new South Africa in 1994.

The Public's Fascination with Celebrities
Psychologists offer varied explanations of why the public becomes impressed—"fascinated" might be the more accurate word—by highly publicized individuals.

Hollywood Glamour
In pretelevision days, the publicity departments of the motion picture studios promoted their male and female stars as glamorous figures that lived in a special world of privilege and wealth. The studios catered to the universal need for fairy tales, which often have a rags-to-riches theme. Dreaming of achieving such glory for themselves, young people with and without talent go to Hollywood to try to crash through the magical gates, almost always in vain.

The Need for Heroes
Many ordinary people leading routine lives also yearn for heroes. Professional and big-time college sports provide personalities for hero worship. Publicists emphasize the performances of certain players, and television sports announcers often build up the stars' roles out of proportion to their actual achievements; this emphasis is supposed to create hero figures for youthful sports enthusiasts to emulate, but the doping scandal of Lance Armstrong and other athletes, including the scandal of Tiger Woods having multiple affairs while married, has somewhat diminished the idea that professional athletes are good role models.

Athletes and Sports
Athletic teams, however, still retain public esteem and loyalty—especially if they are winning. Sports enthusiasts develop a vicarious sense of belonging that creates support for athletic teams. To signify their loyalty, both children and adults gobble up expensive baseball caps, sweatshirts, and other clothing that advertise the team and let others know they are loyal fans. Indeed, a major revenue stream for most professional teams is the sale of merchandise. The NFL teams make about $3 billion annually on merchandise.

The Desire for Entertainment
Still another factor behind the public's fascination is the desire for entertainment. Reading fan magazines or listening to TMZ report on the personal lives and troubles of celebrities gives fans a look behind the curtain of celebrity. Such intimate details provide fuel for discussion among friends or even something to tweet about. And talking about Hollywood's latest couple break-up is certainly more fun than discussing tax reform.

—Wilcox et al., *Public Relations*, pp. 474–477

Look at your score in Exercise 1. Probably you got at least half of the questions right, perhaps more. You can see, then, that previewing does familiarize you with the reading selection and enables you to identify and remember many of its main ideas and details. The following exercise emphasizes how each step in the previewing process gives you useful information about the material you are about to read.

Exercise 2

DIRECTIONS   Preview the reading titled "The Virtual House Call" in Part Six, pages 396–400. Then answer the following questions.

1. What does the subtitle tell you about the article's content? _____

_____

2. Indicate whether each statement is true (T) or false (F).

___ a.   HealthTap seeks to replace traditional doctors.

___ b.   Google searches for medical information may provide disturbing and inaccurate results.

___ c.   A physical exam is now the most critical part of a medical diagnosis.

___ d.   The word *patient* means "one who suffers" in Latin.

Previewing Specific Types of Material

Not all reading materials are organized in the same way, and not all reading materials have the same features or parts. Consequently, you must adjust the way you preview to the type of material you are working with. Figure 6-3 offers suggestions on how to adapt your previewing to suit what you are reading.

Why Previewing Works

Previewing is effective for several reasons.

1. **It helps you get interested in and involved with what you will read.** It activates your thinking. Because you know what to expect, reading the material becomes easier.

FIGURE 6-3
How to Adjust Previewing to the Material

TYPE OF MATERIAL	SPECIAL FEATURES TO CONSIDER
Textbooks	Title and subtitle Preface Table of contents Appendix Glossary
Textbook chapters	Summary Vocabulary list Review and discussion questions
Articles and essays	Title Introductory paragraphs Concluding paragraphs
Research reports	Abstract
Articles without headings	First sentences of paragraphs
Tests and exams	Instructions and directions Number of items Types of questions Point distribution
Reference sources	Table of contents Index
Newspapers	Headline First few sentences Section headings

Tip An *abstract* is a short written statement of the most important ideas in a piece of writing. Here, the word is a noun. Check your dictionary for different meanings of this word as a noun, adjective, and verb.

2. **It provides you with a mental outline of the material you are going to read.** You begin to anticipate the sequence of ideas; you see the relationships among topics; you recognize the author's approach and direction.
3. **It lets you identify what is important, thus establishing an intent to remember.**
4. **It functions as a type of rehearsal that enhances recall because it provides repetition of the most important points.**

Previewing is best used with factual material that is fairly well organized. Knowing this, you can see that previewing is not a good strategy to use when reading materials such as novels, poems, narrative articles, essays, or short stories.

DIRECTIONS   Select a chapter from one of your textbooks. To be practical, choose a chapter that you will be assigned to read in the near future. After previewing it, answer the following questions.

Exercise 3

1. What is the major topic of the chapter?

   _____

2. How does the author subdivide, or break down, this topic?

   _____

3. What approach does the author take toward the subject? (Does he or she cite research, give examples, describe problems, list causes?)

   _____

4. Construct a brief outline of the chapter.

   _____

Making Predictions

Research studies demonstrate that good readers frequently predict and anticipate the contents and organization of the material, both before reading and while they read. For example, from the title of a textbook chapter, you can predict the subject and, often, how the author will approach it. A textbook chapter titled "Schools of Management Thought: Art or Science?" indicates the subject— schools of management—but also suggests that the author will classify the various schools as artistic (creative) or scientific. Similarly, author, source, headings, graphics, photographs, chapter previews, and summaries, all of which you may check during previewing, provide additional information for anticipating content.

Making predictions is an excellent way to expand and broaden your thinking beyond the remembering and understanding levels. Predicting is an opportunity for you to apply your knowledge to new situations (applying), to examine how ideas fit together (analyzing), and to put ideas together in unique ways (creating). For a review of the levels of thinking, see Figure 1-6 on page 33.

Efficient readers frequently make predictions about organization as well as content. That is, they anticipate the order or manner in which ideas or information will be presented. For instance, from a chapter section titled "The History of World Population Growth," you can predict that the chapter will be organized chronologically, moving ahead in time as the chapter progresses. A chapter titled "Behavioral vs. Situational Approaches to Leadership" suggests that the chapter will compare and contrast the two approaches to leadership.

As efficient readers read, they also confirm, reject, or revise their initial predictions. For example, a student who read the heading "Types of Managers" anticipated that the section would describe different management styles. Then he began reading:

TYPES OF MANAGERS

Now that you have an idea of what the management process is, consider the roles of managers themselves. It is possible to classify managers by the nature of the position they hold. This section will review some of the major categories of managers. The next section will identify how these differences affect a manager's job.

The student immediately revised his prediction, realizing that managers would be classified not by style but by the position they hold.

Making predictions and anticipating content and organization are worthwhile because they focus your attention on the material. Furthermore, the process of confirming, rejecting, or revising predictions is an active one—it helps you to concentrate and to understand. Once you know what to expect in a piece of reading, you will find it easier to read.

Exercise 4

DIRECTIONS   Following is an outline of the text in Figure 6-2 on pages 152–153. Place a check mark in front of the statements you predict will appear in each heading or subheading. If possible, also indicate the section in which each statement is most likely to appear. (Indicate by marking 1, 2, 3, 4, or 5 to correspond to the headings and subheadings.)

Article title:	*The Cult of Celebrity*
Heading 1:	What Is a Celebrity?
Heading 2:	The Public's Fascination with Celebrities
Subheading 3:	Hollywood Glamour
Subheading 4:	The Need for Heroes
Subheading 5:	Athletes and Sports
Subheading 6:	The Desire for Entertainment

Statements:

_____   A. Psychologists offer varied explanations of why the public becomes impressed—"fascinated" might be the more accurate word—by highly publicized individuals.

_____   B. In pretelevision days, the publicity departments of the motion picture studios promoted their male and female stars as glamorous figures that lived in a special world of privilege and wealth.

_____   C. Journalists who write for newspapers are rarely as famous or recognized as those who serve as anchors for TV news broadcasts.

_____   D. Sports enthusiasts develop a vicarious sense of belonging that creates support for athletic teams.

_____ E. Individuals such as movie stars, pop music divas, television personalities, and talk show hosts generate a great deal of publicity in the media and on the Web, but today's celebrity status is often only temporary, as there are continually new celebrities who try to take the place of established icons in the public's esteem and interest.

_____ F. Professional and big-time college sports provide personalities for hero worship.

_____ G. Novelist Stephen King can walk down a street anywhere in the United States without being recognized.

DIRECTIONS Preview the reading titled "The Virtual House Call," in Part Six, pages 396–400. Then make a list of topics you predict it will cover. Next, read the selection. Finally, review your list of predictions and place a check mark next to those that were correct. ●

Exercise 5

DIRECTIONS Select a chapter from one of your textbooks. Preview the chapter, and then write a list of predictions about the chapter's content or organization. ●

Exercise 6

DISCOVERING WHAT YOU ALREADY KNOW

Goal 2

Discover what you already know about a topic.

Before reading, take a few minutes to discover what you already know about a topic. Doing so will make learning easier because you will be connecting new information to familiar information already in place. You will find, too, that reading material becomes more interesting once you have connected its topic with your own experience. Comprehension will be easier because you will have already thought about some of the ideas presented in the material.

Suppose you are studying a business textbook and are about to begin reading a chapter on advertising. Before you begin reading the chapter, you should spend a minute or two thinking about what you already know about this topic. Try one or more of the following techniques.

1. **Ask questions and try to answer them.** You might ask questions such as "What are the goals of advertising?" In answering this question, you will realize you already know several objectives: to sell a product, to introduce a new product, to announce sales or discounts, and so on.
2. **Relate the topic to your own experience.** For a chapter section on the construction and design of ads, think about ads you have heard or read recently. What similarities exist? How do the ads begin? How do they end? This process will probably lead you to realize that you already know something about how ads are designed.
3. **Free-associate.** On a sheet of scrap paper, jot down everything that comes to mind about advertising. List facts and questions, or describe ads you have recently heard or seen. This process will also activate your recall of information.

At first, you may think you know very little—or even nothing—about a particular topic. However, by using one of the techniques just listed, you will find that there are very few topics about which you know nothing at all.

Exercise 7

DIRECTIONS   Your instructor has assigned the reading titled "The Cult of Celebrity" in Figure 6-2. Write a list of questions, experiences, or associations that would help focus your mind on the topic of celebrity. (Hint: Think of reasons, regulation, needs, processes, and so forth.) ●

Exercise 8

DIRECTIONS   In Exercise 2 you previewed the article titled "The Virtual House Call." Discover what you already know about house calls and virtual medicine using one of the techniques described in this section. ●

Exercise 9

DIRECTIONS   Select a chapter from one of your textbooks. Preview it, and use one of the techniques described in this section to discover what you already know about the subject of the chapter. ●

Goal 3

Define your purpose for reading.

DEFINING YOUR PURPOSES FOR READING

Have you ever read a complete page or more and then not remembered a thing? Have you wandered aimlessly through paragraph after paragraph, section after section, unable to remember key ideas you just read, even when you were really trying to concentrate? If these problems sound familiar, you probably began reading without a specific purpose in mind. That is, you were not looking for anything in particular as you read. Guide questions can focus your attention and help you pick out what is important.

Developing Guide Questions

Most textbook chapters use boldfaced headings to organize chapter content. The simplest way to establish a purpose for reading is to convert each heading into one or more **guide questions** that will direct your reading. As you read, you then look for the answers. For a section with the heading "The Hidden Welfare System," you could ask the questions "What is the hidden welfare system?" and "How does it work?" As you read that section, you would actively search for answers. For a section titled "Taxonomy of Organizational Research Strategies," you could pose such questions as "What is a taxonomy?" and "What research strategies are discussed and how are they used?" (Note: This step is the "Q" in the SQ3R system, described later in this chapter.)

You may find it helpful to jot down your guide questions in the margins of your texts, next to the appropriate headings. Rereading and answering your questions is an excellent method of review.

Writing guide questions is also useful when reading difficult or lengthy articles and essays that use headings.

Formulating the Right Guide Questions

Guide questions that begin with *What*, *Why*, and *How* are especially effective. *Who*, *When*, and *Where* questions are less useful, because they may lead to simple, factual, or one-word answers. *What*, *Why*, and *How* questions require detailed answers that demand more thought, so they force you to read in greater depth.

For example, a heading in the "The Cult of Celebrities" titled "The Public's Fascination with Celebrities" could be turned into the question "Which celebrities are the public fascinated with?" but it would likely produce a list of names. A more useful question would be "Why is the public fascinated with celebrities?" which would require you to identify reasons.

Copyright © 2017 by Pearson Education, Inc.

DIRECTIONS   The following headings are found in the article titled "The Virtual House Call" on pages 396–400. In the space provided, write a question that would guide your reading.

Exercise 10

1. **HealthTap: A Doctor But Not a Doctor**

   _____

   _____

2. **Trying It Out: One Patient's Experience**

   _____

   _____

3. **Virtual House Calls: The Wave of the Future?**

   _____

   _____

Written Materials Without Headings

In articles and essays without headings, the title often provides the overall purpose, and the first sentence of each paragraph can often be used to form a guide question about the paragraph. In the following paragraph, the first sentence could be turned into a question that would guide your reading.

> Despite its recent increase in popularity, hypnotism has serious limitations that restrict its widespread use. First of all, not everyone is susceptible to hypnotism. Second, a person who does not cooperate with the hypnotist is unlikely to fall into a hypnotic trance. Finally, there are limits to the commands a subject will obey when hypnotized. In many cases, subjects will not do anything that violates their moral code.

From the first sentence you could form the question "What are the limitations of hypnotism?" In reading the remainder of the paragraph, you would easily find its three limitations.

DIRECTIONS   Assume that each of the following sentences is the first sentence of a paragraph within an article that does not contain boldfaced headings. For each sentence, write a guide question.

Exercise 11

1. Historically, there have been three branches of philosophical analysis.

   _____

   _____

2. Scientists who are studying earthquakes attribute them to intense pressures and stresses that build up inside the earth.

_____

_____

3. The way in which managers and employees view and treat conflict has changed measurably over the last 50 years.

_____

_____

4. Perhaps it will be easier to understand the nature and function of empathetic listening if we contrast it with deliberative listening.

_____

_____

5. In addition to the price of a good or service, there are dozens, perhaps hundreds, of other factors and circumstances that affect a person's decision to buy or not buy.

_____

_____

Developing Connection Questions

Connection questions require you to think about content. They force you to draw together ideas and to discover relationships between the material at hand and other material in the same chapter, in other chapters, or in class lectures. Here are a few examples:

- What does this topic have to do with topics discussed earlier in the chapter?
- How is this reading assignment related to the topics of this week's class lectures?
- What does this chapter have to do with the chapter assigned last week?
- What principle do these problems illustrate?

Connection questions enable you to determine whether your learning is meaningful—whether you are simply taking in information or are using the information and fitting it into the scheme of the course. The best times to ask connection questions are before beginning and after you have finished a chapter or each major section.

Exercise 12

DIRECTIONS Turn to Figure 6-2, "The Cult of Celebrity," on pages 152–153. Assume that it is assigned in a communications course in a chapter about the power of television and movies. Read the excerpt and write guide questions that would be useful in guiding your reading. ●

DIRECTIONS Choose a three- to four-page selection from one of your textbooks. Select pages that have already been assigned or that you anticipate will be assigned. For each heading, write guide and connection questions that establish a purpose for reading. Then read the selection and answer your questions. ●

Exercise 13

CHECKING YOUR COMPREHENSION AS YOU READ

Goal 4

Check your comprehension.

For many daily activities, you maintain an awareness of how well you are performing them. In sports such as racquetball, tennis, or bowling, you know if you are playing a poor game; you keep score and deliberately try to correct errors and improve your performance. When preparing a favorite food, you often taste it as you cook to be sure it will turn out as you want. When washing your car, you check to be sure that you have not missed any spots.

A similar type of monitoring or checking should occur as you read. You need to keep track of how well you understand. However, comprehension can be difficult to assess, because it is not always either good or poor. You may understand certain ideas and be confused by others. At times, you may miss certain key ideas and not know you missed them.

Recognizing Comprehension Signals

Read each of the following paragraphs. As you read, be alert to your level of understanding of each.

PARAGRAPH 1

Marriages around the world are either monogamous or polygamous. In Western cultures, marriages are assumed to be **monogamous**—one person is married to another person and the relationship remains exclusive. In some parts of the world, **polygamous** marriages are the accepted form, in which one person is married to multiple husbands or wives. Polygamy is legally practiced in many parts of the world, including the Middle East, South America, Asia, and some parts of Africa. Polygamy is illegal in the United States, although it is still practiced in some states.

—Kunz, *THINK Marriages and Families*, p. 5

PARAGRAPH 2

A pogonophoran lives within an upright tube of chitin and protein that it secretes around itself, with from one to many thousand tentacle-like branchiae protruding from the upper end of the tube. The branchiae are the "beard" of beard worms. Without their tubes many beard worms would look like threads that are badly frayed at one end. The branchiae are often called tentacles, but they absorb gases and are not used to capture solid food. In their typical cylindrical arrangement the branchiae resemble an intestine, complete with microvilli that increase the surface area.

—Harris, *Concepts in Zoology*, p. 573

Did you feel comfortable and confident as you read paragraph 1? Did ideas seem to lead from one to another and make sense? How did you feel while reading paragraph 2? Most likely you sensed its difficulty and felt confused. The paragraph used many unfamiliar words and you could not follow the flow of ideas, so the whole passage didn't make sense.

FIGURE 6-4
Comprehension
Signals

POSITIVE SIGNALS	NEGATIVE SIGNALS
Everything seems to fit and make sense; ideas flow logically from one to another.	Some pieces do not seem to belong; the material seems disjointed.
You understand what is important.	Nothing or everything seems important.
You are able to see where the author is going.	You feel as if you are struggling to stay with the author and are unable to predict what will follow.
You are able to make connections among ideas.	You are unable to detect relationships; the organization is not apparent.
You read at a regular, comfortable pace.	You often slow down or reread.
You understand why the material was assigned.	You do not know why the material was assigned and cannot explain why it is important.
You can express the main ideas in your own words.	You must reread often and find it hard to paraphrase the author's ideas.
You recognize most words or can figure them out from the context.	Many words are unfamiliar.
You feel comfortable and have some knowledge about the topic.	The topic is unfamiliar, yet the author assumes you understand it.

As you read paragraph 2, did you know that you were not understanding it? Did you feel confused or uncertain? Figure 6-4 above lists and compares common signals that may help you assess your comprehension. Not all signals appear at the same time, and not all signals work for everyone. As you study the list, identify those positive signals you sensed as you read paragraph 1 on marriage. Then identify the negative signals you sensed when reading paragraph 2 about pogonophorans.

Exercise 14

DIRECTIONS   Read Figure 6-2, "The Cult of Celebrity" on pages 152–153. Then answer the following questions.

1. How would you rate your overall comprehension? What positive signals did you sense? Did you feel any negative signals? Did you encounter unfamiliar vocabulary?

2. Did you feel at any time that you had lost, or were about to lose, comprehension? If so, go back to that section now. What made that section difficult to read?

3. Do you think previewing and writing guide questions (which you did in Exercise 12) strengthened your comprehension? If so, how? If not, why not? ●

Exercise 15

DIRECTIONS   Select a three- to four-page section of a chapter in one of your textbooks. Read the section, and then answer questions 1 and 2 in Exercise 14. ●

Evaluating Your Comprehension

Sometimes signals of poor comprehension do not come through clearly or strongly enough. In fact, some students think they have understood what they read until they are questioned in class or take an exam. Only then do they discover that their comprehension was incomplete. Other students find that they understand material on a surface, factual level but that they do not recognize more complicated relationships, implied meanings, or applications. Use the following process to determine whether you really understand what you read.

1. **Set checkpoints.** As you preview an assignment, identify reasonable or logical checkpoints: points at which to stop, check, and (if necessary) correct your performance before continuing. Pencil a check mark in the margin to designate these points. These checkpoints should be logical breaking points where one topic ends and another begins or where a topic is broken down into several subtopics.

2. **Use your guide questions.** Earlier in this chapter, you learned how to form guide questions by using boldfaced headings. You can use these same questions to monitor your comprehension while reading. When you finish a section or reach a checkpoint, stop and recall your guide question and answer it mentally or on paper. Your ability to answer your questions will indicate your level of comprehension.

3. **Ask connection questions.** To be certain that your understanding is complete and that you are not recalling only superficial factual information, ask connection questions.

4. **Use internal dialogue.** Internal dialogue—mentally talking to yourself—is an excellent means of monitoring your reading and learning. It involves rephrasing to yourself the message the author is communicating or the ideas you are studying. If you are unable to express ideas in your own words, your understanding is probably incomplete. Here are a few examples of effective internal dialogue.

   - While reading a section in a math textbook, you mentally outline the steps to follow in solving a sample problem.
   - You are reading an essay that argues convincingly that the threat of nuclear war is real. As you finish reading each stage of the argument, you rephrase it in your own words.
   - As you finish each section in a psychology chapter, you summarize the key points.

DIRECTIONS Read "The Virtual House Call" in Part Six on pages 396–400. Answer the guide questions you wrote in Exercise 10, page 159. ●

Exercise 16

DIRECTIONS Choose a section from one of your textbooks. Read it, and then check your understanding by using both guide questions and connection questions. List your questions on a separate sheet of paper. ●

Exercise 17

STRENGTHENING YOUR COMPREHENSION OF TEXT

Goal **5**

Strengthen your comprehension of text.

You have learned how to recognize clues that signal strong or weak understanding of reading material. This section offers some suggestions to follow when you need to strengthen your comprehension.

1. **Analyze the time and place in which you are reading.** If you've been reading or studying for several hours, mental fatigue may be the source of the problem. If you are reading in a place with distractions or interruptions, you may not be able to understand what you're reading. (See the Success Workshop starting on page 82 for suggestions on how to monitor and improve your concentration.)

2. **Rephrase each paragraph in your own words.** You might need to approach complicated material sentence by sentence, expressing each in your own words.

3. **Read aloud sentences or sections that are particularly difficult.** Reading out loud sometimes makes complicated material easier to understand.

4. **Reread difficult or complicated sections.** At times, several readings are appropriate and necessary.

5. **Slow down your reading rate.** On occasion, simply reading more slowly and carefully will provide you with the needed boost in comprehension.

6. **Write guide questions next to headings.** Refer to your questions frequently and jot down or underline answers.

7. **Write a brief outline of major points.** An outline will help you see the overall organization and progression of ideas. (See Chapter 4 for specific outlining techniques.)

8. **Highlight key ideas.** After you've read a section, go back and think about and highlight what is important. Highlighting forces you to sort out what is important, and this sorting process builds comprehension and recall. (Refer to Chapter 4 for suggestions on how to highlight effectively.)

9. **Write notes in the margins.** Explain or rephrase difficult or complicated ideas or sections.

10. **Determine whether you lack background knowledge.** Comprehension is difficult—at times, it is impossible—if you lack essential information that the writer assumes you have. Suppose you are reading a section of a political science text in which the author describes implications of the balance of power in the Third World. If you do not understand the concept of balance of power, your comprehension will break down. When you lack background information, take immediate steps to correct the problem:

   - Consult other sections of your text, using the glossary and index.
   - Obtain a more basic text that reviews fundamental principles and concepts.
   - Consult reference materials (encyclopedias, subject dictionaries, or biographical dictionaries).
   - Ask your instructor to recommend additional sources, guidebooks, or review texts.

Exercise 18

DIRECTIONS   The following three paragraphs are difficult. Assess your comprehension as you read each, paying attention to both positive and negative signals (see Figure 6-4 on page 162.). After you have read each paragraph, list the signals you received and indicate what you could do to strengthen your comprehension.

PARAGRAPH 1

The extension of civil rights was not initiated by government act; civil rights were won through a long and bitter struggle of people determined to seize the citizenship that was their birthright. Deprived of political and business opportunities for a century, bright young black men and women turned to the black church to express their hopes, energies, and aspirations. This was particularly true in the segregated South. But during the 1950s the accumulation of change began to wear the edges of racial separation thin. When a young scholar, Martin Luther King, Jr., returned from Boston University to take up the ministry at Dexter Avenue Baptist Church in 1954 in Montgomery, Alabama, he had no hint that a nationwide civil rights movement would soon swirl around him or that his name would be linked with the great march on Washington of 1963 that would help open the floodgates of integration. What made King one of the most famous Americans of his day was the energy of a suppressed American culture, which he articulated into a momentous political and moral awakening. Its successes were his; its failures revealed his limitations and exposed the deepest barriers to equality in American life.

—Wilson et al., *The Pursuit of Liberty*, p. 422

Positive signals: _____

Negative signals: _____

Strengthen comprehension by: _____

PARAGRAPH 2

In intermediary pricing, cost-plus pricing is the dominant mode among intermediaries in the marketing channel, wholesalers and retailers, where it is called *markup pricing*. These marketers deal with large assortments of products and do not have the resources to develop demand schedules for each item. Channel members' prices are not totally unrelated to demand; they do assign different percentage markups to different items based upon sales experience and estimates of consumer price sensitivity. Wholesalers and retailers will quickly lower prices if an item is not selling. Also, the intermediary's price is based upon a markup on manufacturer's selling price, or discount from manufacturer's suggested retail price. The manufacturer may have researched demand and conducted a competitive analysis before setting the price and discount schedules.

—Kinnear, Bernhardt, and Krentler, *Principles of Marketing*, p. 637

Positive signals: _____

Negative signals: _____

Strengthen comprehension by: _____

PARAGRAPH 3

As noted previously, one of the main motivations for zoologists to study development is that it provides insights regarding taxonomic relationships among groups of animals. In the early 19th century the Estonian biologist Karl Ernst von Baer made a number of observations that suggest such a relationship, although he explicitly rejected any evolutionary implications. What is known as von Baer's law states that embryonic development in vertebrates goes from general forms common to all vertebrates to increasingly specialized forms characteristic of classes, orders, and lower taxonomic levels. Thus the early embryos of all vertebrates, whether fish, frog, hog, or human, all look alike. Later it is possible to tell the human embryo from the fish but not from the hog, and still later one can see a difference between these two mammals.

—Harris, *Concepts in Zoology*, p. 130

Positive signals: _____

Negative signals: _____

Strengthen comprehension by: _____

Exercise 19

DIRECTIONS   Select three brief sections from your most difficult textbook. Choose three of the suggestions for strengthening your comprehension, and list them here. Try out each suggestion on one textbook section. Evaluate and describe the effectiveness of each.

Suggestion   **Evaluation**

1. _____   _____

2. _____   _____

3. _____   _____ ●

Goal 6

Review after reading

REVIEW AFTER READING

Once you have finished reading, it is tempting to close the book, take a break, and move on to your next assignment. If you want to be sure that you remember what you have just read, take a few moments to go back through the material, looking things over one more time to make them stick in your mind.

You can review using some or all of the same steps you followed to preview a textbook chapter (see page 150). Instead of viewing the assignment *before* reading, you are viewing it again *after* reading. Think of it as a "re-view." Review will help you pull ideas together as well as help you retain them for later use on a quiz or exam.

Be sure to test yourself, rather than simply rereading. Use the guide questions you formed after previewing to test your recall. Try to answer each question without looking at the chapter section. Then skim through the section to be sure your answer is correct and complete.

Goal 7

Strengthen your comprehension of visual aids.

STRENGTHENING YOUR COMPREHENSION OF VISUAL AIDS

Highly detailed specific information is often an integral part of course content. For instance, a sociology course may include crime-rate statistics, a chemistry course is concerned with the characteristics of atomic particles, and an art history course focuses on great works of art (painting, sculpture, and architecture).

These kinds of highly specialized information are often presented in graphic form. The term *graphic* or *visual aid* refers to all forms of visual representation of information, including maps, charts, tables, and diagrams. Textbooks in many academic disciplines use graphics to organize and present information. Below is a general strategy for reading graphics.

HOW TO READ A GRAPHIC

1. **Read the graphic at the appropriate time and place.** Look for a reference to the graphic in the text, such as "See Figure 3-1" or "As Exhibit A shows." Look at Figure 6-5 on the next page, which originally appeared in a sociology textbook. The text directs the reader's attention to the graphic by saying "National Map 11-1 shows where a minority majority already exists."

2. **Read the title or caption.** The title will identify the subject and may suggest what relationship is being described. The title of Figure 6-5 clearly identifies the subject of the map: "Where the Minority Majority Already Exists." By reading the caption, you can learn what a "minority majority" is: It is a situation in which minorities comprise a majority of the population.

3. **Determine how the graphic is organized.** Read the column headings or the labels on the horizontal and vertical axis of a graphic. Figure 6-5 is a map that shows all the U.S. states.

(Continued)

4. **Identify the variables.** A variable is something that may be different in different situations (for example, average income in one year versus another year). Decide what is being compared with what or what relationship is being described. In Figure 6-5, the legend identifies the variable being illustrated: "Percentage of total population consisting of African Americans, Hispanics, Asians, Pacific Islanders, or Native Americans."

5. **Anticipate the purpose.** On the basis of what you have seen, predict what the graphic is intended to show. Is its purpose to show change over time, describe a process, compare costs, or present statistics? The purpose of Figure 6-5 is to show areas in the United States in which minorities form a majority of the population.

6. **Determine scale, values, or units of measurement.** The legend that accompanies Figure 6-5 shows that percentages are the scale of measurement.

7. **Study the data to identify trends or patterns.** Note changes, unusual statistics, and any unexplained variations. For example, you may notice that the "minority majority" is clustered in the southern and southwestern United States. Why do you think this might be the case?

8. **Draw connections with the written content.** Take a moment to figure out why the graphic was included and what concepts or key points it illustrates or explains. Figure 6-5 was included in a section titled "Minorities"; the author likely included it to help readers understand the patterns of minority population in the United States.

9. **Make a brief summary note.** In the margin, jot a brief note about the trend or pattern the graphic emphasizes. Writing will crystallize the idea in your mind, and your note will be useful when you review. In the case of Figure 6-5, your summary note might read, "High minority populations are found in the South and Southwest, while New England has the smallest number of minorities."

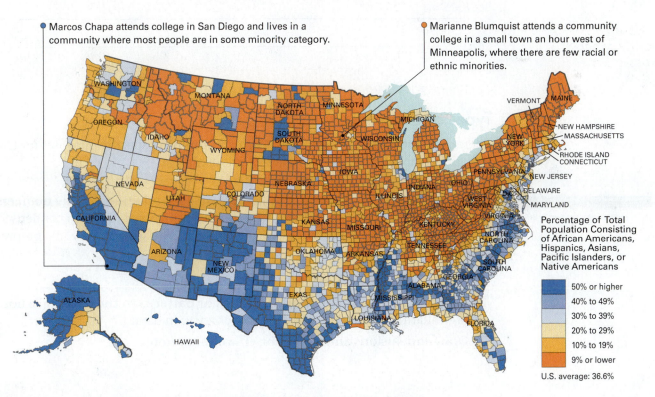

FIGURE 6-5 National Map: Where the Minority Majority Already Exists

Racial and ethnic minorities are now a majority of the population in four states—Hawaii, California, New Mexico, and Texas—as well as in the District of Columbia. At the other extreme, Vermont and Maine have the smallest share (about 6 percent) of minorities. Why do you think states with high minority populations are located in the South and Southwest?

Source: Macionis, *Society: The Basics*, p. 344. Based on U.S. Census Data.

Exercise 20

<blockquote>DIRECTIONS   To answer the following questions, refer to Figure 11-3, "Prejudice and Discrimination: The Vicious Circle" in the sample textbook chapter on page 437.</blockquote>

1. What do the title and caption indicate about the content of the graphic?

   _____

   _____

2. How is the graphic organized? (What is the shape of the graphic and why?)

   _____

   _____

3. What variables are being described?

   _____

   _____

4. Where can you find a description of each stage in the vicious circle?

   _____

   _____

5. Summarize the graphic in a sentence or two.

   _____

   _____

   _____

Types of Graphics

There are many types of visual aids. Each accomplishes specific purposes for the writer, and each describes a particular relationship.

TABLES   A table is an organized display of factual information, usually numbers or statistics. Its purpose is to present large amounts of information in a condensed and systematically arranged form. Use the following tips to increase your comprehension of tables.

1. **Determine how the data are classified or divided.**
2. **Make comparisons and look for trends or patterns in the data.** Take note of similarities, differences, and sudden changes in data.
3. **Draw conclusions and write a brief summary note.**

GRAPHS Bar graphs and line graphs both plot sets of points on a set of axis. These graphs show relationships among variables. Bar graphs make comparisons between quantities or amounts. Line graphs tend to show how a variable evolves over time. Use the following tips to increase your comprehension of graphs.

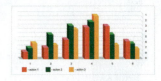

1. **Carefully examine the variables being plotted.** Read the labels to be sure you understand each variable.

2. **Use the colors in the legend to help you determine the relationship between the variables.** Use this information to make comparisons.

3. **Read any notes and captions that accompany the graph.** These may provide further information about the data summarized in the graph.

4. **Once you have determined the relationship between the variables, jot it down in the margin next to the graph.** These notes will be valuable time-savers as you review the chapter.

CHARTS Charts come in many varieties: pie charts (which show whole/part relationships), organizational charts (which show how companies are organized), flowcharts (which show how a process is performed), and pictograms (which use simplified drawings or symbols to show part/whole relationships). Follow a three-step process to read and understand charts:

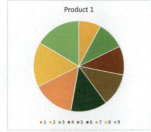

1. **Identify the subject of the chart.** What is being divided or described?

2. **Study its organization.** How is the chart divided? What do the various boxes, arrows, or sections represent?

3. **Look for trends, patterns, or conclusions.** What key points can you take away from the chart? If you are reading a flowchart, describe the process in your own words.

DIAGRAMS Diagrams help explain the relationships between parts; they may also show how processes work. Use the following suggestions to increase your understanding of diagrams.

1. **Switch back and forth between the diagram and the text paragraphs that describe it.**

2. **Get an overview.** Study the diagram and read the corresponding text paragraphs once to discover what process it is describing.

3. **Read both the diagram and text several more times, focusing on the details of the process.** Examine each step or part and understand the progression from one step or part to the next.

4. **Be sure you understand all the vocabulary included in the diagram.** If you don't, seek more information. (You can't fully understand the diagram if you don't understand some of the words used.)

5. **Study the diagram by trying to redraw it without referring to the original.** Include as much detail as possible.

6. **Test your understanding and recall by explaining the process, step-by-step, using your own words.**

MAPS Maps describe relationships and provide information about location and direction. Although most of us think of maps as describing distances and locations, maps also are used to describe placement of geographical and ecological features such as areas of pollution, areas of population density, and political data (voting districts). Use the following tips to aid your comprehension of maps.

1. **Read the caption or title.** This identifies the subject of the map.
2. **Use the legend or key to identify the symbols or codes used.**
3. **Note distance scales.**
4. **Study the map, looking for trends or key points.** Often the text that accompanies the map states the key points that the map illustrates.
5. **Write, in your own words, a statement of what the map shows.**

PHOTOGRAPHS Like other graphics, photographs can be used in place of words to present information. Photographs also are used to spark the reader's interest and, often, to elicit an emotional response or feeling. The caption on a photograph often provides a clue to its intended meaning. As you study a photograph, ask "What is my first overall impression?" and "What details did I notice first?" These questions will help you discover the purpose of the photograph.

INFOGRAPHICS Some visual aids, called **infographics**, combine many different types of visual aids into one mega-graphic. For example, an infographic about a particular country in a tourism textbook may include a time line summarizing the country's history, photos of tourist destinations within the country, a map of the country, and tables and line graphs that show tourist traffic over a number of years. To understand how the infographic presents information, be sure to check out every part of the infographic: top, bottom, right, left, and center. Remember, too, that infographics often provide only an overview of a topic. To fully understand the topic, you may need to find additional information sources.

Exercise 21

DIRECTIONS   To answer these questions, refer to the sample textbook chapter, "Race and Ethnicity," on pages 425–438. Indicate whether each statement is true (T) or false (F).

___ 1. (bar graph on p. 426) More than half of all Hispanic American and African American voters voted for Barack Obama in 2012.

___ 2. (bar graph on p. 426) In general, more men than women voted for Barack Obama in the 2012 presidential election.

___ 3. (photos on p. 428) The author chose to include these six photos as a way of showing that it can be difficult to classify individuals as belonging to a specific race.

___ 4. (Table 11-1 on p. 429) In the United States in 2011, the largest racial or ethnic classification in terms of population was "non-Hispanic European descent."

___ 5. (Table 11-1 on p. 429) In 2011, there were more people of African descent in the United States than people of Hispanic descent.

___ 6. (Figure 11-1 on p. 430) The year in which minorities will become the majority in the United States is 2034.

___ 7. (National Map 11-1 on p. 431) Racial minorities now form a majority of the population in both California and Texas.

___ 8. (National Map 11-1 on p. 431) In no part of Maine do minorities form a majority of the population.

___ 9. (Figure 11-2 on p. 434) According to the figure, the two groups of people most likely to be accepted as a member of the family are Arabs and Muslims.

___10. (Figure 11-3 on p. 437) The purpose of Figure 11-3 is to show that prejudice and discrimination mutually reinforce and lead to each other. ●

A CLASSIC SYSTEM FOR ACTIVE READING: SQ3R

Goal 8

Use and adapt the SQ3R system to fit your needs.

In this chapter you have seen that reading involves a series of skills before, during, and after reading. **SQ3R** is a reading-study system that integrates these skills and provides further strategies for learning and remembering what you read.

Psychologist Francis P. Robinson developed SQ3R to integrate study and review with active reading. Based on principles of learning theory, the SQ3R system was carefully researched and tested and has been used by millions of students. Continuing experimentation has confirmed its effectiveness.

Steps in the SQ3R System

The SQ3R system involves five basic steps that integrate reading and study techniques.

S—SURVEY Try to become familiar with the organization and general content of the material you are to read. The Survey step is often called **previewing**. After you have surveyed or previewed the material, you should know generally what it is about and how it is organized.

Q—QUESTION Try to form questions that you can answer as you read. The easiest way to do this is to turn each boldfaced heading into a question. If the material lacks headings, use the first sentences of a paragraph or two per page and turn them into questions.

R—READ Read the material section by section. As you read each section, look for the answer to the question you formed from the heading of that section.

R—RECITE After you finish each section, stop. Check to see whether you can answer your question for the section. If you can't, look back to find the answer. Then check your recall again. Be sure to complete this step after you read each section.

R—REVIEW When you have finished the whole reading assignment, go back to each heading. Recall your question and try to answer it. If you can't recall the answer, look back and find the answer. Then test yourself again.

The first two steps (Survey and Question) activate your background knowledge and establish questions to guide your reading. The last two steps (Recite and Review) provide a means of monitoring your comprehension and recall. Compared with the usual once-through approach to reading textbook assignments, which offers one chance to learn, SQ3R provides numerous repetitions and increases the amount learned.

Why SQ3R Works

SQ3R offers many advantages over ordinary reading. First, surveying (previewing) gives you a mental organization or structure—you know what to expect. Second, you always feel that you are looking for something specific rather than wandering aimlessly through a printed page. Third, when you find the information you're looking for, it is rewarding; you feel you have accomplished something. And if you can remember the information in the immediate- and long-term recall checks, it is even more rewarding.

Exercise 22

DIRECTIONS   Select a section of one of your other textbooks, including a title and subheadings. Read the section using the SQ3R method. The following SQ3R worksheet will help you get started. Fill in the required information as you go through each step.

SQ3R Worksheet

S—Survey: Read the title of the section, the introduction, and each boldfaced heading.

1. What is the section about?

   _____

   _____

2. What major topics are included?

   _____

   _____

   Q—Question 1: Turn the first heading into a question.

   _____

   _____

R—Read: Read the material that follows the first heading, looking for the answer to your question.

R—Recite: Reread the heading and recall the question you asked. Briefly answer this question in your own words without looking at the section. Check to see whether you are correct.

Q—Question 2: Turn the second heading into a question.

_____

_____

R—Read: Read the material that follows the second heading, looking for the answer to your question.

R—Recite: Briefly answer the question.

Now complete the review step.

R—Review: Look over the entire article by rereading the headings. Try to answer the questions you wrote from the two section headings.

Answer to Question 1:

_____

_____

Answer to Question 2:

_____

_____

Check to see that your answers are correct. ●

Adapting and Revising the SQ3R System

Now that you are familiar with the basic SQ3R system, it is time to modify it to suit your specific needs. Figure 6-6 on the next page lists the steps in the SQ3R method and indicates how you can expand each step to make it work better for you. All of these techniques listed are described in other chapters, as indicated in the table.

One popular modification of the SQ3R system is the addition of a fourth R—"Write"—creating an SQ4R system. SQ4R recognizes the importance of writing, note taking, outlining, and summarizing in the learning process.

Because critical thinking is an important part of learning, many students add an Evaluate step to the SQ3R system. The Review step assures you that you have mastered the material at the knowledge and comprehension levels of thinking.

FIGURE 6-6
Expanding SQ3R

SQ3R STEPS	ADDITIONAL STRATEGIES
Survey	Preview (Chapter 6) Activate your background and experience (Chapter 6) Predict (Chapter 6)
Question	Ask guide questions (Chapter 6)
Read	Highlight and mark (Chapter 4) Check your understanding (Chapter 6) Anticipate thought patterns (Chapter 9)
Recite	Outline (Chapter 4) Summarize (Chapter 4) Map (Chapter 4)
Review	Paraphrase (Chapter 4) Review highlighting, outlining, and mapping (Chapter 4) Self-test (Chapter 13)

An Evaluate step encourages you to sit back and *think* about what you have read. To get started, ask yourself questions such as:

- Why is this information important?
- How can I use it?
- How does it fit with the class lectures?
- How is this chapter related to previously assigned chapters?
- Does the author provide enough evidence to support his or her ideas?
- Is the author biased?
- What are the author's tone and purpose?

CONSIDERING YOUR LEARNING STYLE

Use the characteristics of your learning style to make SQ3R work for you.

- If you are a visual or spatial learner, draw maps or diagrams that show the chapter organization.
- If you are an auditory learner, record your questions as part of the Question step and Recite your answers to them out loud.
- If you are a social learner, study with a classmate and quiz each other during the Recite step.

Exercise 23

DIRECTIONS   Review the results of the Learning Style Questionnaire on pages 22–24. Then write a list of the changes you might make to the SQ3R method for one of your courses. •

Adapting the SQ3R System for Different Academic Disciplines

Because different academic disciplines require different types of learning, they also require different types of reading and study. Therefore, you should develop a specialized study-reading approach for each subject. The chart on the next page lists common academic disciplines, specialized types of learning required, and helpful modifications to the SQ3R system.

To adapt your study-reading system to these courses, ask yourself the following questions:

1. What type of learning is required? What is the main focus of the course? (Often the first chapter of your textbook will answer these questions. The instructor's course outline or syllabus may also be helpful.)
2. What must I do to learn this type of material?

Learn to "read" the instructor of each course. Find out what each expects, what topics and types of information are important, and how your grades are determined. Talk with other students in the course or with students who have already taken the course to get ideas for useful ways of studying.

ADAPTING SQ3R ACROSS THE CURRICULUM			
Discipline	**Kind of Learning**	**Step(s) to Add**	**What to Do**
Mathematics	Sample problems	1. Study the Problems	• Understand what theory or process the problem illustrates. • Work through and review additional practice problems.
Social Sciences	Basic principles and theories, key terminology, problems and viewpoints	1. Highlight/ Write 2. Vocabulary Review	• Highlight reading assignments. • Write outlines. • Create a vocabulary log of new terms.
Sciences	Facts, principles, formulas, and processes	1. Vocabulary Review 2. Write/ Diagram	• Learn common prefixes, roots, and suffixes. • Write study sheets to summarize information. • Draw diagrams of processes; create part/ function diagrams.
Literature	Interpreting, reacting to, and writing about literature	1. Interpret (replaces Recite) 2. React	• Analyze characters, their actions, writer's style, point of view, and theme. • Ask questions such as "What meaning does this have for me?" "How effectively did the writer communicate his or her message?" and "Do I agree with this writer's view of life?"

DIRECTIONS For each of the courses you are taking this term, explain how you will change your study-reading system to meet its characteristics and requirements. ●

Exercise 24

USING COLLEGE TEXTBOOKS
Reading Difficult Textbooks

College textbooks vary in their levels of difficulty. As you advance in your studies, you will likely encounter more difficult texts with more details and complicated concepts. Expressing the ideas of a difficult paragraph in your own words is a particularly useful strategy when reading a difficult text. If you cannot express the main point of a paragraph in your own words, most likely you do not fully understand it.

The following excerpt shows how one student wrote a marginal summary of a difficult concept from her consumer behavior textbook. Because the example clarifies the concept, notice that the student bracketed the example.

Resolving Two Conflicting Attitudes

Attitude-change strategies
A way to help consumers
understand that a negative
attitude they have about a
product may not be in conflict
with another attitude, resulting
in them thinking about the
product more positively.

Attitude-change strategies can sometimes resolve actual or potential conflict between two attitudes. Specifically, if consumers can be made to see that their negative attitude toward a product, a specific brand, or its attributes is really not in conflict with another attitude, they may be induced to change their evaluation of the brand (i.e., moving from negative to positive). For example, Richard is an amateur photographer who has been thinking of moving from his point-and-shoot digital camera to a digital single lens reflex (DSLR) camera in order to take better pictures and to be able to change lenses. However, with the recent improvements in point-and-shoot cameras, Richard is unsure of whether his move to a DSLR camera will be worthwhile. Richard loves the idea of having the ability to change lenses (attitude 1), but he may feel that purchasing a DSLR camera is an unwise investment because these cameras may be supplanted in the near future by newer types of cameras (attitude 2). However, if Richard learns that Olympus and Panasonic are developing "micro four-thirds format" small point-and-shoot size cameras that will offer interchangeable lenses, he might change his mind and thereby resolve his conflicting attitudes.

—Schiffman, *Consumer Behavior*, p. 246

Textbook Exercise 1: Defining A Textbook Passage

Define *attitude-change strategy* in your own words.

FURTHER PRACTICE WITH TEXTBOOK READING
Textbook Exercise 2: Sample Textbook Chapter

1. Preview the entire sample textbook chapter, pages 425–438. Predict what topics you expect to be covered in the chapter.
2. Use one of the strategies on page 157 to discover what you already know about the topics covered in the chapter.
3. Write at least five guide questions that would be useful in reading the chapter.
4. Read Section 11-2, "Prejudice and Stereotypes." Evaluate your comprehension, using the positive and negative signals in Figure 6-4 on page 162.
5. Write marginal summaries of difficult ideas.

Textbook Exercise 3: Your College Textbook

Choose a section from one of your most difficult textbooks. Read the section using the directions listed in Textbook Exercise 2 on the previous page.

SELF-TEST SUMMARY

Goal

What is previewing and how do you do it?

Previewing allows you to become familiar with the reading selection before you begin to read it completely. In previewing, you should note the title and subtitle, the author and source, the introduction or first paragraph, each major heading and the first sentence under it, typographical aids (italics, boldface, maps, pictures, charts, graphs), the summary or last paragraph, and any end-of-chapter or end-of-article materials. Efficient readers make predictions about what they already know about the subject with the clues they pick up during previewing; they continually revise and modify these predictions as they read.

Goal

Why is it valuable to discover what you already know before reading?

Discovering what you already know about a topic before you read will increase your comprehension. Three methods of discovery are questioning, relating to previous experience, and free association.

Goal

How can you define your purpose for reading?

Before reading, establish a purpose by developing guide questions built from boldfaced headings and from first sentences of articles or essays without headings. Ask *What*, *Why*, and *How* questions.

Goal

How can you keep track of comprehension while reading?

Keep track of both positive and negative signals by establishing checkpoints, using guide questions, asking connection questions, and using internal dialogue.

Goal 5

How can you strengthen your comprehension of text?

Strengthen your comprehension by analyzing the time and place you are studying, rephrasing, reading aloud, rereading, slowing down, writing guide questions, outlining, highlighting, writing marginal notes, and assessing background knowledge.

Goal How can you review after reading?	To review after reading use the same steps as you used for previewing. Be sure to test yourself using your guide questions.
Goal How can you strengthen your comprehension of visual aids?	To increase your comprehension of tables, graphs, charts, diagrams, maps, photographs, and infographics, closely examine the visual aid to determine what is being represented. Carefully read the title and caption, going back and forth between the text and the graphic as necessary. To ensure that you understand the graphic, summarize it in a sentence or two.
Goal What is the SQ3R system and how can you adapt it to different needs and academic disciplines?	The SQ3R method is a classic five-step method of study and review. The steps are Survey, Question, Read, Recite, and Review. By building a mental framework on which to fit information, searching for important facts, going through the repetitions involved in the 3 Rs, and feeling rewarded when you find the answers to your questions, you can improve your comprehension and recall of study material. You should adapt the SQ3R method to suit the unique characteristics of various academic disciplines. Considering the focus of the course, the types of learning required, and what you must to do to learn the material will guide you in adapting and expanding the SQ3R system.

APPLYING **YOUR SKILLS**

DISCUSSING THE CHAPTER

1. How well does previewing work for you? If it does not work well, troubleshoot the problem with another student.
2. How do you know when you don't understand what you read? What strategies do you use to improve your understanding?
3. Among the strategies provided in this chapter for improving your comprehension, which seem most helpful? Why? Do you think the strategies should vary from course to course? If so, how? (Use specific examples from courses you are taking or have taken.)
4. What features do your textbooks offer to help you understand what you read? Which features are most helpful? Why?

ANALYZING A STUDY SITUATION

Malcolm's reading assignment this week for his sociology class consists of a newspaper article, a journal article that does not contain a summary, an essay, and a short story. The class is studying the changing structure of the family during the twenty-first century.

1. Describe how Malcolm should preview the newspaper article. What should he be looking for?
2. Describe how Malcolm should preview the journal article.
3. What should Malcolm pay attention to in previewing the essay?
4. The short story was written in 1941 by an American writer. A short story is an unusual assignment in a sociology class. Realizing this, how should Malcolm preview it? What predictions can he make about the story? What should he be looking for as he reads it?
5. Which assignment is most likely to present comprehension problems?
6. How should Malcolm evaluate his comprehension for each reading selection?

WORKING ON COLLABORATIVE PROJECTS

DIRECTIONS   Choose another student with whom to work. Each student should select, from one of his or her textbooks, a chapter that he or she has already read. The students should exchange textbooks, and each should preview the selected chapter. The textbook owner should quiz the textbook previewer about what he or she learned from the chapter by previewing. Then the previewer should make predictions about chapter content and organization. Finally, the owner should confirm or deny each prediction.

Answer Key for Exercise 1
1. F   2. T   3. T   4. F   5. T

Quick Quiz

DIRECTIONS   Write the letter of the choice that best completes each statement in the space provided.

CHECKING YOUR RECALL

_____ 1. The overall topic of a chapter is typically provided in the

   a. title.
   b. first paragraph.
   c. summary.
   d. references.

_____ 2. The first sentence under each boldfaced heading in a chapter typically

   a. gives the author's qualifications.
   b. tells what the section is about.
   c. explains how the author will approach the topic.
   d. announces the author's purpose for writing.

_____ 3. The primary purpose of free association while reading is to

   a. establish your purpose for reading.
   b. distinguish between important and unimportant information.
   c. discover what you already know about the topic.
   d. outline your beliefs about the topic.

_____ 4. The most useful type of guide questions begin with the word

   a. _who._
   b. _when._
   c. _where._
   d. _why._

_____ 5. Making predictions encourages you to do all of the following _except_

   a. apply your knowledge to new situations.
   b. examine how ideas fit together.
   c. put ideas together in new ways.
   d. memorize facts provided by the text.

APPLYING YOUR SKILLS

_____ 6. Lauren uses previewing a chapter to help her identify the most important ideas in the material. In previewing, Lauren

   a. memorizes the important facts.
   b. reads the introduction, each major heading, and the summary.
   c. takes notes on the important points in the chapter.
   d. reads the entire selection carefully.

_____ 7. For her British literature course this semester, Rima is required to read a novel, several poems, three short stories, and selected chapters from a textbook. Of these assignments, the most useful one for Rima to preview would be the

   a. novel.
   b. poems.
   c. short stories.
   d. textbook chapters.

_____ 8. Cory is trying to assess her comprehension of a chapter she has been reading in an anthropology textbook. One positive signal she should look for is whether

   a. everything in the chapter seems important.
   b. she often has to slow down or reread.
   c. the vocabulary is unfamiliar.
   d. she can paraphrase the author's ideas.

_____ 9. Antonio is evaluating his comprehension of a history text. To determine whether he really understands what he has read, Antonio should

   a. read the entire chapter before stopping to assess his level of understanding.
   b. answer guide questions and ask connection questions.
   c. avoid mentally talking to himself in order to keep himself focused on the reading.
   d. skip over information that seems difficult or boring.

_____ 10. Caleb has realized that he needs to strengthen his reading comprehension in his economics class. Caleb should do all of the following _except_

   a. copy word for word sections of the text that are difficult to understand.
   b. consult additional sources if he finds he does not have sufficient background knowledge.
   c. rephrase each paragraph in his own words.
   d. read in a quiet place at a time when he has the energy to concentrate.

Expanding Your Vocabulary

LEARNING GOALS

In this chapter you will learn to

1 Expand your vocabulary.

2 Develop a strategy for learning unfamiliar words.

3 Use context clues.

4 Analyze word parts.

5 Use reference sources.

6 Handle specialized vocabulary.

7 Use systems to build your vocabulary.

LEARNING EXPERIMENT

1 Study the following list of words and meanings (list A) for one to two minutes.

List A

contrive: to plan with cleverness; to devise
comprise: to consist of
revulsion: feeling of violent disgust
retaliate: to return in kind, to get even with
repertoire: a collection of skills or aptitudes; a collection of artistic or musical works to be performed

2 Study list B for one to two minutes. Then, for each word, write a sentence using the word.

List B

ambivalent: uncertain or undecided about a course of action
infallible: incapable of making a mistake
mundane: commonplace, ordinary

relentless: unyielding, unwilling to give in
déjà vu: the impression of having seen or experienced something before

3 Wait two days and then take the following quiz. Cover the two lists above before you begin the quiz.

Match each word in column A with its meaning in column B. Write the letter from column B on the line provided.

Column A	Column B
_____ 1. revulsion	a. to return in kind
_____ 2. comprise	b. undecided
_____ 3. repertoire	c. feeling of violent disgust
_____ 4. contrive	d. feeling of experiencing something before

(Continued)

(*Continued*)

_____	5. retaliate	e. collection of skills or aptitudes
_____	6. ambivalent	f. to consist of
_____	7. relentless	g. ordinary
_____	8. infallible	h. incapable of error
_____	9. déjà vu	i. to create a clever plan
_____	10. mundane	j. unwilling to give in

4 Check your answers using the key at the end of the chapter, page 207.

The Results

Questions 1–5 were based on list A; Questions 6–10 were based on list B. You probably got more questions right for list B than for list A. Why? For list B, you used each word in a sentence. By using each word in a sentence you were practicing it. Practice is a part of a technique known as *rehearsal*, which means going back over material you are attempting to learn.

Learning Principle: What This Means to You

Rehearsal improves both your ability to learn and your ability to recall information. To expand your vocabulary, you should practice using words you identify as important to learn, whether they are part of your general vocabulary or the specialized terminology of your courses. This chapter will help you to identify the words you need to add to your vocabulary and the resources you can use to expand your vocabulary. Your vocabulary is a reflection of you, and a strong vocabulary creates a positive image. Also, a strong vocabulary will make a good impression when you are interviewing for a job.

Goal

Expand your vocabulary.

GENERAL APPROACHES TO VOCABULARY EXPANSION

Expanding your vocabulary requires motivation, a positive attitude, and skills. To improve your vocabulary, you must be willing to work at it. This chapter will focus on the skills you need to build your vocabulary. Before you continue, however, read the following general suggestions for expanding your vocabulary.

Read Widely

One of the best ways to improve your vocabulary is by reading widely and diversely, sampling many different subjects and styles of writing. Through reading, you encounter new words and new uses for familiar words. You also see words used in contexts that you have not previously considered.

College is one of the best places to begin reading widely. As you take elective and required courses, you are exposed to new ideas as well as to the words that express them clearly and succinctly. While you are a student, use your required and elective reading to expand your vocabulary.

Tip *Succinctly* means "expressed well in as few words as possible; concisely."

Use Words You Already Know

Most people think they have just one level of vocabulary and that it can be characterized as large or small, strong or weak. Actually, everyone has at least four levels of vocabulary:

1. Words you use in everyday speech or writing
   Examples: *laptop, leg, lag, lead, leave, lost*
2. Words you know but seldom or never use in your own speech or writing
   Examples: *lethal, legitimate, lawful, landscape, laid-back*

3. Words you've heard or seen before but cannot fully define
   Examples: *logistics, lament, lackadaisical, latent, latitude*
4. Words you've never heard or seen before
   Examples: *lanugo, lagniappe, laconic, lactone, lacustrine*

To build your vocabulary, try to shift as many words as possible from a less familiar to a more familiar category. Start by noticing words. Then question, check, and remember their meanings. Finally, and most important, use these new words often in your speech and writing.

DIRECTIONS In the spaces provided below, list five words that fall under each of the four categories listed above. It will be easy to think of words for category 1. Words for categories 2 through 4 may be chosen from the following list.

Exercise 1

activate	delicate	impartial
alien	delve	impertinent
attentive	demean	liberate
congruent	focus	logic
connive	fraught	manual
continuous	garbanzo	meditate
contort	gastronome	osmosis
credible	havoc	resistance
deletion	heroic	voluntary

Category 1	Category 2	Category 3	Category 4
_____	_____	_____	_____
_____	_____	_____	_____
_____	_____	_____	_____
_____	_____	_____	_____
_____	_____	_____	_____

Look for Five-Dollar Words to Replace One-Dollar Words

Some words in your vocabulary are general and vague. Although they convey meaning, they are not precise, exact, or expressive. Try to replace these one-dollar words with five-dollar words that convey your meaning more specifically. The word *good* is an example of a much-overused word that often has a general, unclear meaning, as in the following sentence:

The movie was so good, it was worth the high admission price.

Try substituting the following words for *good* in the preceding sentence: *exciting, moving, thrilling, scary, inspiring.* Each of these words gives more information than the word *good.*

Build Your Word Awareness

One of the first steps in expanding your vocabulary is to develop word awareness. Get in the habit of noticing new or unusual words when reading and listening. Pay attention to words and notice those that seem useful. Once you begin to notice words, you will find that many of them automatically become part of your vocabulary.

Your instructors are a good resource for new words. Both in formal classroom lectures and in more casual discussions and conversations, many instructors use words that students understand but seldom use. You will hear new words and technical terms that are particular to a specific discipline. Other good sources of new words are textbooks, reading assignments, and reference materials.

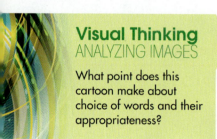

Visual Thinking
ANALYZING IMAGES

What point does this cartoon make about choice of words and their appropriateness?

Frank and Ernest

© 2011 Thaves. Reprinted with permission.

Goal 2

Develop a strategy for learning unfamiliar words.

A STRATEGY FOR LEARNING UNFAMILIAR WORDS

What should you do when you are reading a passage and you come to a word you don't know?

Despite what you might expect, looking up a word in a dictionary is not the answer. In fact, a dictionary should be your last resort—somewhere to turn when all else fails. Instead, first try pronouncing the word aloud. Hearing the word may help you recall its meaning. If pronouncing the word does not help, try to figure out the meaning of the word from its **context**: that is, the words around it in the sentence, paragraph, or passage. Very often, these surrounding words provide various clues that enable you to reason out the meaning of the unknown word. These clues are called **context clues**. You can use four basic types of context clues in determining word meanings: definition, example/illustration, contrast, and logic of the passage.

If a word's context does not provide clues to its meaning, you might try breaking the word into parts. Analyzing a word's parts, which may include its prefix, root, and suffix, also provides clues to its meaning. Finally, if word parts do not help, look up the word in a dictionary. Regardless of the method you use to determine a word's meaning, be sure to record its meaning in the margin of the page. Later, transfer its meaning to a vocabulary log (see p. 204). We discuss all these strategies in the following pages.

Goal 3

Use context clues.

Tip *Synonyms* are words that mean the same or almost the same.

USING CONTEXT CLUES

Definition and Synonym Context Clues

The most obvious type of context clue is an author's direct statement of a word's meaning. Textbook authors often provide definitions when they are aware that a word is new to the reader. Sometimes, words that are about to be defined are shown in boldfaced or italic type. For example, in the first chapter of a chemistry book, the term *chemical reaction* is defined.

A *chemical reaction* is an interaction involving different atoms, in which chemical bonds are formed, or broken, or both.

Some writers signal that they are presenting a definition with expressions such as "Mass *is . . .*" or "Anthropology *can be defined as . . .*" Other writers, however, are less direct and obvious.

Parentheses may be used to give a definition or partial definition of a word, as in the following sentence:

Deciduous trees (trees bearing leaves that are shed annually) respond differently to heat and cold than coniferous trees (trees bearing cones).

An author may use commas or dashes to set off a brief definition within the sentence.

Mendel needed true-breeding plants, plants that showed little variation from generation to generation.

The mean—the mathematical average of a set of numbers—will determine whether grades will be based on a curve.

Finally, an author may simply insert a synonym (a word with a similar meaning) directly within the sentence.

Another central issue, that of the right of a state to withdraw or secede from the Union, was simply avoided.

Exercise 2

DIRECTIONS In each sentence, locate the part of the sentence that gives a definition or synonym of the underlined word. Underline this portion of the sentence.

1. A <u>democracy</u> is a form of government in which the people effectively participate.

2. The amount of heat that it takes to melt one gram of any substance at its melting point is called the <u>heat of fusion</u>.

3. <u>Linoleic acid</u> is an essential fatty acid necessary for growth and skin integrity in infants.

4. When a gas is cooled, it <u>condenses</u> (changes to a liquid) at its condensation point.

5. But neither a monkey nor an ape has thumbs long enough or flexible enough to be completely <u>opposable</u>, able to reach comfortably to the tips of all the other fingers, as is required for our delicate yet strong precision grip. ●

Example/Illustration Context Clues

Authors frequently explain their ideas and concepts by giving specific, concrete examples or illustrations. Many times, you can figure out the meaning of the term from the example. Suppose, for instance, that you frequently confuse the terms *fiction* and *nonfiction* and you are given the following assignment by your instructor: *Select any nonfiction book and write a critical review; you can choose from a wide range of books, such as autobiographies, sports books, how-to manuals, commentaries on historical periods, and current consumer-awareness paperbacks.* From the examples given, you can easily see that *nonfiction* refers to books that are factual, or true.

Tip A *critical review* is a piece of writing that includes an evaluation, statements about the strengths and/or weaknesses of the material being reviewed.

Writers sometimes give you an advance signal that they are going to present an example or illustration. Phrases that signal an example or illustration to follow include *for example, for instance, to illustrate, such as, included are*, and so on. Read the following examples:

Some everyday, common solutions include gasoline, antifreeze, soda water, seawater, vodka, and ammonia.

Specifically, management of a New York bank developed a strategic plan to increase its customers by making them see banks as offering a large variety of services rather than just a few specialized services (for example, cashing checks, putting money into savings accounts, and making loans).

Exercise 3

DIRECTIONS   Read each sentence and write a definition or synonym for each underlined word. Use the illustration/example context clue to help you determine word meanings.

1. Maria enjoys all <u>equestrian</u> sports, including jumping, riding, and racing horses.

   _____

2. Murder, rape, and armed robbery are <u>reprehensible</u> crimes.

   _____

3. Psychological disturbances are sometimes traceable to a particular <u>trauma</u> in childhood. For example, the death of a parent may produce long-range psychological effects.

   _____

4. To <u>substantiate</u> his theory, Watson offered experimental evidence, case study reports, testimony of patients, and a log of observational notes.

   _____

5. Many <u>phobias</u> can seriously influence human behavior; the two most common are claustrophobia (fear of confined spaces) and acrophobia (fear of heights).

   _____

6. <u>Homogeneous</u> groups, such as classes made up entirely of boys, social organizations of people with high IQs, country clubs, and wealthy families, have particular roles and functions.

   _____ ●

Contrast Context Clues

It is sometimes possible to figure out the meaning of an unknown word from a word or phrase in the context that has an opposite meaning. To use a simple example, in the sentence "Sam was thin, but George was obese," a contrast of opposites is set up between George and Sam. The word *but* signals that an opposite or contrasting idea is to follow. By knowing the meaning of *thin* and knowing that George is the opposite of thin, you figure out that *obese* means "not thin" or "fat."

Often when an opposite or contrasting meaning is given, a signal word or phrase in the sentence indicates a change in the direction of the thought.

Common signal words or phrases include *on the other hand, however, although, whereas, but, nevertheless, on the contrary.* Note the following example:

> The Federalists, from their pessimistic viewpoint, believed the Constitution could protect them by its procedures, whereas the more positive Anti-Federalists thought of the Constitution as the natural rights due to all people.

In the preceding example, if you did not know the meaning of the word *pessimistic,* you could figure it out because a word appears later in the sentence that gives you a clue. The sentence is about the beliefs of two groups, the Federalists and the Anti-Federalists. The prefix *anti-* tells you that they hold opposite or differing views, and *whereas* also signals a contrast. If the Federalists are described as pessimistic and their views are opposite those of the Anti-Federalists, who are described as more positive, you realize that *pessimistic* means "the opposite of positive," or "negative."

Here is another example:

> Most members of Western society marry only one person at a time, but in other cultures polygamy is common and acceptable.

From the contrast established between Western society and other cultures, you can infer that *polygamy* refers to the practice of marriage to more than one person at a time.

DIRECTIONS Read each sentence and write a definition or synonym for each underlined word. Use the contrast context clue to help you determine the meaning of the word.

Exercise 4

1. The philosopher was <u>vehement</u> in his objections to the new grading system; the more practical historian, on the other hand, expressed his views calmly and quietly.

   _____

2. The mayor was <u>dogmatic</u> about government policy, but the assistant mayor was more lenient and flexible in his interpretations.

   _____

3. Instead of evaluating each possible solution when it was first proposed, the committee decided it would <u>defer</u> judgment until all possible solutions had been proposed.

   _____

4. The two philosophical theories were <u>incompatible</u>: one acknowledged the existence of free will; the other denied it.

   _____

5. Cultures vary in the types of behavior that are considered socially acceptable. In one culture, a man may be <u>ostracized</u> for having more than one wife, whereas in other cultures, a man with many wives is an admired and respected part of the group.

   _____

Context Clues in the Logic of a Passage

Context is often provided by logic or general reasoning about the content of a sentence or about the relationship of ideas within the sentence. Suppose that before you read the following sentence you did not know the meaning of the word *empirical*.

> Some of the questions now before us are empirical issues that require evidence directly bearing on the question.

From the way *empirical* is used, you know that an empirical issue is one that requires direct evidence. From that information you can infer, or reason, that *empirical* has something to do with proof or supporting facts.

Now suppose that you did not know the meaning of the term *cul-de-sac* before reading the following sentence:

> A group of animals hunting together can sometimes maneuver the hunted animal into a cul-de-sac: out onto a peak of high land, into a swamp or river, or into a gully from which it cannot escape.

From the mention of the places into which a hunted animal can be maneuvered—a gully, a peak, or a swamp—you realize that the hunters have cornered the animal and that *cul-de-sac* means a blind alley or a situation from which there is no escape.

Exercise 5

DIRECTIONS   Read each of the following sentences and write a synonym or definition for each underlined word or term. Look for context clues in the logic of the passage to help you figure out the meaning of each word.

1. Religious or ethical convictions make the idea of capital punishment, in which a life is willingly, even legally, extinguished, a <u>repugnant</u> one.

   _____

2. The former Berlin Wall, originally built with enough force and strength to separate East and West Germany, was <u>impervious</u> to attack.

   _____

3. When the judge pronounced the sentence, the convicted criminal shouted <u>execrations</u> at the jury.

   _____

4. The police officer was <u>exonerated</u> by a police review panel of any possible misconduct or involvement in a case of police bribery.

   _____

5. The editor would not allow the paper to go to press until certain passages were <u>expunged</u> from an article naming individuals involved in a political scandal.

   _____

Exercise 6

DIRECTIONS Each of the following sentences contains an underlined word or phrase whose meaning can be determined from the context. Underline the part of the sentence that contains the clue to the meaning of the underlined words. Then, on the line below, identify what type of context clue you used.

1. Separation of powers is the principle that the powers of government should be separated and dispersed to different parts of the government.

   _____

2. Samples of moon rock have been analyzed by uranium dating and found to be about 4.6 billion years old, or about the same age as Earth.

   _____

3. Like horses, human beings have a variety of gaits; they amble, stride, jog, and sprint.

   _____

4. In the past, malapportionment (large differences in the populations of congressional districts) was common in many areas of the country.

   _____

5. Tremendous variability characterized the treatment of the mentally retarded during the medieval era; in some cases they were treated as innocents, in others persecuted as witches.

   _____

Exercise 7

DIRECTIONS Read each of the following paragraphs. For each underlined word, use context to determine its meaning. Write a synonym or brief definition in the space provided.

1. In the laboratory, too, nonhuman primates have accomplished some surprising things. In one study, chimpanzees compared two pairs of food wells containing chocolate chips. One pair might contain, say, five chips and three chips, the other four chips and three chips. Allowed to choose which pair they wanted, the chimps almost always chose the one with the higher combined total, showing some sort of summing ability. Other chimps have learned to use numerals to label quantities of items and simple sums. Two rhesus monkeys, named Rosencrantz and Macduff, learned to order groups of one to four symbols according to the number of symbols in each group (e.g., one square, two trees, three ovals, four flowers). Later, when presented with pairs of symbol groups containing five to nine symbols, they were able to point to the group with more symbols, without any further training. This is not exactly algebra, but it does suggest that monkeys have a rudimentary sense of number.

   —Wade and Tavris, *Psychology*, p. 337

   a. summing ability _____

   b. numerals _____

   c. order _____

   d. rudimentary _____

Visual Thinking
ANALYZING IMAGES

How is this animal
releasing pheromones?

2. Many animals communicate by chemical signals, which have the unique advantage of <u>persisting</u> for some time after the messenger has left the area. They also have the advantage that they will be detected only by those with receptors that respond to the chemical, so they are less likely to attract predators. Some chemical messages have a hormone-like ability to <u>induce</u> specific behavioral responses in recipients in the same species. Such chemical messages are called <u>pheromones</u>. The best-known pheromones are insect sex attractants, many of which have been isolated and chemically analyzed. The first such pheromone to be studied was bombykol, which is produced in minute amounts by glands near the anus of the female silk moth *Bombyx mori*. The glands from half a million females had to be processed to yield 12 mg of pheromone. (One lab worker was reportedly overheard complaining, "The end is always in sight, but the work is never done.") A single molecule of bombykol is enough to <u>evoke</u> an action potential from the antenna of a male silk moth, and several hundred molecules are enough to make the male fly upwind, toward the female.

—Harris, *Concepts in Zoology*, pp. 408–409

a. persisting _____

b. induce _____

c. pheromones _____

d. evoke _____

3. Certain personal <u>characteristics</u> may explain who among the extremely poor are more likely to become homeless. These characteristics have been found to include chronic mental problems, alcoholism, drug addiction, serious criminal behavior, and physical health problems. Most of the extremely poor do not become homeless because they live with their relatives or friends. But those who suffer from any of the personal <u>disabilities</u> just mentioned are more likely to wear out their welcome as <u>dependents</u> of their parents or as <u>recipients</u> of aid and money from their friends. After all, their relatives and friends are themselves likely to be extremely poor and already living in crowded housing. We should be careful, though, not to <u>exaggerate</u> the <u>impact</u> of personal disabilities on homelessness. To some degree, personal disabilities may be the <u>consequences</u> rather than the cause of homelessness.

—Thio, *Sociology*, p. 235

a. characteristics _____

b. disabilities _____

c. dependents _____

d. recipients _____

e. exaggerate _____

f. impact _____

g. consequences _____

ANALYZING WORD PARTS

Analyzing word parts as a system for learning new vocabulary works not only for courses in which a great deal of new terminology is presented, but also for building your overall, general vocabulary.

Many words in the English language are made up of word parts called prefixes, roots, and suffixes. Think of these as beginnings, middles, and endings of words. These word parts have specific meanings, and when added together, they can help you figure out the meaning of the word as a whole. Let's begin with a few words from biology.

poikilotherm homeotherm endotherm ectotherm

You could learn the definition of each term separately, but learning would be easier and more meaningful if you could see the relationship among the terms.

Each of the four words has as its root *therm,* which means "heat." The meaning of the prefix, or beginning, of each word is given below.

poikilo-	=	changeable
homeo-	=	same or constant
endo-	=	within
ecto-	=	outside

Knowing these meanings can help you determine the meaning of each word.

poikilotherm	=	organism with variable (changeable) body temperature (i.e., cold-blooded)
homeotherm	=	organism with stable (same, constant) body temperature (i.e., warm-blooded)
endotherm	=	organism that regulates its temperature internally (within)
ectotherm	=	organism that regulates its temperature by taking in heat from the environment (outside) or giving off heat to the environment

When you first start using word parts to learn vocabulary, you may not feel that you're making progress; in this case, you had to learn four prefixes and one root to figure out four words. However, these prefixes will help you unlock the meanings of numerous other words, not only in biology but also in related fields and in general vocabulary usage. Here are a few examples of words that include each of the word parts we just analyzed:

therm	**poikilo-**	**homeo- (homo-)**	**ecto-**	**endo-**
thermal	poikilocyte	homeostasis	ectoparasite	endocytosis
thermodynamics	poikilocytosis	homogeneous	ectoderm	endoderm

The remainder of this section will focus on commonly used prefixes, roots, and suffixes in a variety of academic disciplines. In various combinations, these

FIGURE 7-1
A Sample List of
Prefixes

Psychology

neuro– nerves, nervous system   path– feeling, suffering

phob– fear   homo– same

will unlock the meanings of thousands of words. For example, more than 10,000 words begin with the prefix *non-*.

Once you have mastered the prefixes, roots, and suffixes given in this chapter, you should begin to identify word parts that are commonly used in each of your courses. For example, Figure 7-1 shows a partial list made by one student for a psychology course. Keep these lists in your course notebooks or use index cards, as described in Chapter 13.

Before learning specific prefixes, roots, and suffixes, it is useful to be aware of the following points.

1. **In many cases, a word is built on at least one root.**
2. **Words can have more than one prefix, root, or suffix.**

   • Words can be made up of two or more roots (*geo* / *logy*).
   • Some words have two prefixes (*in* / *sub* / ordination).
   • Some words have two suffixes (beauti / *ful* / *ly*).

3. **Words do not always have both a prefix and a suffix.**

   • Some words have neither a prefix nor a suffix (view).
   • Others have a suffix but no prefix (view / *ing*).
   • Others have a prefix but no suffix (*pre* / view).

4. **Roots may change in spelling as they are combined with suffixes.** Some common variations are noted in Figure 7-3 on page 195.
5. **Sometimes you may identify a group of letters as a prefix or root but find that it does not carry the meaning of the prefix or root.** For example, in the word *internal*, the letters *inter* should not be confused with the prefix *inter-*, meaning "between." Similarly, the letters *mis* in the word *missile* are part of the root and are not the prefix *mis-*, which means "wrong" or "bad."

Prefixes

Prefixes, appearing at the beginning of many English words, alter or modify the meaning of the root to which they are connected. In Figure 7-2 on pages 193 and 194, common prefixes are grouped according to meaning.

Exercise 8

DIRECTIONS   Use the prefixes listed in Figure 7-2 to help determine the meaning of the underlined word in each of the following sentences. Write a brief definition or synonym for each. If you are unfamiliar with the root, you may need to check a dictionary.

1. The instances of <u>abnormal</u> behavior reported in the mass media are likely to be extreme.

_____

2. The two theories of language development are not fundamentally <u>incompat-ible</u>, as originally thought.

_____

3. When threatened, the ego resorts to <u>irrational</u> protective measures, which are called defense mechanisms.

_____

4. Freud viewed the <u>interplay</u> among the id, ego, and superego as of critical importance in determining behavioral patterns.

_____

5. The long-term effects of continuous drug abuse are <u>irreversible</u>.

_____

PREFIX	MEANING	SAMPLE WORD
Prefixes indicating direction, location, or placement		
circum-	around	circumference
com-, col-, con-	with, together	compile
de-	away, from	depart
ex-/extra-	from, out of, former	ex-wife
hyper-	over, excessive	hyperactive
inter-	between	interpersonal
intro-/intra-	within, into, in	introduction
mid-	middle	midterm
post-	after	posttest
pre-	before	premarital
re-	back, again	review
retro-	backward	retrospect
sub-	under, below	submarine
super-	above, extra	supercharge
tele-	far	telescope
trans-	across, over	transcontinental
Prefixes referring to amount or number		
bi-	two	bimonthly
equi-	equal	equidistant
micro-	small	microscope
mono-	one	monocle
multi-	many	multipurpose

FIGURE 7-2
Common Prefixes

FIGURE 7-2
(Continued)

PREFIX	MEANING	SAMPLE WORD
poly-	many	polygon
semi-	half	semicircle
tri-	three	triangle
uni-	one	unicycle
Prefixes meaning "not" (negative)		
a-, an-, ab-	not	asymmetrical
anti-	against	antiwar
contra-	against, opposite	contradict
dis-	apart, away, not	disagree
mis-	wrong, bad	misunderstand
non-	not	nonfiction
pseudo-	false	pseudoscientific
un-	not	unpopular

Exercise 9

DIRECTIONS   Write a synonym or brief definition for each of the following under-lined words. Check a dictionary if the root is unfamiliar.

1. a <u>substandard</u> performance _____

2. to <u>transcend</u> everyday differences _____

3. <u>telecommunications</u> equipment _____

4. a <u>hypercritical</u> person _____

5. a <u>retroactive</u> policy _____

6. <u>superconductive</u> metal _____

7. <u>extracurricular</u> activities _____

8. <u>postoperative</u> nursing care _____

9. a blood <u>transfusion</u> _____

10. <u>antisocial</u> behavior _____

11. to <u>misappropriate</u> funds _____

12. a <u>microscopic</u> organism _____

13. a <u>monotonous</u> speech _____

14. a <u>pseudointellectual</u> essay _____

15. a <u>polysyllabic</u> word _____

Roots

Roots carry the basic or core meaning of a word. Hundreds of root words are used to build words in the English language. Thirty of the most common and most useful are listed in Figure 7-3. Knowing the meanings of these roots will assist you

FIGURE 7-3
Common Roots

ROOT	MEANING	SAMPLE WORD
aster, astro	star	astronaut
aud, audit	hear	audible
bio	life	biology
cap	take, seize	captive
chron(o)	time	chronology
corp	body	corpse
cred	believe	incredible
dict, dic	tell, say	predict
duc, duct	lead	introduce
fact, fac	make, do	factory
geo	earth	geophysics
graph	write	telegraph
log, logo, logy	study, thought	psychology
mit, miss	send	dismiss
mort, mor	die, death	immortal
path	feeling, disease	sympathy
phone	sound, voice	telephone
photo	light	photosensitive
port	carry	transport
scop	seeing	microscope
scribe, script	write	inscription
sen, sent	feel	insensitive
spec, spic, spect	look, see	retrospect
tend, tent, tens	stretch, strain	tension
terr, terre	land, earth	territory
theo	god	theology
ven, vent	come	convention
vert, vers	turn	invert
vis, vid	see	invisible
voc	call	vocation

in unlocking the meanings of many words. For example, if you know that the root *dic-* or *dict-* means "tell" or "say," then you have a clue to the meanings of such words as *predict* (to tell what will happen in the future), *contradiction* (a statement that is contrary or opposite), and *diction* (wording or manner of speaking).

Exercise 10

DIRECTIONS   Write a synonym or brief definition for each of the underlined words. Consult Figures 7-2 and 7-3 as necessary.

1. a <u>monotheistic</u> religion _____

2. a <u>subterranean</u> tunnel _____

3. a <u>chronicle</u> of events _____

4. a <u>conversion</u> chart _____

5. <u>exportation</u> policies _____

6. leading an <u>introspective</u> life _____

7. to <u>speculate</u> on the results _____

8. <u>sensuous</u> music _____

9. a <u>versatile</u> performance _____

10. an <u>incredible</u> explanation _____

11. infant <u>mortality</u> rates _____

12. the <u>tensile</u> strength of a cable _____

13. a <u>vociferous</u> crowd _____

14. a logical <u>deduction</u> _____

15. a <u>corporate</u> earnings report _____

Suffixes

Suffixes are word endings that often change the word's part of speech. For example, adding the suffix *-y* to a word changes it from a noun to an adjective and shifts the meaning—for example, *cloud, cloudy.*

Often several different words can be formed from a single root word with the addition of different suffixes. Here is an example:

Root: *class*
       classify
       classification
       classic

Common suffixes are grouped according to meaning in Figure 7-4.

FIGURE 7-4
Common Suffixes

SUFFIX	SAMPLE WORD
Suffixes that refer to a state, condition, or quality	
-able	touchable
-ance	assistance
-ation	confrontation
-ence	reference
-ible	tangible

FIGURE 7-4
(Continued)

SUFFIX	SAMPLE WORD
-ic	aerobic
-ion	discussion
-ity	superiority
-ive	permissive
-ment	amazement
-ness	kindness
-ous	jealous
-ty	loyalty
-y	creamy
Suffixes that mean "one who"	
-ee	employee
-eer	engineer
-er	teacher
-ist	activist
-or	editor
Suffixes that mean "pertaining to" or "referring to"	
-al	autumnal
-hood	brotherhood
-ship	friendship
-ward	homeward

DIRECTIONS Write a synonym or brief definition of each of the underlined words. Consult a dictionary if necessary.

Exercise 11

1. acts of <u>terrorism</u> _____

2. a <u>graphic</u> description _____

3. a <u>materialistic</u> philosophy _____

4. <u>immunity</u> to disease resistance _____

5. <u>impassable</u> road conditions _____

6. a speech <u>impediment</u> _____

7. <u>intangible</u> property _____

8. <u>instinctive</u> behavior _____

9. <u>interrogation</u> techniques _____

10. the communist <u>sector</u> _____

11. obvious <u>frustration</u> _____

12. global conflicts _____

13. in deference to _____

14. piteous physical ailments _____

15. Supreme Court nominee _____ ●

Exercise 12

DIRECTIONS   From a chapter in one of your textbooks, make a list of at least ten words with multiple word parts. Using Figures 7-2, 7-3, and 7-4, define as many as you can. Check the accuracy of your definitions using your book's glossary or a dictionary. ●

Goal 5

Use reference sources.

USING REFERENCE SOURCES

Once you have developed a sense of word awareness and have begun to identify useful words to add to your vocabulary, the next step is to become familiar with the references you can use to expand your vocabulary. While print versions of most reference sources are still available (and can be found in your college's library), most students now use electronic reference materials that are freely available on the Internet.

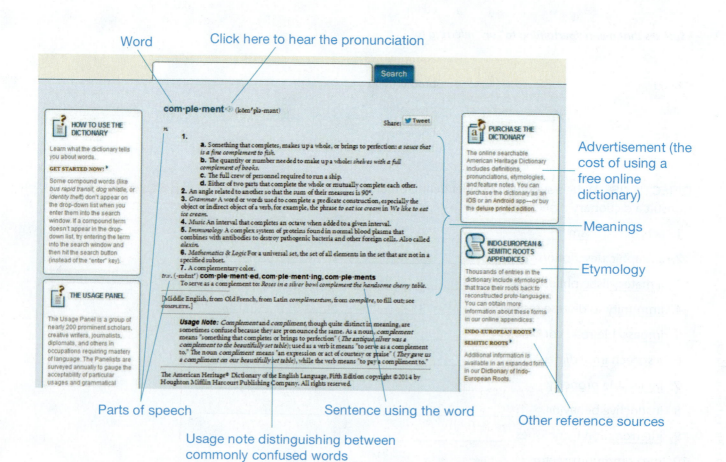

The American Heritage® Dictionary of the English Language, Fifth Edition copyright ©2014 by Houghton Mifflin Harcourt Publishing Company. All rights reserved.

General Dictionaries

Many general dictionaries are available on the Internet and as apps for your tablet or smartphone. Two of the most widely used English print dictionaries, those by Merriam-Webster and American Heritage, have Internet versions. Other dictionary sites, such as Wiktionary.org and Dictionary.com, do not have a print version.

In addition, many word-processing programs, tablets, and e-book readers have built-in dictionaries. By right-clicking or tapping on a word, you can look up its definition.

Online dictionaries have several important advantages over print dictionaries.

- **Audio component.** Many online dictionaries, such as Merriam-Webster and American Heritage, feature an audio component that allows you to hear how the word is pronounced.
- **Multiple dictionary entries.** Some sites, such as Dictionary.com, display entries from several dictionaries at once for a particular word.
- **Tolerance for misspellings.** If you aren't sure of how a word is spelled or you mistype it, several suggested words will be returned.

If you are an ESL student, you may wish to purchase an ESL dictionary. Numerous ESL dictionaries are available in paperback and online editions, including *The Longman Dictionary of Contemporary English.*

Exercise 13

DIRECTIONS   Use the sample dictionary entry on page 198 to complete the following items.

1. Which two parts of speech can the word *complement* be used as?

   _____

2. Find three meanings for *complement* and write a sentence using each.

   _____

3. Based on definition 2, in which college discipline do you think the word *complement* is often used?

   _____

Thesauruses

A **thesaurus**, or dictionary of synonyms, is a valuable reference for locating a precise, accurate, or descriptive word to fit a particular situation. Suppose you are searching for a more precise term for the expression *looked over,* as used in the following sentence:

   My instructor looked over my essay exam.

The thesaurus lists the synonyms for *looked over,* allowing you to choose the word that most closely suggests the meaning you want to convey. Choices include *scrutinized, examined, skimmed,* and so forth. The easiest way to choose a synonym is to test substitute choices in your sentence to see which one is most appropriate. (Check a dictionary if you are not sure of a word's exact meaning.)

Many students misuse the thesaurus by choosing words that do not fit the context. *Be sure to use words only when you are familiar with all their shades of meaning.* Remember, a misused word is often a more serious error than a wordy or imprecise expression.

The most widely used print thesaurus is *Roget's Thesaurus;* it is readily available in an inexpensive paperback edition. The following online thesauruses are also available:

- Roget's Thesaurus
- Merriam-Webster

Free thesauruses are available as apps for tablets and smartphones, also.

Exercise 14

DIRECTIONS   Replace the underlined word or phrase in each sentence with a more descriptive word or phrase. Use a thesaurus to locate your replacement.

1. When Sara learned that her sister had committed a crime, she was <u>sad</u>.

2. Compared with earlier chapters, the last two chapters in my chemistry text are <u>hard</u>.

3. The instructor spent the entire class <u>talking about</u> the causes of inflation and deflation.

4. The main character in the film was a <u>thin</u>, talkative British soldier.

5. We went to see a <u>great</u> film that won the Academy Award for best picture.   ●

Subject Area Dictionaries

Many academic disciplines have specialized dictionaries that list important terminology used in that field. They give specialized meanings and suggest how and when to use a word. For the field of music there is the *New Grove Dictionary of Music and Musicians*, which lists and defines the specialized vocabulary of music. Other subject area dictionaries include *Taber's Cyclopedic Medical Dictionary, A Dictionary of Anthropology*, and *A Dictionary of Economics*. Many of these dictionaries are available in hardbound copies and electronic versions. Your school's library may own the hardcopy, a subscription to the electronic edition, or both.

Exercise 15

DIRECTIONS   List below each course you are taking this term. Using your campus library or the Internet, find out whether a subject area dictionary is available for each discipline. If so, list their titles below.

Course	**Subject Area Dictionary**
_____	_____
_____	_____
_____	_____
_____	_____ ●

Vocabulary Enrichment with Electronic Sources

Many electronic textbooks (e-books, e-readers, etc.) allow you to highlight terminology that is important to learn. You can use this feature to test yourself. For a word you have highlighted, try to recall its definition, and then click on the word and compare your definition with the one that pops up.

Various Web sites are useful for vocabulary building. The Merriam-Webster Web site, for example, offers a word of the day. Wordsmith allows you to sign up to receive a word of the day via e-mail. A variety of other Web sites offer assistance with idioms, frequently confused words, and so forth. Do a Google search to locate useful sites.

LEARNING SPECIALIZED TERMINOLOGY

Goal 6

Handle specialized vocabulary.

Each subject area can be said to have a language of its own—its own set of specialized words that makes it possible to describe and accurately discuss topics, principles, concepts, problems, and events related to the subject area.

One of the first tasks that both college instructors and textbook authors face is the necessity of introducing and teaching the specialized language of an academic field. Often the first few class lectures in a course are introductory. They are devoted to acquainting students with the nature and scope of the subject area and to introducing the specialized language.

The first few chapters in a textbook are introductory, too. They are written to familiarize students with the subject of study and acquaint them with its specialized language. In one economics textbook, 34 new terms were introduced in the first two chapters (40 pages). In the first two chapters (28 pages) of a chemistry book, 56 specialized words were introduced. A sample of the words introduced in each of these texts is given below. Some of the terms are common, everyday words that take on a specialized meaning; others are technical terms used only in that subject area.

New Terms: Economics Text	New Terms: Chemistry Text
capital	matter
ownership	element
opportunity cost	halogen
distribution	isotope
productive contribution	allotropic form
durable goods	nonmetal
economic system	group (family)
barter	burning
commodity money	toxicity

Recognition of specialized terminology is only the first step in learning the language of a course. More important is the development of a systematic way of identifying, marking, recording, and learning the specialized terms. Because new terminology is introduced in both class lectures and course textbooks, it is necessary to develop a procedure for handling the specialized terms in each. (See "Systems for Learning Vocabulary" starting on page 203.)

DIRECTIONS Turn to the section titled "Prejudice and Discrimination" in Part Seven, page 437. Identify as many new terms as you can, and record them in the space provided below.

Exercise 16

Total number of specialized words: _____

Examples of specialized vocabulary: _____

_____

_____

_____

_____ ●

Exercise 17

DIRECTIONS   Select any two textbooks you are currently using. In each, turn to the first chapter and check to see how many specialized terms are introduced. List the total number of such terms. Then list several examples.

Textbook 1: _____   Textbook 2: _____
                title   *title*

Total number of specialized words: ___   Total number of specialized words: ___

Examples of Specialized Words   **Examples of Specialized Words**

1. _____   1. _____

2. _____   2. _____

3. _____   3. _____

4. _____   4. _____

5. _____   5. _____

6. _____   6. _____

7. _____   7. _____ ●

Specialized Terminology in Class Lectures

As a part of your note-taking system, develop a consistent way of separating new terms and definitions from other facts and ideas. You might circle or draw a box around each new term; or, as you edit your notes (make revisions, changes, or additions to your notes after taking them—see Chapter 2), underline each new term in red; or mark "def." in the margin each time a definition is included. The mark or symbol you use is up to you. Be sure to use a system to organize the terms for efficient study. See the section titled "Systems for Learning Vocabulary" starting on the next page.

Specialized Terminology in Textbooks

Textbook authors use various means to emphasize new terminology; these include italics, boldfaced type, colored print, marginal definitions, and a new-terms list or vocabulary list at the beginning or end of each chapter.

While you are reading and highlighting important facts and ideas, you should also mark new terminology. Be sure to mark definitions and to separate them from other chapter content. (The mark or symbol you use is your choice.)

If you encounter a new term that is not defined or for which the definition is unclear, check the glossary at the back of the book for the word's meaning. Make a note of the meaning in the margin of the page.

At the end of each chapter, use the key terms list to test yourself.

SYSTEMS FOR LEARNING VOCABULARY

Goal 7

Use systems to build
your vocabulary.

Here are two effective ways to organize and learn specialized or technical vocabulary.

The Flash Card System

Once you have identified and marked new terminology, both in your lecture notes and in your textbook, the next step is to organize the words for study and review. One of the most efficient and practical ways to accomplish this is the flash card system. You can use flash cards available online or create your own. To create your own, use a 3-by-5-inch index card for each new term. Record the word on the front and its meaning on the back. If the word is particularly difficult, you might also include a guide to its pronunciation. Underneath the correct spelling of the word, indicate in syllables how the word sounds. For the word *eutrophication* (a term used in chemistry to mean "overnourishment"), you could indicate its pronunciation as "you-tro-fi-kay'-shun." On the back of the card, along with the meaning, you might want to include an example to help you remember the term more easily. A sample vocabulary card, front and back, is shown in Figure 7-5.

Use these cards for study, for review, and for testing yourself. Go through your pack of cards once, looking at the front and trying to recall the meaning on the back. Then reverse the procedure; look at the meanings and see whether you can recall the terms. As you go through the pack in this way, sort the cards into two piles: words you know and words you don't know. The next time you review the cards, use only cards in the "don't know" pile for review. This sorting procedure will help you avoid wasting time reviewing words you have already learned. Continue to review the cards until you are satisfied that you have learned each new term. To prevent forgetting, review the entire pack of cards periodically.

Many publishers now provide free electronic flash cards with the Web materials that accompany the textbook. Check the book's preface or Web site for a list of the available study materials.

Several commercial Web sites also enable you to create your own flash cards electronically. These include Cram.com and Quizlet.

FIGURE 7-5
A Sample Vocabulary Card

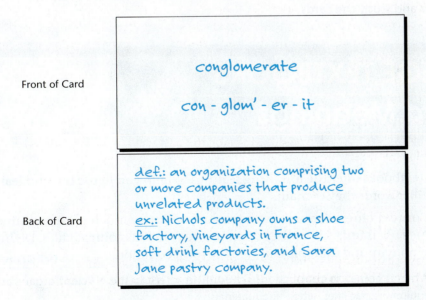

Front of Card

conglomerate

con - glom' - er - it

Back of Card

def.: an organization comprising two or more companies that produce unrelated products.
ex.: Nichols company owns a shoe factory, vineyards in France, soft drink factories, and Sara Jane pastry company.

The Computerized Vocabulary Log

Using a word processing program, create a computer log for each of your courses. Daily or weekly, review textbook chapters and lecture notes and enter specialized and technical terms that you need to learn. Use a three-column format, entering the word in the first column, its meaning in the second, and a page reference in the third. You might subdivide or code your file by textbook chapter so that you can easily find the relevant material when studying for quizzes or exams. A sample is shown in Figure 7-6.

FIGURE 7-6
Sample Vocabulary Log for a Psychology Course

Word	Meaning	Page
intraspecific aggression	attack by one animal upon another member of its species	310
orbitofrontal cortex	region of the brain that aids in recognition of situations that produce emotional responses	312
modulation	an attempt to minimize or exaggerate the expression of emotion	317
simulation	an attempt to display an emotion that one does not really feel	319

You can use your files in several different ways. If you alphabetize the words, you can create a glossary that will serve as a handy reference. Keep a print copy of your vocabulary log handy as you read new chapters and review lecture notes. When studying the words in your file, try scrambling the words to avoid learning them in a fixed order.

Exercise 18

DIRECTIONS Select two or three sets of notes on a particular topic from any course you are taking. Prepare a set of vocabulary cards for the new terms introduced. Review and study the cards. ●

Exercise 19

DIRECTIONS Select one chapter from any of the textbooks you are currently using. Prepare a vocabulary card for each new term introduced in the chapter. Review and study the cards. ●

USING COLLEGE TEXTBOOKS
Locating Word Meanings

Many textbooks offer the following features to help you figure out and learn the unfamiliar words they contain.

1. **Context clues.** Because textbook authors know much of the terminology they use is unfamiliar, they often provide obvious context clues. Definition, synonym, and example clues are the most common.

   Definition

   When it comes to production, **scheduling** refers to the efficient organization of equipment, facilities, labor, and materials.

   —Solomon et al., *Better Business*, p. 323

Synonym

Granulated sugar or crystalline sucrose, called *table sugar*, plays a variety of roles in food systems.

—Bennion and Scheule, *Introductory Foods*, p. 179

2. **Marginal definitions.** Many textbooks include the meanings of unfamiliar terms in the margin next to where each word is first used.

Proteins are one of the three macronutrients and are found in a wide variety of foods. Our bodies are able to manufacture (or *synthesize*) all of the macronutrients. But **DNA**, the genetic material in our cells, dictates the structure only of protein molecules, not of carbohydrates or lipids. We'll explore how our bodies synthesize proteins and the role that DNA plays in this process shortly.

proteins Large, complex molecules made up of amino acids and found as essential components of all living cells.

DNA A molecule present in the nucleus of all body cells that directs the assembly of amino acids into body proteins.

—Thompson and Manore, *Nutrition*, p. 130

Highlight these definitions as you read. Be sure to check them again as you review and study for exams. If there is a lot of terminology to learn, use the index card system described on page 203.

Textbook Exercise 1: Using the Index Card System

Use the index card system to create flash cards for the four key terms introduced in the three excerpts above.

FURTHER PRACTICE WITH TEXTBOOK READING

Textbook Exercise 2: Sample Textbook Chapter

Preview and read "The Social Meaning of Race and Ethnicity" in Part Seven (pp. 427–431), and then create your own vocabulary review list of terms and definitions that would be important to learn for an exam covering that material.

Textbook Exercise 3: Your College Textbook

Choose a textbook chapter that you have been assigned to read for one of your other courses. Locate the vocabulary review list. After you have read the chapter, write a definition for each term listed. (If your textbook does not contain a vocabulary list, prepare your own.)

SELF-TEST SUMMARY

Goal **1**

What can you do to expand your vocabulary?

Develop a sense of word awareness; pay attention to and notice words. Wide reading can expose you to new words and new uses of familiar words. In your speech and writing, try to use more exact and expressive words to convey your meaning more clearly and directly.

Goal **2**

What are some strategies for learning unfamiliar words?

Say the word aloud, analyze the context, break the word into parts, and (when all else fails) use a dictionary.

Goal **3**

What is a context clue and what are the four types of context clues?

The words (context) surrounding an unknown word frequently contain clues that help you figure out the meaning of an unknown word. There are four types of context clues: definition, example/illustration, contrast, and logic of the passage.

Goal **4**

How can learning word parts improve your vocabulary?

Learning word parts enables you to figure out the meaning of an unknown word by analyzing the meanings of its parts—prefixes, roots, and suffixes. Knowing just one word part can help you unlock the meaning of dozens or even hundreds of words.

Goal **5**

Which reference sources are helpful in vocabulary building?

Electronic and printed dictionaries are helpful for quick reference and serious word study. A good thesaurus is an indispensable reference for selecting the best word for a particular situation. Subject area dictionaries are very helpful in locating meanings and understanding the uses of specialized terms in the different academic disciplines.

Goal **6**

How can you identify which specialized terms to learn?

While taking notes and reading textbooks, pay attention to specialized words. When taking lecture notes, distinguish new terms and definitions by circling them, highlighting them, or labeling them in the margins of your notes. Your textbooks make special terms stand out by using italics, bold print, or color. Mark any other terms that are new to you. Consult each chapter's vocabulary list for terms to learn and use your text's glossary as a study aid.

Goal 7

How can you use the flash card system to help you learn new vocabulary?

The flash card system provides an easy and efficient way to learn words. It involves using 3-by-5-inch cards for study, review, and self-testing. Each card should contain a word and its pronunciation on one side and its meaning and an example on the other. Study these cards by looking at one side and then at the other and then reversing the process. Sort them into piles: "words learned" and "words to be learned." Concentrate on the words you haven't learned until you master them all. Keep the words fresh in your memory by reviewing them often and testing yourself frequently.

APPLYING YOUR SKILLS

DISCUSSING THE CHAPTER

1. What are some ways that you learn new vocabulary? Explain the methods that are particularly effective for you in various classes and subject areas.
2. In which academic courses would learning word parts be most useful? In which courses would it be less useful?
3. Which types of context clues are used most frequently in college textbooks?
4. One challenge of accepting a new job is learning the specialized vocabulary used by the people who work in a chosen field, company, or department. What are some ways that a new employee can most effectively deal with and learn new vocabulary?

ANALYZING A STUDY SITUATION

Erika is taking a human anatomy course and is having difficulty understanding and learning all the new vocabulary items. Her instructor uses many specialized words in lectures. Often Erika is unable to spell the words correctly, and sometimes she cannot write down the entire definition.

1. Is there a dictionary you would recommend that Erika use?
2. How can Erika decipher the meaning of some words during lectures?
3. How can Erika separate out these new terms in her lecture notes?
4. How can Erika use word parts to learn the meanings of these words?
5. How can Erika use the glossary in her textbook to help her study for exams?
6. How can Erika use the vocabulary card system to study?

WORKING ON COLLABORATIVE PROJECTS

DIRECTIONS   After listing 20 unfamiliar words and their meanings on the board, the instructor will divide the class into two groups. Group 1 should record each word on an index card, writing the word on the front and its meaning on the back. Group 2 should copy the words in a list on a sheet of notebook paper, writing the meaning to the right of each word. Both groups will be given five minutes to study the words (which have been erased from the board). Members of Group 1 should study by testing themselves using their index cards. Members of Group 2 should study by rereading their lists. During the next class, both groups will take a test on the words. Tally and compare the scores of each group, and discuss what this experiment demonstrates about vocabulary learning.

Answer Key for Learning Experiment
1. c   2. f   3. e   4. i   5. a   6. b   7. j   8. h   9. d   10. g

Quick Quiz

DIRECTIONS   Write the letter of the choice that best completes each statement in the space provided.

CHECKING YOUR RECALL

_____ 1. If you encounter an unfamiliar word when you are reading, the *first* strategy you should try is to

  a. look it up in a dictionary.
  b. pronounce it out loud.
  c. analyze its parts.
  d. figure out its meaning from the words around it.

_____ 2. Teresa read this sentence in her biology class syllabus: "We will study fission—the act of splitting into parts—during our unit on cells." The type of context clue in this situation is

  a. definition.
  b. example.
  c. illustration.
  d. contrast.

_____ 3. All of the following statements about word parts are true *except*

  a. words always have at least one prefix, one root, and one suffix.
  b. roots may change in spelling as they are combined with suffixes.
  c. some words have more than one root.
  d. words can have more than one prefix or suffix.

_____ 4. Specialized vocabulary includes words and phrases that

  a. have a different meaning in another language.
  b. are used in a particular subject area.
  c. must be defined each time they are used.
  d. are used casually in speech.

_____ 5. All of the following characterize a strong vocabulary *except*

  a. substituting long words for short words.
  b. speaking with precise, descriptive language.
  c. using unusual meanings for common words.
  d. applying technical terms in specific disciplines.

APPLYING YOUR SKILLS

_____ 6. Olivia is looking for a synonym for the word *nice*, which she tends to overuse. Which reference work should she consult?

  a. an encyclopedia
  b. a collegiate dictionary
  c. a subject area dictionary
  d. a thesaurus

_____ 7. The tour guide assured us that the trail was safe for travel, but it looked *precarious* to the rest of the group. Which word is the best synonym for *precarious*?

  a. unknown
  b. unsafe
  c. narrow
  d. messy

_____ 8. Detra plans to use the flash card system to help her learn material for a botany course. When she creates her cards, she should be sure to

  a. record as many definitions on each card as possible.
  b. keep the cards in alphabetical order at all times.
  c. include a pronunciation guide for difficult words.
  d. review the whole set of cards every time.

_____ 9. Ron has noticed that his economics instructor often introduces specialized vocabulary in class lectures. When this happens, Ron should

  a. find the term in his text and highlight it.
  b. record the term on a separate list.
  c. disregard the term if he doesn't know what it means.
  d. record and mark the term in his notes.

_____ 10. Martin is *hypersensitive* about his mother's health. Using your knowledge of roots, prefixes and suffixes, you can determine that *hypersensitive* means

  a. considerate
  b. complimentary
  c. overly concerned
  d. indifferent

Understanding Paragraphs

LEARNING GOALS

In this chapter you will learn to

1 Identify the essential elements of a paragraph.

2 Identify the topic of a paragraph.

3 Identify the main idea of a paragraph.

4 Locate topic sentences.

5 Recognize details.

6 Use transitions.

7 Understand unstated main ideas.

LEARNING EXPERIMENT

1 Study list 1 below for a maximum of 15 seconds.

List 1	List 2	List 3	List 4
KQZ	BLT	WIN	DID
NLR	FBI	SIT	THE
XOJ	SOS	LIE	CAT
BTK	CBS	SAW	RUN
YSW	NFL	NOT	OFF

2 Now, cover list 1 with your hand or a piece of scrap paper and write down, in the space provided for list 1, as many items as you can remember.

List 1	List 2	List 3	List 4
_____	_____	_____	_____
_____	_____	_____	_____
_____	_____	_____	_____
_____	_____	_____	_____
_____	_____	_____	_____

3 Follow steps 1 and 2 for each of the other three lists.

4 Check to see how many items you had correct on each of the four lists.

The Results

Did you recall more items on list 2 than on list 1? Why? Did you remember more items on list 4 than on list 3? As you must now realize, after list 1, each list is more meaningful than the one before it. These lists progress from nonsense collections of letters to meaningful letter groups to words and, finally, to words that, when strung together, produce further meaning.

Learning Principle: What This Means to You

You are able to remember information that is meaningful more easily than information that has no meaning. Once you understand how paragraphs are organized, they will become more meaningful and their contents easier to remember. In this chapter you will learn the three essential parts of a paragraph and how they work together to create meaning.

Goal

Identify the essential elements of a paragraph.

THREE ESSENTIAL ELEMENTS OF A PARAGRAPH

Paragraphs are the building blocks of textbooks and essays. A **paragraph** can be defined as a group of related sentences about a single topic. Look for these three essential elements of a paragraph:

1. **Topic**   The one thing a paragraph is about. It is the unifying factor, and every sentence and idea contained in the paragraph is related to the topic.
2. **Main idea**   What the author wants to communicate about the topic. This is the central or most important thought in the paragraph. Every other sentence and idea in the paragraph is related to the main idea. The sentence that expresses this idea is called the **topic sentence**.
3. **Details**   The proof, support, explanation, reasons, or examples that explain the paragraph's main idea.

Each of the following examples contains a group of sentences, but only one has the three essential elements that make it a paragraph. Identify the paragraph.

1. Cats frequently become aggressive when provoked. Some plants require more light than others because of the coloration of their foliage. Some buildings, because of poor construction, waste a tremendous amount of energy.
2. Some plants require more light than others because of the coloration of their foliage. Some plants will live a long time without watering. Plants are being used as decorative items in stores and office buildings.
3. Some plants require more light than others because of the coloration of their foliage. Plants with shades of white, yellow, or pink in their leaves need more light than plants with completely green foliage. For example, a Swedish ivy plant with completely green leaves requires less light per day than a variegated Swedish ivy that contains shades of white, yellow, and green in its leaves.

In the first example, the sentences were unrelated; each sentence was about a different thing, and there was no connection among them.

In the second example, each sentence was about plants—the common topic. However, the sentences together did not prove, explain, or support any particular idea about plants.

In the third example, each sentence was about plants, and all the sentences were about one main idea: that some plants need more light than others because of the coloration of their leaves. Thus, the third example is a paragraph: It has a topic—plants; a main idea—that plants require varying degrees of light due to their coloration; and supporting details—the example of the Swedish ivy. The first sentence of the paragraph functions as a topic sentence.

In order to understand a paragraph, readers must be able to identify the topic, main idea, and details. In the following paragraph, each of these parts is identified.

Main idea | As societies become industrialized, the distribution of workers among various economic activities tends to change in a predictable way. In the early stages, the population is engaged in agriculture and the collection of raw materials for food and shelter. But as technology develops, agricultural workers are drawn into manufacturing and construction. | Topic: distribution of workers

Details

Although the emphasis in this chapter is on reading paragraphs, you will find this information useful in your own writing as well. Just as readers must identify these elements, so must writers structure their paragraphs by using these elements.

HOW TO IDENTIFY THE TOPIC

The **topic** of a paragraph is the subject of the whole paragraph. It is the one thing that the whole paragraph is about. Usually, the topic can be expressed in two or three words. To find the topic, ask yourself this question: What is the one thing the author is discussing throughout the paragraph? Read the following example:

> For years, the loyal Dalmatian has been the trusted companion of firefighters. Few realize that this breed was originally chosen because of the strong bonds that the dogs formed with fire horses, protecting them and keeping them company at the station. The dogs were also expected to rouse the horses at the sound of the alarm bell, then run out and bark a warning at anyone who might be obstructing the fire house exit. The dogs would then chase the fire apparatus all the way to the scene, sometimes barking the whole way. They served the same function, essentially, as the emergency traffic signals located outside many fire stations today and the sirens on fire trucks. When horses were replaced by steam- or gasoline-driven fire engines, many departments opted to keep their beloved mascots. It is not unusual even today to see a proud Dalmatian riding on a fire engine as it races to the scene of an emergency.
>
> —Loyd and Richardson, *Fire and Emergency Services*, p. 12

In the example, the author is discussing one topic—Dalmatian dogs—throughout the paragraph. Notice how many times the word *dogs* is repeated in the paragraph. Frequently, the repeated use of a word serves as a clue to the topic of a paragraph.

DIRECTIONS Read each of the following paragraphs and then select the topic of the paragraph from the choices given.

Exercise 1

1. A reference book for criminal trial lawyers says, "Alibi is different from all of the other defenses . . . because . . . it is based upon the premise that the defendant is truly innocent." The defense of alibi denies that the defendant committed the act in question. All of the other defenses we are about to discuss grant that the defendant committed the act but deny that he or she should be held criminally responsible. Whereas justifications and excuses may produce findings of "not guilty," the defense of alibi claims outright innocence. Alibi is best supported by witnesses and documentation. A person charged with a crime can use the defense of alibi to show that he or she was not present at the scene when the crime was alleged to have occurred. Hotel receipts, eyewitness identifications, and participation in social events have all been used to prove alibis.

   —Schmalleger, *Criminal Justice*, p. 78

   a. types of criminal defenses
   b. criminal responsibility
   c. alibi as a defense
   d. justifications for crimes

2. Earth's magnetic field is known to have reversed polarity many times in our planet's history. The *geographic* North and South Poles have of course remained in place, but the *magnetic* north and south poles have changed polarity continually. Marine geophysicists interpreted the magnetic seafloor patterns as indicating that the rock either solidified during a time when Earth's magnetic field was like it is today (a "positive" value) or solidified at another time, when the field was reversed (a "negative" value). In a way, the formation of these magnetic patterns in rocks is similar to a tape recording: the changes in Earth's magnetic field are the signal,

which is being recorded on two very slowly moving "tapes" that spread in opposite directions from the ridge.

—Ross, *Introduction to Oceanography*, p. 48

    a. polarity of the Earth's magnetic field
    b. patterns of rocks on the seafloor
    c. geographic poles of the Earth
    d. work carried out by marine geophysicists

3. By law, businesses cannot discriminate against people in any facet of the employment relationship. For example, a company cannot refuse to hire someone because of ethnicity or pay someone a lower salary than someone else on the basis of gender. A company that provides its employees with equal opportunities without regard to race, sex, or other irrelevant factors is meeting both its legal and its social responsibilities. Firms that ignore these responsibilities risk losing good employees and leave themselves open to lawsuits.

—Ebert and Griffin, *Business Essentials*, pp. 30–31

    a. employment relationships
    b. employment discrimination
    c. employer ethics
    d. employee rights

4. Why is Buffalo, New York, so much snowier than frigid Winnipeg, Manitoba? Why is Miami, Florida, hot and humid while Tucson, Arizona, is hot and dry? Why does much of India experience monsoons? Why is the daily high temperature in tropical Pacific islands always near 80°F? The answers to all of these questions require an understanding of **climate**, the average weather of a place as measured over many years. The climate of a place includes various measures such as average temperature, average rainfall, and the average number of severe weather events in a given time period such as a month or a year. Climate should be distinguished from *weather*, which can be thought of as the current conditions in terms of temperature, cloud cover, and *precipitation* (rain or snowfall). Put another way, the weather in a place will tell you if you have to shovel snow tomorrow morning, while the climate in a place will tell you if you even need to own a snow shovel.

—Belk and Borden, *Biology: Science for Life*, pp. 392–393

    a. climate
    b. weather
    c. precipitation
    d. temperature

5. Did you know that dark chocolate might actually be a type of health food? Recent large studies that correlate chocolate consumption and health have found that participants who regularly consumed chocolate were less likely to suffer strokes and heart attacks. Cocoa powder (the dark, bitter powder made from the seeds inside cacao pods) contains high concentrations of flavonols, which are powerful antioxidants. Although no controlled studies have been yet done to determine whether eating large quantities of chocolate actually reduces the risk of cancer, strokes, neurological disorders, or heart disease, there would certainly be no shortage of volunteers for this research. Before you begin an uncontrolled study on yourself, however, be aware that the most sinfully delicious chocolates are also high in fat and sugar. But—in moderation—"chocoholics" with a taste for dark chocolate have reason to relax and enjoy!

—Audesirk et al., *Biology*, p. 26

    a. health benefits of chocolate
    b. fat content of chocolate
    c. causes of strokes
    d. effect of flavonols ●

DIRECTIONS For each of the following paragraphs, read the paragraph and write the topic in the space provided. Be sure to limit the topic to a few words.

1. "Diva" is an Italian word that means "goddess" and in the world of opera, it is used to describe that small handful of singers in each generation whose voices and personalities together capture the imagination of opera lovers. Some of the great divas of the last 50 years include Maria Callas, Joan Sutherland, Marilyn Horne, and Leontyne Price. The soprano Maria Callas (1923–1977) attracted an enormous following during her lifetime, and through her recordings, her reputation has grown still greater. She remains one of the top-selling operatic vocalists to this day, more than 30 years after her death. The diva is more than just a singer: she is a phenomenon, a force whose life story fascinates as much as her artistic accomplishments. There is a male counterpart to the diva—the divo—but the image has not sparked nearly the same response in audiences.

—adapted from Bonds, *Listen to This*, p. 307

Topic: _____

2. The characteristic of speed is universally associated with computers. Power is a derivative of speed as well as of other factors such as memory size. What makes a computer fast? Or, more to the point, what makes one computer faster than another? Several factors are involved, including microprocessor speed, bus line size, and the availability of cache. A user who is concerned about speed will want to address all of these. More sophisticated approaches to speed include flash memory, RISC computers, and parallel processing.

—Capron, *Computers*, p. 82

Topic: _____

3. No politician will "ever scrap my social security program." So predicted FDR when he signed the Social Security Act in 1935. He based his confidence on the provisions in the act that linked benefits to payroll deductions. Because workers contributed to the program, they would feel a "right to collect their pensions and unemployment benefits." But Roosevelt could not have imagined just how successful the Social Security program would become as time went on. It now assists more than 50 million Americans, and, over the next two decades, nearly 80 million Americans will be eligible for benefits.

—Goldfield et al., *The American Journey*, p. 733

Topic: _____

4. Earth is sometimes called the *blue planet*. Water more than anything else makes Earth unique. The **hydrosphere** is a dynamic mass of liquid that is continually on the move, evaporating from the oceans to the atmosphere, precipitating back to the land, and running back to the ocean again. The global ocean is certainly the most prominent feature of the hydrosphere, blanketing nearly 71 percent of Earth's surface to an average depth of about 3800 meters (12,500 feet). It accounts for about 97 percent of Earth's water. However, the hydrosphere also includes the freshwater found underground and in streams, lakes, and glaciers.

—Lutgens, Tarbuck, and Tasa, *Essentials of Geology*, p. 13

Topic: _____

5. Let's now deal with the fact that the human eye contains two distinctly different photoreceptor cells. Both rods and cones exist in our retinas, but they are not there in equal numbers. In one eye, there are approximately 120 million rods, but only 6 million cones; rods outnumber cones approximately 20 to 1. Not only are rods and cones found in unequal numbers, but they are not evenly distributed throughout the retina. Cones are concentrated in the center of the retina, at the fovea. Rods are concentrated in a band or ring surrounding the fovea, out toward the periphery

of the retina. These observations have led psychologists to wonder if the rods and cones of our eyes have different functions.

—Gerow, *Essentials of Psychology*, p. 138

Topic: _____

6. Democracy is a means of selecting policymakers and of organizing government so that policy reflects citizens' preferences. Today, the term *democracy* takes its place among terms like *freedom, justice,* and *peace* as a word that seemingly has only positive connotations. Yet the writers of the U.S. Constitution had no fondness for democracy, as many of them doubted the ability of ordinary Americans to make informed judgments about what government should do. Roger Sherman, a delegate to the Constitutional Convention, said the people "should have as little to do as may be with the government." Only much later did Americans come to cherish democracy and believe that all citizens should actively participate in choosing their leaders.

—Edwards, Wattenberg, and Lineberry, *Government in America*, p. 16

Topic: _____

7. When a group is too large for an effective discussion or when its members are not well informed on the topic, a panel of individuals may be selected to discuss the topic for the benefit of others, who then become an audience. Members of a panel may be particularly well informed on the subject or may represent divergent views. For example, your group may be interested in UFOs (unidentified flying objects) and hold a discussion for your classmates. Or your group might tackle the problems of tenants and landlords. Whatever your topic, the audience should learn the basic issues from your discussion.

—Gronbeck et al., *Principles of Speech Communication*, p. 302

Topic: _____

8. It seems obvious that power inequality affects the quality of people's lives. The rich and powerful live better than the poor and powerless. Similarly, power inequality affects the quality of *deviant* activities likely to be engaged in by people. Thus the powerful are more likely to perpetrate profitable crimes, such as corporate crime, while the powerless are more likely to commit unprofitable crimes, such as homicide and assault. In other words, power—or lack of it—largely determines the type of crime people are likely to commit.

—Thio, *Sociology*, p. 181

Topic: _____

9. Automated radio has made large gains, as station managers try to reduce expenses by eliminating some of their on-the-air personnel. These stations broadcast packaged taped programs obtained from syndicates, hour after hour, or material delivered by satellite from a central program source. The closely timed tapes contain music and commercials, along with the necessary voice introductions and bridges. They have spaces into which a staff engineer can slip local recorded commercials. By eliminating disc jockeys in this manner, a station keeps its costs down but loses the personal touch and becomes a broadcasting automaton. For example, one leading syndicator, Satellite Music Network, provides more than 625 stations with their choice of seven different 24-hour music formats that include news and live disc jockeys playing records.

—Agee, Ault, and Emery, *Introduction to Mass Communications*, p. 225

Topic: _____

10. Bone is one of the hardest materials in the body and, although relatively light in weight, it has a remarkable ability to resist tension and other forces acting on it. Nature has given us an extremely strong and exceptionally simple (almost crude), supporting system without giving up mobility. The calcium salts deposited in the

matrix give bone its hardness, whereas the organic parts (especially the collagen fibers) provide for bone's flexibility and great tensile strength.

—Marieb, *Essentials of Human Anatomy and Physiology*, p. 119

Topic: _____

HOW TO FIND THE MAIN IDEA

The **main idea** of a paragraph tells you what the author wants you to know about the topic. The main idea is usually directly stated in one or more sentences within the paragraph. The sentence that states this main idea is called the **topic sentence**. The topic sentence tells what the rest of the paragraph is about. In some paragraphs, the main idea is not directly stated in any one sentence. Instead, the reader must infer, or reason out, the main idea.

To find the main idea of a paragraph, first decide what the topic of the paragraph is. Then ask yourself these questions: What is the main idea—what is the author trying to say about the topic? Which sentence states the main idea? Read the following paragraph:

> The Federal Trade Commission has become increasingly interested in false and misleading packaging. Complaints have been filed against many food packagers because they make boxes unnecessarily large to give a false impression of quantity. Cosmetics manufacturers have been accused of using false bottoms in packaging to make a small amount of their product appear to be much more.

In the preceding paragraph, the topic is false packaging. The main idea is that the Federal Trade Commission is becoming increasingly concerned about false or misleading packaging. The author states the main idea in the first sentence, so it is the topic sentence.

WHERE TO FIND THE TOPIC SENTENCE

Although the topic sentence of a paragraph can be located anywhere in the paragraph, there are several positions where it is most likely to be found. Each type of paragraph has been diagrammed to help you visualize how it is structured.

First Sentence

The most common position of the topic sentence is first in the paragraph. The author states the main idea at the beginning of the paragraph and then elaborates on it.

> The good listener, in order to achieve the purpose of acquiring information, is careful to follow specific steps to achieve accurate understanding. First, whenever possible, the good listener prepares in advance for the speech or lecture he or she is going to attend. He or she studies the topic to be discussed and finds out about the speaker and his or her beliefs. Second, on arriving at the place where the speech is to be given, he or she chooses a seat where seeing, hearing, and remaining alert are easy. Finally, when the speech is over, an effective listener reviews what was said and reacts to and evaluates the ideas expressed.

Usually, in this type of paragraph, the author is employing a *deductive* thought pattern in which a statement is made at the beginning and then supported throughout the paragraph.

Goal 3

Identify the main idea of a paragraph.

Goal 4

Locate topic sentences.

Last Sentence

The second most common position of the topic sentence is last in the paragraph. The author leads or builds up to the main idea and then states it in a sentence at the very end.

> Whenever possible, the good listener prepares in advance for the speech or lecture he or she plans to attend. He or she studies the topic to be discussed and finds out about the speaker and his or her beliefs. On arriving at the place where the speech is to be given, he or she chooses a seat where seeing, hearing, and remaining alert are easy. And when the speech is over, he or she reviews what was said and reacts to and evaluates the ideas expressed. Thus, an effective listener, in order to achieve the purpose of acquiring information, takes specific steps to achieve accurate understanding.

The thought pattern frequently used in this type of paragraph is *inductive*. That is, the author provides supporting evidence for the main idea first and then states it.

Middle of the Paragraph

Sometimes the topic sentence is found in the middle of the paragraph. In this case, the author builds up to the main idea, states it in the middle of the paragraph, and then provides further elaboration and detail.

> Whenever possible, the good listener prepares in advance for the speech or lecture he or she plans to attend. He or she studies the topic to be discussed and finds out about the speaker and his or her beliefs. An effective listener, then, takes specific steps to achieve accurate understanding of the lecture. Furthermore, on arriving at the place where the speech is to be given, he or she chooses a seat where it is easy to see, hear, and remain alert. Finally, when the speech is over, the effective listener reviews what was said and reacts to and evaluates the ideas expressed.

First and Last Sentences

Sometimes an author uses two sentences to state the main idea or states the main idea twice in one paragraph. Usually, in this type of paragraph, the writer states the main idea at the beginning of the paragraph, then explains or supports the idea, and finally restates the main idea at the very end.

> The good listener, in order to achieve the purpose of acquiring information, is careful to follow specific steps to achieve accurate understanding. First, whenever possible, the good listener prepares in advance for the speech or lecture he or she is going to attend. He or she studies the topic to be discussed and finds out about the speaker and his or her beliefs. Second, on arriving at the place where the speech is to be given, he or she chooses a seat where seeing, hearing, and remaining alert are easy. Finally, when the speech is over, he or she reviews what was said and reacts to and evaluates the ideas expressed. Effective listening is an active process in which a listener deliberately takes certain actions to ensure that accurate communication has occurred.

DIRECTIONS   Read each of the following paragraphs and highlight the topic sentence.

1. First, language consists of a large number of *symbols*. The symbols that make up a language are commonly referred to as words. They are the labels that we have assigned to the mental representation of our experiences. When we use the word *chair* as a symbol, we don't use it to label any one specific instance of a *chair*. We use it to represent our concept of what a chair is. Note that, as symbols, words do not have to stand for real things in the real world. With language, we can communicate about owls and pussycats in teacups; four-dimensional, time-warped hyperspace; and a cartoon beagle that flies his doghouse into battle against the Red Baron. Words are used to stand for our cognitions, our concepts, and we have a great number of them.

—Gerow, *Essentials of Psychology*, p. 289

2. Neanderthals first appeared in the European fossil record about 150,000 years ago. Contrary to the popular image of a hulking, stoop-shouldered "caveman," Neanderthals were quite similar to modern humans in many ways. Although more heavily muscled, Neanderthals walked fully erect, were dexterous enough to manufacture finely crafted stone tools, and had brains that, on average, were slightly larger than those of modern humans. Many European Neanderthal fossils show heavy brow ridges and a broad, flat skull, but others, particularly from areas around the eastern shores of the Mediterranean Sea, are somewhat more physically similar to *H. sapiens*.

—Audesirk et al., *Biology*, p. 337

3. Ken Camp, the chief executive officer of Hillenbrand, Inc., has succinctly summed up his company's situation: "We are a very significant player in an industry that isn't growing." Hillenbrand is part of the casket industry, which is facing tough times as a consequence of the falling price of cremations. The overall price of a traditional casket burial exceeds $7,200. In contrast, the price of a cremation service has recently fallen to about $1,300. Today, nearly 400,000 fewer caskets are purchased per year in the United States than were purchased in 2008. Thus, the demand for caskets has declined in response to a decrease in the price of an already lower-priced substitute—cremation. This fact explains why Camp has concluded that the casket industry "isn't growing."

—adapted from Miller, *Economics Today*, p. 69

4. Potatoes that have been exposed to light and turned green contain increased amounts of solanine, a toxin that can cause fever, diarrhea, paralysis, and shock. (Luckily, peeling potatoes usually removes the green layer and the potato can be safely eaten. If it tastes bitter, however, throw it out.) Wild lima beans contain high amounts of cyanogenic glycosides, which can be converted to the poison, cyanide. (Lima beans sold commercially have minimal amounts of this substance, so are safe to eat.) Cassava also contains cyanogenic glycosides and has been known to cause cyanide poisoning in people who eat large amounts of this root vegetable. Raw soybeans contain amylase inhibitors, which are inactivated when cooked or fermented. Thus, many plant foods naturally contain toxins in small amounts, so though they're generally safe to eat, consuming them in very large amounts could be harmful.

—adapted from Blake, *Nutrition and You*, p. 513

5. Nonverbal signals play three important roles in communication. The first is complementing verbal language. Nonverbal signals can strengthen a verbal message (when nonverbal signals match words), weaken a verbal message (when nonverbal signals don't match words), or replace words entirely. The second role for nonverbal signals is revealing truth. People find it much harder to deceive with nonverbal signals. You might tell a client that the project is coming along nicely, but your forced smile and nervous glances send a different message. In fact, nonverbal communication often conveys more to listeners than the words you speak—particularly when they're trying to decide how you really feel about a situation or when they're trying to judge your credibility and aptitude for leadership. The third

role for nonverbal signals is conveying information efficiently. Nonverbal signals can convey both nuance and rich amounts of information in a single instant.

—Bovée and Thill, *Business Communication Today*, p. 54

6. The rate of cooling of an object depends on how much hotter the object is than the surroundings. The temperature change per minute of a hot apple pie will be more if the hot pie is put in a cold freezer than if put on the kitchen table. When the pie cools in the freezer, the temperature difference between it and its surroundings is greater. A warm home will leak heat to the cold outside at a greater rate when there is a large difference in the inside and outside temperatures. Keeping the inside of your home at a high temperature on a cold day is more costly than keeping it at a lower temperature. If you keep the temperature difference small, the rate of cooling will be correspondingly low.

—Hewitt, *Conceptual Physics*, p. 279

7. Many modern computers work solely with two values, 1 or 0. The constraint makes it difficult for a computer to evaluate vague concepts that human beings deal with on a regular basis, such as bright, slow, and light. More and more computers are becoming more capable of handling such vague concepts, thanks to the introduction of fuzzy logic. Unlike the traditional computer logic, fuzzy logic is based on the assignment of a value between 0 and 1, inclusively, that can vary from setting to setting. For example, a camera using fuzzy logic may assign bright a value of 0.9 on a sunny day, 0.4 on a cloudy day, and 0.1 at night.

—Angel et al., *A Survey of Mathematics*, p. 135

8. Because faces are so visible and so sensitive, you pay more attention to people's faces than to any other nonverbal feature. The face is an efficient and high-speed means of conveying meaning. Gestures, posture, and larger body movements require some time to change in response to a changing stimulus, whereas facial expressions can change instantly, sometimes even at a rate imperceptible to the human eye. As an instantaneous response mechanism, it is *the* most effective way to provide feedback to an ongoing message. This is the process of using the face as a regulator.

—Weaver, *Understanding Interpersonal Communication*, p. 220

9. As a result of casual dressing, the men's wear industry has changed. Men's suit sales have decreased, whereas sportswear has enjoyed tremendous growth. In the past, suits represented half of men's wardrobe purchases; now purchases are divided equally among suits, furnishings and accessories, and sportswear. As tailored clothing becomes more casual, the category distinctions become blurred. There is an intermixing of business and leisure wardrobes, such as an Armani suit jacket over jeans.

—Frings, *Fashion*, p. 80

10. During photosynthesis in green plants, as the energy of sunlight falls on the green pigment in the leaves, carbon dioxide and the hydrogens of water are used to make food, and water and oxygen are released. The release of oxygen by those first photosynthesizers was a critical step in the direction of life's development. In a sense, the production of oxygen falls into the "good news–bad news" category. It's good news for us, of course, since we need oxygen, but as oxygen began to become a prevalent gas in the atmosphere, it sounded the death knell for many of the early organisms. This is because oxygen is a disruptive gas, as demonstrated by the process of rusting metal. So, in the early days of life on the planet, many life forms were destroyed by the deadly and accumulating gas.

—Wallace, *Biology: The World of Life*, p. 167 ●

Goal **5**

Recognize details.

RECOGNIZING DETAILS

The **details** in a paragraph are the facts and ideas that prove, explain, support, or give examples of the main idea. Once you have identified the topic and main idea, recognizing the supporting details is a relatively simple matter. The more difficult job is selecting the few primary, or most important, details that clearly support the main idea.

All details in a paragraph are related to, and in some way expand, the paragraph's main idea, but not all these details are crucial to the author's central thought. Some details are just meant to describe; others are meant to provide added, but not essential, information; still others are intended merely to repeat or restate the main idea.

In contrast, the primary supporting details within a paragraph are those statements that carry the primary supporting evidence needed to back up the main idea. To find the primary supporting details in a paragraph, ask yourself the question: What are the main facts the author uses to back up or prove what she or he said about the topic?

In the following paragraph, the topic sentence is highlighted in yellow; the key primary supporting details are highlighted in green. Notice how the highlighted details differ, in the type and importance of the information they provide, from the remaining details in the paragraph.

> Like many animals, humans mark both their primary and secondary territories to signal ownership. Humans use three types of markers: central, boundary, and ear markers. **Central markers** are items you place in a territory to reserve it for you. Examples include a drink at the bar, books on your desk, or a sweater over a library chair. **Boundary markers** serve to divide your territory from that of others. In the supermarket checkout line, the bar placed between your groceries and those of the person behind you is a boundary marker, as are fences, armrests that separate your chair from those on either side, and the contours of the molded plastic seats on a bus. **Ear markers**—a term taken from the practice of branding animals on their ears—are identifying marks that indicate your possession of a territory or object. Trademarks, nameplates, and initials on a shirt or briefcase are all examples of ear markers.
>
> —DeVito, *Essentials of Human Communication*, pp. 109–110

Each highlighted detail identifies and defines one type of marker. The details in the remainder of the paragraph offer examples or explain these markers.

Exercise 4

DIRECTIONS Each of the following statements could function as the topic sentence of a paragraph. After each statement are sentences containing details that may be related to the main idea. Read each sentence and place a check mark beside those with details that can be considered primary support for the main idea statement.

1. *Topic sentence:*

    The development of speech in infants follows a definite sequence or pattern of development.

    Details:

    _____ a. By the time an infant is six months old, he or she can make 12 different speech sounds.

    _____ b. Before the age of three months, most infants are unable to produce any recognizable syllables.

    _____ c. During the first year, the number of vowel sounds a child can produce is greater than the number of consonant sounds he or she can make.

_____ d. During the second year, the number of consonant sounds a child can produce increases.

_____ e. Parents often reward the first recognizable word a child produces by smiling or speaking to the child.

2. _Topic sentence:_

In some parts of the world, famine is a constant human condition and exists for a variety of reasons.

Details:

_____ a. In parts of Africa, people are dying of hunger by the tens of thousands.

_____ b. Famine is partly caused by increased population.

_____ c. Advances in medicine have increased life expectancies, keeping more people active for longer periods of time.

_____ d. Agricultural technology has not made substantial advances in increasing the food supply.

_____ e. Because of the growth of cities, populations have become more dense, and agricultural support for these population centers is not available.

3. _Topic sentence:_

An individual deals with anxiety in a variety of ways and produces a wide range of responses.

Details:

_____ a. Anxiety may manifest itself in such physical symptoms as increased heart activity and labored breathing.

_____ b. Fear, unlike anxiety, is a response to real or threatened danger.

_____ c. Psychologically, anxiety often produces a feeling of powerlessness, or lack of direct control over the immediate environment.

_____ d. Temporary blindness, deafness, and loss of the sensation of touch are examples of extreme physical responses to anxiety.

_____ e. Some people cannot cope with anxiety and are unable to control the neurotic behavior associated with anxiety.

4. _Topic sentence:_

An individual's status or importance within a group affects his or her behavior in that particular group.

Details:

_____ a. High-status individuals frequently arrive late at social functions.

_____ b. Once a person achieves high status, he or she attempts to maintain it.

_____ c. High-status individuals demand more privileges.

_____ d. Low-status individuals are less resistant to change within the group structure than persons of high status.

_____ e. There are always fewer high-status members than low-status members in any particular group.

5. *Topic sentence:*

An oligopoly is a market structure in which only a few companies sell a certain product.

Details:

_____ a. The automobile industry is a good example of an oligopoly, although it gives the appearance of being highly competitive.

_____ b. The breakfast cereal, soap, and cigarette industries, although basic to our economy, operate as oligopolies.

_____ c. Monopolies refer to market structures in which only one company produces a particular product.

_____ d. Monopolies are able to exert more control and price fixing than oligopolies.

_____ e. In the oil industry, because there are only a few producers, each producer has a fairly large share of the sales. ●

DIRECTIONS Read each paragraph and identify the topic and the main idea. Write each in the space provided. Then underline the key supporting details.

1. Have you ever snacked on baby carrots? Did you know at the time that you were eating a functional food? A **functional food** is one that has been shown to have a positive effect on your health beyond its basic nutrients. Baby carrots are a functional food because they are rich in beta-carotene, which, in addition to being a key source of vitamin A, helps protect your cells from damaging substances that can increase your risk of some chronic diseases such as cancer. In other words, the beta-carotene's function goes beyond its basic nutritional role as a source of vitamin A, because it may also help fight cancer. Oats are another functional food because they contain the soluble fiber beta-glucan, which has been shown to lower cholesterol levels. This can play a positive role in lowering the risk for heart disease.

—Blake, *Nutrition and You*, p. 52

Topic: _____

Main idea: _____

2. There are a number of reasons why there has been an increase in the demand for nurses, not the least of which is the aging of the U.S. population. Older people use hospitals more and have chronic ailments that require more nursing. Moreover, as hospitals reduce the length of stay of patients, people who are discharged earlier than in previous years need more home care, usually provided by nurses. At the same time as demand has been rising, the supply of nurses has decreased somewhat. The age distribution of women between 18 and 24 has decreased in the past decade. Because this is the group from which nurses traditionally come, there have been fewer potential nurses. In addition, women have more alternatives in the labor market than they did years ago.

—Miller, *Economics Today*, p. 84

Topic: _____

Main idea: _____

_____

3. Surveys by telephone, particularly those that are locally based, are used extensively by research firms. The telephone survey has four major advantages: (1) The

feedback is immediate, (2) the telephone is a more personal form of communication, (3) it's less intrusive than interviewers going door to door, and (4) the response rate, if the survey is short and handled by skilled phone interviewers, can reach 80 to 90 percent. The major disadvantage of telephone surveys is the difficulty in getting access to telephone numbers. In many urban areas, as many as one-third to one-half of all numbers are unlisted. Although researchers can let a computer program pick numbers through random dialing, this method is not as effective as actually knowing who is being called. Another barrier is convincing respondents that a legitimate poll or survey is being taken. Far too many salespeople, and even charitable organizations, attempt to sell goods or get donations by posing as researchers.

—Wilcox and Camea, *Public Relations*, p. 145

Topic: _____

Main idea: _____

4. Put in simple terms, pronunciation means saying a word the way it should be said. Pronunciation is not always an easy task, and several characteristics of the English language make the task even harder. First, sometimes a letter in a word is silent; for instance, the *w* in *sword* and the *t* in *often*. Remember, you cannot always tell how to pronounce a word just by looking at it. When you are not sure you are saying a word correctly, consult a standard dictionary. Second, there are many ways to pronounce the same vowel in our language. For example, consider the six pronunciations of the letter *o* for the following words: *do, no, dot, oar, woman,* and *women.* Even some words that are spelled alike can require different pronunciations depending on the form they take. For instance, the word *read* as in "Read the same passage you read yesterday." Third, correct pronunciation requires knowing how to accent words of more than one syllable. This is more difficult in some cases than in others. While the word *contact* is accented the same regardless of whether it is used as a noun, verb, adverb, or adjective, the similar word *contract* has the accent on the first syllable when used as a noun but on the second syllable when used as a verb.

—Koch, *Speaking with a Purpose*, p. 110

Topic: _____

Main idea: _____

5. The role of the pharmacist is extensive and varies significantly depending on the practice setting. For example, in a community pharmacy setting the pharmacist might counsel patients about over-the-counter remedies, whereas in a hospital pharmacy setting the pharmacist might advise physicians about the best drugs to prescribe for certain indications. The primary jobs of all pharmacists are to dispense medications prescribed by authorized medical professionals and provide vital information to patients about medications and their use. Pharmacists also monitor the health and progress of patients in response to drug therapy to ensure that the medications being used are safe and effective.

—Johnston, *Pharmacy Technician*, p. 13

Topic: _____

Main idea: _____

6. Most extinction occurs gradually, one species at a time. The rate at which this type of extinction occurs is referred to as the *background extinction rate*. However, Earth has seen five events of staggering proportions that killed off massive numbers of species at once. These episodes, called mass extinction events, have occurred at widely spaced intervals in Earth history and have wiped out 50–95% of our planet's species each time. The best-known mass extinction occurred 65 million years ago and brought an end to the dinosaurs (although birds are modern representatives of dinosaurs).

—Withgott and Brennan, *Environment*, p. 148

Topic: _____

Main idea: _____

7. In a public speaking situation, just as the speaker and the listener have ethical obligations, so does the critic. First, the ethical critic separates personal feelings about the speaker from the evaluation of the speech. A liking for the speaker should not lead you to give positive evaluations of the speech, nor should dislike for the speaker lead you to give negative evaluations. Second, the ethical critic separates personal feelings about the issues from an evaluation of the validity of the arguments. Recognize the validity of an argument even if it contradicts a deeply held belief; at the same time, recognize the flaws of an argument even if it supports a deeply held belief. Third, the ethical critic is culturally sensitive and doesn't negatively evaluate customs and beliefs simply because they differ from her or his own. Conversely, the ethical critic does not positively evaluate a speech just because it supports her or his own cultural beliefs and values.

—DeVito, *Essentials of Human Communication*, p. 278

Topic: _____

Main idea: _____

8. Each state is governed by a separate and unique constitution that spells out the basic rules of that state's political game. Every state elects a governor as its chief executive officer, and most states have a legislature with two chambers like Congress (except for Nebraska, which only has a senate). However, the states endow their governors with different powers and organize and elect their legislatures differently. Each state's constitution was written under unique historical conditions and with a unique set of philosophical principles in mind. Each is unique in its length and provisions. Some are modern documents; others were written over 100 years ago. The differences among these documents also reflect the diversity—social, economic, geographic, historic, and political—of the states.

—Edwards, Wattenberg, and Lineberry, *Government in America*, p. 653

Topic: _____

Main idea: _____

_____

9. Each year, the government's Department of Housing and Urban Development conducts a national survey of cities and towns to find out how many people in the United States are homeless. The 2011 survey found about 636,000 people living in shelters, in transitional housing, and on the street on a single night in January. But, the government estimates, a much larger number—approximately 1.6 million people—are homeless for at least some time during the course of the year. As with earlier estimates of the homeless population, critics claimed that the HUD estimate undercounted the homeless, who may well have numbered several million people. Some estimates suggest that as many as 3 million people are homeless for at least one night in a given year. In addition, they add, evidence suggests that the number of homeless people in the United States is increasing.

—Macionis, *Society: The Basics*, p. 270

Topic: _____

Main idea: _____

10. Gentrification refers to the movement of middle-class people into rundown areas of a city. They are attracted by the low prices for large houses that, although deteriorated, can be restored. A positive consequence is an improvement in the appearance of some urban neighborhoods—freshly painted buildings, well-groomed lawns, and the absence of boarded-up windows. However, a negative consequence is that the

poor residents are displaced by the more well-to-do newcomers. Tension between the gentrifiers and those being displaced is widespread.

—Henslin, *Essentials of Sociology*, p. 402

Topic: _____

Main idea: _____ ●

Goal 6

Use transitions.

TRANSITIONS

Transitions are linking words or phrases used to lead the reader from one idea to another. Transitions make clear the connection between a paragraph's primary details. If you see the phrase *for instance* at the beginning of a sentence, then you know that an example will follow. When you see the phrase *on the other hand*, you can predict that a different, opposing idea will follow. In the next chapter, you will see that transitional words also signal the author's organization.

Figure 8-1 presents a list of commonly used transitions and indicates what they tell you. If you get in the habit of recognizing transitions, you will see that they often guide you through a paragraph, helping you to read it more easily.

In the following paragraph, notice how the highlighted transitions lead you from one important detail to the next.

No discussion of communication in the workplace can omit a discussion of sexual harassment, one of organizations' major problems today. How can you avoid sexual harassment behaviors? You can avoid conveying messages that might be considered sexual harassment by following these suggestions. First, begin with the assumption that others at work are not interested in your sexual advances, sexual stories and jokes, or sexual gestures. Second, listen and watch for negative reactions to any

FIGURE 8-1
Common Transitions

TYPE OF TRANSITION	EXAMPLES	WHAT THEY TELL THE READER
Time sequence	first, later, next, finally	The author is arranging ideas in the order in which they happened.
Illustration	for example, for instance, to illustrate, such as	An example will follow.
Listing	first, second, third, last, another, next	The author is marking or identifying each major point (sometimes these may be used to suggest order of importance).
Continuation	also, in addition, and, further, another	The author is continuing with the same idea and is going to provide additional information.
Contrast	on the other hand, in contrast, however	The author is switching to a different, opposite, or contrasting idea than previously discussed.
Comparison	like, likewise, similarly	The writer will show how the previous idea is similar to what follows.
Cause–effect	because, thus, therefore, since, consequently	The writer will show a connection between two or more things, how one thing caused another, or how something happened as a result of something else.
Summation	thus, in short, to conclude	The writer will state or restate his or her main point.

sex-related discussion. Use the suggestions and techniques discussed throughout this book (such as perception checking and critical listening) to become aware of such reactions. When in doubt, find out; ask questions, for example. Third, avoid saying or doing anything you think your parent, partner, or child would find offensive in the behavior of someone with whom she or he worked.

—adapted from DeVito, *Human Communication*, p. 256

However, not all paragraphs contain such obvious transitions, and not all transitions serve as such clear markers of major details.

Exercise 6

DIRECTIONS Circle each transition used in the paragraphs in Exercise 5. ●

UNSTATED MAIN IDEAS

Occasionally, a writer does not directly state a paragraph's main idea in a topic sentence. Instead, he or she leaves it up to the reader to infer, or reason out, the main idea. A paragraph with an **unstated main idea** contains only details or specifics that are related to a given topic. To read this type of paragraph, start as you would for paragraphs with stated main ideas. Ask yourself the question for finding the topic: What is the one thing the author is discussing throughout the paragraph? Then try to think of a sentence about the topic that all the details included in the paragraph would support.

Read the paragraph in the following example. First, identify the topic. Then study the details and think of a general statement that all the details in the paragraph would support or prove.

Goal 7

Understand unstated main ideas.

> Suppose a group of plumbers in a community decide to set standard prices for repair services and agree to quote the same price for the same job. Is this ethical? Suppose a group of automobile dealers agree to abide strictly by the used-car Kelly Blue Book prices on trade-ins. Is this ethical? Two meat supply houses serving a large university submit identical bids each month for the meat contract. Is this ethical?

Tip *Price fixing* is an illegal agreement in which companies in the same industry charge the same price for specific items or services. (Note: Here, *fix* does *not* mean "repair.")

This paragraph describes three specific instances in which there was agreement to fix prices. Clearly, the author's main idea is whether price fixing is ethical, but that main idea is not directly stated in a sentence anywhere within the passage.

Exercise 7

DIRECTIONS In the following paragraphs the main idea is not directly stated. Read each paragraph, identify the topic, and write it in the space provided. Then write a sentence that expresses the main idea of the passage.

1. What do a cast-iron skillet, the salt on an icy road, and the copper pipes in some houses have in common? They're made from some of the same minerals that play essential roles in your body. From iron to sodium to copper, these rocky substances occur as part of the earthen world around you and are necessary for your day-to-day functioning. Along with another essential nutrient, water, minerals help chemical reactions take place in your cells, help your muscles contract, and keep your heart beating.

—Blake, *Nutrition and You*, p. 258

Topic: _____

Main idea: _____

2. According to the most recent statistics, more than 100,000 people in the United States are shot in murders, assaults, suicides, accidents, or by police intervention each year. More than 33,000 died from gun violence last year, whereas many who survived experienced significant physical and emotional repercussions.

The presence of a gun in the home triples the risk of a homicide there. The presence of a gun in the home increases suicide risk by more than five times.

—adapted from Donatelle, *Health: The Basics*, p. 105

Topic: _____

Main idea: _____

3. A number of companies face the issue of religion in the workplace. On the one hand, some employees feel they should be able to express their beliefs in the workplace and not be forced to "check their faith at the door" when they come to work. On the other hand, companies want to avoid situations in which openly expressed religious differences cause friction between employees or distract employees from their responsibilities. To help address such concerns, firms such as Ford, Intel, Texas Instruments, and American Airlines allow employees to form faith-based employee support groups as part of their diversity strategies. In contrast, Procter & Gamble is among the companies that don't allow organized religious activities at their facilities.

—adapted from Thill and Bovée, *Excellence in Business Communication*, p. 73

Topic: _____

Main idea: _____

_____

4. The world population of domesticated animals raised for food rose from 7.2 billion animals to 24.9 billion animals between 1961 and 2008. Most of these animals are chickens. Global meat production has increased fivefold since 1950, and per capita meat consumption has doubled. The United Nations Food and Agriculture Organization (FAO) estimates that as more developing nations go through the demographic transition and become wealthier, total meat consumption will nearly double by the year 2050.

—Withgott and Brennan, *Environment*, p. 267

Topic: _____

Main idea: _____

5. A number of ideas are being tested for how cancers get going in the first place, but a common thread that runs through these ideas is that, for cells to be brought to a cancerous state, two things are required: Their accelerators must get stuck and their brakes must fail. The control mechanisms that *induce* cell division must become hyperactive, and the mechanisms that *suppress* cell division must fail to perform. There are normal genes that induce cell division, but that when *mutated* can cause cancer; these are the stuck-accelerator genes, called oncogenes. Then there are genes that normally suppress cell division, but that can cause cancer by acting like failed brakes. These are tumor suppressor genes. Note that *both* kinds of genes must malfunction for cancer to get going.

—Krogh, *A Brief Guide to Biology*, p. 148

Topic: _____

Main idea: _____

6. Severe punishment may generate such anxiety in children that they do not learn the lesson the punishment was designed to teach. Moreover, as a reaction to punishment that they regard as unfair, children may avoid punitive parents, who therefore will have fewer opportunities to teach and guide the child. In addition, parents who use physical punishment provide aggressive models. A child who is regularly slapped, spanked, shaken, or shouted at may learn to use these forms of aggression in interactions with peers.

—Newcombe, *Child Development*, p. 354

Tip *Induce* means "to cause a change."

Tip To *suppress* means "to prevent something from growing or developing."

Tip Something that is *mutated* is changed so that it is different from organisms of the same type (a genetic change).

Topic: _____

Main idea: _____

7. In 1920 there was one divorce for every seven marriages in the United States. Fifty years later the rate had climbed to one divorce for every three marriages, and today there is almost one divorce for every two marriages. The divorce rate in the United States is now the highest of any major industrialized nation, while Canada is in a rather distant second place.

> —Coleman and Cressey, *Social Problems*, p. 130

Topic: _____

Main idea: _____

8. The use of the court system to resolve business and other disputes can take years and cost thousands, if not millions, of dollars in legal fees and expenses. In commercial litigation, the normal business operations of the parties are often disrupted. To avoid or lessen these problems, businesses are increasingly turning to methods of **alternative dispute resolution (ADR)** and other aids to resolving disputes. The most common form of ADR is *arbitration*. Other forms of ADR are *negotiation, mediation, conciliation, minitrial, fact-finding,* and using a *judicial referee.*

> —Goldman, *Paralegal Professional*, p. 222

Topic: _____

Main idea: _____

_____

9. People's acceptance of a product is largely determined by its package. The very same coffee taken from a yellow can was described as weak, from a dark brown can too strong, from a red can rich, and from a blue can mild. Even our acceptance of a person may depend on the colors worn. Consider, for example, the comments of one color expert: "If you have to pick the wardrobe for your defense lawyer heading into court and choose anything but blue, you deserve to lose the case. . . ." Black is so powerful it could work against the lawyer with the jury. Brown lacks sufficient authority. Green would probably elicit a negative response.

> —DeVito, *Messages*, p. 153

Topic: _____

Main idea: _____

10. Most animals can survive for several weeks with no nutrition other than water. However, survival without water is limited to just a few days. Besides helping the body disperse other nutrients, water helps dissolve and eliminate the waste products of digestion. Water helps to maintain blood pressure and is involved in virtually all cellular activities.

> —Belk and Borden, *Biology: Science for Life*, p. 46

Topic: _____

Main idea: _____

DIRECTIONS   Turn to the reading "The Ocean's Plastic Problem" on pages 382–384. Read each paragraph and identify the topic and main idea. Then place brackets around the topic and underline the sentence that expresses the main idea. If the main idea is unstated, write a brief statement of the main idea in the margin. ●

Exercise 8

Exercise 9

DIRECTIONS   Select a three-page section from a textbook that you have been assigned to read. After reading each paragraph, place brackets around the topic and then underline the sentence that states the main idea. If any paragraph has an unstated main idea, write a sentence in the margin that summarizes the main idea. Continue reading and marking until you have completed the three pages. ●

USING COLLEGE TEXTBOOKS
Locating Main Ideas

Textbook authors present their ideas clearly and directly in order to make them easy to understand and learn. You will find that paragraphs in college textbooks usually have clearly stated main ideas. Very often, too, the topic sentence is placed first or early in the paragraph to guide you through the paragraph.

Because textbooks are designed to teach, they contain numerous features to help you locate main ideas.

1. **Marginal labels.** Some textbooks, such as the one excerpted below, label key ideas. Others provide focus or review questions after major sections to enable you to check your recall of important information.

Key Concept

Music as a forum for rebellion Popular music has often served younger generations as a way to express and encourage rebellion against existing social rules and norms. Music helps express the emotions people feel about their lives.

Social Meaning: Music and Rebellion

Music—particularly music as a form for mass media—has served each generation as a *forum for rebellion* against the status quo. As rock spread into a variety of subgroups defined by varying ethnic backgrounds, cultures, and classes, its breakthroughs and barriers in the recording industry represented cultural tension, not merely a change in musical form.

—Donatelle, *Health*, p. 107

Textbook Exercise 1: Finding the Main Idea

Underline the main idea in the paragraph titled "Social Meaning: Music and Rebellion." Use the "Key Concept" to guide you.

2. **Boldfaced headings and subheadings within a chapter.** These announce the topics to be discussed in each section and point you to main ideas. When you finish reading a section, turn its heading into a question and be sure you can recall the answer.

Here is a list of headings from a biology chapter on nutrients.

> # Nutrients of Life
>
> 13.1 Biomolecules Are Produced and Utilized in Cells
> 13.2 Carbohydrates Give Structure and Energy
> 13.3 Lipids Are Insoluble in Water

—Audesirk et al., *Biology*, p. 301

Notice that together these headings form an outline of the key ideas of the section, showing the progression of ideas. Here is a question you might ask based on heading 13.1 above:

- What are biomolecules and how are they produced?

Textbook Exercise 2: Understanding Headings and Subheadings

Write study questions for headings 13.2 and 13.3.

3. **Chapter summary.** A chapter summary is a list of main ideas covered in a chapter. Read the summary before you read the chapter to get an overview of the ideas you will be expected to learn. Study it after reading the chapter to review and to test your recall of main ideas. In this text, a question–answer format is used to enable you to test your mastery of the learning goals stated at the beginning of the chapter.

   The sample below shows part of a chapter summary. Notice how each summary bullet clearly states a main idea.

> ## 15.2 What Causes Evolution?
>
> Evolutionary change is caused by mutation, gene flow, small population size, nonrandom mating, and natural selection.
>
> - Mutations are random, undirected changes in DNA composition. Although most mutations are neutral or harmful to the organism, some prove advantageous in certain environments. Mutations are rare and do not change allele frequencies very much, but they provide the raw material for evolution.
> - Gene flow is the movement of alleles between different populations of a species. Gene flow tends to reduce differences in the genetic composition of different populations.

—Audesirk et al., *Biology*, p. 301

Textbook Exercise 3: Understanding Chapter Summaries

Three more bulleted points follow the second bullet point about gene flow. What do you predict these three bulleted points will summarize?

FURTHER PRACTICE WITH TEXTBOOK READING

Textbook Exercise 4: Sample Textbook Chapter

Using the section called "The Social Meaning of Race and Ethnicity" (pages 427–431), highlight the topic sentence of each paragraph. If the topic sentence is unstated, write a sentence stating the main idea.

Textbook Exercise 5: Your College Textbook

Choose a textbook chapter that you have been assigned to read for one of your other courses. For the first five pages, highlight the topic sentence of each paragraph. If the topic sentence is unstated, write a sentence stating the main idea.

SELF-TEST SUMMARY

Goal **1**

What are the essential elements of a paragraph?

A paragraph is a group of related sentences about a single topic. It provides explanation, support, or proof for a main idea (expressed or unexpressed) about a particular topic. A paragraph has three essential elements.

a. Topic: the one thing the entire paragraph is about
b. Main idea: a direct statement or an implied idea about the topic
c. Details: the proof, reasons, or examples that explain or support the paragraph's main idea

Goal **2**

How do you identify the topic of a paragraph?

The topic of a paragraph is the subject of the whole paragraph. Usually, the topic can be expressed in two or three words. To find the topic, ask yourself: What is the one thing the author is discussing throughout the whole paragraph?

Goal **3**

How do you find the main idea of a paragraph?

The main idea tells you what the author wants you to know about the topic. It is often stated directly in the topic sentence. To find the main idea, ask yourself: What is the author trying to say about the topic?

Goal **4**

Where is the topic sentence of a paragraph most likely to be found?

A topic sentence expressing the main idea of the paragraph may be located anywhere within the paragraph. It most commonly appears first or last but can also appear in the middle, or both first and last.

Goal **5**

What are supporting details?

Supporting details are facts and ideas that explain, support, or give examples of the main idea. It is helpful to distinguish primary supporting details from less important supporting details.

Goal **6**

What are transitions?

Transitions are linking words or phrases used to lead the reader from one idea to another. Transitions clarify the connections between ideas.

Goal **7**

How do you recognize an unstated main idea?

To find an unstated main idea, read the paragraph while asking yourself: What is the one thing the author is discussing throughout the whole paragraph? Then, think of a general statement about the topic that covers all of the ideas that support it.

APPLYING YOUR SKILLS

DISCUSSING THE CHAPTER

1. Do newspaper articles use topic sentences? Why or why not?
2. Are topic sentences used in fiction? Why or why not?
3. Why would a writer choose not to explicitly state the main idea in a paragraph?
4. What are some guidelines a writer could use to know when to start a new paragraph?
5. How are the paragraphs typically organized in magazines? Web pages? Newspaper articles?

ANALYZING A STUDY SITUATION

Irina is having trouble distinguishing topic sentences from details in her sociology textbook. Imagine that you are Irina's study partner and that she has asked you for help. You have decided that the best way to help her is to explain by using some sample paragraphs.

1. Using "Ethical Dilemnas Surround Those Willing to Sell, Buy Kidneys on the Black Market" in Part Six, page 392, select several paragraphs you could use as samples.
2. Outline the advice you will give Irina about distinguishing topic sentences from details.

WORKING ON COLLABORATIVE PROJECTS

DIRECTIONS   Working in pairs, exchange the textbook sections you chose in Exercise 9. Review and critique each other's marking.

Quick Quiz

DIRECTIONS Write the letter of the choice that best completes each statement in the space provided.

CHECKING YOUR RECALL

_____ 1. The topic of a paragraph can be defined as the
   a. subject of the paragraph.
   b. most specific fact in the paragraph.
   c. noun that is the subject of the first sentence.
   d. author's point of view.

_____ 2. The three essential elements of a paragraph are its
   a. proof, reasons, and examples.
   b. topic, main idea, and details.
   c. main idea, topic sentence, and transitions.
   d. topic, transitions, and examples.

_____ 3. The best clue to the topic of a paragraph can be found in the paragraph's
   a. organization.
   b. transitional words.
   c. repeated use of a word.
   d. types of details.

_____ 4. The details of a paragraph are intended to
   a. restate the main idea.
   b. appear before the main idea.
   c. explain or support the topic sentence.
   d. indicate the topic of the next paragraph.

_____ 5. The phrase "to illustrate" indicates the type of transition known as
   a. cause–effect.
   b. example.
   c. comparison.
   d. summation.

APPLYING YOUR SKILLS

_____ 6. Erika is having difficulty identifying topic sentences in the paragraphs she reads. One helpful fact Erika should remember is that the topic sentence of a paragraph is most commonly the
   a. first sentence.
   b. second sentence.
   c. middle sentence of the paragraph.
   d. last sentence.

_____ 7. Antonio is reading a paragraph in which the author has stated the main idea of the paragraph at both the beginning and the end of the paragraph. In this situation, Antonio should expect that
   a. the first statement is more important than the last.
   b. the last statement is more important than the first.
   c. the sentences in between are all examples.
   d. one sentence is a restatement of the other.

_____ 8. You are reading a paragraph in which the author has left the main idea unstated. Which of the following questions can help you find the main idea of the paragraph?
   a. Does the author reveal any bias?
   b. Does the author express an opinion?
   c. Are there any examples in the paragraph?
   d. What does the author want me to know about the topic?

_____ 9. Sofia is reading a paragraph with this topic sentence: "One unwelcome result of the increase in sexual activity is a high incidence of teenage pregnancies." Of the following sentences, the detail that does not belong in this paragraph is:
   a. An epidemic of teenage pregnancies has captured national attention.
   b. Nearly one million teenage girls become pregnant each year.
   c. About 30 percent of all teenage girls become pregnant once.
   d. Teenage boys are traditionally unable to assume financial responsibility.

_____ 10. Diedre is reading a paragraph that arranges ideas in the order in which they happened. Diedre is correct if she identifies this type of pattern as
   a. comparison.
   b. time sequence.
   c. continuation.
   d. listing.

Following Thought Patterns

LEARNING GOALS

In this chapter you will learn to

1 Use textbook chapter organization.

2 Recognize types of supporting information.

3 Identify organizational patterns.

LEARNING EXPERIMENT

1 Study the following five diagrams for a minute. Then cover the diagrams with your hand and draw as many of them as you can recall.

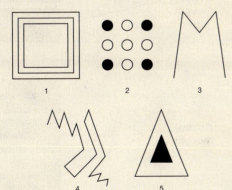

2 Compare your drawings with the original diagrams.

The Results

Did you get the first, second, third, or fifth drawing correct? Why didn't you get the fourth one correct?

Diagram 4 had no organization or pattern; the other four diagrams had an organization that you could identify.

Learning Principle: What This Means to You

You are able to remember information better if it is organized or if you can detect a pattern. The experiment above demonstrated that you can recall a diagram more easily if you can detect a pattern. The same principle applies to ideas. If you can recognize how a writer has organized ideas, you will be able to remember them more easily.

In college you will read a variety of materials; however, most of what you read will be textbooks, which are unique, highly organized information sources. This chapter focuses on important features of textbook chapters: (1) their overall structure or progression of ideas, (2) the types of details used to support each idea, and (3) organizational patterns (how the ideas fit together).

Goal ❶

Use textbook chapter organization.

THE ORGANIZATION OF TEXTBOOK CHAPTERS

A textbook is made up of parts, each successively smaller and more limited in scope. As a general rule, the whole text is divided into chapters; each chapter may be divided by headings into sections and subsections, and each subsection is divided into paragraphs. Each of these parts has a similar structure. Just as each paragraph has a main idea and supporting information, each subsection, section, or chapter has its own key idea and supporting information.

Locating the Controlling Idea and Supporting Information

The controlling idea in a textbook section is the broad, general idea the writer is discussing throughout the section. It is the central, most important thought that is explained, discussed, or supported throughout the section. It is similar to the main idea of a paragraph but is a more general, more comprehensive idea that takes several paragraphs to explain. The controlling idea, then, is developed or explained throughout the section (see Figure 9-1).

Tip *Comprehensive* means "including everything that's necessary."

On page 235, read the section in Figure 9-2, "Learning," from a chapter in a biology book titled *Biology: The Network of Life*. (Note: Ellipses [. . .] indicate places where text has been omitted from the original.)

Note that paragraph 1 of the section introduces the subject: learning. The paragraph then defines learned behavior and states that only recently has it been studied in animals. The last sentence of the first paragraph states the controlling idea of the section: there are five categories of learning. The subheadings divide the remaining text, and each identifies one category of learning. Each group of paragraphs under a subheading explains one category of learning (its central thought). In the first subsection, on imprinting, the third sentence in paragraph 1 states the section's central thought.

FIGURE 9-1
Organization of a Textbook Section

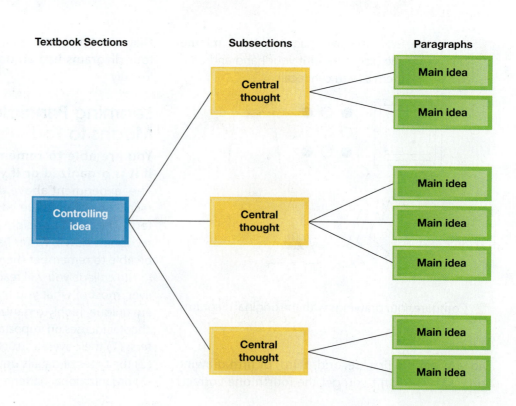

FIGURE 9-2
Excerpt from *Biology: The Network of Life*

LEARNING

Learned behavior occurs when animals change their responses as a result of experience. Psychologists did a considerable amount of the early work on learning. They have primarily been concerned with human learning, and even when their research has been on animals, it has been with an eye toward using animals to understand human behavior. More recently, biologists have focused directly on animal learning. Although studies on learning have been carried out on a relatively small number of species, a vast amount of information has been generated. Scientists now recognize five major categories of learning: imprinting, habituation, associative learning, latent learning, and insight.

Imprinting

Imprinting is a highly specialized form of learning. In many species, it takes place during the early stages of an animal's life, when attachment to parents, the family, or a social group is critical for survival. Imprinting is a process whereby a young animal forms an association or identification with another animal, object, or class of items. . . .

Young animals are not completely indiscriminate in what they follow. For example, a mallard duckling will follow a moving object for the first two months after hatching. It will show a preference, however, for yellow-green objects . . .

Imprinting is an important form of learning because it has both short-term effects on the immediate parent–offspring relationship and long-term effects that become evident in adult animals. For example, lack of imprinting has been shown . . .

Habituation

Habituation is a simple form of learning . . .

Associative Learning

Habituation is learning that results in the loss of a response that is not relevant or useful to the animal. Associative learning, in contrast, is . . .

Latent Learning . . .

Insight . . .

—Mix, Farber, and King

This example shows that the subheadings divide the section into five parts, or subsections. The section titled "Learning" begins with a general discussion of the subject and is divided into five smaller topics. This progression of ideas from large to small, general to particular, is typical of most textbooks. When you are familiar with and can follow this progression, your textbooks will seem more logical and systematic and will be easier to read.

Exercise 1

DIRECTIONS   Turn to "Linking Up: 21st Century Social Networking" in Part Six on page 416 of this text and complete the following instructions.

1. Where is the controlling idea of this article expressed? Express it in your own words it.

2. The dark-print headings divide the reading into three parts. Write a sentence expressing the main point of each part. ●

Exercise 2

DIRECTIONS   Read the article "Some Possible Consequences of Global Warming" in Part Six on page 385, taken from a geology textbook. Complete the following activities.

1. Circle the subject the article discusses.

2. Highlight the controlling idea.

3. Underline the topic sentence of each paragraph. ●

Exercise 3

DIRECTIONS   From one of your textbooks, choose a three- to four-page section that you have already read and answer the following questions.

1. What is the overall topic or subject discussed in this section?

2. What is the controlling idea?

3. Is the section divided by subheadings? If so, underline the central thought in each subsection. ●

Goal 2

Recognize types of supporting information.

TYPES OF SUPPORTING INFORMATION

Authors use various types of supporting information to explain the controlling idea of a textbook section. Recognizing these types of supporting information is the key to understanding *how* the author develops and connects ideas.

Examples

An example shows how a principle, concept, problem, or process works or can be applied in a real situation. Usually a writer gives an example in order to make an idea practical and understandable. In the following paragraph, notice how the writer explains the concept of objectivity by giving a specific example.

> The first concept in a sociologist's repertoire should be objectivity, the foundation for all sociological research. For sociologists, **objectivity** is the ability to conduct research without allowing personal biases or prejudices to influence them. They must put their own opinions and preconceived notions aside to study human behavior objectively. Being objective may seem simple, but it can be very difficult in practice. We all have our own opinions and prejudices, which can skew an objective point of view. For example, if you're studying the implication of ethics violations among NBA referees, your research might be swayed if you feel a particular referee has treated your favorite team unfairly. In that case, it's probably unwise to start this study after a bad call just cost your team a playoff game.
>
> —Carl, *THINK Sociology*, p. 31

As you read examples, be sure to look for the connection between the example and the concept it illustrates. Remember that examples are important only for the ideas they illustrate.

Reasons

Certain types of main ideas are most easily explained by giving reasons. Especially in argumentative and persuasive writing, you will find that a writer supports an opinion, belief, or action by discussing why it is appropriate. In the following paragraph, the writer gives reasons *why* people postpone having children.

> Even more popular than a childfree lifestyle is the option to postpone having children. The National Survey of Families and Households (NSFH) found that the majority of 19- to 39-year-olds who didn't have children were planning to have them in the future. Postponing parenting often follows naturally from wanting to first complete higher education, establish one's self professionally, and achieve financial stability, all of which may also cause both women and men to postpone marriage.
>
> —Kunz, *THINK Marriages and Families*, p. 134

You can see that the writer offers three reasons why people postpone having children: wanting to complete higher education, wanting to establish a career, and wanting to become financially stable.

Description

An author uses description to help you visualize the appearance, organization, or composition of an object, a place, or a process. Descriptions are usually detailed and are intended to help you create a mental picture of what is being described. Read the following description of how movement is depicted in a particular thirteenth-century sculpture.

Tip In this context, *composition* means "the different parts that make up a single thing."

> To give lifelike feeling, artists often search for ways to create a sense of movement. Sometimes movement itself is the subject or a central quality of the subject. One of the world's most appealing depictions of movement is that of the Dancing Krishna, portraying a moment in India's ancient legend of the god Krishna when Krishna, as a playful child, has just stolen his mother's butter supply and now dances with glee. Bronze provides the necessary strength to hold the dynamic pose as the energy-radiating figure stands on one foot, counterbalancing arms, legs, and torso.
>
> —Preble, Preble, and Frank, *Artforms*, p. 60

You should be able to visualize the pose depicted in this bronze sculpture and even, perhaps, Krishna's facial expression. Each detail contributes a bit of information that, when added to other bits, reveals the object's appearance.

Facts and Statistics

Another way to support an idea is to include facts or statistics that provide information about the main or controlling idea. Read the following paragraph, and notice how facts and statistics are used to support the idea that some people cannot digest milk products.

> Is it difficult for you to imagine life without milk, ice cream, or even pizza? Although some people consider these foods to be staples of the U.S. diet, they are not enjoyed by most of the world's population. Why? About 75% of people worldwide, including 25% of people in the United States, lose the ability to digest lactose, or milk sugar, in early childhood. Roughly 75% of African Americans, Hispanics, and Native Americans, as well as 90% of Asian Americans, experience **lactose intolerance**.
>
> —Audesirk et al., *Biology*, p. 106

When reading factual support or explanations, remember these questions: *What? When? Where? How?* and *Why?* They will lead you to the important facts and statistics contained in the passage.

Citation of Research

In many fields of study, authors support their ideas by citing research that has been done on the topic. Authors report the results of surveys, experiments, and research studies in order to substantiate theories or principles or to support a particular viewpoint. The following excerpt from a psychology textbook reports the results of research about nonverbal communication. The name and date in parentheses in the last sentence provide a citation, or information that tells readers where to find the full research study. Complete source information for the research study appears in either an end-of-chapter or end-of-book reference list.

> We humans are remarkably good at "reading" (correctly interpreting) cues about emotion, acquiring information from even minimal bodily signs. For instance, in one study researchers attached 13 small lights to the bodies of each of two professional dancers and had them perform dances that conveyed fear, anger, grief, joy, surprise, and disgust. Undergraduate students who later watched videos of the dances were able to recognize the intended emotions, even when the dancers performed in the dark so that only the lights were visible (Dittrich et al.,1996).
>
> —Kosslyn and Rosenberg, *Introducing Psychology*, p. 257

When reading research reports, keep the following questions in mind. They will help you see the relationship between the research results and the author's controlling idea.

1. Why was the research done?
2. What did it show?
3. Why did the author include it?

Exercise 4

DIRECTIONS   Read the following passages and identify the type of supporting information or detail that is used in each.

1. Three ceramic jars made in different villages in the late nineteenth and early twentieth centuries illustrate similarities and variations within the regional pottery style of the Pueblo peoples of New Mexico. The jars are similar in size and shape, but are different in surface decoration, with each bearing a design that is typical of the pottery produced by the artists of its Pueblo.

   The jar from Acoma Pueblo is decorated in large swaths—the brick-red elements seem to wander over the entire surface, draping over the shoulders of the jar like a garland. This undulating form divides the pot into irregularly shaped large areas.

   On the Zuni jar the design is divided by vertical lines into sections in which other lines define circular triangular areas.

   In San Ildefonso Pueblo, Maria Martinez and her husband developed another distinctive style. The San Ildefonso jar has contrasting curvilinear and rectilinear shapes. This jar also features the subtle contrast of matte black and shiny black areas.

   —Preble, Preble, and Frank, *Artforms*, pp. 98–99

Type of detail: _____

2. For couples who have decided that biological childbirth is not an option, adoption provides an alternative. About 50,000 children are available for adoption in the United States every year. This is far fewer than the number of couples seeking adoptions. By some estimates, only 1 in 30 couples receives the child they want.

On average, couples spend 2 years and $100,000 on the adoption process. Increasingly, couples are choosing to adopt children from other countries. In 2008, U.S. families adopted over 17,400 foreign-born children. The cost of intercountry adoption varies from approximately $10,000 to more than $30,000, including agency fees, dossier and immigration processing fees, and court costs. However, it may be a good alternative for many couples, especially those who want to adopt an infant rather than an older child.

—Donatelle, *Health*, p. 186

Type of detail: _____

3. <u>Polls</u> help political candidates detect public preferences. Supporters of polling insist that it is a tool for democracy. With it, they say, policymakers can keep in touch with changing opinions on the issues. No longer do politicians have to wait until the next election to see if the public approves or disapproves of the government's course. If the poll results suddenly turn, government officials can make corresponding midcourse corrections. Indeed, it was George Gallup's fondest hope that polling could contribute to the democratic process by providing a way for public desires to be felt at times other than elections.

Critics of polling, by contrast, think it makes politicians more concerned with following than leading. Polls might have told the constitutional convention delegates that the Constitution was unpopular, or told Jefferson that people did not want the Louisiana Purchase. Certainly they would have told William Seward not to buy Alaska, known widely at the time as "Seward's Folly." Polls may thus discourage bold leadership.

—Edwards, Wattenberg, and Lineberry, *Government in America*, p. 156

> **Tip** A *poll* is a survey of a selected group of people that is designed to reveal the opinion(s) of a much larger group. (Polls usually ask interviewees about political candidates, issues, or products.)

Type of detail _____

4. Venetian portraitist Rosalba Carriera made dozens of works with pastels in the early eighteenth century. Her *Portrait of a Girl with a Bussola* shows her sensitivity to the medium. The hard, fine-grained pastels in common use at that time give the finished work a smooth surface that makes possible fine color shadings. Because of the artist's light, deft touch with short strokes of the pastel, the work resembles an oil painting in its appearance, an effect promoted by the very smooth paper. Carriera was in demand to make pastel portraits throughout Germany, France, and North Italy until poor eyesight forced her retirement in 1746.

—Frank, *Artforms*, p. 112

Self-Portrait as Winter is another fine example of Carriera's pastel works.

Visual Thinking
ANALYZING IMAGES

How does the inclusion of the photograph make the paragraph easier to read?

Type of detail: _____

5. One reason why Americans seemed constantly on the move was their devotion to automobiles. In the postwar decades the automobile entered its golden age. During the booming 1920s, when the car became an instrument of mass transportation, about 31 million autos were produced by American factories. During the 1950s, 58 million rolled off the assembly lines; during the 1960s, 77 million. Gasoline consumption first touched 15 billion gallons in 1931; it soared to 35 billion gallons in 1950 and to 92 billion in 1970.

—Carnes and Garraty, *The American Nation*, p. 826

Type of detail: _____

6. A consumer's national origin is often a strong indicator of his preferences for specific magazines or TV shows, foods, apparel, and choice of leisure activities. Marketers need to be aware of these differences and sensitivities. Even overseas American restaurants must adapt to local customs. For example, in the Middle East, rules about the mixing of the sexes and the consumption of alcohol are quite strict. Chili's Grill & Bar is known simply as Chili's, and the chain offers a midnight buffet during Ramadan season, when Muslims are required to fast from dawn to dusk. McDonald's in Saudi Arabia offers separate dining areas for single men and women and children. Booths must have screens because women can't be seen eating meat.

—Solomon, Marshall, and Stuart, *Marketing: Real People, Real Choices*, p. 202

Type of detail: _____

7. The first stage of the purchase decision process is problem recognition. It occurs when a person perceives a difference between some ideal state and his or her actual state at a given moment. Consider, for example, a student who is in the market to rent an apartment. For her, the problem-recognition stage may have started when she decided that her dorm was too noisy or perhaps after an argument with her roommate. For a product like shampoo, problem recognition may occur when a consumer sees his favorite brand on sale, or it may be triggered when he notices that the bottle in his shower is almost empty.

Problem recognition may occur gradually. Several weeks may have passed before our student realized how much the noise in the dorm was bothering her. Sometimes, it occurs very quickly. When standing in the check-out line at the grocery store you see your favorite movie star on the cover of *People* and impulsively buy the magazine, you have experienced nearly instantaneous problem recognition. In fact, you have gone through virtually the entire purchase decision process in a matter of moments.

—Kinnear, Bernhardt, and Krentler, *Principles of Marketing*, p. 180

Type of detail: _____

8. Ice Age glaciers had significant effects on the landscape. For example, as the ice advanced and retreated, animals and plants were forced to migrate. This led to stresses that some organisms could not tolerate. Hence, a number of plants and animals became extinct. Other effects of Ice Age glaciers involved adjustments in Earth's crust due to the addition and removal of ice and sea-level changes associated with the formation and melting of ice sheets. The advance and retreat of ice sheets also led to changes in the routes taken by rivers. In some regions, glaciers acted as dams that created large lakes. When these ice dams failed, the effects on the landscape were profound.

—Lutgens, Tarbuck, and Tasa, *Essentials of Geology*, p. 261

Type of detail: _____

9. When the government sets out to measure the size of the labor force or the number of unemployed, its statisticians obviously cannot interview every single worker or potential worker. Survey data must be used. Although the survey technique is extensive—consisting of almost 60,000 households in almost 2,000 counties and cities in all 50 states and the District of Columbia—it is imperfect. One of the main reasons, argue some economists, is because of the *underground economy*. The underground economy consists of individuals who work for cash payments without paying any taxes. It also consists of individuals who engage in illegal activities such as prostitution, gambling, and drug trafficking.

Some who are officially unemployed and are receiving unemployment benefits do nonetheless work "off the books." Although they are counted as unemployed by the BLS, they really are employed. The same analysis holds for anyone who works and does not report income earned. The question, of course, is, How big is the underground economy? If it is small, the official unemployment statistics may still be adequate to give a sense of the state of the national economy. Various researchers have come up with different estimates of the size of the underground economy. Professor Peter Guttman believes that it is at least 10 percent of the size of the national economy. Other researchers have come up with estimates ranging from 5 to 15 percent. In dollars and cents that may mean that the underground economy represents between $300 billion and $900 billion a year. How many members of the true labor force work in this economy and their effect on the true unemployment rate is anyone's guess.

—Miller, *Economics Today*, p. 147

Type of detail: _____

10. Most U.S. urban areas have experienced ozone alerts. The American Lung Association estimates that one-third of the U.S. population lives in counties that exceed recommended concentrations of ozone. Ozone is a powerful oxidizing agent and is highly reactive. This makes it a severe irritant to the respiratory system. Episodes of high ozone levels correlate with increased hospital admissions and emergency room visits for respiratory problems. At low levels, it causes eye irritation. Repeated exposure can make people more susceptible to respiratory infection, cause lung inflammation, aggravate asthma, decrease lung function, and increase chest pain and coughing. Ozone is particularly damaging to children. The WHO estimates that 80% of all deaths attributed to air pollution occur among children.

—Hill, McCreary, and Kolg, *Chemistry for Changing Times*, p. 370

Type of detail: _____

RECOGNIZING ORGANIZATIONAL PATTERNS

Goal 3

Identify organizational patterns.

You have seen that textbook sections are structured around a controlling idea and supporting information and details. The next step in reading these materials effectively is to become familiar with how information is organized. By identifying how the key details in a paragraph or passage form a pattern, you are making them more meaningful to you and, as a result, making them easier to remember. Once you recognize that a paragraph or passage follows a particular pattern, its organization becomes familiar and predictable.

Six organizational patterns are commonly used in textbooks: definition, time sequence and process, comparison–contrast, cause–effect, classification, and listing/enumeration. A chart that summarizes these patterns is shown in Figure 9-3. To help you visualize each pattern, a diagram is presented for each as they are explained.

FIGURE 9-3
Summary of
Organizational Patterns

PATTERN	CHARACTERISTICS
Definition	Explains the meaning of a term, phrase, or concept; often consists of class, category or group; distinguishing characteristics; and explanation
Time sequence, Process	Describes events, processes, procedures
Comparison–contrast	Discusses similarities and/or differences among ideas, theories, concepts, objects, or people
Cause–effect	Describes how one or more things cause or are related to another
Classification	Explains by dividing a topic into parts or categories
Listing/Enumeration	Organizes lists of information: characteristics, features, parts, or categories

For each pattern, particular words and phrases are used to connect details and lead from one idea to another. These words are called **transitional words** because they make a transition, or change, and indicate the direction or pattern of thought. Figure 9-13 on page 253 gives examples of transitional words used with each organizational pattern.

Definition

The definition pattern defines and explains the meaning of a term or concept. Definition is one of the most obvious patterns, and you will find it widely used in textbooks.

Suppose you were asked to define the word *comedian* for someone unfamiliar with the term. First, you would probably say that a comedian is a person who entertains. Then you might distinguish a comedian from other types of entertainers by saying that a comedian is an entertainer who tells jokes and makes others laugh. Finally, you might mention as examples the names of several well-known comedians. Although you may have presented it informally, your definition would have followed the standard pattern. The first part of your definition tells what general class or group the term belongs to (entertainers). The second part tells what distinguishes the term from other items in the same class or category. The third part includes further explanation, characteristics, examples, or applications.

This pattern can be mapped or visualized as follows:

FIGURE 9-4
Typical Pattern of a Definition

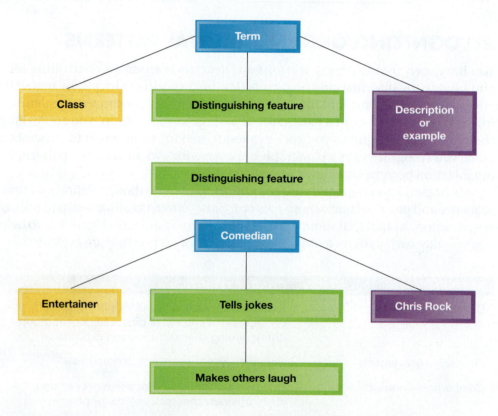

Read the following definition of *fossils* taken from a geology textbook.

Fossils are the remains or traces of prehistoric life. They are basic and important tools for interpreting the geologic past. Knowing the nature of the life forms that existed at a particular time helps researchers understand past environmental conditions.

Further, fossils are important time indicators and play a key role in correlating rocks of similar ages that are from different places. Common examples of fossils include such objects as teeth, bones, and shells.

— Lutgens, Tarbuck, and Tasa, *Essentials of Geology*, p. 426

This definition has three parts: (1) the general class is stated first, (2) the distinguishing characteristics are then described, and (3) further explanation and examples are given. When reading definitions, be sure to look for each of these parts. Passages that define often use transitional words and phrases such as:

TRANSITIONS FOR THE DEFINITION PATTERN

refers to	can be defined as
means	consists of
is	

Copyright © 2017 by Pearson Education, Inc.

DIRECTIONS   Define each of the following terms by identifying the class to which it belongs and describing its distinguishing characteristics.

Exercise 5

1. adolescence

2. automated teller machine (ATM)

3. cable television

4. computer

5. advertising ●

Time Sequence and Process

One of the clearest ways to describe events, processes, procedures, and development of theories is to present them in the order in which they occurred. The event that happened first appears first in the passage; whatever occurred last is described last in the passage. (Sometimes this order is reversed.)

The time sequence pattern can be visualized or mapped as follows:

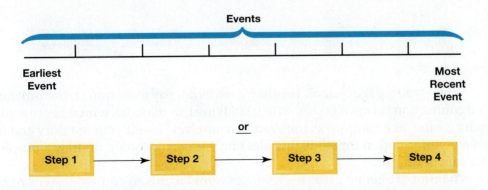

FIGURE 9-5
Typical Patterns of Time Sequence and Process

The first drawing is often called a **time line**, the second a **process diagram**. Time sequence focuses on events that may or may not be related, while process is concerned with the relationships among events as they progress through time. Material presented in terms of a time sequence is relatively easy to read because you know what order the writer will follow. (For more on time lines and process diagrams, see Chapter 4.)

Notice in the following example how the writer describes the process of communication among members of an organization.

> **Conversation**, whether face-to-face or online, takes place in five steps: opening, feedforward, business, feedback, and closing. Of course, there are variations in the process; when reading about the process of conversation, therefore, keep in mind the wide range of forms in which conversation can take place.
>
> The first step in conversation is the opening, which usually involves some kind of greeting. In face-to-face conversation, greetings can be verbal or nonverbal but are usually both. In most computer communication, the greetings are verbal with perhaps an emoticon or two thrown in. Verbal greetings include, for example, verbal salutes, initiation of the topic, and personal inquires. Nonverbal greetings include waving, smiling, shaking hands, and winking (and their emoticon equivalents).
>
> In the second step of conversation, you usually give some kind of feedforward in which you seek to accomplish a variety of functions. One function is to open the channels of communication. An example would be "Haven't we met before?" or "Nice day, isn't it?" In e-mail you give feedforward simply by sending the message, which tells the other person that you want to communicate.
>
> The third step is the business, or the substance and focus, of the conversation. Business is a good term for this stage, because it emphasizes that most conversations are directed at achieving some goal. You converse to fulfill the general purposes of interpersonal communication: to learn, relate, influence, play, or help.
>
> In the fourth step of conversation, feedback, you reflect back on the conversation. You normally do this immediately in face-to-face conversation and in your response to a previous e-mail. You say, for example, "So, you may want to send Jack a get-well card," or "Wasn't that the dullest meeting you ever went to?"
>
> The fifth and last step of the conversation process is the closing, the goodbye. Like the opening, the closing may be verbal or nonverbal but usually is a combination of both. Just as the opening signals access, the closing signals the intention to end access. The closing usually also signals some degree of supportiveness—for example, you express your pleasure in interacting ("Well, it was good talking with you").
>
> —DeVito, *Essentials of Human Communication*, pp. 131–133

This excerpt could be mapped or visualized as follows:

When reading sequential, organized material, pay attention to the order of and connection between events. When studying this material, remember that the order is often as important as the events themselves. To test your memory and to prepare information for study, list ideas in this correct order, or draw a process diagram or time line.

The time sequence pattern uses transitional words to connect events or to lead you from one step to another. The most frequently used words are presented in the following box.

TRANSITIONS FOR THE TIME SEQUENCE AND PROCESS PATTERNS

first	before	following
second	after	last
later	then	during
next	finally	when
as soon as	meanwhile	until

Copyright © 2017 by Pearson Education, Inc.

Exercise 6

DIRECTIONS For each of the following topic sentences, make a list of transitional words you expect to be used in the paragraph.

1. Advertising has appeared in magazines since the late 1700s.

2. Large numbers of European immigrants first began to arrive in the United States in the 1920s.

3. The first step in grasping a novel's theme is reading it closely for literal content, including plot and character development.

4. After Columbus left Spain, strong winds blew his ships into the middle of the Atlantic.

5. The life cycle of a product consists of the stages a product goes through from when it is created to when it is no longer produced. ●

Comparison–Contrast

Many fields of study involve the comparison of two sets of ideas, theories, concepts, or events. These comparisons usually examine similarities and differences. In anthropology, one kinship category might be compared with another; in literature, one poet might be compared with another; in biology, one species might be compared with another. You will find that the comparison–contrast pattern appears regularly in the textbooks used in these fields. The comparison–contrast pattern can be visualized or mapped in several ways. For material that considers both similarities and differences, the maps below are effective.

TOPICS A AND B

Similarities	Differences
_____	_____
_____	_____
_____	_____

For example:

PROFESSOR MILLER AND PROFESSOR WRIGHT

Similarities	Differences
both require class attendance	Miller assigns term paper
both give essay exams	Wright demands class participation
both have a sense of humor	age

For material that focuses primarily on differences, you might use the following:

	TOPIC A	TOPIC B
Feature 1	_____	_____
Feature 2	_____	_____
Feature 3	_____	_____

For example:

Feature	*Professor Smith*	*Professor Jones*
teaching style	lecture	discussion
class atmosphere	formal	casual
type of exam	multiple choice	essay

A comparison–contrast pattern can be organized in three ways. A writer comparing two artists, X and Y, could use any of the following forms of organization:

1. Discuss the characteristics of artist X and those of artist Y, and then summarize their similarities and differences.
2. Consider their similarities first, and then discuss their differences.
3. Consider both X and Y together for each of several characteristics. For instance, discuss the use of color by X and Y, then discuss the use of space by X and Y, and then consider the use of proportion by X and Y.

Some comparison–contrast paragraphs focus primarily on similarities or, as shown in the paragraphs and map below, concentrate primarily on differences.

In the battle to ratify the Constitution, proponents of the Constitution enjoyed great advantages over the unorganized opposition. Their most astute move was the adoption of the label **Federalist**. The term cleverly suggested that they stood for a confederation of states rather than for the creation of a supreme national authority. In fact, they envisioned the creation of a strong centralized national government capable of fielding a formidable army. Critics of the Constitution, who tended to be somewhat poorer, less urban, and less well educated than their opponents, cried foul, but there was little they could do. They were stuck with the name **Antifederalist**, a misleading term that made their cause seem a rejection of the very notion of a federation of the states.

The Federalists recruited the most prominent public figures of the day. In every state convention, speakers favoring the Constitution were more polished and better prepared than their opponents. The nation's newspapers threw themselves overwhelmingly behind the new government, whereas few journals even bothered to carry Antifederalist writings.

The Antifederalists were deeply suspicious of political power. They demanded direct, personal contact with their representatives and argued that elected officials should reflect the character of their constituents as closely as possible. According to the Antifederalists, the Constitution favored the wealthy.

Federalists mocked their opponents' localist perspective. The Constitution deserved support precisely because it ensured that future Americans would be represented by "natural aristocrats," those possessing greater insight, skills, and training than the ordinary citizen. These talented leaders were not tied to the selfish needs of local communities.

—Brands et al., *American Stories*, pp. 175–177

DIFFERENCES

Federalists	Antifederalists
Name suggested federation of states	Misleading name suggested rejection
Well educated, richer, urban	Less well educated, poorer, less urban
Recruited popular public figures to speak	Speakers were less well prepared and less polished
Newspapers supported them	Few newspapers carried Antifederalist writings
Believed in natural aristocrats	Suspicious of political power

Transitional words indicate whether the passage focuses on similarities, differences, or both.

TRANSITIONS FOR THE COMPARISON–CONTRAST PATTERN

Similarities		Differences	
also	too	unlike	nevertheless
similarly	as well as	despite	however
like	both	instead	in spite of
likewise		on the other hand	

DIRECTIONS For each of the following topic sentences, predict the content of the paragraph. Will it focus on similarities, differences, or both? Also, if you predict that the passage will discuss both similarities and differences, predict the organization of the paragraph that will follow. (Identify the type of organization by its number in the list on page 246 for the comparison–contrast pattern.)

Exercise 7

1. Two types of leaders can usually be identified in organizations: informal and formal.

   Content: _____ *Organization:* _____

2. The human brain is divided into two halves, each of which is responsible for separate functions.

   Content: _____ *Organization:* _____

3. Humans and primates, such as gorillas and New World monkeys, share many characteristics but are clearly set apart by others.

   Content: _____ *Organization:* _____

4. Interpersonal communication is far more complex than large group communication.

   Content: _____ *Organization:* _____

5. Sociology and psychology both focus on human behavior.

   Content: _____ *Organization:* _____

Cause–Effect

Understanding any subject requires learning *how* and *why* things happen. In psychology it is not enough to know that people are often aggressive; you also need to know why and how people show aggression. In physics it is not enough to know the laws of motion; you also must understand why they work and how they apply to everyday experiences.

The cause–effect pattern arranges ideas according to why and how they occur. This pattern is based on the relationships between or among events. Some passages discuss one cause and one effect. For example, the omission of a command causes a computer program to fail. This single cause–effect relationship can be visualized or mapped as follows:

FIGURE 9-6
A Simple Cause–Effect Pattern

Most passages, however, describe multiple causes or effects. Some may describe the numerous effects of a single cause, such as unemployment producing an increase in crime, family disagreements, and diminishing self-esteem, as in the following map:

FIGURE 9-7
A Complex Cause–Effect Pattern

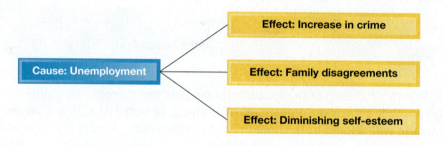

Other passages may describe the numerous causes of a single effect, such as higher unemployment, greater poverty, and decreased police protection causing a high crime rate, as in the following map:

FIGURE 9-8
Multiple Causes of a Single Effect

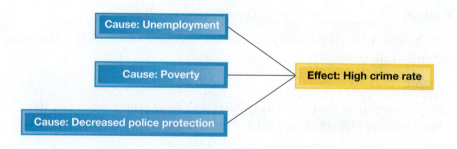

Still other passages may present multiple causes and effects, such as unemployment and poverty producing an increase in crime and in family disputes, as in the following map:

FIGURE 9-9
Multiple Causes and Effects

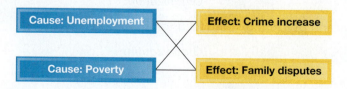

Read the following passage, which is taken from a biology text, and determine which of the following patterns is used:

- single cause–single effect
- single cause–multiple effects
- multiple causes–single effect
- multiple causes–multiple effects

Then draw a diagram in the margin describing this relationship.

> Rabies is caused by a virus that spreads through animal saliva. In the "furious" form of the disease, the virus is passed on by means of one animal biting another, thus injecting its saliva into the second animal. Not surprisingly, one of the things the virus does is affect salivary tissue in an infected animal's head and neck. This ensures that there is plenty of saliva to be transmitted. The virus also inhibits swallowing in an infected animal, which ensures more saliva. Finally, the virus affects the animal's central nervous system in such a way as to bring about the famous behavioral change in infected animals—frenzied, unprovoked attacks on other animals.
>
> —Krogh, *A Brief Guide to Biology*, p. 406

The paragraph offers three effects of a rabid animal biting another. Numerous effects, then, result from a single cause.

When you read and study ideas organized in a cause–effect pattern, focus on the connection between or among events and determine which of the four cause–effect patterns is used. Transitional words can help you determine the cause–effect relationship.

TRANSITIONS FOR THE CAUSE–EFFECT PATTERN

Causes	Effects
because	consequently
because of	as a result
since	one result is
one cause is	therefore
one reason is	thus

DIRECTIONS From the following list of section headings from an American government textbook, predict which sections will be developed using the cause–effect pattern. Place a check mark in front of those you select.

Exercise 8

_____ 1. How Public Policies Affect Income

_____ 2. Explaining the Decline of Isolationism in America

_____ 3. Tasks of Political Parties

_____ 4. The Affirmative Action Issue

_____ 5. Political Parties: How Party Loyalty Shifts

_____ 6. Why Bureaucracies Exist

_____ 7. The Organization of National Political Parties

Classification

If you were asked to describe types of computers, you might mention desktop, laptop, and tablet. By dividing computers into major categories, you are using a pattern known as **classification**. The classification pattern divides a broad topic into categories.

This pattern is widely used in many academic subjects. For example, a psychology text might explain human needs by classifying them into two categories: primary and secondary. In a chemistry textbook, various compounds may be grouped and discussed according to common characteristics, such as the presence of hydrogen or oxygen. The classification pattern divides a topic into parts on the basis of common or shared characteristics.

Here are a few examples of topics and the classifications or categories into which each might be divided:

- Movies: comedy, horror, mystery
- Motives: achievement, power, affiliation, competence
- Plant: leaves, stem, roots, flower

You can visualize the classification patterns as follows:

FIGURE 9-10
A Classification Pattern

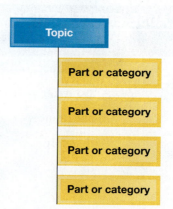

Note how the paragraph that follows classifies the various types of cancers.

The name of the cancer is derived from the type of tissue in which it develops. Carcinoma (carc = cancer; omo = tumor) refers to a malignant tumor consisting of epithelial cells. A tumor that develops from a gland is called an adenosarcoma (adeno = gland). Sarcoma is a general term for any cancer arising from connective tissue. Osteogenic sarcomas (osteo = bone; genic = origin), the most frequent type of childhood cancer, destroy normal bone tissue and eventually spread to other areas of the body. Myelomas (myelos = marrow) are malignant tumors, occurring in middle-aged and older people, that interfere with the blood-cell-producing function of bone marrow and cause anemia. Chondrosarcomas (chondro = cartilage) are cancerous growths of cartilage.

—Tortora, *Introduction to the Human Body*, p. 56

You can visualize or map this classification paragraph as follows:

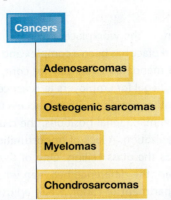

FIGURE 9-11
A Sample
Classification

TRANSITIONS FOR THE CLASSIFICATION PATTERN

several kinds	first	finally
one type	second	can be classified as
another type		

DIRECTIONS For each of the following topic sentences, supply three pieces of information that might be contained in the paragraph.

Exercise 9

1. There are blogs designed for almost every possible interest and every conceivable type of person.

2. Due, in part, to our complicated economic system, a number of different types of taxes are levied.

3. There are several different types of resources a person can turn to when experiencing financial difficulties.

4. There are many types of diet plans; the wise dieter evaluates the benefits of each.

5. Stress comes from a wide variety of situations; however, each situation falls into one of three primary sources. ●

Listing/Enumeration

Many types of information in textbooks have no inherent order or connection. Lists of facts, characteristics, parts, or categories can appear in any order. In these cases, writers use a pattern called *listing* or *enumeration*. In this pattern, the information is often loosely connected with a topic sentence or controlling idea: "There are several issues to be considered . . ." or "There are three problems that may occur when . . ." and so forth. You can visualize or map the listing pattern as follows:

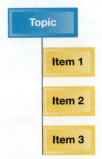

FIGURE 9-12
A Listing Pattern

Read the following paragraph, observing how the pattern proceeds from one type of issue to another.

> Gender issues are prevalent in the workplace. Perceptions, roles, and treatment of men and women in the workplace has been a complex and at times contentious issue. The Equal Pay Act of 1963 mandated equal pay for comparable work and the Civil Rights Act of 1964 made it illegal for employers to practice sexism, or discrimination on the basis of gender. Another significant issue is access to opportunities. Although women now hold half of all managerial positions, the ratio shrinks dramatically the higher you look in an organization. A lack of opportunities to advance into the top ranks is often referred to as the glass ceiling. One of the most complicated issues of all is the gender pay gap, the difference between what women and men earn. According to the U. S. Department of Labor, when adjusted for individual choices, the pay gap is roughly 5 to 7 percent.
>
> —adapted from Bovée and Thill, *Business in Action*, p. 243

One key to reading and studying the list/enumeration pattern is to be aware of how many items are enumerated so you can check your recall of them. It is also helpful to note whether the information is listed in order of importance, frequency, size, or any other characteristic. Doing so will help you organize the information for easier recall.

Transitional words are very useful in locating items in a list. As a writer moves from one item in a list to another, he or she may use transitional words to mark or identify each point.

TRANSITIONS FOR THE LISTING/ENUMERATION PATTERN

one	first
another	second
also	finally
too	for example
for instance	in addition

Exercise 10

DIRECTIONS   For each of the following topic sentences, supply three pieces of information that might be contained in the paragraph.

1. There are a number of factors wise consumers must consider in deciding which credit card to apply for.

2. Humans have more than just five senses; within the broad category of touch, there are many different kinds of sensation that can be felt.

3. The species of mammals contains many widely different kinds of animals.

4. Scientists find life hard to define, except by describing its characteristics.

5. Because the purpose of a résumé is to sell the qualities of the person writing it, it should include several important kinds of information. ●

Mixed Patterns

Many sections and passages combine one or more patterns. In defining a concept or idea, a writer might explain a term by comparing it with something similar or familiar. In describing an event or process, a writer might include reasons for or causes of an event or might explain why the steps in a process must be followed in the prescribed order.

Read the following paragraph and determine which two patterns are used.

> **Noise** is anything that distorts the message and prevents the listeners from receiving your message as you intended it to be received. It's revealing to distinguish noise from "signal." In this context the term *signal* refers to information that is useful to you, information that you want. Noise, on the other hand, is what you find useless; it's what you do not want. So, for example, an e-mail list that contained lots of useful information would be high on signal and low on noise; if it contained lots of useless information, it would be high on noise and low on signal. Spam is high on noise and low on signal, as is static on the radio, television, or telephone. Noise may be physical (others talking loudly, cars honking, illegible handwriting), physiological (hearing or visual impairment, speech disorders), psychological (preconceived ideas, wandering thoughts), or semantic (misunderstood meanings).
>
> —DeVito, *The Essential Elements of Public Speaking*, p. 8

This paragraph defines the terms *noise* and *signal*. The terms are also compared. Therefore, the paragraph combines a definition pattern with a comparison–contrast pattern.

When reading mixed patterns, do not be overly concerned with identifying or labeling each pattern. Instead, look for the predominant pattern that shapes the overall organization.

Figures 9-3 and 9-13 present a review of the organizational patterns and transitional words commonly used with each pattern. On exams, especially essay exams, you will find questions that require you to organize information in terms of one or more of the organizational patterns. (Refer to Chapter 14 for more information on essay exam questions.)

THOUGHT PATTERN		TRANSITIONAL WORDS
Definition		refers to, means, can be defined as, consists of, is
Time sequence and Process		first, second, later, before, next, as soon as, after, then, finally, meanwhile, following, last, during, when, until
Comparison–contrast	*Similarities:*	also, similarly, like, likewise, too, as well as, both
	Differences:	unlike, on the other hand, instead, despite, nevertheless, however, in spite of
Cause–effect	*Causes:*	because, because of, since, one cause is, one reason is
	Effects:	consequently, as a result, one result is, therefore, thus
Classification		several kinds, one type, another type, first, second, finally, can be classified as
Listing/Enumeration		one, another, also, too, for instance, first, second, finally, for example, in addition

FIGURE 9-13
Summary of Transitional Words

Exercise 11

DIRECTIONS Assume that each of the following sentences or groups of sentences is the beginning of a textbook section. On the basis of the information contained in each, predict what organizational pattern is used throughout the passage. Look for transitional words to help you identify the pattern.

1. In large businesses, clerical jobs are usually very specialized in order for the work to be accomplished in the most efficient manner. As a result, clerical work is very often routine and highly repetitive. _____

2. There are clear limitations to population growth and the use of natural resources. First, the food supply could be exhausted as a result of water, mineral, and soil depletion. _____

3. Unlike the statues of humans, the statues of animals found at Stone Age sites are quite lifelike. _____

4. When a patient enters a mental hospital, he is carefully tested and observed for 24 hours. Then a preliminary decision is made concerning medication and treatment. _____

5. One shortcoming of the clinical approach in treating mental illness is that definitions of normal behavior are subjective. Another shortcoming of the approach is that it assumes that when a patient has recovered, he will be able to return to his previous environment. _____

6. Most of the world's news is transmitted by Western news agencies. Third World nations regard this dominance as oppressive and feel that action must be taken to develop their communication networks. _____ ●

Exercise 12

DIRECTIONS Read each of the following passages and identify the main organizational pattern used in each.

1. TAMPERING WITH GENES, OR GENETIC ENGINEERING? Genetic engineering, as the name implies, involves manipulating genes to achieve some particular goal. Some people object to the entire idea of tailoring molecules with such profound implications for life. Where could it lead? Would we have the wisdom not to unleash something terrible on the earth?

   Perhaps the greatest threat of recombinant techniques, some would say, lies in [their] very promise. The possibilities of such genetic manipulation seem limitless. For example, we can mix the genes of anything—say, an ostrich and a German shepherd. This may bring to mind only images of tall dogs, but what would happen if we inserted cancer-causing genes into the familiar *E. coli* that is so well adapted to living in our intestines? What if the gene that makes botulism toxin, one of the deadliest poisons known, were inserted into the DNA of friendly *E. coli* and then released into some human population? One might ask, "But who would do such a terrible thing?" Perhaps the same folks who brought us napalm and nerve gas.

   Another, less cynical concern is that well-intended scientists could mishandle some deadly variant and allow it to escape from the laboratory. Some variants have been weakened to prevent such an occurrence; but we should remember that even though smallpox was "eradicated" from the earth, there were two minor epidemics in Europe caused by cultured experimental viruses that had escaped from a lab. One person died of a disease that technically didn't exist.

   —Ferl, Wallace, and Sanders, *Biology: The Realm of Life*, pp. 252–253

Organizational pattern: _____

2. **SCHOOL ATTENDANCE AND NUTRITION** School attendance can affect a child's nutrition in several ways. In the hectic time between waking and getting out the door, many children minimize or skip breakfast completely. School children who don't eat breakfast are more likely to do poorly on schoolwork, have decreased attention spans, and have more behavioral problems than their peers who do eat breakfast. Public schools are required to offer low-cost school breakfasts; taking advantage of these breakfasts can help children avoid hunger in the classroom. Another consequence of attending school is that, with no one monitoring what they eat, children do not always consume enough food. They may spend their lunch time talking or playing with friends rather than eating. They might not like the foods being served as part of the school lunch, and even homemade lunches that contain nutritious foods may be left uneaten or traded for less nutritious fare.

—Thompson and Manore, *Nutrition for Life*, p. 355

Organizational pattern: _____

3. There are three primary categories of stress that people report when they experience stage fright. *Physical sensations* make up the first category of stress that can occur when we are preparing to speak. The exact physical sensations vary from person to person, of course, but almost everyone experiences some degree of physical discomfort or uneasiness when speaking in front of others. The second category of stress includes *emotional responses* that can be experienced before, during, and after the speaking performance. They can include feelings of fear, loss of control, panic, anxiety, shame, and anger. The final category is the *psychological responses* of stress that can be experienced when delivering a speech. They include loss of memory, negative self-talk, jumbled thought patterns, nervous repetition of words or phrases, and the use of verbal pauses, such as "ah," "um," and "you know."

—Fujishin, *The Natural Speaker*, p. 21

Organizational pattern: _____

4. Many will contests involve written wills. The contesters allege things such as mental incapacity of the testator at the time the will was made, undue influence, fraud, or duress. To prevent unwarranted will contests, a testator can use a **videotaped will** to supplement a written will. Videotaping a will that can withstand challenges by disgruntled relatives and alleged heirs involves a certain amount of planning. A written will should be prepared to comply with the state's Statute of Wills. The video session should not begin until after the testator has become familiar with the document. The video should begin with the testator reciting the will verbatim. Next, the lawyer should ask the testator questions to demonstrate the testator's sound mind and understanding of the implications of his or her actions. The execution ceremony—the signing of the will by the testator and the attestation by the witnesses—should be the last segment on the film. The videotape then should be stored in a safe place.

—Goldman, *Paralegal Professional*, p. 561

Organizational pattern: _____

5. In a two-year study of more than 25 different communities, Jonathan Kozol observed public schools in the United States and noted that not all schools are created equal. Kozol saw that urban schools frequently lacked basic supplies necessary to teach: Playgrounds often had little or no equipment, chemistry labs were missing beakers and test tubes, and students had to share textbooks. Meanwhile, suburban schools often had a surplus of supplies and staff. Kozol pointed out that while these two systems often turned out different qualities of education,

the major cause for this disparity rested in the structures that supported the educational systems. Property values and taxes are higher in the suburbs, so their schools receive more funding than urban schools. This extra financial support allows suburban schools to purchase up-to-date materials and hire ample staff for the students. Unfortunately, because most urban schools are underfunded, the students who need the most help actually get the least, which adds to the endless cycle of educational inequality. Is this really "equal opportunity"?

—Carl, *THINK Sociology*, p. 127

Organizational pattern: _____

6. COUNCILS AND COMMITTEES   Councils and committees are advisory groups found in many different kinds of societies. We have briefly mentioned councils among the Shavante, Tetum, and Qashgai. They meet in public and are usually made up of informally appointed elders. *Committees* differ from councils in that they meet privately. Moreover, whereas councils are typical of simpler political organizations, committees are more characteristic of states. But the two kinds of groups can and often do coexist within the same political organization. When this occurs, councils are superior to committees, whose tasks and powers are delegated to them by councils.

Councils tend to be consensus-seeking bodies, while committees are more likely to achieve agreement by voting (although either kind of body may reach decisions in either way). Consensus seeking is typical of small social groups whose members have frequent personal interaction. Once a council or committee increases to more than about 50 members, decision by consensus is no longer possible. Voting is typical of larger groups whose members do not see much of one another in daily life and who owe their main allegiance not to other group members but to people (perhaps many millions) outside the council or committee. Members may in fact represent these outside people, as is the case with the U.S. Congress.

—Hicks and Gwynne, *Cultural Anthropology*, p. 304

Organizational pattern: _____

7. Sociologist Louis Wirth defined a **minority group** as people who are singled out for unequal treatment and who regard themselves as objects of collective discrimination. Worldwide, minorities share several conditions: Their physical or cultural traits are held in low esteem by the dominant group, which treats them unfairly, and they tend to marry within their own group. These conditions tend to create a sense of identity among minorities (a feeling of "we-ness"). In many instances, a sense of common destiny emerges.

Surprisingly, a minority group is not necessarily a *numerical* minority. For example, before India's independence in 1947, a handful of British colonial rulers discriminated against tens of millions of Indians. Accordingly, sociologists usually refer to those who do the discriminating not as the majority but, rather, as the **dominant group**, for they have the greater power, privileges, and social status.

—Henslin, *Essentials of Sociology*, p. 226

Organizational pattern: _____

8. The Founders selected a presidential system of government for the United States. Most democracies in developed countries, however, have chosen a parliamentary system. In such a system the chief executive, the prime minister, is selected by the legislature, not the voters. The prime minister is a member of the legislature, elected from one district as a member of parliament. The majority party, or the largest bloc of votes in the legislature if there is no majority party, votes its party leader to be prime minister. Unlike the president, the prime minister may remain in power for a long time—as long as his or her party or coalition has a majority of the seats and supports the leader.

Presidents and prime ministers govern quite differently. Prime ministers never face divided government, for example. Since they represent the majority party or coalition, they can almost always depend on winning on votes. In addition, party discipline is better in parliamentary systems than in the U.S. Parties know that if the prime minister should lose on an important vote, the government might have to call elections under circumstances unfavorable to the majority. As a result, members of parliament almost always support their leaders.

So why does the United States maintain a presidential system? The Founders were concerned about the concentration of power, such as that found in the prime minister. Instead, they wanted to separate power so that the different branches could check each other.

—Edwards, Wattenberg, and Lineberry, *Government in America*, p. 398

Organizational pattern: _____

9. A **hangover** is your body's way of saying, "Don't do that to me again." After heavy drinking, individuals can experience the unpleasant symptoms of a hangover, ranging from a pounding headache, fatigue, nausea, and increased thirst to a rapid heartbeat, tremors, sweating, dizziness, depression, anxiety, and irritability. Alcohol contributes to the symptoms of a hangover in several ways. Alcohol is a diuretic, so it can cause dehydration, and thus, electrolyte imbalances. It inhibits the release of antidiuretic hormone from your pituitary gland, which in turn causes your kidneys to excrete water, as well as electrolytes, in your urine. Vomiting and sweating during or after excessive drinking will further contribute to dehydration and electrolyte loss. Dehydration also increases your thirst and can make you feel lightheaded, dizzy, and weak. Increased acid production in the stomach and secretions from the pancreas and intestines can cause stomach pain, nausea, and vomiting.

—Blake, *Nutrition and You*, p. 318

Organizational pattern: _____

10. Blood is critical to maintaining life, as it transports virtually everything in our bodies. Blood is actually a tissue, the only fluid tissue in our bodies. It is made up of four components. **Erythrocytes**, or red blood cells, are the cells that transport oxygen. **Leukocytes**, or white blood cells, protect us from infection and illness. **Platelets** are cell fragments that assist in the formation of blood clots and help stop bleeding. **Plasma** is the fluid portion of the blood and enables blood to flow easily through the blood vessels.

—Thompson and Manore, *Nutrition for Life*, p. 205

Organizational pattern: _____

USING COLLEGE TEXTBOOKS
Identifying Patterns

Because patterns can help you comprehend and recall what you read, it is especially helpful to identify them when reading textbooks. Textbook chapter titles and the major headings within a chapter provide important clues about the pattern(s) used in the chapter.

1. **Chapter titles.** Chapter titles often suggest how the writer will organize the ideas contained in the chapter. For example, for a chapter titled "Islam: From Its Origins to 1300" in a Western civilization textbook, you can predict that, overall, a chronological order will be used. Here are a few more chapter titles. Can you predict the pattern?

> # 6 Your Reproductive Choices

—Donatelle, *Health*, p. 158

Textbook Exercise 1: Predicting Patterns in Chapter Titles

Predict the pattern of this chapter. _____

> # The Process of Fitting *into* Society

—Carl, *Think Sociology*, pp. 82–83

Textbook Exercise 2: Predicting Patterns in Chapter Titles

Predict the pattern of this chapter. _____

> # The History of Life   Chapter **17**

—Audesirk et al., *Biology*, p. 317

Textbook Exercise 3: Predicting Patterns in Chapter Titles

Predict the pattern of this chapter. _____

2. **Chapter headings.** Headings within a chapter form an outline of the chapter content. Headings often suggest the pattern of the material to follow. If you see a heading titled "Events Leading Up to the Thirty Years' War" you expect a cause and effect pattern to be used. Below are several headings from different textbooks. Can you identify the pattern each suggests?

> ## Consumer Involvement and Passive Learning   211
> Definitions and Measures of Involvement   211

—Schiffman, *Consumer Behavior*, p. xi

Textbook Exercise 4: Predicting Patterns in Chapter Headings

Predict the pattern of this chapter. _____

> ### Types of Business Ownership 19–21
>
> Sole Proprietorship   19
> Partnership   20
> Corporation   20

—Poatsy, *Better Business*, p. v

Textbook Exercise 5: Predicting Patterns in Chapter Headings

Predict the pattern of this chapter. _____

> ### CULTURAL DIFFERENCES
>
> Individualist and Collectivist Cultures
> High- and Low-Context Cultures
> Masculine and Feminine Cultures
> High- and Low-Power-Distance Cultures
> High- and Low-Ambiguity-Tolerant Cultures

—DeVito, *Interpersonal Messages*, p. v

Textbook Exercise 6: Predicting Patterns in Chapter Headings

Predict the pattern of this chapter. _____

FURTHER PRACTICE WITH TEXTBOOK READING

Textbook Exercise 7: Sample Textbook Chapter

Identify the pattern(s) used in the following two sections: "Measuring Prejudice: The Social Distance Scale" (p. 433) and "Theories of Prejudice" (p. 435).

Textbook Exercise 8: Your College Textbook

Choose a textbook chapter that you have been assigned to read for one of your other courses. Analyze its title and study the headings. After you have read the chapter, make a list of the patterns used in the chapter.

SELF-TEST
SUMMARY

Goal **1**

Why is it important to become familiar with the organization of your textbooks?

Textbooks are highly organized sources of information. Becoming familiar with their organization and structure and learning to follow the writer's thought patterns are important textbook reading skills. A textbook is divided into parts: chapters, sections, subsections, and paragraphs. Although each is successively smaller in size and more limited in scope, each follows a similar organization and is built around a single idea with details that support and explain it.

Goal **2**

What types of supporting information are used in textbooks?

Textbook writers explain ideas by providing various types of supporting information: examples, reasons, description, facts and statistics, and citation of research.

Goal **3**

Why is it helpful to recognize the pattern of organization of a paragraph or passage you are reading?

The organizational patterns are definition, time sequence and process, comparison–contrast, cause–effect, classification, and listing/enumeration. By paying close attention to the transitional words and phrases used to connect ideas and lead from one idea to another, you can usually identify the pattern being used. When you recognize that what you are reading follows a specific pattern, you will be better able to follow the ideas being presented and to predict what will be presented next. You will find that you have connected the important details so that recalling one idea will help you recall the others, and as a result, it will be easier to learn and remember them.

APPLYING | YOUR SKILLS

DISCUSSING THE CHAPTER

1. Choose a particular academic discipline, such as biology or psychology. Which organizational patterns do you think are used most frequently in that discipline? Why?
2. Think about the various essay examinations you've taken in recent months. Which types of supporting information did you use to explain the controlling idea of your answer? How can you improve your ability to organize an essay question on an examination?
3. Compare the organization of several textbooks. How are the texts organized similarly? How are they different? Which style seems best suited for the topic each text presents?

4. How do Web sites, television shows, radio programs, and documentary films organize information presented? Which type of organization is most typical in each medium?
5. What type of supporting evidence is typically found in each of the media listed in question 4? How do you know when supporting evidence is sufficient?

ANALYZING A STUDY SITUATION

Suzanne is writing a research paper on "male and female language" for her sociology class. She has collected a great deal of information through research and interviews, but she is having difficulty organizing it. Some of the subtopics on which she has collected information are listed below.

SUBJECT OF PAPER:

Male and Female Language

SUBTOPICS:

- Research studies on use of language in adolescent, sex-separate peer groups
- Men's language patterns
- Women's language patterns
- Stages of language development in infants and children
- Physical differences in areas of men's and women's brains that control language functioning
- Types of games children play and how they involve language

1. What possible *overall* organizational pattern could her paper follow?
2. What organizational pattern(s) might she follow in developing the section of her paper that deals with each of the topics above?
3. What types of details do you anticipate that Suzanne will include to develop each subtopic?

WORKING ON COLLABORATIVE PROJECTS

DIRECTIONS Locate and mark, in one of your textbooks or in Part Seven of this text, several paragraphs that are clear examples of thought patterns discussed in this chapter. Write the topic sentence of each paragraph on a separate index card. Once your instructor has formed small groups, choose a group "reader" who will collect all the cards and read each sentence aloud. Groups should discuss each and predict the pattern of the paragraph from which the sentence was taken. The "finder" of the topic sentence should then confirm or reject the prediction and quote sections of the paragraph if necessary.

Quick | Quiz

DIRECTIONS Write the letter of the choice that best completes each statement in the space provided.

CHECKING YOUR RECALL

_____ 1. The controlling idea in a textbook section is similar to the main idea of a paragraph *except* that the
   a. paragraph's main idea is more general.
   b. paragraph's main idea is more comprehensive.
   c. textbook section's controlling idea relies on fewer supporting details.
   d. textbook section's controlling idea takes several paragraphs to explain.

_____ 2. The type of supporting evidence that presents the findings or opinions of respected scholars in the discipline is
   a. citation of research.
   b. facts and statistics.
   c. reasons.
   d. description.

_____ 3. The type of supporting information that is used primarily to create a mental picture consists of
   a. research evidence.
   b. comparisons.
   c. reasons.
   d. description.

_____ 4. The primary purpose of an example is to
   a. support ideas with facts and statistics.
   b. highlight differences between two ideas.
   c. illustrate how an idea can be applied to a real situation.
   d. help the reader visualize a process.

_____ 5. Transitional words and phrases such as *on the other hand* and *however* suggest the organizational pattern called
   a. comparison–contrast.
   b. cause–effect.
   c. listing.
   d. time sequence.

APPLYING YOUR SKILLS

_____ 6. For Louise's biology paper, she wants to explain the various stages that a polliwog goes through before becoming a frog. The best way for her to present this information would be to use a
   a. time sequence pattern.
   b. cause–effect pattern.
   c. classification pattern.
   d. definition pattern.

_____ 7. Dean is writing a research paper using the cause–effect organizational pattern. Of the following topics, the one Dean is most likely to write is
   a. measurement of personality traits.
   b. sources of stress.
   c. limitations of objective tests.
   d. classification of mental disorders.

_____ 8. Mykaela is attempting to identify organizational patterns in articles she is reading for her economics class. To help her identify the comparison–contrast pattern, Mykaela should look for
   a. the meaning of a term or phrase.
   b. events, processes, and procedures.
   c. differences among similar situations.
   d. "if . . . then" relationships.

_____ 9. Miguel wrote a paper in which he stated that several factors, including an aging population, the rise of the Internet, and the rise of cable TV are responsible for the shrinking subscriber base for newspapers. The cause–effect pattern that Miguel used in his paper was
   a. single cause–single effect.
   b. multiple causes–single effect.
   c. single cause–multiple effects.
   d. multiple causes–multiple effects.

_____ 10. Kelli is writing an article for the college newspaper listing the wide variety of activities available on campus. Kelli is using listing as the organizational pattern for this information because the list
   a. has no inherent order or connection.
   b. is based on the relationships between events.
   c. has its own specialized terminology.
   d. focuses primarily on why and how things happen.

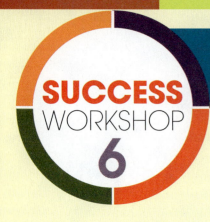

SUCCESS WORKSHOP 6

THINK CRITICALLY ABOUT COURSE CONTENT

Did You Know?

⟳ In 2012, 20.5 percent of bachelor's degrees were awarded in the business disciplines, 9.8 percent in the social sciences, 8 percent in the health-related professions, 6 percent in education, 5.6 percent in psychology, and 2.7 percent in the liberal arts and humanities.[1]

⟳ Courses vary in difficulty and complexity. Some require hands-on skills, such as studio art courses. Others, such as nursing courses, require field participation.

Regardless of your major, you will likely take courses across the curriculum, from literature through science. How can you apply your skills to different courses in different areas of study?

WHY IS EACH COLLEGE COURSE UNIQUE?

Each academic discipline and course requires a unique system of study; each takes a specialized approach to the study of the world around us. To illustrate, let's consider how various disciplines might approach the study of human beings.

- A **psychologist** might study the human needs that are fulfilled by various human behaviors.

- A **historian** might research the historical importance of human decisions—for example, a government's decision to enter a war or form an alliance with another country.

- A **biologist** or nurse would be concerned with human bodily functions (breathing, heart rate, body temperature, and so on).

- An **artist** might consider a human being as an object of beauty and record a person's flexible muscular structure and meaningful facial expressions on canvas.

Each academic discipline, then, approaches a given object, topic, or event with a different focus or perspective. Because each discipline is unique, each requires you to adapt your reading, learning, and study strategies.

---

[1] https://nces.ed.gov/programs/digest/d13/tables/dt13_322.10.asp

HOW DO I ADAPT MY SKILLS TO EACH OF MY COLLEGE COURSES?

One of your primary goals in this course should be to learn how to adapt your skills to each of your academic courses. In your first few years of college, you are likely to encounter disciplines with which you have no prior experience. Economics, political science, geology, or organic chemistry may be new to you. To adapt your existing study techniques, use the following suggestions.

1. ***Spend more time than usual reading and studying.*** Until you feel more confident in the course or discipline, overlearn by reading and reviewing the assignments multiple times.

2. ***Organize the same information in several different ways.*** For example, in an anthropology course, you might learn events and discoveries chronologically (according to occurrence in time) as well as comparatively (according to similarities and differences among various discoveries). In an accounting course, you might organize information by procedures as well as by controlling principles.

3. ***Use several methods of learning.*** Because you are not sure which reading and study techniques will be most effective, try several methods at once. For example, you might highlight textbook information (to promote factual recall) as well as write outlines and summaries (to interpret and consolidate ideas). You might also draw diagrams that map the relationships among concepts and ideas. Then select the techniques that work best for you in each course.

4. ***Look for similarities between new subject matter and other academic fields that are familiar to you.*** If similarities exist, you may be able to modify or adapt existing learning approaches and strategies to fit your new field of study.

5. ***Establish an overview of the field.*** Spend time studying the table of contents of your textbook; it provides an outline of the course. Look for patterns, progression of ideas, and recurring themes, approaches, or problems.

6. ***Obtain additional reference materials, if necessary.*** Some college textbooks delve into a subject immediately, providing only a brief introduction or overview in the first chapter. If your text does this, spend an hour or so online or in the library getting a more comprehensive overview of the field.

   - Read or skim several online encyclopedia entries in your field of study, taking notes if necessary.

   - Check the library's online catalog to see how the subject is divided.

   - Locate two or three introductory texts in the field. Study the table of contents of each and skim the first chapter.

HOW CAN I PRACTICE ADAPTING MY SKILLS?

Select two courses that you are taking this term. Think about how you read and study for those two courses. Do you use different reading and study techniques in each? Which strategies are working best for you in the first course? Would any of these strategies work equally well in the other course? Why or why not? What are the similarities between the two courses? What are the differences?

HOW DO I ANALYZE THE DEMANDS OF EACH OF MY COURSES?

The single best way to prepare for each of your college courses is to analyze the demands each will place on you using the following tips.

1. ***Talk to your advisor before registration.*** Your advisor can look at your academic record and advise you on which courses you are ready to take. He or she might also provide advice on which instructors are the best match for your learning style.

2. ***Read the course catalog.*** Your school's course catalog contains course descriptions that will help you determine which courses may be more challenging and which will be less so. Try to balance easier and more difficult courses within each term. Be sure you are taking required courses before you attempt to register for higher-level courses.

3. ***Visit the instructor's Web page.*** This will give you an overview of the instructor's interests and typical assignments.

4. ***Be sure you are prepared technologically.*** Determine which technologies your instructor will use. Will you need a specific Web browser, an account for a campus course management system, an access code for an online e-book or course pack? Which types of software will you be required to purchase and use? Does the instructor expect that you will enter the class proficient in a particular software package, such as SPSS (which is frequently used in statistics and psychology courses)?

5. ***Talk with other students to determine what will make you successful in the instructor's class.*** For example, ask whether the instructor values class participation. Does he place a lot of weight on the term paper? Does she grade on a curve or drop the lowest grade?

6. ***Conduct a full course analysis using the questions that follow.*** Then use the course analysis to create your reading and study schedule for the term.

Conducting a Course Analysis

1. What level of math, if any, is required for success in the course?
2. How much memorization (for example, of key terms and processes) is required?
3. How is the course organized—chronologically, thematically, topically, comparatively, or some other way?
4. How much writing is required?
5. How much reading is required? What types of reading materials must I acquire beyond the textbook?
6. What types of collaborative activity, if any, are required?
7. Does the course require a lab period?
8. How much creativity is required?
9. What additional resources (a tutoring center, exam review sessions, etc.) are available outside the class?

10. Will the instructor accept extra-credit assignments?
11. What makes the course different from other courses you've taken? What makes it unique?
12. Will I benefit from joining a study group with other classmates?
13. Does the course require an ongoing (or end-of-term) project or community involvement?
14. How much of the course requires me to learn theory (as opposed to facts)?
15. How will the instructor assess how well I have mastered the course content?

ANALYZING A COURSE

Using the 15 questions listed earlier, conduct a course analysis for a course you want or need to take next term. Be sure to answer all 15 questions. Based on the information you uncovered, answer the following questions:

1. Will the course be fairly easy, very challenging, or somewhere in between?

_____

2. Do you feel prepared to take the course right now, or will you feel prepared at the end of the current term?

_____

3. What possible weaknesses will you need to overcome before taking the course?

_____

4. Which reading and study skills will be particularly useful in this course?

_____

5. How much of the course content do you have some familiarity with? How much will you need to learn from scratch?

_____

ADAPT!

Analyze the demands of each course.

   Determine what will make you successful.

      Acquire reference materials as necessary.

         Prepare yourself technologically.

            Talk to your advisor.

Evaluating the Author's Message

LEARNING GOALS

In this chapter you will learn to

1 Make valid inferences.

2 Evaluate author and source credibility.

3 Distinguish between fact and opinion.

4 Identify the author's purpose.

5 Recognize bias.

6 Analyze tone.

7 Analyze arguments.

8 Evaluate data and evidence.

9 Think critically about graphics.

LEARNING EXPERIMENT

1 Read the following paragraph on school voucher systems and highlight important ideas.

In the late 1960s, a new idea began to receive considerable publicity. It was vintage USA: If there were more competition among schools, perhaps schools would be better. After all, people were entitled to more freedom in choosing where their children would be educated. This idea inspired proposals for voucher plans. Public schools have a virtual monopoly on public funds for education, and children attend schools depending, for the most part, on where they live. A voucher plan can change this situation. In a sense, parents, not schools, receive public money. They receive it in the form of a *voucher*, which they use to pay for their children's attendance at the schools of their choice. The schools receive money from the government in return for the vouchers. The greater the number of parents who choose a particular school, the more money it receives. The idea is to force the public schools to compete with each other, and with private and parochial schools, for "customers." Presumably, good schools would attract plenty of students, and poor schools would be forced either to improve or close.

—Thio, *Sociology*, pp. 376–377

2 Read the following paragraph on homeschooling and then answer the questions that follow, either alone, as part of a classroom discussion group, or with a friend or classmate.

There has been phenomenal growth in the number of children who receive their formal education at home. In the late 1970s there were only about 12,500 such children, but today the number has soared to more than 500,000 and is still increasing rapidly. Before 1994, most of the home-schooling parents were fundamentalist Christians who believed that religion was either abused or ignored in the public school. But today two thirds of the families reject public education for secular reasons: poor teaching, crowded classrooms, or lack of safety. Many of the older children, though, enroll in public schools part time, for a math class or a chemistry lab, or for after-school activities such as football or volleyball. Most home-schooling parents have some college education, with median incomes between $35,000 and $50,000. Over 90 percent are white.

—Thio, *Sociology*, p. 377

a. What are the advantages and disadvantages of homeschooling for the child?
b. What credentials should parents be required to have in order to teach their own children?
c. Do you think a homeschooled child would learn as much or more than a traditionally schooled child? Why or why not?

3 On which topic—voucher systems or homeschooling—do you feel you would be better prepared to write a paper, make a speech, or lead a discussion group?

The Results

You most likely feel better prepared to work with the topic of homeschooling. Why? Because the discussion questions that you answered after reading stimulated your thinking and opened up your mind to new ideas. By discussing the topic of homeschooling, you used the principle of elaboration.

Learning Principle: What This Means to You

Elaboration, or thinking about and reacting to what you read, helps you to remember more of what you read and prepares you to write about and discuss the ideas. This chapter will show you how to improve your critical reading skills by reacting to and analyzing what you read. You will learn to make inferences, ask critical questions, analyze arguments, and evaluate sources. By mastering these skills, you will learn to handle exam questions, class discussions, and written assignments that demand critical reading and thinking more effectively.

MAKING INFERENCES AS YOU READ

Goal

Make valid inferences.

The photograph shown on the next page was taken from a psychology textbook. What do you think is happening in the photo? What events may have led up to this situation? What might each of the two individuals be feeling?

To answer these questions, you used what you see in the photo to make reasonable guesses. The process you went through is called making an inference. An **inference** is a reasoned guess about what you don't know based on what you do know. We all make inferences throughout our daily lives. If a friend is late, you may predict that she was delayed in traffic, especially if you know that she often encounters traffic. If you see a seated man frequently checking his watch, you can infer that he is waiting for someone who is late.

As you read, you also need to make inferences frequently. Authors do not always directly state exactly what they mean. Instead, they may only hint at or suggest an idea. You have to reason out or infer the meaning an author intends

(but did not say) on the basis of what he or she did say. For instance, suppose a writer describes a character as follows:

> Agnes' eyes appeared misty, her lips trembled slightly, and a twisted handkerchief lay in her lap.

From the information the author provides, you may infer that Agnes is upset and on the verge of tears. Yet the writer does not say this directly. Instead, the author implies her meaning through the description she provides.

How to Make Inferences

There are no specific steps to follow in making inferences. Each inference depends on the situation and the facts provided as well as on your knowledge and experience with the situation. Below are a few general suggestions for making inferences.

MAKING INFERENCES	
Suggestions	**Make Inference by Asking these Questions**
Understand the directly stated meaning first.	• What is the topic? • What is the main idea? • What are the supporting details? • What is the organizational pattern?
Add up the facts.	• What is the author trying to suggest through the stated information? • What do all the facts and ideas point to or add up to? • For what purpose did the author include these facts and details?
Use clues provided by the writer.	• Is descriptive language used? • Do you notice emotionally charged words? • Do certain words have positive or negative connotations?

(Continued)

Suggestions	Make Inference by Asking these Questions
Make a logical inference.	• Is your inference consistent with all available facts? • It is logical and plausible?
Verify your inference.	• Do you have sufficient evidence to support your inference? • Have you overlooked equally possible or more likely inferences?

DIRECTIONS   Read the following passages and then answer the questions. The answers are not directly stated in the passage; you will have to make inferences in order to answer the questions.

Exercise 1

Passage A

A Bridge of Music

Charley Garfield tells a story about waiting his turn for the toll on the Bay Bridge in Oakland, California. As he's inching his way up to the tollbooth, he hears loud music coming from up ahead. Looking around for the offending car, the music gets louder as Charley gets closer to paying.

Then Charley realizes that the music is coming from his tollbooth and the attendant is smiling right at him. Not only is he smiling, he's dancing in the booth, pausing briefly only to take money from each driver, then resuming his outrageous movements.

When Charley finally hands the smiling attendant his money, he shouts over the thumping music, "Why are you dancing?"

"I'm having a party!" the attendant shouts over the loud music.

"But you're at work."

"I know, but you see the other tollbooths? They're all like coffins," the attendant says to Charley. "Just look at their faces—they're all dead."

"So why are you smiling?"

"Because I've got a great job here. My office has windows on all four walls. And I've got a view of the San Francisco Bay!" The car in back of Charley honked a second time, so he said goodbye to the smiling attendant.

—Fujishin, *Natural Bridges*, p. 54

1. In the first paragraph, what does Charley's reaction seem to be to the music coming from up ahead?
2. What language does the attendant use to describe the other tollbooths? What does he mean by these descriptions?
3. Explain why the attendant is smiling and dancing to music in his tollbooth.

Passage B

Is laughter the best medicine?

Lucy went to the hospital to visit Emma, a neighbor who had broken her hip. The first thing Lucy saw when the elevator door opened at the third floor was a clown, with an enormous orange nose, dancing down the hall, pushing a colorfully decorated cart. The clown stopped in front of Lucy, bowed, and then somersaulted to the nurses' station. A cluster of patients cheered. Most of them were in wheelchairs or on crutches. Upon asking for directions, Lucy learned that Emma was in the "humor room," where the film *Blazing Saddles* was about to start.

Since writer Norman Cousins's widely publicized recovery from a debilitating and usually incurable disease of the connective tissue, humor has gained new respectability in hospital wards around the country. Cousins, the long-time editor of the *Saturday Review,* with the cooperation of his physician, supplemented his regular medical therapy with a steady diet of Marx Brothers movies and *Candid Camera* film clips. Although he never claimed that laughter alone effected his cure, Cousins is best remembered for his passionate support of the notion that, if negative emotions can cause distress, then humor and positive emotions can enhance the healing process.

—Zimbardo and Gerrig, *Psychology and Life*, p. 501

1. In paragraph one, the author states that Lucy ran into the clown. For what reason is the author suggesting the clown is there?
2. What kind of movie is *Blazing Saddles*?
3. What kind of treatment did Emma's hospital use?
4. How does the author imply that humor assists in healing? ●

Goal 2

Evaluate author and source credibility.

EVALUATING AUTHOR AND SOURCE CREDIBILITY

You usually assume that your course textbook is timely, reliable, and authoritative—but you can't assume that about other sources you read, especially materials that you find online. The Internet has no editor; anyone can post anything on it. Not all sources are equal in accuracy, scholarship, or completeness. In fact, some sources may be inaccurate, and some may be purposely misleading. Other sources that were once respected are now outdated or have been discredited by more recent research. Use the following suggestions to evaluate sources:

1. **Assess the author's authority.** In textbooks and standard reference books such as encyclopedias and dictionaries, you can assume the publisher has chosen competent authors. However, when using other source materials, it is important to find out whether the author is qualified to write on the subject. Does he or she have a degree or experience in the field? What is the author's present position or university affiliation? This information may appear in the preface or on the title page of a book. In magazine or journal articles, a brief paragraph at the end of the article or on a separate page in the journal may summarize the author's credentials. Web-based materials often have an "About the Author" section. Be cautious of any materials that supply no information about the writer.

2. **Check the copyright or posting date.** In print sources, the date the source was published or revised is indicated on the back of the title page. On Web sites, the date of posting is generally provided. Especially in rapidly changing fields such as computer science, the timeliness of your sources is important. Using outdated sources can make a research paper incomplete or incorrect. Consult at least several current sources, if possible, to discover recent findings and new interpretations. Be cautious of any Web source that does not provide a posting date or any print publication without a copyright date.

3. **Look for footnotes, endnotes, or a list of references. These suggest the author consulted other sources and is presenting reliable information.** By appraising the sources the author cites (footnotes and bibliography), you also can judge the author's competence.

4. **Identify the intended audience.** For whom is the work intended? Some sources are written for children, others for young adults, and others for a

general-interest audience. The intended audience will suggest the level of detail, as well as the standards used to prepare it.

5. **Verify one source against other sources.** If you find information that seems questionable, unbelievable, or disputable, verify it by locating the same information in several other reputable sources. Ask your reference librarian for assistance, if necessary. If you do verify the information in other sources, then you can be reasonably confident that the information is acceptable. You cannot, however, assume that it is correct—only that it is one standard or acceptable approach or interpretation.

6. **Look for a <u>consensus</u> of opinion.** As you read differing approaches to or interpretations of a topic, sometimes it is difficult to decide what source(s) to accept. When you encounter differing opinions or approaches, the first thing to do is locate additional sources; in other words, do more reading. Eventually, you will discover the consensus.

> **Tip** *Consensus* means "an opinion that everyone in a group can agree with or accept."

7. **Ask critical questions.** Consider whether the material is fact-based or opinion-based. Question the author's purpose, the use of generalizations, any basic assumptions, and the type of evidence presented. (For more on these topics, see Chapter 11).

Suppose you were doing a research paper on the economic advantages of waste recycling. You found that each of the following sources contained information on recycling. Which do you predict would contain the type of information that would be most useful in writing a term paper?

- An article in *USA Today* titled "Stiffer Laws for Waste Recycling"
- A newspaper opinion piece titled "Why I Recycle"
- A brochure published by the Waste Management Corporation explaining the benefits of recycling to its potential customers
- An article on BusinessWeek.com titled "Factors Influencing an Economic Boom: Recycling and Waste Management"

The *USA Today* article is limited to discussing laws that regulate recycling and will not focus on its advantages. The newspaper opinion piece is likely to contain a single, personal viewpoint rather than factual information. The brochure may be biased (see p. 280), because it was written to convince potential customers that they need the company's services. The best source will be the article on BusinessWeek.com. It is concerned with the economic effects of recycling and is likely to contain fairly detailed factual information.

DIRECTIONS For each situation described, predict how useful and appropriate the following sources will be. Rate each as "very appropriate," "possibly useful," or "not appropriate."

Exercise 2

1. *Situation:* You are collecting information for a research paper on food cravings for your health and nutrition class.
   Source: A *Time* magazine article on American eating habits

2. *Situation:* You are preparing a presentation on flea markets for your public speaking class.
   Source: A book titled *Junk and Collectibles: The History of Flea Markets*

3. *Situation:* You are writing a letter to the editors of your local newspaper opposing the construction of a chemical waste treatment plant in your neighborhood; you need evidence about possible dangers.
   Source: The Human Ecologist, a periodical dealing with environmental health issues

4. *Situation:* You are shopping for a used car.
    Source: A classified ad for a pre-owned Toyota

5. *Situation:* You are writing a paper evaluating whether the lumber industry acts responsibly toward the environment.
    Source: A newsletter published by the Sierra Club, a group devoted to environmental protection ●

Exercise 3

DIRECTIONS   What critical questions would you ask when evaluating each of the following sources?

1. An article in *The New York Times* reporting a dramatic increase in domestic violence in the United States

    _____

    _____

2. An article written by an executive of a large home mortgage company describing effective and ineffective business management strategies

    _____

    _____

3. An essay on juvenile street gangs reporting a high incidence of emotional disturbance among gang members (Other articles, using other sources, report a much lower rate.)

    _____

    _____

4. An article, published in an advertising trade journal, titled "Teenage Drinking: Does Advertising Make a Difference?"

    _____

    _____

5. An article in *TV Guide* focusing on TV reality shows titled "Should Producers Pay More Attention to the Moral Messages?"

    _____

    _____ ●

Evaluating Internet Sources

Although the Internet contains a great deal of valuable information and resources, it also contains rumor, gossip, hoaxes, and misinformation. In other words, you must be particularly careful when using Internet sources. Here are some guidelines to follow when evaluating Internet sources.

DETERMINE THE WEB SITE'S PURPOSE   There are millions of Web sites and they vary widely in purpose. Table 10-1 on the next page summarizes five primary types of Web sites.

TABLE 10-1 Types of Web Sites

TYPE	PURPOSE AND DESCRIPTION	DOMAIN	SAMPLE SITES
Informational	To present facts, information, and research data. May contain reports, statistical data, results of research studies, and reference materials.	.edu or .gov	http://www.haskins.yale.edu/ http://www.census.gov/
News	To provide current information on local, national, and international news. Often supplements print newspapers, periodicals, and television news programs.	.com or .org	http://news.yahoo.com/ http://www.theheart.org
Advocacy	To promote a particular cause or point of view. Usually concerned with a controversial issue; often sponsored by nonprofit groups.	.com or .org	http://www.goveg.com/ http://www.bradycampaign.org/
Personal	To provide information about an individual and his/her interests and accomplishments. May list publications or include the individual's résumé.	Varies . . . may contain .com, .org, .biz, .edu, .info May contain a tilde (~)	http://www.jessamyn.com/ http://www.johnfisher.biz/resume.html http://www.maryrussell.info/ http://www.plu.edu/~chasega/
Commercial	To promote goods or services. May provide news and information related to products.	.com, .biz, .info	http://websitebuilding.biz/ http://www.alhemer.com/ http://www.vintageradio.info/

EVALUATE THE WEB SITE'S CONTENT To evaluate a site's content, use the same guidelines you would use to evaluate any other source. Ask and answer the following questions:

- **Does the Web site provide useful, relevant, credible information written by experts or provided by reputable organizations?** Read biographical information about the authors to determine their credentials. If no author is credited or no information is provided about the author, proceed with caution.
- **Is the information presented in a way that you can understand?**
- **Are sources cited?** The citation of sources is essential for academic credibility. Be wary of any Web site that provides evidence, examples, or statistics without citing the original sources.
- **Does the Web site provide complete information and data on the topic?** If the information is incomplete, you will need to find a more thorough treatment of the topic elsewhere.
- **Who sponsors the Web site, and is the sponsor biased?**
- **If opinions are offered, are they clearly presented as opinions?** Web sites that disguise their opinions as facts are not trustworthy.
- **Does the writer make unsubstantiated assumptions or base ideas on misconceptions?** If so, the information presented may not be accurate.
- **Is the content well written?** If the author did not take the time to present ideas clearly, he or she may not have taken time to collect accurate information, either.
- **Are the links relevant and current?** If the links do not work or the sources appear unreliable, you should question the reliability of the entire site.

EVALUATE THE WEB SITE'S TIMELINESS   Although the Web is well known for providing up-to-the-minute information, not all Web sites are current. Evaluate a site's timeliness by checking the following dates:

- The date on which the Web site was published (put up on the Web) or revised
- The date when the document you are using was added
- The date when the links were last checked

In many disciplines, timely information is essential. Out-of-date Web sites may have been accurate at the time they were published but may no longer be helpful. When that is the case, search for a better, more timely source of information.

Goal 3

Distinguish between fact and opinion.

DISTINGUISHING BETWEEN FACT AND OPINION

When working with any source, try to determine whether the material is factual or an expression of opinion. **Facts** are statements that can be verified—that is, proved to be true or false. **Opinions** are statements that express feelings, attitudes, or beliefs and are neither true nor false. Here are a few examples of each:

Facts

1. More than one million teenagers become pregnant every year.
2. The costs of medical care increase every year.

Opinions

1. Government regulation of our private lives should be halted immediately.
2. By the year 2050, most Americans will not be able to afford to retire.

Facts that are taken from a reputable source or verified can be accepted and regarded as reliable information. Opinions, on the other hand, are not reliable sources of information and should be carefully evaluated. Look for evidence that supports the opinion and indicates that it is reasonable. For example, opinion 2 above is written to sound like a fact, but look closely. What basis does the author have for making that statement?

Some authors are careful to signal the reader when they are presenting an opinion. Watch for words and phrases such as:

apparently	this suggests	in my view	one explanation is
presumably	possibly	it is likely that	according to
in my opinion	it is believed	seemingly	

Other authors do just the opposite; they try to make opinions sound like facts, as in opinion 2 above.

In the following excerpt from a psychology textbook, notice how the author carefully distinguishes factual statements from opinion by using qualifying words and phrases (highlighted).

Some research has suggested that day care can have problematic effects on children's development. For example, studies indicate that children who begin day care as infants are more aggressive, more easily distracted, less considerate of their peers, less popular, and less obedient to adults than children who have never attended day care or haven't attended for as long.

Other studies have found that day care is associated with adaptive behaviors. For example, researchers have reported that children who attend day care develop social and language skills more quickly than children who stay at home, although the children who don't attend day care catch up in their social development in a few years. Poor children who go to day care are likely to develop better reading and math skills than poor children who stay at home.

—Uba and Huang, *Psychology*, p. 323

Other authors mix fact and opinion without making clear distinctions. This is particularly true in the case of **informed opinion**, which is the opinion of an expert or authority. Thomas Friedman represents expert opinion on globalization, for example. Textbook authors, too, often offer informed opinion, as in the following statement from an American government text:

The United States is a place where the pursuit of private, particular, and narrow interests is honored. In our culture, following the teachings of Adam Smith, the pursuit of self-interest is not only permitted but actually celebrated as the basis of the good and prosperous society.

—Greenberg and Page, *The Struggle for American Democracy*, p. 186

The authors of this passage have reviewed the available evidence and are providing their expert opinion on what the evidence indicates about American political culture. The reader is free to disagree and offer evidence to support an opposing view.

DIRECTIONS   Read each of the following statements and identify whether it sounds like fact, opinion, or informed opinion.

Exercise 4

_____ 1. United Parcel Service (UPS) is the nation's largest package delivery service.

_____ 2. United Parcel Service (UPS) will become even more successful because it uses sophisticated management techniques.

_____ 3. UPS employees are closely supervised; new drivers are accompanied on their rounds, and time logs are kept.

_____ 4. The best way to keep up with world news is to read the newspaper.

_____ 5. A community, as defined by sociologists, is a collection of people who share some purpose, activity, or characteristic.

_____ 6. The mayor of our city is an extraordinarily honest person.

_____ 7. To a dieter, food is a four-letter word.

_____ 8. According to a leading business analyst, most television advertising is targeted toward high-spending consumer groups.

_____ 9. Americans spend $13.7 billion per year on alternative medicine and home remedies.

_____ 10. A survey of Minnesota residents demonstrated that lotteries are played most frequently by those who can least afford to play. ●

Exercise 5

DIRECTIONS   Read or reread "Some Possible Consequences of Global Warming" in Part Six on page 385. Underline four statements of informed opinion contained in the excerpt. ●

Exercise 6

DIRECTIONS   Using one of your own textbooks from another course, identify three statements of fact and three statements of informed opinion. ●

Goal 4

Identify the author's purpose.

IDENTIFYING THE AUTHOR'S PURPOSE

Author's purpose refers to the reason(s) a writer has for writing. Here are a few examples: Textbook authors write to inform and present information. Advertising copywriters write to sell products or services. Comic strip writers write to amuse, entertain, or provide social commentary. Essay writers write to inform, describe, or persuade.

Recognizing an author's purpose can also provide a means of evaluating the material. Ask yourself: How effectively did the author accomplish what he or she set out to accomplish?

For many types of material, the author's purpose is obvious. You know, for example, that the directions on a toy carton are written to tell you how to assemble it and that an advertisement is written to sell a product or service. Other times, the author's purpose is less obvious. To find the author's purpose, use the suggestions in the following table.

HOW TO IDENTIFY THE AUTHOR'S PURPOSE		
What to Consider	**Questions to Ask**	**Example**
Consider the source of the material.	• Is the source specific and detailed? • To whom do the examples appeal? • Are the ideas complex and sophisticated or obvious and straightforward? • Is the language simple or difficult?	A review of a rock concert that appeared in *Rolling Stone* would be quite different in style, content, and purpose from an article that appeared in *Popular Music & Society*.
Consider the intended audience.	• To what interest level, age, sex, occupational, or ethnic groups would this material appeal?	An article about a musical rock group appearing in *Teen Vogue* may be written to encourage concert attendance or increase the group's popularity.
Consider the point of view (the perspective from which the material is written)	• Is the point of view objective (factual) or subjective (showing emotion and feeling)? • Are both sides of an issue shown, or does the writer present or favor only one side?	A rock concert may be described quite differently by a music critic, a teenager, and a classical music fan, each with different attitudes and opinions expressed.

(Continued)

What to Consider	Questions to Ask	Example
Consider what the writer may be trying to prove.	• Is the material written to persuade you to accept a particular viewpoint or take a particular action?	A rock concert promoter may write to encourage concert attendance; a music critic may argue that the group has copied the style of another group.

DIRECTIONS   For each of the following passages, identify the author's purpose.

Exercise 7

Passage 1

Quotation by Jay Leno

For the first time ever, overweight people outnumber average people in America. Doesn't that make overweight the average then? Last month you were fat, now you're average—hey, let's get a pizza!

—Jay Leno, http://www.workinghumor.com/quotes/jay_leno.shtml

Purpose: _____

_____

Passage 2

Self-Help Books

You can find a self-help book for every problem, from how to toilet train your children to how to find happiness, but you must distinguish good ones from useless ones. To begin with, good self-help books do not promise the impossible. This rules out books that promise perfect sex, total love, or high self-esteem in 30 days. (Sorry.) Truly helpful books are not based on the author's pseudo-scientific theories, armchair observations, or personal accounts. People who have survived difficulties can tell inspirational stories, of course, but an author's own experience and vague advice to, say, "find love in your heart" or "take charge of your life" won't get you far. In contrast, when self-help books propose a specific, step-by-step empirically supported program for the reader to follow, they can actually be as effective as treatment administered by a therapist—if the reader follows through with the program.

—adapted from Wade, Tavris, and Garry, *Psychology*, p. 612

Purpose: _____

_____

Passage 3

Life in the Universe

What about the existence of intelligent life that could communicate with us? Some scientists argue that as a result of natural selection, the evolution of intelligence is inevitable wherever life arises. Others point to the history of life on Earth—consisting of at least 2.5 billion years, during which all life was made up of single-celled organisms—to argue that most life in the universe must be "simple and dumb." It is clear from our explorations of the solar system that none of the sun's other planets host intelligent life. The nearest sun-like stars that could host an Earth-like planet,

> Alpha Centauri A and B, are over 4 light years away—nearly 40 trillion miles. With current technologies, it would take nearly 50,000 years to reach the Alpha Centauri stars, and there is certainly no guarantee that intelligent life would be found on any planets that circle them. For all practical purposes, at this time in human history, we are still unique and alone in the universe.
>
> —Belk and Borden, *Biology: Science for Life*, p. 41

Purpose: _____

_____

Goal 5

Recognize bias.

BEING ALERT FOR BIAS

Bias refers to an author's partiality, inclination toward a particular viewpoint, or prejudice. A writer is biased if she or he takes one side of a controversial issue and does not recognize opposing viewpoints. Perhaps the best example of bias occurs in advertising. A magazine advertisement for a new snack cracker, for instance, describes only positive selling features: taste, low cholesterol, convenience, and crunch. The ad does not recognize the cracker's negative features: that it's high in calories, high in fat, and high in carbohydrates. Sometimes the writer is direct and forthright in expressing his or her bias; other times, the bias is less obvious.

Read the following passage about city life:

> Having lived in small towns and mega-metropolises, I can say with complete conviction that I am a huge fan of the city—but only as a place to visit. Would I actually live in a big city again? Not on your life! I will admit, some of the best meals I've ever had were prepared by top-tier chefs in places like Atlanta, New York, and Chicago, but those happen to be the very same cities where I experienced blatant price gouging and food poisoning in all its stomach-churning glory. And yes, the seemingly endless choices provided by a big city—where to live, where to shop, where to dine, etc.—can be exhilarating, especially if you have a short attention span and don't mind spending an insane amount of time stuck in traffic on your way to and from those destinations. Mass transit? Oh, you mean the crowded and foul-smelling train, where I have been harassed by aggressive panhandlers on countless occasions, relieved of my wallet once, and delayed twice by poor souls who threw themselves onto the tracks. Thanks, but no thanks.

In this passage, the author's bias against living in a big city is clear. The author's choice of words—*price gouging, stomach-churning, insane, crowded, foul-smelling, harassed,* and *aggressive*—reveals a negative attitude. Note, too, that the author's selection of details is biased; any positive aspects of city life are mentioned only as a way to emphasize the downsides of big cities.

RECOGNIZING BIAS

To identify bias, apply the following steps:

1. **Pay attention to emotional language.** Does the author use numerous positive or negative terms to describe the subject?
2. **Notice descriptive language.** What impression is created? How does the author make you feel?
3. **Look for opposing viewpoints.** Does the author present or ignore disadvantages, limitations, and alternative solutions?

DIRECTIONS Read each of the following statements, and place a check mark in front of any that reveal bias.

Exercise 8

_____ 1. Hydrogen is by far the best choice for an alternative fuel.

_____ 2. Intelligent design should not be taught in schools along with evolution.

_____ 3. In 1913, Arthur Whynne created the first crossword puzzle.

_____ 4. The Swim to Stay Fit Program gives students an excellent way to get in shape.

_____ 5. A third of all students today buy their back-to-school items online. ●

DIRECTIONS Describe the author's bias in each of the following statements.

Exercise 9

1. Those clamoring to shut down the farmers, however, should look hard at the prospect of a prairie full of subdivisions and suburban pollution: car exhaust, lawn and garden fertilizers, woodstoves, sewage. Certainly, the smoke from field burning is an annoyance, particularly to the hard-hit Sandpoint area, and to some it's a health hazard. But the benefits the sturdy farmers produce 50 weeks of the year shouldn't be dismissed casually.

—Oliveria, "Burning Will Go; That's Not All Good," _Spokesman Review_

2. Cruises are one of the best buys in vacationing today. Prices have not increased in over a decade yet the amenities on board have improved year after year. And the service is second to none. Passengers are pampered by employees at every turn; by the pool, in the many dining rooms, in the casino, and in their cabins, with a steward on call 24 hours a day.

—adapted from Cook, Yale, and Marqua, _Tourism: The Business of Travel_, p. 245

3. While world leaders once again pledged to help Africa, the many poor people in another part of the developing world, Latin America, attract little notice. There is a reason for that oversight: all but a wretched pair (Haiti and Nicaragua) of Latin American countries are officially classed as "middle-income" and all (except Cuba) are democracies. Latin America is less of a stain on the world's conscience.

—"Not Always With Us," _The Economist_

4. NASCAR can't make vague rules. This bunch of young racecar drivers is high-strung and emotional. They're hot-headed, and they react to everything quickly. They don't have the wisdom and patience of an older driver. They are young men who are wired to the max. They're coiled up like a snake all the time, and they're ready to strike at anybody or anything.

—Waltrip, "Calling Dr. Phil: NASCAR Needs Black-and-White Penalties," _FOXSports.com_ ●

DIRECTIONS Read the following passage. Underline words and phrases that reveal the author's bias.

Exercise 10

The Deception of Green Energy

If good intentions were all that were necessary to create "green" power, we would have so much of it today that we would not need to use coal, oil, natural gas, or nuclear power. Of course, it is also true that if wishes were horses, beggars would ride.

In the last decade or so, the federal government has poured tens of billions of dollars into "green" energy projects. The results have neither noticeably reduced our dependence on foreign oil, nor cleaned our air and water of pollutants. They have not even made a dent in the atmospheric buildup of greenhouse gases. What we *have* accomplished by using up all of these scarce resources on solar, wind, and battery power is a convincing demonstration that while green energy may make for great politics, it also makes for lousy environmental and economic policy.

—Miller, Benjamin, and North, *The Economics of Public Issues*, p. 138 ●

Goal 6

Analyze tone.

ANALYZING THE AUTHOR'S TONE

In speech, a speaker's tone of voice often reveals his or her attitude toward the subject and contributes to the overall message. **Tone** is also evident in writing, and it also contributes to meaning. Recognizing an author's tone is important because tone can reveal feelings, attitudes, or viewpoints not directly stated by the author. Many human emotions can be communicated through tone—disapproval, hate, admiration, disgust, gratitude, and forcefulness are examples. An author's tone is achieved primarily through word choice and stylistic features such as sentence pattern and length.

A list of words frequently used to identify tone are shown in the table below.

WORDS FREQUENTLY USED TO DESCRIBE TONE				
abstract	condemning	flippant	irreverent	playful
absurd	condescending	forgiving	joyful	reverent
amused	convincing	formal	loving	righteous
angry	cynical	frustrated	malicious	sarcastic
apathetic	depressing	gentle	melancholic	satiric
arrogant	detached	grim	mocking	sensational
assertive	disapproving	hateful	nostalgic	serious
awestruck	disrespectful	humorous	objective	solemn
bitter	distressed	impassioned	obsequious	sympathetic
caustic	docile	incredulous	optimistic	tragic
celebratory	earnest	indignant	outraged	uncomfortable
cheerful	excited	indirect	pathetic	vindictive
comic	fanciful	intimate	persuasive	worried
compassionate	farcical	ironic	pessimistic	

Read the following passage, paying particular attention to the feeling it creates.

The McDonaldization of Society

The significance of the McDonald's restaurants that dot the United States—and, increasingly, the world—goes far beyond quick hamburgers, milk shakes, and salads. As sociologist George Ritzer says, our everyday lives are being "McDonaldized." The McDonaldization of society does not refer just to the robotlike assembly of food.

This term refers to the standardization of everyday life, a process that is transforming our lives. Want to do some shopping? Shopping malls offer one-stop shopping in controlled environments. Planning a trip? Travel agencies offer "package" tours. They will transport middle-class Americans to ten European capitals in fourteen days. All visitors experience the same hotels, restaurants, and other scheduled sites—and no one need fear meeting a "real" native. Want to keep up with events? *USA Today* spews out McNews—short, bland, non-analytical pieces that can be digested between gulps of the McShake or the McBurger.

—adapted from Henslin, *Sociology*, p. 177

Here the author's tone is concerned and indignant. He is unhappy about what he sees as the standardization of everyday life.

IDENTIFYING TONE

Use the following tips and questions to identify the author's tone:

1. **Consider how the material makes you feel.** What emotions surface?
2. **Study the author's word choice.** Does he or she use words that provoke strong feelings? Which words and phrases have positive or negative associations or connotations? (See p. 301 for more about connotative language.)
3. **Study how the author writes.** Is the material straightforward and factual or does the writer play with language, use sarcasm or humor, or use figurative language? (See p. 302 for more about figurative language.)

DIRECTIONS   Describe the tone of each of the following passages.

Exercise 11

An Important Order

1. The caller's voice does not hold together well. I can tell he is quite old and not well. He is calling from Maryland.

   "I want four boxes of the Nut Goodies," he rasps at me after giving me his credit card information in a faltering hurry.

   "There are 24 bars in each box," I say in case he doesn't know the magnitude of his order. Nut Goodies are made here in St. Paul and consist of a patty of maple cream covered with milk chocolate and peanuts. Sort of a Norwegian praline.

   "OK, then make it five boxes but hurry this up before my nurse gets back."

   He wants the order billed to a home address but sent to a nursing home.

   "I've got Parkinson's," he says. "I'm 84."

   "OK, sir. I think I've got it all. They're on the way." I put a rush on it.

   "Right. Bye," he says, and in the pause when he is concentrating God knows how much energy on getting the receiver back in its cradle, I hear a long, dry chuckle.

   One hundred and twenty Nut Goodies.

   Way to go, buddy.

   —Swardson, *City Pages*

Tone: _____

_____

Corporations and Global Warming

2. There is evidence that even some of the most serious polluters on the planet, American corporations, now understand that global warming is increasing at such a rapid rate, and is so hazardous to human life, that government regulation is

necessary. However, many large national and multinational corporations have yet to "find religion." The terrible explosion of British Petroleum's oil rig in the Gulf of Mexico in 2010, killing eleven workers and spewing thousands of gallons of oil into the sea every day for months, provides ominous evidence that many corporations need not only national but international regulation. Otherwise, the profits they crave may drive most of the species of the earth (including humans) to extinction.

—adapted from Suppes and Wells, *The Social Work Experience*, p. 53

Tone: _____

_____

3. What You Need

You need a large wooden frame and enough space to accommodate it. Put comfortable chairs around it, allowing for eight women of varying ages, weight, coloring, and cultural orientation. It is preferable that this large wood frame be located in a room in a house in Atwater or Los Banos or a small town outside Bakersfield called Grasse. It should be a place that gets a thick, moist blanket of tule fog in the winter and be hot as blazes in the summer. Fix plenty of lemonade. Cookies are a nice complement.

When you choose your colors, make them sympathetic to one another. Consider the color wheel of grammar school—primary colors, phenomena of light and dark; avoid antagonism of hues—it detracts from the pleasure of the work. Think of music as you orchestrate the shades and patterns; pretend that you are a conductor in a lush symphony hall; imagine the audience saying *Ooh* and *Ahh* as they applaud your work.

—Otto, *How to Make an American Quilt*

Tone: _____

_____

Exercise 12

DIRECTIONS   Read the article titled "Ethical Dilemmas Surround Those Willing to Sell, Buy Kidneys on the Black Market" in Part Six on p. 392 and complete the following items.

1. Evaluate the source of the article.
2. Identify two statements of fact and two statements expressing opinion.
3. What was the author's purpose in writing the article?
4. Is the author biased?
5. Write two or three words that describe the author's tone. ●

Goal 7

Analyze arguments.

ANALYZING ARGUMENTS

An argument has three essential parts: issue, claim, and support.

First, an argument must address an **issue**—a problem or controversy about which people disagree. Abortion, gun control, animal rights, capital punishment, and drug legalization are all examples of issues. Second, an argument must take a position on an issue. This position is called a **claim**. An argument may claim that capital punishment should be outlawed or that medical use of marijuana should be legalized. Finally, an argument offers **support** for the claim. Support consists of reasons and evidence that the claim is reasonable and should be accepted. An argument may also include a fourth part—a **refutation**. A refutation considers opposing viewpoints and attempts to disprove or discredit them.

Here is an example: baseball players' use of steroids is an issue. A claim could be made that baseball players' use of steroids is unhealthy and unfair to other players, and that owners and players need to take the issue seriously. Support for the claim could include reasons why steroid use is unhealthy and unfair. An opposing viewpoint may be that steroid use creates enhanced performance, which makes the game more fun and competitive. This argument could be refuted by providing evidence that fans dislike extraordinary feats of performance and would prefer to see the game played without the use of performance-enhancing drugs.

For most issues, more than one claim is possible. For example, on the issue of gun control, here are three possible claims:

- All handguns should be legal.
- No handguns should be legal.
- Some handguns should be legal for certain individuals.

In short, an **argument** takes one position on an issue and provides reasons and evidence that its claim is sound or believable.

DIRECTIONS   For each of the following issues, identify at least two claims and write a sentence expressing each.

Exercise 13

1. Immigration laws restricting entry into the United States

_____

_____

2. Drug testing in the workplace

_____

_____

3. Smoking in public places

_____

_____

DIRECTIONS   For each of the following essay titles, predict the issue and claim that the essay addresses.

Exercise 14

1. "Organic Farming: Quality and Environmental Care"
2. "Park Neighbors Applaud Curfew"
3. "Limited Access Limits Votes of Disabled"
4. "Global Warming Linked to Hurricanes"
5. "Solar Energy: An Energy Alternative Whose Time Has Come" ●

Types of Support

Three common types of support for arguments are reasons, evidence, and emotional appeals. A **reason** is a general statement that supports a claim. It explains why the writer's viewpoint is reasonable and should be accepted. In an argument opposing steroid use by baseball players, two primary reasons are

- It is unhealthy.
- It is unfair.

Evidence consists of facts, statistics, experiences, comparisons, and examples that demonstrate why the claim is valid. To support the claim that steroids are unhealthy, a writer could offer medical facts that demonstrate that steroids are dangerous to one's health. Alternatively, the writer could provide an example of a player who used steroids and describe his health problems.

Emotional appeals are ideas that are targeted toward needs or values that readers are likely to care about. Needs include physiological needs (food, drink, shelter) and psychological needs (sense of belonging, sense of accomplishment, sense of self-worth, sense of competency). In an argument against steroid use, the writer could appeal to a reader's sense of fairness—players should not be allowed to succeed by using drugs rather than natural talent. The writer could also appeal to the reader's sense of nostalgia by mentioning baseball traditions that are being corrupted. An argument favoring gun control may appeal to a reader's need for safety, while an argument favoring restrictions on sharing personal or financial information may appeal to a reader's need for privacy and financial security.

Exercise 15

DIRECTIONS   Identify the type(s) of evidence used to support each of the following brief arguments.

1. Many students have part-time jobs that require them to work late afternoons and evenings during the week. These students are unable to use the library during the week. Therefore, library hours should be extended to weekends.

2. Because parents have the right to influence their children's sexual attitudes, sex education should take place in the home, not at school.

3. No one should be forced to inhale unpleasant or harmful substances. That's why the ban on cigarette smoking in public places was put into effect in our state. Why shouldn't there be a law to prevent people from wearing strong colognes or perfumes, especially in restaurants, since the sense of smell is important to taste? ●

Goal 8

Evaluate data and evidence.

EVALUATING DATA AND EVIDENCE

Once you have understood a writer's argument by identifying what is asserted and how, the next step is to evaluate the soundness, correctness, and worth of the reasons and evidence that support the assertion. As a critical reader, your task is to assess whether the evidence is sufficient to support the claim. Let's look at a few types of evidence that are often used.

FACTS Be sure the facts are verifiable and taken from a reliable source.

PERSONAL EXPERIENCE Writers often substantiate their ideas through experience and observation. Although a writer's personal account of a situation may provide an interesting perspective on an issue, personal experience should not be accepted as proof. The observer may be biased or may have exaggerated or incorrectly perceived a situation.

EXAMPLES Examples can illustrate or explain a principle, concept, or idea. To explain what aggressive behavior is, your psychology instructor may offer several examples: fighting, punching, and kicking. Examples alone are not enough to prove the concept or idea they illustrate, as in the following passage:

> The American judicial system treats those who are called for jury duty unfairly. It is clear from my sister's experience that the system has little regard for the needs of those called as jurors. My sister was required to report for jury duty the week she was on vacation. She spent the entire week in a crowded, stuffy room waiting to be called to sit on a jury and never was called.

The sister's experience does sound unfair, but by itself it does not prove anything about the entire judicial system.

STATISTICS Many people are impressed by statistics—the reporting of figures, percentages, averages, and so forth—and assume that they are irrefutable proof of an assertion. Actually, statistics can be misused, misinterpreted, or used selectively to give a biased, subjective, or inaccurate picture of a situation. Always approach statistical evidence with a critical, questioning attitude.

COMPARISONS AND ANALOGIES Comparisons and analogies serve as illustrations and are often used in argument. Their reliability depends on how closely the comparison corresponds, or how similar it is, to the situation to which it is being compared. For example, Martin Luther King, Jr., in his famous letter from the Birmingham jail, compared nonviolent protesters to a robbed man. To evaluate this comparison, you would need to consider how the two are similar and how they are different.

APPEAL TO AUTHORITY A writer may quote a well-known person or expert on the issue. Unless the well-known person is knowledgeable or experienced with the issue, his or her opinion is not relevant. Whenever experts are cited, be certain that they offer support for their opinions.

CAUSE–EFFECT RELATIONSHIPS A writer may argue that when two events occurred in close sequence, one caused the other. In other words, a writer may assume a cause–effect relationship when none actually exists. For example, suppose unemployment decreased the year a new town mayor was elected. The mayor may claim she decreased unemployment. However, the decrease may have been caused by factors the mayor was not involved with, such as a large corporation opening a branch in the town and creating new jobs.

Relevance and Sufficiency of Evidence

Once you have identified the evidence used to support an argument, the next step is to decide whether the writer has provided enough of the right kind of evidence to lead you to accept the claim. This is always a matter of judgment; there are no easy rules to follow. You must determine (1) whether the evidence provided is relevant and directly supports the statement and (2) whether sufficient evidence has been provided.

Suppose an article in your campus newspaper urges the elimination of mathematics as a required course at your college. As evidence, the article offers the following:

> Mathematics does not prepare us for the job market. In today's world, calculators and computer programs have eliminated the need for the study of mathematics.

This evidence neither directly supports the assertion nor provides sufficient evidence. First, calculators and computer programs do not substitute for an understanding of mathematical principles. Second, the writer does nothing to substantiate his idea that mathematics is irrelevant to the job market. The writer should provide facts, statistics, expert opinion, or other forms of documentation.

Exercise 16

DIRECTIONS　For each of the following statements, discuss the type or types of evidence that you would need in order to support and evaluate the statement.

1. Parents must accept primary responsibility for the health and safety of their children.
2. Apologizing is often seen as a sign of weakness, especially among men.
3. There has been a steady increase in illegal immigration over the past 50 years.
4. More college women than college men agree that euthanasia should be legal.
5. Car advertisements sell fantasy experiences, not a means of transportation. ●

Reading an Argument

When reading arguments, use the following steps:

READING ARGUMENTS

1. **Identify the issue.** What controversial question or problem does the argument address?

2. **Identify the claim/position, idea, or action the writer is trying to persuade you to accept.** Often, a concise statement of this key point appears early in the argument or in the introduction of a formal essay. The author often restates this key point within or at the end of the article or essay. What is stated? What is implied or suggested?

3. **Read the entire article or essay completely, more than once if necessary.** Underline key evidence that supports the author's claim.

(Continued)

4. **Evaluate the types of evidence provided.** Does the author offer statistics, facts, or examples? Is the evidence relevant and sufficient?

5. **Observe whether the author recognizes opposing viewpoints—ideas that those who disagree with the claim may hold.** Also note whether the author refutes those viewpoints (explains why they are wrong).

6. **Watch for conclusions.** Words and phrases such as *since, thus, therefore, accordingly, it can be concluded, it is clear that, it follows that*, and *hence* are signals that a conclusion is about to be given.

7. **Write a brief outline of the argument, listing its key points,** or annotate and highlight the article during and after reading.

Now read the following brief argument, using the marginal annotations to help you see how the argument is structured. The issue discussed in the argument is undocumented immigrant children in the United States. The author takes the position that undocumented immigrant children need and deserve government support.

Undocumented Children Need Charitable Help

The justified outrage over detained minors in California, Oklahoma and Texas has focused the nation's attention on what is only the tip of the iceberg. While the number of apprehended, unaccompanied Central American children could reach 90,000 this year, an estimated 1 million undocumented children already live among us.

Background information identifies the extent of the problem

But this is not just a Southwestern story. In New York and other cities with large immigrant communities, newly arrived children are desperate for medical attention, legal services, and help finding family members.

Statement of claim

Ask pediatrician Alan Shapiro, medical director of Children's Health Fund's Montefiore-based medical programs for highly disadvantaged kids in New York City. In cooperation with Catholic Charities New York, he recently co-founded Terra Firma, an innovative medical-legal partnership designed to meet the complex medical, psychosocial, and legal needs of unaccompanied minors. "Their life experience is marked by multiple traumas in their home countries, on their journey north and here in the U.S.," Shapiro explains. "As a society, it is our responsibility to heal them, not to compound the trauma."

Expert opinion offered as evidence

"Tomás," a teenage boy participating in a support group at Terra Firma's south Bronx clinic, recently showed Shapiro a photo of a relative who had been killed as punishment for not joining a Central American gang. When the pediatrician asked who else has seen anyone killed, all hands were raised. Needless to say, this is part of a humanitarian crisis rooted in severe international poverty.

Predictably, Tomás suffered from severe post-traumatic stress disorder, which in his case manifested as depression, frequent nightmares and insomnia. But thanks to the care he (and the other kids lucky enough to have found Terra Firma) is receiving, Tomás is now going to school, learning English, and working.

Example used to illustrate the issue

But what about the tens of thousands of other young unaccompanied immigrants who need help and a chance to grow up without fear and with a plausible opportunity to, one day, live normal lives?

Reason: medical-legal services are limited

First, many more service programs are needed to deal with the immediate medical-legal crises facing these kids. In fact, right now, excellent care is being provided by the U.S. Public Health Service and other private, voluntary efforts around the country. But they are only dealing with a fraction of the need.

Policy changes that could address the issue

In addition, there are two domestic policy changes that could alleviate massive suffering: include undocumented children of all ages in Obamacare and make targeted changes to immigration law that will create a safe haven for kids like Tomás.

Reason why services are needed

When, in 2010, the Affordable Care Act excluded undocumented immigrants from the provision mandating health insurance for all, a major gap was created in the safety net for 1 million children, most of whom already shouldered unconscionable health risks because of severe poverty. We are only beginning now to tabulate the exorbitant cost of leaving so many uninsured—billions of dollars in emergency room visits and even more from missed opportunities in preventive care. Some states have dealt with this challenge on their own.

Example used to demonstrate that more state laws are needed

In New York, for instance, children are covered under the state Child Health Plus program regardless of immigration status. But this is not the case in most states.

Opposing viewpoint is recognized and refuted using an example

And for those worried about runaway health care costs, it must be noted that care for children represents a minimal percentage of our nation's health care budget, and, furthermore, costs spike when you don't treat kids. Confronting tuberculosis before it spreads, for example, not only saves money for that child's care but for that of all of his or her schoolmates who might otherwise catch the disease.

Possible solution is offered

Immigration advocates have put forth some common sense ideas that could shield vulnerable children through a few relatively straight-forward strategies. For example, the courts or Congress could revise eligibility rules for asylum to include those fleeing gang violence, now at epidemic proportions in El Salvador, Honduras and Guatemala.

Restatement of claim

Yes, we do have a crisis involving vulnerable children now in the U.S., but we have the capacity to do the right thing—if we have the will to act quickly and respond effectively. Isn't that the American way?

—Redlener, *USA Today*, June 25, 2014

Exercise 17

DIRECTIONS Read the argument below, paying particular attention to the type(s) of evidence used. Then answer the questions that follow.

Vaccine Opt-Outs Put Public Health at Risk

Measles, which once killed 450 children each year and disabled even more, was virtually eliminated in the United States 14 years ago by nearly universal use of the MMR vaccine. But the disease is making a comeback, fueled by a growing anti-vaccine movement and misinformation that is spreading like a contagious disease. Already this year, 115 measles cases have been reported in the USA, compared with 189 for all of last year.

The numbers might sound small, but they are the leading edge of a dangerous trend. When vaccination rates are very high, as they still are in the nation as a whole, everyone is protected. Diseases such as polio, smallpox and measles are wiped out. This "herd immunity" protects the most vulnerable, including those who can't be vaccinated for medical reasons, infants too young to get vaccinated and people on whom the vaccine doesn't work.

But herd immunity works only when nearly the whole herd joins in. When some refuse vaccinations and seek a free ride, immunity breaks down and everyone is more vulnerable.

That's exactly what's happening in small clusters around the country from Orange County, Calif., where 22 measles cases were reported this month, to Brooklyn, N.Y., where a 17-year-old—intentionally not vaccinated—sparked an outbreak last year in an orthodox Jewish community where many families reject vaccines.

A 2008 measles outbreak in San Diego showed how many can be put at risk by the selfish decisions of a few. The outbreak started with one intentionally unvaccinated 7-year-old and spread to 11 other children, also not vaccinated. In less than a week, the infected youngsters exposed more than 800 other people to the disease at school, at a clinic, a swimming class, a grocery store and on a flight to Hawaii.

The anti-vaccine movement was sparked by a 1998 study in a British medical journal linking the MMR vaccine to autism. That study has been thoroughly debunked. But its hold on worried parents has only grown. Fears extend to other vaccines, as well.

Whooping cough numbers have been on the rise thanks in part to resistance that has persisted for decades. In that case, the opposition is driven by a real but very small risk. Those who refuse to take that risk selfishly inflict it on others.

Making matters worse are state laws that make it too easy to opt out of what are supposed to be mandatory vaccines for all children entering kindergarten. Seventeen states allow parents to get a "philosophical exemption," sometimes just by signing a paper saying they personally object to a vaccine. Others define religious exemptions too broadly. In Oregon, they can include almost any belief or practice.

Several states are moving to tighten laws by adding new barriers to opting out. Last year, Oregon added a small hurdle. A similar measure was moving through Colorado's Senate last week. But neither does enough to limit exemptions.

Parents ought to be able to opt out for strictly defined medical or religious reasons. But personal opinions? Not good enough. Everyone enjoys the life-saving benefits vaccines provide, but they'll exist only as long as everyone shares in the risks.

—USA Today, April 13, 2014

1. What is the issue? _____

2. What is the claim? _____

   _____

3. What types of evidence are used? _____

   _____

4. Is the evidence convincing? _____

5. Is there sufficient evidence? Why or why not? _____

   _____

   _____

6. What action is called for? _____

   _____

Think critically about graphics.

THINKING CRITICALLY ABOUT GRAPHICS

As we saw in Chapter 6, graphics and visual aids are common in popular and academic materials. Graphics and visual aids offer as much opportunity for critical thinking and analysis as text (word-based) materials do. Just as words can mislead, so too can visual aids. For example, a writer may include a photograph that elicits a strong emotional reaction as part of an argument essay, or a politician may post on his Web site data that presents only one side of the story.

To understand how graphics can mislead, look at Table 10-2, which summarizes the government's recommended dietary guidelines for a moderately active 23-year-old man. The table may seem straightforward; it provides clear recommendations for a daily diet. However, a closer reading of the table may bring up several questions, including:

TABLE 10-2 Daily Dietary Guidelines, 23-Year-Old Male (Moderately Active)

➢ Grains	10 ounces
➢ Vegetables	3.5 cups
➢ Fruits	2.5 cups
➢ Dairy	3 cups
➢ Protein foods	7 ounces

Source: USDA

- How is each of the food groups defined? For example, what exactly are "protein foods"? What kinds of protein foods are appropriate and healthy for a vegetarian who does not eat meat?
- How should the diet be adjusted if someone suffers from allergies? For example, some people are allergic to dairy foods or grains. What should they eat instead?
- Are the categories too broad? For example, certain fruits are fairly low in calories, while others (such as bananas) are very high in calories. Eating 3.5 cups of bananas per day would give you many more calories than 3.5 cups of strawberries. So, is the diet appropriate for someone who is trying to lose weight?

To find answers to these questions, you would need to read the text that accompanies the table and possibly conduct additional research.

Figure 10-1 on the next page presents the information in Table 10-2 graphically. But note that the presentation is misleading. The figure shows small icons to represent each ounce of grain or protein, or each cup of vegetables, fruits, or dairy. Because all the icons are the same size, you might think that one ounce of grain = one cup of vegetables = one ounce of protein food. But the icons represent different units that are *not* equivalent, because one cup does not equal one ounce. In fact, one cup equals *eight* ounces.

Grains: 10 ounces

FIGURE 10-1
Daily Dietary Guidelines, 23-Year-Old Male (Moderately Active)

Vegetables: 3 ½ cups

Fruits: 2 ½ cups

Dairy: 3 cups

Protein foods: 7 ounces

When viewing photographs, it is important to study their context. How is the image used, and could a different image have been used to make an opposing point? Consider the two photos in Figure 10-2 below. Which photo would you use to illustrate the following paragraph?

> The use of cell phones is out of control. Research shows that the average person checks his or her cell phone—get this—150 times a day. The first thing most people do when they get out of bed in the morning is reach for the cell phone. This wouldn't be so bad if people were using the cell phone as a tool to improve their productivity. But a cell phone is nothing but a way of wasting valuable time that would be better spent working, studying, or spending time with family or friends. The obsession is such that people endanger themselves and innocent people every single day by texting while driving. What is it about a text saying "hi, how r u" that can't wait until the car is parked? In 2011, 23 percent of all auto accidents were caused by texting while driving. A car accident is a high price to pay to send a text, but more than a third of the population doesn't care; they admit to texting while driving, and they don't apologize for it because they think it doesn't interfere with their driving at all.

Clearly, the photo showing a woman taking her eyes off the road while texting would be the much better choice. By choosing this photo, the author can reinforce his argument. The photo's content makes it difficult for readers to reject the author's key points.

But there's more than one side to the cell-phone controversy, of course. While cell phones are sometimes used irresponsibly, they are extremely helpful in many circumstances. An argument in favor of cell phones might point to their usefulness in calling for help when a car breaks down—an argument that would be nicely supported by the other photo in Figure 10-2.

As you examine photos, carefully gauge your emotional reaction. How does the photo make you feel? What type of reaction does it elicit? Perhaps the photo of the woman made you think, "She's so selfish and stupid," while the photo of the man made you think, "Poor guy; good thing he had his cell phone with him." Determine why the author has chosen the photo and ask yourself whether it influences you as you read.

FIGURE 10-2
Photos: The Pros and Cons of Cell Phones

DIRECTIONS   Use the sample textbook chapter in Part Seven to answer the following questions.

1. Examine the bar graph that appears on page 426 of the sample textbook chapter. In what ways could this graph be improved? How might the graph mislead you if you don't read the text that accompanies it?
2. Examine the photo on page 436. What is your emotional reaction to the photo? Which side of the Trayvon Martin/George Zimmerman controversy does the photo illustrate? ●

USING COLLEGE TEXTBOOKS
Critical Thinking Questions

Textbooks contain information on a variety of topics and issues, many of which demand critical thinking and evaluation. Many textbooks include features that ask students to think critically, evaluate chapter content, and make connections to their other coursework and their own lives. For instance, critical thinking questions are designed to help you process and apply the information you have learned. In the excerpt below from an environmental studies textbook, the question requires readers to fully understand factors that influence population growth.

> **5. THINK IT THROUGH**   India's prime minister puts you in charge of that nation's population policy. India has a population growth rate of 1.6% per year, a TFR [total fertility rate] of 2.7, a 49% rate of contraceptive use, and a population that is 71% rural. What policy steps would you recommend, and why?

—Withgott and Brennan, *Environment*, p. 222

Textbook Exercise 1: Understanding Critical Thinking Questions

Based on the information provided in the above "Think It Through" feature, do you think India wants to increase or decrease its population? Explain.

The following example, taken from a communication textbook, requires the reader to understand how groups function and then apply the information to real situations in his or her own life. By thinking about the information in terms of real examples, students get a deeper understanding of chapter content.

> **THINKING CRITICALLY   About Members and Leaders**
> 1. **Group Role in Interpersonal Relationships.** Can you identify roles that you habitually or frequently serve in certain groups? Do you serve these roles in your friendship, love, and family relationships as well?

2. **Groupthink.** Have you ever been in a group when groupthink was operating? If so, what were its symptoms? What effect did groupthink have on the process and conclusions of the group?

—DeVito, *Human Communication*, p. 240

Textbook Exercise 2: Answering Critical Thinking Questions

Answer the five questions above and at the bottom of page 295. Note that you will need to research the definition of *groupthink* before you can do so.

FURTHER PRACTICE WITH TEXTBOOK READING

Textbook Exercise 3: Sample Textbook Chapter

In the sample textbook chapter, the author provides journal entries under selected headings: "March 3, Dallas, Texas" (p. 430) and "November 19, Jerusalem, Israel" (p. 432). What is the purpose of these journal entries?

Textbook Exercise 4: Your College Textbook

Choose a textbook chapter that you have been assigned to read for one of your other courses. Read the chapter, and then answer the critical thinking questions at the end. If your textbook chapter does not have any, then write your own questions and answer them.

SELF-TEST SUMMARY

Goal 1 What is an inference?	An inference is a reasoned guess about what you do not know based on information that you do have. Inferences should be logical, plausible, and supported by evidence.
Goal 2 Why is it important to evaluate author and source credibility?	Not all sources are reliable or trustworthy; and, not all authors are qualified to write about their subjects. From an unqualified author or unreliable source you may get incomplete or incorrect information. It is particularly important to examine the credibility of Web sources, because the Web has no editor. Anyone can post anything on the Internet at any time.
Goal 3 What is the difference between facts and opinions?	Facts are statements that can be verified as correct. Opinions express feelings, attitudes, and beliefs and are neither true nor false.

Goal 4 How can you identify an author's purpose?	You can identify an author's purpose by considering the source of the material, the intended audience, the author's viewpoint, and any persuasive statements the author makes.
Goal 5 What is bias?	Bias refers to an author's partiality or inclination to express only one viewpoint.
Goal 6 What is tone?	Tone is an expression of the author's attitude toward his or her subject.
Goal 7 What are the three parts of an argument?	An argument addresses an issue, takes a position or makes a claim, and presents reasons and evidence to support the position. Some arguments also offer a refutation that considers opposing viewpoints and attempts to discredit them.
Goal 8 What are seven types of evidence?	Evidence includes facts, personal experience, examples, statistics, comparisons and analogies, appeals to authority, and cause–effect relationships. Each should be carefully evaluated.
Goal 9 Why is it important to think critically about graphics?	Just as words can be used to mislead, so too can graphics and visual aids. For this reason, all visual aids should be evaluated and examined critically.

APPLYING YOUR SKILLS

DISCUSSING THE CHAPTER

1. Think about editorials that you've read in your school or local paper. What makes a great editorial? What makes a poor editorial? What techniques can a writer use to present his or her argument and supporting evidence in an editorial?
2. Why is making inferences helpful in college studies? What subjects most frequently require you to make inferences?
3. What types of evidence are typically used in academic materials related to the topics you are studying? What types of questions should you ask when dealing with these various types of evidence?

ANALYZING A STUDY SITUATION

Ian is taking a business course in which he is studying forms of business ownership: sole proprietorships, partnerships, corporations, cooperatives, syndicates, and joint ventures. He read and highlighted his textbook and attended all class lectures. To prepare for an essay exam, Ian made a study sheet summarizing the characteristics of each form of ownership. When Ian read the following exam question, he knew he was in trouble.

Exam Question

Suppose you are the sole proprietor of a successful car wash. The owner of a competing car wash suggests that you form a partnership. Another competitor suggests that you enter into a joint venture to explore expansion opportunities. And a major car wash chain offers you a management position and stock in the corporation if you sell out. Write an essay explaining what factors you would consider in making a decision.

1. What levels of thinking did Ian use in preparing for the exam?
2. Why was Ian in trouble? That is, what types of thinking does the question demand?
3. How should Ian have prepared for the exam?

WORKING ON COLLABORATIVE PROJECTS

DIRECTIONS   Bring to class a brief (two- or three-paragraph) newspaper article, editorial, film review, etc. Working in groups of three or four students, each student should read his or her piece aloud or distribute copies. The group should discuss and evaluate (1) the source of the material, (2) the author's qualifications, (3) whether more facts or opinions are represented, (4) the author's purpose, (5) any bias, and (6) the tone of the passage. Your group should choose one article and submit your findings to the class or instructor.

Quick Quiz

DIRECTIONS Write the letter of the choice that best completes each statement in the space provided.

CHECKING YOUR RECALL

_____ 1. A fact is a statement that
   a. can be verified.
   b. is true.
   c. has no proof.
   d. expresses an opinion.

_____ 2. Statistics must be evaluated primarily because they may
   a. include too many facts.
   b. have appeared in another source first.
   c. have been manipulated.
   d. be based on another person's research.

_____ 3. All of the following questions indicate a higher level of thinking _except:_
   a. What are the author's qualifications?
   b. Is the material fact or opinion?
   c. What is the literal meaning of the material?
   d. What is the author's purpose?

_____ 4. One characteristic of biased writing is that it
   a. analyzes examples in great detail.
   b. favors a particular viewpoint.
   c. presents evidence objectively.
   d. consists primarily of untrue statements.

_____ 5. The author's position in an argument can best be described as the
   a. author's paraphrase of the issue.
   b. author's collection of relevant evidence.
   c. idea the author wants you to agree with.
   d. concept the author is refuting.

APPLYING YOUR SKILLS

_____ 6. Antonio arrived several minutes late for his sociology class and discovered the room empty and dark. He decided that the class must have been canceled and went to the library instead. In this situation, Antonio reached his decision by making
   a. an informed opinion.
   b. an inference.
   c. a generalization.
   d. a connotation.

_____ 7. In her research on homeschooling, Raquel has encountered the following statements. The one that is an example of an opinion is:
   a. Over half a million children are homeschooled annually.
   b. Homeschooled children completely miss out on all the normal social advantages that a child in public school gets every day.
   c. Most parents who homeschool their children have had at least one year of college.
   d. Most homeschooling parents are middle-class, with median incomes between $35,000 and $50,000.

_____ 8. Robert has a literature assignment in which he has to identify Jane Austen's tone in _Persuasion_. In this assignment, he will be looking specifically for Austen's
   a. feelings about her subject.
   b. purpose for writing.
   c. style of writing.
   d. use of historical information.

_____ 9. Analise wants to identify bias in the articles she has found while researching the need for increased security in courtrooms. Analise can assume an article is biased when the author
   a. presents both sides of a controversial issue.
   b. includes numerous facts and statistics as evidence.
   c. attempts to appeal to a general-interest audience.
   d. uses primarily positive or negative terms to describe the subject.

_____ 10. Trevor has been asked to evaluate the argument presented by the author of an article on the use of the atomic bomb in World War II. As a critical reader, Trevor should evaluate an argument primarily by deciding whether the
   a. author's ideas agree with his own.
   b. evidence is relevant and sufficient.
   c. author's personal experience is interesting and believable.
   d. supporting details are presented dramatically.

Evaluating Authors' Techniques

LEARNING GOALS

In this chapter you will learn to

1. Recognize and interpret connotative language.

2. Recognize and interpret figurative language.

3. Identify missing information.

4. Identify generalizations.

5. Analyze assumptions.

6. Recognize manipulative language.

LEARNING EXPERIMENT

1 Read each of the following statements.

_____ 1. The governor of our state is a loose cannon.

_____ 2. They say that the economy is booming and will show further improvement over the next year.

_____ 3. The tendency to prefer products and people from one's own culture over those from other cultures is known as ethnocentrism.

_____ 4. Politicians are a greedy, lazy bunch.

_____ 5. People in glass houses shouldn't throw stones.

_____ 6. Senator Whiner's foreign policies were criticized and then defeated.

2 Place a check mark in front of each of the above statements that you think is true, for which you do not need further information, and which you could safely use in a research paper, provided that it came from a reliable source and you documented that source.

The Results

Did you check only statements 3 and 6? If so, your choices show that you are a questioning, critical thinker. All of the other statements are not usable. You need further explanation, evidence, or more information before you can accept them as reliable.

Learning Principle: What This Means to You

Reading with a critical eye and a questioning attitude is an important skill, not just in college but also in the workplace and beyond. This chapter will show you how to recognize the various techniques writers can use to mislead, misguide, or even deceive a reader. You will learn how to spot emotional language, interpret figurative language, spot missing information, examine generalizations and assumptions, and study manipulative language.

PAYING ATTENTION TO CONNOTATIVE LANGUAGE

If you were wearing a jacket that looked like leather but was made of man-made fibers, would you prefer it be called *fake* or *synthetic?* Would you rather be part of a *crowd* or a *mob?* Would you rather be called *thin* or *skinny?*

Each of these pairs of words has basically the same meaning. A *crowd* and a *mob* are both groups of people. Both *fake* and *synthetic* refer to something man-made. If the words have similar meanings, why did you choose *crowd* rather than *mob* and *synthetic* rather than *fake?* While the pairs of words have similar primary meanings, they carry different shades of meaning; each creates a different image or association in your mind. This section explores these shades of meaning, called *connotative meanings.*

All words have one or more standard meanings, called **denotative meanings**. Think of them as the meanings or definitions listed in the dictionary. **Connotative meanings** include the feelings and associations that accompany a word. For example, the denotative meaning of *sister* is a female sibling. However, the word carries many connotations. For some, *sister* suggests a playmate with whom they shared their childhood. For others the term may suggest an older sibling who watched over them.

Connotations can vary from individual to individual. The word *dog* to dog lovers suggests a loyal and loving companion. To those who are allergic to dogs, however, the word *dog* connotes discomfort and avoidance—itchy eyes, a runny nose, and sneezes.

Writers and speakers use connotative meanings to stir your emotions or to bring to mind positive or negative associations. Suppose a writer is describing how someone drinks. The writer could choose words such as *gulp, sip, slurp,* or *guzzle.* Each creates a different image of the person drinking. Connotative meanings, then, are powerful tools of language. When you read, be alert for meanings suggested by the author's word choice. When writing or speaking, be sure to choose words with appropriate connotations.

DIRECTIONS For each of the following pairs of words, underline the word with the more positive connotation.

Exercise 1

1. suspicious	curious	
2. simple	plain	
3. shove	nudge	
4. immature	youthful	
5. mistake	blunder	
6. welcome	allow	
7. junk	salvage	
8. enthusiastic	fanatic	
9. timid	shy	
10. easygoing	lazy ●	

Exercise 2

DIRECTIONS   For each word listed, write a word that has similar denotative meaning but a negative connotation. Then write a word that has a positive or neutral connotation. Consult a dictionary or thesaurus, if needed.

Word	Negative Connotation	Positive or Neutral Connotation
Example: slow	sluggish	gradual
1. large	_____	_____
2. persuade	_____	_____
3. characteristic	_____	_____
4. uncommon	_____	_____
5. work	_____	_____
6. protect	_____	_____
7. toss	_____	_____
8. lecture	_____	_____
9. obtain	_____	_____
10. smart	_____	_____ •

Exercise 3

DIRECTIONS   Discuss the differences in the connotative meanings of each of the following sets of words. Consult a dictionary, if necessary.

1. **refuge:** retreat—shelter—hideout
2. **original:** unusual—strange—creative
3. **sensitive:** responsive—thin-skinned—emotional
4. **enemy:** adversary—opponent—rival
5. **tolerant:** permissive—liberal—soft
6. **routine:** regular—predictable—boring
7. **trick:** prank—feat—hoax
8. **complaint:** protest—criticism—gripe
9. **fascinate:** charm—hypnotize—seduce
10. **careful:** cautious—particular—fussy •

Goal 2

Recognize and interpret figurative language.

EXAMINING FIGURATIVE LANGUAGE

Figurative language makes a comparison between two unlike things that share a common characteristic. If you say that your apartment looks like a tornado struck it, you are comparing two unlike things—your apartment and the effects of a tornado. Figurative language makes sense creatively or imaginatively, but not literally. You mean that the apartment is messy and disheveled, not that a tornado appeared in your living room. Figurative language is a powerful tool that allows writers to create images or paint pictures in the reader's mind. Figurative language also allows writers to suggest an idea without directly stating it. If you say the mayor bellowed like a bear, you are suggesting that the mayor was animal-like, loud, and forceful, but you have not said so directly. By planting the image of bearlike behavior, you have communicated your message to your reader.

There are three primary types of figurative language—similes, metaphors, and personification. A **simile** uses the words *like* or *as* to make the comparison:

> The computer hums like a beehive.
>
> After 5:00 P.M. our downtown is as quiet as a ghost town.

A **metaphor** states or implies the relationship between the two unlike items. Metaphors often use the word *is*.

> The computer lab is a beehive of activity.
>
> After 5:00 P.M. our downtown is a ghost town.

Personification compares humans and nonhumans according to one characteristic, attributing human characteristics to ideas or objects. If you say "the wind screamed its angry message," you are giving the wind the human characteristics of screaming, being angry, and communicating a message. Here are some other examples:

> The sun mocked us with its relentless glare.
>
> After two days of writer's block, she felt her pen start dancing across the page.

Because figurative language is a powerful tool, be sure to analyze the author's motive for using it. Often, a writer uses figurative language as a way of describing rather than telling. A writer could say "The woman blushed" (telling) or "The woman's cheeks filled with the glow of a fire" (describing). Other times, figurative language is a means of suggesting ideas or creating impressions without directly stating them. When evaluating figurative language, ask the following questions:

- Why did the writer make the comparison?
- What is the basis or shared characteristic of the comparison?
- Is the comparison accurate?
- What images does the comparison suggest? How do these images make you feel?
- Is the comparison positive or negative?
- Are several different interpretations possible?

DIRECTIONS Label each statement as a simile, metaphor, or personification. Then, explain the comparison made in each.

Exercise 4

1. The rain moved like a curtain across the lake.
2. At the busy playground, the child was glued to her mother's side.
3. Every time the locker room door opened, a pungent bouquet of dirty socks, wet towels, and sweaty boys smacked us in the face.
4. The roast beef was as tough as an old boot.
5. After hours of delays, the weary passengers were herded like sheep through the airport and onto a hotel shuttle bus. ●

DIRECTIONS Discuss how the writers of each of the following passages use figurative language to create a specific impression.

Exercise 5

1. Aliens have invaded Hollywood. Helped by new computer graphics technology that has simplified the creation of weird-looking extraterrestrials, the silver screen is now crawling with cosmic critters eager to chow down on us, abduct us, or just tick us off as they total our planet. Why are aliens suddenly infesting the local

multiplex? Partly it's because after the collapse of the Soviet Union, Hollywood had to hunt around for a new source of bad guys. But our own space program has also convinced many among the popcorn-eating public that visiting other worlds will be a walk in the park for any advanced species.

—Bennett, Shostak, and Jakosky, *Life in the Universe*, p. 2

2. A frequent objection is that poetry ought not to be studied at all. In this view, a poem is either a series of gorgeous noises to be funneled through one ear and out the other without being allowed to trouble the mind, or an experience so holy that to analyze it in a classroom is as cruel and mechanical as dissecting a hummingbird.

—Kennedy and Gioia, *Literature: An Introduction to Fiction, Poetry, and Drama*, p. 454

3. Thick as a truck at its base, the Brazil-nut tree rises 10 stories to an opulent crown, lord of the Amazon jungle. It takes the tree a century to grow to maturity; it takes a man with a chain saw an hour to cut it down. "It's a beautiful thing," nods Acelino Cardoso da Silva, a 57-year-old farmer. "But I have six hungry people at home. If the lumberman turns up, I'll sell."

—Margolis, "A Plot of Their Own," *Newsweek* ●

Exercise 6

DIRECTIONS　Convert each of the following statements to an expression of figurative language.

Example: The daffodils bloomed. The daffodils covered the hillside like a bright yellow blanket.

1. People cried at the movie.
2. I was embarrassed.
3. We ate too much.
4. The fireworks were beautiful.
5. It snowed a lot last night. ●

Goal ③

Identify missing information.

WATCHING FOR MISSING INFORMATION

Most writers are honest and straightforward in conveying their meaning; however, some writers use techniques to mislead or manipulate the reader. Writers mislead by omission. They may omit essential details, ignore contradictory evidence, or selectively include only details that favor their position. They may also make incomplete comparisons, use the passive voice, or use unspecified nouns and pronouns.

Suppose, in describing homeschooling, a writer states, "Many children find homeschooling rewarding." But what is the author not telling us? If the author does not tell us that some children find homeschooling lonely and feel isolated from their peers, the author is not presenting a fair description of homeschooling. The writer has deliberately omitted essential details that a reader needs to understand homeschooling.

Suppose the same writer describes a research study that concludes that homeschooled children excel academically. To be fair, the writer should also report that other studies have demonstrated that homeschooled children do not differ in academic achievement from traditionally educated students. In this case, the writer has ignored contradictory evidence, reporting only evidence that he or she wants the reader to know.

One way writers avoid revealing information is to use a particular sentence structure, called *passive voice*, that does not identify who performed a specified action. In the sentence *The bill was paid*, you do not know who paid the bill. Here are a few more examples of the passive voice. In each, notice what information is missing.

> The tax reform bill was defeated.
>
> The accounting procedures were found to be questionable.
>
> The oil spill was contained.

Another way writers avoid revealing information is to use nouns and pronouns that do not refer to a specific person or thing. The sentence *They said it would rain by noon* does not reveal who predicted rain. The sentence *It always happens to me* does not indicate what always happens to the writer. Here are a few more examples:

> They say the enemy is preparing to attack.
>
> Anyone can get rich with this plan; many people have already.
>
> Politicians don't care about people.

To be sure you are getting full and complete information, ask the questions in the box below.

HAS ANYTHING BEEN OMITTED?

Be sure to ask . . .	To find out if . . .	Then you may need to . . .
What hasn't the author told me?	The author has deliberately omitted important information in an attempt to cover up or mislead.	Do additional research on the topic.
Did the author report details selectively?	The author favors a particular viewpoint.	Determine the author's bias. Compare the source with a source presenting an alternative viewpoint.
Is there contradictory evidence that was not reported?	The author has presented both sides of an issue fairly.	Obtain additional sources that discuss both sides of an issue. If the writer presents only one viewpoint, read sources presenting the opposite or alternative viewpoints.
What additional information may be helpful or important?	The author has covered all aspects of the problem or issue, or given just a quick overview.	Read a source that is more comprehensive and detailed.

DIRECTIONS For each of the following statements, indicate what information might be missing.

Exercise 7

1. They were denied health insurance.
2. Ticket prices have doubled this year.

3. Anyone can get a fake I.D.
4. Our schools are safer.
5. Real estate prices are inflated in parts of the country. ●

Goal 4

Identify
generalizations.

BEING ALERT FOR GENERALIZATIONS

Suppose you are reading an article that states, "Artists are temperamental people." Do you think that every artist who ever painted a portrait or composed a song is temperamental? Can you think of exceptions? This statement is an example of a **generalization**, which is a statement about an entire group (artists) based on known information about part of the group (artists the writer has met or observed). A generalization requires a leap from what is known to a conclusion about what is unknown. Generalizations may be expressed using words such as *all*, *always*, *none*, or *never*. Some statements may imply but not directly state that the writer is referring to the entire group or class. The statement "Artists are temperamental people" suggests but does not directly state that all artists are temperamental. Here are a few more generalizations:

> Rich people are snobs.
>
> Chinese food is never filling.
>
> Pets are always troublesome.

The ability to generalize is a valuable higher-level thinking skill. Many generalizations lead to valuable insights and creative problem-solving. However, generalizations made without sufficient evidence may be dangerous and misleading. The key to evaluating generalizations is to evaluate the type, quality, and amount of evidence given to support them. Here are a few more generalizations. What type of evidence would you need to be convinced that each is or is not true?

> College students are undecided about future career goals.
>
> All fast food lacks nutritional value.
>
> Foreign cars always outperform similar American models.

For the generalization about college students, you might need to see research studies about college students' career goals, for example. And then, even if some studies did conclude that many college students are undecided about their career goals, it would not be fair to conclude that every single student is undecided. If no evidence is given, then the generalization is not trustworthy and should be questioned.

You can also evaluate a generalization by seeing whether the author provides specifics about the generalization. For the statement "Pets are always troublesome," ask what kind of pets the author is referring to—a pet potbellied pig, an iguana, or a cat? Then ask what is meant by troublesome—does it mean the animal is time-consuming, requires special care, or behaves poorly?

Another way to evaluate a generalization is to try to think of exceptions. For the generalization *Medical doctors are aloof and inaccessible*, can you think of a doctor you have met or heard about who was caring and available to his or her patients? If so, the generalization is not accurate in all cases.

DIRECTIONS Read each of the following statements and place a check mark before each generalization.

_____ 1. Motorcyclists are thrill-seekers.

_____ 2. Houses are not built like they used to be.

_____ 3. In the United States, hurricane season lasts from June 1 to November 30.

_____ 4. Cars equipped with diesel engines are about 25 percent more efficient than regular cars.

_____ 5. People who visit the seedy side of town are looking for trouble. ●

DIRECTIONS Read the following paragraphs and underline each generalization.

1. Students who attend coeducational middle and high schools are at a disadvantage. Teenage boys and girls always learn better in single-sex classrooms, without the constant distraction of the opposite sex.
2. Travelers are fed up with their treatment by the airlines. Flight delays occur even in good weather, and overbookings leave passengers scrambling to find another flight. On top of the inconvenience, tickets cost a fortune.
3. Motorists never give pedestrians the right of way. Once they get behind the wheel of a car, people believe that they own the road; yielding to someone on foot would never occur to someone driving a car. ●

DIRECTIONS For each of the following generalizations, indicate what questions you would ask and what types of information you would need to evaluate the generalization.

1. No one writes letters anymore.
2. The weather is always perfect in San Diego.
3. All of the instructors at the college are dedicated to helping students.
4. People who work at home have a better quality of life.
5. Cosmetic surgery is only for the very wealthy and the very vain. ●

EXAMINING THE AUTHOR'S ASSUMPTIONS

Goal 5

Analyze assumptions.

Suppose a friend asks you, "Have you stopped cheating on your girlfriend?" This person, perhaps not a friend after all, is making an assumption. He or she is assuming that you are cheating. An **assumption** is an idea or principle the author accepts as true and makes no effort to prove or substantiate. Usually, it is a beginning or premise on which the writer bases the remainder of the statement. Assumptions often use words such as *since*, *if*, or *when*. Here are a few more examples:

• You're not going to make that mistake again, are you? (The assumption is that you have already made the mistake at least once.)
• When you're mature, you'll realize you made a mistake. (The assumption is that you are not mature now.)
• You are as arrogant as your sister. (The assumption is that your sister is arrogant.)

Each of the previous statements makes no attempt to prove or support the hidden assumption; it is assumed to be true.

Authors who make assumptions often fail to prove or support them. For example, an author may assume that television encourages violent behavior in children and proceed to argue for restrictions on TV viewing. Or a writer may assume that protests against a government are wrong and suggest legal restrictions on how and when protests may be held. If a writer's assumption is wrong or unsubstantiated, then the statements that follow from the assumption should be questioned. If television does not encourage violent behavior, for example, then the suggestion to restrict viewing should not be accepted unless other reasons are offered.

Exercise 11

Tip *Dwindling* means "decreasing."

Imperative means "very important to do immediately."

Converting means "changing."

DIRECTIONS   Read each of the following statements and then circle those choices that are assumptions made by the writer of the statement.

1. Since fossil-fuel resources are dwindling, it is imperative that we begin converting to nuclear energy now.

    a. It can be accurately predicted when fossil fuels will run out.
    b. People who oppose nuclear power are not realistic.
    c. Nuclear power is the only alternative to fossil fuels.

2. Many cultural treasures, such as paintings and other artifacts, were wrenched from their country of origin during times of war; these national treasures should be returned and displayed in their rightful homes.

    a. These artifacts were taken forcibly and illegally.
    b. Some artifacts were taken in an effort to safeguard them from damage.
    c. There is an appropriate and safe place for artifacts to be displayed in their country of origin.

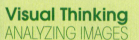

Visual Thinking
ANALYZING IMAGES

Why would the author have chosen this image to support her assertion?

FIGURE A Noted rapper Ja Rule awaits a hearing.

3. Hip-hop music and gangsta rap encourage violence and criminal behavior; therefore, these types of music should be subject to government censorship.

    a. It is the government's responsibility to censor music.
    b. Criminal behavior is a result of hip-hop music and gangsta rap.
    c. Other forms of entertainment feature violence and criminal behavior. ●

Exercise 12

DIRECTIONS   For each statement listed below, identify at least one assumption.

1. Musicians should let their songs be downloaded for free. The profits they make more than make up for any losses they may have from fans' file sharing.
2. Adding essay items to standardized tests will make the tests impossible to grade objectively.
3. Sports teams should be banned from using Native American names or references; teams such as the Braves and the Redskins are showing extreme disrespect to Native Americans.

4. Shopping online is the most efficient way to purchase clothing and other household items.

5. Sodas and other carbonated beverages have no place in our schools; school vending machines should contain bottled water only. ●

WATCHING FOR MANIPULATIVE LANGUAGE

Goal 6

Recognize manipulative language.

Writers can shape their readers' thinking and response to their message by the language they choose to express that message. Writers use a variety of language manipulation techniques to achieve a particular effect, to communicate their message in a particular way, and to appeal to specific groups of people. These techniques include clichés, allusions, and euphemisms.

Clichés

A **cliché** is a tired, overused expression. Here are a few examples:

> Curiosity killed the cat.
>
> Bigger is better.
>
> Absence makes the heart grow fonder.
>
> He is as blind as a bat.

These everyday expressions are so overused that they no longer carry a specific meaning. They have become pat expressions, often used by writers without much thought or creativity. Because the expressions are so common, many readers tend to accept them at face value rather than evaluate their meaning and appropriateness. When you recognize a cliché, ask yourself the following questions:

- Why did the writer use the cliché?
- Why did the writer not use a fresh, original expression instead?

Numerous clichés may suggest that the writer has not thought in depth about the topic or has not made the effort to express ideas in an interesting and unique way. When evaluating a writer's use of cliché, ask the following questions:

- **Is the author trying to gloss over details by using a cliché?** Clichés often oversimplify a complex situation. In trying to decide which courses to register for, a student may say, "Don't put off till tomorrow what you can do today." Actually the student *could* register today, but it may be better to wait until he or she has had time to think, do research, and talk to others about course selection.
- **Is the author trying to avoid directly stating an unpopular or unpleasant idea?** After describing recent acts of terrorism, suppose a writer concludes with the cliché, "What will be, will be." What does this cliché really say? In this context, the cliché suggests (but does not directly state) that nothing can be done about terrorism.
- **Is the cliché fitting and appropriate?** A writer may admonish students not to spend their financial aid loan before they receive it, by saying, "Don't count your chickens before they hatch." The writer's audience would be better served if the writer had explained that loan checks are often delayed, and that spending money before it is received may cause serious financial problems.
- **What does the use of clichés reveal about the author?** A writer who packs an article full of clichés is not aware that readers usually prefer fresh, descriptive information rather than standard clichés.

The grammar and spell-checking functions of word-processing programs typically include features that can help you check your own writing for clichés, colloquialisms, and jargon. From the "Tools" menu, select "Spelling and Grammar," "Options," and "Settings." You'll find these options under "Style."

Exercise 13

DIRECTIONS   For each of the following clichés, explain its meaning and then think of a situation in which it would be untrue or inappropriate.

1. There's no time like the present.
2. No pain, no gain.
3. Don't judge a book by its cover.
4. Every cloud has a silver lining.
5. If you can't take the heat, get out of the kitchen. •

Exercise 14

DIRECTIONS   Replace each of the following clichés with more specific information that fits the context of the sentence.

1. Joe had worked at the firm for a year but he was still low man on the totem pole.
2. The councilman promised to turn over a new leaf after he was convicted of bribery and extortion.
3. We wanted to sell our house quickly, so when our agent brought a prospective buyer we put all our cards on the table.
4. The caterers were two hours late and the band was awful, but the straw that broke the camel's back was seeing the guest of honor's name misspelled on the cake.
5. The new teacher may seem strict but she has a heart of gold. •

Allusions

Allusions are references to well-known religious, literary, artistic, or historical works or sources. For example, a writer may refer to a biblical verse, a character in a famous poem or novel, a line in a well-known song, or a historical figure such as Napoleon or George Washington. An allusion makes a connection or points to similarities between the author's subject and the reference. Writers usually assume that educated readers will recognize and understand their allusions. Here are a few examples of allusions:

- A writer describes a person as having the patience of Job. In the Bible, Job is a righteous man whose faith was tested by God.
- An article on parental relationships with children refers to the Oedipus complex. Oedipus was a figure in Greek mythology who unknowingly killed his father and married his mother. He blinded himself when he discovered what he had done. The Oedipus complex is controversial but refers to a child's unconscious sexual desires.

If you encounter an allusion you do not understand, check it on the Internet using a search engine such as Google or a reference such as Wikipedia by typing in the key words of the allusion.

Allusions can make writing interesting and connect the present to the past. Some authors, however, may include numerous literary or scholarly allusions to give their writing the appearance of scholarship. Do not be overly impressed by a writer's use of allusions, particularly obscure ones. A writer may use allusions to divert readers' attention from the lack of substantive detail or support. When evaluating a writer's use of allusions, ask the following questions:

- What does the allusion mean?
- Why did the author include the allusion?
- What does the allusion contribute to the overall meaning of the work?

DIRECTIONS   For each of the following statements, explain the meaning of the allusion.

| **Exercise 15** |

1. The investigation into city politics has opened a Pandora's box.
2. The cruise ship appeared Brobdingnagian next to the fishing boat.
3. Thanks to a good Samaritan, our flat tire was changed and we were on our way again in less than an hour.
4. The latest cell phones have a Big Brother aspect to them, allowing parents to constantly monitor their children's locations and activities.
5. When it comes to investing, my brother-in-law certainly has the Midas touch. ●

Euphemisms

What do these sentences have in common?

> He suffered combat fatigue.
>
> The company is downsizing.
>
> Capital punishment is controversial.

Each uses an expression called a **euphemism**, a word or phrase that is used in place of a word that is unpleasant, embarrassing, or otherwise objectionable. The expression *combat fatigue* is a way to refer to the psychological problems of veterans caused by their experiences in war, *downsizing* replaces the word *firing*, and *capital punishment* is a substitute for *death penalty*.

Euphemisms tend to downplay something's importance or seriousness. They are often used in politics and advertising. They can be used to camouflage actions or events that may be unacceptable to readers or listeners if bluntly explained. For example, the phrase *casualties of war* may be used instead of the phrase *dead soldiers* to lessen the impact of an attack. To say that a politician's statement was *at variance with the truth* is a less forceful way of saying that the politician lied.

Use the following questions to evaluate an author's use of euphemisms:

1. **What is the subject being discussed?** State it in everyday, straightforward, and direct language.
2. **How does the euphemism alter your perception of the situation?** Does it seem less harsh, severe, ugly, or serious?
3. **Why did the author use the euphemism?** Determine how the euphemism advances the writer's position and whether it reveals bias.

DIRECTIONS   For each of the underlined euphemisms, write a substitution that does not minimize or avoid the basic meaning of the term.

| **Exercise 16** |

1. Her grandmother <u>passed away</u> after a long illness.
2. Several ferryboat passengers experienced severe <u>motion discomfort</u> and became violently ill.
3. They finally made the difficult decision to have their dog <u>put to sleep</u>.
4. Because of our financial status, we bought a <u>pre-owned</u> vehicle. ●

Exercise 17

DIRECTIONS   Read "Ethical Dilemmas Surround Those Willing to Sell, buy Kidneys on the Black Market" in Part Six on page 392 and complete each of the following tasks.

1. Identify at least five words that have strong connotative meanings.
2. Identify at least two generalizations.
3. Is there any information the author might have purposefully omitted?
4. What assumptions does the author make? ●

USING COLLEGE TEXTBOOKS
Using Critical Thinking Features

Many textbooks contain information, features, or boxed inserts that discuss issues and problems related to chapter content. Their purposes are to demonstrate how chapter content can be applied to practical situations and to ask thought-provoking questions that will lead students to think critically. Here is a sampling of some critical thinking features.

TAKING A **CLOSER LOOK**

What does it say about American cultural values and norms when it is assumed that if a baby is left unattended it will be abducted and harmed? Can you think of other behaviors that might be considered deviant by American cultural standards, but perfectly acceptable in another country?

—Thompson and Hickey, *Society in Focus*, p. 167

Textbook Exercise 1: Understanding Critical Thinking Features

Answer the questions posed in the above "Taking a Closer Look" feature.

STOP AND STRETCH

One possible consequence of global warming is a decrease in the overall ice cover at the North Pole. Less ice is not only an effect of warming, it is likely to increase the rate of warming. Why?

—Belk, *Biology*, p. 399

Textbook Exercise 2: Answering Critical Thinking Questions

Based on the "Stop and Stretch" above, what is another possible consequence of global warming?

What Do You Think?

What implications do developments in global health have for people living in the United States today? What international programs, policies, or services might help control the world's health problems in the next decade? Are there actions that individuals can take to help?

—Donatelle, *Health*, p. 12

Textbook Exercise 3: Making Connections with Critical Thinking Questions

How does the development of a serious disease (such as Ebola) in a distant country eventually affect the United States?

FURTHER PRACTICE WITH TEXTBOOK READING

Textbook Exercise 4: Sample Textbook Chapter

Read the box titled "Thinking About Diversity: Race, Class and Gender—Hard Work: The Immigrant Life in the United States" (p. 432 in the sample textbook chapter). Then answer the "What Do You Think?" questions that appear at the end of the box.

Textbook Exercise 5: Your College Textbook

Choose a textbook chapter that you have been assigned to read for one of your other courses. Read any boxes and summarize their content. If your textbook chapter does not have any, then write a proposal for one.

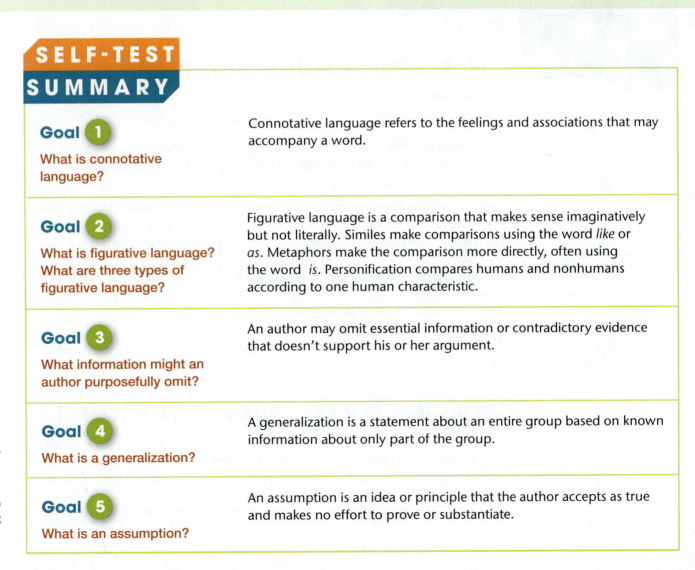

SELF-TEST SUMMARY

Goal 1 What is connotative language?	Connotative language refers to the feelings and associations that may accompany a word.
Goal 2 What is figurative language? What are three types of figurative language?	Figurative language is a comparison that makes sense imaginatively but not literally. Similes make comparisons using the word *like* or *as*. Metaphors make the comparison more directly, often using the word *is*. Personification compares humans and nonhumans according to one human characteristic.
Goal 3 What information might an author purposefully omit?	An author may omit essential information or contradictory evidence that doesn't support his or her argument.
Goal 4 What is a generalization?	A generalization is a statement about an entire group based on known information about only part of the group.
Goal 5 What is an assumption?	An assumption is an idea or principle that the author accepts as true and makes no effort to prove or substantiate.

Goal 6

What are clichés, allusions, and euphemisms?

A cliché is a tired, overused expression. An allusion is a reference to a well-known religious, literary, artistic, or historical work or source. A euphemism is a word or phrase used in place of a word that is unpleasant, embarrassing, or otherwise objectionable.

APPLYING   YOUR SKILLS

DISCUSSING THE CHAPTER

1. Discuss the types of publications in which you might expect a writer to purposefully omit information.
2. Create a figurative expression to describe one characteristic of a close friend.
3. Brainstorm a list of clichés that you are tired of hearing and would like to avoid using in your speech and writing.
4. Create a list of connotative meanings that may exist for one of the following words: *birthday, patriotism, paycheck*, or *dinner*.

ANALYZING A STUDY SITUATION

Analyze the following situation and answer the questions below.

An English instructor gave his class the following assignment:

Locate three articles on a current controversial issue. One of the three must express a different viewpoint from the other two. Write a two-page paper that critically evaluates each article.

One student in the class located three articles on censorship but did not know how to approach the assignment. He summarized each article and then wrote a paragraph describing how one article differed from the other two. The instructor refused to accept and grade this student's paper, saying that he had not completed the assignment.

1. Why was the student's paper unacceptable?
2. How should he have approached the assignment?
3. On what bases or using what criteria might the student have evaluated the articles?

WORKING ON COLLABORATIVE PROJECTS

DIRECTIONS   Each student should bring a copy of a current popular magazine to class. Form groups of three students, select one magazine, and choose a feature article. Examine it for each of the topics covered in this chapter. Analyze why each was included and its possible effect on unsuspecting readers. Report your findings to the class, beginning with a brief summary of the article.

Quick Quiz

DIRECTIONS Write the letter of the choice that best completes each statement in the space provided.

CHECKING YOUR RECALL

_____ 1. The standard, dictionary meaning of a word is known as its

  a. connotative meaning.
  b. denotative meaning.
  c. figurative meaning.
  d. inferred meaning.

_____ 2. A generalization can be defined as a

  a. principle or idea that an author accepts as true and makes no effort to prove.
  b. comparison between two unlike things that share one common characteristic.
  c. statement expressing feeling, attitudes, or beliefs that are neither true nor false.
  d. statement about a whole group based on information about part of the group.

_____ 3. An author who uses the passive voice may be trying to avoid

  a. identifying who performed a particular action.
  b. explaining incomplete comparisons.
  c. including contradictory evidence.
  d. revealing details that favor one position.

_____ 4. An assumption can be defined as an idea or principle that the author

  a. attempts to disprove.
  b. approaches logically.
  c. disagrees with.
  d. accepts as true without attempting to prove.

_____ 5. Figurative language compares

  a. several images.
  b. two unlike things.
  c. many similar things.
  d. several descriptive images.

APPLYING YOUR SKILLS

_____ 6. The statement "The cousins fought like cats and dogs" is an example of

  a. an allusion.
  b. a cliché.
  c. a euphemism.
  d. jargon.

_____ 7. The statement "He's more indecisive than Hamlet" is an example of

  a. a euphemism.
  b. denotative language.
  c. jargon.
  d. an allusion.

_____ 8. The statement "The soldier was wounded by friendly fire" is an example of

  a. a euphemism.
  b. a cliché.
  c. jargon.
  d. a generalization.

_____ 9. A word or expression with a negative connotation that describes an intelligent person is

  a. intellectual.
  b. scholar.
  c. egghead.
  d. wise guy.

_____ 10. Of the following statements, which is a generalization?

  a. "I learned more than I ever expected to in this course."
  b. "That course was my favorite."
  c. "Dr. Fassell is a biology professor."
  d. "All of the instructors at the college are dedicated to helping students."

POLISH YOUR ACADEMIC IMAGE

Did You Know?

⊃ A recent study asked instructors why they think students succeed or fail. Faculty indicated that student success is based on students' having good time-management skills, being motivated, asking for help, and having goals and reasons for attending college.[1]

All of these predictors of student success are evident in the way a student behaves in class. In other words, success is tied to presenting a positive academic image.

WHAT ACADEMIC IMAGE DOES A SUCCESSFUL STUDENT PROJECT?

Imagine that you are a teacher meeting a class of students for the first time. Look at the students in the photos on the next page from the teacher's point of view. Next to each photo, write your first impressions of how each student will approach his or her coursework. Ask yourself:

- Who do you think will participate in class?

- Who will turn in careful, neatly organized work?

- Who will be early, on time, or late for class?

- Who will come to your office to ask questions when he or she doesn't understand an assignment? Whom will you never see there?

- Who will tell you the dog ate his or her homework?

Be prepared to discuss your reasoning. Now take a few moments and brainstorm a list of observable behaviors that characterize a successful student. Be prepared to share and discuss your list with the class.

---

[1] http://cop.hlcommission.org/cherif.html

WHAT ACADEMIC IMAGE DO YOU PROJECT?

Now that you have brainstormed ideas about student behavior, let's turn the focus inward. The following questionnaire will help you assess your academic image and identify behaviors you need to change.

	Always	Sometimes	Never
1. I ask and answer questions in class.	❏	❏	❏
2. I make eye contact with my instructor during class.	❏	❏	❏
3. I speak to my instructors when I see them on campus.	❏	❏	❏
4. I turn in neat, carefully done assignments using formal English.	❏	❏	❏
5. I make myself known to instructors by speaking to them before or after class.	❏	❏	❏
6. I attend all classes and explain any necessary lengthy absences to my instructors.	❏	❏	❏
7. I avoid texting or talking with classmates while the instructor is talking.	❏	❏	❏
8. I come to class before the instructor and stay until class is dismissed.	❏	❏	❏
9. I try to stay alert to show that I am interested.	❏	❏	❏
10. I sit in class with other students who demonstrate a positive academic image.	❏	❏	❏

If you answered "Sometimes" or "Never" to more than one or two questions, you should work on improving your academic image.

WHY IS A POSITIVE ACADEMIC IMAGE IMPORTANT?

When you meet someone new, how do you figure out what he or she is like? Usually you try to understand others by the way they act—their behavior. Your instructors do the same.

How can your instructor tell that you are interested in the course material? She can watch for behaviors that usually go along with interest—asking questions when you want to know more or don't understand something, answering questions that she asks, paying attention to what she says, and taking notes. If you visit her office for help, she knows you are serious about doing well in her class.

If you talk to your classmates or surf the Web instead of paying attention to your instructor, she will likely decide you are not interested in the class.

Instructors respect and appreciate students whose behaviors are professional, positive, and courteous. They respond well to students who want to learn and do well in their classes.

In short: A positive academic image gives you a head start on the road to academic success.

WHAT IS ACADEMIC INTEGRITY?

Academic integrity means presenting your own work fairly and honestly; this includes class assignments, exams, projects, and papers. It means you avoid cheating and presenting the work of others as your own (also called plagiarism). For more about plagiarism, see Chapter 4.

HOW CAN I IMPROVE MY ACADEMIC IMAGE?

For each response of "Sometimes" or "Never" you gave in the academic image questionnaire, write a new statement about how you can change your everyday behaviors in class and on campus to improve your academic image. What will help your instructors think of you as a serious, hardworking, responsible student? (Remember what things look like from the front of the room!)

1. I will _____

_____

2. I will _____

_____

3. I will _____

_____

4. I will _____

_____

HOW CAN I SUSTAIN MY POSITIVE ACADEMIC IMAGE?

The key to sustaining your new behaviors is to practice them until they become habits. Take time each day to mentally assess your academic image and behaviors. Has your instructor noticed the change in your behavior? Are you earning better grades? Do you notice the academic behavior of others? If so, you are well on your way to an excellent academic image. But don't sit back and think that you have arrived; take a few minutes every week or two to reflect on the following questions:

Am I communicating with my instructors?

- Do I talk to instructors before or after class?
- Do I take advantage of my instructors' office hours or willingness to answer questions via e-mail?
- Have I explained any attendance problems to my instructors?

Am I participating in my classes?

- Am I making eye contact with my instructors?
- Do I ask and answer questions in class?
- Do I show my interest and motivation in class?
- Do I sit near the front of the class?
- Do I focus on the lecture or classroom discussion instead of checking my phone or surfing the Web?

Am I turning in good-quality work?

- Do I submit neat and complete assignments?
- Do I always include my name and the date, course title, and section number on my assignments?
- Do I word-process all my papers?

Am I projecting a successful academic image?

IMAGE!

Integrity

  Motivation

    Attention

      Good Work

        Energy

SUCCESS WORKSHOP 8

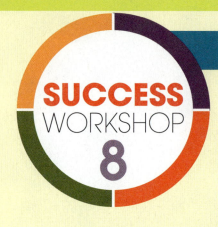

Learning to handle the many demands of college life can be stressful, especially if you are trying to raise a family or work a job at the same time. If you learn to manage stress, you will find that your life becomes more enjoyable and productive, and your grades will likely improve.

WHAT IS STRESS?

Stress is a state of mental or emotional strain that results from demanding circumstances. Stress affects people of all ages, but it is especially prevalent in the young adult years, when individuals are trying to balance the multiple aspects of their lives. There always seems to be too much to do, but never enough time.

WHAT ARE THE SYMPTOMS OF STRESS?

The symptoms of stress can be emotional, physical, or both.

Emotional Symptoms

- Feeling rushed or mentally exhausted
- Difficulty concentrating
- Being short-tempered
- Feeling listless or unfocused

Physical Symptoms

- Headaches
- Fatigue

[1] American College Health Association. National College Health Assessment. http://www.acha-ncha.org/docs/ACHA-NCHA-II_ReferenceGroup_ExecutiveSummary_Spring2013.pdf

[2] Keith A. King, Meha Singh, Amy Bernard, Ashley L. Merianos, and Rebecca A. Vidourek, "Employing the Health Belief Model to Examine Stress Management Among College Students," *American Journal of Health Studies* 27, no. 4 (2012): 192–203.

- Queasiness or indigestion
- Weight loss or weight gain
- Difficulty sleeping

IDENTIFYING YOUR LEVEL OF STRESS

Before continuing with this workshop, complete the stress questionnaire below to help you identify your level of stress.

STRESS QUESTIONNAIRE

Respond to each of the following statements by checking "Yes," "No," or "Sometimes" in the boxes provided and then adding up the total for each column. If you answered "Yes" to more than three or four items, or "Sometimes" to more than four or five items, you may be experiencing stress. Evaluate the pattern of your responses. Look at the questions to which you answered "Yes" or "Sometimes." Some questions deal with physical habits; others focus on organizational skills. By evaluating your answers, you will be better able to identify your own stress indicators.

	Yes	No	Sometimes
1. I feel as if I don't have enough time in a week to get everything done.	❑	❑	❑
2. I worry about money regularly.	❑	❑	❑
3. I have recently begun to smoke or use alcohol, or I have increased my use of either.	❑	❑	❑
4. I have more conflicts and disagreements with friends and/or family than I used to.	❑	❑	❑
5. I am having difficulty staying involved with social, religious, or academic activities.	❑	❑	❑
6. I seem to get colds and other minor illnesses (headaches, upset stomachs) more frequently.	❑	❑	❑
7. I find myself confused or listless.	❑	❑	❑
8. My usual level of physical activity or exercise has decreased.	❑	❑	❑
9. Small problems seem overwhelming.	❑	❑	❑
10. I seldom find time to do some fun things each week.	❑	❑	❑
11. I find myself unable to meet deadlines and am losing track of details (appointments, chores, promises to friends, and so on).	❑	❑	❑
12. I spend time worrying about grades.	❑	❑	❑
Total	_____	_____	_____

ANALYZING THE CAUSES OF YOUR STRESS

Rate each of the following causes of stress as High, Medium, or Low for you. Then compare your ratings with those of a classmate. Brainstorm ways of eliminating or controlling each stressor.

Source	Rating
Job	_____
Friends	_____
Family (spouse, parents, children)	_____
Academic course work	_____
Health, fitness, and nutrition	_____
Financial problems	_____
Sleep	_____

HOW CAN YOU MANAGE STRESS?

You can take direct, positive action to reduce and manage your stress. The following tips will help.

Get enough sleep. The amount of sleep a person needs is highly individual. Discover how much you need by noticing patterns. For several weeks, analyze how well your day went and consider how much sleep you had the night before. Then adjust your schedule to make sure you get the right amount of sleep each night.

Exercise regularly and notice stress as it is happening. Exercising three times a week for about 15 minutes each time is a good way to release general stress. When you find yourself getting tense—for example, when your shoulders or neck start tightening—take a few minutes immediately to stretch or go for a brief walk.

Eat regular, healthy meals. Give yourself time to eat three meals a day. For snacks in between, eat fruit or vegetables. Avoid a diet heavy in fats, and try to eat balanced meals rather than junk food. (But do not deny yourself an occasional treat as a reward for accomplishing a task or goal.)

Reduce or eliminate smoking and drinking alcohol. Check with a counselor at the student health center for a program that will help you.

Learn to say no to unreasonable requests from friends and family. Explain your schedule to your family, and make sure they understand your academic goals. Then when you need to turn down unreasonable requests, they will understand why.

Take breaks and breathe deeply. Constantly pushing yourself compounds stress. Slow down and do nothing for a brief period, even if just for five minutes. If you practice deep breathing on your breaks, you will relax even more. Breathe in through your nose; then breathe out completely through your mouth.

HOW CAN YOU USE POSITIVE THINKING TO DECREASE STRESS?

When you feel as if you don't have enough time in your day to get everything done, don't think negatively—"I'll never be able to get all this done!" Instead think positively—"It's going to feel great to accomplish this!"

- **Visualize success.** Imagine yourself getting everything done in an orderly, systematic way.

- **Focus on the benefits of completing each task.** How will completing each task help you or others?

- **Develop a plan or schedule that will allow you to get everything done.**

- **Interact with others.** Problems often seem smaller and more manageable after you've talked about them.

- **Refocus your attention on others occasionally.** You might shop for an elderly relative, tutor a classmate, or volunteer at a soup kitchen or animal shelter. Once you take your mind off yourself and you see others with problems, your own problems will often seem more manageable.

- **Make fewer choices.** Stress tends to increase when you are responsible for making a large number of decisions. To reduce stress, eliminate some of the daily decisions that consume your time and energy. Instead of deciding what to cook, eat, or order for dinner each night, decide on the menu for the whole week all at once. Alternatively, make every Monday pasta night, every Tuesday chicken night, and so forth. With fewer decisions to make, you'll feel less pressured and have more time to think about important decisions.

- **Reduce the clutter.** Get organized and keep everything in its place. You won't waste time looking for misplaced objects or devote hours to cleanup blitzes.

MANAGING STRESS!

Say no when you don't have the time to take on more responsibility.

 Take a moment to sit and relax.

  Refocus your attention and energy to their best use.

   Eat healthy meals and snacks.

    Sleep as many hours as you need to.

     Spend time with family and friends.

12

Working with Other Academic Sources

LEARNING GOALS

In this chapter you will learn to

1 Read nontextbook assignments.

2 Read periodicals.

3 Read nonfiction and scholarly books.

4 Read academic sources.

LEARNING EXPERIMENT

1 Select and summarize a chapter from one of your textbooks.

2 At the library, find a periodical article and a chapter in a nonfiction or scholarly book that cover the same topic as your textbook chapter.

3 Summarize the article and the book chapter, and evaluate the author's tone and use of data and evidence (see p. 282, Chapter 10).

4 Compare how each of these three different sources covers the same basic topic. What are the strengths and weaknesses of each source? How does consulting all three sources give you a more complete picture of your topic?

The Results

Textbooks give a straightforward, basic overview of information necessary to learn about a discipline or skill. Authors who are writing for nonstudent audiences have more flexibility when it comes to tone, data, and evidence. Nontextbook sources complement the basic understanding you get from a textbook.

Learning Principle: What This Means to You

Applying your critical reading skills to other sources in addition to textbooks will broaden your understanding of an academic subject area. Knowing how to identify useful and authoritative sources will encourage you to keep learning about topics that interest you.

BEYOND TEXTBOOKS: OTHER ACADEMIC SOURCES

Goal 1

Read nontextbook assignments.

You probably have discovered that your reading assignments are not limited to textbooks; many of your professors require that you read magazine, journal, and newspaper articles. Some professors distribute reading lists and direct you to read a specified number of articles or write a specified number of abstracts. Others post links to readings on your class course management system or place materials on reserve in the library.

It is important to learn to read academic sources beyond textbooks because:

- Textbooks are written for students and are a good introduction to a field; however, many professors expect you to go beyond your textbook to find further information or explore related issues.
- Reading serious and scholarly books and periodicals about your field of study introduces you to what professionals in the field are thinking about and working on.
- Textbooks are not generally accepted as sources for research papers. You will need to consult other kinds of sources when you do research for your course work.

Reading academic sources is very different from reading textbooks. It differs in the following ways:

- **Level of retention and recall.** When reading textbooks, your goal is usually a high level of retention and recall of all assigned material. In reading other sources, however, complete retention is not always necessary. You may be searching for evidence to support an argument, reading widely to gain overall familiarity with a subject, or locating a particular statistic.
- **Format and organization.** While textbooks follow a consistent format and organization, research and reference sources differ widely in format. Consequently, you must adapt your reading strategy to suit the nature of the material.

This chapter presents a systematic approach to locating, reading, and evaluating academic sources. Often your instructor assigns or guides you to specific academic sources.

HOW TO LOCATE SOURCES

When it is up to you to locate your own sources, use the following general guidelines:

1. **Consult with your reference librarian to determine the best sources available.** Many libraries have access to data banks or online services that identify all possible sources on a given topic. (Some libraries charge a fee for this service.) The librarian can show you all the main sources, both print and online, for your topic. Check the library's Web site; there might be an online guide or tutorial for undertaking research in your subject.
2. **Read an encyclopedia entry to get an overview of the subject.** Both general and specialized encyclopedias for specific subjects are available in print and online.
3. **Check the library's online catalog to see how your topic is subdivided.** Start your search by using keywords. Once you find a subtopic that looks useful, check the subject headings for that item. Use those subject headings to do a more specific search that narrows in on your topic.

(Continued)

4. **Consider your purpose and the type of information you need.** If you need an overview of a topic, choose a more general source. If you need detailed information, choose a specialized source.

5. **Consult your instructor if you're not sure whether your source is appropriate.** Your reference librarian can then direct you toward more suitable sources if necessary.

There is a wide variety of academic sources, each with a specific purpose and use. These are summarized in Table 12-1. Most of these sources are now available online; many still offer print versions, too.

TABLE 12-1
Types of Reference Sources

SOURCE	PURPOSE AND USE
Reference book (encyclopedia, directory)	Provides authoritative background and overview; useful when starting out on a new topic to become familiar with key names, dates, and concepts; usually lists sources for further reading
Scholarly nonfiction book—monograph	One author's detailed treatment of a subject using his or her own research, ideas, and informed opinions supported with those of others. Often it refutes opposing viewpoints and offers points for consideration.
Scholarly nonfiction book—edited collection	A group of essays centered around a common theme or idea, each providing a specific viewpoint or theory
Periodical: magazine	Provides articles on current topics of interest for a broad audience; can give a simplified treatment of a scholarly topic
Periodical: scholarly journal	Provides articles written by experts and researchers in a specific field; often contains original research studies
Primary sources	Original documents that give a first-person account of an era or event (e.g., letters and diaries)

Exercise 1

DIRECTIONS Using Table 12-1 as a guide, identify what type of source would be useful in each of the following situations.

1. You are giving a presentation on the Oregon Trail and you want to include a firsthand account from one of the pioneers traveling West.
2. For your political science class, you need to prepare for a debate on the United States' use of the atomic bomb in WWII, but you hardly know anything about this topic.
3. You need a lot of in-depth information and analysis from an expert on Abraham Lincoln for your history research paper.
4. An online class requires you to contribute your thoughts on current events once per week; you need a source that will keep you up-to-date on a variety of topics without overwhelming you with too much detail.
5. One of your professors has assigned a research paper for which you need studies that show how a vegan diet affects diabetes. ●

Goal 2
Read periodicals.

PERIODICALS: MAGAZINES AND SCHOLARLY JOURNALS

Periodicals include both popular press magazines, such as *Time, Sports Illustrated,* and *In Style,* and scholarly publications, such as *The Journal of Sociology* and *Marine Ecology.* Magazines and scholarly journals differ in the ways shown in Table 12-2.

MAGAZINES	SCHOLARLY JOURNALS
Broad audience, often the general public	Specialized audience, such as professionals
Information and entertainment	Research, theories, ideas, detailed analysis
Colorful, photographs, graphics	Black and white, charts, graphs, tables
Advertising	Little or no advertising
Commercial publisher	Published by a professional organization or educational institute
Writers are journalists or enthusiasts; they are paid for their articles.	Authors are experts in the field—researchers, professors; they are not paid for their articles.

TABLE 12-2
Comparing Magazines and Scholarly Journals

Visual Thinking
APPLYING SKILLS

Which of these periodicals are trustworthy and reliable sources of information? What standards would you use to evaluate them?

In many classroom situations, magazines are not considered appropriate sources because their articles are written by journalists for a general audience and do not provide the depth necessary for academic investigation. For example, an article in a magazine about healthy eating may mention a study about eating pomegranates for good health. The original study, originally published in an academic journal, described the details of the method, participants, data, and findings. Perhaps it was a study of only five senior citizens in Sweden who ate only pomegranates for a month and didn't get a cold during that time. Looking at the original study would help you discover firsthand how relevant the data are, while the journalist takes the data and makes her own interpretation to fit her article.

However, a magazine article might be appropriate when you need an easy-to-read overview of a complicated topic before you start your research. For example, there are many complicated technical studies that deal with aspects of climate change, but a magazine article might provide a good overview of all the issues.

The Structure of Articles and Essays

An article or essay begins with a **title** and is usually followed by an **introduction** that presents the thesis statement (or controlling idea). Then one or more paragraphs are devoted to each supporting idea. The main part of the essay or article, often called the **body**, presents ideas and information that support the thesis statement. A **conclusion** makes a final statement about the subject and draws the article or essay to a close.

You can visualize or map the organization of an article or essay as follows.

The Structure of an Essay

PARTS   FUNCTIONS

Title   **Title**   1. Can suggest the subject
                                               2. Can create interest

Introduction   **Thesis Statement**   1. Identifies the topic
                                               2. Presents the thesis statement
                                               3. Interests the reader
                                               4. Provides background
                                               5. Defines terms

         Supporting Idea (Paragraph 2)

         Supporting Idea (Paragraph 3)   1. Supports and explains the
                                                  thesis statement
Body   2. Presents each main
                                                  supporting point in a
                                                  separate paragraph
         Supporting Idea (Paragraph 4)   3. Provides, in each
                                                  paragraph, details that make
                                                  each main point
                                                  understandable
         Supporting Idea (Paragraph 5)

Conclusion   **Final Paragraph**   1. Reemphasizes the thesis
                                                  statement (does not merely
                                                  restate it)
                                               2. Draws the essay to a close

Note: There is no set number of paragraphs that an essay contains. This model shows six paragraphs, but in actual essays the number will vary greatly.

Exercise 2

DIRECTIONS Assume your sociology instructor assigns the essay "Ethical Dilemmas Surround Those Willing to Sell, Buy Kidneys on the Black Market" (Part Six, p. 392). Read it and then answer the following questions.

Introduction:

1. How does the author try to interest you in the subject?
2. What is the subject of the essay?
3. What is the author's thesis?

Body:

4. What main supporting ideas does the author offer to support the thesis?

Conclusion:

5. How does the author conclude the essay? ●

The Structure of Scholarly Articles

Many scholarly articles, especially those that report research conducted by the author, follow a similar format and often include the following parts. Different journals may use different headings to organize their articles, or they may not label all sections with headings.

- **Abstract.** An abstract is a brief summary of the article and its findings. It is sometimes labeled "Summary." It usually appears at the beginning of the article, following the title and author. Read the abstract to get an overview of the article. It can help you determine whether the study or report contains the information you need.
- **Summary of Related Research.** Many research articles begin by summarizing research that has already been done on the topic. Authors will cite other studies and briefly report their findings. This summary brings you up to date on the most current research and may suggest why the author's study or research is necessary. In some journals this rationale may appear in a section titled "Statement of the Problem."
- **Methodology.** In this section the author describes his or her research. For experimental research, you can expect it to include purpose, description of the population studied, sample size, procedures, and statistical tests applied.
- **Results.** Results and findings of the research are presented in this section.
- **Implications, Discussion, and Conclusion.** Here the author explains what the results mean and presents possible implications and conclusions.
- **Further Research.** Based on their findings, some authors conclude the article by suggesting additional research that is needed to further explain the problem or issue being studied.

NONFICTION AND SCHOLARLY BOOKS

Goal 3

Read nonfiction and scholarly books.

Many professors assign papers that require you to analyze a topic or literary work deeply and with reference to its history. For example, you might be asked to evaluate the way that Russia has developed into a country with a market economy. This topic will require the use of several scholarly nonfiction books that deal with different aspects of the topic, such as the history of Russia and the Soviet Union, the political and social factors that led to the change, the political and economic theories in play, and the current situation. To make sure you are using appropriate scholarly nonfiction, use the guidelines below.

HOW TO IDENTIFY APPROPRIATE SCHOLARLY NONFICTION SOURCES

1. **What are the author's credentials?** Look for information on the author. What are his or her educational background and current college or university affiliation? What awards has he or she won and what other books has he or she written?
2. **Who is the publisher?** Look at who published the book. Is it an educational institution or a professional organization?
3. **Is the writing style serious, sophisticated, or complicated?** Skim through a few chapters. Use the index to find topics of interest.
4. **Does the author cite his or her sources?** Is there a bibliography or list for further reading? Do these sources seem scholarly?

Finding What You Need in a Serious Nonfiction or Scholarly Book

Textbooks have a lot of useful features to help you find, summarize, memorize, and work with information, such as chapter-review questions, glossaries, and so on. Books written for the serious general reader or for a scholarly audience do not have most of these helpful features. To find the information you need in a nonfiction or scholarly book, look for the following:

- Table of contents
- Index
- Notes, bibliographies, lists of works cited
- Illustrations

Exercise 3

DIRECTIONS   You have located each of the following books for a research paper on how diet affects cancer risk. Explain why you think each book is or is not a serious or scholarly work.

1. *Nutrition and Cancer Prevention: New Insights into the Role of Phytochemicals*
2. *Health Education Ideas and Activities: 24 Dimensions of Wellness for Adolescents*
3. *Nutrition in the 21st Century*
4. *Nutrition for Dummies*
5. *The Clinical Guide to Oncology Nutrition* ●

Goal 4

Read academic sources.

HOW TO READ ACADEMIC SOURCES

Let's assume you have located five articles and books for a psychology assignment on the psychological effects of terrorism on its victims. How should you proceed?

1. **Analyze the assignment.** Listen carefully as your professor announces the assignment; he or she often provides important clues about how to read the sources you locate. If the purpose of an assignment is to present new and important topics not covered in your text, then you know that a high level of recall is required. If an assignment's purpose is to expose you to alternative points of view on a controversial issue, then key ideas are needed but highly factual recall is not as important.
2. **Preview the sources.** Use previewing to determine which sources are useful for your assignment. (Previewing is discussed in detail in Chapter 6.) Eliminate any sources that are outdated. Next, glance through the table of contents to get an overall idea of the material covered by each source. Check the index to determine how extensively the source treats your specific topic. Select only those sources that provide a comprehensive treatment of your topic. Once you have identified these sources, randomly select a sample page in each and skim it to get a "feel" for the source. Pay particular attention to the level of difficulty. Is the source too basic, containing little more information than your course textbook? Or is the source too complicated? Does it assume extensive background knowledge of the subject, such as an extensive knowledge of psychoanalysis, for example?
3. **Determine how the sources are organized.** Use the sections titled "The Structure of Articles and Essays" (p. 327) and "The Structure of Scholarly Articles" (p. 328) to guide you.
4. **Select a level of comprehension that suits your purpose and the task.** Comprehension is not an either/or situation. Rather, comprehension is a continuum, and many levels of understanding are possible. An extremely high level of comprehension is necessary if you are reading a critical interpretation of a poem for an English literature paper, for example. Each detail is important. However, a lower level of comprehension is appropriate for reading excerpts

TABLE 12-3 Strategies for Reading Academic Sources

ASSIGNMENT	PURPOSE	READING STRATEGIES	RETENTION STRATEGIES
Historical novel for American history course.	To acquaint you with living conditions of the period being studied.	Read rapidly, noting trends, patterns, characteristics; skip highly detailed descriptive portions.	Write a brief synopsis of the basic plot; make notes (including some examples) of lifestyles and living conditions (social, religious, political, as well as economic).
Essay on exchange in Moroccan bazaars (street markets) for economics course.	To describe system of barter.	Read for main points, noting process, procedures, and principles.	Underline key points.
Article titled "What Teens Know About Birth Control" assigned in a maternal care nursing course.	To reveal attitudes toward, and lack of information about, birth control.	Read to locate topics of information, misinformation, and lack of information; skip details and examples.	Prepare a three-column list: information, misinformation, and lack of information.

from a biography assigned for an American history course. Here, you would not be expected to recall each descriptive detail or bit of conversation.

5. **Choose a reading strategy.** Depending on the purpose of the assignment and the necessary level and type of recall, your reading choices range from a careful, thorough reading to skimming to obtain an overview of the key ideas presented. Table 12-3 above lists examples of assignments and their purposes and suggests possible reading and retention strategies for each. The table shows how strategies vary widely to suit the material and the purpose for which it was assigned.

DIRECTIONS Summarize how you would approach each of the following academic assignments. What would be your purpose? What reading and study strategies would you use?

Exercise 4

1. Reading a *Time* magazine article about a recent incident of terrorism for a discussion in your political science class
2. Reading two articles that present opposing opinions and evidence about the rate of the spread of AIDS throughout Third World countries
3. Reading a recent journal article on asbestos control to obtain current information for a research paper on the topic
4. Reading a case study of a child with autism for a child psychology course
5. Reading Microsoft's end-of-the-year statement for stockholders for a business class studying public relations strategies ●

Using Skimming and Scanning to Read Academic Sources

For reading assignments that require lower levels of comprehension, you can afford to read some parts and skip others. Two reading strategies will be helpful—skimming and scanning.

Skimming is a technique in which you selectively read and skip in order to find only the most important ideas. Skimming is similar to previewing; you look at the parts that carry the most important ideas: titles, headings, introductions, conclusions, and so forth. Here are a few situations in which you might skim academic sources.

- Reading a section of a reference book that you are consulting for a research paper. If you have already collected most of your basic information, you might skim through additional references, looking only for new information not discussed in sources you have used before.
- Sampling a 15-item supplementary reading list for a sociology class. Your instructor has encouraged you to review as many of the items as possible. You anticipate that the final exam will include one essay question that is related to these readings. Clearly, you cannot read every entry, but you can skim a reasonable number.

Scanning is a technique for quickly looking through reading material to locate a particular piece of information—a fact, a date, a name, a statistic. Every time you use a dictionary to find a particular word, you are scanning. If you look up the population of the United States, you are scanning.

Exercise 5 | **DIRECTIONS**   Choose one of the nontextbook readings in Part Six, beginning on p. 378. Skim the reading and write a brief summary including the main point and most important information. Then check the accuracy of your summary by reading the selection more closely. ●

USING COLLEGE TEXTBOOKS
Adapting Your Learning Style by Reading Further

Textbooks often include material to assist you in studying or exploring topics of interest. The following features are particularly useful for adapting your textbook reading and study to suit your learning style.

1. **For Further Reading.** Authors sometimes include lists of books or articles related to a chapter's content so that you can explore a topic in greater detail. You can also use the references as a starting point for your own research.

For Further Reading

Baum, Matthew A. *Soft News Goes to War: Public Opinion and American Foreign Policy in the New Media Age*. Princeton, NJ: Princeton University Press, 2003. A path-breaking examination of how people learn about major foreign policy events from entertainment news shows like *Oprah* and *Dateline*.

Davis, Richard. *Typing Political: The Role of Blogs in American Politics*. New York: Oxford University Press, 2009. A comprehensive assessment of the growing role played by political blogs and their relationship with the mainstream media.

—Edwards et al., *Government in America*, p. 223

Textbook Exercise 1: Using For Further Reading Lists

Look up reviews of the above two books on Amazon.com. Which would you rather read? Which would be more helpful if you were writing a research paper about blogs? Which would be more helpful if you were writing a paper about celebrities' involvement with politics?

2. **Web Site Links.** Many textbooks have companion Web sites associated with them that include videos, MP3 files, study guides, sample tests, and more. These offer different methods of learning as well as additional information and valuable study aids.

> ## Succeed with MySociologyLab
>
> **Experience, Discover, Observe, Evaluate**
> MySociologyLab is designed just for you. Each chapter features a pre-test and post-test to help you learn and review key concepts and terms.
> Experience sociology in action with dynamic visual activities, videos and readings to enhance your learning experience. Complete the following activities at **www.mysoclab.com**.

—Thompson and Hickey, *Society in Focus*, p. 325

Textbook Exercise 2: Using Online Materials

Explore online materials available for one topic covered in this textbook. Try out the materials and write a paragraph evaluating their usefulness. Which do you find most useful? Why?

> ## Relevant Web Sites
>
> **http://alcoholism.about.com/od/abuse/**
> Comprehensive domestic abuse site that provides a potential abuse screening quiz, various personalized stories of abuse by victims, and information on the association of drinking and spousal abuse and the effect on children and adults of witnessing repeated domestic abuse.
> **http://www.elderabusecenter.org/**
> National Center on Elder Abuse site that is a gateway for information on elder abuse, neglect, and exploitation.

—Withgott and Brennan, *Environment*, p. 106

Textbook Exercise 3: Using Web Sites for Research

Do a Web search to find three credible sources of information about some type of abuse. Refer to Chapter 10 for information on how to evaluate the quality of a Web site.

FURTHER PRACTICE WITH TEXTBOOK READING

Textbook Exercise 4: Sample Textbook Chapter

The "Making the Grade" feature found at the end of the sample textbook chapter (p. 438) refers several times to "MySocLab" (short for "MySociologyLab"). Note the use of icons for Read, Explore, and Watch. What types of resources do you think might be included for each of these sections?

Textbook Exercise 5: Your College Textbook

Choose a textbook that you are using in one of your other courses. Use one of the additional materials the textbook offers to correspond with a current assignment. Evaluate how effective and helpful these materials are. Which, if any, are particularly well suited to your learning style?

SELF-TEST SUMMARY

Goal 1

How is reading other academic sources different from reading textbooks?

The high level of retention and recall usually needed for textbooks may not be necessary for other academic sources. Consult with a reference librarian first to find the main online and print sources for your topic. Read an encyclopedia entry for an overview of the subject. Check the library's online catalog to see how the subject is subdivided. Consider your purpose and the type of information you need, and consult your instructor to verify the appropriateness of a source.

Goal 2

How do scholarly periodicals differ from popular periodicals?

Popular periodicals, such as magazines, target a broad audience, often the general public. Scholarly articles focus on a specialized audience; these articles usually include an abstract; a summary of related research; methodology; results; implications, discussion, and conclusion; and suggestions for further research.

Goal 3

What are common uses of scholarly nonfiction sources?

Scholarly nonfiction sources are often used to research context and literary criticism.

Goal 4

How should you read academic sources?

Analyze the purpose of the assignment. Use previewing to determine which sources are useful for the assignment. Determine how each source is organized. Select a level of comprehension that suits both your purpose and the tasks that will follow your reading. Choose a reading strategy appropriate to the assignment.

APPLYING YOUR SKILLS

DISCUSSING THE CHAPTER

1. Suppose you were asked to write a paper for a sociology class on the effects of social media (Facebook, Twitter, Instagram, etc.). Would you use popular magazines or scholarly sources, or both, to learn about the topic? Explain your answer.
2. In what situations or for what topics would a scholarly journal be a more appropriate source than a magazine article?
3. When researching a topic, when might you consider locating a nonfiction book on your topic, instead of journal or magazine articles?

ANALYZING A STUDY SITUATION

Kerry has been assigned a four-page research paper for her business class, and she has decided to write about ethics in the workplace. For this class, she also has to read and summarize two articles on current events in business each week. In addition, she is expected to read a case study on public relations strategies, which was the topic of this week's lecture, and be prepared to discuss it in class.

1. For her research paper, Kerry went to the library and found several print and online sources, including magazine and journal articles, encyclopedia entries, and reference books. In fact, she found too many sources and now she feels overwhelmed. What should she do to narrow her topic and determine which sources are appropriate for her paper?
2. Kerry found four articles that seem to fit the current-events assignment, but they are all from popular magazines. What steps should Kerry take to evaluate the quality of the sources? Where else should she look for material for this assignment?
3. To help her prepare for the class discussion on the case study, what reading strategies would you suggest for Kerry? What level of retention would be most appropriate for this assignment?

WORKING ON COLLABORATIVE PROJECTS

DIRECTIONS Working with another student, select and skim one of the readings in Part Six of this text. Then question each other on the main ideas the article presents.

Quick Quiz

DIRECTIONS   Write the letter of the choice that best completes each statement in the space provided.

CHECKING YOUR RECALL

_____ 1. One way that reading other academic sources is different from reading textbooks is that other academic sources

  a. follow a consistent format.
  b. always require a high level of recall and retention.
  c. differ widely in format and organization.
  d. can only be found online.

_____ 2. In comparison to magazines, scholarly journals typically feature

  a. a broad audience made up of the general public.
  b. an emphasis on information and entertainment.
  c. unpaid authors who are experts in the field.
  d. colorful photographs and graphics.

_____ 3. An abstract can be defined as a

  a. group of essays centered around a common theme.
  b. brief summary of an article and its findings.
  c. statement of related research that has already been done on a topic.
  d. description of the procedures and tests used in an author's research.

_____ 4. The technique for looking quickly through reading material to locate a particular piece of information is known as

  a. skimming.   c. scanning.
  b. sampling.   d. previewing.

_____ 5. When you are evaluating academic sources, you should do all of the following *except*

  a. verify the author's qualifications.
  b. check the copyright date for timeliness.
  c. look for a consensus of opinion.
  d. accept statistical figures without question.

APPLYING YOUR SKILLS

_____ 6. Gus is writing a research paper on the theme of family in *The Adventures of Huckleberry Finn*. The reference source that would provide

him with a group of critical essays centered around Mark Twain's work is

  a. a monograph.
  b. a specialized encyclopedia.
  c. a popular press magazine.
  d. an edited collection in a scholarly nonfiction book.

_____ 7. For a research paper in biology, Tashayla chose to write about wildlife migration and located a scholarly article on the subject. The section of the article that would give Tashayla a detailed description of the author's research methods is the

  a. summary.
  b. statement of the problem.
  c. methodology.
  d. conclusion.

_____ 8. As part of a sociology project, Claire has located several articles and reference books on language and communication in animals. Her first step in reading these academic sources should be to

  a. analyze the purpose of the assignment.
  b. eliminate any sources that seem outdated.
  c. determine how each source is organized.
  d. create a bibliography for each of her sources.

_____ 9. Which of the following would be considered the least scholarly?

  a. *Encyclopedia Britannica*
  b. *Webster's New World Dictionary*
  c. *The American Journal of Medicine*
  d. *People* magazine

_____ 10. Javier has found several interesting articles about carbon offsetting that he plans to use in a research paper. In evaluating the sources, it is important that he ask all of the following questions *except*

  a. Is the author qualified to write on the subject?
  b. Which sources share my opinions on the subject?
  c. For whom is the work intended?
  d. How current is the source?

Preparing for Exams

LEARNING GOALS

In this chapter you will learn to

1 Organize how you study.

2 Figure out what to study.

3 Pull together information.

4 Review for objective and essay exams.

5 Test yourself to evaluate your learning.

LEARNING EXPERIMENT

Imagine you are taking a statistics class and must learn to calculate the median of a set of numbers.

1 Read the following passage defining the term *median*.

Because it can be affected by extremely high or low numbers, the mean is often a poor indicator of central tendency for a list of numbers. In cases like this, another measure of central tendency, called the **median**, can be used. The *median* divides a group of numbers in half; half the numbers lie above the median, and half lie below the median.

Find the median by listing the numbers *in order* from *smallest* to *largest*. If the list contains an *odd* number of items, the median is the *middle number*.

If a list contains an *even* number of items, there is no single middle number. In this case, the median is defined as the mean (average) of the *middle two* numbers.

2 Applying the definition explained here, find the median of each of the following groups of numbers.

17, 24, 6, 9, 10, 2, 44
7, 13, 9, 4

Which step was more useful in helping you learn how to calculate the median of a set of numbers?

The Results

Most students find step 2 more useful. Why? In step 1 all you do is read. In step 2 you apply the explanation to two sets of numbers. Step 2 forces you to use and apply the information contained in step 1. By practicing computing the median, you come to understand it.

Learning Principle: What This Means to You

One of the best ways to prepare for a test is to simulate the test conditions. To prepare for an exam, then, practice answering the types of questions you think will be on the test. Do not just read or reread as

step 1 required you to do. This chapter will show you ways to study by simulating test conditions for both objective and essay tests. You will also learn how to organize your review, identify what to study, analyze and synthesize information, prepare study sheets, and practice self-testing.

Goal

Organize how you study.

ORGANIZING YOUR STUDY AND REVIEW

Students frequently complain that they spend large amounts of time studying for exams and do not get the grades they think they deserve. Often the problem is that although they did study, they did not study effectively. The first thing to do, then—well in advance of the exam—is to get organized.

Organize Your Time

1. **Schedule several review sessions at least a week in advance of an exam.** Set aside specific times for daily review, and incorporate them into your weekly schedule. If you are having difficulty with a particular subject, set up extra study times.
2. **Spend time organizing your review.** Make a list of all chapters, notes, handouts, electronic assignments, and supplementary materials that need to be reviewed. Divide the material, planning what you will review during each session.
3. **Reserve time the night before the exam for a final, complete review.** Do not study new material during this session. Instead, review the most difficult material, checking your recall of important facts or information for possible essay questions.

Find Out About the Exam

To prepare effectively for an exam, you need to know as much as possible about it.

1. **Find out whether it will be objective, essay, or a combination of both.** If your instructor does not indicate the type of exam when announcing the date, ask during or after class.
2. **Be sure you know what material the exam will cover.** Usually your instructor will announce the exam topics or give the time span that the exam will cover.
3. **Find out what your instructor expects of you and how your exam will be evaluated.** Some instructors expect you to recall text and lecture material; others want you to recall, discuss, analyze, or disagree with the ideas and information they have presented. You can usually tell what to expect by the way quizzes have been graded or classes have been conducted.

Attend the Class Before the Exam

Be sure to attend the class prior to the exam. During this class, the instructor may give a brief review of the material to be covered or offer last-minute review suggestions. Have you ever heard an instructor say, "Be sure to look over . . ." prior to an exam? Also, listen carefully to how the instructor answers students' questions; these answers will provide clues about what the exam will emphasize.

Consider Studying with Others

Depending on your learning style, it may be helpful to study with another person or with a small group of classmates, either in person or online. Be sure to weigh the following advantages and disadvantages of group study. Then decide whether group study suits your learning style.

Group study can be advantageous for the following reasons:

1. **Group study helps you to become actively involved with the course content.** Talking about, reacting to, and discussing the material aids learning. If you have trouble concentrating or staying focused when studying alone, group study may be useful.
2. **One of the best ways to learn something is to explain it to someone else.** By using your own words and thinking of the best way to explain an idea, you are analyzing it and testing your own understanding. The repetition involved in explaining something you already understand also strengthens your learning.

Group study can, however, have disadvantages.

1. **Unless everyone is serious, group study sessions can turn into social events in which very little studying occurs.**
2. **Studying with the wrong people can produce negative attitudes that will work against you.** For example, the "None of us understands this and we'll all fail" attitude sometimes rears its ugly head.
3. **By studying with someone who has not read the material carefully or attended classes regularly, you will waste time reviewing basic definitions and facts that you already know, instead of focusing on more difficult topics.**

DIRECTIONS Plan a review schedule for an upcoming exam. Include material you will study and when you will study it. ●

Exercise 1

IDENTIFYING WHAT TO STUDY

In preparing for an exam, review every source of information—textbook chapters and lecture notes—as well as sources sometimes overlooked, such as old exams and quizzes, the instructor's handouts, course outlines, and outside assignments. Talking with other students about the exam can also be helpful.

Goal 2

Figure out what to study.

Textbook Chapters

You must review all chapters that were assigned during the period covered by the exam or that are related to the topics covered by the exam. Review of textbook chapters should be fairly easy if you have kept up with weekly assignments, used your own variation of a study-reading system, and marked and underlined each assignment.

Lecture Notes

In addition to textbook chapters, review all relevant notes. This, too, is easy if you have used the note-taking and editing system presented in Chapter 2.

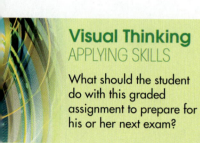

Visual Thinking
APPLYING SKILLS

What should the student do with this graded assignment to prepare for his or her next exam?

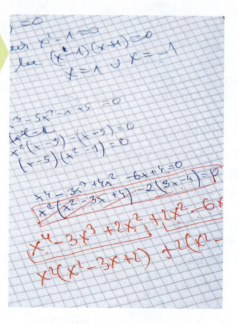

Previous Exams and Quizzes

Be sure to keep all old tests and quizzes, which are valuable sources of review for longer, more comprehensive exams. Most instructors do not repeat the same test questions, but old quizzes list important facts, terms, and ideas. A comprehensive final exam will probably test your recall of the same information through different types of questions.

LOOK FOR PATTERNS OF ERROR Pay particular attention to items that you got wrong; try to see a pattern of error.

1. **Are there certain topics on which you lost most of your points?** If so, review these topics.
2. **Are you missing questions at a particular level of thinking?** Use a grid like the one shown in Figure 13-1 to analyze what type of questions you are getting wrong. If you discover, for example, that you are getting knowledge and comprehension questions wrong, include more factual review in your study plans. If you are missing numerous synthesis questions, you need to focus more on drawing connections between and among your study topics.

FIGURE 13-1
Sample Grid for
Analysis of Errors

LEVEL OF QUESTION	EXAM 1 WRONG ANSWERS	EXAM 2 WRONG ANSWERS	EXAM 3	EXAM 4	EXAM 5
Remembering	0	1			
Understanding	2	0			
Applying	7	5			
Analyzing	1	2			
Evaluating	1	0			
Creating	0	0			

IDENTIFY THE LEVELS OF THINKING YOUR INSTRUCTOR EMPHASIZES The grid shown in Figure 13-2 on the next page can be used to identify the level of thinking your instructor requires on exams. For example, some instructors emphasize application; others focus on analysis and synthesis. You can see that the exam analyzed in Figure 13-2 emphasized understanding and application questions.

LEVEL OF THINKING	EXAM 1 QUESTION NUMBERS	EXAM 2 QUESTION NUMBERS
Remembering	5, 8, 25	
Understanding	1, 3, 18, 19, 21, 22, 24	
Applying	2, 6, 7, 10, 11, 12, 14, 16, 20	
Analyzing	4	
Evaluating	13, 17	
Creating	9, 15, 23	

FIGURE 13-2
Sample Grid for Determining Your Instructor's Emphasis

To discover your instructor's emphasis, go through a previous exam, question by question, identifying and marking each question's type in the grid. Once you have discovered your instructor's emphasis, adjust your study methods accordingly. Include more factual review if knowledge and comprehension are emphasized. Be sure to consider practical situations and uses if application questions are frequently asked.

Instructors' Handouts

Instructors frequently distribute duplicated sheets of information, such as summary outlines, lists of terms, sample problems, maps and charts, or explanations of difficult concepts. Any material that an instructor prepares for distribution (whether paper-based or uploaded to a course Web site) is bound to be important. As you review these materials throughout the course, date them and label the lecture topic to which they correspond. Keep them together in a computer file or in a folder at the front of your notebook so that you can refer to them easily.

Outside Assignments

Out-of-class assignments might include problems to solve, library research, written reactions or evaluations, lectures or movies to attend, videos to watch, or Web activities to complete. Because of the limited number of assignments that can be given in a course, instructors choose only those that are most valuable. You should therefore keep your notes on assignments together for easy review.

Talk with Other Students

Talking with classmates can help you identify the right material to learn. By talking with others, you may discover a topic that you have overlooked or recognize a new focus or direction.

DIRECTIONS Construct a grid like the one shown in Figure 13-2. Use it to analyze the level(s) of thinking your instructor emphasized on one of your previous exams. ●

Exercise 2

ANALYZING AND SYNTHESIZING INFORMATION

Goal **3**

Pull together information.

Once you have identified what material to learn, the next step is to draw together, analyze, and synthesize the information. **Synthesis** is an important critical thinking skill because it allows you to see connections among ideas. In your close study of chapters and lecture notes, it is easy to get lost in details and lose sight of major themes or processes. When concentrating on details, you can miss significant points and fail to see relationships. Exams often measure your awareness of concepts and trends as well as your recall of facts, dates, and definitions. The following suggestions will help you learn to synthesize information.

Get a Perspective on the Course

To avoid focusing too narrowly on details and to obtain perspective on the course material, step back and view the course from a distance. Imagine that all your notes, textbook chapters, outlines, and study sheets are arranged on a table and that you are looking down on them from a peephole in the ceiling. Then ask yourself: What does all that mean? When put together, what does it all show? Why is it important?

Look for Relationships

Try to see how facts are related. In learning the periodic table of chemical elements, for example, you should do more than just learn names and symbols. You should understand how elements are grouped, what properties the elements in a group share, and how the groups are arranged.

Look for Patterns and the Progression of Thought

Try to see why the material was covered in the order in which it was presented. How is one class lecture related to the next? To what larger topic or theme are several lectures connected? For class lectures, check the course outline, course Web site, or syllabus that was distributed at the beginning of the course. Because it lists major topics and the order in which they will be covered, your syllabus will be useful in discovering patterns.

Similarly, for textbook chapters, try to focus on the progression of ideas. Study the table of contents to see the connections between chapters you have read. Often chapters are grouped into sections based on similar content.

Watch for the progression or development of thought. Ask yourself: What is the information presented in this chapter leading up to? What does it have to do with the chapter that follows? Suppose that in psychology you had covered a chapter on personality traits and next were assigned a chapter on abnormal behavior. You would want to know what the two chapters have to do with each other. In this case, the first chapter on personality establishes the standards or norms by which abnormal behavior is determined.

Interpret and Evaluate

Once you have identified the literal content, stop, react, and evaluate its use, value, and applications. Ask yourself: What does this mean? How is this information useful? How can this be applied to various situations?

Prepare Study Sheets

The study sheet system is a way of organizing and summarizing complex information by preparing a mini-outline. It is useful for reviewing material that is interrelated, or connected, and needs to be learned as a whole rather than as separate facts. Types of information that should be reviewed on study sheets include:

1. Theories and principles
2. Complex events with multiple causes and effects
3. Controversial issues—pros and cons
4. Summaries of philosophical issues
5. Trends in ideas or data
6. Groups of related facts

FIGURE 13-3
A Sample Study Sheet

	Problem-Focused Approach	Emotion-Focused Approach
Purpose	solving the problem causing stress	changing or managing the emotions the problems caused
Example	learning about a disability and how to live with it	expressing grief and anger to get them out of your system
How it is accomplished	1. define the problem 2. learn about the problem and how to fix it 3. take steps to fix the problem	1. reappraisal 2. comparisons 3. avoidance 4. humor

Look at the sample study sheet in Figure 13-3, which was created by a student preparing for a psychology exam that would cover a chapter on stress. Note that the study sheet organizes information on two approaches to coping with stress and presents that information in a form that permits easy comparison.

To prepare a study sheet, first select the information to be learned. Then outline the information, using as few words as possible. Group together important points, facts, and ideas related to each topic.

Exercise 3

DIRECTIONS   Prepare a study sheet for the section titled "Theories of Prejudice," which begins on page 435 in Part Seven. ●

Exercise 4

DIRECTIONS   Prepare a study sheet for a topic you are studying in one of your courses. Include all the information you need to learn in order to prepare for an exam. ●

REVIEWING FOR OBJECTIVE AND ESSAY EXAMS

Goal **4**

Review for objective and essay exams.

The methods and procedures you use to learn and to remember information depend on the type of exam for which you are preparing. You would study and learn information differently for a multiple-choice test than for an essay exam.

Exams can be divided into two basic types: objective and essay. **Objective tests** include short-answer questions in which you choose one or more answers from several possibilities, or supply a word or phrase to complete a statement. Multiple-choice, true/false, matching, and fill-in-the-blank questions appear on objective tests. In each of these, the questions are constructed so that the answers you choose are either right or wrong; scoring is completely objective, or free from judgment.

Essay tests require you to answer questions in your own words. You have to recall information, organize it, and present it in an acceptable written form. The skills involved in writing a good essay answer are different from those involved in recognizing the correct answer among several choices or recalling a word or phrase.

Review for Objective Tests

Objective tests usually require you to recognize the right answer. On a multiple-choice test, for example, you have to pick the correct answer from the choices given. On matching tests, you have to recognize which two items go together. One goal in reviewing for objective tests, then, is to become so familiar with the course material that you can recognize and select the right answers.

USE HIGHLIGHTING AND MARKING Your highlighting of reading assignments can be used in several ways for review.

1. **Reread your highlighting in each chapter.**
2. **Read the chapter's boldfaced headings and form a question for each, as you did in the Question step in the SQ3R system (see p. 172).**
3. **Try to answer your question; then check your highlighting to see whether you were correct.**
4. **Review special marks you may have included.** For example, if you marked new or important definitions with a particular symbol, then you should go through the chapter once and note these terms, checking your recall of their meanings.

USE THE RECALL CLUES IN YOUR LECTURE NOTES Your recall clues are an important tool for reviewing lecture content.

1. **Go back through each set of lecture notes and check your recall by using the marginal recall clue system (see p. 55).**
2. **Test yourself by asking questions and trying to remember answers.** Mark in red ink (or, on a computer screen, highlight in red) things you have trouble remembering.
3. **Use ink or highlighting of a different color the second time you go through your notes, marking information you still can't recall.**

USE STUDY AIDS Use all study sheets, outlines, summaries, and organizational charts and diagrams that you have prepared to review and learn course content. Also use any online quizzing materials provided by the publisher to help you test your knowledge. To learn the information on a study sheet or outline, follow these steps:

1. **Read through it several times.**
2. **Take the first topic, write it on a sheet of paper, and see whether you can fill in the information under the topic on your study sheet or outline.**
3. **If you can't recall all the information, test yourself until you have learned it.**
4. **Continue in this way with each topic.**

USE THE FLASH CARD SYSTEM The flash card system, while old-fashioned, is an effective way of reviewing for objective tests. You can create your own using 3-by-5-inch index cards (or just small sheets of paper) or use an online program to create them. Write part of the information on the front, the remainder on the back. To review the dates of important events, write the date on the front, the event on the back; to review vocabulary, put each term on the front of a card and its definition on the back. See the sample flash cards shown in Figure 13-4, which were made by a student preparing for an objective exam in biology.

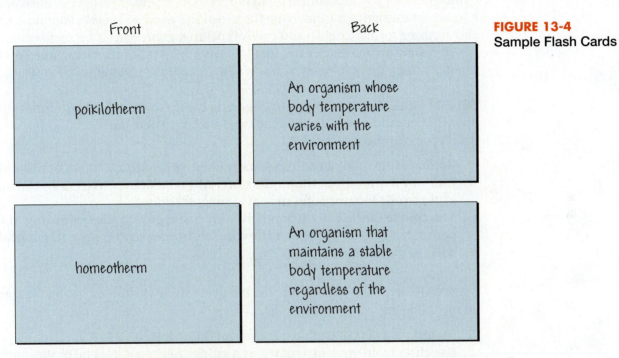

Front   Back

poikilotherm

An organism whose body temperature varies with the environment

homeotherm

An organism that maintains a stable body temperature regardless of the environment

FIGURE 13-4
Sample Flash Cards

To study these cards, follow these steps:

1. **Look at the front of each and try to remember what is written on the back.** Then turn the card over to see whether you are correct.
2. **As you go through your pack of cards, sort them into two stacks—those you know and those you don't.**
3. **Then go back through the stack of those you don't know, study each, and retest yourself, again sorting the cards into two stacks.**
4. **Continue this procedure until you are satisfied that you have learned all the information.**
5. **Go through your cards in this manner two or three times a day for three or four days before the exam.**
6. **On the day of your exam, do a final, once-through review so that the information is fresh in your mind.**

The flash card system is more appropriate for learning brief facts than for reviewing concepts, ideas, and principles or for understanding sequences of events, theories, and cause–effect relationships. For this reason, it works best when you are studying for objective tests that include short-answer questions such as fill-in-the-blanks. Note, too, that the online materials that accompany your textbooks may have ready-made flash cards that you can use to study and learn.

Exercise 5

DIRECTIONS   Prepare a set of flash cards (at least 20) for a chapter or section of a chapter you are studying in one of your courses. Then learn the information on the cards, using the study techniques described on the previous page. ●

Review for Essay Exams

Essay exams demand extensive recall. Starting with a blank sheet of paper, you are required to retrieve from your memory all the information that answers the question. Then you must organize that information and express your ideas about it in acceptable written form. Note the use of the word *acceptable*; you must write clearly, using formal English and correct spelling, grammar, and punctuation.

To review for an essay exam, first identify topics that may be included on the exam. Then predict actual questions and write outline or rough-draft answers.

SELECT PROBABLE TOPICS   In choosing topics to study, you attempt to predict what questions will be included on the exam. There are several sources from which you can choose topics.

1. **Boldfaced textbook headings usually identify important topics or subtopics.**
2. **End-of-chapter discussion questions and recall clues written in the margins of your lecture notes may also suggest topics.**
3. **The course outline distributed by your instructor at the beginning of the course (and often posted on the course's home page) frequently contains a list of major topics.**

STUDY THE TOPICS SELECTED   To effectively study the topics you have chosen, do the following.

1. **Identify aspects of each topic that might be tested.**
2. **Use clues from your instructor as a guideline.** What does he or she emphasize? Causes and effects? Events? Research? Theories? Historical significance? Similarities and differences?

Once you have identified what to study, it is time to self-test: that is, to write and answer sample questions.

Goal 5

Test yourself to evaluate your learning.

PREPARING FOR SELF-TESTING

Self-testing is a study strategy that uses writing to discover and relate ideas. It involves writing possible exam questions and drafting answers to them. This activity combines the use of factual recall with interpretation and evaluation.

Constructing potential test questions is fun and challenging and can be done with a classmate or in groups. It is usually best to write answers yourself, however, to get maximum benefit from the technique. After writing, compare and discuss your answers with classmates or members of your study group. If you prefer to work alone, be sure to verify your answers by referring to your text and/or lecture notes.

What kinds of questions you ask depends on the type of material you are learning as well as on the type or level of analysis your instructor expects. Sample questions for various types of material that you may be required to study are listed in Figure 13-5 on the next page.

TYPE OF MATERIAL	QUESTIONS
Reports of research studies and experiments	What was the purpose of the study? What are the important facts and conclusions? What are its implications? How can these results be used?
Case studies	What is the case intended to illustrate? What problems or limitations does it demonstrate? To what other situations might this case apply?
Models	How was the model derived? What are its applications? What are its limitations? Do other models of the same process exist?
Current events	What is the significance of the event? What impact will this have in the future? Is there historical precedent?
Supplementary readings	Why did your instructor assign the reading? How is it related to course content? What key points or concepts does the reading contain? Does the reading present a particular viewpoint?
Sample problems	What processes or concepts does the problem illustrate? What is its unique feature? How is it similar to and different from other problems?
Historical data (historical reviews)	Why were the data presented? What trends or patterns are evident? How is this information related to key concepts in the chapter or article?
Arguments	Is the argument convincing? How is the conclusion supported? What persuasive devices does the author use? Do logical flaws exist? Is the author's appeal emotional?
Poetry	What kinds of feelings does the poem evoke? What message or statement is the poet making? How does the poet use language to create feelings?
Essays	What is the author's purpose? What thought patterns are evident? How does the author support his or her key point (thesis)?
Short stories	What does the title mean? Beyond the plot, what does the story really mean? (What is the theme?) What comments does it make about life? How do the plot, setting, and tone contribute to the overall meaning?

FIGURE 13-5
Questions to Provoke Thought

Many students who use self-testing as a review strategy are pleasantly surprised when they take their first exam: they discover that some (or many!) of their questions actually appear on the exam. This discovery boosts their confidence during the exam and saves them time as well.

Creating Effective Self-Testing Questions

To construct and answer possible test questions, use the following hints.

1. Do not waste time writing multiple-choice or true/false questions. They are time-consuming to write, and you know the answer before you start.
2. Matching tests are useful, but they should be limited to information that requires only factual recall.
3. Open-ended questions that require full-sentence answers are best because they tend to require more levels of thought.
4. Consult Figure 13-5 on the previous page for ideas on how to word your questions.
5. You are interested in long-term retention of information, so it is best to write the questions one day and answer them a day or two later.

Apply Levels of Thinking

As you prepare your list of questions, ask questions that you think your instructor might ask. Be sure to predict questions at all levels of thinking.

APPLYING LEVELS OF THINKING

Preparing for Essay Exams and Levels of Thinking

Level of Thinking	What to Ask
Knowing and Understanding	These levels require recall of facts; remembering dates, names, definitions, and formulas falls into these categories. The five "W" questions—*Who? What? Where? When?* and *Why?*—are useful to ask.
Applying	This level of thinking requires you to use or apply information. The following two questions best test this level: In what practical situations would this information be useful? What does this have to do with what I already know about the subject?
Analyzing	Analysis involves seeing relationships. Ask questions that test your ability to take ideas apart, find cause–effect relationships, and discover how things work.
Evaluating	This level involves making judgments and assessing value or worth. Ask questions that challenge sources, accuracy, long-term value, importance, and so forth.
Creating	This level involves pulling ideas together. Ask questions that force you to look at similarities and differences.

Write Outline or Rough-Draft Answers

Once you have identified possible exam questions, the next step is to practice answering them.

1. **Collect and organize the information you would include in your answer.**
2. **Do not take the time to write out full, complete sentences.**
3. **Write your answer in brief note or outline form, listing the information you would include.**

USE KEY-WORD OUTLINES As a convenient way to remember what your draft answer includes, make a key-word outline of your answer. For each item in your draft, identify a key word that will trigger your memory of that idea. Then list and learn these key words. Together, these words form a mini-outline of topics and ideas to include in an essay on this topic. A key-word outline is shown in Figure 13-6. It is a mini-outline for the study sheet shown in Figure 13-3 on page 343.

Problem vs. Emotion

Purpose

Example

How accomplished

FIGURE 13-6
A Sample Key-Word Outline

Now Test Yourself

Now that you have written questions that you expect will be on the exam, you are ready to write the answers. By testing yourself before the instructor tests you, you are preparing in a realistic way for the exam. If you were entering a marathon race, you would prepare for the race by running—not by playing golf. The same is true of test taking; you should prepare for a test by testing yourself—not by simply rereading chapters or pages of notes. Use the following suggestions as you write the answers to the questions you've prepared.

1. **As you answer your questions, respond in complete sentences.** Writing complete sentences usually involves more careful and deliberate thought and therefore leads to more effective learning. It is also good practice for the exam itself, where your writing skills will count.
2. **Take time to review and critique your answers.** This process will also contribute to learning.
3. **Rewrite any answers that you found to be poor or incomplete.** This repetition will facilitate learning.
4. **Save your answers, and review them once again the evening before the exam.**
5. **Time yourself.** Make sure you can answer the question in the time allotted for the exam.

You can also test yourself in any of the following ways:

1. **Use recall clues for your lecture notes.** (See Chapter 2, p. 55.)
2. **Draw and label maps.** (See Chapter 4, p. 112.)
3. **Write partially completed outlines.** Fill in the blanks from memory.
4. **Use vocabulary cards.** (See Chapter 7, p. 203.)
5. **Work with a classmate, testing each other by making up sample questions and answering them.**

Predicting and answering possible examination questions is effective for several reasons. Predicting forces you to analyze the material, not just review it. Drafting answers forces you to express ideas in written form. Through writing, you will recognize relationships, organize your thoughts, and discover the best way to present them.

DIRECTIONS Write a list of questions that might be asked on an exam covering one of the chapters that you have already read in this text. Answer them and then verify the correctness of your answers by consulting the chapter. ●

Exercise 6

Exercise 7

DIRECTIONS   Assume you are preparing for an essay exam in one of your courses. Predict several questions that might be asked for one textbook chapter and write them in the space provided. Try to write questions that require different levels of thinking.

_____

_____

_____

_____

_____ ●

Exercise 8

DIRECTIONS   Choose one of the essay exam questions that you wrote in Exercise 7. Prepare a study sheet that summarizes the information on the topic. Then reduce that information on your study sheet to a key-word outline. ●

USING COLLEGE TEXTBOOKS
Using In-Chapter Self-Test Questions

To help you learn chapter content, many textbooks include self-test questions interspersed throughout the chapters and/or at the end of chapters. Often, the answers to these questions are provided somewhere in the chapter or at the end of the book. The goal of these questions is to help you test your knowledge as you proceed through the chapter. Once you can answer the questions correctly, you will know that you are ready to proceed to the next section of the chapter.

To use self-test questions, answer them after you complete the section that immediately precedes them. If you are unable to answer the question, this is a signal that you need to go back and reread the section. Mark in your notes that this is a section you had difficulty with, and review the material accordingly.

> **SO FAR . . .**
> 1. Under the biological species concept, species are defined by their _____ behavior.
> 2. Two factors always play a part in allopatric speciation: first, the development of _____ and second, the development of one or more _____.

—Krogh, *Biology*, p. 334

Textbook Exercise 1: Understanding Self-Test Questions

True or False? The "So Far" feature above tests your knowledge of biological vocabulary.

CONCEPT CHECK

1. Fission and fusion are opposite processes, yet each releases energy. Isn't this contradictory?
2. To get a release of nuclear energy from the element iron, should iron undergo fission or fusion?

CHECK YOUR ANSWERS

1. No, no, no! This is contradictory only if the same element is said to release energy by both fission and fusion. Only the fusion of light elements and the fission of heavy elements result in a decrease in nucleon mass and a release of energy.
2. Neither, because iron is at the very bottom of the "energy valley." Fusing a pair of iron nuclei produces an element to the right of iron on the curve, in which the mass per nucleon is higher. If you split an iron nucleus, the products will lie to the left of iron on the curve and again have a higher mass per nucleon. So no energy is released. For energy release, "decrease mass" is the name of the game—any game, chemical or nuclear.

—Suchocki, *Conceptual Chemistry*, p. 145

Textbook Exercise 2: Using Self-Test Questions and Answers

Here, the author provides answers immediately following the questions. What are the pros and cons of this approach? Where do you typically like to see answers provided?

TESTING YOUR COMPREHENSION

1. In what ways are campus sustainability efforts relevant to sustainability efforts in the broader society?
2. Describe one way in which campus sustainability proponents have addressed each of the following areas: (1) recycling and waste reduction, (2) "green" building, and (3) water conservation.

—Withgott and Brennan, *Environment*, p. 688

Textbook Exercise 3: Analyzing Self-Test Questions

Suppose both of these questions appeared on an essay examination. Which one do you think is "easier"? Which one would take longer to answer, and why?

SAMPLE TEST QUESTIONS

These multiple-choice questions are similar to those found in the test bank that accompanies this text.

1. Which of these statements is *true* of marriages in all cultures?
   a. Marriage is a legal union between one man and one woman.

> b. Marriage is a voluntary union between two parties.
> c. Marriage establishes rights and obligations related to gender.
> d. Marriage is only legally recognized if individuals are over the age of 16.
> 2. Which of these is *not* a current trend in modern households?
>   a. fewer marriages
>   b. fewer children
>   c. delayed marriage
>   d. more nuclear families

—Kunz, *Think Marriage and Families*, p. 21

Textbook Exercise 4: Answering Self-Test Questions

Try to answer these questions based on your own observations and experiences. For the correct answers, see the bottom of page 355.

FURTHER PRACTICE WITH TEXTBOOK READING

Textbook Exercise 5: Sample Textbook Chapter

After reading the entire chapter, "Race and Ethnicity" in Part Seven, convert the five learning objectives (11.1, 11.2, 11.3, 11.4 and 11.5) on page 425 into questions and then answer them.

Textbook Exercise 6: Your College Textbook

Choose a textbook you are currently using. Read a chapter and then answer the self-test questions throughout the chapter or at the end to evaluate your understanding of the material. If the chapter does not have questions, write questions and then answer them.

SELF-TEST SUMMARY

Goal

How can you get organized to study and review for exams?

Organizing for study and review requires planning and scheduling your time so that you can review all the material carefully and thoroughly. You should begin at least a week before the exam to plan what material you will study each day and at what specific times you will study, and you should plan time for a complete review the evening before the exam. Find out about the exam's format and what material it will cover. Attending the last class before the exam can provide you with useful hints, and group study can be helpful for certain individuals and circumstances.

Goal 2

How can you identify what to study?

To identify what to study, it is important to review all of your sources of information. Review all textbook chapters assigned, your lecture notes, exams and quizzes you have taken, classroom handouts, and notes on outside assignments. From these sources and discussion with other students, you will arrive at the topics most likely to be covered on the exam.

Goal 3

How can you organize facts and ideas and synthesize them into a meaningful body of information to be studied?

To synthesize the information presented in a course, it is helpful to "step back" and examine the larger picture. Look at relationships between ideas, note patterns in the course syllabus and your textbook's table of contents, and see past the details to the use, value, and application of this information. Preparing study sheets or mini-outlines can help in this process.

Goal 4

How can you best learn and memorize the information for objective and essay exams?

For objective exams, you should review all highlighting and marking, the recall clues in your lecture notes, and any study aids you have prepared throughout the course. By using the flash-card system and testing yourself, you can be sure you have learned all the important facts and ideas. For essay exams, you should begin by predicting probable exam questions. Next, you should study the topics selected by preparing a study sheet from which you can review and write a clear, concise essay. Finally, prepare a key-word outline or mini-outline that will guide you when writing answers to the questions you predicted.

Goal 5

Why should you practice testing yourself before you take an exam?

Self-testing uses writing to discover and relate ideas, combining factual recall with interpretation and evaluation. By writing possible exam questions, you identify important information that will likely be on the test. By writing the answers, you will recognize relationships, organize your thoughts, and discover the best way to present them. You can then bring all this knowledge to the table when you take the real exam.

APPLYING YOUR SKILLS

DISCUSSING THE CHAPTER

1. Under what conditions have study groups been effective in helping you study?
2. What are some ground rules your group could establish to help ensure your valuable time is spent well?
3. Review several previous exams, quizzes, or tests from one of your courses. Discuss whether and how this review was beneficial.

ANALYZING A STUDY SITUATION

Kimberly is taking a psychology course in which grades are based on four multiple-choice exams. Each exam contains 50 items worth two points and is machine scored. When exams are returned, students receive their answer sheets but do not receive the questions themselves. On the first exam, Kimberly earned 68 points, which is a high D grade. For the second exam, she spent more time studying but only earned 72, a C–. When Kimberly visited her instructor in her office and asked for advice on how to improve her grade, the instructor handed Kimberly copies of the first two exams and said, "Spend a half hour or so with each of these; I'm sure you'll discover what's going wrong."

1. What things should Kimberly look for in the exams?
2. What kinds of notes should she make, if any, about the exams?
3. How should Kimberly use each of the following in preparing for her next multiple-choice exam?
   - flash cards
   - lecture notes
   - summaries of textbook chapters

WORKING ON COLLABORATIVE PROJECTS

DIRECTIONS   Each student should write five essay questions based on one of the readings included in Thematic Group C, "Internet and Communication," in Part Six, pages 408– 421. Working in groups of three or four students, compare and evaluate your questions, revise several strong ones, and categorize each question using the six levels of thinking described in Chapter 1 on page 33. Finally, choose one question to submit to the class. After each group has presented its question, the class will identify the level(s) of thinking that each question demands and discuss which is the hardest and which is the easiest.

Quick Quiz

DIRECTIONS Write the letter of the choice that best completes each statement in the space provided.

CHECKING YOUR RECALL

_____ 1. As you prepare for an exam, you should do all of the following *except*

a. spend time organizing your review.
b. skip the class prior to the exam so you can study.
c. find out what type of exam it will be.
d. set aside specific times for daily review.

_____ 2. The best reason to review previous exams and quizzes before an exam is to

a. try to identify important facts, terms, and ideas.
b. look for questions that will be repeated on the exam.
c. eliminate some areas of study.
d. replace extensive textbook review.

_____ 3. A common mistake students make when studying for an exam is to

a. begin reviewing too far ahead of the exam.
b. study with other students.
c. look for relationships among ideas.
d. fail to interpret facts and details.

_____ 4. A study sheet is most similar to

a. a mini-outline.
b. an organizational chart.
c. a self-test.
d. a learning journal.

_____ 5. Of the following review situations, flash cards would be most useful for

a. comparing Thoreau and Whitman for a literature class.
b. studying the theory of relativity in physics.
c. learning definitions for an anatomy and physiology class.
d. studying the events leading up to America's involvement in Vietnam for a history class.

APPLYING YOUR SKILLS

_____ 6. By looking at old exams, Evan has determined that his marketing instructor tends to emphasize essay questions at the application level of thinking. Therefore, Evan should predict essay questions that ask students to

a. recall facts, dates, names, and definitions.
b. use information in practical situations.
c. find cause–effect relationships.
d. assess the long-term value of the information.

_____ 7. Alicia is studying her American government textbook before an exam. If she wanted to find out the textbook's progression of ideas, she would probably consult the text's

a. appendix.
b. preface.
c. table of contents.
d. first chapter.

_____ 8. Sheri has analyzed her patterns of error on history exams and discovered that she frequently gets knowledge and comprehension questions wrong. One way she should adjust her study methods is to focus more on

a. connections between topics.
b. factual review.
c. practical situations and uses.
d. out-of-class assignments.

_____ 9. Keith is preparing for an essay exam in his world history class. The first step Keith should take is to

a. identify topics that may be included on the exam.
b. predict actual questions.
c. write sample essay answers.
d. create a key-word outline.

_____ 10. Spencer is preparing for an essay test. He should use a key-word outline to

a. trigger his memory of ideas he wants to include in an essay.
b. serve as a guide for study and review.
c. organize his study.
d. test his understanding of a topic.

Answers to Sample Test Questions on page 352:
1. b 2. d

CHAPTER

14

Taking Exams

LEARNING GOALS

In this chapter you will learn to

1 Use tips for taking exams.

2 Use strategies to perform better on objective exams.

3 Use strategies to perform better on standardized tests.

4 Use strategies to perform better on essay exams.

5 Control test anxiety.

LEARNING EXPERIMENT

1 Here is a multiple-choice test item from a psychology exam:

Modern psychological researchers maintain that the mind as well as behavior can be scientifically examined primarily by

   a. observing behavior and making inferences about mental functioning.

   b. observing mental activity and making inferences about behavior.

   c. making inferences about behavior.

   d. direct observation of behavior.

If you know the correct answer, circle it now.

2 If you did not know the correct answer, use your reasoning skills to determine the best answer and circle it.

Hints:
1. Which choices do *not* refer to both the mind and behavior? (Answer: choices c and d)
2. Which choice contains an activity that cannot be easily done? (Answer: b—mental activity

cannot be observed without specialized medical equipment.)

The Results

Using the hints above, you probably were able to eliminate choices b, c, and d.

Learning Principle: What This Means to You

Although you probably did not know the correct answer, you were able to figure it out. **When taking exams, trust your reasoning skills to help you figure out correct answers.** In this chapter you will learn how to sharpen your reasoning skills for all types of exams. The manner in which you approach an exam, how you read and answer objective questions, and how carefully you read, organize, and write your answers to an essay exam all influence your grade. This chapter discusses each of these aspects of becoming test-wise and also considers a problem that interferes with many students' ability to do well on exams: test anxiety.

356

GENERAL SUGGESTIONS FOR TAKING EXAMS

Goal **1**

Use tips for taking exams.

The following suggestions will help you approach classroom exams in an organized, systematic way.

Bring Necessary Materials

When going to any exam, be sure to take along any materials you might be asked or allowed to use. Be sure you have extra pens and pencils in case you must make a drawing or diagram (or fill in a Scantron sheet). Take scrap paper—you may need it for computing figures or outlining essay answers. Take along anything you have been allowed to use throughout the semester, such as a pocket or graphing calculator, conversion chart, or reference work. If you are not sure whether you may use these items, ask the instructor or proctor.

Get There on Time

Arrive at the exam room on time, or a few minutes early, to get a seat and get organized before the instructor arrives. If you are late, you may miss instructions and feel rushed as you begin the exam. If you arrive too early (15 or more minutes ahead), you risk anxiety induced by panic-stricken students questioning each other, trading last-minute memory tricks, and worrying about how difficult the exam will be.

Sit at the Front of the Room

The best place to sit in an exam room is the front. There you often receive the test first and get a head start. There, also, you are sure to hear directions and corrections and easily read any changes written on the board. Finally, it is easier to concentrate at the front of the room. At the back, you are exposed to distractions, such as a student dropping papers or the person in front who is already two pages ahead of you.

Preview the Exam

Before you start to answer any of the questions, take a minute or two to quickly page through the exam, noting the directions, the length, the types of questions, and the general topics covered. Previewing provides an overview of the whole exam and helps eliminate the panic you may feel if you are unsure of the answers to the first few questions.

Plan Your Time

After previewing the exam, you will know the number and types of questions included. You should then estimate how much time you will spend on each part of the exam. The number of points each section is worth (the point distribution) should be your guide. For example, if one part of an exam has 20 multiple-choice questions worth one point each and another part has two essays worth 40 points each, you should spend much more time answering the essay questions than working through the multiple-choice items. If the point distribution is not indicated on the test, you may want to ask the instructor about it.

As you plan your time, allow three to four minutes at the end of the exam to review what you have done, answer questions you skipped, and make any necessary corrections or changes.

To keep track of time, wear a watch or use the countdown function on your phone. Many classrooms do not have wall clocks, or you may be sitting in a position where the clock is difficult to see.

If you were taking an exam with the following distribution of questions and points, how would you divide your time? Assume the total exam time is 50 minutes.

Type of Question	Number of Questions	Total Points
Multiple-choice	25 questions	25 points
True/false	20 questions	20 points
Essay	2 questions	55 points

You should probably divide your time like this:

Previewing	1–2 minutes
Multiple-choice	12 minutes
True/false	10 minutes
Essay	23 minutes
Review	3–4 minutes

Because the essays are worth twice as many points as either of the other two parts of the exam, you should spend double the time on the essay portion.

Exercise 1

DIRECTIONS For each of the exams described below and on page 359, estimate how you would divide your time.

1. Time limit: 75 minutes

Type of Question	Number of Questions	Total Points
Multiple-choice	20 questions	40 points
Matching	10 questions	10 points
Essay	2 questions	50 points

How would you divide your time?

Previewing	_____ minutes
Multiple-choice	_____ minutes
Matching	_____ minutes
Essay	_____ minutes
Review	_____ minutes

2. Time limit: 50 minutes

Type of Question	Number of Questions	Total Points
True/false	15 questions	30 points
Fill in the blank	15 questions	30 points
Short answer	10 questions	40 points

How would you divide your time?

Previewing	_____ minutes
True/false	_____ minutes
Fill in the blank	_____ minutes
Short answer	_____ minutes
Review	_____ minutes ●

Read the Questions Carefully

Most instructors word their questions so that the expected answer is clear. A common mistake is to read more into the question than is asked for. To avoid this error, read the question several times, paying attention to how it is worded. If you are uncertain what is asked for, try to relate the question to the course content. Don't assume hidden meanings or trick questions.

Taking an Exam on a Computer

Some instructors are now giving tests by computer. Use the following tips for taking computerized exams:

1. Don't wait until the due date to take the exam. Last-minute computer problems or connection issues may force you to miss the deadline.
2. Avoid technical problems and glitches by taking the exam on a computer you are familiar with. Close all other programs so nothing interferes with the exam's operation or interrupts your thought.
3. Wait until the exam is fully loaded on your computer before you start working on it.
4. Read the instructions closely to be sure you move forward and backward correctly, use the right format for entering responses, and submit your final answers properly.
5. If you are uncomfortable with computerized exams, ask if a print exam is available.

HINTS FOR TAKING OBJECTIVE EXAMS

Goal

When taking objective exams—those with true/false, matching, short-answer, fill-in-the-blank, or multiple-choice questions—remember the following hints, which may net you a few more points.

Use strategies to perform better on objective exams.

General Hints for Objective Exams

1. **Read the directions.** Before answering any questions, read the directions. Often an instructor may want the correct answer marked in a particular way (underlined rather than circled). The directions may contain crucial information that you must know in order to answer the questions correctly. Consider the following two sets of directions on the next page. If you did not read them properly, you could lose a considerable number of points.

True/False Directions

Read each statement. If the statement is true, mark a T in the blank to the left of the item. If the statement is false, add and/or subtract words in such a way as to make the statement true.

Multiple-Choice Directions

Circle all the choices that correctly complete the statement.

Without reading the true/false directions, you would not know that you should correct incorrect statements. Without reading the multiple-choice directions, you would not know that you are to choose more than one answer.

2. **Leave nothing blank.** Before turning in your exam, review it to be sure you have answered every question. If you have no idea about the correct answer to a question, guess—you might be right. On a true/false test, your chances of being correct are 50 percent; on a four-choice multiple-choice question, your odds are 25 percent.

3. **Look for clues.** If you encounter a difficult question, choose what seems to be the best answer, mark the question so that you can return to it, and keep the item in mind as you go through the rest of the exam. Sometimes you will see some piece of information later in the exam that reminds you of a fact or idea. At other times you may notice information that, if true, contradicts an answer you have already chosen.

4. **Don't change answers without good reason.** When reviewing your exam answers, don't make a change unless you have a specific reason for doing so. If a later test item made you remember information for a previous item, by all means make a change. If, however, you are just having second thoughts about an answer, leave it alone. Your first guess is usually the best one.

Hints for Taking True/False Tests

1. **Watch for words that qualify or change the meaning of a statement; often, just one word makes it true or false, as in the following oversimplified example.**

   False: *All* dogs are white.

   True: *Some* dogs are white.

   On college true/false exams, you will find that one word often determines whether a statement is true or false.

   All paragraphs must have a stated main idea.

   Spelling, punctuation, and handwriting *always* affect the grade given to an essay answer.

   When taking notes on a lecture, try to write down *everything* the speaker says.

   Also watch for words that specify degree (*usually, commonly*), quantity (*most, several*), or change in amount (*increase, reduce*). Overlooking these words may cost you several points on an exam.

2. **Read two-part statements carefully.** Occasionally, you may find a statement with two or more parts. In answering these items, remember that both or all parts of the statement must be true in order for the entire statement to

be true. If part of the statement is true and another part is false, then mark the statement false.

> The World Health Organization (WHO) has been successful in its campaign to eliminate smallpox and malaria.

Although it is true that WHO has been successful in eliminating smallpox, malaria is still a world health problem and has not been eliminated. Because only part of this statement is true, it should be marked false.

3. **Look for negative and double-negative statements.** Test items that use negative words or word parts can be confusing. Words such as *no, none, never, not,* and *cannot* and prefixes such as *in-, dis-, un-, it-,* and *ir-* are easy to miss and always affect the meaning of the statement. Make it a habit to underline or circle negative statements in items as you read.

Statements that contain two negatives, such as the following, are even more confusing.

> It is not unreasonable to expect returning veterans to continue to suffer post-traumatic stress disorder years after their discharge.

In reading these statements, remember that two negatives cancel out each other. "Not unreasonable," then, can be interpreted to mean "reasonable."

If you encounter such statements, rephrase them in your own words; then you will probably know the correct answer.

4. **Make your best guess.** When all else fails and you are unable to reason out the answer to an item, use these three last-resort rules of thumb:

   - **Absolute statements tend to be false.** Because there are very few things that are always true and for which there are no exceptions, your best guess is to mark statements that contain words such as *always, all, never,* or *none* as false.
   - **Mark any item that contains unfamiliar terminology or facts as false.** If you've studied the material thoroughly, trust that you would recognize as true anything that was a part of the course content.
   - **When all else fails, it is better to guess true than false.** It is more difficult for instructors to write false statements than true statements. As a result, many exams have more true items than false items.

DIRECTIONS The following true/false test is based on content presented in the reading "Linking Up: 21st-Century Social Networking" in Part Six on page 416. Read each item. In the space provided at the left, indicate whether the statement is true or false by marking *T* for true and *F* for false. Then find and underline the single word that, if changed or deleted, could change the truth or falsity of the statement.

Exercise 2

_____ 1. Digital natives can be defined as the last group up who grew up with digital technologies and the Internet already in place.

_____ 2. Digital natives seldom practice multitasking.

_____ 3. Some marketers hire college students to promote their products and services.

_____ 4. The development of professional blog sites has made it difficult for independent bloggers to contribute to the public debate on an issue.

_____ 5. The evolution of the blogosphere reveals how slowly technology creates change. ●

Hints for Taking Matching Tests

Matching tests require you to select items in one list that can be paired with items in a second list. Use the following tips to complete matching tests.

1. **Before answering any items, glance through both lists to get an overview of the subjects and topics.** Next, try to discover a pattern. Are you asked to match dates with events, terms with meanings, people with accomplishments?
2. **Answer the items you are sure of first, lightly crossing off items as you use them.**
3. **Don't choose the first answer you see that seems correct; items later in the list may be better choices.**
4. **If the first column consists of short words or phrases and the second is made up of lengthy definitions or descriptions, save time by "reverse matching."** That is, look for the word or phrase in column 1 that fits each item in column 2.

Hints for Taking Short-Answer Tests

Short-answer tests require you to write a brief answer, usually in list or sentence form. Here is an example:

List three events that increased U.S. involvement in the Vietnam War.

In answering short-answer questions, be sure to do the following.

1. **Use point distribution as a clue to how many pieces of information to include.** For a nine-point item asking you to describe the characteristics of a totalitarian government, give at least three ideas.
2. **Plan what you will say before starting to write.**
3. **Use the amount of space provided, especially if it varies for different items, as a clue to how much you should write.**

Hints for Taking Fill-in-the-Blank Tests

Items that ask you to fill in a missing word or phrase within a sentence require recall of information rather than recognition of the correct answer. It is important, therefore, to look for clues that will trigger your recall.

1. **Look for key words in the sentence, and use them to decide what subject matter and topic the item covers.**
2. **Decide what type of information is required.** Is it a date, name, place, or new term?
3. **Use the grammatical structure of the sentence to determine the type of word called for.** Is it a noun, verb, or qualifier?

Hints for Taking Multiple-Choice Tests

Multiple-choice exams are among the most frequently used types of exams and are often the most difficult. The following suggestions should improve your success in taking multiple-choice tests.

1. **Read all choices first, considering each.** Do not stop with the second or third choice, even if you are sure that you have found the correct answer. Remember, on most multiple-choice tests, your job is to pick the *best* answer, and the last choice may be better than the preceding answers.

2. **Be alert for questions that include combinations of previously listed choices.** See the following test item:

> Among the causes of slow reading is (are)
>
> a. lack of comprehension.
> b. reading word by word rather than in phrases.
> c. poorly developed vocabulary.
> d. making too few fixations per line.
> e. a and b
> f. a, b, and c
> g. a, b, c, and d

The addition of choices that are combinations of previous choices tends to be confusing. Treat each choice, when combined with the stem, as a true or false statement. As you consider each choice, mark it true or false. If you find more than one true statement, select the choice that contains the letters of all the true statements you identified.

3. **Use logic and common sense.** Even if you are unfamiliar with the subject matter, it is sometimes possible to reason out the correct answer. The following item is taken from a sociology exam:

> Prejudice and discrimination are
>
> a. harmful to our society because they waste our economic, political, and social resources.
> b. helpful because they ensure against attack from within.
> c. harmful because they create negative images of the United States in foreign countries.
> d. helpful because they keep the majority pure and united against minorities.

Through logic and common sense, it is possible to eliminate choices b and d. Prejudice and discrimination are seldom, if ever, regarded as positive, desirable, or helpful, because they are inconsistent with democratic ideals. Having narrowed your answer to two choices, a and c, you can see that choice a offers a stronger, more substantial reason why prejudice and discrimination are harmful. What other countries think of the United States is not as serious as the waste of economic, political, and social resources.

4. **Study any items that are very similar.** When two choices seem very close and you cannot choose between them, stop and examine each. First, try to express each in your own words. Then analyze how they differ. Often this process will lead you to recognize the correct answer.

5. **Look for qualifying words.** As in true/false tests, the presence of qualifying words is important. Because many statements, ideas, principles, and rules have exceptions, you should be careful when evaluating items that contain such words as *best, always, all, no, entirely,* and *completely,* all of which suggest that something is always true, without exception. Also be careful of statements that contain such words as *none, never,* and *worst,* which allow for no exceptions. Items containing words that provide for some level of exception or qualification are more likely to be correct; a few examples are *often, usually, less, seldom, few, more,* and *most.*

In the following example, note the use of italicized qualifying words:

> In most societies
>
> a. values are *highly* consistent.
> b. people *often* believe and act on values that are contradictory.
> c. *all* legitimate organizations support the values of the majority.
> d. values of equality *never* exist alongside prejudice and discrimination.

In this question, items c and d contain the words *all* and *never*, suggesting that those statements are true without exception. Thus, if you did not know the answer to this question based on content, you could eliminate items c and d on the basis of these qualifiers.

6. **Be alert for questions that require application of knowledge or information.** You may be asked to analyze a hypothetical situation or to use what you have learned to solve a problem. Here is an example taken from a psychology test:

> Carrie is uncomfortable in her new home in New Orleans. When she gets dressed up and leaves her home and goes to the supermarket to buy the week's groceries, she gets nervous and upset and thinks that something is going to happen to her. She feels the same way when walking her four-year-old son Jason in the park or playground.
> Carrie is suffering from
>
> a. shyness.
> b. a phobia.
> c. a personality disorder.
> d. hypertension.

In answering questions of this type, start by crossing out unnecessary information that can distract you. In the preceding example, distracting information includes the woman's name, her son's name, where she lives, and why she goes to the store.

7. **Answer the question using your own words.** If a question concerns steps in a process or the order in which events occur, or any other information that is likely to confuse you, ignore the choices and use the margin or scrap paper to jot down the information as you can recall it. Then select the choice that matches what you wrote.

8. **Avoid selecting answers that are unfamiliar or that you do not understand.** A choice that looks complicated or uses difficult words is not necessarily correct. If you have studied carefully, a choice that is unfamiliar to you is probably incorrect.

9. **Pick the choice that seems most complete.** As a last resort, when you do not know the answer and are unable to eliminate any of the choices as wrong, guess by picking the one that seems complete and contains the most information. This is a good choice because instructors are always careful to make the best answer completely correct and recognizable. Such a choice often becomes long or detailed.

10. **Make educated guesses.** In most instances, you can eliminate one or more of the choices as obviously wrong. Even if you can eliminate only one choice, you have increased your odds of being correct on a four-choice item from 1 in 4 to 1 in 3. If you can eliminate two choices, you have improved your odds to 1 in 2, or 50 percent. Don't hesitate to play the odds and make a guess—you may gain points.

Goal 3

Use strategies to perform better on standardized tests.

HINTS FOR TAKING STANDARDIZED TESTS

At various times in college, you may be required to take a standardized test, which is a commercially prepared, timed test used nationally or statewide to measure skills and abilities. Your score compares your performance with that of large numbers of other students throughout the state or the country. The SAT and ACT are examples of standardized tests. Many graduate schools require a standardized test as part of their admission process. Following are a few suggestions for taking this type of test.

1. **Most standardized tests are timed, so the pace you work at is critical.** Work at a fairly rapid rate, but not so fast as to make careless errors.
2. **Don't plan on finishing the test.** Many of the tests are designed so that no one finishes.
3. **Don't expect to get everything right.** Unlike classroom tests or exams, you are not expected to get all of the answers correct.
4. **Find out if there is a penalty for guessing.** If there is none, then use the last 20 or 30 seconds to randomly fill in an answer for each item that you have not had time to answer. The odds are that you will get one item correct for every four items that you guess.
5. **Get organized before the timing begins.** Line up your answer sheet and test booklet so you can move between them rapidly without losing your place.

HINTS FOR TAKING ESSAY EXAMS

Goal 4

Use strategies to perform better on essay exams.

Essay questions are usually graded on two factors: what you say and how you say it. It is not enough, then, simply to include the correct information. The information must be presented in a logical, organized way that demonstrates your understanding of the subject you are writing about. There can be as much as one whole letter grade difference between a well-written essay and a poorly written essay, even though both contain the same basic information. This section offers suggestions for getting as many points as possible on essay exams.

Read the Question

For essay exams, reading the question carefully is the key to writing a correct, complete, and organized answer.

READ THE DIRECTIONS FIRST The directions may tell you how many essays to answer and how to structure your answer, or they may specify a minimum or maximum length for your answer.

STUDY THE QUESTION FOR CLUES The question usually includes three valuable pieces of information. First, the question tells you the *topic* you are to write about. Second, it contains a *limiting word* that restricts and directs your answer. Finally, the question contains a *key word* or phrase that tells you how to organize and present answers. Read the essay question in this example.

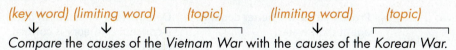

(key word) *(limiting word)* *(topic)* *(limiting word)* *(topic)*
Compare the *causes* of the *Vietnam War* with the *causes* of the *Korean War.*

In this example you have two topics—the Vietnam War and the Korean War. The question also contains a limiting word that restricts your discussion of these topics and tells you what to include in your answer. In this sample question, the limiting word is *causes*. It tells you to limit your answer to a discussion of events that started, or caused, each war. Do not include information about events of the war or its effects. The key word in the sample question is *compare*. It means you should consider the similarities, and possibly the differences, between the causes of the two wars.

Several key words and phrases used in essay questions are listed in Figure 14-1 on the next page. Some essay questions require only knowledge and

FIGURE 14-1
Key Words Used in
Essay Questions

KEY WORDS	EXAMPLE	INFORMATION TO INCLUDE
Understanding		
Discuss	Discuss Tamoxifen as a treatment for cancer.	Consider important characteristics and main points.
Enumerate	Enumerate the reasons for U.S. withdrawal from Vietnam.	List or discuss one by one.
Define	Define thermal pollution and include several examples.	Give an accurate meaning of the term with enough detail to show that you really understand it.
Applying		
Illustrate	State Boyle's law and illustrate its use.	Explain, using examples that demonstrate or clarify a point or idea.
Analyzing		
Compare	Compare the causes of air pollution with those of water pollution.	Show how items are similar as well as different; include details or examples.
Contrast	Contrast the health-care system in the United States with the health-care system in England.	Show how the items are different; include details or examples.
Explain	Explain why black Americans are primarily city dwellers.	Give facts, details, or reasons that make the idea or concept clear and understandable.
Describe	Describe an experiment that tests whether plants are sensitive to music.	Tell how something looks or happened, including how, who, where, and why.
Justify	Justify former President Carter's attempt to rescue the hostages in Iran.	Give reasons that support an action, event, or policy.
Evaluating		
Evaluate	Evaluate the strategies our society has used to treat mental illness.	React to the topic in a logical way. Discuss the merits, strengths, weaknesses, advantages, or limitations of the topic.
Criticize	Criticize the current environmental controls to combat air pollution.	Make judgments about quality or worth; include both positive and negative aspects.
Prove	Prove that ice is a better cooling agent than water.	Demonstrate or establish that a concept or theory is correct, logical, or valid.
Creating		
Trace	Trace the history of legalized prostitution in Nevada.	Describe the development or progress of a particular trend, event, or process in chronological order.
Summarize	Summarize the arguments for and against offering sex education courses in public schools.	Cover the major points in brief form; use a sentence-and-paragraph form.

comprehension, but most require the higher-level thinking skills of applying, analyzing, evaluating, and creating.

Watch for Questions with Several Parts

A common mistake that students make is failing to answer all parts of an essay question, perhaps because they get involved with answering the first part and forget about the remaining parts. Questions with several parts come in two forms. The most obvious form is as follows:

> For the U.S. invasion of Afghanistan, discuss the
>
> a. causes.
> b. immediate effects.
> c. long-range political implications.

A less obvious form that does not stand out as a several-part question is the following:

> Discuss *how* the Equal Rights Amendment was developed and *why* it aroused controversy.

When you find a question of this type, underline or circle the limiting words to serve as a reminder.

Make Notes as You Read

As you read a question the first time, you may begin to formulate an answer. To keep track of your ideas, jot down a few key words that will bring these thoughts back when you are ready to organize your answer.

DIRECTIONS   Read each of the following essay questions. For each question, underline the topic(s), circle the limiting word(s), and place a box around the key word(s).

Exercise 3

1. Discuss the long-term effects of the trend toward a smaller, more self-contained family structure.

2. Trace the development of monopolies in the late nineteenth and early twentieth centuries in America.

3. Explain one effect of the Industrial Revolution on each of three of the following:

   a. transportation
   b. capitalism
   c. socialism
   d. population growth
   e. scientific research

4. Discuss the reason that, although tropical plants have very large leaves and most desert plants have very small leaves, cacti grow equally well in both habitats.

5. Describe the events leading up to the War of 1812.

6. Compare and contrast the purpose and procedures in textbook marking and lecture note taking.

7. Briefly describe a complete approach to reading and studying a textbook chapter that will enable you to handle a test on that material successfully.

8. List four factors that influence memory or recall ability and explain how each can be used to make study more efficient.

9. Summarize the techniques a speaker or lecturer may use to emphasize the important concepts and ideas in a lecture.

10. Explain the value and purpose of the previewing technique and list the steps involved in previewing a textbook chapter. ●

Exercise 4

DIRECTIONS   Write ten possible essay questions for a course you are taking. *Be sure to write at least one question at each level of thinking.* ●

Organize Your Answer

As mentioned earlier, a well-written, organized essay often gets a higher grade than a carelessly constructed one. Read each of these sample responses to an essay question and notice how they differ. Each essay was written in response to this question on a psychology final exam: *Describe the stages involved in the memory process.*

Example 1

Memory is important to everybody's life. Memory has special ways to help you get a better recollection of things and ideas. Psychologists believe that memory has three stages: encoding, storage, and retrieval.

In the encoding stage, you are putting facts and ideas into a code, usually words, and filing them away in your memory. Encoding involves preparing information for storage in memory.

The second stage of memory is storage. It is the stage that most people call memory. It involves keeping information so that it is accessible for use later in time. How well information is stored can be affected by old information already stored and newer information that is added later.

The third step in memory is retrieval, which means the ability to get back information that is in storage. There are two types of retrieval—recognition and recall. In recognition, you have to be able to identify the correct information from several choices. In recall, you have to pull information directly from your memory without using the recognition type of retrieval.

Example 2

Memory is very complicated in how it works. It involves remembering things that are stored in your mind and being able to pull them out when you want to remember them. When you pull information out of your memory it is called retrieval. How well you can remember something is affected by how you keep the information in your mind and how you put it in. When keeping, or storing, information you have to realize that this information will be affected by old information already in your memory. Putting information in your memory is called encoding, and it means that you store facts and ideas in word form in your memory. Information stored in your memory can also be influenced by information that you add to your memory later.

There are two ways you can retrieve information. You can either recognize it or recall it. When you recognize information you are able to spot the correct information among other information. When you recall information you have to pull information out of your head. Recall is what you have to do when you write an essay exam.

While these two essays contain practically the same information, the first will probably receive a higher grade. In this essay, it is easy to see that the writer knows that the memory process has three stages and knows how to explain each. The writer opens the essay by stating that there are three stages and then devotes one paragraph to each of the three stages.

In the second essay, it is not easy to identify the stages of memory. The paragraphs are not organized according to stages in the memory process. The writer does not write about one stage at a time in a logical order. Retrieval is mentioned first; then storage and retrieval are discussed further. At the end, the writer returns to the topic of retrieval and gives further information.

Here are a few suggestions to help you organize your answer.

1. **Think before you start to write.** Decide what information is called for and what you will include.
2. **Make a brief word or phrase outline of the ideas you want to include in your answer.**
3. **Study your word outline and rearrange its order.** You may want to put major topics and important ideas first and less important points toward the end, or you may decide to organize your answer chronologically, discussing events early in time near the beginning and mentioning more recent events near the end. The topic you are discussing will largely determine the order of presentation.
4. **If the point value of the essay is given, use that information as a clue to how many separate points or ideas may be expected.** For an essay worth 25 points, for example, discussion of five major ideas may be expected.
5. **Use correct paragraph form.** Be sure to write your answers in complete, correct sentences and include only one major point in each paragraph. Each paragraph should have a main idea, usually expressed in one sentence. The remainder of the paragraph should explain, prove, or support the main idea you state. Also, use correct spelling and punctuation.
6. **Begin your answer with a thesis statement.** Your first sentence should state what the entire essay is about and suggest your approach to it. If a question asks you to discuss the practical applications of Newton's three laws of motion, you might begin by writing, "Newton's laws of motion have many practical applications." Then you should proceed to name the three laws and their practical applications, devoting one paragraph to each law.
7. **Make your main points easy to find.** State each main point at the beginning of a new paragraph. For lengthy answers or multipart questions, you might use headings or the same numbering used in the question. Use space (skip a line) to divide your answers into different parts.
8. **Include sufficient explanation.** Instructors often criticize essay answers because they fail to explain or support ideas fully. Make sure your answers convince your instructor that you have learned the material. Remember to explain, define, and give examples. Too much information is better than too little.
9. **Avoid opinions and judgments.** Unless the question specifically asks you to do so, do not include your personal reaction to the topic. When you are asked to state your reactions and opinions, include reasons to support them.

10. **Make your answer readable.** An instructor cannot help having personal reactions to your answer. Try to make those reactions positive by handing in a paper that is as legible and easy to read as possible.

11. **Proofread your answer.** Before rereading your essay, read the question again. Then check to see that you have included all necessary facts and information and that you have adequately explained each fact. Add anything you feel improves your answer. Then reread the essay a second time, checking and correcting all the mechanical aspects of your writing.

If You Run Out of Time

Despite careful planning, you may run out of time before you finish writing one of the essays. If this happens, try to jot down the major ideas that you would discuss fully if you had time. Often, your instructor will give you partial credit for this type of response, especially if you mention that you ran out of time.

If You Don't Know the Answer

Despite careful preparation, you may forget an answer. If this should happen, do not leave a blank page; write something. Attempt to answer the question—you may hit upon some partially correct information. The main reason for writing something is to give the instructor a chance to give you a few points for trying. If you leave a blank page, your instructor has no choice but to give you zero points. Usually when you lose full credit on one essay, you are automatically unable to get a high passing grade.

Exercise 5

DIRECTIONS   Organize and write a response to one of the following essay questions.

1. Six organizational patterns are commonly used in textbook writing: comparison–contrast, definition, time sequence, cause–effect, classification, and enumeration. Discuss the usefulness of these patterns in predicting and answering essay exam questions.

2. Describe three strategies that have improved your reading skills. Explain why each is effective.

3. Describe your approach to time management. Include specific techniques and organizational strategies that you have found effective. ●

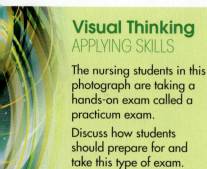

Visual Thinking
APPLYING SKILLS

The nursing students in this photograph are taking a hands-on exam called a practicum exam.

Discuss how students should prepare for and take this type of exam.

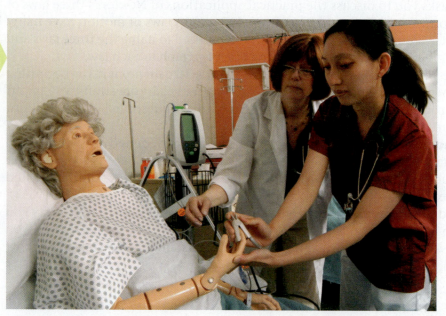

CONTROLLING TEST ANXIETY

Goal 5

Control test anxiety.

Do you get nervous and anxious just before an exam begins? If so, your response is normal; most students feel some level of anxiety before an exam. In fact, research indicates that some anxiety is beneficial and improves your performance by sharpening your attention and keeping you alert. However, very high levels of anxiety can interfere with test performance.

Test anxiety is a complicated psychological response to a threatening situation, and it may be related to other problems and past experiences. The following suggestions are intended to help you ease test anxiety. If these suggestions do not help, the next step is to discuss the problem with a counselor.

Be Sure Test Anxiety Is Not an Excuse

Many students say they have test anxiety when actually they have not studied and reviewed carefully or thoroughly. The first question, then, that you must answer honestly is this: Are you in fact *unprepared* for the exam, and do you therefore have every reason to be anxious?

Get Used to Test Situations

Psychologists who have studied anxiety use processes called "systematic desensitization" and "simulation" to reduce test anxiety. Basically, these are ways of becoming less sensitive to or disturbed by tests by putting yourself in test-like conditions. Here are a few ways you can use these processes to reduce test anxiety.

1. **Become familiar with the building and room in which the test will be given.** Visit the room when it is empty and take a seat. Visualize yourself taking a test there.
2. **Develop practice or review tests.** Treat them as real tests, and work on them in situations as similar as possible to real test conditions.
3. **Practice working with time limits.** Set an alarm clock or countdown timer and work only until it rings.
4. **Take as many tests as possible, even though you dislike them.** Always take advantage of practice tests and make-up exams. Buy a review book for the course you are taking or a workbook that accompanies your text. Treat each section as an exam, and have someone else correct your work.

Control Negative Thinking

Major factors that contribute to test anxiety are self-doubt and negative thinking. Just before and during an exam, test-anxious students often think, "I won't do well." "I'm going to fail." "What will my friends think of me when I get a failing grade?" This type of thinking predisposes you to failure; you are telling yourself that you expect to fail. By thinking in this way, you undermine your own chances for success.

One solution to this problem is to send yourself positive rather than negative messages, such as, "I have studied hard and I deserve to pass." "I know that I know the material." "I know I can do it!" And remember, being well prepared is one of the best ways to reduce test anxiety.

Compose Yourself Before the Test Begins

Don't take an exam on an empty stomach; you will feel queasy. Have something light or bland to eat. Some students find that a brisk walk outside before going to an exam helps to reduce tension.

Before you begin the test, take 30 seconds or so to calm yourself, to slow down, and to focus your attention. Take several deep breaths, close your eyes, and visualize yourself calmly working through the test. Remind yourself that you have prepared carefully and have every reason to do well.

Answer Easy Questions First

To give yourself an initial boost of confidence, begin with a section of the test that seems easy. This will help you to work calmly, and you will prove to yourself that you can handle the test.

USING COLLEGE TEXTBOOKS
Using Headings to Create Practice Tests

Before you take a test in class, it is helpful to prepare yourself by taking practice tests. If your textbook does not contain sample essay questions or detailed review questions, you can create practice essay tests on your own.

To write your own practice essay exam questions, study the headings in the chapter you will be tested on. Think about the topics and concepts presented and write some possible questions that require you to understand, apply, or analyze the facts contained in the section. You can write full answers, create outlines of your answers, or both. Here is an example of the questions one student wrote for a section of his sociology textbook.

Textbook: *THINK* Sociology

Headings	Essay Questions

Headings

AGING AND HEALTH

The Graying of Society 208

Health Defined 211
    Social Epidemiology 211
Health in the United States: Living
    off the Fat of the Land 213 •
    Childhood Obesity 213
    Stigmatization of the Obese 214
    Obesity and Race 214
Health Care 215
    The Uninsured 215 •Costs
    of Services 215 •Health
    Care: An International
    Comparison 215 •Health Care
    and the Elderly—Medicare 216
Aging: The Graying of the United
    States 216
    Aging and Demographic
    Change in the United State 216
    The "Sandwiched" Generation 217
    Concerns About Aging 219

Essay Questions

Discuss the impacts of obesity on the United States. How have these changed in recent years?
Explain how the aging population in the United States is affecting society.

—Carl, *THINK Sociology,* p. vii

Textbook Exercise 1: Creating Test Questions

Identify at least three other possible exam questions based on the outline on the previous page.

FURTHER PRACTICE WITH TEXTBOOK READING

Textbook Exercise 2: Sample Textbook Chapter

For the section titled "Prejudice and Stereotypes" in Part Seven, pages 432–436, predict two possible essay questions.

Textbook Exercise 3: Your College Textbook

Choose a textbook that you are currently using in one of your other courses and select a chapter. Predict an essay question for each main heading in the chapter.

SELF-TEST SUMMARY

Goal 1
How can you improve the way you take exams?

You can improve your exam grades by approaching tests in a systematic, organized manner. This involves bringing the necessary materials to the exam, arriving on time, choosing a seat at the front of the room, previewing the exam, planning the time you will devote to various sections of the exam, and reading the questions carefully.

Goal 2
What can you do to improve your performance on objective exams?

When taking any type of objective exam, read the directions carefully, leave nothing blank, and look for clues that will help you recall the information. When taking true/false tests, you should also read two-part statements carefully and be aware of negative words or word parts. When you have no idea of the answer, mark extreme statements and those that contain unfamiliar terms as false and all others as true.

For multiple-choice tests, make educated guesses by reading the choices carefully, narrowing them down by using reasoning power, paying attention to qualifying words, and considering the choices in light of what you know about the topic. When all else fails, eliminate unfamiliar or confusing items and choose an answer that seems complete.

When taking short-answer tests, use the point distributions and the amount of space provided to determine how much to write, and plan what to write beforehand.

For fill-in-the-blank tests, decide what kind of information is being asked for by the key words in, and grammatical structure of, the sentence.

Goal 3
How should you approach standardized tests?

When taking a standardized test, maintain a rapid but careful pace and don't be upset if you don't finish the test or don't know all the answers. Before testing, find out if there is a penalty for guessing. Get organized before you begin the test.

Goal 4

What can you do to improve your performance on essay exams?

When taking an essay exam, first examine the question carefully, reading the directions, noting all parts, and looking for clues that signal exactly what type of response your instructor wants. Essay answers should be carefully organized and written in an easy-to-read form. Include a topic sentence in each paragraph, use numbering and headings when appropriate, include enough information to prove your point, and state opinions and judgments only when the question asks for them. Take pains to make your answer legible, and carefully proofread for accuracy, grammar, and mechanics. If you run out of time or your memory fails, you may be able to earn some credit by jotting down an outline or writing something relevant on the page.

Goal 5

How can you control test anxiety?

Too much test anxiety can negatively affect your performance on exams. You can relieve anxiety by being prepared for the exam; becoming familiar with the testing location, conditions, and time limits; controlling negative thoughts; taking time to compose yourself near the start of the exam; and beginning with the easy questions for an initial boost of confidence.

APPLYING YOUR SKILLS

DISCUSSING THE CHAPTER

1. What techniques do you use to overcome test anxiety? What techniques are particularly effective for various types of examinations?
2. What types of exams are the least stressful for people with each learning style? What can people do to become more relaxed when taking various types of examinations?
3. Why do professors use various types of objective and essay tests in order to evaluate student learning? From the professor's perspective, what are the advantages and disadvantages of using each type of examination?
4. Why do you think a person's first guess on a multiple-choice test item is usually the best one?

ANALYZING A STUDY SITUATION

Maria is taking an American history course. The instructor announced that the next exam will cover only three chapters on the Constitution—its origins, history, and current applications and interpretations. Further, students are allowed to use their textbook and both lecture and study notes during the exam. As most students breathed a sigh of relief, the instructor cautioned, "It's not as easy as you think!" Still, many students in the class are not preparing for this exam at all. Maria knows she should prepare, but she is uncertain about what to do.

1. What type of questions (multiple-choice, true/false, short-answer, or essay) do you think Maria's exam will contain?
2. Why would the instructor allow students to bring materials to the exam? What types of learning is she emphasizing? What is she not emphasizing?
3. How should Maria prepare for this exam?

WORKING ON COLLABORATIVE PROJECTS

DIRECTIONS   Each member of the class should write an answer to the following essay question, which is based on the reading "Linking Up: 21st Century Social Networking" in Part Six, page 416.

> Social networking widely influences human communication and interaction. Discuss at least three ways social networking has created change or innovation.

Working in pairs, compare your answers, noting the strengths and weaknesses of the essays. Then rewrite and combine your answers to produce a stronger or more nearly complete response.

Quick Quiz

DIRECTIONS Write the letter of the choice that best completes each statement in the space provided.

CHECKING YOUR RECALL

_____ 1. The best way to approach an exam is to
  a. plan to arrive at least 30 minutes before the exam begins.
  b. sit near the back of the class.
  c. bring only a pencil with you.
  d. preview the exam before you answer any questions.

_____ 2. Neil's history exam has a total of 100 points, divided as follows: ten multiple-choice questions worth 20 points, five short-answer questions worth 20 points, five true/false questions worth 10 points, and one essay question worth 50 points. Based on this information, Neil should plan to spend almost half of his time on the
  a. true/false questions.
  b. short-answer questions.
  c. multiple-choice questions.
  d. essay question.

_____ 3. One thing to remember when taking an objective exam is that
  a. the directions for all objective tests are the same.
  b. you should leave difficult questions blank.
  c. absolute statements tend to be true.
  d. your first guess is usually the best one.

_____ 4. An example of a limiting word in a true/false statement is
  a. _always_.
  b. _however_.
  c. _when_.
  d. _because_.

_____ 5. On a multiple-choice test, the qualifying word most likely to indicate a correct statement is
  a. _always_.
  b. _usually_.
  c. _best_.
  d. _worst_.

APPLYING YOUR SKILLS

_____ 6. All of the following suggestions can help improve your performance on multiple-choice exams _except_
  a. choosing the answer that seems most complete.
  b. using logic and common sense.
  c. answering the item first in your own words.
  d. choosing the answer that is unfamiliar to you.

_____ 7. Graham is taking a standardized test for admission to college. One thing he should know about this type of test is that
  a. it is most important that he finish the test.
  b. he is expected to get most of the answers correct.
  c. he should guess on all the items he doesn't know, regardless of how the test is scored.
  d. he should work at a fairly quick rate because the test is probably timed.

_____ 8. In order to reduce test anxiety, you should try to do all of the following _except_
  a. become familiar with the testing location.
  b. avoid taking practice tests.
  c. control negative thinking.
  d. practice working within time limits.

_____ 9. Of the following essay exam questions, the one that asks you to give reasons that support an idea is:
  a. Define symbiosis and give several examples.
  b. Enumerate the strategies our society uses to deal with homelessness.
  c. Justify President George W. Bush's invasion of Iraq.
  d. State Boyle's law and illustrate its use.

_____ 10. When you are writing an essay exam answer, you should typically try to do all of the following _except_
  a. begin with a thesis statement.
  b. use correct paragraph form.
  c. provide sufficient explanation.
  d. include your personal reaction to the topic.

Thematic Readings

THEME A Controversies in Science

Science and controversy often go hand in hand. The controversies frequently center around a single question: "How far should we let science go?" For example, if human cloning becomes possible, should society embrace the idea? Is it ethical to transplant animal organs (such as a pig's heart) into a human body? What are the limits of science and medicine? In this thematic section, you will read about three current controversies in science. "Shades of Grey in the Ethics of Designer Babies" (p. 379) asks whether parents should be allowed to select their children's genes to create children who are mentally, athletically, or otherwise superior. "The Ocean's Plastic Problem" (p. 382) examines a perennial problem: the pollution caused by plastic. "Some Possible Consequences of Global Warming" (p. 385) looks at the science of global warming, outlining some of the ways that higher temperatures can affect Earth and its people.

A-1   Shades of Grey in the Ethics of Designer Babies

Anjana Ahuja

One might hope society would recoil at selecting the perfect shade embryo, writes Anjana Ahuja.

1 As a guide to improbable gifts, the Neiman Marcus roll call of fantasy Christmas presents takes some beating. There is the $35,000, 5-foot tall cocktail-shaking machine made from cast iron, which looks more likely to leave the recipient hospitalized than intoxicated. Those aspiring to impractical extravagance will surely covet the $65,000 outdoor peacock sculpture hand-crafted from silk flowers and crystals.

2 In the decades to come, science is likely to acquire the power to deliver its own improbable gift: the genetically perfect baby. A gathering storm of social factors—more families being created through fertility treatment, partly because of delayed parenthood, coupled with the rise of genetic screening—means that the potential to choose a healthy embryo is already here. An embryo's **genome** can be read like a bar code, revealing the presence—or hopefully absence—of genetic disease.

genome
complete genetic code

3 But as biologists unravel more about how genes also contribute to intelligence, talent, and beauty, academics have begun to ask: why stop at genetic selection for health when you can have genetic selection for success? The promise of a handsome jaw, a generous IQ, and a statuesque height offers a child a head start over his peers before he has even left the womb.

4 That was the opening salvo at a conference on reproduction last week, organized by the Progress Educational Trust. Julian Savulescu, professor of practical ethics at Oxford University, argued that parents should be free to use technology to select advantageous physical and intellectual

traits in their offspring. That might include gender, IQ, height—and even skin color. His belief is underpinned by two quite reasonable arguments: that couples are entitled to procreative freedom; and that the overriding duty of a parent is to do what is in a child's best interests.

5   In the United Kingdom, sex selection for social reasons is forbidden. Couples cannot choose whether to have a boy or a girl, except if there is a risk of inheriting a rare gender-linked, life-limiting disease. Prof. Savulescu disagrees: "I don't see why the state or any other group should tell me what kind of child I should have. The Nazis interfered with reproductive freedoms, and the current regime [banning sex selection] is closer to **eugenics** than my own view." And if the world does treat the light-skinned more favorably, the professor says, it is reasonable to want a light-skinned child so that they can have a better life.

eugenics
the controversial science of improving the human population by controlled breeding

6   One might hope that society would recoil at the thought of a couple producing several embryos and then selecting the perfect shade, as if from a Dulux palette. Sadly, such technology is likely to find favor in India, where gender selection is already available in private clinics, usually favoring boys (there is female infanticide for the poor). There, dark skins are associated with the lowest **castes**; light skins with wealth and "good" marriage. People reportedly spend more money on skin-whitening creams than on Coca-Cola.

caste
social class in India

7   Newspaper marriage columns and dating Web sites are full of men yearning for fair-skinned maidens (women seem less fussy). One tale emerged recently of a woman who had married into a paler family and was seeking the sperm of a white donor in order to "color-match" her baby to her in-laws. There is an Indian parenting Web site that runs "how to use skin bleach" tutorials.

8   The social pressure to lighten up has led to the campaign Dark is Beautiful, featuring actress and director Nandita Das. Ms. Das has lambasted her homeland's biggest movie star, Shah Rukh Khan, for promoting lightening creams.

abhor
detest

9   If we **abhor** choosing a baby's skin color, we should also condemn such products as Fair and Handsome, the "fairness cream" that Mr. Khan endorses. In fact, it is one of Hindustan Unilever's best-selling brands in India. The creams also sell well in Britain, where there is clearly a willing market.

10   Perhaps, when it comes to reproductive genetic choice, we instinctively dislike the prospect of some children being advantaged by birth. Well, what technology threatens tomorrow, class and wealth can deliver today. Rich, well-connected parents pack their kids off to the best schools and sign them up for piano, ballet, and Mandarin. These thoroughbreds will go to good universities, intern at banks and glossy magazines, and marry in socially exclusive circles.

11   And with direct-to-consumer genetic testing already here— 23andMe, a genomics research company, was launched in the UK last week—the future is closer than you think. Skin color is largely controlled by genes that code for the pigment melanin, and they are already being investigated.

12   I admire Prof. Savulescu for having the courage to make an unpopular case—though the freedom to select risks reinforcing discrimination

against the short, the ugly, the dark, and the stupid. (I write as one who ticks at least two of those boxes.)

13   But more than that, I adore the rich, chaotic diversity of the human gene pool. I want the future to be black, white, brown, and all the shades in between. Give me the blondes, the brunettes, and—while you can—the redheads. Go on, throw in the bald ones too. Show me the **introverts and the extroverts**, the musical and the tone deaf, the happy and the melancholy, the short and the tall.

14   My two children, born to a dark mother and a pale father, have turned out as different in skin color, looks, and temperament as it is possible for them to be. And—unlike that oversized, overpriced cocktail shaker—it has all come as a wonderful surprise.

—Ahuja, ft.com, Dec. 5, 2014

introverts and extroverts
shy people and outgoing people

REVIEWING THE READING

DIRECTIONS   Write the letter of the choice that best completes each statement in the space provided.

Checking Your Comprehension

_____   1. The tone of this selection is best described as

a. academic.

b. nostalgic.

c. subjective.

d. humorous.

_____   2. The author wrote this selection in order to

a. discuss a controversial issue and offer her opinion about it.

b. convince parents to customize their unborn children's genes.

c. criticize doctors who offer embryo-altering therapies.

d. argue for laws that would make eugenics illegal.

_____   3. In India, darker skin is associated with

a. celebrities.

b. priests and other religious figures.

c. wealth.

d. the lower classes.

_____   4. The author believes that

a. skin-lightening creams and other "lightening" products should be outlawed.

b. the children of the wealthy already have the advantages that rich people can buy for their children.

c. Prof. Savulescu's beliefs about embryo enhancement violate the laws of medical ethics.

d. skin color ultimately does not matter in terms of a child's social prospects and chances in life.

_____ 5. The author fears the reinforcement of "discrimination against the short, the ugly, the dark, and the stupid" (paragraph 12). Which of those words definitely describes the author?

    a. short

    b. ugly

    c. dark

    d. stupid

Checking Your Vocabulary

_____ 6. The word _recoil_ in the subheading under the title means

    a. be interested in.

    b. be disgusted by.

    c. cheer.

    d. dismiss.

_____ 7. The word _covet_ (paragraph 1) means

    a. desire.

    b. pay for.

    c. laugh at.

    d. admire.

_____ 8. A synonym for _yearning for_ (paragraph 7) is

    a. avoiding.

    b. helping.

    c. wanting.

    d. marrying.

_____ 9. To _lambaste_ (paragraph 8) is to

    a. celebrate.

    b. enrich.

    c. suggest.

    d. criticize.

_____ 10. A synonym for _melancholy_ (paragraph 13) is

    a. pessimistic.

    b. sad.

    c. average.

    d. downtrodden.

A-2   The Ocean's Plastic Problem

Cami Tellez

1   In her recent excursion to the Arctic, Dr. Rachel Obbard, assistant professor at the Thayer School of Engineering at Dartmouth College, noted an accumulation of plastic debris in the Arctic Ocean. A specialist in polar ice, Obbard was concerned about the volume of micro-plastic inside the ice of perhaps one of the most pristine areas of the planet.

2   Most people are aware of the dangers of wildlife being caught in debris near land, but Obbard has determined the rippling effects that our "plastic footprint" has had in even the most remote areas of the world.

3   The use of plastic has increased dramatically over the past ten years. During that same ten-year period, scientists who study ocean currents began to notice a similar and disturbing phenomenon: the five major oceans act as whirling conveyor belts, carrying plastic debris, often invisible to the naked eye, into every main current of the ocean. Since this micro-plastic cannot be detected, it is almost impossible to quantify and record. Most of this micro-plastic ends up frozen when submerged in Arctic waters.

4   Recent experiments by scientists like Obbard have demonstrated that ice cores in the Arctic Ocean have three orders of magnitude more particles than some counts of plastic in the Great Pacific Garbage Patch, a gyre of marine debris particles in the North Pacific Ocean that is recognized by scientists as one of the highest levels known of plastic particulate suspended in the upper water column.

5   For most of the 20th century, plastic waste in the ocean was considered a simply aesthetic problem with no economic consequences. Recently, however, United Nations Environmental Programmes ("UNEP") determined that plastic pollution costs the world over $13 billion in global damages, although scientists have disputed that this number is a gross undervaluation. As the melting of the ice caps progresses, scientists have estimated that more than 1 trillion pieces of plastic will enter the world's ocean in the next ten years.

6   While we may be able to put a price on the economic risks that the plastic debris has caused our society, the damage we have caused to the environment is incalculable. All around the Arctic animals have fallen prey to the dangers of plastic accumulation. Furthermore, because it takes hundreds of years for plastic to decompose, plastic has also affected animals that are not fooled initially by consuming plastic debris or trapped by "ghost nets." Fish consume food that is tainted by plastic in the water, which then affects commercial fishing industries for years after in Arctic regions. In Arctic sea canyons, plastic bags sink to the seafloor of underwater canyons and may deter gas exchanges, thus making the water low in oxygen. Plastic particles absorb high concentrations of gas such as PCB and DDT, increasing these gases in the ocean by thousands of magnitudes.

7   Should humans consume fish and marine life that have been exposed to this change of environment, it may result in cancer, fetus malformation, and impaired reproductive ability. Indigenous populations in the Arctic are especially prone to these health risks, given that their diet consists primarily of fish harvested from the Arctic.

8   On a global scale, though there has been little to no response from Asian and Arab countries concerning the issue of dumping plastic into the world's oceans, the West has been somewhat receptive to changing its behavior. UNEP has partnered with various organizations around the world to raise general awareness about dumping debris into the ocean

and has sponsored ocean cleanups around the world. It has also begun to track the waste in various oceans so that it can monitor the severity of the situation.

9   Additionally, some international agreements address the problem. For instance, the EU's Marine Strategy Framework Directive indicates that by 2020 it hopes to improve the marine environment in oceans that feed directly into the Arctic. Despite the murky and unclear world of marine waste control, there has been an influx of support and interest from newer generations on how we can solve this growing problem. Approaches include Boyan Slat's Ocean Cleanup invention and the Surfrider Foundation's powerful activist network. Setbacks aside, there is still hope within individuals worldwide that we can live in a world with clean oceans.

— http://www.worldpolicy.org/blog/2014/09/11/oceans-plastic-problem

REVIEWING THE READING

DIRECTIONS   Write the letter of the choice that best completes each statement in the space provided.

Checking Your Comprehension

_____   1. The greatest concentration of micro-plastic can be found in

   a. the Great Pacific Garbage Patch.
   b. the waters surrounding Asian and Arab countries.
   c. ice cores in the Arctic Ocean.
   d. abandoned fishing nets off the coast of California.

_____   2. The impact of plastic debris includes all *except* the following:

   a. Fishermen have lost thousands of dollars worth of equipment damaged by plastic debris.
   b. Plastic pollution costs the world billions of dollars in damages.
   c. Animals are harmed by plastic debris.
   d. Humans who consume animals affected by plastic debris may have health and reproductive issues.

_____   3. The spread of plastic debris is accomplished by

   a. the moon's gravitational pull on Earth.
   b. plate tectonics that affect the oceans.
   c. ocean currents that carry the debris far and wide.
   d. the Earth's movement around the sun.

_____   4. Marine life that is not harmed by plastic debris or ghost nets may be affected by

   a. fishermen illegally fishing for protected fish species or other marine life.
   b. ocean cleanup efforts that remove elements necessary to sustain marine life.
   c. chemicals released into the oceans to speed up the decomposition of plastic debris.
   d. the extended decomposition process of plastic debris.

5. Over the next ten years, the world's oceans will experience an enormous increase in the amount of plastic debris due to

a. an expected shift in ocean currents.

b. an increase in the use of plastics across the globe.

c. the melting of polar ice caps.

d. the refusal of some nations to take seriously the issue of polluting the world's oceans with plastic.

Checking Your Vocabulary

_____ 6. *Debris* (paragraph 1) means

a. plant-based material.

b. scattered fragments.

c. animal bones.

d. geological data.

_____ 7. *Pristine* (paragraph 1) means

a. uncorrupted.

b. remote.

c. polluted.

d. frigid.

_____ 8. Something that is *aesthetic* (paragraph 5)

a. pertains to global affairs.

b. pertains to a sense of beauty.

c. pertains to disposal.

d. pertains to the environment.

_____ 9. An item that is *tainted* (paragraph 6) is

a. absorbed.

b. preyed upon.

c. contaminated.

d. trapped.

_____ 10. The word *indigenous* (paragraph 7) means

a. foreign.

b. marine.

c. aging.

d. native.

A-3 Textbook Excerpt: Some Possible Consequences of Global Warming

Frederick K. Lutgens

carbon dioxide
greenhouse gas responsible for global warming

1 What consequences can be expected if the **carbon dioxide** content of the atmosphere reaches a level that is twice what it was early in the twentieth century? Because the climate system is complex, predicting the distribution of particular regional changes can be speculative. It is not

yet possible to pinpoint specifics, such as where or when it will become drier or wetter. Nevertheless, plausible scenarios can be given for larger scales of space and time.

2   The magnitude of the temperature increase will not be the same everywhere. The temperature rise will probably be smallest in the tropics and increase toward the poles. As for precipitation, the models indicate that some regions will experience significantly more precipitation and runoff, whereas others will experience a decrease in runoff due to reduced precipitation or greater evaporation caused by higher temperatures.

IPCC
Intergovernmental Panel on Climate Change

3   Table 1 summarizes some of the most likely effects and their possible consequences. The table also provides the **IPCC's** estimate of the probability of each effect.

TABLE 1 Twenty-First-Century Climate Trends

PROJECTED CHANGES AND ESTIMATED PROBABILITY*	EXAMPLES OF PROJECTED IMPACTS
Higher maximum temperatures; more hot days and heat waves over nearly all land areas (*virtually certain*)	Increased incidence of death and serious illness in older age groups and urban poor. Increased heat stress in livestock and wildlife. Shift in tourist destinations. Increased risk of damage to a number of crops. Increased electric cooling demand and reduced energy supply reliability.
Higher minimum temperatures; fewer cold days, frost days, and cold waves over nearly all land areas (*virtually certain*)	Decreased cold-related human morbidity and mortality. Decreased risk of damage to a number of crops and increased risk to others. Extended range and activity of some pest and disease vectors. Reduced heating energy demand.
Increases in frequency of heavy precipitation events over most areas (*very likely*)	Increased flood, landslide, avalanche, and debris flow damage. Increased soil erosion. Increased flood runoff could increase recharge of some floodplain aquifers. Increased pressure on government and private flood insurance systems and disaster relief.
Increases in area affected by drought (*likely*)	Decreased crop yields. Increased damage to building foundations caused by ground shrinkage. Decreased water-resource quantity and quality. Increased risk of wildfires.
Increases in intense tropical cyclone activity (*likely*)	Increased risks to human life, risk of infectious-disease epidemics, and many other risks. Increased coastal erosion and damage to coastal buildings and infrastructure. Increased damage to coastal ecosystems, such as coral reefs and mangroves.

*Virtually certain indicates a probability of 99–100 percent, very likely indicates a probability of 90–99 percent, and likely indicates a probability of 66–100 percent.

Source: Based on the Fifth Assessment Report. Climate Change 2013: The Physical Science Basis, Summary for Policy Makers.

Sea-Level Rise

4   A significant impact of a human-induced global warming is a rise in sea level. As this occurs, coastal cities, wetlands, and low-lying islands could be threatened with more frequent flooding, increased shoreline erosion, and saltwater encroachment into coastal rivers and aquifers.

5   How is a warmer atmosphere related to a rise in sea level? One significant factor is thermal expansion. Higher air temperatures warm the adjacent upper layers of the ocean, which in turn causes the water to expand and sea level to rise.

6   The second factor contributing to global sea-level rise is melting glaciers. With few exceptions, glaciers around the world have been retreating at unprecedented rates over the past century. Some mountain glaciers have disappeared altogether. A recent 18-year satellite study showed that the mass of the Greenland and Antarctic Ice Sheets dropped an average of 475 gigatons per year. (A gigaton is 1 billion metric tons.) That is enough water to raise sea level 1.5 millimeters (0.05 inch) per year. The loss of ice was not steady but was occurring at an accelerating rate during the study period. Each year over the course of the study period, the two ice sheets lost a combined average of 36.3 gigatons more than they did the year before. During the same span, mountain glaciers and ice caps lost an average of slightly more than 400 gigatons per year. Research indicates that sea level has risen about 25 centimeters (9.75 inches) since 1870, with the rate of sea-level rise accelerating in recent years.

7   Scientists realize that even modest rises in sea level along a gently sloping shoreline, such as the Atlantic and Gulf coasts of the United States, will lead to significant erosion and severe and permanent inland flooding. If this happens, many beaches and wetlands will be eliminated, and coastal civilization will be severely disrupted. Low-lying and densely populated places such as Bangladesh and the small island nation of the Maldives are especially vulnerable. The average elevation in the Maldives is 1.5 meters (less than 5 feet), and its highest point is just 2.4 meters (less than 8 feet) above sea level.

8   Because sea-level rise is a gradual phenomenon, coastal residents may overlook it as an important contributor to shoreline erosion problems. Rather, the blame may be assigned to other forces, especially storm activity. Although a given storm may be the immediate cause, the magnitude of its destruction may result from the relatively small sea-level rise that allowed the storm's power to cross a much greater land area.

Increasing Ocean Acidity

9   The human-induced increase in the amount of carbon dioxide in the atmosphere has some serious **implications** for ocean chemistry and for marine life. Recent studies show that about one-third of the human-generated carbon dioxide currently ends up in the oceans. The additional carbon dioxide lowers the ocean's pH, making seawater more acidic. The pH scale is shown and briefly described in Figure 1.

implications
consequences

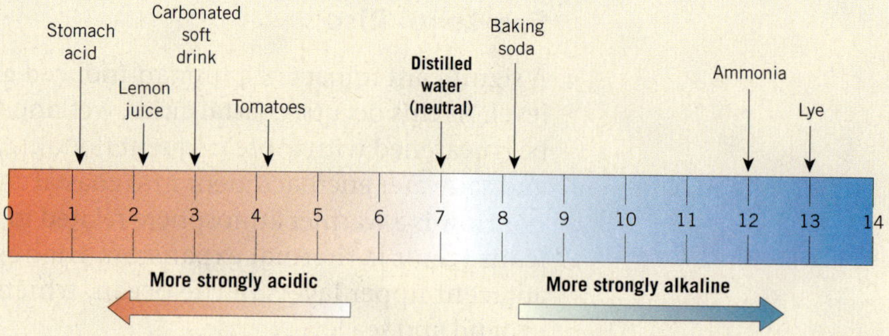

FIGURE 1

The pH scale This is the common measure of the degree of acidity or alkalinity of a solution. The scale ranges from 0 to 14, with a value of 7 indicating a solution that is neutral. Values below 7 indicate greater acidity, whereas numbers above 7 indicate greater alkalinity. It is important to note that the pH scale is logarithmic; that is, each whole number increment indicates a tenfold difference. Thus, pH 4 is 10 times more acidic than pH 5 and 100 times (10×10) more acidic than pH 6.

Stomach acid
Lemon juice
Carbonated soft drink
Tomatoes
Distilled water (neutral)
Baking soda
Ammonia
Lye

0 1 2 3 4 5 6 7 8 9 10 11 12 13 14

More strongly acidic ← 　　　　→ More strongly alkaline

10   When atmospheric CO_2 dissolves in seawater (H_2O), it forms carbonic acid (H_2CO_3). This lowers the ocean's pH and changes the balance of certain chemicals found naturally in seawater. In fact, the oceans have already absorbed enough carbon dioxide for surface waters to have experienced a pH decrease of 0.1 pH units since preindustrial times, with an additional pH decrease likely in the future. Moreover, if the current trend in carbon dioxide emissions continues, by the year 2100, the ocean will experience a pH decrease of at least 0.2 pH units, which represents a change in ocean chemistry that has not occurred for millions of years. This shift toward acidity and the resulting changes in ocean chemistry make it more difficult for certain marine creatures to build hard parts out of calcium carbonate. The decline in pH thus threatens a variety of calcite-secreting organisms as diverse as microbes and corals, which concerns marine scientists because of the potential consequences for other sea life that depend on the health and availability of these organisms.

The Potential for "Surprises"

11   You have seen that climate in the twenty-first century, unlike in the preceding 1000 years, is not expected to be stable. Rather, a constant state of change is very likely. Many of the changes will probably be gradual environmental shifts, **imperceptible** from year to year. Nevertheless, the effects, accumulated over decades, will have powerful economic, social, and political consequences.

12   Despite our best efforts to understand future climate shifts, there is also the potential for "surprises." This simply means that, due to the complexity of Earth's climate system, we might experience relatively sudden, unexpected changes or see some aspects of climate shift in an unexpected manner. The report *Climate Change Impacts on the United States* describes the situation like this:

13   Surprises challenge humans' ability to adapt, because of how quickly and unexpectedly they occur. For example, what if the Pacific Ocean warms in such a way that **El Niño** events become much more extreme? This could reduce the frequency, but perhaps not the strength, of hurricanes along the East Coast, while on the West Coast, more severe winter storms, extreme precipitation events, and damaging winds could become common. What if large quantities of methane, a potent greenhouse gas currently frozen in icy Arctic tundra and sediments, began to be released to the atmosphere by warming, potentially creating an

imperceptible
undetectable

El Niño
climate condition that leads to warmer weather in certain parts of the world

amplifying "feedback loop" that would cause even more warming? We simply do not know how far the climate system or other systems it affects can be pushed before they respond in unexpected ways.

14   There are many examples of potential surprises, each of which would have large consequences. Most of these potential outcomes are rarely reported, in this study or elsewhere. Even if the chance of any particular surprise happening is small, the chance that at least one such surprise will occur is much greater. In other words, while we can't know which of these events will occur, it is likely that one or more will eventually occur.[1]

15   The impact on climate of an increase in atmospheric carbon dioxide and **trace** gases is obscured by some uncertainties. Yet climate scientists continue to improve our understanding of the climate system and the potential impacts and effects of global climate change. Policymakers are confronted with responding to the risks posed by emissions of greenhouse gases, knowing that our understanding is imperfect. However, they are also faced with the fact that climate-induced environmental changes cannot be reversed quickly, if at all, due to the lengthy time scales associated with the climate system.

—Lutgens, *Essentials of Geology*, pp. 550–554

trace
small amount

REVIEWING THE READING

DIRECTIONS   Write the letter of the choice that best completes each statement in the space provided.

Checking Your Comprehension

_____   1. The author wrote this selection in order to

   a. secure government funding for alternative energies, such as wind and solar power.

   b. educate the reader about the possible effects of global warming.

   c. help the reader understand how changes in water acidity affect life on Earth.

   d. criticize developing (poor) nations for their carbon dioxide emissions.

_____   2. In which of the following regions of the globe will temperatures likely rise the most?

   a. at the Equator

   b. in the tropics

   c. along the coast

   d. at the North and South Poles

_____   3. Which of the following is *not* a possible effect of sea-level rise?

   a. saltwater encroachment into coastal rivers and aquifers

   b. increased shoreline erosion

   c. droughts at high elevations

   d. more frequent flooding of coastal cities

[1] National Assessment Synthesis Team, *Climate Change Impacts on the United States: The Potential Consequences of Climate Variability and Change* (Washington, DC: U.S. Global Research Program, 2000), p. 19.

_____ 4. According to Table 1 (p. 386), which of the following is the LEAST likely climate trend in the twenty-first century?

    a. higher minimum temperatures

    b. increases in intense tropical cyclone activity

    c. higher maximum temperatures

    d. increases in frequency of heavy precipitation events over most areas

_____ 5. Ultimately, carbon dioxide makes ocean water more _____, which affects ocean animals' ability to build hard shells.

    a. acidic

    b. dense

    c. alkaline

    d. evaporative

Checking Your Vocabulary

_____ 6. A synonym for _magnitude_ (paragraph 2) is

    a. size.

    b. width.

    c. change.

    d. quality.

_____ 7. In Table 1 (p. 386), the words _morbidity_ and _mortality_ mean rates of

    a. depression and hunger.

    b. mental illness and stiffness.

    c. poverty and stress.

    d. disease and death.

_____ 8. An _aquifer_ (paragraph 4) is an underground source of

    a. metals.

    b. salt.

    c. heat.

    d. water.

_____ 9. The word _unprecedented_ (paragraph 6) means

    a. unlikely.

    b. unheard of.

    c. impossible.

    d. increasing.

_____ 10. _Tundra_ (paragraph 13) is

    a. snow.

    b. water sources.

    c. frozen ground.

    d. icebergs.

Understanding Your Textbook

_____ 11. An outline of this selection would be titled "Some Possible Consequences of Global Warming," and its three main subheadings would be: "Sea-Level Rise," "_____," and "The Potential for 'Surprises.'"

    a. Twenty-First Century Climate Trends
    b. The pH Scale
    c. Examples of Projected Impacts
    d. Increasing Ocean Acidity

_____ 12. Figure 1 on page 388 indicates that a neutral value is _____, _____ is highly alkaline, and _____ is highly acidic.

    a. 0, lemon juice, baking soda
    b. 1, distilled water, a tomato
    c. 7, lye, stomach acid
    d. 14, baking soda, a carbonated soft drink

MAKING CONNECTIONS

1. Of the issues discussed in this section, which do you consider the most serious? The least serious? Why?
2. Each of the selections explores a problem, but none of the authors offers solutions to the problem. Why do you think this is the case? Choose one of the issues and list at least three possible solutions (even if they are only starting points).
3. List and explain at least two other current scientific controversies not discussed in these readings. Why are they controversial, and what are both sides of the argument?
4. Compare the tone in each of the readings. Which has the strongest author viewpoint? Which seem more balanced?
5. How does the authors' choice of supporting details affect your response to each reading? Which reading did you find most compelling? Why?

WHAT DO YOU THINK?

DIRECTIONS   On a separate sheet of paper, write about any four of these five choices.

1. After reading these selections, you decide to eliminate plastic from your life. How would you compensate? Do you think living without plastic would be difficult?
2. Suppose you are expecting a child. What three qualities would you want your child to have? Why?
3. As part of a senior project, you must volunteer for an environmental organization. Which one would you choose, and why? (You may want to conduct some Web research before you answer.)
4. Name at least three things that you can do to prevent plastic from getting into the ocean.
5. What signs of global warming have you seen or experienced? Or do you think that claims of global warming have been exaggerated?

THEME B	Health Issues

Some people believe that money can buy happiness, but it can't buy health. As many sick people learn the hard way, good health is a human being's most precious commodity. Because good health is so important, many governments spend huge amounts of money on doctors and medical care, and medical care itself is often controversial. The readings in this section focus on issues in health and medicine. "Ethical Dilemmas Surround Those Willing to Sell, Buy Kidneys on the Black Market" (p. 392) looks at the market for human organs and asks whether living people should be allowed to sell their organs to people who want to buy them. "The Virtual House Call" (p. 396) asks whether an online consultation with a doctor can be more effective than a time-consuming, expensive visit to a doctor's office—and what the answer means for society and medical practice. "Self-Help on the Web: Proceed with Caution" (p. 402) discusses a common occurrence—people searching for medical information on the Web—and offers suggestions for evaluating medical information found online.

B-1   Ethical Dilemmas Surround Those Willing to Sell, Buy Kidneys on the Black Market

Michelle Castillo

1 There's no denying that there is a shortage of organ donations in the United States. Government estimates show 18 people die each day waiting for a transplant, and every 10 minutes someone is added to the transplant list.

2 The need for kidneys is especially high. In 2013, there were 98,463 people waiting for a new kidney in the United States, the most requested organ by far. By November, only 9,708 kidney transplants had been completed.

3 The beauty of kidney donation compared to other organs is that people are born with two of them, making possible donation from a living person. Other organs, like hearts, can only be donated from recently deceased individuals. But, the fact that people can live a normal life with one kidney has helped the black market kidney trade to flourish.

4 "Kidneys come in pairs, and we do know that people live with one kidney and seem to do okay, and when the surgery's done right, removing a kidney is a very safe procedure. Although deaths do occur," said Dr. Arthur Caplan, the director of the division of medical ethics at NYU Langone Medical Center.

5 "We all say, 'Oh everybody does fine, it's pretty minor,'" Caplan, who served as co-director of a United Nations/Council of Europe study on organ trafficking, continued. "You sometimes wonder, if it's so minor then how come so many kidney surgeons have two kidneys? Why aren't they giving up a kidney? The data shows that you can do okay, but if you do get a kidney injury or something happens, you are in trouble.

Your biological life insurance is gone . . . if you had diabetes in your family and you got it later, or you had hypertension/high blood pressure, it isn't so clear that we know what the long-term implications are for having one kidney."

6   Some argue that if the donor is made aware of all the potential risks and still consents, he or she should be free to sell a kidney. Advocates say if people are able to sell other body parts like hair or eggs, they should be allowed to get money for their organs.

7   And recent research suggests paying for organs could reduce societal health care costs long-term. A study showed that if people were able to pay $10,000 for a living kidney donation, medical costs—such as related to dialysis treatments—would go down overall and patients would get additional quality years of life compared to the current system.

8   However, the practice of getting paid for an organ is illegal everywhere except Iran.

9   In 2009, Levy Izhak Rosenblum pled guilty to the first-ever proven case of organ trafficking in the United States. The Newark, N.J. resident admitted that he helped get U.S. residents organs from donors in Israel for $120,000 or more. Rosenblum's lawyers argued that he was saving lives, and that both parties were fully aware of the risks and complications that came with transplants, donations and living with one kidney.

10   An HBO documentary, *Tales from the Organ Trade*, follows one case of a Canadian man who went to the black market to procure a kidney and the doctor and **nephrologist** who helped perform the procedure. It also tells the story of the donor, an Eastern European woman, who says she was fully aware of what she was doing when she agreed to sell her kidney.

nephrologist
person who studies kidneys and kidney functions

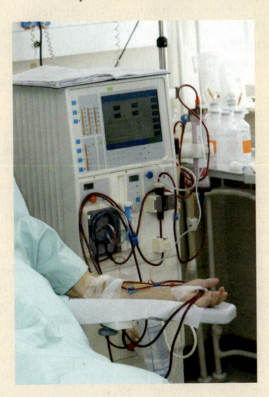

11   Director, writer and producer Ric Esther Bienstock admitted that when she first learned about the black-market organ trade, she was dubious about the practice. As she met more people and learned about the toll dialysis takes on a person, she started to understand why people were willing to do something illegal to obtain a kidney. She also began to understand why some impoverished individuals were more than willing to part with their organs in order to better their lives.

12   "The act itself—suddenly it wasn't as clear cut for some of those people," she explained. "I began to think, maybe selling a kidney isn't the worst thing in the world unless we solve the problem of desperation on both sides of the equation."

contemplated
thought about

13　Thirty-five year old Toronto resident Mary Jo Vradis admitted she **contemplated** getting an organ from the black market before getting a kidney three years ago. She had been on dialysis since she was 24, and her grandmother, mother, and brother all suffered from kidney problems.

14　"When you're suffering, you tend to do research to see how you can make your life better," she said. "You're always looking for different options."

15　It took nine years for her to get a legal transplant from a cadaver. Vradis said if she had to do it again, she doesn't think she could wait that same amount of time and would definitely go for the first kidney offered—legal or not—no matter what the cost.

16　Part of her problem was that she found two living donors who were willing to give her their kidneys for free, but the current system wasn't set up to support them, she said. One of her friends was told he would be denied life insurance if he donated the kidney. Another woman was a single mother, and would not be financially able to support her family if she took time off for the operation. Current laws prevent recipients from providing any payment.

17　"Why shouldn't they get paid for their time and their efforts?" Vradis argued. "They have to take off work. They're going to have to recover, and they're going to have expenses. There's a lot of people who I think would do it and I think money is a problem. You aren't allowed to pay for people, but why can't you pay at least for their expenses?"

18　Caplan believes that a payment system raises a red flag because many of those who are willing to sell their kidneys tend to be poor. If the kidney is removed and transplanted in an unregulated country, there are higher risks of complications for both parties. The donor might also suffer additional problems, and because they are poor to begin with, they might not have the resources to treat their new medical conditions.

19　"Who's going to run down and sell a kidney who has a job and is relatively well off?" Caplan said. "It's going to be poor people who do it, and around the world it's the poorest of the poor who do it. So, aren't you really taking advantage of their poverty to get a body part?"

20　Bienstock traveled to the Philippines, and found an entire town where people had willingly sold their kidneys for cash. While the majority of them ended up squandering their earnings, there was one man who improved his family's life with the money.

unduly
excessively

21　But, she disagrees with the notion that people are **unduly** forced into selling their kidneys because of their financial situation. While poverty may be the main motivation, this doesn't mean that they can't comprehend what they are giving up to give educated consent.

22　"Of course they're coerced by their own poverty, but just because they work in mines or clean our toilets doesn't mean by definition that they are incapable of making a decision," Bienstock argued.

23　Both Caplan and Bienstock believe that the current opt-in system of organ donations should be changed to an opt-out. Now, Americans select on their driver's licenses if they'd like to donate their organs, but they're calling for a system where everyone by default is a donor. The bioethicist noted that data show that most people are willing to be an organ donor, so the system should be changed, so the few who are against it can have their decision respected.

24   "When countries do that, they get more organs," Caplan said. "Instead of getting into all these wars about 'is the market okay,' 'am I going to exploit poor people' and 'can you sell your body parts,' why don't we try to shift to a default to donation?"

25   However, Bienstock believes that even if everyone registered to donate, the demand for all organ donations will remain unmet. She feels if we regulated the black market, more donors would be correctly informed about the risks and undergo the proper medical and psychological screenings that would be necessary to donate an organ.

26   "Yes, it's illegal, but the black-market organ trade is also populated by all these people who are law-abiding," she pointed out. "Something else is driving people to do it other than money. The people who are selling kidneys, they are also getting a payoff in **altruism**."

—Castillo, CBS News, Nov. 1, 2013

altruism
selflessness

REVIEWING THE READING

DIRECTIONS   Write the letter of the choice that best completes each statement in the space provided.

Checking Your Comprehension

_____ 1. The organs that are most needed for transplants are

    a. lungs.

    b. livers.

    c. hearts.

    d. kidneys.

_____ 2. The only country in which it is legal for a living person to sell an organ is

    a. the United States.

    b. the United Kingdom.

    c. Iran.

    d. Israel.

_____ 3. A key argument against legalizing organ trade is that

    a. doctors should not extend human life beyond that intended by nature.

    b. most of those who sell organs are poor and desperate.

    c. the prices of organs are much too high.

    d. it is difficult to match organs between people of different racial or ethnic backgrounds.

_____ 4. Many of those in the Philippine town populated by people who'd sold organs had

    a. wasted the money they received when they sold their organ.

    b. died slowly and painfully.

    c. risen to become members of the middle class.

    d. become outcasts in their community.

_____ 5. According to the authorities quoted in the article, Arthur Caplan and Ric Esther Bienstock, a key way to increase the availability of organs in the United States is to

   a. have doctors require their patients to sign organ-donation forms.
   b. eliminate laws that forbid organ sales.
   c. create an organ bank among family members.
   d. move to an opt-out system on U.S. drivers' licenses.

Checking Your Vocabulary

_____ 6. The word *deceased* (paragraph 3) means

   a. sick.
   b. dead.
   c. diagnosed.
   d. hospitalized.

_____ 7. Another word for *implications* (paragraph 5) is

   a. suggestions.
   b. questions.
   c. consequences.
   d. benefits.

_____ 8. People who are *advocates* (paragraph 6) are _____ a particular viewpoint.

   a. in favor of
   b. arguing against
   c. neutral about
   d. extremely angry about

_____ 9. *Impoverished* (paragraph 11) means

   a. desperate.
   b. intelligent.
   c. charitable.
   d. poor.

_____ 10. A *cadaver* (paragraph 15) is a

   a. donor.
   b. corpse.
   c. doctor.
   d. seller of human organs.

B-2   The Virtual House Call

James Hamblin

algorithm
calculations performed
by a computer

1 What if you could text a doctor with a medical question at any time of day and get a quick, thoughtful response? No more haphazard Googling (*swollen feet allergies; tick stuck in ear access to brain?*). No more sifting through random message boards. No more WebMD **algorithms**

suggesting that a vague stomachache might be the first sign of a terminal skin disorder.

2 As a patient, I'd say that sounds great. As a doctor, I'd say that sounds at best unsustainable, and at worst disastrous. The average primary-care physician has about 2,300 patients. He or she would never sleep. But Ron Gutman, a Silicon Valley entrepreneur, would say that's a business opportunity. Since he founded HealthTap four years ago, the Web site has grown into an interactive community of more than 60,000 licensed U.S. physicians, who answer user questions for free. More than 10 million people visit the site every month. Now the company has added a service called Prime, whereby a subscriber can talk immediately with a licensed doctor by phone, tablet, or computer; using voice, text, or video; at any time of day or night; as many times as he or she might like; in sickness and in health, for better or for worse. For this, a person pays $99 a month.

hypochondriac
person who is abnormally anxious about his or her health

dire
serious

3 Is this a vanity service for wealthy **hypochondriacs**, or a harbinger of a coming revolution in health-care delivery? Possibly both. If some basic needs were addressed remotely, doctors could focus on more **dire** cases during their busy office hours. Patients could ask simple questions without needing to take an afternoon off work for an office visit. As of last year, only 12 percent of Americans had ever texted or e-mailed with a doctor, according to a survey conducted for *The Atlantic*. But about a third of people under 30 were open to having their primary communication with their doctors be online.

HealthTap: A Doctor but Not a Doctor

4 HealthTap is not, at least for now, trying to take over for anyone's doctor. It is instead trying to supplement standard primary care. Specifically, it is trying to sell you on the idea of not ever having to wait for health-care advice. Upon hearing the story of an untimely fall from a horse or seeing a photo of a child's post-water-park rash, the doctor on call might tell you to sit tight, or make an appointment to see someone in person, or run to the ER.

5 Doctors on HealthTap are paid for the time they spend conducting one-on-one consultations with patients, but they aren't paid for answering questions submitted by anonymous users via the Web site. Why do they do it? "I think doctors are great people, in general," Gutman told me. Being a doctor, I found that explanation reassuring. But physicians also participate in HealthTap for reasons not unlike the ones that motivate restaurants to post professional photos on Yelp and the CIA to join Twitter: they want

to gain credibility and construct the dreaded but increasingly necessary *online presence*. Online presence is mentioned nowhere in the Hippocratic oath. But it can, Gutman says, help doctors "build a name and get speaking engagements, or just advance their careers."

6   One doctor with an enviable online presence is Keegan Duchicela. HealthTap's doctor-rating system gives him five out of five stars; he is also ranked first among HealthTap doctors nationwide for his knowledge of "insurance" and third for "abscessed tooth." His profile boasts that his answers have been **corroborated** by other doctors 5,803 times, that patients have given him "thanks" 12,555 times, and that he has saved 25 users' lives. (Whenever a doctor answers a question via the service, a pop-up box asks the patient whether the answer helped him, made him feel good, or saved his life. The number of "lives saved" by a given doctor indicates the number of people who checked that box. By this curious logic, HealthTap figures that its doctors have collectively saved 16,336 lives.)

corroborated
confirmed

7   On the basis of all this information, if you were in search of a family-medicine physician in Northern California, you might well seek out Duchicela, who practices in the Bay Area and teaches doctors-in-training at a Stanford-affiliated residency program. Especially in the tech-obsessed South Bay, Duchicela says, if a doctor doesn't have an online presence, "patients think, *Are you still using leeches?*"

8   In keeping with his enthusiasm for new doctoring platforms, he was among the first to jump on board when Prime launched. When he can spare the time, he picks up a shift, during which he generally hears from a handful of patients. He can log in from anywhere, has to do almost none of the bureaucratic paperwork that burns physicians out, and gets to meet and help interesting people in that predictable, finite, and instantly gratifying way that typifies Internet interactions.

Trying It Out: One Patient's Experience

9   I wanted to experience a HealthTap consultation from a patient's perspective, so I waited for something to happen to me. The editor of this magazine suggested I get myself punched in the face. I turned that over in my mind. Luckily, my throat started to feel scratchy. The next morning, it was legitimately sore. Jackpot.

10   "Would you like to speak with a doctor?," HealthTap prompted. Yes. "Is this an emergency?" No. Next, the site allotted me 150 characters to explain my problem: "Sore throat for two days, getting worse, no other symptoms."

11   Within 30 seconds, I was in the virtual presence of Dr. Vicken Poochikian. He was **bespectacled** and white-haired, sitting in front of a painting in what may have been his home or office. He wore a sweater over his collared shirt, and a white coat over that. He must have been someplace colder than where I was.

bespectacled
wearing eyeglasses

12   Pleasantries were brief.

13   "Are your bowels doing okay?" he asked. Doctors are trained to ask these all-encompassing questions as part of a traditional examination, even if the patient clearly states that he has no other symptoms.

14   "Yes."

15   "Do you have coughing?"

16   "No."

17   And so on, until Poochikian was satisfied that I indeed had no other symptoms. I inquired about antibiotics (knowing that they weren't yet medically warranted); he said it was too soon. I was ready to shine a flashlight in my mouth and lean over my computer's camera, but I wasn't asked to do so. He suggested that I stay hydrated, take it easy, and call back in a couple of days if I wasn't feeling better. Immediately after we disconnected, he documented our encounter for a record that will follow me through future HealthTap visits. His notes were to the point, in sharp contrast to the tedious documentation required in most electronic-medical-record systems. His account of my exam, in its entirety, read: "Common cold symptoms. On video he didn't really look sick or in any distress."

Virtual House Calls: The Wave of the Future?

cursory
quick

emblematic
representative

18   This **cursory** exam is **emblematic** of a larger trend in medicine: physical examination has become less central to diagnosis than it once was. To some extent, this is because of increased reliance on tests and imaging. Doctors are less and less concerned with honing their stethoscope skills, because echocardiograms are readily available. Tapping on a sore stomach tells a doctor something, but rarely as much as a CT scan does. And to some extent, this change has been a matter of necessity. The average medical appointment now allows a doctor little time to interrogate or thoroughly examine a person, or really get to know him.

19   That may also be the most significant limitation of a service like HealthTap Prime. Under the current model, doctors don't see patients on an ongoing basis. As a result, a patient is inevitably getting advice from a doctor who, because she hasn't seen what he looks like when he's not sick, can't tell whether he really "looks sick"—a gut valuation that remains crucial to effective primary care.

20   Yet, with the American Association of Medical Colleges projecting a national shortage of more than 90,000 doctors by 2020—especially in rural areas—there simply may not be enough doctors to provide this kind of ongoing care. Telemedicine could play a crucial role in addressing basic needs, particularly in settings where long-term relationships don't come into play, like emergency rooms. Already, to take one example, a company called Avera Health makes physicians in cities available via video to hospitals in small towns, where they are remotely helping to staff emergency rooms overnight. (They work in concert with people who are on-site. So, for instance, a nurse might perform hands-on work at the direction of an onscreen doctor until a local doctor can arrive.)

21   For his part, Duchicela hopes that HealthTap and similar platforms will allow for continuous doctor–patient relationships in the future. He already brings up e-mail etiquette when teaching his

medical residents, and he imagines their training evolving to include instruction in telemedicine—say, how to evaluate a mole via smartphone. He also hopes to one day use video service to supplement care for his regular patients. He might initially treat someone in person, but answer follow-up questions and give reassurance via the camera on his phone.

22   And really, providing peace of mind may be the most important thing any doctor does. "It's kind of funny: we're most anxious when we're not feeling well; we need immediate gratification more than any other time," Ron Gutman told me. "The only place we're expected to have a waiting room anywhere, outside of the DMV, is the doctor's office. We're trained, as health-care consumers, that we need to be patient. It's not a coincidence that we are called patients."

23   It is a coincidence, actually. I looked it up. *Patient* (the noun) comes from the Latin for "one who suffers." But he might be on to something.

—Hamblin, *The Atlantic*, Nov. 2014

REVIEWING THE READING

DIRECTIONS   Write the letter of the choice that best completes each statement in the space provided.

Checking Your Comprehension

_____   1. The author wrote this selection primarily to

    a. explore the benefits and drawbacks of HealthTap, a new way for patients to interact with doctors.

    b. explain why HealthTap is a serious threat to medical care in the United States.

    c. describe his own negative experiences as a patient with HealthTap.

    d. criticize the U.S. government for allowing health care and prescription medications to be so costly.

_____   2. Suppose you are a subscriber to HealthTap Prime. You can do all of the following *except*

    a. talk immediately with a doctor at any time of day.

    b. have unlimited access to doctors whenever you want them.

    c. decrease the amount of medical insurance you carry.

    d. use voice, text, or video to talk with doctors.

_____   3. Doctors take part in HealthTap for all of the following reasons *except*

    a. to do a general service to people.

    b. to gain credibility and to boost their online presence.

    c. to get speaking engagements or advance their careers.

    d. to fulfill mandatory continuing-education requirements.

_____ 4. According to the author, why have in-person examinations become faster and less personal?

    a. Today's doctors are more concerned with money than they are with patients' health.

    b. Doctors rely much more on tests and imaging, and less on patient interaction, to make a diagnosis.

    c. The U.S. health-care system requires doctors to take on more patients than they can realistically handle.

    d. Most ailments are easily diagnosed with just a few questions, so doctors are trying not to waste time.

_____ 5. The supporting details provided in the selection include all of the following _except_

    a. numbers and statistics.

    b. the author's personal experience.

    c. expert opinions.

    d. data tables.

Checking Your Vocabulary

_____ 6. A synonym for _haphazard_ (paragraph 1) is

    a. dangerous.

    b. possible.

    c. random.

    d. unlucky.

_____ 7. The word _harbinger_ (paragraph 3) means

    a. substitute.

    b. sign.

    c. downfall.

    d. excuse.

_____ 8. The word _enviable_ (paragraph 6) means

    a. desirable.

    b. massive.

    c. growing.

    d. visible.

_____ 9. A synonym for _tedious_ (paragraph 17) is

    a. precise.

    b. electronic.

    c. demanding.

    d. boring.

_____ 10. An _echocardiogram_ (paragraph 18) is a machine that measures

    a. blood sugar.

    b. brain waves.

    c. heartbeat.

    d. hormone levels.

B-3   Textbook Excerpt: Self-Help on the Web: Proceed with Caution

Lillian Burke and Barbara Weill

1   Tens of millions of adults search the Web for health-related information. Some people visiting health-related Web sites may just be doing academic research or seeking to learn. However, many are looking for a diagnosis, treatment, and cure. The numbers of sites either providing advice or linking to sites that provide advice are too numerous to list. Many sites include disclaimers stating in general that, although they attempt to include only accurate information, they are not responsible for the validity of the information presented. The disclaimer may further advise that a medical professional be consulted before any treatment is either started or discontinued. There are sites devoted to almost any disease, condition, treatment, and drug. You can find self-help for depression, stress, addiction, and almost any personal problem you can name. You do not even need to name your problem. One site shows you a human body and invites you to click where it hurts. You are then presented with a list of possible body parts and their possible diseases. If you continue to click, you will be linked to sites that can provide you with information and advice, from "how to treat your own . . ." to where to go for professional help.

2   Information is not the only online health-related resource. A possibly dangerous development is the availability of both prescription and nonprescription drugs on the Web. The sale of drugs over the Internet is virtually unregulated. A person can log on in one state, find a pharmacy in another state, and "consult" (over telecommunications lines) with a doctor, who will then write a prescription, which will be filled through the mail. The prescriptions are signed by physicians whose "examination" of the "patient" may consist of a review of a short questionnaire. This is illegal in some states. Under federal law "dispensing prescription drugs without a valid physician order is a violation of the FDCA [Federal Food, Drug, and Cosmetics Act]." Nonprescription drugs are also available.

3   In 2010, Google launched its **Body Browser**. From an Internet window, the user can look into the human body, rotate it, and zoom in or out. The user can peel back layers and look at bones, muscles, or blood vessels. You can focus on one organ or the whole body.

Support Groups on the Web

4   The Web provides online support. There are support groups for hospitalized children, for people with cancer and other diseases, and for patients' families and caregivers. Newsgroups, e-mail discussion groups, and live chat groups are available that link people with health- or disease-related interests. **Starbright World** is a network linking 30,000 seriously ill children in 100 hospitals and many homes in North America. Children in the network can play games, chat, and send and receive e-mail. They can also get medical information. Children and teenagers suffering with

asthma use Starbright World to discuss their experiences with others in similar situations.

5   Support groups exist for virtually every illness. When Dr. Ken Mott, a public health physician, was diagnosed with cancer, he had to travel to receive the treatment he needed. Illness can be isolating. Being in a strange city can compound the isolation. But Dr. Mott, like many other patients, found support and community on the World Wide Web. "Physical disability and pain . . . physical and emotional isolation occur . . . [and] the . . . side effects of treatment . . . leave victims susceptible to depression and withdrawal. But on the Internet and through e-mail I find dimensions of communication for emotional and psychological support that you may not have imagined." It is especially helpful for people with rare diseases. Takayasu arteritis occurs in between 1.2 and 2.6 people per million scattered over the world, making it virtually impossible to form face-to-face support groups. Yet, now the Internet is being used to build a community and disseminate information and give support.

6   For people isolated by illness or disability, special social networks may be their only social connections. Although these people are less likely to have Internet access, when they do access the Internet, it may become their whole social world—a lifeline, according to a woman with multiple sclerosis. Some of the bigger patient networks include PatientsLikeMe, Health Central, Inspire, CureTogether, and Alliance Health Network. Diabetic Connect has 140,000 members. Other networks are started by patients and are much smaller. Nin was started by a person with lupus in 2008. Currently, it has 2,300 members. People use these networks to share experiences with others who know how they feel. Friends and doctors, unless they are living with disabilities, don't understand. The networks are used to share experiences, to get tips on coping with the disease, "to get a real-life perspective," and just "to interact with people without worrying about the stigma of the disease." The networks are clear that they are not a substitute for medical advice. However, a recent Pew study found that "just 2% of adults living with chronic disease report being harmed by following medical advice found on the Internet." According to some research, "emotions can be contagious." If the people on your network are negative about the disease, you can become negative; on the other hand, you can catch a positive attitude too.

Judging the Reliability of Health Information on the Internet

7   Anyone can offer information on the Web, with possibly dangerous results. A compliance officer at the FDA related one instance, "A physician was browsing the Web when he came across a site that contained a fraudulent drug offering ... the person who maintains the site claimed he had a cure for a very serious disease, and advised those with the disease to stop taking their prescription medication. Instead they were told to buy the product he was selling, at a cost of several hundred dollars." Web sites can be run by anyone. More and more sites providing medical information are being operated by unidentified sources, vendors,

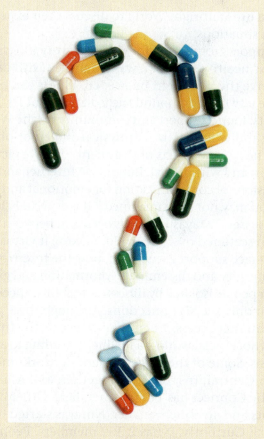

and manufacturers; many sites are produced by patients. Judging the reliability of a Web site can be difficult. The U.S. Department of Health and Human Services has established a site called http://healthfinder.gov to help guide people toward reliable sources of information.

8   The American Medical Association advises users to judge Web sites as critically as they would judge printed information. The major concern of people using the Web for medical information is privacy. Even though most sites have stated privacy policies, a study found that most do not adhere to them. Users have no way of knowing this. The actual content of the site should be judged on the following criteria: Is there information on the author, and is the author reliable? Are the sources of information clear and reliable? Are the sources of funding revealed? Are there any conflicts of interest; for example, does the author or site receive money from any source interested in steering the user toward a particular treatment? Is the information up-to-date? Conflicts of interest bearing on money received from a drug or device company are the most important information to reveal. This does not necessarily make the information invalid. However, you should be very careful using that information and should find backup from another source.

9   Even reliable sites can provide partial information to doctors as well as to patients. According to one physician, the Web is as attractive to physicians as it is to patients. But even the best sites are incomplete at best. A MEDLINE search produces abstracts of articles, not the articles themselves. The abstract states the conclusion of a study, for example, that a heart drug was found to be effective, but that is not enough information. The abstract leaves out the necessary details: Who were the participants and how were they selected? What other medications were they taking? How was the data analyzed? Who designed and financed the study?

10   Reliable sites do exist. The Virtual Hospital was a comprehensive and authoritative site, maintained by the University of Iowa. The information it collected continues to be available on the Internet at http://www.uihealthcare.com/vh/. It provides information for patients and health care providers. Its information is provided by health care professionals. Material is presented in a multimedia format and is organized both

by type of information (e.g., textbook) and by problem. A health care provider can read a chapter on upper respiratory conditions and view a video clip of the condition. The Virtual Hospital provides information for patients on disease prevention, including immunizations, diet, and cancer screening. Reliable information is also available through **Medscape**, which provides a collection of medical journals online.

—Burke and Weill, *Information Technology for the Health Professions*, pp. 248–250

REVIEWING THE READING

DIRECTIONS Write the letter of the choice that best completes each statement in the space provided.

Checking Your Comprehension

_____ 1. Which of the following best states the implied main idea of paragraph 1?

    a. Many different types of health-related Web sites provide medical information in a variety of formats.

    b. The Internet has become the main source of medical information for most adults.

    c. Diagnosis and treatment of specific illnesses are much easier when doctors use the Web.

    d. Even if you don't know your symptoms, the Internet can still help you solve your medical problems.

_____ 2. Which application, discussed in the selection, allows users a close-up look at all the parts of the human body?

    a. Starbright World

    b. Body Browser

    c. PatientsLikeMe

    d. MEDLINE

_____ 3. Which paragraph in the reading provides details in the form of critical thinking questions that people can use to evaluate medical Web sites?

    a. paragraph 5

    b. paragraph 7

    c. paragraph 8

    d. paragraph 10

_____ 4. The Nin network was founded as an online support group for people with

    a. multiple sclerosis.

    b. cancer.

    c. lupus.

    d. diabetes.

5. The authors wrote this selection primarily to
   a. provide information about the information in medical databases.
   b. explore the pros and cons of using the Web for medical information or support.
   c. encourage doctors to move more of their medical practices online.
   d. explain how to evaluate the content of Web sites.

Checking Your Vocabulary

6. The word *validity* (paragraph 1) means
   a. reliability.
   b. confidentiality.
   c. quantity.
   d. readability.

7. A synonym for *susceptible to* (paragraph 5) is
   a. vulnerable to.
   b. suffering from.
   c. free of.
   d. in a state of confusion about.

8. The word *disseminate* (paragraph 5) means
   a. write.
   b. spread.
   c. question.
   d. steal.

9. A synonym for *stigma* (paragraph 6) is
   a. origin.
   b. shame.
   c. result.
   d. cure.

10. The word *abstract* (paragraph 9) means
    a. quite complicated.
    b. vague and difficult to understand.
    c. a medical topic.
    d. a brief summary of an article.

Understanding Your Textbook

11. The authors use boldfaced type to indicate
    a. key terms you should remember.
    b. useful Internet resources.
    c. essential statistics.
    d. critical thinking questions.

_____ 12. Suppose you are annotating paragraph 9. Which of the following would be the most useful annotation?

    a. physicians & patients

    b. reliable Web sites

    c. MEDLINE abstracts: questions to ask

    d. participants & data

MAKING CONNECTIONS

1. For one of the issues discussed in this section, identify what information you would need to understand the issue more fully. If you were to write a paper or speech on this issue, where would you look for more information?

2. Which of these readings is or are applicable to your life? Which seem further removed from your daily existence?

3. Why is each of these topics considered controversial? What other topics could have been included in a section on health-related controversies?

4. Compare the tone used in each of the readings. Which uses the most objective language? Which uses subjective or slanted language?

5. Consider the different types of supporting details each author used. Which details were most convincing and why?   ●

WHAT DO YOU THINK?

DIRECTIONS On a separate sheet of paper, write about any four of these five choices.

1. If you had the opportunity to sell one of your organs for a large amount of money, would you do so? Why or why not?

2. Have you ever looked for medical information on the Web and been frightened by what you found? Describe your experience.

3. Do you think it is wrong for a wealthy person to offer to buy an organ from a person who is poor? Why or why not?

4. When you visit a doctor, do you feel that he or she spends time with you and knows you well? Or do you feel rushed during an office visit? Write briefly about your relationship with your doctor.

5. "Self-Help on the Web: Proceed with Caution" lists several valuable pointers for evaluating information you find on the Web. Provide at least two more suggestions for evaluating the reliability or credibility of Web information.   ●

THEME C   Internet and Communication

In just under two decades, the Internet has revolutionized the world, and wireless technologies are improving daily. Of course, the Internet has advocates and detractors. Advocates note how the Internet has improved lives; detractors think the Internet has taken the place of human interaction and is becoming too powerful and too all-consuming. The readings in this section look more closely at Internet- and communication-related issues. "What Happens When Kids Don't Have Internet at Home" (p. 408) explores the digital divide: the fact that many poor families cannot afford Internet service. "Don't Let Developing Countries Lag Behind in the Smartphone Revolution" (p. 413) looks at the smartphone revolution around the globe and makes a case for providing inexpensive Internet access to people in developing (poor) countries. "Linking Up: 21st-Century Networking" (p. 416) examines the dominance of social media in many facets of life, from friendship through business, journalism, and political activism.

C-1   What Happens When Kids Don't Have Internet at Home?

Rachel Monahan

Roughly half of low-income families nationwide lack access to the Web in their houses.

1   KENT, Wash.—As students stream off the school buses here, the typical end-of-day scene unfolds with a twist.

2   Thrown over the kids' shoulders are sleek black laptop bags with the name of their district emblazoned on them.

3   As part of an effort to bridge the so-called digital divide—the gap between rich and poor when it comes to access to technology—the Kent School District has for six years given every student a laptop, beginning in seventh grade.

4   But some of these students don't need to carry the bags home—because they can't get online there. It's a problem that districts are increasingly facing as they turn to technology to revolutionize their teaching.

5   In Kent, about 9 percent of students, or roughly 2,500 kids, can't access the Internet once they go home, district surveys show. Many of them are the poorest students, the very ones district officials believe would benefit from more exposure to technology to help them catch up to their more advantaged peers.

6   "If you do this well, in the process what you're going to do is widen that gap, not close it," said Thuan Nguyen, Kent School District's assistant superintendent.

7   With the laptops, the district has shifted its instruction away from standard approaches to homework, such as reading textbooks or completing worksheets, Nguyen said. "Once you've converted the curriculum, the material, it's more project-based learning. You kind of need the Internet for all those pieces to work well. If you're not able to provide that last level of connectivity, you've now widened the gap in terms of what kids can do, not to mention the expectation around that."

8   The Federal Communications Commission voted Thursday to increase funding for the federal e-rate program, which provides money for school districts to access the Internet, by $1.5 billion for a total of $3.9 billion annually. It's unlikely, however, that the funding will help districts expand access outside of school walls.

9   Roughly half of low-income families nationwide lack Internet service. Kent, a city between Seattle and Tacoma of 124,000 people and whose 27,000-student district covers parts of six other towns and some rural areas, clearly is ahead of the curve in trying to address this problem of equity; most recently, it installed Wi-Fi hotspots at three community centers in public housing. But these efforts have been **fraught** with difficulties, showing how hard it may be for other districts to close the digital divide.

10   "The theory is that if we can create not just a digital school district but a digital community, then we can create the **infrastructure** to eliminate the equity issue in terms of access—to content and knowledge and information," said Edward Lee Vargas, the former superintendent for Kent who recently went to the White House to argue that schools' federal technology dollars should be permitted to go toward funding out-of-school Internet connections for low-income kids.

11   "It becomes a civil rights issue," said Vargas, who led the district for five years until last month. "They're being denied equal access to knowledge and information that are part of education in the 21st century."

12   As the Obama administration pushes schools to modernize their technology, Kent stands out for its innovations and offers lessons about what challenges other districts may face. Besides its laptop program and wireless Internet access at every school, the district has upgraded its broadband speed to two gigabits—ahead of the Obama administration's goals for schools to have one gigabit per second by 2017.

13   But Kent isn't a wealthy district. Last year, 52 percent of students qualified for free and reduced lunch, and many are new immigrants. Forty percent speak a language other than English at home, district officials said, while 18 percent are enrolled in bilingual instruction. Perhaps because of the influence of the tech industry in the Seattle area nearby, however, voters have embraced the district's efforts to bolster its technology. Kent has had a dedicated technology levy since 2000. And voters have stuck with it, renewing it each time, most recently to expand a one-to-one program into the elementary schools, meaning each child in kindergarten through sixth grade will also have access to a computer.

14   To keep pace with the technology being introduced into the classroom, the school district has pushed to bring Internet access to parts of the community where it is needed.

* * *

fraught
filled with

infrastructure
the basic structures needed for a society to operate

15   On a Wednesday night in October in the Birch Creek community center, high school and middle school students came to shoot hoops, go to Girl Scout meetings, and do their online homework assignments.

16   A dozen students clustered around laptops set up on heavy-duty folding tables near an Internet kiosk the school district had installed two years earlier. The kiosk resembles an ATM and includes a wireless Internet hotspot, as well as a built-in computer with a touch screen that any community member can use to access news on the district and that parents can use to access a district program called Skyward, which provides grades and attendance records for kids.

17   Muhsin Shamdeen, a 12-year-old seventh grader and aspiring professional skateboarder, was working on a letter to President Barack Obama about Christopher Columbus, with help from a community center staffer.

18   Using an online version of SparkNotes (her teacher had suggested consulting the guide), Ayan Mohamed, a 15-year-old sophomore immigrant from Somalia, sat working on an end-of-quarter essay.

19   In class the computer helps when there's something confusing, Mohamed said, pointing to a page she had pulled up explaining some research relevant to an essay she was working on. "You can look it up right there," she noted. The paper happened to be about technology's impacts and disappointments as portrayed by the books they'd read for the course.

20   The kiosks, in theory, won't cost the district any money in the long run. They sold for $7,000 upfront, but the district hopes to recover the money by income from business partners who'll get to advertise on them. And they're located in places already wired for the Internet, so there's no ongoing expense for the district.

21   The kiosk program is novel, but it has a couple wrinkles. For example, while the kiosk was working that evening, it had just been put back online for the first time in two weeks. Before then, the system had gone down, likely after it was unplugged during a cleaning. Still, it turned out the outage hadn't been much of an impediment because Kent Youth and Family Services, which runs programs for students at the Birch Creek community center, had installed a separate Wi-Fi network there a year and a half ago. (The other two community centers had Wi-Fi set up two months ago.)

fickle
unreliable

22   Of course, overlap isn't a terrible issue to have when it comes to **fickle** Wi-Fi networks—but it's a situation the district's technology chief was wholly unaware of, calling it "good feedback," when he learned about it from me. The kiosk is, after all, a pilot for the district that's designed to iron out the kinks before being put up all around town.

23   Still, if the idea is to reach kids who don't have access after school hours, students point to another challenge: Unlike their peers in, say, public housing, the kids without Internet access at home generally live scattered across the district.

24   "Until we find a way to provide free Internet access, there's always going to be some measure of the population left behind; we have a long way to go to solving this problem," said Christopher Mitchell, who directs a Minneapolis-based initiative that advocates for community-based broadband networks.

25   Mitchell also called a Comcast program that offers low-income families across the country inexpensive—though highly inefficient—Internet access "an incredibly self-serving approach to get better publicity while doing the bare minimum." The program is exceptionally popular in Kent—in part because the district has been very effective at promoting it.

26   All Kent schools provide Wi-Fi, which is accessible from the parking lot. Early in the laptop program, Nguyen, the assistant superintendent, recalled showing up to schools late or early to see cars parked, presumably so families could get online before and after school. Inside, students would hover over their laptops, their faces glowing.

27   But as community access to the Internet has expanded, that's happening less.

—Monahan, *The Atlantic*, Dec. 12, 2014

REVIEWING THE READING

DIRECTIONS   Write the letter of the choice that best completes each statement in the space provided.

Checking Your Comprehension

_____ 1. Which term is used to describe the gap between rich and poor when it comes to access to technology?

    a. the technology gap

    b. the digital divide

    c. the 1% phenomenon

    d. the cranial chasm

_____ 2. About what percentage of low-income families nationwide lack Internet service?

    a. 10%

    b. 25%

    c. 50%

    d. 75%

_____ 3. All of the following paragraphs use numbers and statistics as supporting details *except* paragraph

    a. 5.

    b. 9.

    c. 10.

    d. 13.

_____ 4. The Kent school district expects that Internet kiosks will not cost the school district any money in the long run because

a. the federal government will pay for the kiosks.

b. local businesses will pay for the kiosks through advertising dollars.

c. new laws will require parents to provide Internet service in the home.

d. students will pay for the costs of the kiosks by paying a per-hour usage fee.

_____ 5. The author wrote this selection primarily to

a. argue for more computer-based instruction in public schools across the country.

b. explore the problems of the digital divide and explore some possible solutions.

c. persuade local politicians to provide free Internet kiosks in public-housing projects.

d. motivate readers to donate laptops to their local school districts.

Checking Your Vocabulary

_____ 6. The word _emblazoned_ (paragraph 2) means

a. displayed.

b. written.

c. removed.

d. forced.

_____ 7. A _curriculum_ (paragraph 7) comprises the _____ studied in school.

a. subjects

b. values

c. works of literature

d. social norms

_____ 8. The word _equity_ (paragraph 9) means

a. wealth.

b. age.

c. fairness.

d. technology.

_____ 9. A synonym for _novel_ (paragraph 21) is

a. book.

b. costly.

c. fictional.

d. new.

_____ 10. The word _impediment_ (paragraph 21) means

a. advantage.

b. obstacle.

c. incentive.

d. expense.

C-2 Don't Let Developing Countries Lag Behind in the Smartphone Revolution

Nathan Eagle

Smartphone penetration and affordable data stimulate development, so collaboration is needed to reduce costs

In June 2013 Google revealed plans to use solar panels attached to balloons to bring the Internet to those without web access.

sustainability
the ability to maintain a certain rate or level of accomplishment

1 Internet access was a 20th-century luxury, but it is a 21st-century necessity that is increasingly important to enabling sustained economic development for much of the world.

2 In the latest draft of the United Nations' **sustainability** goals beyond 2015, universal Internet access sits alongside education and health at the core of a future development agenda. The aim is to "strive to provide universal and affordable access to the Internet in LDCs [least developed countries] by 2020."

3 Universal Internet access is an enormous undertaking, yet thanks to the dynamics of the mobile market, progress is being made. The falling cost of smartphones is driving rapid uptake in the developing world. Around 725 million smartphones were sold in 2012, nearly 1 billion in 2013, and sales are expected to exceed 1 billion for the first time in 2014. Most of this year's 1 billion-plus smartphones will ship to emerging-market consumers: 283 million in China, 225 million in India, 47 million in Brazil, and 46 million in Indonesia.

4 In these countries, it is possible to buy an Android smartphone for around $30. These low-cost smartphones are already changing people's lives in real, quantifiable ways. Examples are everywhere: from business, to education, to health.

5 M-Pesa users in rural Kenya report that they have increased income by 30% by using mobile payment technology. In India, over 5 million people are learning via Bharti Airtel's mEducation platform. In Tanzania, patients in isolated rural communities are diagnosed by dermatologists in Dar es Salaam, all through a smartphone app.

aggregated
consolidated, total

6   In the future, smartphone users will also provide development agencies with vital, actionable data. User behavior can be analyzed to reveal patterns and provide insight. Health organizations can analyze search patterns to gauge when an influenza outbreak is coming; **aggregated** social media reports can provide early warning of a natural disaster. This data, used properly, can add considerable value to health and emergency services.

7   Bring enough people online, and this all becomes possible. But to what extent can the United Nations—or any organization—make universal Internet access happen?

8   In the developing world, governments have started to recognize the value of the mobile Internet, and have acted to make smartphones more affordable. In Ghana, government officials recently voted to remove import **duties** on smartphones, effectively slashing the cost of all devices by 35%. It will be interesting to see if this is as effective as the rebate scheme that Malaysia's government has operated since 2012, which has provided discounted smartphones for millions of low-income youths.

duties
taxes

9   However, while smartphones are undoubtedly cheaper, the total cost of ownership is keeping many people offline. Right now, the biggest barrier is data cost.

10   In the developing world, there are few unlimited data plans—most smartphone users pay for online access in increments, with pre-paid vouchers. The problem is that these data plans are prohibitively expensive.

11   According to our recent analysis of data collected by McKinsey, the average 500MB data plan costs the equivalent of five days work in some countries. In India, an individual earning the minimum wage would have to work 18 hours to earn enough money to get online. In Nigeria, more than 28 hours. In Brazil and Mexico, the average 500MB smartphone plan costs the equivalent of 34 hours of minimum wage work.

12   It's no surprise that smartphone owners are reluctant to pay the price. Last year, a Nielsen study of 10,000 smartphone users in India found that 50% had deactivated the Internet capability of their phone.

13   The fact that so many people can have access to a life-changing technology such as a smartphone, but cannot afford the basic functionality that makes it so empowering, is a serious issue.

14   While governments act to cut device costs, most of the work to remove data costs is being done by actors in the private sector. Internet.org—an **NGO** backed by Facebook, among others—recently launched a mobile app in Zambia, Tanzania, and Kenya, providing free access to basic Internet services. Google's Project Loon may seem slightly far-fetched, but its scheme to beam down a kind of universal WiFi from balloons in the stratosphere is seeing positive results.

NGO
non-governmental
organization

15   These are both ambitious and promising initiatives, yet to achieve significant progress by 2020, the United Nations must engage with the mobile landscape as it exists today. With the aim to improve Internet access in developing countries, Jana has partnered with 237 operators in 102 international markets. These are the actors that control the cost of

data, and their involvement will be vital to achieving the goal of affordable Internet access by 2020 and closing the information gap between the developed and developing worlds.

—Eagle, *The Guardian*, Dec. 18, 2014

REVIEWING THE READING

DIRECTIONS Write the letter of the choice that best completes each statement in the space provided.

Checking Your Comprehension

_____ 1. Which of the following is *not* one of the United Nations' sustainability goals?

    a. health

    b. education

    c. income equality

    d. universal Internet access

_____ 2. The selection use the phrases "LDCs" (paragraph 2), "emerging markets" (paragraph 3), and "developing world" (paragraph 8) to mean

    a. countries where smartphones are more popular than landlines.

    b. Third World countries that are not yet economically developed.

    c. a younger generation of people using Internet-based technologies.

    d. the extension of wireless technologies into space.

_____ 3. In which country has the government provided discounted smartphones for low-income youths?

    a. Kenya

    b. Malaysia

    c. Tanzania

    d. Brazil

_____ 4. For most of the world's poor people, the biggest barrier to using smartphones is

    a. the cost of the phone itself.

    b. government regulation of smartphones.

    c. the cost of data plans.

    d. a fear and distrust of technology.

_____ 5. The author wrote this selection to

    a. provide data and statistics about Internet usage for a general audience.

    b. reveal the differences between the "haves" and "have nots" with regard to Internet data plans.

    c. argue that the Internet makes a greater impact in poor countries than in rich countries.

    d. support the U.N. goal of universal and affordable Internet access.

Checking Your Vocabulary

_____ 6. The word *undertaking* (paragraph 3) means
  a. project.
  b. funeral ceremony.
  c. disaster.
  d. expense.

_____ 7. *Dermatologists* (paragraph 5) study
  a. eyesight.
  b. skin.
  c. hair.
  d. education.

_____ 8. As used in paragraph 6, the word *gauge* means
  a. determine.
  b. prevent.
  c. allow.
  d. worry.

_____ 9. A synonym for *increments* (paragraph 10) is
  a. government assistance.
  b. savings.
  c. wages.
  d. segments.

_____ 10. The *stratosphere* (paragraph 14) lies
  a. just beneath Earth's surface.
  b. in remote locations that have no Internet access.
  c. above Earth, in space.
  d. at the North Pole.

C-3   Textbook Excerpt: Linking Up: 21st-Century Social Networking

J. Charles Sterin

1 Online social networking has quickly become a mainstay among members of the millennial generation and represents a new form of social culture that takes place entirely online. Who is actually participating in online social networking, and what are the trends?

Digital Natives

2 In a 2008 study to determine social network usage conducted by RapLeaf, then a leading Web 2.0 social networks tracking organization, of the 175 million people in its database, 49.3 million of whom actually participated in the study, approximately 90 percent of the respondents were from the United States. RapLeaf's study also found that while the overall rates of use of and participation in new media and the Internet are

roughly equal between young men and young women, young women far outnumber young men as participants on major social networking sites such as Facebook, Twitter and Tumblr. This trend is changing, however, as the percentage of male users is growing rapidly.

3   **Digital natives**, the first generation to grow up in a world where digital technologies and the Internet were already in place, stay connected to cyberspace during a large part of their waking hours each day. They create for themselves multiple digital identities that simultaneously "live" in parallel with their real-world identities and with each other. Using the power of the Internet, digital natives are creating their own virtual society and virtual culture populated by online relationships that are largely hidden from their parents and teachers.

4   By 2007, almost 90 percent of teenagers in the United States were online for a significant portion of each day, seven days a week—and this percentage has grown to just about 100 percent today. Digital natives view their online lives not as separate lives, but rather as a seamless continuation of their real-world lives. They are also heavily involved in and naturally **adept** at digital multitasking. They often utilize multiple Internet sites for homework, research and entertainment and talk with as many as a dozen online "friends" at the same time. When they are away from their computers, they are on cell phones and tablets, text messaging, accessing the Web and maintaining their online relationships on multiple sites. Some become so good at multitasking that they are uncomfortable being out of the digital loop for even short periods of time.

adept
skilled

Social Networking in Business

Twitter's incredible speed allowed it to break the news of the devastating earthquake in China in 2008 before any other media outlet managed to do so.

5   Many large businesses have begun to use Twitter as an alternative to e-mail and text messaging. Even government agencies have started to use Twitter as an alternative form of communication for emergency first responders during forest fires or other natural disasters.

6   Social networking sites such as Facebook, LinkedIn and Twitter can also be very valuable for businesses. Advertising and marketing firms, as well as **venture capital** groups, are flocking to social networking sites in an effort to identify and target like-minded consumers who share important demographics. Some firms are hiring independent marketing reps—often college students—who apply their social networking skills to promote products and services to the firms' "friends" and "followers," usually without disclosing that they are being paid to make these promotional posts. Other companies are using social networking sites to track employee job performance, monitor employee ethical standards and even predict employee turnover rates. Many corporations use social

venture capital
money invested in companies that have the potential for strong growth

networking sites more openly. Nike, for example, tracks social networking sites and bloggers to see whose posts most influence the sales of their athletic shoes.

Life Blogging

7 Generally, Twitter's major use is **life-blogging**, wherein millions of individuals share the highlights, and often the minutia, of their daily lives with a circle of online "friends" in a very public forum. Life-bloggers, also called life-loggers, use new media technologies—computers and tablets, digital cameras and Internet photo-sharing sites such as Pinterest—to document and openly share their daily lives in an ongoing personal reality show.

8   An example of life blogging is Facebook's Timeline. The Timeline feature allows Facebook users to highlight photos and posts of life events, from important **milestones** to the **minuscule** details of one's day-to-day activities. Originally, the Timeline feature was optional, but in 2012, Facebook made it an automatic part of the "walls" of all of Facebook's 800 million users. Timeline aggregates information about each user's Web activities across Websites and tablet apps, not just on Facebook, which raised the alarm of Web privacy advocates and the angst of many Facebook users.

9   The ability for anyone to build a database clone of his or her life is now more possible than we think—but is it of practical use? One might argue that just because new media technologies allow us to do extraordinary things, it does not always mean that the results have practical value. According to the opposite view, users are regularly finding new and innovative ways to use new media such as Twitter and Pinterest to benefit everyday life or to support political and social causes.

Activism and Citizen Journalism

10 On both the national and international fronts, activists have effectively used Twitter to organize rallies and coordinate street protests: in China, during the 2008 Summer Olympics; in Moldova, in April 2009 after suspected **rigged** elections restored the Communist Party to power; and in Iran, during the June 2009 presidential elections.

11   Closer to home, in March 2008, on the fifth anniversary of the U.S. invasion of Iraq, antiwar protesters used blogging sites and Twitter to coordinate numerous demonstrations around the United States. Additional public support was solicited via text messaging. Potential protesters were able to sign up to receive live updates of the organizers' activities as well as responses from the media and authorities. Videos of aggressive police action against some of the activists, as well as the crowd's reactions, were filmed. These videos quickly found their way onto YouTube and such Web-based video news services as the American News Project (ANP); the ANP then sent out hundreds of thousands of e-mails alerting its viewer base to the story. Within a few hours, the mainstream news media picked up these videos, and they appeared as feature stories on CNN, MSNBC and others.

milestones
key events

minuscule
tiny

rigged
fraudulently manipulated

12   The rapid evolution of the blogosphere demonstrates how fast technologies and trends can change in the new media world of the 21st century. Since the blogosphere first appeared in 1994, tens of thousands of citizen journalists have come to dominate it. Their presence in the blogosphere was motivated by their desire to bypass paths traditionally open only to professional journalists and the wish for the public to respond to their voices. By the 2004 presidential election, the leading blog-based Internet journalists had gained so much influence in the culture that they were given press credentials for both the Democratic and Republican national conventions and were admitted to the White House pressroom. Yet by 2008, the blogosphere had largely moved away from its roots as a **populist** free-for-all of public expression, becoming dominated by advertising-supported blogs. These blogs are populated by professional writers, journalists and political pundits—many of them employed by mainstream media organizations. The emergence of such "professional" blog sites has made it difficult, but not impossible, for individual independent bloggers to attract audiences, gain advertiser support and keep their voices being heard in the public debate and the mass media marketplace of ideas.

populist
in favor of ordinary
people

—Sterin, *Mass Media Revolution*, pp. 190–191, 195–197

REVIEWING THE READING

DIRECTIONS   Write the letter of the choice that best completes each statement in the space provided.

Checking Your Comprehension

_____ 1. The term used to define people who have grown up in a world where the Internet and other digital technologies are already in place is

    a. millennials.

    b. digital natives.

    c. Facebookers.

    d. friendsters.

_____ 2. Which of the following statements is *not* true of the millennial generation?

    a. Almost all of them are online every day.

    b. They create multiple digital identities that live alongside their real-world identities.

    c. They share their online/virtual worlds with parents and teachers.

    d. Some are very uncomfortable being offline for even short periods of time.

_____ 3. Facebook's "Timeline" is an example of

    a. life blogging.

    b. citizen journalism.

    c. product promotion by advertisers.

    d. political activism.

_____ 4. The author wrote this selection primarily to

    a. criticize society's obsession with the Internet.

    b. encourage more young people to develop an "Internet presence."

    c. stir up political action against repressive governments.

    d. explore some of the ways social media is used today.

_____ 5. The tone of the selection is best described as

    a. inflammatory.

    b. skeptical.

    c. sarcastic.

    d. balanced.

Checking Your Vocabulary

_____ 6. The word *mainstay* (paragraph 1) means

    a. trend.

    b. central component.

    c. advantage.

    d. time waster.

_____ 7. A synonym for *seamless* (paragraph 4) is

    a. smoothly combined.

    b. hidden.

    c. educational.

    d. overwhelming.

_____ 8. The word *demographics* (paragraph 6) means

    a. population.

    b. levels of schooling.

    c. characteristics.

    d. likes and dislikes.

_____ 9. The word *minutia* (paragraph 7) means

    a. trivial details.

    b. statistics.

    c. triumphs.

    d. challenges.

_____ 10. A synonym for *pundits* (paragraph 12) is

    a. bloggers.

    b. experts.

    c. political parties.

    d. journalists.

Understanding Your Textbook

_____ 11. The photo and caption accompanying the reading (p. 417) indicate that the first media outlet to break the news of the devastating 2008 China earthquake was

    a. Tumblr.

    b. Facebook.

    c. LinkedIn.

    d. Twitter.

_____ 12. An outline of this reading selection would use all of the following as key headings *except*
   a. Digital Natives.
   b. The Blogosphere.
   c. Social Networking in Business.
   d. Activism and Citizen Journalism.

MAKING CONNECTIONS

1. What is each author implying about access to the Internet? That is, what do the authors see as the role of the Internet in people's personal and business lives?
2. Compare the tone of each reading. Which is the most formal and academic? Which is the most journalistic?
3. Which of these readings engage in *advocacy*—that is, which are arguing a particular point of view? Explain.
4. What would the benefits of universal Internet access be? Would there be any drawbacks?
5. Suppose you decided to begin blogging about your life. On which aspects of your life would you focus—that is, which areas of your life do you think people would find most interesting?

WHAT DO YOU THINK?

DIRECTIONS   On a separate sheet of paper, write about any four of these five choices.

1. Do you think local communities have the responsibility to purchase laptops and Internet access for all students? Why or why not?
2. Suppose the Internet and wireless technology did not exist. List at least five ways your life would change. Would any of these changes be positive?
3. In reading C-3, "Linking Up: 21st–Century Social Networking," paragraph 6 talks about businesses paying students to advertise or "talk up" their products on social media. Do you think this practice is ethical? Why or why not?
4. Choose one of the social media discussed in these readings (e.g., Twitter, Facebook, Tumblr, LinkedIn) and describe your experiences with it.
5. Do you think Internet-based communication has changed the way people interact in person? If so, how? Are these changes positive, negative, or neutral?

Discipline: Sociology

Course: Introduction to Sociology

Sociology is the study of human society. Many students choose an introductory sociology course to satisfy their social science requirement. Introductory sociology is a wide-ranging course that covers many topics, including culture, groups and organizations, economics and politics, family and religion, health and medicine, education, and race and ethnicity.

This part of *College Reading and Study Skills* provides you with a series of activities that you are likely to encounter in a typical introductory sociology course. These activities include

- Reading a textbook chapter
- Preparing for a lecture
- Participating in class
- Writing about the reading
- Taking quizzes and exams on the topics covered in the textbook

The textbook chapter reprinted on pages 425–438 originally appeared in *Society: The Basics*, 13th edition, by John J. Macionis. The reprinted selection comes from Chapter 11, "Race and Ethnicity." As you read, note the ways the author connects sociological concepts to readers' lives.

> *Note: As you complete the activities in this part, you will be using the SQ3R method described in Chapter 6. The writing activities add a fourth R, React, to the SQ3R method.*

PREPARING FOR THE LECTURE

Your instructor tells your class that she will devote all of next week to the topics of race, ethnicity, stereotypes, prejudice, and discrimination, all of which receive a great amount of attention in the media. She assigns the chapter reprinted on pages 425–438 and asks you to come to class prepared to discuss it.

You check the course syllabus and see that your instructor plans to spend Monday and Tuesday lecturing. On Thursday, the class will break into small groups that will work together to review the sociological concepts, examples, and applications that are discussed in the chapter.

ACTIVITY 1	Previewing the Text (Survey)

After previewing the textbook selection, answer the following questions.

1. Which two main topics will the chapter cover?_____

2. A _____ is a socially constructed category of people who share biologically transmitted traits that members of a society consider important.

3. Which term means "a shared cultural heritage"? _____

4. A _____ is any category of people distinguished by physical or cultural difference that a society sets apart and subordinates.

5. Which event may have reduced social acceptance of Arabs and Muslims in the United States? _____

6. Which four theories of prejudice does the text discuss? _____

   _____

7. Which term is used for the unequal treatment of various categories of people?

   _____

ACTIVITY 2	Previewing the Visual Aids (Survey)

Preview the visual aids included with the textbook selection, and then answer the following questions.

1. The visual aid on page 426 indicates the percentage of men and women in various ethnic groups who voted for _____ in the presidential election of 2012.

2. True or false: The six photos on page 428 are making the point that it can be difficult to determine a person's race based on his or her appearance. _____

3. Table 11-1 on page 429 indicates that the highest number of people in the United States are of _____ descent. The second highest number of people are of _____ descent.

4. According to Figure 11-1 on page 430, the year by which minorities will form a majority of the entire U.S. population is _____.

5. True or false: According to National Map 11-1 on page 431, in no part of Maine or Vermont do racial and ethnic minorities make up the majority of the population (50 percent or higher). _____

6. Figure 11-3 on page 437 portrays the _____ of prejudice and discrimination.

ACTIVITY 3	Working with Textbook Features to Help Increase Your Comprehension (Survey)

Examine the features included in the textbook selection and think about how you can use them to help you study and learn. Answer the following questions.

1. What is the purpose of the "Learning Objectives" listed on page 425 and then repeated in the "Making the Grade" feature on page 438? _____

   _____

2. The chapter includes a "Seeing Ourselves" map on page 431. The purpose of this map is to provide a snapshot of life in which country?

   _____

3. Notice the "diary entries," labeled "March 3, Dallas, Texas" on page 430 and "November 19, Jerusalem, Israel," on page 432. What is the purpose of these entries?

   _____

   _____

4. Which textbook feature is intended to stimulate critical thinking? _____ Which aspect of this feature asks for students' opinions on contemporary topics? _____

_____

5. Which textbook feature, found at the end of the chapter, helps students review important terms and concepts, while also providing additional study tools? _____

6. The chapter review on page 438 makes reference to "MySocLab." What do you think MySocLab is? _____

_____

ACTIVITY 4	Activating Background Knowledge (Survey and Question)

As you complete your preview of the chapter, activate your background knowledge by thinking about the following questions.

1. What do you consider your race to be? To which ethnic group or groups do you belong?

2. Do you believe that people prefer to develop friendships and romantic relationships with those who are most similar to them? Why or why not?

3. Do you consider yourself a part of any minority groups? If so, on which bases is the minority group defined (for example, language, skin color, sexuality, height, and so on)?

4. Do you think that any groups in the United States are subject to particularly high levels of discrimination? If so, which groups?

5. What are the races and ethnicities of the people who live in your neighborhood or town?

READING THE ASSIGNMENT

Now that you have previewed the textbook selection and activated your background knowledge, read the selection.

ACTIVITY 5	Asking Questions About the Reading (Question, Read, and Recite)

As you read each heading, turn it into a question or questions that you think the section will answer. Write these questions in the margin. For example, for the heading titled "Measuring Prejudice: The Social Distance Scale" on page 433, you might ask the questions "What is the social distance scale? How is it measured?" After you read each section, look away from the page and try to answer the questions you wrote down.

11 Race and Ethnicity

((• **Listen** to **Chapter 11** in **MySocLab**

LEARNING OBJECTIVES

11.1 Explain the social construction of race and ethnicity.

11.2 Describe the extent and causes of prejudice.

11.3 Distinguish discrimination from prejudice.

11.4 Identify examples of pluralism, assimilation, segregation, and genocide.

11.5 Assess the social standing of racial and ethnic categories of U.S. society.

the Power of Society

to shape political attitudes

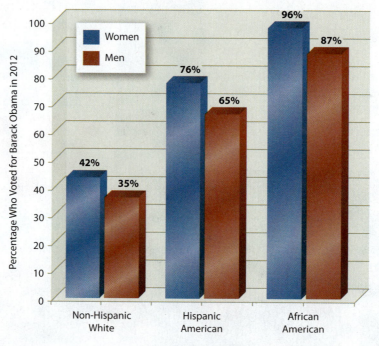

Source: Center for American Women and Politics (2012)

Is our choice to cast a vote for a particular candidate a purely "personal" decision? In the 2012 presidential election, just 42 percent of non-Hispanic white women and 35 percent of non-Hispanic white men voted for Barack Obama. But Hispanic Americans and especially African Americans supported him overwhelmingly, ensuring his victory. The political choices people make when they vote in elections are not simply personal but also reflect race, ethnicity, and other societal factors.

Chapter Overview

This chapter explains how race and ethnicity are created by society. The United States is a nation as racially and ethnically diverse as any in the world. Here and elsewhere, both race and ethnicity are not only matters of difference but also dimensions of social inequality.

On a cool November morning in New York City, the instructor of a sociology class at Bronx Community College is leading a small-group discussion of race and ethnicity. He explains that the meaning of both concepts is far less clear than most people think. Then he asks, "How do you describe yourself?"

Eva Rodriguez leans forward in her chair and is quick to respond. "Who am I? Or should I say *what* am I? This is hard for me to answer. Most people think of race as black and white. But it's not. I have both black and white ancestry in me, but you know what? I don't think of myself in that way. I don't think of myself in terms of race at all. It would be better to call me Puerto Rican or Hispanic. Personally, I prefer the term 'Latina.' Calling myself Latina says I have a mixed racial heritage, and that's what I am. I wish more people understood that race is not clear-cut."

This chapter examines the meaning of race and ethnicity. There are now millions of people in the United States who, like Eva Rodriguez, do not think of themselves in terms of a single category but as having a mix of ancestry.

The Social Meaning of Race and Ethnicity

11.1   Explain the social construction of race and ethnicity.

As the opening to this chapter suggests, people often confuse race and ethnicity. For this reason, we begin with some basic definitions.

Race

A **race** is *a socially constructed category of people who share biologically transmitted traits that members of a society consider important.* People may classify one another racially based on physical characteristics such as skin color, facial features, hair texture, and body shape.

Racial diversity appeared among our human ancestors as the result of living in different geographic regions of the world. In regions of intense heat, for example, humans developed darker skin (from the natural pigment melanin) as protection from the sun; in regions with moderate climates, people have lighter skin. Such differences are literally only skin deep because human beings the world over are members of a single biological species.

The striking variety of physical traits found today is also the product of migration; genetic characteristics once common to a single place (such as light skin or curly hair) are now found in many lands. Especially pronounced is the racial mix in the Middle East (that is, western Asia), historically a crossroads of migration. Greater physical uniformity characterizes more isolated people, such as the island-dwelling Japanese. But every population has some genetic mixture, and increasing contact among the world's people ensures even more blending of physical characteristics in the future.

Although we think of race in terms of biological elements, race is a socially constructed concept. It is true that human beings differ in any number of ways involving physical traits, but a "race" comes into being only when the members of a society decide that some physical trait (such as skin color or eye shape) actually *matters.*

race a socially constructed category of people who share biologically transmitted traits that members of a society consider important

ethnicity a shared cultural heritage

CHAPTER 11   Race and Ethnicity

The range of biological variation in human beings is far greater than any system of racial classification allows. This fact is made obvious by trying to place all of the people pictured here into simple racial categories.

Because race involves social definitions, it is a highly variable concept. For example, the members of U.S. society consider racial differences more important than people of many other countries. We also tend to "see" three racial categories—typically, black, white, and Asian—while people in other societies identify many more categories. People in Brazil, for example, distinguish between *branca* (white), *parda* (brown), *morena* (brunette), *mulata* (mulatto), *preta* (black), and *amarela* (yellow) (Inciardi, Surratt, & Telles, 2000).

In addition, race may be defined differently by various categories of people within a society. In the United States, for example, research shows that white people "see" black people as having darker skin than black people do (Hill, 2002).

The meanings and importance of race not only differ from place to place but also change over time. Back in 1900, for example, it was common in the United States to consider people of Irish, Italian, or Jewish ancestry as "nonwhite." By 1950, however, this was no longer the case, and such people today are considered part of the "white" category (Loveman, 1999; Brodkin, 2007).

Today, the Census Bureau allows people to describe themselves using more than one racial category (offering six single-race options and fifty-seven multiracial options). Our society officially recognizes a wide range of multiracial people (U.S. Census Bureau, 2012).

Racial Types

Scientists invented the concept of race more than a century ago as they tried to organize the world's physical diversity into three racial types. They called people with lighter skin and fine hair *Caucasoid*, people with darker skin and coarse hair *Negroid*, and people with yellow or brown skin and distinctive folds on the eyelids *Mongoloid*.

Sociologists consider such terms misleading at best and harmful at worst. For one thing, no society contains biologically "pure" people. The skin color of people we might call "Caucasoid" (or "Indo-European," "Caucasian," or more commonly "white") ranges from very light (typical in Scandinavia) to very dark (in southern India). The same variation exists among so-called "Negroids" ("Africans" or more commonly "black" people) and "Mongoloids" ("Asians"). In fact, many "white" people (say, in southern India) actually have darker skin than many "black" people (the Aborigines of Australia). Overall, the three racial categories differ in just 6 percent of their genes, and there is actually more genetic variation *within* each category than *between* categories. This means that two people in the

Read in **MySocLab Document:** *The Souls of Black Folk* by W.E.B. Du Bois

Race and Ethnicity   **CHAPTER 11**

European nation of Sweden, randomly selected, are likely to have at least as much genetic difference as a Swede and a person in the African nation of Senegal (Harris & Sim, 2002; American Sociological Association, 2003; California Newsreel, 2003).

So how important is race? From a biological point of view, the only significance of knowing people's racial category is assessing the risk factors for a few diseases. Why, then, do societies make so much of race? Such categories allow societies to rank people in a hierarchy, giving some people more money, power, and prestige than others and allowing some people to feel that they are inherently "better" than others. Because race may matter so much, societies may construct racial categories in extreme ways. Throughout much of the twentieth century, for example, many southern states labeled as "colored" anyone with as little as one thirty-second African ancestry (that is, one African American great-great-great-grandparent). Today, the law allows parents to declare the race of a child (or not) as they wish. Even so, most members of U.S. society are still very sensitive to people's racial backgrounds.

A Trend toward Mixture

Over many generations and throughout the Americas, the genetic traits from around the world have become mixed. Many "black" people have a significant Caucasoid ancestry, just as many "white" people have some Negroid genes. Whatever people may think, race is not a black-and-white issue.

Today, people are more willing to define themselves as multiracial. On the most recent U.S. Census survey for 2011, 8.7 million people described themselves by checking two or more racial categories. In 2011, 6 percent of children under the age of five were multiracial compared to less than 1 percent of people age 65 and older.

Ethnicity

Ethnicity is *a shared cultural heritage*. People define themselves—or others—as members of an *ethnic category* based on common ancestry, language, or religion that gives them a distinctive social identity. The United States is a multiethnic society. Even though we favor the English language, more than 60 million people (21 percent of the U.S. population) speak Spanish, Italian, German, French, Chinese, or some other language in their homes. In California, about 44 percent of the population does so (U.S. Census Bureau, 2012).

With regard to religion, the United States is a predominantly Protestant nation, but most people of Spanish, Italian, and Polish descent are Roman Catholic, and many of Greek, Ukrainian, and Russian descent belong to the Eastern Orthodox Church. More than 5.2 million Jewish Americans have ancestral ties to various nations around the world.

TABLE 11–1 Racial and Ethnic Categories in the United States, 2011

Racial or Ethnic Classification*	Approximate U.S. Population	Share of Total Population
Hispanic descent	**52,045,277**	**16.7%**
Mexican	33,557,922	10.8%
Puerto Rican	4,885,294	1.6%
Cuban	1,891,014	0.6%
Other Hispanic	11,605,686	3.7%
African descent	**40,750,746**	**13.1%**
Nigerian	275,174	0.1%
Ethiopian	192,045	0.1%
Somalian	131,894	<
Other African	40,151,633	12.9%
Native American descent	**2,547,006**	**0.8%**
American Indian	2,064,928	0.7%
Alaska Native Tribes	121,883	<
Other Native American	360,195	0.1%
Asian or Pacific Island descent	**16,270,474**	**5.2%**
Chinese	3,520,150	1.1%
Asian Indian	2,908,204	0.9%
Filipino	2,538,325	0.8%
Vietnamese	1,669,447	0.5%
Korean	1,449,876	0.5%
Japanese	756,898	0.2%
Cambodian	253,830	0.1%
Other Asian or Pacific Islander	3,173,744	1.0%
West Indian descent	**2,768,024**	**0.9%**
Arab descent	**1,822,447**	**0.6%**
Non-Hispanic European descent	**197,510,927**	**63.4%**
German	47,392,523	15.2%
Irish	34,520,787	11.1%
English	25,696,424	8.2%
Italian	17,460,857	5.6%
Polish	9,447,939	3.0%
French	8,596,126	2.8%
Scottish	5,412,820	1.7%
Dutch	4,441,071	1.4%
Norwegian	4,398,767	1.4%
Other non-Hispanic European	42,483,926	13.6%
Two or more races	**8,721,818**	**2.8%**

*People of Hispanic descent may be of any race. Many people also identify with more than one ethnic category. Therefore, figures total more than 100 percent.
Source: U.S. Census Bureau (2012).

CHAPTER 11 Race and Ethnicity

The population of Muslim men and women is generally estimated at between 2 and 3 million and is rapidly increasing due to both immigration and a high birthrate (Pew Research Center, 2011; ARDA, 2012).

Like race, the concept of "ethnicity" is socially constructed, becoming important only because society defines it that way. For example, U.S. society defines people of Spanish descent as "Latin," even though Italy has a more "Latin" culture than Spain. People of Italian descent are not viewed as Latin but as "European" and therefore less different from the point of view of the European majority (Camara, 2000; Brodkin, 2007). Like racial differences, the importance of ethnic differences can change over time. A century ago, Catholics and Jews were considered "different" in the mostly Protestant United States. This is much less true today.

Keep in mind that race is constructed from *biological* traits and ethnicity is constructed from *cultural* traits. However, the two often go hand in hand. For example, Japanese Americans have distinctive physical traits and, for those who hold to a traditional way of life, a distinctive culture as well. Table 11–1 on page 342 presents the most recent data on the racial and ethnic diversity of the United States.

On an individual level, people play up or play down cultural traits, depending on whether they want to fit in or stand apart from the surrounding society. Immigrants may drop their cultural traditions or, like many people of Native American descent in recent years, try to revive their heritage. For most people, ethnicity is more complex than race because they identify with several ethnic backgrounds. Rock-and-roll legend Jimi Hendrix was African American, white, and Cherokee; news anchor Soledad O'Brian considers herself both white and black, both Australian and Irish, and both Anglo and Hispanic.

minority any category of people distinguished by physical or cultural difference that a society sets apart and subordinates

Minorities

March 3, Dallas, Texas. *The lobby of just about any hotel in a major U.S. city presents a lesson in contrasts: The majority of the guests checking in are white; the majority of hotel employees who carry luggage, serve food, and clean the rooms are racial or ethnic minorities.*

As defined in Chapter 10 ("Gender Stratification"), a **minority** is *any category of people distinguished by physical or cultural difference that a society sets apart and subordinates.* Minority standing can be based on race, ethnicity, or both. As shown in Table 11–1, non-Hispanic white people (63 percent of the total) are still a majority of the U.S. population. But the share of minorities is increasing. Today, minorities are a majority in four states (California, New Mexico, Texas, and Hawaii) and in more than half of the country's 100 largest cities. By 2011, a majority of the births in the United States were racial and ethnic minorities. This fact—coupled to the effects

Diversity Snapshot

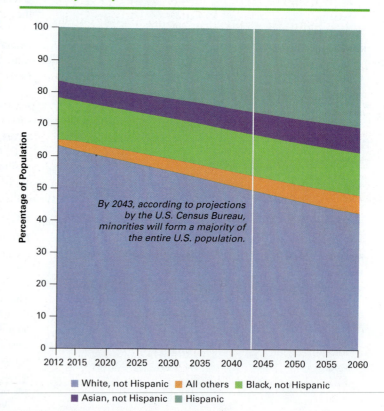

By 2043, according to projections by the U.S. Census Bureau, minorities will form a majority of the entire U.S. population.

Legend:
- White, not Hispanic
- All others
- Black, not Hispanic
- Asian, not Hispanic
- Hispanic

FIGURE 11–1 The Coming Minority Majority

According to projections from the Census Bureau, the United States will have a minority majority in the year 2043, less than thirty years from now. By that time, as the figure shows, the white, non-Hispanic population will actually decline, as the number of Asian Americans, African Americans, and especially Hispanic Americans increases. What changes do you expect this trend will bring to the United States?

Source: U.S. Census Bureau (2012).

Seeing Ourselves

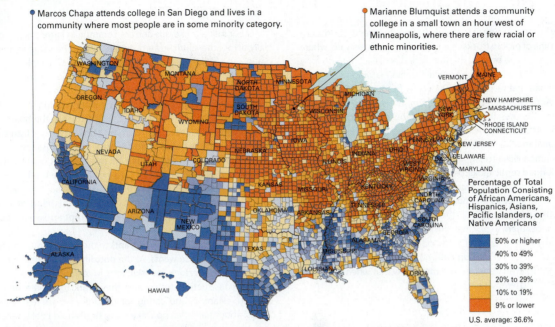

Explore the percentage of minority people in your local community and in counties across the United States in **MySocLab**

Marcos Chapa attends college in San Diego and lives in a community where most people are in some minority category.

Marianne Blumquist attends a community college in a small town an hour west of Minneapolis, where there are few racial or ethnic minorities.

Percentage of Total Population Consisting of African Americans, Hispanics, Asians, Pacific Islanders, or Native Americans

- 50% or higher
- 40% to 49%
- 30% to 39%
- 20% to 29%
- 10% to 19%
- 9% or lower

U.S. average: 36.6%

NATIONAL MAP 11–1 Where the Minority Majority Already Exists

Racial and ethnic minorities are now a majority of the population in four states—Hawaii, California, New Mexico, and Texas—as well as in the District of Columbia. At the other extreme, Vermont and Maine have the smallest share (about 6 percent) of minorities. Why do you think states with high minority populations are located in the South and Southwest?

Source: U.S. Census Bureau (2012).

of immigration—means that the minority share of the population will steadily increase. By 2043, according the U.S. Census Bureau (2012), minorities are likely to form a majority of the entire U.S. population. Figure 11–1 on page 343 shows how this trend is projected to unfold over time. National Map 11–1 shows where a minority majority already exists.

Minorities have two important characteristics. First, they share a *distinctive identity*, which may be based on physical or cultural traits. Second, minorities experience *subordination*. As the rest of this chapter shows, U.S. minorities typically have lower income, lower occupational prestige, and limited schooling. These facts mean that class, race, and ethnicity, as well as gender, are overlapping and reinforcing dimensions of social stratification. The Thinking About Diversity box on page 345 profiles the struggles of recent Latin American immigrants.

Of course, not all members of any minority category are disadvantaged. Some Latinos are quite wealthy, certain Chinese Americans are celebrated business leaders, and African Americans are among our nation's political leaders. But even job success rarely allows individuals to escape their minority standing. As described in Chapter 4 ("Social Interaction in Everyday Life"), race or ethnicity often serves as a *master status* that overshadows personal accomplishments.

Minorities usually make up a small proportion of a society's population, but this is not always the case. Black South Africans are disadvantaged even though they are a numerical majority in their country. In the United States, women represent slightly more than half the population but are still struggling for all the opportunities and privileges enjoyed by men.

Watch in **MySocLab**
Video: *Sociology on the Job: Race and Ethnicity*

CHAPTER 11 Race and Ethnicity

Thinking About Diversity: Race, Class, and Gender

Hard Work: The Immigrant Life in the United States

Early in the morning, it is already hot on the streets of Houston as a line of pickup trucks snakes slowly into a dusty yard, where 200 laborers have been gathering since dawn, each hoping for a day's work. The driver of the first truck opens his window and tells the foreman that he is looking for a crew to spread boiling tar on a roof. Abdonel Cespedes, the foreman, turns to the crowd, and after a few minutes, three workers step forward and climb into the back of the truck. The next driver is looking for two experienced housepainters. The scene is repeated over and over as men and a few women leave to dig ditches, spread cement, hang drywall, open clogged septic tanks, or crawl under houses to poison rats.

As each driver pulls into the yard, the foreman asks, "How much?" Most offer $5 an hour. Cespedes automatically responds, "$7.25; the going rate is $7.25 for an hour's hard work." Sometimes he convinces them to pay that much, but usually not. The workers, who come from Mexico, El Salvador, and Guatemala, know that dozens of them will end up with no work at all this day. Most accept $5 or $6 an hour because they know that when the day is over, $50 is better than nothing.

These immigrants gather on a New York City street corner every morning hoping to be hired for construction work that pays about $60 a day with no benefits.

Labor markets like this one are common in large cities, especially across the southwestern United States. The surge in immigration in recent years has brought millions of people to this country in search of work, and most have little schooling and speak little English.

Manuel Barrera has taken a day's work moving the entire contents of a store to a storage site. He arrives at the boarded-up building and gazes at the mountains of heavy furniture that he must carry out to a moving van, drive across town, and then carry again. He sighs when he thinks about how hot it is outside and realizes that it is even hotter inside the building. He will have no break for lunch. No one says anything about toilets. Barrera shakes his head: "I will do this kind of work because it puts food on the table. But I did not foresee it would turn out like this."

The hard truth is that immigrants to the United States do the jobs that no one else wants. At the bottom level of the national economy, they perform low-skill jobs in restaurants and hotels and on construction crews, and they work in private homes cooking, cleaning, and caring for children. Across the United States, about half of all housekeepers, household cooks, tailors, and restaurant waiters are men or women born abroad. Few immigrants make much more than the official minimum wage ($7.25 in 2012), and rarely do immigrant workers receive any health or pension benefits. Many well-off families take the labor of immigrants as much for granted as their air-conditioned cars and comfortable homes.

What Do You Think?

1. In what ways do you or members of your family depend on the low-paid labor of immigrants?

2. Do you favor allowing the 11.5 million people who entered this country illegally to earn citizenship? What should be done?

3. Should the U.S. government act to reduce the number of immigrants entering this country in the future? Why or why not?

Sources: Booth (1998), Tumulty (2006), U.S. Department of Homeland Security (2012), and U.S. Department of Labor (2012).

Prejudice and Stereotypes

11.2 Describe the extent and causes of prejudice.

November 19, Jerusalem, Israel. We are driving along the outskirts of this historical city—a holy place to Jews, Christians, and Muslims—when Razi, our taxi driver, spots a small group of Falasha—Ethiopian Jews—on a street corner. "Those people over there," he points as he speaks, "they are different. They don't drive cars. They don't want to improve themselves. Even when our country offers them schooling, they don't take it." He shakes his head at the Ethiopians and drives on.

prejudice a rigid and unfair generalization about an entire category of people

stereotype a simplified description applied to every person in some category

Prejudice is *a rigid and unfair generalization about an entire category of people.* Prejudice is unfair because *all* people in some category are described as the same, based on little or no direct evidence. Prejudice may target people of a particular social class, sex, sexual orientation, age, political affiliation, physical disability, race, or ethnicity.

Prejudices are *prejudgments* that can be either positive or negative. Our positive prejudices tend to exaggerate the virtues of people like ourselves, and our negative prejudices condemn those who differ from us. Negative prejudice can be expressed as anything from mild dislike to outright hostility. Because such attitudes are rooted in culture, everyone has at least some prejudice.

Prejudice often takes the form of a **stereotype** (*stereo* is derived from a Greek word meaning "solid"), *a simplified description applied to every person in some category.* Many white people hold stereotypical views of minorities. Stereotyping is especially harmful to minorities in the workplace. If company officials see workers only in terms of a stereotype, they will make assumptions about their abilities, steering them toward certain jobs and limiting their access to better opportunities (Kaufman, 2002).

Minorities, too, stereotype whites and other minorities (T. W. Smith, 1996; Cummings & Lambert, 1997). Surveys show, for example, that African Americans are more likely than whites to express the belief that Asians engage in unfair business practices and Asians are more likely than whites to criticize Hispanics for having too many children (Perlmutter, 2002).

Measuring Prejudice: The Social Distance Scale

One measure of prejudice is *social distance,* how closely people are willing to interact with members of some category. In the 1920s, Emory Bogardus developed the *social distance scale* shown in Figure 11–2 on page 347. Bogardus (1925) asked students at U.S. colleges and universities to look at this scale and indicate how closely they were willing to interact with people in thirty racial and ethnic categories. People express the greatest social distance (most negative prejudice) by declaring that a particular category of people should be barred from the country entirely (point 7); at the other extreme, people express the least social distance (most social acceptance) by saying they would accept members of a particular category into their family through marriage (point 1).

Bogardus (1925, 1967; Owen, Elsner, & McFaul, 1977) found that people felt much more social distance from some categories than from others. In general, students in his surveys expressed the most social distance from Hispanics, African Americans, Asians, and Turks, indicating that they would be willing to tolerate such people as co-workers but not as neighbors, friends, or family members. Students expressed the least social distance from those from northern and western Europe, including English and Scottish people, and also Canadians, indicating that they were willing to include them in their families by marriage.

What patterns of social distance do we find among college students today? A recent study using the same social distance scale reported three major findings (Parrillo & Donoghue, 2005):[1]

1. **Student opinion shows a trend toward greater social acceptance.**   Today's students express less social distance from all minorities than students did several decades ago. Figure 11–2 shows that the mean (average) score on the social distance scale declined from 2.14 in 1925 to 1.93 in 1977 and 1.44 in 2001. Respondents (81 percent of whom were white) showed notably greater acceptance of African Americans, a category that moved up from near the bottom in 1925 to the top one-third in 2001.

---

[1]Parrillo and Donoghue dropped seven of the categories used by Bogardus (Armenians, Czechs, Finns, Norwegians, Scots, Swedes, and Turks), claiming they were no longer visible minorities. They added nine new categories (Africans, Arabs, Cubans, Dominicans, Haitians, Jamaicans, Muslims, Puerto Ricans, and Vietnamese), claiming that these are visible minorities today. This change probably encouraged higher social distance scores, making the trend toward decreasing social distance all the more significant.

Student Snapshot

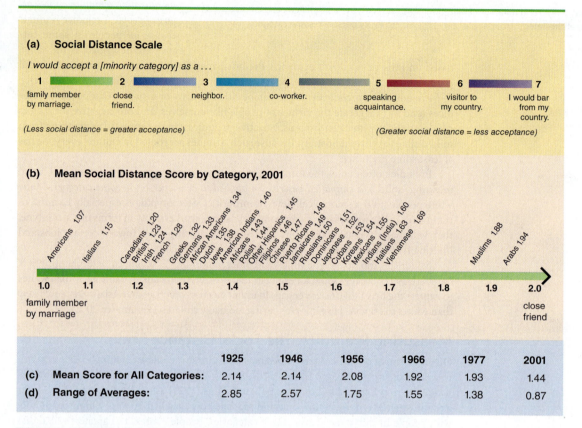

FIGURE 11–2 Bogardus Social Distance Research

The social distance scale is a good way to measure prejudice. Part (a) illustrates the complete social distance scale, from least social distance at the far left to greatest social distance at the far right. Part (b) shows the mean (average) social distance score received by each category of people in 2001. Part (c) presents the overall mean score in specific years (the average of the scores received by all racial and ethnic categories). These scores have fallen from 2.14 in 1925 to 1.44 in 2001, showing that students express less social distance toward minorities today than they did in the past. Part (d) shows the range of averages, the difference between the highest and lowest scores in given years (in 2001, for instance, it was 0.87, the difference between the high score of 1.94 for Arabs and the low score of 1.07 for Americans). This figure has also become smaller since 1925, indicating that today's students tend to see fewer differences between various categories of people.

Source: Parrillo and Donoghue (2005).

2. **People see less difference between various minorities.**   The earliest studies found the difference between the highest- and lowest-ranked minorities (the range of averages) equal to almost three points on the scale. As the figure shows, the most recent research produced a range of averages of less than one point, indicating that today's students see fewer differences between various categories of people.

3. **The terrorist attacks of September 11, 2001, may have reduced social acceptance of Arabs and Muslims.**   The most recent study was conducted just a few weeks after September 11, 2001. Perhaps the fact that the nineteen men who attacked the World Trade Center and the Pentagon were Arabs and Muslims is part of the reason that students ranked these categories last on the social distance scale. However, not a single student gave Arabs or Muslims a 7, indicating that they should be barred from the country. On the contrary, the 2001 mean scores (1.94 for Arabs and 1.88 for Muslims) show higher social acceptance than students in 1977 expressed toward eighteen of the thirty categories of people studied.

Racism

For a closer look at studies of race and intelligence, **Read More** in **MySocLab**, *Does Race Affect Intelligence?*

racism the belief that one racial category is innately superior or inferior to another

A powerful and harmful form of prejudice, **racism** is *the belief that one racial category is innately superior or inferior to another*. Racism has existed throughout world history. Despite their many achievements, the ancient Greeks, the peoples of India, and the Chinese all regarded people unlike themselves as inferior.

Racism has also been widespread throughout the history of the United States, where ideas about racial inferiority supported slavery. Today, overt racism in this country has decreased because more people believe in evaluating others, in Martin Luther King Jr.'s words, "not by the color of their skin but by the content of their character."

Even so, racism remains a serious social problem, as some people think that certain racial and ethnic categories are smarter than others. As studies have shown, however, racial differences in mental abilities result from environment rather than biology (Sowell, 1994, 1995).

Theories of Prejudice

Where does prejudice come from? Social scientists provide several answers to this question, focusing on frustration, personality, culture, and social conflict.

Scapegoat Theory

Scapegoat theory holds that prejudice springs from frustration among people who are themselves disadvantaged (Dollard et al., 1939). For instance, take the case of a white woman who is frustrated by the low pay she receives from her assembly-line job in a textile factory. Directing hostility at the powerful factory owners carries the obvious risk of being fired; therefore, she may blame her low pay on the presence of minority co-workers. Her prejudice does not improve her situation, but it is a relatively safe way to express anger, and it may give her the comforting feeling that at least she is superior to someone.

scapegoat a person or category of people, typically with little power, whom people unfairly blame for their own troubles

A **scapegoat**, then, is *a person or category of people, typically with little power, whom people unfairly blame for their own troubles*. Because they have little power and thus are usually "safe targets," minorities often are used as scapegoats.

Authoritarian Personality Theory

Theodor Adorno and colleagues (1950) considered extreme prejudice a personality trait of certain individuals. This conclusion is supported by research showing that people who show strong prejudice toward one minority are usually intolerant of all minorities. These *authoritarian personalities* rigidly conform to conventional cultural values and see moral issues as clear-cut matters of right and wrong. People with authoritarian personalities also view society as naturally competitive and hierarchical, with "better" people (like themselves) inevitably dominating those who are weaker (all minorities).

Adorno and his colleagues also found the opposite pattern to be true: People who express tolerance toward one minority are likely to be accepting of all. They tend to be more flexible in their moral judgments and treat all people as equals.

Adorno thought that people with little schooling and those raised by cold and demanding parents tend to develop authoritarian personalities. Filled with anger and anxiety as children, they grow into hostile, aggressive adults who seek out scapegoats.

Culture Theory

A third theory claims that although extreme prejudice may be found in some people, some prejudice is found in everyone. Why? Because prejudice is part of the culture in which we all live and learn. The Bogardus social distance studies help prove the point. Bogardus found that students across the country had much the same attitudes toward specific racial and ethnic categories, feeling closer to some and more distant from others.

More evidence that prejudice is rooted in culture is the fact that minorities express the same attitudes as white people toward categories other than their own. Such patterns suggest that individuals hold prejudices because we live in a "culture of prejudice" that has taught us all to view certain categories of people as "better" or "worse" than others.

CHAPTER 11 Race and Ethnicity

discrimination unequal treatment of various categories of people

institutional prejudice and discrimination bias built into the operation of society's institutions

Conflict Theory

A fourth explanation proposes that prejudice is used as a tool by powerful people to oppress others. Anglos who look down on Latino immigrants in the Southwest, for example, can get away with paying the immigrants low wages for long hours of hard work. Similarly, all elites benefit when prejudice divides the labor force along racial and ethnic lines and discourages them from working together to advance their common interests (Geschwender, 1978; Olzak, 1989; Rothenberg, 2008).

According to another conflict-based argument, made by Shelby Steele (1990), minorities themselves encourage *race consciousness* to win greater power and privileges. Because of their historical disadvantage, minorities claim that they are victims entitled to special consideration based on their race. This strategy may bring short-term gains, but Steele cautions that such thinking often sparks a backlash from whites or others who oppose "special treatment" on the basis of race or ethnicity.

Discrimination

(11.3) Distinguish discrimination from prejudice.

Closely related to prejudice is **discrimination**, *unequal treatment of various categories of people. Prejudice* refers to *attitudes,* but *discrimination* is a matter of *action.* Like prejudice, discrimination can be either positive (providing special advantages) or negative (creating obstacles) and ranges from subtle to extreme.

Institutional Prejudice and Discrimination

We typically think of prejudice and discrimination as the hateful ideas or actions of specific people. But Stokely Carmichael and Charles Hamilton (1967) pointed out that far greater harm results from **institutional prejudice and discrimination,** *bias built into the operation of society's institutions,* including schools, hospitals, the police, and the workplace. For example, researchers have found that banks reject home mortgage applications from minorities at a higher rate than those from white people, even when income and quality of neighborhood are held constant (Gotham, 1998; Blanton, 2007).

According to Carmichael and Hamilton, people are slow to condemn or even recognize institutional prejudice and discrimination because it often involves respected public officials and long-established traditions. A case in point is *Brown* v. *Board of Education of Topeka,* the 1954 Supreme Court decision that ended the legal segregation of schools. The principle of "separate but equal" schooling had been the law of the land, supporting racial inequality by allowing school segregation. Despite this change in the law, half a century later, most U.S. students still attend schools in which one race overwhelmingly predominates (KewalRamani et al., 2007). In 1991, the courts pointed out that

Watch in **MySocLab**
Video: *The Basics: Race and Ethnicity*

In 2012, seventeen-year old Trayvon Martin was shot and killed by twenty-eight-year old George Zimmerman, who was the coordinator of his Florida community's neighborhood watch program. From the outset, questions arose about whether racial bias played a part in the shooting. Eventually, Zimmerman was charged with murder, and in 2013 a jury found him not guilty. The high level of national concern over this event—especially within the African American community—suggests that many believe race continues to shape the operation of the U.S. criminal justice system.

Race and Ethnicity   **CHAPTER 11**

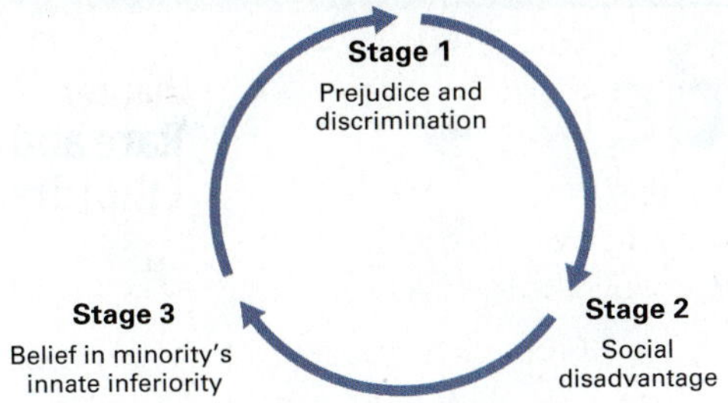

neighborhood schools will never provide equal education as long as our population is segregated, with most African Americans living in central cities and most white people and Asian Americans living in suburbs.

Prejudice and Discrimination: The Vicious Circle

Prejudice and discrimination reinforce each other. The Thomas theorem, discussed in Chapter 4 ("Social Interaction in Everyday Life"), offers a simple explanation of this fact: *Situations that are defined as real become real in their consequences* (Thomas & Thomas, 1928; Thomas, 1966:301, orig. 1931).

Applying the Thomas theorem, we understand how stereotypes can become real to people who believe them and sometimes even to those who are victimized by them. Prejudice on the part of white people toward people of color does not produce *innate* inferiority, but it can produce *social* inferiority, pushing minorities into low-paying jobs, inferior schools, and racially segregated housing. Then, as white people interpret that social disadvantage as evidence that minorities do not measure up, they unleash a new round of prejudice and discrimination, giving rise to a vicious circle in which each perpetuates the other, as shown in Figure 11–3.

Stage 1
Prejudice and discrimination

Stage 2
Social disadvantage

Stage 3
Belief in minority's innate inferiority

Stage 1: Prejudice and discrimination begin, often as an expression of ethnocentrism or an attempt to justify economic exploitation.

Stage 2: As a result of prejudice and discrimination, a minority is socially disadvantaged, occupying a low position in the system of social stratification.

Stage 3: This social disadvantage is then interpreted not as the result of earlier prejudice and discrimination but as evidence that the minority is innately inferior, unleashing renewed prejudice and discrimination by which the cycle repeats itself.

FIGURE 11–3 Prejudice and Discrimination: The Vicious Circle

Prejudice and discrimination can form a vicious circle, thereby perpetuating themselves.

Making the Grade

The Social Meaning of Race and Ethnicity

11.1 Explain the social construction of race and ethnicity.

📖 **Read** the **Document** in **MySocLab**   ✳️ **Explore** the **Map** in **MySocLab**

👁️ **Watch** the **Video** in **MySocLab**

Race refers to socially constructed categories based on biological traits a society defines as important.
- The meaning and importance of race vary from place to place and over time.
- Societies use racial categories to rank people in a hierarchy, giving some people more money, power, and prestige than others.
- In the past, scientists created three broad categories—Caucasoids, Mongoloids, and Negroids—but there are no biologically pure races.

Ethnicity refers to socially constructed categories based on cultural traits a society defines as important.
- Ethnicity reflects common ancestors, language, and religion.
- The importance of ethnicity varies from place to place and over time.
- People choose to play up or play down their ethnicity.
- Societies may or may not set categories of people apart based on differences in ethnicity.

race a socially constructed category of people who share biologically transmitted traits that members of a society consider important
ethnicity a shared cultural heritage
minority any category of people distinguished by physical or cultural difference that a society sets apart and subordinates

Prejudice and Stereotypes

11.2 Describe the extent and causes of prejudice.

Prejudice is a rigid and unfair generalization about a category of people.
- The social distance scale is one measure of prejudice.
- One type of prejudice is the **stereotype**, an exaggerated description applied to every person in some category.
- **Racism**, a very destructive type of prejudice, asserts that one race is innately superior or inferior to another.

There are four **theories of prejudice**:
- **Scapegoat theory** claims that prejudice results from frustration among people who are disadvantaged.
- **Authoritarian personality theory** (Adorno) claims that prejudice is a personality trait of certain individuals, especially those with little education and those raised by cold and demanding parents.
- **Culture theory** (Bogardus) claims that prejudice is rooted in culture; we learn to feel greater social distance from some categories of people.
- **Conflict theory** claims that prejudice is a tool used by powerful people to divide and control the population.

prejudice a rigid and unfair generalization about an entire category of people
stereotype a simplified description applied to every person in some category
racism the belief that one racial category is innately superior or inferior to another
scapegoat a person or category of people, typically with little power, whom people unfairly blame for their own troubles

Discrimination

11.3 Distinguish discrimination from prejudice.

👁️ **Watch** the **Video** in **MySocLab**

Discrimination refers to actions by which a person treats various categories of people unequally.
- Prejudice refers to *attitudes*; discrimination involves *actions*.
- **Institutional prejudice and discrimination** are biases built into the operation of society's institutions, including schools, hospitals, the police, and the workplace.
- Prejudice and discrimination perpetuate themselves in a vicious circle, resulting in social disadvantage that fuels additional prejudice and discrimination.

discrimination unequal treatment of various categories of people
institutional prejudice and discrimination bias built into the operation of society's institutions

REVIEWING THE READING ASSIGNMENT

Now that you have read the textbook selection, you should reread it at least once (and perhaps more than once) in order to strengthen your comprehension and knowledge.

| ACTIVITY 6 | Highlighting or Annotating the Reading (Review) |

After you have read the complete textbook selection once, decide whether highlighting or annotating is your preferred review strategy. Then, on your second reading, highlight or annotate the selection to help you review the selection before the lecture (or before a quiz or examination).

| ACTIVITY 7 | Learning Vocabulary (Review) |

This textbook selection includes a number of vocabulary terms, including *race, ethnicity, minority, prejudice, stereotype,* and *discrimination*. These key terms are indicated by **boldface type** in the selection. List at least three ways you can study and learn these vocabulary words.

_____

_____

_____

ATTENDING THE LECTURE AND PARTICIPATING IN CLASS

No two professors will emphasize the exact same materials in their lectures. This is true for several reasons. First, professors have a wide range of interests. Second, instructors often complain that the term is much too short to cover everything they'd like to talk about. For that reason, they have to pick and choose the topics they will cover in class. Often, they rely on the textbook to fill in the gaps.

We asked several sociology professors to share their strategies for teaching the material in the "Race and Ethnicity" textbook selection that you just read. Here are some of their responses:

"Even though this is a social science course, I want students to understand that race has nothing to do with biology and everything to do with social definitions. For this reason, I focus quite a bit on the early part of the chapter, but I expect students to have read the entire chapter before my first lecture on the topic."

"I have begun to flip my classroom. By this, I mean that I expect students to come to class with a basic understanding of key terms and concepts. Then, I use our class time to answer questions and help students through the areas they are having difficulty with. A student who comes to class without reading the assignment is at a tremendous disadvantage."

"While I love sociology, I understand that most of my students are not going to become sociologists. For this reason, I try to focus more on the ways that students can apply sociology to their everyday lives. I think it's important that they understand their own prejudices, so I ask them to complete a social-distance survey like the one on page 434. I then use that as a basis for class discussion. I also want students to understand how their community fits into the United States as a whole, so I spend a lot of time with the national map on page 431."

ACTIVITY 8   Participating in Class (Question)

Prepare a list of five questions that you would ask in class about the selection. Compare these with your classmates' questions. Did many of you ask the same or similar questions? What purposes might these questions serve, other than stimulating classroom discussion?

_____

_____

ACTIVITY 9   Classroom Activity—Working with Visuals (Question)

Several of the figures in this textbook selection are intended to be interactive. In a group of three to five classmates, brainstorm answers to the questions that appear at the end of Figure 11-1 (page 430) and National Map 11-1 (page 431). Present your responses to the class. Did the groups come up with similar answers?

ACTIVITY 10   Classroom Activity—Critical Thinking (Question)

Working with a group of three to five classmates, answer the questions that appear at the end of the "Thinking About Diversity: Race, Class, and Gender" box on page 432.

WRITING ABOUT THE READING

Students often have two purposes for writing in response to a reading. The first purpose is to help them learn the material better. Many studies have shown that writing greatly aids comprehension. The second purpose is to react to the reading. Reactions can be informal (journal entries, freewriting, and so on) or formal (paragraphs, essays, or longer papers on a specific topic). Sometimes the instructor assigns a specific topic or a specific question to which students must respond. Other times, students must come up with their own topic.

ACTIVITY 11   Paraphrasing (Review and React)

Choose one of the following activities to complete.

1. Paraphrase the section titled "A Trend toward Mixture" on page 429.

2. Paraphrase the section titled "Culture Theory" on page 435.

3. Paraphrase the section titled "Prejudice and Discrimination: The Vicious Circle" on page 437.

ACTIVITY 12   Summarizing (Review and React)

Choose one of the following activities to complete.

1. Write a summary of the section titled "Race" on pages 427–429.

2. Write a summary of the section titled "Ethnicity" on pages 429–430.

3. Write a summary of the box titled "Hard Work: The Immigrant Life in the United States" on page 432.

4. Write a summary of the section titled "Institutional Prejudice and Discrimination" on pages 436–437.

ACTIVITY 13   Outlining (Review and React)

Prepare an outline of the reading selection.

ACTIVITY 14   Freewriting (Journal Entry) (React)

When you *freewrite*, you sit down and just begin writing. Freewriting is an informal way of responding to a reading. It allows you to begin exploring your ideas and reactions without worrying about grammar, punctuation, or spelling. Many writers find that freewriting is an excellent way to begin getting their thoughts on paper. A *journal* is a notebook in which you record ideas, reactions, and freewrites. React to the textbook selection by freewriting on one of these topics:

1. skin color

2. ethnic traditions or holidays

3. the lives of recent immigrants in the United States

4. stereotypes about a particular group of people

5. affirmative action or other race-based governmental programs

ACTIVITY 15   Writing Paragraphs and Essays (React)

Write a paragraph or essay in which you answer one of the following questions, found in the "Thinking About Diversity" box on page 432.

1. In what ways do you or members of your family depend on the low-paid labor of immigrants?

2. Do you favor allowing the 11.5 million people who entered this country illegally to earn citizenship? What should be done?

3. Should the U.S. government act to reduce the number of immigrants entering this country in the future? Why or why not?

ACTIVITY 16   Brainstorming Research Topics (React)

In many courses, you will be asked to write a long paper (perhaps as long as ten pages). For these papers, you are often expected to choose your own topic. Based on the reading, brainstorm a list of five possible topics you might like to research and write about. Then revisit your list and choose the topic you like best. Why did you eliminate the other topics? Why did you choose the specific topic that you selected?

TAKING QUIZZES

To make sure students read and understand the assignment, instructors often give quizzes based on the reading selection. These quizzes usually focus on the reading's key points or main ideas. The goal of these quizzes is not to trick students but rather to make sure they have read and understood the selection. For this reason, the quiz questions usually focus on key (vocabulary) terms and concepts. If you have read the selection, it should be easy to do well on the quiz.

ACTIVITY 17   Quiz: Section 11.1, The Social Meaning of Race and Ethnicity, pages 427–431

Select the best answer for each question. Hints are provided to help you think about each question and answer it correctly.

_____ 1. The term _____ refers to a socially constructed category of people who share biologically transmitted traits that members of a society consider important.

  a. ethnic group
  b. race
  c. phenotype
  d. minority

Hint: Review the key terms and definitions that appear in the margins.

_____ 2. Which of the following was *not* one of the original groups of people identified by early scientists who studied race?

  a. Mongoloid
  b. Caucasoid
  c. Negroid
  d. Trapezoid

Hint: Review the material under the heading "Racial Types" and look for key terms in italics.

_____ 3. What is the only real significance of knowing a person's racial category?

  a. to match a person to his or her country of origin
  b. to assess risk factors for a few diseases
  c. to create communities of people who share the same race
  d. to identify racial differences in IQ and academic achievement

Hint: This key point is embedded in the text. The instructor is asking this question because the answer is essential to an understanding of race.

_____ 4. Which of the following is *not* commonly used to identify the members of an ethnic group?

  a. religion
  b. language
  c. common ancestry
  d. skin color

Hint: Review the material under the heading "Ethnicity."

_____ 5. Which of the following statements is *not* true?

  a. By definition, minority groups experience subordination.
  b. The distinctive identity of minority groups may be based on physical or cultural traits.
  c. All the members of any minority group are economically disadvantaged.
  d. Minorities often, but not always, make up a small portion of a society's population.

Hint: Notice that this question is really four true/false questions. You must read all four answers and determine whether each is true or false. Then use the process of elimination to determine the correct answer.

ACTIVITY 18	Quiz: Section 11.2, Prejudice and Stereotypes, pages 432–436

Indicate whether each statement is true (T) or false (F).

_____ 1. Prejudice by definition makes a negative judgment.

_____ 2. Stereotypes do not allow for individual differences.

_____ 3. Minority groups are not capable of prejudice or stereotypes.

_____ 4. Bogardus's research showed that students expressed the least social distance from people from Canada and from western and northern Europe.

_____ 5. In general, today's students demonstrate higher social distance from all minorities than students did several decades ago.

_____ 6. The events of 9/11 may have reduced social acceptance of Muslims and Arabs in the United States.

_____ 7. A racist is someone who believes in the inherent superiority of a particular racial category.

_____ 8. Differences in mental abilities result from environment, not biology.

_____ 9. Adorno believed that extreme prejudice is tied to authoritarian personality traits.

_____ 10. Conflict theory holds that most cultures subscribe to some form of cultural prejudice against specific groups.

ACTIVITY 19	Quiz: Section 11.3, Discrimination, pages 436–437

Indicate whether each statement is true (T) or false (F).

_____ 1. Institutional racism refers to the type of racism found in mental institutions and prisons.

_____ 2. *Prejudice* refers to attitudes and beliefs, while *discrimination* refers to action.

_____ 3. The case of *Brown* v. *Board of Education of Topeka* ended the legal racial segregation of schools.

_____ 4. The racial segregation of schools in the United States is now a thing of the past.

_____ 5. Prejudice and discrimination reinforce each other in a vicious circle.

ACTIVITY 20	Vocabulary

Match the word in Column A with its definition in Column B.

COLUMN A	COLUMN B
_____ 1. scapegoat	a. a measure of how closely people are willing to interact with members of some category
_____ 2. racism	b. a shared cultural heritage
_____ 3. discrimination	c. a rigid and unfair generalization about an entire category of people

COLUMN A	COLUMN B
_____ 4. stereotype	d. bias built into the operation of society's institutions
_____ 5. minority	e. a socially constructed category of people who share biologically transmitted traits that members of a society consider important
_____ 6. race	f. a person or category of people, typically with little power, whom people unfairly blame for their own troubles
_____ 7. institutional prejudice and racism	g. unequal treatment of various categories of people
_____ 8. prejudice	h. a simplified description applied to every person in some category
_____ 9. ethnicity	i. any category of people distinguished by physical or cultural difference that a society sets apart and subordinates
_____ 10. social distance	j. the belief that one racial category is innately superior or inferior to another

TAKING THE EXAM

Exams are often an important part of determining your grade. While some exams feature mostly objective (true/false, multiple-choice, short-answer, fill-in-the-blank) questions, many require writing.

ACTIVITY 21   Brainstorming Essay Exam Questions

Use the heading structure of the reading to prepare a list of three possible exam questions. (Note: If you used the SQ3R method, you have already brainstormed these questions and practiced answering them.)

ACTIVITY 22   Taking an Essay Exam

Select one of the following questions and answer it. Because all exams have a time limit, make sure you can answer this question fully in fifteen minutes or less.

1. Review Figure 11-2, which summarizes the Bogardus social distance research. Based on the figure, write five conclusions based on Bogardus's research. Specifically,
   (a) What does the phrase "mean score for all categories" mean? How did it change between 1925 and 2001?
   (b) What does the phrase "range of averages" mean, and how did it change between 1925 and 2001?
   (c) What does a score of 1.0 mean; and what would a score of 7.0 mean?
   (d) How might the categories that achieved the lowest levels of social distance be described and classified?
   (e) What is the relationship between social distance and greater acceptance?

2. The terms _race_ and _ethnicity_ are often confused. What does each term mean? How are the terms similar, and how are they different?

3. What is the difference between prejudice and discrimination? Provide examples to support your answer.

4. Identify and explain four theories that have been proposed to explain prejudice. Which of these theories do you most favor? Explain.

5. Describe the vicious circle of prejudice and discrimination, using an example to support your answer. How is this vicious circle tied into institutional prejudice and racism?

CREDITS

PHOTO CREDITS

Cover: Mark Skalny/Shutterstock; **p. 6:** Monkey Business/Fotolia; **p. 7:** Kmiragaya/Fotolia; **p. 10:** Carlos Santa Maria/Fotolia; **p. 17:** Tor Eigeland/Alamy; **p. 30:** Blend Images/SuperStock; **p. 40:** Michaeljung/Shutterstock; **p. 46:** Tetra Images/SuperStock; **p. 71:** Radius/SuperStock; **p. 78:** mtkang/Shutterstock; **p. 82:** CandyBox Images/Fotolia; **p. 95:** Science Photo/Fotolia; **p. 128:** Oneinchpunch/Fotolia; **p. 132:** WavebreakmediaMicro/Fotolia; **p. 169 (top to bottom):** Yes Man/Fotolia; Pongam/Fotolia;: Pongam/Fotolia; Okea/Fotolia; Nikolya/Fotolia; **p. 170:** Cartographer/Fotolia; **p. 184:** Bob and Tom Thaves/Cartoonist Group; **p. 190:** Tom Reichner/Shutterstock; **p. 239:** Self-Portrait as Winter. Carriera, Rosalba Giovanna (1657–1757). Pastel on paper. Rococo. 1731. Italy, Venetian School. Dresden State Art Collections. Age Fotostock.; **p. 270:** Monkey Business/Fotolia; **p. 293 (top to bottom):** Timmary/Fotolia; Luigi Giordano/Fotolia; Tom Gough/Fotolia; Jiri Hera/Fotolia; Joe Gough/Fotolia; **p. 294 (left):** Voyagerix/Fotolia; **p. 294 (right):** Tommaso79/Shutterstock; **p. 308:** Marc A. Hermann/Pool/Reuters; **p. 317 (left):** Kevin Radford/Purestock/SuperStock; **p. 317 (right):** Image Source/SuperStock; **p. 317 (bottom):** Tetra Images/SuperStock; **p. 320:** Ermolaev Alexander/Shutterstock; **p. 327:** Richard Levine/AGE Fotostock; **p. 340:** Worker/Shutterstock; **p. 370:** Martin Heitner/Purestock/SuperStock; **p. 379:** Monkey Business/Shutterstock; **p. 383:** Beror/Shutterstock; **p. 393:** Picsfive/Shutterstock; **p. 397:** Asierromero/Fotolia; **p. 404:** Puckillustrations/Fotolia; **p. 408:** Janice Wiggins; **p. 413:** DPA Picture Alliance/Alamy; **p. 417:** Teh Eng Koon/AFP/GettyImages; **p. 425:** Joseph Sohm/Newscom; **p. 427:** CREATISTA/Shutterstock; **p. 428 (bottom left):** Charles O'Rear/Corbis; **p. 428 (bottom middle):** Paul W. Liebhardt; **p. 428 (bottom right):** Buddy Mays/Alamy; **p. 428 (top left):** Paul Matthew Photography/Shutterstock; **p. 428 (top middle):** Sanjay Deva/Shutterstock; **p. 428 (top right):** Owen Franken/Corbis; **p. 432:** Joe Raedle/Getty Images; **p. 436:** EPA/Peter Foley/Landov; **p. 438:** Cheryl Diaz Meyer/Dallas Morning News/Corbis.

TEXT CREDITS

Chapter 1

p. 35: Gronbeck, Bruce E., et al., *Principles of Speech Communication*, 11th brief ed. New York: HarperCollins College Publishers, 1992, pp. 217–218.

p. 38: Belk, Colleen and Virginia Borden Maier, *Biology: Science for Life with Physiology*, 3e, Upper Saddle River: Pearson, 2010.

p. 39: Macionis, John J., *Society: The Basics*, 13th Ed., © 2015, pp. viii, 339, 343, 344, 347, 350. Reprinted and electronically reproduced by permission of Pearson Education, Inc., New York, NY.

Chapter 2

p. 59: Thompson, Janice J.; Manore, Melinda, *Nutrition for Life*, 1st Ed., © 2007. Reprinted and electronically reproduced by permission of Pearson Education, Inc., New York, NY.

Chapter 3

p. 73: Carl, John D., *THINK Sociology*, 1st Ed., © 2010, Pearson Education, Inc.

Chapter 4

pp. 86–87: Devito, Joseph A., *The Interpersonal Communication Book*, 8th ed. New York: Longman, 1998, p. 266.

p. 88: Wade, Carole and Carol Tavris, *Psychology*, 4th ed. New York: HarperCollins College Publishers, 1996, pp. 124–125.

p. 89: Ross, David A., *Introduction to Oceanography*. New York: HarperCollins College Publishers, 1995, p. 239.

p. 89: Wallace, Robert A., *Biology: The World of Life*, 5th ed. Glenview, IL: Scott, Foresman, 1987, p. 443.

p. 89: U.S. Constitution. United States Congress.

pp. 90–91: Thio, Alex, *Sociology*, 4th ed. © Pearson Education (New York: HarperCollins College Publishers, 1996) 1996, p. 181.

p. 91: DeVito, Joseph A., *The Interpersonal Communication Book*, 9th ed. New York: Longman, 2001.

p. 92: Wallbank, T. Walter, et al., *Civilization Past and Present*, 8th ed. New York: HarperCollins College Publishers, 1996.

p. 93: DeVito, Joseph A., *Essentials of Human Communication*, 6th Ed., © 2008, pp. 109–110, 125, 131–133. Reprinted and electronically reproduced by permission of Pearson Education, Inc., New York, NY.

pp. 93–94: Campbell, Bernard G. and James D. Loy, *Humankind Emerging*, 7th ed. New York: HarperCollins College Publishers, 1996.

p. 94: Thio, Alex, *Sociology: A Brief Introduction*, 7th ed., p. 105. © 2009. Printed and electronically reproduced by permission of Pearson Education, Inc., Upper Saddle River, New Jersey.

p. 95: Marieb, Elaine N., *Essentials of Human Anatomy & Physiology*, 9th ed. San Francisco: Pearson Benjamin Cummings, 2009.

p. 96: McCarty, Marilu Hurt, *Dollars and Sense: An Introduction to Economics*, 8th ed. Reading, MA: Addison-Wesley, 1997.

p. 99: Lynch, April; Barry Elmore, Jerome Kotecki, *Choosing Health*, 2nd Ed., San Francisco: Pearson Benjamin Cummings, 2014.

p. 100: Blake, Joan Salge, *Nutrition & You*. San Francisco: Pearson Benjamin Cummings, 2008, p. 329.

pp. 102–103: Donatelle, Rebecca J., *Health: The Basics, Green Edition*, 9th Ed., © 2011. Reprinted and electronically reproduced by permission of Pearson Education, Inc., New York, NY.

pp. 102–103: Donatelle, Rebecca J., *Health: The Basics*, 4th Ed., © 2001, pp. 282, 346. Reprinted and electronically reproduced by permission of Pearson Education, Inc., New York, NY.

pp. 103–104: Solomon, Michael R. and Elnora W. Stuart, *Marketing: Real People, Real Choices*, 2nd ed., p. 135, © 2000. Printed and electronically reproduced by permission of Pearson Education, Inc., Upper Saddle River, New Jersey.

p. 105: Thompson, Janice J.; Manore, Melinda, *Nutrition for Life*, 1st Ed., © 2007. Reprinted and electronically reproduced by permission of Pearson Education, Inc., New York, NY.

p. 107: Thompson, Janice J.; Manore, Melinda, *Nutrition for Life*, 1st Ed., © 2007. Reprinted and electronically reproduced by permission of Pearson Education, Inc., New York, NY.

pp. 107–108: Donatelle, Rebecca J., *Health: The Basics*, 4th Ed., © 2001, pp. 282, 346. Reprinted and electronically reproduced by permission of Pearson Education, Inc., New York, NY.

p. 108: Donatelle, Rebecca J., *Health: The Basics, Green Edition*, 9th Ed., © 2011. Reprinted and electronically reproduced by permission of Pearson Education, Inc., New York, NY.;

p. 109: Christopherson, Robert W., *Geosystems: An Introduction to Physical Geography*, 4th ed. Upper Saddle River, NJ: Prentice Hall, 2000, p. 470.

p. 109: Barlow, Hugh D., *Criminal Justice in America*. Upper Saddle River, NJ: Prentice Hall, 2000, p. 439.

p. 109: Solomon, Michael R. and Elnora W. Stuart, *Marketing: Real People, Real Choices*, 2nd ed., p. 135, © 2000. Printed and electronically reproduced by permission of Pearson Education, Inc., Upper Saddle River, New Jersey.

p. 110: Donatelle, Rebecca J., *Health: The Basics*, 4th Edition, Upper Saddle River, New Jersey: Pearson Education, Inc., 2001, p. 338.

p. 110: Macionis, John J., *Society: The Basics*, 13th Ed., © 2015, pp. viii, 339, 343, 344, 347, 350. Reprinted and electronically reproduced by permission of Pearson Education, Inc., New York, NY.

p. 111: Donatelle, Rebecca J., *Health: The Basics*, 4th Edition, Upper Saddle River, NJ: Pearson Education, Inc., 2001, p. 41

p. 116: Berman, Louis and J. C. Evans, *Exploring the Cosmos*, 5th ed. Boston: Little Brown, 1986, p. 145.

p. 119: Curry, Tim, Robert Jiobu, and Kent Schwirian, *Sociology for the Twenty-First Century*, 2nd ed. Upper Saddle River, NJ: Prentice Hall, 1999.

p. 120: Levens, Michael P, *Marketing: Defined, Explained, Applied*, 1st Ed., © 2010, p. 223. Reprinted and electronically reproduced by permission of Pearson Education, Inc., New York, NY.

p. 121: Badasch, Shirley A. and Doreen S. Chesebro, *Health Science Fundamentals*, 1st ed., p. 356, © 2009. Printed and electronically reproduced by permission of Pearson Education, Inc., Upper Saddle River, New Jersey.

p. 122: Frings, Gini Stephens, *Fashion: From Concept to Consumer*, 9th Ed., © 2008, pp. 80, 158. Reprinted and electronically reproduced by permission of Pearson Education, Inc., New York, NY.

p. 122: Belk, Colleen M.; Borden Maier, Virginia, *Biology: Science for Life with Physiology*, 3rd Ed. © 2010, pp. 30–31, 78, 364, 399. Reprinted and electronically reproduced by permission of Pearson Education, Inc., NewYork, NY.

p. 122: Kennedy, X. J.; Gioia, Dana, *Literature: An Introduction to Fiction, Poetry, Drama, and Writing*, 11th Ed., © 2010, p. 258. Reprinted and electronically reproduced by permission of Pearson Education, Inc. New York, NY.

p. 123: Ciccarelli, Saundra K., J. Noland White, *Psychology: An Exploration*, 3rd Ed., Pearson Education, Inc., 2013, p. 484.

Chapter 5

p. 128: Katz, Jane, *Swimming for Total Fitness: A Progressive Aerobic Program*. Garden City, NY: Dolphin Books/Doubleday, 1981, p. 99.;

p. 142: Frings, Gini Stephens, *Fashion: From Concept to Consumer*, 9th Ed., © 2008, pp. 80, 158. Reprinted and electronically reproduced by permission of Pearson Education, Inc., New York, NY.

p. 142: Thill, John V. and Courtland L. Bovée, *Excellence in Business*, 9th ed. Upper Saddle River,© Bovee and Thill LLC, 2010. NJ: Pearson Prentice Hall, 2010, p. 355.

p. 142: Withgott, Jay H.; Brennan, Scott R., *Environment: The Science Behind the Stories*, 4th Ed., © 2011. Reprinted and electronically reproduced by permission of Pearson Education, Inc., New York, NY.

Chapter 6

p. 151: Solomon, Michael R., Greg W. Marshall, and Elnora W. Stuart, *Marketing: Real People, Real Choices*, 4th ed. Upper Saddle River, NJ: Pearson Prentice Hall, 2006, p. 25–27.

pp. 152–153: Wilcox, Dennis L. and Glen T. Cameron, *Public Relations: Strategies and Tactics*, 9th ed. Boston: MA: Pearson Allyn & Bacon, 2010, p. 474–477.

p. 153: Carl, John D., *THINK Sociology*, 1st Ed., © 2010. Reprinted and electronically reproduced by permission of Pearson Education, Inc., New York, NY.

p. 161: Kunz, Jenifer, *THINK Marriages and Families*, 1st Ed., © 2011. Reprinted and electronically reproduced by permission of Pearson Education, Inc., New York, NY.

p. 161: Harris, C. Leon, *Concepts in Zoology*, 2nd ed. © Pearson Education, Inc, Published by New York: HarperCollins College Publishers, 1996, p. 573.

pp. 164–165: Wilson, R. Jackson, et al., *The Pursuit of Liberty: A History of the American People*, 3rd ed., Vol. 2. New York: HarperCollins College Publishers, 1996, p. 422.

p. 165: Kinnear, Thomas C., Kenneth L. Bernhardt, and Kathleen A. Krentler, *Principles of Marketing*, 4th ed., p. 637. © 1995. Printed and electronically reproduced by permission of Pearson Education, Inc., Upper Saddle River, New Jersey.

p. 165: Harris, C. Leon, *Concepts in Zoology*, 2nd ed. © Pearson Education, Inc. Published by New York: HarperCollins College Publishers, 1996, p. 573.

p. 167: Macionis, John J., *Society: The Basics*, 13th Ed., © 2015, pp. viii, 339, 343, 344, 347, 350. Reprinted and electronically reproduced by permission of Pearson Education, Inc., New York, NY.

p. 168: Mix, Michael C., Paul Farber, and Keith I. King, *Biology: The Network of Life*, 1st Edition, p. 165. © 1992. Printed and electronically reproduced by permission of Pearson Education, Inc., Upper Saddle River, New Jersey.

p. 176: Schiffman, Leon and Leslie Kanuk, *Consumer Behavior*, 10th ed., p. 246. © 2010. Printed and electronically reproduced by permission of Pearson Education, Inc., Upper Saddle River, New Jersey.

Chapter 7

p. 189: Wade, Carole and Carol Tavris, *Psychology*, 6th ed. Upper Saddle River, NJ: Prentice Hall, 2000

p. 190: Harris, C. Leon, *Concepts in Zoology*, 2nd ed. © Pearson Education, Inc, Published by New York: HarperCollins College Publishers, 1996, p. 573.

p. 190: Thio, Alex, *Sociology*, 5th ed. New York: Longman, 1998.

p. 198: Copyright © 2011 by Houghton Mifflin Harcourt Publishing Company. Reproduced by permission from *The American Heritage Dictionary of the English Language*, Fifth Edition.

p. 204: Solomon, Michael R., Mary Anne Poatsy and Kendall Martin, *Better Business*, Upper Saddle River, NJ: Pearson Prentice Hall, 2010

p. 205: Bennion, Marion and Barbara Scheule, *Introductory Foods*, 14th Ed., Upper Saddle River, NJ: Pearson Prentice Hall, 2014, p. 14.

p. 205: Thompson, Janice and Melinda Manore, *Nutrition: An Applied Approach*, 2nd ed. San Francisco: Pearson Benjamin Cummings, 2009.

Chapter 8

p. 211: Schmalleger, Frank, *Criminal Justice: A Brief Introduction*, 10th Ed., Pearson Education, Inc., 2013, p. 78.

p. 211: Loyd, Jason B. and James D. Richardson, *Fundamentals of Fire and Emergency Services*. Upper Saddle River, NJ: Pearson Prentice Hall, 2010, p. 12.

pp. 211–212: Ross, David A., *Introduction to Oceanography*. New York: HarperCollins College Publishers, 1995, p. 48.

p. 212: Audesirk, Gerald; Audesirk, Teresa; Byers, Bruce E., *Biology: Life on Earth*, 9th Ed., Pearson Education, Inc., 2011, p. 26.

p. 212: Ebert, Ronald J. and Ricky W. Griffin, *Business Essentials*, 8th ed. Upper Saddle River, NJ: Pearson Prentice Hall, 2011, pp. 30–31.

p. 212: Belk, Colleen and Virginia Borden, *Biology: Science for Life*, 2nd ed. San Francisco: Pearson Benjamin Cummings, 2006, pp. 392–393.

p. 213: Bonds, Mark Evan, *Listen to This*, 3rd Ed., Pearson Education, Inc., 2014, p. 307.

p. 213: Goldfield, David and Carl Abbott, *The American Journey*, 7th Ed., Pearson Education, Inc., 2013.

p. 213: Capron, H. L., *Computers: Tools for an Information Age*, Brief Edition. New York: Addison Wesley Longman Publishing Company, 1998, p. 82.

p. 213: Lutgens, Frederick K., Edward J. Tarbuck, and Dennis Tasa, *Essentials of Geology*, 10th ed. Upper Saddle River, NJ: Pearson Prentice Hall, 2009, p. 13.

pp. 213–214: Gerow, Josh R., *Essentials of Psychology: Concepts and Applications*, 2nd ed. New York: HarperCollins College Publishers, 1996, p. 138.

p. 214: Edwards, George C.; Wattenberg, Martin P.; Lineberry, Robert L., *Government in America: People, Politics, and Policy*, 12th Ed., © 2006, p. 16. Reprinted and electronically reproduced by permission of Pearson Education, Inc., New York, NY.

p. 214: Gronbeck, Bruce E., et al., *Principles of Speech Communication*, 12th brief ed. New York: HarperCollins College Publishers, 1995, p. 302.

p. 214: Thio, Alex, *Sociology*, 4th ed. © Pearson Education (New York: HarperCollins College Publishers, 1996) 1996, p. 181.

p. 214: Agee, Warren K., Phillip H. Ault, and Edwin Emery, *Introduction to Mass Communications*, 12th ed. New York: Longman, 1997, p. 225.

pp. 214–215: Marieb, Elaine N., *Essentials of Human Anatomy and Physiology*, 5th ed. Menlo Park, CA: Benjamin/Cummings, 1997, p. 119.

p. 217: Miller, Roger Leroy, *Economics Today*, 8th ed. New York: HarperCollins College Publishers, 1994, p. 69.

p. 217: Marieb, Elaine N., *Essentials of Human Anatomy and Physiology*, 5th ed. Menlo Park, CA: Benjamin/Cummings, 1997, p. 119.

p. 217: Audesirk, Gerald; Audesirk, Teresa; Byers, Bruce E., *Biology: Life on Earth*, 9th Ed., © 2011, pp. 160, 301, 317, 337. Reprinted and electronically reproduced by permission of Pearson Education, Inc., New York, NY.

p. 217: Blake, Joan Salge, *Nutrition and You*, 1st Ed., © 2008, pp. 52, 318, 513. Reprinted and electronically reproduced by permission of Pearson Education, Inc., New York, NY.

pp. 217–218: Bovée, Courtland and John V. Thill, *Business Communication Today*, 9th ed., p. 54, © Bovee and Thill, LLC, 2008. Printed and electronically reproduced by permission of Pearson Education, Inc., Upper Saddle River, New Jersey.

p. 218: Angel, Allen R., Christine D. Abbott and Dennis C. Runde, *A Survey of Mathematics with Applications*, 9th Ed., Pearson Education, Inc., 2012, p. 135.

p. 218: Hewitt, Paul G., *Conceptual Physics*, 8th ed. Reading, MA: Addison Wesley Longman, 1998, p. 279.

p. 218: Weaver II, Richard, *Understanding Interpersonal Communication*, 7th ed. New York: HarperCollins College Publishers, 1996, p. 220.

p. 218: Frings, Gini Stephens, *Fashion: From Concept to Consumer*, 9th Ed., © 2008, pp. 80, 158. Reprinted and electronically reproduced by permission of Pearson Education, Inc., New York, NY.

p. 218: Wallace, Robert A., *Biology: The World of Life*, 7th ed. Menlo Park, CA: Benjamin/Cummings, 1997, p. 167.

p. 219: DeVito, Joseph A., *Essentials of Human Communication*, 6th Ed., © 2008, pp. 109–110, 125, 131–133. Reprinted and

electronically reproduced by permission of Pearson Education, Inc., New York, NY.

p. 221: Blake, Joan Salge, *Nutrition and You*, 1st Ed., © 2008, pp. 52, 318, 513. Reprinted and electronically reproduced by permission of Pearson Education, Inc., New York, NY.

p. 221: Miller, Roger Leroy, *Economics Today*, 8th ed. New York: HarperCollins College Publishers, 1994, p. 84.

pp. 221–222: Wilcox, Dennis L. and Glen T. Cameron, *Public Relations: Strategies and Tactics*, 9th ed. Boston: MA: Pearson Allyn & Bacon, 2010, p. 145.

p. 222: Koch, Arthur, *Speaking with a Purpose*, 7th ed. Boston, MA: Pearson Allyn and Bacon, 2007, p. 110.

p. 222: Johnston, Mike, *The Pharmacy Technician: Foundations and Practices*. Upper Saddle River, NJ: Pearson Prentice Hall, 2009, p. 13.

p. 222: Withgott, Jay and Scott Brennan, *Environment: The Science Behind the Stories*, 4th ed. San Francisco: Pearson Benjamin Cummings, 2011, p. 59.

p. 223: Macionis, John J., *Society: The Basics*, 5th Ed., Pearson Education, Inc., 2000, p. 270.

p. 223: DeVito, Joseph A., *Essentials of Human Communication*, 6th Ed., © 2008, p. 278. Reprinted and electronically reproduced by permission of Pearson Education, Inc., New York, NY.

p. 223: Edwards III, George C., Martin P. Wattenberg, and Robert L. Lineberry, *Government in America: People, Politics, and Policy*, 12th Edition, p. 653, © 2006. Pearson Education, Inc., Upper Saddle River, New Jersey.

pp. 224–225: DeVito, Joseph A., *Human Communication: The Basic Course*, 12th ed. Boston, MA: Pearson Allyn & Bacon, 2012, p. 256.

pp. 224–225: Henslin, James M., *Essentials of Sociology: A Down-to-Earth Approach*, 7th ed. © James Henslin, Boston, MA: Pearson Allyn & Bacon, 2007. p. 402.

p. 225: Blake, Joan Salge, *Nutrition & You*. San Francisco: Pearson Benjamin Cummings, 2008, p. 258.

pp. 225–226: Donatelle, Rebecca J., *Health: The Basics, Green Edition*, 9th Ed., © 2011. Reprinted and electronically reproduced by permission of Pearson Education, Inc., New York, NY.

p. 226: Thill, John V. and Courtland L. Bovée, *Excellence in Business*, 9th ed. © Upper Saddle River, NJ: Pearson Prentice Hall, 2010, p. 355.

p. 226: Withgott, Jay H.; Brennan, Scott R., *Environment: The Science Behind the Stories*, 4th Ed., © 2011. Reprinted and electronically reproduced by permission of Pearson Education, Inc., New York, NY.

p. 226: Krogh, David, *A Brief Guide to Biology*. Upper Saddle River, NJ: Pearson Prentice Hall, 2007, p. 148.

p. 226: Newcombe, Nora, *Child Development: Change Over Time*, 8th ed. New York: HarperCollins College Publishers, 1996, p. 354.

p. 227: Coleman, James William and Donald R. Cressey, *Social Problems*, 6th ed. New York: HarperCollins College Publisher, 1996, p. 130.

p. 227: Goldman, Thomas F.; Cheeseman, Henry R., *The Paralegal Professional*, 3rd Ed., © 2011, p. 393. Reprinted and electronically reproduced by permission of Pearson Education, Inc., New York, NY.

p. 227: DeVito, Joseph A., *Messages: Building Interpersonal Communication Skills*, 3rd ed. New York: HarperCollins College Publishers, 1996, p. 153.

p. 227: Belk, Colleen and Virginia Borden, *Biology: Science for Life*, 2nd ed. San Francisco: Pearson Benjamin Cummings, 2006, p. 46.

p. 228: Folkerts, Jean, et al., *The Media in Your Life: An Introduction to Mass Communication*, Boston: Allyn and Bacon, 2007, p. 204.

p. 228: Audesirk, Gerald; Audesirk, Teresa; Byers, Bruce E., *Biology: Life on Earth*, 9th Ed., © 2011, pp. 160, 301, 317, 337. Reprinted and electronically reproduced by permission of Pearson Education, Inc., New York, NY.

p. 229: Audesirk, Gerald; Audesirk, Teresa; Byers, Bruce E., *Biology: Life on Earth*, 9th Ed., © 2011, pp. 160, 301, 317, 337. Reprinted and electronically reproduced by permission of Pearson Education, Inc., New York, NY.

Chapter 9

p. 235: Mix, Michael C., Paul Farber, and Keith I. King, *Biology: The Network of Life*. (New York: HarperCollins, 1997);

p. 236: Carl, John D., *THINK Sociology*, 1st Ed., © 2010. Reprinted and electronically reproduced by permission of Pearson Education, Inc., New York, NY.

p. 237: Preble, Duane, Sarah Preble, and Patrick Frank, *Artforms: An Introduction to the Visual Arts*, 9th ed. New York: Longman, 2008, p. 60.

p. 237: Kunz, Jenifer, *THINK Marriages and Families*, 1st Ed., © 2011. Reprinted and electronically reproduced by permission of Pearson Education, Inc., New York, NY.

p. 237: Audesirk, Gerald; Audesirk, Teresa; Byers, Bruce E., *Biology: Life on Earth*, 9th Ed., © 2011, pp. 160, 301, 317, 337. Reprinted and electronically reproduced by permission of Pearson Education, Inc., New York, NY.

p. 238: Kosslyn, Stephen M., and Robin S. Rosenberg, *Introducing Psychology: Brain, Person, Group*, 4th Ed., Pearson Education, Inc., 2011, p. 257.

p. 238: Preble, Duane, Sarah Preble, and Patrick Frank, *Artforms: An Introduction to the Visual Arts*, 6th ed. New York: Longman, 1999, p. 60.

pp. 238–239: Donatelle, Rebecca J., *Health: The Basics, Green Edition*, 9th Ed., © 2011. Reprinted and electronically reproduced by permission of Pearson Education, Inc., New York, NY.

p. 239: Edwards III, George C., Martin P. Wattenberg, and Robert L. Lineberry, *Government in America: People, Politics, and Policy*, 12th Edition, p. 156, © 2006. Pearson Education, Inc., Upper Saddle River, New Jersey.

p. 239: Frank, Patrick, *Artforms: An Introduction to the Visual Arts*, 9th ed. Upper Saddle River, NJ: Pearson Prentice Hall, 2009, p. 112.

p. 239: Carnes, Mark C. and John A. Garraty, *The American Nation: A History of the United States*, 12th ed. New York: Pearson Longman, 2006, p. 826.

p. 240: Solomon, Michael R., Greg W. Marshall, and Elnora W. Stuart, *Marketing: Real People, Real Choices*, 4th ed. Upper Saddle River, NJ: Pearson Prentice Hall, 2006, p. 202.

p. 240: Kinnear, Thomas C., Kenneth L. Bernhardt, and Kathleen A. Krentler, *Principles of Marketing*, 4th ed., p. 180. © 1995. Printed and electronically reproduced by permission of Pearson Education, Inc., Upper Saddle River, New Jersey.

p. 240: Lutgens, Frederick K., Edward J. Tarbuck, and Dennis Tasa, *Essentials of Geology*, 10th ed. Upper Saddle River, NJ: Pearson Prentice Hall, 2009, p. 261.

pp. 240–241: Miller, Roger Leroy, *Economics Today*, 8th ed. New York: HarperCollins College Publishers, 1994, p. 147.

p. 241: Hill, John W, Doris K Kolb and Terry Wade McCreary, *Chemistry for Changing Times*, 13th Ed., Pearson Education, Inc., 2013, p. 370.

pp. 242–243: Lutgens, Frederick K., Edward J. Tarbuck, and Dennis Tasa, *Essentials of Geology*, 10th ed. Upper Saddle River, NJ: Pearson Prentice Hall, 2009, p. 426.

p. 244: DeVito, Joseph A., *Essentials of Human Communication*, 6th Ed., © 2008, pp. 109–110, 125, 131–133. Reprinted and electronically reproduced by permission of Pearson Education, Inc., New York, NY.

p. 246: Brands, H. W., et al., *American Stories: A History of the United States, Vol. 1*. New York: Pearson Longman, 2009, pp. 175–177.

p. 249: Krogh, David, *A Brief Guide to Biology*. Upper Saddle River, NJ: Pearson Prentice Hall, 2007, p. 406.

p. 250: Tortora, Gerard J., *Introduction to the Human Body: The Essentials of Anatomy and Physiology*, 2nd ed. New York: HarperCollins College Publishers, 1991,.

p. 252: Bovee, Courtland L. and John V Thill, *Business in Action*, 6th Ed., Upper Saddle River: NJ, Pearson Education, Inc., 2014, p. 243.

p. 253: DeVito, Joseph A., *The Essentials of Public Speaking*, 3rd ed. Boston, MA: Pearson Allyn and Bacon, 2009, p. 8.

p. 254: Ferl, Robert J., Robert A. Wallace, and Gerald P. Sanders, *Biology: The Realm of Life*, 3rd ed. New York: HarperCollins College Publishers, 1996, pp. 252–253.

p. 255: Thompson, Janice J.; Manore, Melinda, *Nutrition for Life*, 1st Ed., © 2007. Reprinted and electronically reproduced by permission of Pearson Education, Inc., New York, NY.

p. 255: Fujishin, Randy, *The Natural Speaker*, 6th ed. Boston, MA: Pearson Allyn and Bacon, 2009, p. 21.

p. 255: Goldman, Thomas F.; Cheeseman, Henry R., *The Paralegal Professional*, 3rd Ed., © 2011, p. 393. Reprinted and electronically reproduced by permission of Pearson Education, Inc., New York, NY.

pp. 255–256: Carl, John D., *THINK Sociology*, 1st Ed., © 2010. Reprinted and electronically reproduced by permission of Pearson Education, Inc., New York, NY.

p. 256: David Hicks, Margaret Gwynne, *Cultural Anthropology*, 2nd ed. New York: HarperCollins College Publishers, 1996.

p. 256: Henslin, James M.,*Essentials of Sociology: A Down-to-Earth Approach*, 7th ed. Boston, MA: Pearson Allyn & Bacon, 2007.

pp. 256–257: Edwards III, George C., Martin P. Wattenberg, and Robert L. Lineberry, *Government in America: People, Politics, and Policy*, 12th Edition, p. 156, © 2006. Pearson Education, Inc., Upper Saddle River, New Jersey.

p. 257: Blake, Joan Salge, *Nutrition and You*, 1st Ed., © 2008, pp. 52, 318, 513. Reprinted and electronically reproduced by permission of Pearson Education, Inc., New York, NY.

p. 257: Thompson, Janice J.; Manore, Melinda, *Nutrition for Life*, 1st Ed., © 2007. Reprinted and electronically reproduced by permission of Pearson Education, Inc., New York, NY.

p. 258: Schiffman, Leon and Leslie Kanuk, *Consumer Behavior*, 10th ed., p. xi. © 2010. Printed and electronically reproduced by permission of Pearson Education, Inc., Upper Saddle River, New Jersey.

p. 258: Audesirk, Gerald; Audesirk, Teresa; Byers, Bruce E., *Biology: Life on Earth*, 9th Ed., © 2011, pp. 160, 301, 317, 337. Reprinted and electronically reproduced by permission of Pearson Education, Inc., New York, NY.

p. 258: Carl, John D., *THINK Sociology*, 1st Ed., © 2010. Reprinted and electronically reproduced by permission of Pearson Education, Inc., New York, NY.

p. 258: Donatelle, Rebecca J., *Health: The Basics, Green Edition*, 9th Ed., © 2011. Reprinted and electronically reproduced by permission of Pearson Education, Inc., New York, NY.

p. 259: DeVito, Joseph A., *Interpersonal Messages: Communication and Relationship Skills*, 2nd ed. Boston, MA: Pearson Allyn & Bacon, 2011.

p. 259: Poatsy, Mary Anne and Kendall Martin, *Better Business*. Upper Saddle River, NJ: Pearson Prentice Hall, 2010.

Chapter 10

p. 268: Thio, Alex, *Sociology*, 5th ed. New York: Longman, 1998.

p. 268: Loyd, Jason B. and James D. Richardson, *Fundamentals of Fire and Emergency Services*. Upper Saddle River, NJ: Pearson Prentice Hall, 2010.

p. 269: Thio, Alex, *Sociology*, 5th ed. New York: Longman, 1998.

p. 271: Fujishin, Randy, *Natural Bridges: A Guide to Interpersonal Communication*, Boston: MA, Pearson Education, Inc., 2011.

pp. 271–272: Zimbardo, Philip G. and Richard J. Gerrig, *Psychology and Life*, 18th ed. Upper Saddle River: Pearson Education, Inc. 2008.

p. 274: Scott R. Brennan, *Environment: The Science Behind the Stories*, 1st Edition, © 2005. Reprinted by permission of Pearson Education, Inc., Upper Saddle River, NJ.

pp. 276–277: Uba, Laura and Karen Huang, *Psychology*, New York: Longman Pearson, 1999, p. 323.

p. 277: Greenberg, Edward S. and Benjamin I. Page, *The Struggle for Democracy*, 10th Ed., Boston, MA: Longman Pearson, 2011, p. 186.

p. 279: WorkingHumor.com.

p. 279: WorkingHumor.com

pp. 279–280: Belk, Colleen and Virginia Borden, Biology: *Science for Life*, 2nd ed. San Francisco: Pearson Benjamin Cummings, 2006.

p. 281: Oliveria, D.F., "Burning Will Go: That's Not All Good," *Spokesman Review*, July 24, 2002.

p. 281: Cook, Roy A., Laura J. Yale, and Joseph J. Marqua, *Tourism: The Business of Travel*, 2nd ed. Upper Saddle River, NJ: Prentice Hall, 2002.

p. 281: "Not Always With Us", *The Economist*, June 1, 2013.

p. 281: Waltrip, Darrell, "Calling Dr. Phil: NASCAR Needs Black and White Penalties," FOXSports.com, September 2005.

pp. 281–282: WorkingHumor.com

pp. 282–283: WorkingHumor.com

p. 283: Swardson, Roger, "Greetings from the Electronic Plantation," *City Pages*, October 21, 1992.

pp. 283–284: WorkingHumor.com

p. 284: Otto, Whitney, *How to Make an American Quilt*. New York: Villard Books, 1991.

pp. 289–290: Redlener, Irwin, "Undocumented Children Need Charitable Help: Children need high-quality health care regardless of citizenship," *USA Today Magazine*, June 25 © 2014 Time Inc. Used under license.

pp. 290–291: Editorial Board, "Vaccine opt-outs put public health at risk: Our view," *USA Today*, April 13 © 2014 Gannett. All rights reserved. Used by permission and protected by the Copyright Laws of the United States. The printing, copying, redistribution, or retransmission of this Content without express written permission is prohibited.

p. 295: Withgott, Jay H.; Brennan, Scott R., *Environment: The Science Behind the Stories*, 4th Ed., © 2011. Reprinted and electronically reproduced by permission of Pearson Education, Inc., New York, NY.

pp. 295–296: DeVito, Joseph A., *Human Communication: The Basic Course*, 12th ed. Boston, MA: Pearson Allyn & Bacon, 2012.

Chapter 11

pp. 303–304: Bennett, Jeffrey, Seth Shostak, and Bruce Jakosky, *Life in the Universe*. San Francisco: Addison Wesley, 2003.

p. 304: Kennedy, X. J. and Dana Gioia, *Literature: An Introduction to Fiction, Poetry, and Drama*, 3rd ed. New York: Longman, 2003.

p. 304: Margolis, Mac, "A Plot of Their Own," *Newsweek*, January 21, 2002.

p. 312: Reprinted by permission from *Society in Focus: An Introduction to Sociology*, 7th ed., by William E. Thompson and Joseph V. Hickey.

p. 312: Belk, Colleen M.; Borden Maier, Virginia, *Biology: Science for Life with Physiology*, 3rd Ed., © 2010, pp. 30–31, 78, 364, 399. Reprinted and electronically reproduced by permission of Pearson Education, Inc., New York, NY.

p. 312: Donatelle, Rebecca J., *Health: The Basics, Green Edition*, 9th Ed., © 2011. Reprinted and electronically reproduced by permission of Pearson Education, Inc., New York, NY.

Chapter 12

p. 332: Edwards, George C.; Wattenberg, Martin P.; Lineberry, Robert L., *Government in America: People, Politics, and Policy*, 15th Ed., © 2011, p. 240. Reprinted and electronically reproduced by permission of Pearson Education, Inc., New York, NY.

p. 333: Reprinted by permission from *Society in Focus: An Introduction to Sociology*, 7th ed., by William E. Thompson and Joseph V. Hickey.

p. 333: Withgott, Jay H.; Brennan, Scott R., *Environment: The Science Behind the Stories*, 4th Ed., © 2011. Reprinted and electronically reproduced by permission of Pearson Education, Inc., New York, NY.

Chapter 13

p. 350: Krough, David, *Biology: A Guide to the Natural World*, 4th Ed., © 2009, p. 334. Reprinted and electronically reproduced by permission of Pearson Education, Inc., New York, NY.

p. 351: Suchocki, John, *Conceptual Chemistry*, 4th ed., p. 145, © 2011. Printed and electronically reproduced by permission of Pearson Education, Inc., Upper Saddle River, New Jersey.

p. 351: Withgott, Jay H.; Brennan, Scott R., *Environment: The Science Behind the Stories*, 4th Ed., © 2011. Reprinted and electronically reproduced by permission of Pearson Education, Inc., New York, NY.

pp. 351–352: Kunz, Jenifer, *THINK Marriages and Families*, 1st Ed., © 2011. Reprinted and electronically reproduced by permission of Pearson Education, Inc., New York, NY.

Chapter 14

p. 372: Carl, John D., *THINK Sociology*, 1st Ed., © 2010. Reprinted and electronically reproduced by permission of Pearson Education, Inc., New York, NY.

Part Six

pp. 379–381: Ahuja, Anjana, "Shades of Grey in the Ethics of Designer Babies," *Financial Times*, December 5, 2014. Reprinted with permission of The Financial TImes.

pp. 382–384: Tellez, Cami, "The Ocean's Plastic Problem," www.worldpolicy.org, September 11, 2014. http://www.worldpolicy.org/blog/2014/09/11/oceans-plastic-problem.

pp. 385–390: Lutgens, Frederick K.; Tarbuck, Edward J.; Tasa, Dennis G., *Essentials of Geology*, 12th Ed., © 2015, p. 553. Reprinted and electronically reproduced by permission of Pearson Education, Inc., New York, NY.

pp. 392–395: Castillo, Michelle, "Ethical Dilemmas Surround Those Willing to Sell, Buy Kidneys on the Black Market," *CBS News*, November 1, 2013. Reprinted with permission.

pp. 396–400: Hamblin, James, "The Virtual House Call," © 2014 The Atlantic Media Co., as first published in *The Atlantic Magazine*. All rights reserved. Distributed by Tribune Content Agency, LLC.

pp. 402–405: Burke, Lilian; Barbara Weill, *Information Technology for the Health Professions*, 4th Ed., Pearson Education, Inc., 2012.

pp. 408–411: Monaha, Rachel, "What Happens When Kids Don't Have Internet At Home?" © 2015 The Atlantic Media Co., as first published in *The Atlantic Magazine*. All rights reserved. Distributed by Tribune Content Agency, LLC.

pp. 413–415: Eagle, Nathan, "Don't Let Developing Countries Lag Behind in the Smartphone Revolution," *The Guardian*, December 18, 2014. Reprinted with permission.

pp. 416–419: Sterin, J. Charles, *Mass Media Revolution*, 2nd Ed., © 2014, pp. 190–191, 195–197. Reprinted and electronically reproduced by permission of Pearson Education, Inc., New York, NY.

Part Seven

pp. 425–438: Macionis, John, J., *Society: The Basics,* 13th Ed., ©2015, p. 340–350. Reprinted and electronically reproduced by permission of Pearson Education, Inc., New York, NY.

p. 426: Macionis, John J., *Society: The Basics,* 13th Ed., © 2015, pp. viii, 339, 343, 344, 347, 350. Reprinted and electronically reproduced by permission of Pearson Education, Inc., New York, NY.

p. 430: Macionis, John J., *Society: The Basics,* 13th Ed., © 2015, pp. viii, 339, 343, 344, 347, 350. Reprinted and electronically reproduced by permission of Pearson Education, Inc., New York, NY.

p. 431: Macionis, John J., *Society: The Basics,* 13th Ed., © 2015, pp. viii, 339, 343, 344, 347, 350. Reprinted and electronically reproduced by permission of Pearson Education, Inc., New York, NY.

p. 434: Macionis, John J., *Society: The Basics,* 13th Ed., © 2015, pp. viii, 339, 343, 344, 347, 350. Reprinted and electronically reproduced by permission of Pearson Education, Inc., New York, NY.

p. 437: Macionis, John J., *Society: The Basics,* 13th Ed., © 2015, pp. viii, 339, 343, 344, 347, 350. Reprinted and electronically reproduced by permission of Pearson Education, Inc., New York, NY.

INDEX